REWRITING
MAYA RELIGION

REWRITING MAYA RELIGION

Domingo de Vico, K'iche' Maya Intellectuals, and the *Theologia Indorum*

Garry G. Sparks

UNIVERSITY PRESS OF COLORADO
Louisville

Published by University Press of Colorado
245 Century Circle, Suite 202
Louisville, Colorado 80027

Manufactured in the United States of America

The University Press of Colorado is a proud member of the Association of University Presses.

The University Press of Colorado is a cooperative publishing enterprise supported, in part, by Adams State University, Colorado State University, Fort Lewis College, Metropolitan State University of Denver, Regis University, University of Colorado, University of Northern Colorado, University of Wyoming, Utah State University, and Western Colorado University.

∞ This paper meets the requirements of the ANSI/NISO Z39.48–1992 (Permanence of Paper)

ISBN: 978-1-60732-969-5 (cloth)
ISBN: 978-1-60732-970-1 (ebook)
https://doi.org/10.5876/9781607329701

Library of Congress Cataloging-in-Publication Data

Names: Sparks, Garry, author.
Title: Rewriting Maya religion : Domingo de Vico, k'iche' Maya intellectuals, and the Theologia indorum / Garry G. Sparks.
Description: Louisville : University Press of Colorado, [2019] | Includes bibliographical references and index.
Identifiers: LCCN 2019020036 | ISBN 9781607329695 (cloth) | ISBN 9781607329701 (ebook)
Subjects: LCSH: Vico, Domingo de, 1485-1555. Theologia indorum. | Catholic Church—Doctrines. | Quich?e language—Texts. | Theology, Doctrinal. | Indians of Mexico—Religion.
Classification: LCC PM4231.Z77 S63 2019 | DDC 897/.423—dc23
LC record available at https://lccn.loc.gov/2019020036

Cover illustration: *Theologia Indorum*, folio 1 verso, Garrett-Gates Mesoamerican Manuscripts, no. 177 (C0744.01); Manuscripts Division, Department of Rare Books and Special Collections, Princeton University Library.

El pensamiento y la acción de los dominicos de San Esteban en América mostraron que la lucha por la libertad y la dignidad de todos los pueblos es el camino hacia la verdad. Y el único medio: la palabra.

The thought and action of the Dominicans of San Esteban in America demonstrated that the struggle for the freedom and dignity of all peoples is the way toward the truth. And the only means: the word.

—A WALL INSCRIPTION ON THE SECOND-FLOOR OF THE COURTYARD OF SAN ESTEBAN DE SALAMANCA, SPAIN

Contents

Note on Orthography and Pronunciation

Since the arrival of Europeans to the historic Maya region of Mesoamerica, various orthographies based on Latin script have been developed for writing the Mayan languages. With the exception of some direct quotes rendered in a colonial or other missionary alphabet, all Maya words in this book are written in the Unified Maya Alphabet (UMA)—the legally official orthography for all the Mayan languages of Guatemala since 1987 as developed, applied, and modified since then by the Mayan Language Academy of Guatemala (Academia de Lenguas Mayas de Guatemala [ALMG]). Based on a 2006 decision of the ALMG, vowels are not maked here as long or short, nor as tense or relaxed.

DOI: 10.5876/9781607329701.c000a

Colonial (Parra, 1540s)	*UMA (ALMG, 1987)*	*Phonetics*	
a	a	<a:>, <ä>	long, short, tense, and relaxed
b	b’	<ɓ>	implosive like the <p> in “gulp”
ch	ch	<tʃ>	similar to <ch> in English
4h / qh	ch’	<tʃ’>	glottalized <ch> like in “catch”
e	e	<e:>, <ë>	long, short, tense, or relaxed
i	i	<i:>, <ï>	long, short, tense, or relaxed
h	j	<χ>	similar to <h> in English
c / qu	k	<k>	similar to <k> in English
4 / q / g / ¢	k’	<k’>	glottalized <k>
l	l	<l>	similar to <l> in English
m	m	<m>	similar to <m> in English
n	n	<n>	similar to <n> in English
o	o	<o:>, <ö>	long, short, tense, or relaxed
p	p	<p>	similar to <p> in English
k	q	<q>	similar to <k> further in the throat
ε	q’	<q’>	like a “glug” sound of pouring
r	r	<r>	similar to <r> in English
z / ç	s	<s>	similar to <s> in English
t	t	<t>	similar to <t> in English
tt	t’	<t’>	similar to <t> in “bottle” in Britian
tz	tz	<ts>	similar to <ts> in “beets”
4, / tz	tz’	<ts’>	glottalized <ts>
u / v	u	<u:>, <ü>	long, short, tense, or relaxed
v / uh	w	<w>	similar to <w> in English
x	x	<ʃ>, <š>	similar to <sh> in English
y	y	<j>	similar to <y> in English

REWRITING
MAYA RELIGION

Introduction

(Re)Reading a First Coauthored Paper Trail

There are, in fact, very few times in human history when two or more sizably significant groups of people encounter each other and neither has any actual idea who, or even what, the other group is. At the turn of the sixteenth century, Europeans sailing from the east had no idea where they really were or what, let alone who, they were encountering. And the indigenous peoples of the Americas had no idea what had just washed up on their shores. While an encounter with the radically cultural and religious others is not new within the history of Christian writings, the arrival of mendicant missionaries—Franciscans and Dominicans—to Mesoamerica is unique because it provoked and now provides a paper trail authored by both of the voices of the culture contact: western Christianity, from late medieval and early modern Iberia, and to a lesser degree their indigenous American hosts, resisters, and converts. As is apparent in the earliest Christian literature, such as the letters of Paul of Tarsus (written ca. 40s–ca. 60s CE), Christian thought has always addressed, in some way, the intersection between aspects of cultures and claims of a Christian identity. Yet the encounter between Hispano-Catholicism and Mesoamerican worldviews—including Maya religion—is one of the earliest incidents, if not *the* earliest incident, to include contemporaneous *minority* reports by survivors of Christendom or colonial Christianity.

The landing of the first sustained presence of explicitly Christian missionaries on the *terra firma* of the Americas' mainland until the arrival, implementation, and enforcement of the Catholic Reformation occupies the period roughly between

DOI: 10.5876/9781607329701.c000b

1519 and 1572. In Mesoamerica, it circumscribes a relatively brief but highly distinct moment in the radical shifting of religious reflection. Such periods of first contact or encounter mark foundational moments for religious ecologies and for the critical and comparative study of religious thought and practice. During such contentious moments, the communities that engaged often felt compelled to translate or even reconfigure their religious systems and traditions. Whether real or imagined, the perception of crisis by a community often motivates its members, especially its highly reflective thinkers—local intellectuals—to make otherwise assumed or deeply implicit understandings more explicit and accessible, to restate what had often been assumed and left "unsaid." During such seminal periods of interreligious or even intrareligious encounters—be they militant or conversational, or accompanied with coercive or persuasive force—communities reflect upon, assess, reassess, clarify, and re-present their claims about their discernment of explicit but also implicit religious meanings and values.

The early decades of first encounters between indigenous Americans and Europeans are often, and rightly, described in terms of the use of coercive force, with the stereotypical image of Spaniards landing with a sword in one hand and a crucifix in the other. The use of persuasive force by both Iberian arrivals and indigenous peoples, often mutually albeit rarely equally, is less appreciated. During these early decades, Dominicans argued for the removal of Spanish armed forces (though often also relied on them) and even questioned the Crown's rightful use of force within emerging theories of rights and natural law developed largely by Dominican theologians—theories informed, in part, by the maltreatment of Native American peoples and concern for their defense. And during these early decades the first explicit Christian theology to be composed in either North or South America was written, the *Theologia Indorum* by Friar Domingo de Vico, O.P. Originally most likely written in the Highland Mayan language of K'iche', it was soon translated into various other Highland Mayan languages but never into Latin or fully into Spanish or any other European language. It was completed just a year prior to Vico's murder, and still remains the longest single work on any topic to have been written in a Native American language. And yet, within only a couple of decades, it seems to have been broken up into smaller works that were continuously copied and used by both local mendicant priests and literate Highland Maya over the course of the next centuries and eventually misidentified and wrongly cataloged in European and US colonial manuscript collections. Likewise, its principal author, Domingo de Vico, all but vanished from the later histories and studies of the colonial Americas, Mesoamerica, Catholicism, religion in general, or Highland Maya language and literature. Except for a handful of scholars, even among Mesoamericanists, the mention of the name "Vico" usually refers to the Italian humanist Giambattista Vico

(1668–1744). Domingo de Vico and his writings among the Highland Maya of Guatemala have largely fallen into the fault lines between the late medieval period and early modernity, and between the "Old" and "New Worlds."

However, explicit and implicit traces of Vico's linguistic, ethnographic, and theological work can be found in many of the later writings by colonial-period mendicants among the Highland Maya of Guatemala. By the early nineteenth century, amid the political and ideological battles between Liberals and Conservatives in the region, clerical and Maya paper trails thin out and any evidence of the continued influence of Vico's work wanes. Furthermore, all surviving copies of his writings managed to migrate out of Guatemala, mainly to France and the United States. But by the late twentieth century, trends within Latin American social and theological movements were building on a foundation that Vico laid centuries prior, though unknowingly by many of those invested in these theological movements or even by the outside scholars who are studying them. Such movements include liberation theology and inculturation theology, including the strand of Christian theology, now produced by indigenous Americans who constructively engage non-Christian native rituals, narratives, and symbols, called Indian theology (*teología india*) in general or Maya theology (*teología mayense*) by specifically Maya Catholics. The significance of recovering and tracing the legacy of Vico and his *Theologia Indorum* directly affects the study of early modernity and Mesoamerica but also extends latently into studies of religious movements among present-day Maya and other indigenous Americans.

Perhaps ironically in the light of the stereotypical portrayals of sixteenth-century mendicant missionaries entering the Americas, Asia, and Pacific Islands, the earliest surviving documents that mention Vico or his *Theologia Indorum* are not Spanish but rather Maya texts, by Highland Maya authors, in Highland Mayan languages, mostly addressing a Highland Maya readership. Coincidentally, the period, place, and even language in which Vico wrote the Americas' first Christian theology are the same as some of the first postcontact writings by any indigenous Americans, including one of the most important—the Popol Wuj.[1] Vico and many of the Maya authors learned from each other and drew from similar prehispanic Maya sources for their respective works. Furthermore, many of the first entirely native Maya writings—that is to say, writings almost entirely in an indigenous language, by indigenous authors, and primarily if not exclusively for an indigenous audience—constructively engaged with and reacted against not simply a generic hegemon of Christendom but rather specifically the *Theologia Indorum*.[2] While most of these early Highland Maya texts take the form of legal genres and provide insights into their local social structures and concerns, they are also intermeshed with their religious worldview and may also be read as highly localized and even kinship-based theologies. Therefore, the early Highland Maya literature (along with that by non-Maya) must be engaged before even beginning to fully recover, reconstruct, and understand Vico and his theological project. Conversely, any reading of the early postcontact texts by Guatemala Maya (as well as those by many fellow and later clergy in the region) will not unpack the fuller force of their respective arguments or appreciate their use of Maya and mendicant sources without first understanding Vico and the *Theologia Indorum*.

HOW TO LEARN TO STOP WORRYING AND ENGAGE THEOLOGY

Too often narrowly misunderstood as apologetic, dogmatic, doctrinal, or confessional by scholars outside of religious studies, "theology" in a broader sense of the term may be understood as simply a community's metadiscourse on its own religious worldview. "Religion" is here defined as a community's articulation of its meanings and values, manifested through speech, symbols, and practices (including ceremonial rites or rituals and quotidian ethics). Religion also entails discernment of what community members understand by the "proper" selection and ordering of those meanings and values from all other possibilities, as well as reflexive and critical discernment of criteria by which they understand how such reflection, selection, and ordering ought to occur. In this respect, the interdisciplinary field of religious studies involves the rigorous, critical, analytical, and reflective examination of understandings of what may be qualified as "the religious" and its relations with other, often intermeshed realms of life, particularly when represented by written evidence.

However, within this broader, perhaps more Aristotelian (i.e., pre-Christian, observational, survey-based approach) understanding of *theos-logia,* or "talk about god," the historically Catholic (and Eastern Orthodox) understanding of theology also implies engagement with not only canonized scriptural information—the Bible—but also with authoritative understandings that have been "handed down"—*traditio,* or tradition.[3] On one hand, this Christian intellectual tradition—in the strict sense of the term—includes the officialized voices in texts that postdate those of the New Testament. Those voices have come from local, regional, and empire-wide synods and councils since late antiquity, and include influential letters, treatises, lectures, sermons, and dialogues. The Festal letter of Bishop Athanasius of Alexandria of 367 CE, for example, played a decisive role in standardizing or "canonizing" the twenty-seven books that would be the New Testament.[4] By the Council of Trent (1545–1563), the Catholic Church explicitly spelled out that scripture and "tradition" were mutually informative and equally authoritative, in contrast with the Protestant position of *sola scriptura*. The apparent problem of internal consistency—that these various sources did not necessarily seem to agree among themselves—was not lost on medieval theologians. Like in his *Sic et Non,* Peter Abelard developed a philosophical theology that prioritized the use of reason, especially from pre-Christian Greco-Roman philosophies. His approach became foundational within the later "school men" movement, or scholasticism, along with Peter Lombard's *Sententiae* or *Four Books of Sentences,* which was eventually established as the standard text of the medieval curriculum. On the other hand, "handed down" truths were also practices, such as the liturgical traditions of rites and rituals, as well as increasingly standardized hymns, prayers, and verbal formulas. *Lex orandi lex credendi* ("the law of praying is the law of believing" or "what is prayed is what is to be believed") summarizes the understanding by late antiquity that previous ritual performances and practices served both as precedents and authoritative reservoirs for thought. The production of Catholic theology and its assent within the Catholic Church as "proper" or "straight" opinion, *ortho-doxa,* requires the engagement of an accumulated corpus of intellectual as well as devotional histories.

Recent ethnohistorical studies of indigenous Mesoamerican-authored pastoral material has involved an assessment of the extent to which early colonial texts present orthodox, heterodox, or even heretical positions—that is, an assessment of the extent to which they are indigenous Mesoamerican Catholicisms. Such an evaluation is beyond the scope of this book.[5] For one, understandings of what constitutes and qualifies as "orthodox" or "heterodox" in Catholicism, especially by the turn of the sixteenth century, was precisely what was up for debate within most of western and central Europe.[6] The canons of the Tridentine Catholic Church took decades to permeate and be interpreted, applied, and enforced throughout Europe, let alone the Americas. Furthermore, the identification of theology in the indigenous Mesoamerican record ought not to necessarily consist of *whether* the construals and content align with widely notable Christian understandings but *how* they came about and the extent to which they engaged sources of the Catholic "tradition." Therefore, the occasional referring to these native texts as articulations of a Highland Maya or K'iche'an Catholicism is not a doctrinal evaluation in this book but rather is merely indicative of a religious identity in the throes of emerging dialogically with a particular strand of Catholic thought and practices conveyed and translated during a particular period. The fact that Maya authors may have produced their theology without the fuller engagement of the Catholic tradition, as Vico and his Dominican colleagues did, may be a distinguishing hallmark of the Maya theology, namely its hyperlocality, its highly if not also limited local and particularized discursive ecology.

Within the history of Christianity little to no paper trail exists to tell about, for example, the firsthand experiences of Nestorian Christians in China, Arian

Christians among the Germanic peoples of central Europe, or Scotti Christians from Ireland among the Jutes and Saxons in the British Isles. While "dialogues" with, or responses to, religious and cultural others help compose some of the earliest Christian literature in late antiquity—such as the Pauline epistles in the Christian scriptures or Justin Martyr's *Dialogue with Trypho*—contemporaneous replies or counterarguments are absent. For example, there is no written record by the Athenian elites regarding their reactions to Paul of Tarsus (such as portrayed in Acts 17:16–34) nor a text by the Jewish Trypho that presents his version of his debate with Justin Martyr (assuming that Trypho was not merely a literary foil created by Justin Martyr for demonstrating his Christian philosophy's superiority). And even where early direct arguments against Christian ideas have survived—such as one of the earliest and most detailed, Celsus's *On the True Doctrine* (ca. 178 CE)—they have mostly been preserved within, and thus filtered through, Christian apologetic literature. Just as historically significant, we have no contemporaneous corresponding Christian reply. For example, Origen of Alexandria wrote his response to Celsus's critique, *Contra Celsum* (ca. 248 CE), long after Celsus had died.[7] Obviously, Jewish and Greco-Roman religious texts of late antiquity occasionally commented on Christians or Christianity, as in the mention by the Roman governor Pliny the Younger, the Jewish Roman historian Flavius Josephus, and the Roman historians Tacitus and Suetonius. However no contemporaneous reply or intertextual dialogue between Christian and non-Christian writings exists.[8] Similarly, notable examples from the early and middle medieval periods—such as the Synod of Whitby in 663 CE regarding Celtic Christianity or the ninth-century *Hêliand* epic narrative that depicts Christ as a Saxon tribal chief—point out perennial efforts and concerns in contextualizing a Christianity during its spread from the wider Mediterranean region into northern Europe.[9] But it was not until the 1945 discovery of the Nag Hammadi cache of noncanonical or "Gnostic" Christian texts in Egypt that primary sources of dissenting positions against a gradually emerging Christian orthodoxy, or "straight teaching," became critically appreciated.[10]

And the same holds true in Asia. Through trade with and threat from the Mongolian Empire in the thirteenth century, western Latin Christianity became abruptly aware of an Asian Christianity beyond the Eastern Orthodox churches of Russia, Asia Minor, and North Africa. However, aside from a sparse archaeological record and some liturgical elements, little scholarly work focuses on surviving written accounts (such as the 781 CE Xi'an or Sian-fu Stele), apart from the Franciscan mission to the Mongolian territory in present-day Russia.[11] To paraphrase the historians' adage: Christian theology—in general but especially during these periods—is written and preserved by the victors. The thoughts of a "losing side" are rarely documented, copied, or archived and thus are lost to the ravages of time and corrosive environments, not to mention failing memories, let alone intentionally suppressive politics like bonfires. In part, this is what makes notable and valuable the documents written in Highland Mayan languages by both Catholic clergy and indigenous elites, beginning in the mid-sixteenth century.

Yet, the legacies of such moments from contact zones exist not only in the paper trail of religious treatises and tracts but also in the mythic narratives, symbols, and practices (both ceremonial and quotidian) inherited into the present. Modern resources of archaeology (and the tendancy of interpreting unearthed Classic-era Maya carvings or murals with myths later written down in the Popol Wuj, or vice versa) and ethnography (and the tendancy of interpreting the myths of the sixteenth-century Popol Wuj with studies of present-day prayers and ceremonies of Maya daykeepers, *ajq'ijab'*, or vice versa) harbor perspectives from cultural and religious others by juxtaposing the vantages of multiple constituencies, especially where documents by indigenous authors do survive. This written record can then be further read in a dialogical mode with the assistance of present-day native speakers of the indigenous languages in which the documents were written. Native speakers sometimes can explicate subtle nuances and multiple layers of meaning from a text. For example, literal translation of an early idiomatic phrase commonly found in many of the mendicants' Maya writings—*q'anal raxal*—as "yellowness and greenness" will not get a reader far toward understanding it as referring to "abundance." Noting its meaning, let alone multiple meanings, in the various colonial dictionaries on Mayan languages written by mendicants helps to elucidate at least what maybe they thought they were trying to say, at least at a particular time, such as "gloria." But in finding this exact phrase in ancient, precontact, Maya hieroglyphic (technically logosyllabic with some syllabogramatic features) texts, in autonomously written colonial-era Maya documents, and in contemporary Highland Maya ceremonial or ritual discourse (such as during a *kotz'i'j* fire-offering ceremony or in the prayers germane to the 260-day sacred calendar), conceptual waypoints can be established by which further meanings may be diachronically trafficked "upstream" or "downstream."

Many of the mendicant texts in Mesoamerican languages were written by more than one person—usually a European priest working in a local language as a *lengua* aided if not led by literate native amanuenses or *ladinos*, such as identified by William Hanks.[12] Likewise, many notarial and quasi-notarial texts were written by committees of indigenous elites for their own purposes. Reading these documents collaboratively today pairs a compositional with an exegetical strategy. Dennis Tedlock, along with *ajq'ij*, or daykeeper, Andrés Xiloj Peruch translated the most significant Maya text, the Popol Wuj, through this kind of dialogical mode. So have, in varying degrees, Allen Christenson's translations of the Popol Wuj, Dennis

Tedlock's translation of the *Rab'inal Achi*, and Judith Maxwell and Robert Hill's translation of the *Kaqchikel Chronicles*—namely the *Kiwujil Xajila'* (or *Xajil Chronicle*) and *Xpantzay Cartulary*. In this respect, Domingo de Vico's *Theologia Indorum*—a mendicant text written in various Mayan languages—has been treated here in the same dialogical mode as Mayanists have treated the early postcontact Maya texts written in Mayan languages. In other words, the translation and interpretation of Vico's theology that undergirds the analysis of this book was carried out, first, with extensive consultation of colonial-period grammar guides (*artes*) and dictionaries or lexicons (*vocabularios*) on the various K'iche'an languages written by clergy who worked in the Guatemalan highlands, including two possibly written by Vico. Second, Vico's work was analyzed by working extensively with present-day Highland Maya elders who are not only native K'iche' writers and speakers but also masters of the high register of K'iche'an ritual and ceremonial discourse.

Furthermore, recent translations and critical studies of early postcontact central and southern Mesoamerican indigenous texts—such as by Louise Burkhart, David Tavárez, William Hanks, Timothy Knowlton, and Mark Christensen—have entailed a tight comparative methodology of native language competency (and thus philological analysis as part of the New Philology movement in ethnohistory) and correspondence between those indigenous language texts (Yukatek, Nahuatl, etc.) paired with Franciscan literature either imported from Europe and translated into native languages or written originally in those languages during the outset of Spanish colonialism. The multiple and even seemingly conflicting set of entextualized meanings of an author or group of authors is understood to reside not within the words of the text but rather in a discursive relationship between the various composing texts—in this case both mendicant and Maya—in a domain of what Hanks calls "intertextuality."[13] Examination of the *Theologia Indorum* as well as notable early Highland Maya texts is treated here in this vein of intertextual analysis as it has been developed initially with the Lowland Maya literature of Mexico but that until recently has not been applied to the earlier Highland Maya literature of Guatemala.

The present volume may be read as a companion to a separate book—*The Americas' First Theologies: Early Sources of Post-Contact Indigenous Religion*—which consists of original English translations from K'iche', Q'eqchi', and Kaqchikel of many of the exemplary sections of the *Theologia Indorum* and Highland Maya texts examined here.[14] Whereas that edition of fuller translations invites readers to conduct their own intertextual and comparative study, this book consists of ethnohistorical and intertextual analysis of the *Theologia Indorum* and its author, sources, production, reception and impact among fellow mendicants and K'iche'an Maya. It then revisits some of the earliest postcontact indigenous literature, particularly the theological dimensions within their legal writings, to indicate where the legacy of the *Theologia Indorum* may still be implicitly noted.

APPROACH TO AN ETHNOHISTORY OF CHRISTIANITIES

The present study is significantly distinct in two ways. First, it attends to some of the rare texts written in indigenous American languages prior to the paradigmatic changes that occurred in both the Americas and Europe by the end of the sixteenth century. As is explained in greater detail in chapters 1 and 2, the first few decades (ca. 1520s–ca. 1580s) of initial contact between indigenous peoples of the Americas and Catholic clergy consists of a distinct, even unique, intellectual period—designated herein as the "late postclassic" period of the Maya—which is perhaps more transformative than any epoch that followed, with the possible exception of the late twentieth century. Second, almost all the examinations of the indigenous-language writings from this early period approach them primarily from the interdisciplinary—namely historical and anthropological—understandings of Latin American studies, Mesoamerican studies, Maya studies, and the like. Only secondarily, and as intellectually warranted, do they derive their understanding from a fuller comparative history of Christian thought and practices, such as from the interdisciplinary fields of religious studies or history of religions. Where these previous studies are thick in excavating the dialogicality, heteroglossia, and intertextuality of the indigenous Mesoamerican texts, they are often thin in noting and appreciating the heteroglossia and intertextuality within the history of the Catholic literature. There is therefore room to grow the recognition of conflicting Christian influences in postcontact Maya literature, the distinctiveness of late medieval Catholicism in "the Spains" prior to King Felipe II, or the various, specific, and often competing strands of Hispano-Catholicism (or "Catholicisms") that arrived in respective waves to the Americas.

Significant gains have often been made in reexamining the role and diversity of agency among indigenous peoples following the turn of the sixteenth century. However, portrayals of the European others—namely Hispano-Catholicism—are too often flattened, superficial, and homogeneous, if not monolithic. Too much scholarship on postcontact indigenous America in the aftermath of the arrival of Christian missionaries uncritically perpetuates the missionary authors' party line that there was only one singular Catholicism, or one understanding of "orthodoxy." Ironically, for the period of the sixteenth-century Reformations, which began well before, in the fifteenth century, that was precisely the set of questions at issue: what is a correct, proper, "straight" understanding of Christianity?; what is universal or "catholic"?[15] Mendicant missionaries arriving to the Americas did not have definitive answers so much as an ethos of rigorous critique and experimentation. Those who thought they did have incontrovertible answers might have seen their once "orthodox" positions deemed "heterodox," or vice versa, decades later.

Although recent efforts in cultural and postcolonial studies, ethnohistory, and the like have striven to reexamine this early period of encounters with an augmented critical appreciation for indigenous peoples' agency and reasoning, and a less Eurocentric portrayal, the scales of analysis often do not become balanced but tilted too far to the opposite side. Too often, more detailed descriptions of the historically disenfranchised come at the expense of nuanced descriptions of the historical victors. To compensate for centuries of quasi-hagiographies about Christian missionaries in the Americas, recent scholarship too often has caricatured missionaries. Figures like the famous "defender of the Indians," Bartolomé de las Casas, are relegated to the status of anomalies rather than being interrogated as voices of a possibly larger, critical, contentious cohort in and from Iberia. The critique, though, of modern empires did not come about sequentially well-after their establishment but consecutively amidst their forging. Furthermore, critiques of specifically the emerging Spanish Empire were not simply anti-Catholic in origin (such by the competing British Empire) but, on the contrary, were often initiated from within Hispano-Catholicism; just as, conversely, many of the clerical and theological apologists for the *Conquista* built their cases on justifications for the previous *Reconquista*. The voices of Iberian Catholicim were several and varied, provoking a range of responses in return from the many groups and strata of the indigenous peoples.

On the one hand, it is necessary to attend to the distinctiveness of the first fifty to sixty years of the encounter between Europe and the Americas, namely the years through the 1580s. This period encompasses the years before the arrival of the Spanish Inquisition in 1571 and the Jesuits in 1572, and the subsequent disempowerment and replacement of mendicant clergy with Jesuits and secular clergy (especially locally born clergy from wealthy *criollo* families). Important too are the implementations of the Catholic Reformation by the Third Synod of Mexico in 1585, the shift from the Julian to the Gregorian calendar in 1584, and, most important, the loss of nearly 90 percent of the indigenous population by the 1580s.[16] On the other hand, it is also necessary to attend to the distinctions between the various indigenous Americans and their receptions of the varieties of Catholic clergy, specifically the clergies' different theological methodologies and language ideologies prior to the Catholic Reformation.[17]

In general, Scotist and voluntaristic nominalism led Franciscans educated in convents to believe that a sign could not be readily separated from its referent, and thus a word in one language could never truly substitute for a word in another language. Franciscans in New Spain, for example—most of whom were strict

Observants heavily influenced by Joachim of Fiore's millenarianism rather than Conventuals—believed that local terms and images intimately bound with their non-Christian particulars could not be simply incorporated into Christian use without risking confusion or, even worse, heresy. With religious terms, for example, Franciscans in Guatemala promoted the incorporation of loanwords from Latin or Spanish into Mayan languages. In contrast, Thomistic scholasticism and the emphasis on analogical thinking allowed Dominicans to believe that a concept was autonomous from the word that expressed it.[18] Especially in southern New Spain, Dominicans, educated in the humanistic Thomism of the early Salamanca school, thought that local terms, images, or neologisms from non-Christianized cultures could be used to speak and write about Christian concepts.[19] While the mendicant orders were exceptional linguists and authors of the first grammars and dictionaries of Mesoamerican languages, their differing semiotic ideologies—that is, their theories of how signs related to meanings, referents, or other signs including words, material objects, and gestures—inflected their discernment of analogical relationships between the various cultures or language groups and their ability to configure local construals of the Christian god.

In this sense, different applications of humanism affected the Christian educational and devotional writings in Native American languages.[20] For example, among missions to the Highland Maya, Franciscans promoted the use of a K'iche'anized form of "Dios," *Tyox*, for "God," rather than use a Maya term. Furthermore, they translated many local religious terms and images, like *k'ab'awil* in K'iche' Maya, to mean false divinities or "idolatries."[21] In contrast, Dominicans working among the Highland Maya used ethnographic and linguistic research to find terms they could appropriate. One of their initial proposals was *k'ab'awil* for "pure divinity." In other words, for Dominicans, as distinct from Franciscans, the term *k'ab'awil* was understood not only to refer to the stone or wooden effigies used in Maya rituals but also to be an indigenous term for "God."[22]

However, with his work among the Highland Maya, the Dominican friar Domingo de Vico went further than any other clergy, even up to today, in writing the first explicit, original Christian theology in the Americas. For a theologian like Vico, educated at Salamanca soon after Francisco de Vitoria, O.P., introduced the theology of Thomas Aquinas as the curricular standard, theological claims regarding predicates for the Catholic god fell into three basic modes: univocal or positive statements (such as synonymous claims, like "God's essence is Being"), equivocal or negative statements (such as claims addressing opposition, like "God is *not* finite or, thus, is *in*finite"), and analogical statements (positive claims made in terms of similarity-in-difference). For Vico and others facing the challenge of how to translate recondite teachings of Christianity into radically other languages, cultures, and religions, these three kinds of statements, along with the conventional modes of biblical exegesis—especially historical (or conventionally "literal"), allegorical, and tropological (or moral) interpretations[23]—served as their immediate models for cultural translation between Hispano-Catholicism and the worlds of the Americas. Similar to how Aquinas in the thirteenth century sought common ground between the then known different religions by drawing on Jewish and Muslim sources, Vico explicitly turned toward Maya myth and religious discourse in his theological compendium or *summa* for his K'iche'an audience.

Ironically, due to the development of a Latin-based script for Mayan languages and literature for literate Maya, like Vico's *Theologia Indorum*, K'iche'an elites quickly wrote their own texts. To the extent to which Highland Maya texts in the colonial script engaged missionary materials—such as catechisms, sermons, lessons, biblical dramas, and so on—their late postclassic (ca. 1520s–ca. 1580s) documents illustrate a larger, longer conversation that evinces active Maya involvement in the reshaping and maintaining of their religiosity and wider conceptual world.[24] Furthermore, in general, they offer insight from the Maya perspective on their prehispanic social order, elite genealogies, calendrics, history, and cosmogony.[25]

Written between 1554 and 1558, the Popol Wuj in particular has become an increasingly influential text since the 1850s rediscovery of Dominican friar Francisco Ximénez's early eighteenth-century manuscripts. Archaeologists use it as a lens to interpret scenes depicted on ancient murals and pottery; ethnohistorians comb it for indigenous understandings of society, time, and the cosmos; Latin American authors have been inspired by its nonlinear and fantastical narratives; postcolonial theorists cite it as evidence of native resistance to European hegemony since the sixteenth century; and present-day Native American activists—many within the Catholic and Protestant churches—use it as a core text in current Maya religious and social movements. As Mexican author Carlos Fuentes stated, many Maya and non-Maya consider the Popol Wuj the Maya Bible.[26] However, except for recent trends in liberal Latin American theology—such as inculturation theology or "Indian" theology (*teología india*)—the influence of Maya religious narratives on Christian theologians has either been ignored in academic studies of religion or assumed not to have occurred.

While recent scholarship acutely notes the impact of Hispano-Catholicism on Highland Maya, and often their resistance to it in early postcontact Maya texts like the Popol Wuj, too few have begun to consider the diverse ways that indigenous religious narratives influenced early articulations of Christian ideas in the region, as evidenced in the texts by missionaries in local languages addressed primarily to native audiences. While written slightly before the Popol Wuj, Vico's *Theologia Indorum* strategically used Highland Maya names from local stories, legends, and myths to translate a doctrine of his god and the afterlife in authoritative and eloquent Maya discourse. In this regard, critical study of Vico's theological tome for Highland Maya—who, in turn, wrote the first postcontact native literature—helps to fill in some gaps and provide a hyperlocal perspective during this unique period between the 1520s and 1580s. If analyzed intertextually, the written sources authored by various mendicant missionaries and Mesoamerican elites provide a unique glimpse into a colonial encounter. Though this meeting is traditionally construed as a tale of power imbalance or an overt clash, reevaluating these texts reminds us that this was an encounter that defied prefabricated cultural categories or ready-made interpretations from any specific side at the time.

The approach taken here is twofold. First is to situate Vico and his text within the wider context of the intellectual and sociocultural currents within western European Christian thought as well as read and examine as a Mayanist the *Theologia Indorum*. This includes the transition between the late medieval and early modern periods as well as the ethnohistorical framing, dialogical mode, sociolinguistic and philological (specifically from the New Philology movement) attentiveness, and intertextual analysis Mayanists have developed and employed to study Maya texts like the Popol Wuj, such as the *Xajil Chronicle* (or *Kiwujil Xajila'* or *Annals of the Kaqchikel*), *Lord of Rab'inal* (or *Rab'inal Achi*), *Books of Chilam Balam*, and *Title of Totonicapán* and various other notarial documents. The second approach is to read and examine a wider body of early postcontact Highland Maya literature, including notarial or legal documents, as theology; that is to say, as implicit or explicit Maya articulations of their religious worldview during a contentious period of reconfiguration for and by them.

As is examined in greater detail in the subsequent chapters, what holds these two seemingly distinct bodies of literature—mendicant and Maya—together from the vantage point of some mendicant authors, especially those like Domingo de Vico who were products of the first Salamanca school, is an understanding of analogical relations aimed to establish commensurability between, on one hand, the familiar and unfamiliar, not only from human understanding towards an understanding of the divine—what is wholly Other—but also, on the other hand, between cultures and religions, between cultural and religious others.

The textual evidence is less clear from the Highland Maya perspective as to how these two sets of writings hold together. The lack of clarity stems from a shifting accommodation to Hispano-Catholicism that Maya authors demonstrated—an integration in which the Maya did not simply meld mendicant messages with their prehispanic understandings but, rather, strategically treated them as a new historical font on which to justify key features of their traditional world and ways.

Ironically, the Highland Maya arrived at and stabilized their process of accommodation at the period when the Catholic Church was beginning to put an end to its own process of creative and constructive engagement with indigenous religiosity. But, thirdly, what holds these two families of religious documents together from the vantage of religious studies is their intertextuality—that they were all written at roughly the same time, drew from many of the same sets of narratives and discourses (though not always in the same ways), and can be aligned and read as at least implicit responses to each other, dialogically.

THE HYPERLOCAL (VS. THE TRANSLOCAL)

For various political and social factors that exceed the scope here, the decades of early contact with Hispano-Catholicism in the sixteenth and the later decades of the twentieth centuries (consisting of a new Maya awareness or renaissance) are highly analogous, especially in terms of texts produced by Maya. In this respect, the elaboration of written reflections with religious content by Maya in these two moments resembles some recent trends of news production referred to as *hyperlocal media*, signifying news produced by citizen-reporters with little formal training in journalism. Appearing historically in low-cost print or increasingly on online form, hyperlocal newspapers are produced in single-room operations, often someone's home, by one person or small team with tight profit margins. Costs—if not covered out-of-pocket as a labor of love—come from low subscription rates that are *de facto* donations or ads from local businesses or community activists. In addition to low production quality, traditional lines between descriptive reporting and normative editorializing are blurred, as stories draw from crowd-sourced materials that focus on issues of major concern exclusively for a targeted constituency but that might seem insignificant to outsiders. Communicating to and from a highly limited demographic, the full significance and meaning of hyperlocal issues in these endogamous texts are virtually inaccessible to outsiders not familiar with the deeper, historical backstories, which are left as unspoken and obvious to insiders. While used to appreciate the uniqueness of, say, tribal newspapers on US reservations, hyperlocality can be extended to describe the autochthonous theology produced by Maya since the sixteenth century.

While difficult to trace, the term *hyperlocal* emerged in the 1980s among journalists and by 1991 referred specifically to television news coverage and content focused on particular locales, such as at the level of neighborhood communities.[27] By the middle of the first decade of the new century (2005–2008), the use of the term shifted to refer to websites and blogs that dealt almost exclusively with community news either by amateur "citizen reporters" or with the funding of and on platforms by major media brands, such as the *Washington Post*'s LoudounExtra .com for that northern Virginia suburb. Other notable ventures by established print newspapers into this niche area also included the *Local* by the *New York Times*, *Triblocal* by the *Chicago Tribune*, and the *Patch* by AOL. Most of these were deemed failures by 2009–2010, due to limited markets and lack of financial sustainability.[28] Nevertheless, the attention, interest, and promotion of these first two types or waves of hyperlocal news continues to gain traction with, for example, the Hyperlocal Newsroom and Summer Academy of New York University's Arthur L. Carter Journalism Institute.

A third type or wave of hyperlocal discourse arose but declined almost as rapidly by 2012: the internationally outsourced and foreign written but US locally focused production of aggregated news. Namely, the company Journatic, also invested in by the Tribune Company, used overseas journalists in places like the Philippines to pseudonymously write copy about US neighborhoods based on aggregated internet searches or RSS feeds that newspapers in the United States then purchased and printed under false bylines.[29] A July exposé by National Public Radio's program *This American Life* resulted in an investigation into and subsequent waning of Journatic, but ventures like it indicated the merger of two basic earlier trends: (1) the concentrated aggregation of highly localized information begun by websites like Craigslist .com and H2OTown.com, and (2) the drive of global news corporations to survive by seeking profits online in perceivably untapped specialty markets.

As a metadiscourse term like "globalization," "hyperlocal" can have germane applicability within the human sciences, including religious studies, beyond its originating context, comparable to the recent decade's wider appropriation of "glocalization" beyond its coining by Japanese marketing agencies and businesses.[30] In this respect, as listed by Sarah Hartley of Wordpress.com but echoed by other media reporters in stories in the *New York Times* and National Public Radio's program *On the Media*, all three of these kinds of hyperlocalism share common characteristics:[31] (1) a narrow geography or demographic domain ranging from 10,000 to 50,000 people and their shared immediate concerns, issues, values, and internal conflicts; (2) articulation by and gravitation around texts, almost irrespective of the formal levels of education or training of the authors; and (3) acute focus on a scope of concern and extent of arguments and claims that are not construed to speak to a wider audience.

Although still highly undertheorized, "hyper-" in this sense is not merely a diminutive to mean "smaller" but rather is an intensifier that augments the role and value of the immediate, concrete particulars of a community or constituency. In contrast to understandings of "localism" or "popular" culture as theorized initially by the Frankfurt school and now by cultural studies, hyperlocalism is not necessarily a balancing of power to the pressures of global dynamics nor is it merely another or extended locus of resistance, but, rather, it is agnostic to them. This means that, while hyperlocality specifies an additional, smaller, and closer type of intense local connectivity—and thus is not isolated or inoculated from global dynamics—its internal dynamics are not primarily reactions against or responses to outside, wider forces, issues, or concerns. The hyperlocal perspective almost exclusively experiences and interprets the pinch and impinging of wider influences, for good and for ill, as microlocally appropriated in and through radically endogamous texts.

Most important, hyperlocal discourse is not limited to either indigenous American populations in the United States or to social or political texts, like newspapers. Rather, it extends throughout the Americas and includes other types of discourse, such as the moral and the religious. Among the Highland Maya, in particular, recent ethnographic and linguistic scholarship on the moral and religious discursive practices at the hamlet or village level has focused on how wider, common, translocal genres, terms, and images mean differently in various communicative ecologies.[32] One example, as studied by linguistic anthropologist Robin Shoaps, is the production and ritualized use of the annual "Testament of Judas" during the Holy Week festivities among the Sakapultek Maya.[33] This is pseudonymously typed and photocopied communication—most likely by an unknown committee rather than an individual—as an annual open letter to the whole town by "Judas Iscariot" prior to the public hanging of his effigy in front of the Catholic church. It circulates as a moral chastisement of the previous year's scandals—a public shaming of individuals littered with profanity, puns in stereotypical Mayan-inflected Spanish, and clever if not also poetically bawdy turns of local phrases virtually unintelligible to an outsider unfamiliar with the innumerous backstories and local Sakapultek dialect. While seemingly a mere parody of a Catholic epistle or encyclical, and thus not a simple appropriation of and resistance to Hispano-Catholic hegemony and religious global dynamics since the 1520s, this unique tradition within a Highland Maya community actually plays a vital role in the town's unique, deeper, and possibly prehispanic tradition of moral discourse through public advice-giving (*pixab'*) and scolding-gossip (*yajanek*).[34] Seen this way, "hyperlocal" helps specify the scope or range of a communicative ecology, one that is simultaneously very narrow (in terms of audience and authorial appeal) and intense (in terms of multivariegated voices, or heteroglossia, and domains of references, or signification) but not removed from wider, translocal dynamics.

Seemingly an isolated, contemporary example, the unique practice of Sakapultek Maya's annual "Testament of Judas" nonetheless represents a hyperlocal scope of a communicative ecology and, more specifically, the advantage of understanding this text as hyperlocal theology. The particular use or construal of Judas Iscariot and the epistolary genre means differently than it does in any other Catholic liturgical context in Europe or Latin America, historically or presently. Previous underappreciation by social scientists and clergy alike as local superstition, *costumbre*, folk Catholicism, internalized oppression due to colonialism, or popular resistance to historical dominant Ladino culture left Sakapultek Maya religious and moral reasoning largely ignored unless seen as suitable for the scholars' (post)modern or the Church's dogmatic agenda.

To this extent, various types or parts of Maya texts not readily recognized as explicitly religious or moral—or dismissed as mere regurgitations of Catholic religious or moral teachings—may instead be read as a type of theology or as having theological import for and by the Highland Maya in their various communicative ecologies. The Maya authors of these texts may not have much if any formal theological education, especially compared to clergy or academic theologians. However, they still critically, analytically, and constructively reflected upon and evaluated how their world "is" and what they understood it "ought" to be, and how to close the gap between the "is" and the "ought." The extent of such theological claims may not have much traction beyond the immediate world and worldview of the audience of a speaker's family or village, and there may be little to no expectation that a text may last more than a single occasion or couple of generations. The force or appeal of a hyperlocal moral or religious argument, for many Highland Maya, draws more from within their worldview, from a sense of "tradition" or understanding of what has always been done rather than from resources perceived as alien and thus inappropriate for wider comprehension.

Ethnohistorians have noted the extent to which the bulk of early indigenous Mesoamerican postcontact literature consists of notarial documents, and have culled through these texts for political, social, and historical insights from the native perspectives. Yet, little research has gone into why indigenous authors leaned so heavily into Iberian legal genres for their own writings. Presumably, native Mesoamericans were exposed initially and more heavily by their mendicant teachers to pastoral and doctrinal genres, such as sermons, catechisms, dramas and other forms of narrative. However, few indigenous texts take these forms. Again, presumably, as many Mesoamericanists have pointed out, native peoples already had well-established genres, many of which aligned with the legal genres that were introduced by Spanish colonial authorities and that were required of native elites if they were to maintain their status, land, and privileges.

The legal genres served as antecedents to those used later by postcontact native elites. A shift in legal discourse from privileges (*fueros*) to rights (*derechos*) is one of the hallmarks between the late medieval and early modern periods. The boundary between legal and theological concerns was most porous when this shift was occurring in the sixteenth century at places like the University of Salamanca, driven by Thomists like Francisco de Vitoria, his correspondents like Las Casas, and their students like Domingo de Vico and other mendicant missionaries to Mesoamerica. As is touched upon further in chapter 2, indigenous Americans drew upon Iberian sources and mixed them with their own in order to defend their rights, in part because mendicants shared their concerns and taught them many of those genres, legal theories, and lines of argument.[35] And they taught them, not in addition to or aside from, but rather as integral to their theology.

When read as hyperlocal theologies, early sixteenth-century Highland Maya literature—such as the Popol Wuj; notarial texts such as wills (*testamentos* or *memorias*) and land deeds (*títulos*); the earliest known indigenous drama (such as *Lord of Rab'inal*); and indigenous chronicles (such as the *Annals of the Kaqchikel*)—illuminates the levels of autochthonous moral thinking and the reconfiguring of Maya religiosity and worldview during the period of first contact. It does so without reducing their religious or theological construals to simply political, economic, or sociocultural foci and motives, and by transcending dyadic or binary options that limit indigenous thought and agency to merely passive victimhood or reactionary resistance. As texts that engaged, drew from, and implicitly or directly responded to mendicant writings, Highland Maya literature constitutes the earliest indigenous theological writings in the Americas. Many of the texts demonstrate autochthonous contextualizations of Hispano-Catholic claims, narratives, and symbols, not for the wider Church, but for their immediate Maya audience. In contrast to the efforts of mendicant missionaries working among indigenous Americans to articulate universalized religious truths, Highland Maya elites were more concerned with what was theologically true within and for their hyperlocal milieu.

CHAPTER SUMMARY

Through intertextual analysis between contemporaneous early Dominican and Highland Maya writings in K'iche'an languages, the present volme recovers and reconstructs the first original Christian theology written in the Americas, the *Theologia Indorum* by Domingo de Vico. Analysis situates the book's features but also throws light on Vico's sources and influences, construals and claims, and methodology within a transatlantic milieu at the fault line of the late medieval and early modern periods. It traces his book's impact not so much in translocal venues beyond central Guatemala but rather in the highly localized texts—hyperlocal theologies—produced by Maya elites. More broadly, the contention argued throughout is that both of these sets of texts not only can but should be read as theologies—as metadiscourse on their respective religious worlds—although explicitly and translocally for the Dominicans like Vico and more implicitly and hyperlocally for the K'iche'an Maya authors. Furthermore, it is argued that neither set of texts, mendicant or Maya, can be fully understood and appreciated simply on its own terms and its own respective "indigenous" sources (i.e., late medieval and early modern European for the Catholic missionary and ancient Mesoamerican for the Maya) but rather also via their various relations to each other.

However, this volume is therefore less about the dispossession of indigenous Mesoamerican peoples through the collaboration of Christian clergy with imperial Spain than it is about how scholars—Mayanists, those in religious studies, social scientists, historians and ethnohistorians—have often managed their own dispossession of the Maya as well.[36]

In this sense, indigenous Mesoamericans and Catholic missionaries have more than a single story each and, thus, the first two chapters present ethnohistorical and historical contexts. Such narrative contexts often begin the story of first encounters in Europe, explaining the prior conditions of Iberian, including Christian, thought and culture. However, since the story of the *Theologia Indorum* takes places almost exclusively in the Guatemalan highlands, it seems only fitting that the reader is presented with the background beginning with ancient K'iche'an Maya prior to contact with Europeans. Notably, in addition to being based on findings by non-Maya—such as colonial-era documents by clergy and administrators, the archaeological record of the region, linguistic analysis, ethnographies, and so on—the core of the admittedly thin presentation of the postclassic Highland Maya world is based on their own records, which begin within only a couple of decades of the arrival of Iberians, and many of which also show the influence of the *Theologia Indorum*. Along the way, this context argues for a revised set of historical rubrics regarding the Highland Maya, including postponing the application of the term "colonial" until the middle of the seventeenth century (rather than the early sixteenth century) and, correspondingly, extending the preceding "late postclassic" period of the Maya. As many of the documents indicate, from neither the Maya nor the European perspective was it certain until the end of the sixteenth century that the new arrivals and their religion were successfully planted in the Americas to stay. Many of the colonial institutions, considered as expansions, applications, and adaptions of European structures—like the parish—were to not arrive for another few decades after contact. Many historians of the Highland Maya have argued that the local authority of elites did not so much end as transition gradually over time.[37]

This book is divided into three parts, with the specific aims of (1) providing contextual background for scholars of indigenous Mesoamerica or religious studies and history of religions (namely history of Christian thought), or nonspecialists in either, but also suggesting a new historical periodization as conventionally understood, (2) recovering the lost record of Domingo de Vico and his work and gesturing to the reasons for this loss, and (3) tracing the explicit and implicit influence of Vico's theology in the early K'iche'an literature and possibly that of the present-day Maya. Specifically, chapter 1 presents ethnohistorical context about the Highland Maya that contends that the transition from a precontact native "old world" into a colonial "new world" was not as sudden as often imagined. The early impact of epidemic diseases, efforts at relocating and reorganizing local communities, repartitioning lands to new and alien lords, and the destruction of indigenous material culture (including religion) certainly should not be underestimated, but neither should the continuation of indigenous agency, reasoning, and creativity. Given the deep historical consciousness evinced in the early native literature, the extent that they continued to vastly outnumber Europeans in the early decades, and the difficulties Iberians had in holding and administering terrain like the highlands of Guatemala, the permanence of the new arrivals and the changes they brought were not necessarily seen then as a done deal. Many Mesoamerican epics of previous arrivals of foreigners, such as various waves of Nahuas into the Maya highlands, indicate that those earlier invaders themselves eventually became assimilated or K'iche'anized as much as they impacted K'iche' institutions of governance, ritual, and aesthetics, for example. Furthermore, between 1553 and 1921 the Highland Maya of Guatemala instigated at least twenty-five documented, major armed uprisings against colonial and state structures that they considered forms of social, economic, and political, if not also foreign, oppression.[38]

Chapter 2 presents historical background regarding Iberia, its historical multireligious milieu, and what made the Christianity that flourished and migrated initially to the Americas stand out as what may be called Hispano-Catholicism—a Christianity that historically shared features with the wider Latin Catholicism of western and central Europe but that was also distinct from Catholicism outside of Iberia, especially in contrast to those strands that became identified with Protestantism beginning in the 1520s. Of particular focus is the development of a Dominican school of thought that drew from a *longue durée* of intellectual tradition for approaching the religious others. Dominican thought consequently had roots in the medieval era of the Mediterranean region on both sides of the Pyrenees but became distinctively influenced by the final decades of the *Reconquista*, during the development of arguably the first European nation-state with the marriage between the holdings of Aragon and Castile. In the intellectual realm, the resources of humanism combined with Thomistic scholasticism in northern Iberia, notably at the University of Salamanca, where seminal Dominican thinkers were informed and influenced by written accounts and returned clergy from the Americas that reported on indigenous languages, cultures, religions, and histories as well as the treatment, or mistreatment, of natives.

These two first chapters, then, hope to point out how the understanding of terms like "Old World" and "New World" ought to be less geocultural phrases. Instead of referring to contemporaneous Europe and the Americas, respectively as has been usual in the colonial European and Eurocentric literature, descriptively the understanding should rather be of authentically historical phrases in *both* the Americas *and* Europe prior to and then after contact. The conceptualization should be about how postcontact indigenous thought in the Americas and postcontact Hispano-Catholic thought in both the Americas and Iberia emerged as transatlantic, if not also transpacific, phenomena.[39]

Building initially from chapter 2, the second part of this volume, beginning with the third chapter, provides a biography of Friar Domingo de Vico. It is a brief sketch, since little is mentioned of him in the surviving written records. Notably, however, a significant amount of the surviving early literature that mentions Vico, including some of the oldest documentation, is not in Hispanic but rather Maya writings. For this reason, chapter 3 presents more of an "ethnobiography"—that is, to reconstruct an image of the life and work of Vico, with a heavy reliance on indigenous sources. The chapter also, therefore, introduces many of the important Maya and mendicant texts contextualizing not only Vico's life but also his work, namely his *magnum opus,* the *Theologia Indorum,* with a critical assessment of his wider possible written corpus. It thus not only pairs his life and his work but also considers texts by him, about him, and eventually influenced by the construals and interpretive methodology of his work.

Chapters 4 and 5 focus almost exclusively on the *Theologia Indorum,* although not topically, as culled from various parts of his treatise. Rather, the chapters are attentive to the order and manner that he presented his arguments, the mendicant and the Highland Maya sources that he drew upon, and the methods by which he did so. Chapter 4 is the result of reconstructing the text from reidentification and critical assessment of the various surviving partial manuscripts now in scattered archives of the United States and Europe. In part, based on analysis of Vico's structure of his work, his European sources, and comparison with contemporaneous texts used and produced by mendicants in the region, chapter 4 argues for a reassessment of Vico's theology as a *summa*—a theological compendium that incorporates other, non-Christian worldviews and aligns them, or at least accounts for them, analogically, with a Hispano-Catholic worldview. Chapter 5 then examines Vico's theological method and how he engaged Highland Maya theogony and cosmogony, together with his strategic use of writing the *Theologia Indorum* in the high register poetry, or parallelism, of Maya moral and ritual discourse to convey a Christianity. In addition to his method and rhetoric, chapter 5 focuses on Vico's construals or doctrines of god, cosmology, effigies, ritual practices, theological anthropology, and moral reasoning; on how he constructs and conveys these basic religious construals based on what he specifically draws upon, reconfigures, and rejects from Maya religion;

and on how, in turn, that reconfigures the Christianity communicated to the first indoctrinated K'iche'an Maya.

Finally, the third part, beginning with chapters 6 and 7, examines the impact and legacy of the *Theologia Indorum* almost immediately as apparent in some of the earliest and most significant postcontact literature by indigenous Americans. It also further elaborates on the reciprocal relationship between Vico's theology and the hyperlocal theologies of the Highland Maya. Whereas chapters 4 and 5 examine how early mendicant ethnographies on Maya culture and religion became source material for Vico in the production of his theology, chapters 6 and 7 examine how K'iche' and Kaqchikel Maya elites used the *Theologia Indorum* as a touchstone for judiciously incorporating or countering not just Hispano-Catholicism in general but specifically Vico's text. Chapter 6 examines the implied use, chiefly as an argumentative foil, of the *Theologia Indorum* by the K'iche' composer-redactors of the Popol Wuj, one of the most important indigenous American texts. In addition to clarifying perennial questions regarding the Popol Wuj—the influence of a Christianity on and within this set of stories—this intertextual analysis also helps to circumscribe and trace the gradual, initially partial, highly local reception of the *Theologia Indorum* among both fellow mendicant clergy and Highland Maya. Chapter 7 continues this intertextual analysis with a critical assessment of all of the surviving Highland Maya documents that explicitly or even implicitly used the *Theologia Indorum* to present a reception ethnohistory of Vico's theology. It also reexamines the initial heavy Maya authorial influence on Vico, mainly that of Diego Reynoso (a *popol winaq*, or member of the prehispanic K'iche' ruling council) and aides and students of Vico.

Placed within the histories and panorama of Christian thought, the *Theologia Indorum* can be identified, on one hand, as a protoliberal theology in terms of its theological method—that is, the extent to which it strategically and constructively placed traditional Christian sources, such as canonical scripture and historically established teachings, in a mutually informative relationship with non-Christian sources, in this case Highland Maya theogony and ceremonial authority, discourse, and practices. On the other hand, Vico's book is in general doctrinally conservative, with the explicit femininity of the Christian god being a notable exception. Furthermore, from the sensibilities of postmodernity and its suspicion of metanarratives and universals along with an emphasis on the significance of context of many present-day scholars—perhaps ironically akin to the nominalism harbored generally by early Franciscans in Mesoamerica—the semiotics of Vico and the rest of the Dominican school that functioned based on a distinction between form and content may now seem also conservative if not also naive in its understandings of signification and how meaning means. It is not the aim of this book to construct a hagiography of Domingo de Vico or to present an *apologia* for the *Theologia Indorum* or even for the first Catholic clergy, especially Dominicans and their approach, in New Spain or the rest of the Americas. Nor is it to draw too simplistic a contrast between early Franciscans and Dominicans or to rebalance the amount of literature on each.[40] In many respects their differences in Catholic worldview had much more to do with when and where they received their formal education, theological and otherwise, than it did with which religious order they belonged to (or not, in the case of secular clergy) or whether they went to New Spain rather than to the Andean region (although that also made for differences among the Dominicans).[41]

Instead, the aim of this book is to illustrate how critical understandings of some of the earliest indigenous American literature must be enhanced by an equally thorough historical understanding of the different—often contested if not also conflictive—contemporaneously emerging strands of Catholicism, especially in the intellectually and popularly contentious period around the turn of the sixteenth century. In turn, too, historical understanding must extend to how the encounter with the indigenous peoples of the Americas affected the development of those Catholic strands within hyperlocal and also translocal spheres and, most likely, not only at particular moments but also through tracings thereafter, despite various attempts to limit such effects. The Highland Maya writings are among the oldest postcontact autochthonous literature in all of the Americas and, while assuming the genre of notarial documents, they interweave religious thoughts throughout their arguments. The early indigenous arguments were thus not merely sociopolitical claims about the status, power, and privileges of local elites but were also religious and theological arguments about how they understood their world, the origins of that world, and their privileged if not also tragic place in it. Arguments are better understood when juxtaposed with their contextual counterarguments and the intellectual sources, often shared, that each drew upon to be crafted. Finally, although later Christian and Maya discourse can only precariously inform earlier texts, establishing the specifics of how some early postcontact Maya diversely engaged a Christianity can lay a thicker ethnohistorical foundation for later studies on subsequent and current indigenous theologies and their arguments for indigenous rights within Mesoamerica, as among the Maya today.

PART 1

Historical Contexts of the Old Worlds

1

Mesoamericans Shape a New World

K'iche' Maya 101

They [the Hero Twins] descended into Xib'alb'a,
    quickly they descended the face of a stepped cliff.
They passed then
    into the changing of the rivers
        and canyons.
Just through the birds they passed by,
    the ones called throng birds.
They passed over then along Pus River
        and along Blood River,
    intended as traps for them by those of Xib'alb'a.
But they were not bothered,
    and just on their blowguns they passed over them.
They went on to then arrive
        at the four-way crossroads,
but [unlike their father and uncle] they knew then about the roads of Xib'alb'a:
        the Black Road,
        the White Road,
        the Red Road, and
        the Green Road
[and, thus, were not defeated like those before them].[1]

DOI: 10.5876/9781607329701.c001

Xeqej chi Xib'alb'a,
    lib'aj chi' xeqaj chuwa kumuk
Xe'ik'ow chiwi k'ut
    chi upam jal ja'
        siwan.
Xa chuxo'l tz'ikin xe'ik'ow wi,
    are ri tz'ikin molay kib'i'.
Xe'ik'ow chi k'ut pa Puj Ya'
        pa Kik' Ya';
    ch'akb'al ta ke chi kik'u'x Xib'alb'a.
Mawi xikiyikow,
    xa chi rij wub' xe'ik'ow wi.
Xe'el chi k'u apanoq
        pa kajib' xalq'at b'e,
xa xketa'm wi k'ut kib'e Xib'alb'a:
        Q'eqab'e,
        Saqib'e,
        Kaqab'e,
        Raxab'e.

PRODUCTION OF THEOLOGY AT A CROSSROADS, A *XALQ'AT B'E*

Cosmogonic narratives of indigenous peoples of the Americas typically address the origins, structures, and dynamics of the cosmos and all the worlds and other phenomena within it. A common narrative involves a set of twins as culture heroes who finish setting in place the "proper" cosmological order in preparation for humanity. As told in its oldest and most extant form by any indigenous American group, the Popol Wuj, or "Book of the Council," by the K'iche' Maya and quoted above, tells of the Hero Twins' journey into the otherworld, Xib'alb'a, and of their arrival at a four-way crossroads, a *kajib' xalq'at b'e*. Previous travelers, such as their own father and uncle—Jun Junajpu and Wuqub' Junajpu, respectively—had also traveled to Xib'alb'a but chose the wrong path and were thus defeated. Like them, the Hero Twins—Jun Ajpu and Xb'alanke—had to choose a "correct" way at the crossroads.[2] Since the choice of their father and uncle, for example, had introduced corporeal death into the cosmos, the Hero Twins' choice at the crossroads likewise involved great risk.[3]

Similar to the predicament of the Hero Twins, the Highland Maya of Guatemala and Mexico, like other indigenous peoples of the Americas, have often found themselves at a set of crossroads as they have negotiated, and continue to negotiate, the intersections between their indigenous cultural or religious practices and those inherited or adopted from a Christianity, an intersectionality that involves risks theologically, politically, socially, and economically. Variants of a Christianity have been present throughout modern Maya history, beginning with Hispano-Catholicism after the turn of the sixteenth century, and later with various strands of Protestantism, including later charismatic Christianity, by the turn of the twentieth century.

Despite that long religious juxtaposition, studies among the Maya have only recently begun to reveal the risks that Maya have made at such crossroads between Christianity and their indigenous worldview, which since the 1990s is increasingly referred to as Maya Spirituality (*kojb'al* in K'iche').[4] Furthermore, studies of religious, political, and wider cultural movements by contemporary Maya, while quick to make connections from the prehispanic Maya or to upstream ethnographic data back through the colonial era, often fail to develop a fuller context of the decades of first contact based on the surviving records. Indigenous agency and reasoning is often portrayed as either ending or at least permanently corrupted by the early 1500s—a degradation catalyzed in large part by Christian missionaries. Indeed, non-Christian Maya religiosity like *kojb'al* has been denigrated since the sixteenth century by Hispano-Catholic and later Protestant missionaries as "idolatry," "paganism," or "sorcery."

As survivors of ethnocide since the 1520s and of genocide in the 1970s and 1980s, the Maya of Guatemala, including Maya Christians, have often questioned the adequacy of Christian resources for and responses to those two violent bookends of modern Maya history.[5] Since the arrival of Europeans, Maya have interpreted such events and made their claims in part from the conceptual and symbolic resources of what may now be referred to as *kojb'al*. In the past few decades, Highland Maya intellectuals have advocated for an affirming and constructive construal of *kojb'al* as the distinct religious conventions identified by Highland Maya that continue to serve as a reservoir of Maya thought in general and as the core of an indigenous social movement. Maya "spirituality" and its notions of space, time, purpose, authority, agency, language, and culture continue to operate among present-day Highland Maya. Yet the Maya assert that they do not have a "religion" but rather a "spirituality" because they do not yet have a "theology," conceived as metadiscourse on "the religious," broadly identified but still more narrowly as the formal, highly systemic (e.g., doctrinal or dogmatic), apologetic, or confessional thought in the advocacy of a particular religion. Ironically, even those present-day non-Christian Maya intellectuals and their non-Maya allies active in the Maya Movement often implicitly understand religious terms like "theology" as distinctively Christian categories.

In fact, it may simply be impossible to study any Native American religion as unengaged with a postcontact Christianity. With rare exception—as in some of the archaeological records and precontact writings that survived the bonfires and time—all Native American religious texts (written and verbal), symbols, and practices are postcontact. They and their interpretations are affected and infused—for good and for ill, enriched and corrupted, by indigenous practitioners and nonnative scholars—with at least Christianity if not also strands of Islam, Judaism, native west African, or Asian Pacific religions. And even those ancient precontact records can only be read and heard—again, by indigenous practitioners and nonnative scholars alike—through postcontact eyes loaded with one's own implied presuppositions of what qualifies as a "god" versus a "spirit"; or an animism or shamanism versus a kind of monotheism or a polytheistic pantheon; or informed by childhood catechism or Sunday School lessons if not the cultural dominance of Christianty; or post-Renaissance knowledge of Greco-Roman myths; or anti-Spanish imperial "black legend" histories; or even contemporary social science theories, such the latent trinitarianism in the semiotics of Charles Sanders Peirce. Critical study of religion of indigenous peoples in the Americas requires critical understanding of the development of Christianities, and study of Christianities in the Americas requires appreciative and detailed understanding of the worlds of the indigenous peoples of the Americas.

Yet, until recently, continuities or discontinuities between present-day, distinctively non-Christian Maya ceremonial practices and discourse often regarded as "traditional" have received mostly sociocultural and ethnographic study but little historiographic study, except for some analyses that relate current Maya traditionalism to a limited sample of precolumbian and early colonial texts, such as the Popol Wuj. Even less study is devoted to the lengthy, complex, and often mutual engagement between Maya traditionalism and Christianities. Furthermore, often when the history of engagement between a Christianity, such as a Catholicism, and a non-Christianized culture is examined, the analysis begins from the senders' side, usually Europe, in this case Iberia, rather than the recipients' side, in this case Mesoamerica. Implicitly, then, the effort for a more balanced if not also transatlantic understanding is undermined. For this reason, the present analysis of the engagement between indigenous Americans and Hispano-Catholicism begins with a presentation of the Highland Maya, particularly the K'iche' and the wider K'iche'an branch of the Maya, specifically for readers unfamiliar with studies on Mesoamerica and more specifically the Highland Maya.[6] While various studies try to construct a description of the distinct particularities of Maya religion, they too often do so with any of several misleading presuppositions. One is to proceed as if there was only ever one religion, or even in essence one Christianity, in Iberia. Another presumption is that key particularities of religion remained static enough over time and geography to validate comparisons of ancient classic Lowland Maya texts and images with centuries-later postcontact Highland Maya writings or modern ethnographies on the Maya. Synchronic comparison of Lowland Maya texts with linguistically and culturally different early postcontact Mesoamerican peoples, including the Highland Maya, raises methodological difficulties as well. In this sense, writings on native Mesoamerican religions risk creating anachronistic and homogenous protrayals consisting largely of analyses of forms—similar use of etymologically related words, images, and patterns, for example—rather than specifying *how* the *meanings* of such construals shifted temporally, ecologically, and linguistically for a people and among peoples even prior to contact with a Christianity. Due to the precariousness of the evidence regarding specifically postclassic Highland Maya religion leading up to the period of first contact with Hispano-Catholicism, contextual background here is thus largely limited to the social, cultural, and political rather than the religious.

Beyond presenting a basic overview of the Highland Maya, especially for nonspecialists, this first chapter also introduces two perspectival reorientations regarding this period as part of the larger argument for recognizing the role, agency, and contribution by indigenous Mesoamericans in early modern religious thought. First, conventional use of the terms "Old World" and "New World" stem from modern historiography's Eurocentric orientation and, thus, refer respectively to Eurasia and Africa on one side and the Americas, especially as they became European colonies, on the other side. Here I argue for another understanding. Prior to 1492, both the indigenous peoples of the Americas and Europeans lived in their respective old or previous worlds. Postcontact, Native Americans and Europeans engaged in various attempts—via intermarriage, warfare, trade, and so on—to interpret, translate, and respond to, each other.[7] After the initial decades of contact between Native Americans and Europeans, neither of their respective older, precontact worlds would ever be the same. Although trade was not always equal, through the exchange of populations, ideas, crops, artistic styles, diseases, technologies, and values Native Americans, Europeans, Africans, Pacific Islanders, and Asians created transatlantic and transpacific new worlds, if not new world. For this reason, understanding the domains of and the dynamics within and between the hyperlocal and the translocal may be more meaningful categories for reading religious histories.

Second, and more specific to the Maya of Mesoamerica, this chapter argues for a more nuanced understanding of the postclassic era of the Maya. While, as "postclassic," this third historical moment of the Maya is traditionally delineated by the decline of the monumental city-states in the lowlands around 900 CE on the one hand and the arrival of non-American peoples—mostly Iberians but also enslaved Africans—into the region beginning in the 1520s on the other, the documentary evidence from both the Maya and missionaries illustrates a strong, continued, and autonomous agency on the part of the Maya for at least an additional century.

The Spanish colonial administration and the ecclesial structures of the Tridentine Catholic Church (after the Council of Trent between 1545–1563) took firm hold not until the mid-seventeenth century, aided in large part by a near-90 percent population loss among the Maya from imported epidemics but also warfare and trafficked enslavement. The recognition of the role and value of the Maya through this later date then means that the colonial era of the Maya did not begin in the 1520s but rather in the 1650s. Unquestionably, the Highland Maya eventually began to change under the impact of, for example, military campaigns by Spanish-led forces; razing of major population centers, like the K'iche' capital of Q'umarkaj; execution of indigenous regents, as among the K'iche' and Kaqchikel; social reorganization, with the establishment of new mendicant mission towns (*reducciones* or *congregaciones*) or districts (*barrios*) for native peoples near new Spanish towns and local native administrative councils (*cabildos*); and the introduction of different languages, cultural and religious practices, and technologies, including alphabetic writing. At least initially, such social change was not necessarily much different than other times when the Highland Maya were impacted by the different religious, sociopolitical, aesthetic, technological, and linguistic institutions of other native Mesoamericans, such as by the proverbial Toltecs in the thirteenth century. Engagement with religious, cultural, and linguistic others and resultant sociocultural changes were not new dynamics for the Highland Maya.

Furthermore, until the mid-seventeenth century it was not a foregone conclusion that the Spaniards were there to stay, that indigenous military resistance would not eventually overcome this new occupation. In fact, the Spaniards would not defeat the last Maya polity—the Itza' around Lake Petén Itzá[8]—until the 1690s, and the Highland Maya of Guatemala would still launch no fewer than twenty-five separate local rebellions against nonindigenous colonial and national administrations.[9] The Highland Maya texts engaged here and discussed in greater detail with regards to the *Theologia Indorum* in the final two chapters date from the historical period in which native Mesoamericans learned the mendicant alphabet for their indigenous languages and wrote texts responding to but also incorporating Hispano-Catholicism. These texts represent not so much the early colonial as the late postclassic period. Through this modestly expanded understanding of the postclassic era, this chapter serves to sketch the early "new world" milieu of indigenous Mesoamericans.

THE "MAYA" AND THEIR OLD WORLD

The Maya in Mesoamerican History

Maya history does not begin with Christopher Columbus's "discovery" of a boat of what were most likely Yukatek Maya merchant traders off the coast of present-day

Honduras in 1502, or with the subsequent landings in the Yucatán region by Spanish *conquistadores* such as Francisco Hernández de Córdova in 1517 or Hernán Cortés in 1519 as recorded by the first Spanish nonreligious chronicler.[10] Rather, Maya history in this strict sense begins with the first decipherable long-count date written in a Maya hand. Archaeological evidence, however, indicates settlement and continued material development much, much earlier in areas like the Copán Valley of Honduras beginning around 1100 BCE. By 300 BCE scenes of the Maya cosmogonic narratives, some later versions of which were also written into the Popol Wuj, appeared in depictions on monumental structures in Izapa of southern Chiapas, Mexico.[11]

As a designation for a people, the term "Maya" has patchy currency among previous chroniclers, current social scientists, and Maya activists. For purposes here the term pertains to (1) a distinct linguistic family in general and subsequent languages within it and (2) the historical demographic shifts by these speakers and related changes in material culture in the archaeological record. Linguistically, the term "Maya" has often had both a narrower and a wider use. In the narrower sense of the word, "Maya" refers specifically to the Yukatek speakers, largely located in the Yucatán Peninsula of Mexico. In addition to inhabiting a relatively large amount of land in Mesoamerica, Yukatek was also one of the languages of the dominant governing polities when the first seventeen Europeans arrived in the area from a 1511 shipwreck, of whom only two survived—Gonzalo Guerrero and Gerónimo de Aguilar.[12] Guerrero reportedly married into Yukatek society, acquired significant status and wealth, and eventually fought and died with the Yukatek in a struggle against Spanish forces. In contrast, the Yukatek enslaved Aguilar who, in 1519, eventually managed to join Cortés's troops once they too landed on the coast. His time in Lowland Maya captivity made Aguilar an invaluable instrument, as his ability to speak Yukatek could now facilitate a linguistic half of Cortés's interactions with the Mexica (later also referred to as the Aztec) and other Nahuatl speakers.[13] However, this communication between the Spaniards and the Nahua also depended on the work of Malinalli Tenepatl (Cortés's Nahua consort), who constituted the other linguistic half; she translated between Yukatek and Nahuatl as Aguilar could only translate between Yukatek and Castilian until within six months she learned enough Spanish.[14]

Aside from the Yukatek's historic size and political and military power in the area at the time of contact, as well as the role of an accidental Castilian-Yukatek speaker, Aguilar, for negotiating such contacts, Yukatek Maya language and culture was also later virtually treated as the norm in the twentieth century in early anthropological, archaeological, and epigraphic studies of ancient Maya civilizations. The use of the Yukatek language in excavations of Lowland Maya sites located in and around current Yukatek speakers and in the cracking of the Maya code of the glyphic script was further reinforced by the existence of some of the few early Maya books written in a Mayan language but with a Latin-based script, a corpus referred to as the nine *Books of Chilam Balam,* or "prophecies of the jaguar priests," as well as the *Rituals of the Bacabs* and some other notarial texts in Yukatek.[15] Finally, in addition to the glyphic writing carved on classic-era buildings and monuments found in lowland archaeological sites and the Latin-based orthography of seventeenth-century Yukatek manuscripts, the importance of Yukatek Maya also appears with the only four Maya books written in glyphs known to have survived the book-burnings of the sixteenth century: the Dresden Codex, Paris Codex, Madrid Codex, and Grolier Codex. As this litany of emphases makes clear, "Mayan language" or "ancient Maya civilization" has often meant either specifically just the Yukatek Maya, or only the Lowland Maya of present-day western Honduras, Belize, El Petén of Guatemala, and the Mexican states of Quintana Roo, Yucatán, Campeche, Tabasco, and eastern Chiapas.

In the wider sense of the word, though, "Maya" refers to a unique macrofamily of languages historically and presently spoken in southern Mexico, Guatemala, Belize, western Honduras, and northern El Salvador. While hypothetically there once existed a single proto-Maya language, over the course of centuries thirty-one distinct languages or "linguistic communities" evolved and are presently spoken in the wider region, including Wastek, a distantly separated Mayan language north of Veracruz, Mexico (see table 1.1). Today, some of these languages—such as Yukatek in the Maya lowlands or K'iche' in the Maya highlands—have easily over a million speakers and include several distinct dialects within each of them. However, many other of these languages have so few modern speakers that they are on the verge of extinction within the next generation. Despite the literary propensity to call these language groups "dialects," these languages are, at their most proximate, as similar as Castilian is to Catalan, and, at their most distinct, as different as Norwegian is from Italian. Likewise, the dialects within the Mayan languages, such as the six or seven spoken within K'iche' Maya, can be as distinct as Hyperion or "Queen's English" is from Ebonics (or US "inner-city vernacular"), or as similar as English spoken by a Minnesotan and a Texan.

However, in general, the linguistic macrofamily of Maya divides into five large or "greater" branches: Greater Yukatekan, Greater Ch'olan, Greater Q'anjob'alan, Greater K'iche'an, and Mamean.[16] Where the dominant languages during the ancient classic era of the Maya (ca. 200 CE–ca. 900 CE)—and thus the languages of the glyphs in the large lowland city-states—were primarily Ch'olan and Yukatekan, speakers of the K'iche'an branch of languages (see lines 25–34 in bold in table 1.1) came to politically dominate the highlands in the centuries just prior to contact with Europeans and produced some of the most significant texts during the time of early contact. Within this branch of Greater K'iche'an languages, a smaller, more closely related group of speakers of K'iche'an languages—K'iche', Kaqchikel, Achi (or Eastern K'iche'), and to a lesser extent Tz'utujil—dominated the postclassic era, especially after 1200 CE. Therefore, for the purposes of this book, and in terms of language family, "K'iche'an" refers to the Greater K'iche'an branch of the Maya, and in terms of sociopolitical history, "K'iche'an" refers to the peoples of the various postclassic Maya polities. The more specific uses of the term "K'iche'"—namely the Nima K'iche' (Great K'iche') clan and Ajaw K'iche' (Lord K'iche') lineage within the Q'umarkaj confederation—are further clarified below when the polity and history of the Western K'iche' ruling from Q'umarkaj are discussed.

In general, Mayanists have divided the history of the Maya people and the Maya region into two parts: (1) "prehispanic," "precolumbian," or "precontact" Maya refers to the period prior to the arrival of Spaniards and other Europeans in the early sixteenth century, and (2) "Hispanic," "colonial," or "postcontact" Maya distinguish the era after the *Conquista* in which joint Spanish and central Mexican forces (composed of Nahua, Mixtec, Zapotec, and other indigenous allied peoples from north of Guatemala) entered and administratively took over the Maya region. Scholarship by ethnohistorians, postcolonial theorists, and Maya activists in the recent decades has attempted to redress this Hispanocentric approach to the history of the Maya by reexamining and reappreciating sixteenth- and seventeenth-century documents written by Highland and Lowland Maya.[17] By focusing closely on a few of these Highland Maya texts, the aim here is to cooperate further in this correction by arriving at a new understanding of the sixteenth century in light of Maya and mendicant relations and their theological production.

As a Mesoamerican people, the Maya shared in a set of cultural traits concentrated in the areas of present-day central and southern Mexico, Guatemala, Belize, and western Honduras and El Salvador, but with commonalities spread thinner as far south as present-day Costa Rica and as far north as the southwestern United States. Among these traits are a 260-day ritual calendar; a dietary and farming complex centered on maize, beans, and squash; monumental plazas, causeways, large carvings, and multileveled residential and ceremonial compounds; recreational and ceremonial ball games; money based on precious metals, stones, feathers, and cacao; and extensive trade networks. The various peoples of Mesoamerica had differing levels of stratified and specialized social structures, systems of literacy and numeracy, and material technology. The first phases of settlement patterns in the region constitute the preclassic era, in which a group or artistic style called the Olmec moved along the southern basin of the Gulf of Mexico, across the Isthmus of Tehuantepec, and along the Pacific coastline of Guatemala to Costa Rica.[18] By around 250 CE significantly large and highly organized Maya populations in the eastern lowland tropics had began to build sizable city-states which, at their height

Table 1.1. Mayan languages and areas where presently spoken*

Language	*Area Spoken*
1. Wastek (Huastec, Tenek)	Mexico (San Luis Potosí, Veracruz)
2. Chicomuseltek (Chicomuceltec)	Mexico (Chiapas, extinct)
3. Yukatek (Yucatec, Maya)	Mexico (Yucatán Peninsula region)
4. Lakantun (Lacandón)	Mexico (eastern Chiapas)
5. Itza' (Itzá, Itzaj)	Guatemala (El Petén)
6. Mopan (Mopán)	Guatemala (El Petén) and Belize
7. Ch'ol	Mexico (Tabasco and Chiapas)
8. Ch'ontal (Yocotán)	Mexico (Tabasco)
9. Ch'orti' (Chortí)	southeastern Guatemala, western Honduras
10. Ch'olti	(extinct)
11. Tzotzil (Tsotsil, Quelén)	Mexico (Chiapas)
12. Tzeltal (Tseltal)	Mexico (Chiapas)
13. Mocho' (Motozintlec, Cotoque)	Mexico (Chiapas)
14. Tusantek (Tuzantec)	Mexico (Chiapas, extinct)
15. Popti' (Jacaltec)	Guatemala (Huehuetenango)
16. Akatek (Acatec)	Guatemala (Huehuetenango)
17. Q'anjob'al (Kanjobal, Conob)	Guatemala (Huehuetenango)
18. Tojolob'al (Tojolobal, Chaneabal)	Mexico (Chiapas)
19. Chuj	Guatemala (Huehuetenango)
20. Mam	Guatemala (Huehuetenango)
21. Tek (Tectitec, Teco)	Guatemala (Huehuetenango)
22. Awakatek (Aguatepec, Aguacatec)	Guatemala (Huehuetenango)
23. Chalchitek	Guatemala (Huehuetenango)
24. Ixil	Guatemala (El Quiché)
25. Q'eqchi' (Kekchí)	Guatemala (Verapaces)
26. Uspantek (Uspantec)	Guatemala (El Quiché)
27. Poqomchi' (Pocomchí)	Guatemala (Verapaces)
28. Poqomam (Pocomám)	Guatemala (southeastern)
29. K'iche' (Quiché, Kiché)	Guatemala (El Quiché)
30. Achi (Rab'inal)†	Guatemala (Verapaces)
31. Sipakapenese (Sipacapa)	Guatemala (San Marcos)
32. Sakapultek (Sacapultec)	Guatemala (El Quiché)

continued on next page

TABLE 1.1—*continued*

Language	*Area Spoken*
33. **Kaqchikel** (Cakchiquel)	Guatemala ("old capital cities" region)
34. **Tz'utujil** (Tzutuhil)	Guatemala (Atitlán)

Sources: Coe (1992, 48); Kaufman (1974, 85); England (1994, 4; 1999, 7–9); Oxlajuj Keej Maya' Ajtz'iib' (OKMA) (1997, 15–29); Academia de Lenguas Mayas de Guatemala (ALMG): http://www.almg.org.gt/index.php?option=com_content&view=article&id=12&Itemid=7 (as of January 2010).

* Greater K'iche'an languages are indicated in bold.

† Linguistically Achi is an eastern dialect of K'iche', however given both the strong historical political separation between the Western and Eastern K'iche' (Achi) and the distinct literary tradition of Achi (e.g., the prehispanic dance drama *Rab'inal Achi*), Achi (also occasional listed as Achi') is recognized as a distinct language or "linguistic community" by the ALMG.

during the apex of the classic era, ranged in populations from 30,000 to 500,000 for an average of 50,000 people per polis.[19]

This demographic growth accompanied expansion in social and political structures and technologies. In addition to the invention of a concept of zero and a vigesimal, or twenty-based, number system, the Maya developed an elaborate writing system with distinct symbols for both phonemes and basic concepts; this double system ensured that members of both dominant lowland languages—Yukatek and Ch'olan—could read the same inscriptions on monuments.[20] These classic texts provide evidence of highly developed religion and organizational structures. Found on large stone-carved monuments, ceremonial pottery, pieces of jade and bone, and folding-screen codices, or books, these inscriptions are of characters and events in the Maya cosmogonic stories, and the terms found in the writing—for instance the use of the emblem glyph for *ajaw* ("lord") in various titles for historic persons or legendary divinities—indicates the emergence of specialized civic and religious offices of leadership during this time.[21] For sets of complex reasons that archaeologists continue to debate—ranging from overpopulation and overproduction, environmental exhaustion and calamity, famine and nutrition-deficiency-based diseases, and increased territorial expansion, competition, and warfare for resources—construction of these Lowland Maya city-states ceased by 900 CE, though the population did not.

The Highland Maya and the Making of a Postclassic Era

With rare exception, such as the construction of the early city-state of Kaminal Juyu', which now lies underneath present-day Guatemala City, and some sites toward the southern Pacific coast, like Tak'alik Ab'aj, little significant material development occurred during the classic era in the Maya highlands of what are now Guatemala and Chiapas, Mexico, in contrast to the lowlands of either the Pacific coast or the Caribbean basin.[22] The proverbial decline or "fall" of the Lowland Maya around 900 CE appears to have relieved the Highland Maya populations of the pressure of growing and exporting foodstuffs to increasingly demanding lowland consumers and, thus, created a political vacuum that local highland leaders began to fill in the new postclassic era. This is not to say, however, that Lowland Maya civilization ceased. On the contrary, major Lowland Maya city-states in the Yukatek region, such as Chichén Itzá, Mayapán, Izamal, Maní, and T'ho, may have waned in the late classic period but were on the rise again by 1200 CE, sporting strong central Mexican cultural influences in their artistic styles, architecture, ceremonial dress, Nahuatl loanwords and concepts, and thus also most likely sociopolitical and religious ideas. The reemergence of some lowland sites corresponded to the new emergence of the Highland Maya during this era.

The archaeological record of highland sites along with later sixteenth-century written K'iche' sources, such as the Popol Wuj and *Title of Totonicapán*, and Kaqchikel sources such as the *Xajil Chronicle* (also known as the *Kiwujil Xajila'*, *Annals of the Kaqchikel*, *Memorial of Sololá*, or *Memorial of Tecpán Atitlán*), all tell of a small but significant wave of migration from the eastern lowlands into the western highlands of the Maya region from "across the waters," from a place called Tulan, Tollan, or Tula, probably around 1200 CE.[23] Comparative linguistic and archaeological evidence, however, indicates that K'iche'an speakers migrated from the northwestern area of the highlands as far back as 2700 BCE but had separated from the proto-Maya linguistically by 1600 BCE to became a distinct language group by 1000 BCE, and arrived in their current territory of the west-central highlands of Guatemala as early as 600 BCE.[24] A large base of locally speaking K'iche' people, therefore, preexisted the arrival of those smaller groups of people described as coming later "from the east."[25] While an ancient Mesoamerican site called Tula does exist in northern Mexico, the mythical Tulan referred to in the Highland Maya texts as a place of origin most likely does not reach that far back in time or far away to a specific city. Tulan may mean "place of the cattail reeds" in the central Mexican language of Nahuatl. However, the name is more probably a general term for an urban area, with implied reference back to the earliest cities, such as the Olmec settlements of La Venta and San Lorenzo along the marshes of present-day Tabasco, Mexico, between the Nahua- and Maya-speaking regions.[26] Someone from an urban area—from a "tulan" or "tollan"—could be referred to as a "toltec," which described the central Mexican, Nahuatl-speaking wave of merchant-soldier-settlers who arrived and influenced the rebuilding of some of the older Lowland Maya city-states in the early postclassic period.

In addition to increased artistic, archaeological, social, political, and linguistic influences into the Lowland Maya region from central Mexico, a confluence of religious understandings also occurred. Through redaction and source criticism of the archaeological record, sixteenth- and seventeenth-century Maya documents, and modern ethnography, Dutch ethnohistorian Ruud van Akkeren has argued that two distinct religious complexes combined during the period.[27] The first and older religious tradition for the Lowland Maya region was symbolically, ritually, and mythically oriented around maize. The second religious tradition, brought down from the north from less-maize-reliant cultures like the various Nahua peoples of central Mexico, was more oriented symbolically, ritually, and mythically around the Sun. Together, these initially different Mesoamerican religious systems did not so much replace or displace each other in the Maya lowlands, but rather enfolded and augmented the meaning of the stories about the domain of the gods in the fashioning of the cosmos and in sustaining human life—be they narratives regarding the divine "birth," "death," and "rebirth" of the cosmic Sun or of terrestrial crops, or enacted in the rituals of the Maya theater-state, such as ball games, fire offerings, or bloodletting rites.

Beginning in the late classic period and continuing into the early postclassic period, three identifiable waves of Toltec or epi-Toltec migrants followed the Usumacinta River from the lowland region into the highlands to settle among the K'iche'an peoples. The so-called Toltecs provided the K'iche' Maya with models for social and political structure, consolidation, and gradual expansion.[28] The reemergence of some lowland cities in the Yucatán Peninsula suggests the Toltec leadership of the Lowland Maya sent emissaries to the Highland K'iche'an Maya. K'iche'an texts possibly make references to Toltec cities such as Chichen Itzá, Mayapán and Copán as a specific "Tulan," and to the Laguna de Términos or the Usumacinta River as possibly one of the major bodies of water crossed "in the east."[29] Where the arrival of a leadership class of Maya influenced by the Toltec movement from the north previously marked a distinction for Mayanists between the early postclassic period and the late postclassic period, the production of K'iche'an texts in the sixteenth century that help shed light on the postclassic era in general constitutes a mild reorientation. The milestone of 1200 CE in Highland Maya history, therefore, marks instead the transition between the early postclassic period and a newly designated period—the middle postclassic period—so that the "late postclassic period" better designates the transition in the wake of European arrival beginning in the 1520s (see table 1.2).

As stated in the beginning of this chapter, previous historians have distinguished between the early postclassic period (ca. 900 CE–ca. 1200 CE) and the late postclassic period (ca. 1200 CE–1524 CE), thereby implying that Maya intellectual

Table 1.2. Modified historical divisions of the Maya

Historical Eras/Periods	*Estimated Years*
Paleo-Indian Era	ca. 20,000 BCE–ca. 8000 BCE
Archaic Era (end of the proto-Maya)	ca. 8000 BCE–ca. 2000 BCE
Preclassic (or Formative) Era	
Early Preclassic Period	ca. 2000 BCE–ca. 900 BCE
Middle Preclassic Period	ca. 900 BCE–ca. 300 BCE
Late Preclassic Period	ca. 300 BCE–ca. 200 CE
Classic Era	
Early Classic Period	ca. 200 CE–ca. 600 CE
Late Classic Period	ca. 600 CE–ca. 900 CE
Postclassic Era	
Early Postclassic Period	ca. 900 CE–ca. 1200 CE
Middle Postclassic Period	**ca. 1200 CE–ca. 1500 CE**
Late Postclassic Period*	**ca. 1500 CE–ca. 1650 CE**
Colonial Era	
Colonial Period	ca. 1650 CE–ca. 1820 CE
Neocolonial Period	ca. 1820 CE–ca. 1950 CE
Pan-Maya Movement or Maya Renaissance	ca. 1950 CE–present

* Also conventionally labeled the "Conquest" of the Maya and early colonial period.

influence and autonomous agency ended with the arrival of Europeans. However, as argued here, the Maya and mendicant textual evidence indicates a continued, albeit decreasing, Maya cultural independence through at least the middle of the seventeenth century. As signaled in bold in table 1.2, that cultural continuity warrants the extension of the "late postclassic period" until at least the 1650s and the creation of a new understanding of the preceding period, between ca. 1200 CE and ca. 1500 CE, better designated as the "middle postclassic period."

The K'iche' Maya and the Middle Postclassic Period

After building a series of semifortified settlements southward through the northeastern Guatemalan highlands into the central highlands and eventually to the heads of the Motagua River, by 1200 CE the acculturated so-called Toltec influenced the formation of local leadership among those K'iche' concentrated in a new urban area on a set of plateaus referred to by archaeologists as the K'iche' Basin or *Q'umarkaj* in K'iche' and later as *Utatlán* in Nahuatl especially after the arrival of the Spaniards and their Nahua allies in the 1520s.[30] Between roughly 1225 and 1325 CE the K'iche' confederation developed by incorporating preexisting clans or tribal groups into an increasingly complex and stratified political and social administration and by expanding in all four geographic directions to acquire additional territory, peoples, and material resources. Within later K'iche'an writings regarding this period of expansion and consolidation, a new national narrative of the elite genealogies of regents and their deeds was grafted onto the older corpus of Maya cosmogonic narratives, integrating elements from local groups along with those of a Toltec heritage. For example, by 1425 CE the main K'iche' regent—*ajpop* ("keeper of the mat")—was named after the amalgamated Nahua mythical and historical characters of the Plumed Serpent (*Quetzalcoatl* in Nahuatl, *K'uk'ulk'aan* in Yukatek, and *Q'ukumatz* in K'iche'). Extraordinary powers were attributed to the K'iche' regent Plumed Serpent, who was listed as the sixth or seventh direct descendent from the first humans created out of maize dough by the divine grandmother Xmukane and the principal creator deity, the Framer and Former (*Tz'aqol B'itol*). He was also credited with establishing the new capital city for the K'iche' nation—Q'umarkaj. Though Q'umarkaj was newly constructed, its name ("Place of Rotten Cane," or "Place of the Old Reeds") alluded to Tulan, the legendary primal city "Place of the Cattail Reeds." Q'umarkaj's layout (which overlies seven caves, as is also said of other ancient mythical and actual Mesoamerican capitals) and architecture (which included temples, plazas, ball courts, and causeways) articulated its legitimacy by such harkening back to older exemplary cities.[31]

The main sixteenth-century histories written by the Highland Maya, such as the Popol Wuj, emphasize that the K'iche' nation, though based in Q'umarkaj, was actually composed of the Western K'iche' in the center but also the Eastern K'iche' or Achi in Rab'inal to the east, the Mam and smaller groups to the north, the Kaqchikel to the south, and the Tz'utujil to the west between Lake Atitlán and the Pacific coast. Most of these groups are referred to as *winaq,* roughly translated as a "people" or "nation," within both the K'iche' texts and the other Maya people's surviving texts of the sixteenth century, such as the *Xajil Chronicle*.[32] The sixteenth-century highland texts mention three distinct subgroups of the K'iche' *winaq* at the time of the migrations from the lowlands, and refer to these groups as *amaq'ib'* (roughly "tribes").[33] Corroborating archaeological and linguistic evidence indicates that the three subgroups—the Nima K'iche' ("Great K'iche'"), the Tamub' ("Drummers"), and the Ilokab' ("Seers")—were preexisting K'iche' speakers who then consolidated around 1200 CE close to the archaeological site known as Jakawitz.[34] Each of these three tribes contains a composing set of moieties, and each moiety consists of two major lineages or clans. The lineages, in turn, inherited the civic and ritual titles, emblems, and authority of the major ruling offices, as well as geographic territory; by the 1520s, there were at least twenty-four titles held by twenty-three royal houses or dominant lineages (see table 1.3).

Of the three *amaq'ib'*, the Nima K'iche' or Great K'iche' eventually dominated political and religious control of the Q'umarkaj-based nation. Within the Nima K'iche,' the Kaweq (*Kaweqib'* in the plural) lineage or clan in particular consistently managed to occupy the top two offices of *ajpop* ("regent") and *ajpop k'amja* ("vice regent") (see table 1.3 in bold). However, the other three major lineages within the Nima K'iche' *amaq'*—the Nija'ib,' Ajaw K'iche,' and Saqik'—along with the Kaweqib' divided the bulk of the highest-ranking offices among themselves, legitimating their claims mythically by tracing genealogies in which three of the four groups descended directly from three of the four primary couples, the first ancestors created out of maize dough by the Framer and Former.[35]

Each of these four major lines affiliated with one of four spiritual protectors or tutelary spirits: Tojil, Awilix, Jakawitz, and Nik'aqaj Taq'aj. Although scholarly and popular literature on the Highland Maya often refers to these protectors as "gods," here this term is generally avoided because it is not used in the Maya texts, it is especially loaded with Judeo-Christian-Islamic connotations, and it is one of the principal concepts that early mendicant missions to Mesoamerica, like that of Domingo de Vico, set out to explore and unpack in their focus on an indigenous doctrine of god, as detailed in the following chapters. Regardless, in conjunction with specific political offices, each of the four major lineages also held the priesthood or title of the ritual specialist dedicated to one of the four spiritual protectors of the Western K'iche' nation. For example, the Kaweqib' held the office of *ajtojil* (literally "he of Tojil," "keeper of Tojil," or the Tojil priest), the Nija'ib' held the office of *ajawilix* (the priest for Awilix), the Ajaw K'iche' held the office of *ajakawitz* (the priest for Jakawitz), and the Saqik' held the office of *ajtz'utuja* (the priest for the Tz'utu Ja).

The major lineages or clans within the Tamub' and Ilokab' held other positions on the ruling council, such as *q'alel* ("judges"), *ajtzij* ("heralds"), and *nim ch'okoj* ("dramatists") (see table 1.3 in bold). These last two sets of offices, considered the most knowledgeable about legendary histories and national genealogies, most likely became the principal authors, transcribers, and redactors of the sixteenth-century K'iche'an texts like the Popol Wuj, *Title of Totonicapán*, and *Lord of Rab'inal*.[36] Furthermore, while not able to claim direct descent from the first generation of human beings in the Maya cosmogonic myth, lineages of the Tamub' also held offices entrusted to the top two dominant tutelary spirits: an *ajtojil* of the Kaweqib' and an *ajawilix* of the Nija'ib' (see table 1.3 in bold). In this respect, a distribution of religious or ceremonial offices among the principal ruling houses dovetailed or overlapped with the distribution of administrative offices.

Table 1.3. Divisions within the polity of the Western K'iche' *winaq* (nation)

First Eight Ancestors	*Tutelary Deity*	*Tribe*	*Moiety*	*Lineage*	*Offices, Titles, Ranks**
B'alam Kitze' and Kaja Paluna	Tojil	Nima K'iche'	Kaweqib'-Ajaw K'iche'	Kaweqib'	**Ajpop**
					Ajpop K'amja
					Nima Rajpop Achij
					Ch'uti Rajpop Achij
					Nim Ch'okoj
					Ajtojil
					Ajq'ukumatz
					Popol Winaq Chituy
					Lolmet Kejnay
					Popol Winaq Pajom
					Tepew Yaki
Majukutaj and Tz'ununi Ja	Jakawitz	Nima K'iche'	Kaweqib'-Ajaw K'iche'	Ajaw K'iche'	**Ajtzij Winaq**
					Lolmet
					Nim Ch'okoj
					Ajakawitz
B'alam Aq'ab' and Chomi Ja	Awilix	Nima K'iche'	Nija'ib'-Saqik'	Nija'ib'	**Q'alel**
					Ajtzij Winaq
					Q'alel K'amja
					Nima K'amja
					Uchuch K'amja
					Nim Ch'okoj
					Ajawilix
					Yakolatam
					Lolmet Ye'oltux
Ik'i B'alam and Kaq'ixa Ja	Nik'aqaj Taq'aj or Tz'utu Ja	Nima K'iche'	Nija'ib'-Saqik'	Saqik'	**Ajtz'utuja**
					Q'alel
	Tojil (Awilix)	Tamub'	Eq'o'amaq'	K'opichoj	**Ajtzij Winaq**
					K'okutum
					Makwil Tuch
					Saqrij Tum
					Saqrij Kamachal
					Q'aleyol
					Nim Ch'okoj
					Uchuch K'amja

continued on next page

Table 1.3—*continued*

First Eight Ancestors	*Tutelary Deity*	*Tribe*	*Moiety*	*Lineage*	*Offices, Titles, Ranks**
	Tojil (Awilix)	Tamub'	Eq'o'amaq'	Kochoja'n	Q'aletam Ajpop K'amja **Ajawilix** Julajuj
	Tojil	Tamub'	Qaqoj	Majkinalo	**Q'alel** **Ajtzij Winaq** Q'alel K'amja Nima K'amja Nima Pop Ajwajxaq **Nim Ch'okoj** Ajyakola
	Tojil	Tamub'	Qaqoj	K'oq'anawil	**Ajtojil** Ajyatas Julajuj Ajyakola
	Tojil	Ilokab'	Chiyatoj-Chiyatz'ikin	Roqche'	**Q'alel** **Ajtzij Winaq** Utzampop
	Tojil	Ilokab'	Chiyatoj-Chiyatz'ikin	Kajib' Aj	**Q'alel** **Ajtzij Winaq**
	Tojil	Ilokab'	Yolchitun-Yolchiramaq'	Sik'a Xuwanija	**Q'alel** **Ajtzij Winaq**
	Tojil	Ilokab'	Chipel-Kanmuq'el	Wukmil	

Sources: Ayer Ms 1515, fols. 35v–36r, 37v, 43v, 45r; Carmack (1981b, 157–163; 2001b, 196–197, modified); Carmack and Weeks (1981, 330, figure 4); Mondloch and Carmack (2018, 321–322).

* Ranks or titles discussed throughout are listed in **bold**.

In the capital city complex of Pa Ismachi' and Q'umarkaj on the plateaus of the K'iche' Basin in 1350 CE, the placement of administrative palaces and temples dedicated to the spiritual protectors symbolized the nexus of the sociopolitical with the religious life. It also represented in the integration of the wider cultural elements of the K'iche' and other local non-K'iche'an Maya with Toltec influences. The strategic placement of temples and courts articulated an architectural network of checks and balances between the various *amaq'ib'* and respective lineages. For example, the main plaza of Q'umarkaj locates the main temples of three of the four tutelary spirits or deities at (such as Jakawitz in the south) or facing toward their respective cardinal directions (such as Tojil in the west facing east and Awilix in the east facing west) with the main council hall of the Kaweqib' in the north and a round temple in the middle of the large plaza square dedicated to Tepew Q'ukumatz, the "Sovereign Plumed Serpent." The Kaweqib', in addition to holding the title of *ajtojil* ("keeper of Tojil"), also held the office of the priest for the Plumed Serpent, or *ajq'ukumatz* (see table 1.3 in bold). Various levels of city planning, from capital complexes to the smallest neighborhood plazas and outlying towns, repeat this organizational pattern.[37] In other words, in both the smaller residential plazas within urban Q'umarkaj and in the main plazas of other surrounding towns, temples to the main tutelary spirits—especially Tojil—were built and celebrated with corresponding ceremonies entrusted to designated lineage-officeholders.[38]

Under the leadership of Q'ukumatz's successor, *Ajpop* K'iq'ab', the K'iche' confederation reached its apex in the mid-fifteenth century. At this point, the nation encompassed virtually all the Guatemalan highlands, included the Pacific coastline, and reached as far north into present-day southern Chiapas, Mexico. Between the regencies of *Ajpop* Q'ukumatz and *Ajpop* K'iq'ab', the K'iche' and affiliated groups composed a multilingual confederacy that also included other K'iche'an groups and other non-K'iche' Highland Maya—such as the Mam and Ixil—as well as non-Maya Nahuatl speakers to the south, referred to as the *Yaki* (later known as the *Pipil* after the 1520s).[39] According to various sixteenth-century K'iche'an texts like the *Xajil Chronicle* (or *Annals of the Kaqchikel*), the Popol Wuj, the *Title of the K'oyoy*, a set of early writings by the Nija'ib', parts of the *Xpantzay Cartulary* like the "Wars of the Sotz'il and the Tuquche'," and other such notarial documents along with archaeological evidence of the area, the half-century 1400–1450 CE was especially prosperous for the K'iche' confederacy.[40] The emergence of a Highland Maya realm that extended beyond a significant city-state paralleled the rise of the Mexica, or Aztec, realm and their capital of Tenochtitlán between ca. 1350 and ca. 1520 CE. With the Nima K'iche' based in Q'umarkaj, Tamub' based in Pa Ismachi', and Ilokab' based in Pa Ilokab', their political configuration echoed the contemporaneous Mexica Triple Alliance in the north.[41]

Ironically, this period of growth and enrichment was bookended by two moments of internal violence. First, around 1400 CE, *Ajpop* K'oka'ib', Q'ukumatz's father and predecessor, was assassinated in a revolt by one of the other leading lineages, the Ilokab'; and around 1450 CE younger members of *Ajpop* K'iq'ab's own household overthrew him and exacerbated tensions between the other governing lineages within the K'iche' confederacy. Second, in addition to this *coup d'état*, the expansion program and integrity of the confederation began to unravel. To the east, in a battle documented in the only existing prehispanic play, the *Lord of Rab'inal*, the Eastern K'iche' or Achi of Rab'inal militarily defeated the Western K'iche' of Q'umarkaj and permanently established the former's sociopolitical independence. To the south, aided by the unseated former regent K'iq'ab', the Tz'utujil and Kaqchikel Maya rebelled against Q'umarkaj's new leadership and established their own respective capital cities of Chi Ya' (near present-day Santiago Atitlán) and Iximche' (near present-day Tecpán).[42] By the time the Spanish-led combined military force of Europeans, Nahuas, Zapotecs, and Mixtecs entered the old realm of the Western K'iche' in early 1524, the K'iche' polity of Q'umarkaj was on the wane and the newer Kaqchikel polity had begun to dominate the Tz'utujil, Poqom, Xinka, and Yaki.[43]

Postclassic Highland Maya cities like Q'umarkaj and Iximche' had ceramics, carvings, murals, and multitiered buidings. However, compared with their distant kin in the lowlands of the Yucatán Peninsula or even of the ancient Guatemalan Pacific coastline, the earlier K'iche'an Maya of the classic (ca. 250 CE–ca. 900 CE) or preclassic eras (prior to ca. 250 CE) built few ancient metropolitan city-states and left few of the major archaeological sites with monumental architecture or inscribed glyphic texts on walls, stelae, elaborately painted ceramics, or carved jade.[44] Nor did they write any known hieroglyphic books, so their languages today are not as useful for deciphering the ancient Maya script. They did, however, write; and because of their early postcontact writings—arguably among the first sixteenth-century texts written exclusively by indigenous authors, in indigenous languages, for their indigenous audience—ethnohistorians, in large part, can reconstruct the preceding sociopolitical narrative—that is, histories based on indigenous sources. Helpfully, unlike their textual Mexican peers or *títulos primordiales* by Nahua, Mixtec, and other native elites farther north, the Highland Maya authors tended not to backdate their documents to make them appear more ancient, and thereby more authoritative, than they were, but instead their documents have reliable composition and copy dates attributed to them.

Curiously, though, with rare exceptions, such as the Popol Wuj or even the *Rab'inal Achi*, the clear majority of indigenous Mesoamerican literature in general, and Highland Maya literature in particular, was composed not of religious material but rather of modified variations of European notarial genres. Rather than draw from and customize the pastoral genres introduced by clergy—such as sermons, doctrinal lessons, and devotional dramas—Highland Maya authors borrowed from and customized the then-new legal genres brought from Iberia, such as wills (*testamentos*), affidavits (*autos*), land titles or deeds (*títulos*), bills of sale (*cédulas*), legal charges or orders (*despachos de ámparos*), rulings (*real ámparos*), or treatises or contracts (*convenios*). They did so in a way that used the notarial genre as a macroformat or housing within which they could still employ many of their prehispanic indigenous genres, namely cartographic histories or pictorial narrative maps (*lienzos*), accounts of events in the lives of important people *(res gestae)*, and annals or historical entries listed by continuous year-counts or calendrical cycles.[45]

On one hand, the popularity of the notarial genres among early Highland Maya authors could be due to many of the same factors and concerns that led other Mesoamerican elites to write these kinds of documents. Their historic elite powers, privileges, and properties were under attack and these documents were part of the means to defend them recognized by the new European authorities. On the other hand, these regions were under heavy evangelization efforts of Dominicans in particular. Much of Dominican theology—including understanding of human nature, the design and dynamics of the natural world, the normative will of the Christian god, the planned course of cosmic and human history as discerned through biblical interpretations, and thus also the normative understanding of human society, peace, and true justice—involved an increasingly elaborate theory of natural law and legal discourse. Translations of K'iche'an religiously ethical terms found in both the early postcontact writings and present-day moral discourse of Maya elders tends to focus on the theological meanings—such as "sin" for *mak*, "prohibitions" for *awas*, "counsel" for *pixab'*, or "word" for *tzij*—yet these same K'iche'an terms also have legal import—"norms" (*mak* and *awas*), "judgments" (*pixab'*), and "truth" (*tzij*).

For both the Highland Maya and the Dominicans, legal construals, discourse, and genres were intimately bound with religious ones. This was especially the case for those Dominicans who studied at the University of Salamanca, and it stood them in contrast to other clergy, such as Franciscans from various convents outside of Salamanca, Augustinians especially from Valladolid, and even seculars not from Salamanca. Thus, just as Dominicans affected by the encounter with indigenous American peoples would also make legal arguments,[46] many of these early Mesoamerican texts can and should also be read as indigenous theologies. Within the histories of Christian thought, most of the earliest theologies were defenses or apologetics, and in the first century they largely took epistolary form, such as the cases of Paul of Tarsus or the Johannine community. Later came philosophical dialogues, such as with Justin Martyr, and even explicit genres of legal defense, especially in the Latin Roman west. The early Mesoamerican texts from an emerging Maya Catholicism thus fit into wider intellectual histories on both sides of the Atlantic.

CONCLUSION: TRANSITIONS TO A NEW LATE POSTCLASSIC MAYA

Militarily the Spaniards managed, intentionally and unintentionally, to take advantage of both the recent internal divisions within the Western K'iche' leadership and the competition between the once dominant K'iche' of Q'umarkaj and other newly independent and emergent Highland Maya nations, specifically the Kaqchikel of Iximche'. As with their military victory over the Mexica farther north in Tenochitlán only a couple years earlier in 1521, the Spaniards employed a divide-and-conquer strategy that pitted Highland Maya factions against each other and imported central Mexican factions that had been vying for greater influence in the Highland Maya regions for decades prior. As reflected in the early Highland Maya writings, this arrival was only the latest in a centuries-long history of migrations and layerings of peoples, bringing their languages, cultures, and particular religious narratives and practices into the highlands from the Pacific coastline and the eastern lowlands, and from the north. As is discussed later regarding the Popol Wuj, the arrival of mendicant missionaries seems to have provided a warrant and a new technology—alphabetic script—for the Maya to document their worldview, but it did not necessarily yet generate a competing religion. In fact, while qualitatively distinct in many respects, the Popol Wuj is only one of an estimated forty extant autochthonous K'iche'an texts written by Highland Maya elites within the first several decades of engagement with Christian missionaries. Such early postcontact writings constitute an indigenous textual response that has often been overburdened by non-indigenous accounts.[47] Or as current intellectuals and writers like Chimamanda Ngozi Adichie might phrase it: despite efforts by K'iche' elites to collect and redact together various narratives, the prehispanic and early postcontact Maya never had only a single story. This early written evidence, often used by ethnohistorians to piece together a prehispanic series of events, illustrates that, for the sixteenth-century Highland Maya, incorporating other religious symbols, rites, terms, and concepts within their own indigenous theological complex was nothing new.

Over this sociopolitical, linguistic, and religious landscape came the additional complex of Catholicism, specifically from Iberia and, more specifically, by diverse kinds and waves of mendicant clergy. Competition was already tense between secular clergy and religious (regular) clergy on one hand, as well as between the various religious orders of regular clergy—namely between the mendicant orders of Dominicans and Franciscans—on the other hand. To limit frictions among the clergy, the Highland Maya region was apportioned into separate domains. To the Dominicans were given the central K'iche'-speaking highlands and northward into Chiapas; the Eastern K'iche'-, Q'eqchi'-, and Poqom-speaking areas on the eastern slopes; and a limited number of far northern Kaqchikel towns close to the K'iche' region, including the eastern area of Lake Atitlán. The Franciscan domains were the main Kaqchikel-speaking region of the southern highlands, most of the region around Lake Atitlán, and the Pacific coastline, including much of the far western highland slopes, which also spoke K'iche'. In addition to political factions along generational lines that pitted young rebellious leaders against older established governors, precontact Maya were divided by competion between lineages, including their respective historic allies. The competing kinship units often shared ritual devotion to a tutelary spirit or "god," which exacerbated growing linguistic divisions between emerging Maya national identities. The arrival of distinct generations of Catholic mendicants and their schools of thought into an unstable indigenous politico-religious mix of this kind compounded the highly local ecologies of the Highland Maya with new and translocal means to engage each other and an increasingly wider world. It is a brief historical overview and breakdown of the diversity within this Catholicism that the next chapter addresses.

2

Mendicants Shape a New World

Transatlantic Catholicisms

é encima de ciertas sepulturas y enterramientos, cruces, las cuales diz que tienen entre sí en mucha veneración, trabajaréis de *inquerir e saber por todas las vías que ser pudiere, e con mucha diligencia e cuidado, la significación de por qué las tienen, porqué hayan tenido o tengan noticia de Dios* nuestro Señor y que en ella padeció hombre alguno, y sobre esto pornéis mucha vigilancia y de todo, por ante vuestro escribano, tomaréis muy entera relación . . . Ternéis mucho cuidado de *inquerir e saber por todas las vías e formas que pudiéredes si los naturales de las dichas islas o de algunas dellas tengan alguna seta, o creencia o rito o ceremonia en que ellos crean, o en quien adoren, o si tienen mezquitas, o algunas casas de oración o ídolos o otras cosas semejantes, e si tienen personas que administren sus ceremonias, así como alfaquíes o otros ministros*; y de todo muy por estenso traeréis ante vuestro escribano muy entera relación, que se la pueda dar fe.

and over the certain tombs and graves [on Cozumel], *there are crosses* of which it is said that among them *there is reverence*. You must work to *investigate and know by all means what this could be, and with much diligence and care what meaning that they have, why they might or would have news of God* our Lord and the suffering of some man. And over this you should be very vigilant and with everything before your scribe take a detailed account . . . Take much care to *investigate and know by all means and forms as to whether the natives of these islands [Mexico] have some religion, beliefs, rites, or ceremonies in which they believe or in whom they worship, or if they have "mosques" or some houses of prayer, or wise men or other ministers.* And with everything take extensive note in front of your scribe for a detailed account so that if may be faithful.[1]

DOI: 10.5876/9781607329701.c002

INTO THE 1520S

Despite conventional depictions of a singular, monolithic, homogenous Christianity—especially of Catholicism and particularly of Catholicism in Spain by the sixteenth century—the histories of the composing influences and, thus, strands of a Christianity even beginning in its first few decades reveal a wide amount of diversity. The diversity of Catholicism, if not Catholicisms, found in the written records of Mesoamerica may be due to the encounter with the various and complex indigenous cultures of the region but did not originate as a result from it.[2] In fact, despite apologetic claims of uniformity by European Christian writers leading up to, through, and in the wake of the Council of Trent (1545–1563), the effort to successfully define, sustain, and defend such an ideal was the perennial anxiety of the age because so much of the historical, intellectual, and practical reality was so different both on the ground and in the universities. And the encounter with the Americas forever augmented those differences.

Many scholars on the development of Christianity among indigenous Americans are well versed in the local languages, cultures, and social and political histories. Nevertheless, understandings of histories of Christian thought, practices, and institutions, both leading up to and during the sixteenth century, are often too thin for a descriptively balanced portrayal of the transmissions—including conceptual translations—and local receptions of a Christianity. Therefore, this second contextual chapter aims to provide a general yet detailed background on the development of Hispano-Catholicism—Catholicisms in Iberia—specifically geared to those interested in how it bore on Mesoamerica beginning in the 1520s. Many early mendicant missionaries emerged from a Hispano-Catholicism that was far from being a homogeneous or monolithic "orthodoxy." Those missionaries who went to the Americas and Asia embodied long traditions of attempting to integrate diverse religious realities into coherent wholes rather than merely suppress them. Failure to situate mendicant texts written in indigenous American languages within the varied and at times competing intellectual strands of Christianity risks misreading them and, in turn, misunderstanding the Catholicisms that developed among their indigenous recipients.

THE IBERIANS, THEIR OLD WORLD HISPANO-CATHOLICISMS, AND TRACING A PREMODERN RELIGIOUS LANDSCAPE

The sociocultural landscape of Europe is certainly no less complex than that of Mesoamerica in this period, and there are more historical writings than are available on the Maya. In addition to the various waves of Celtic, Carthaginian, Hellenist, Roman, and non-Indo-European peoples such as the Basques, Christian roots in the Roman territory of Hispania appear to date to at least around 180–188 CE with Bishop Irenaeus of Lyons's reference to "those churches which have been planted... do not believe or hand down anything different... in Spain."[3] The late first-century *First Epistle of Clement* refers to Paul of Tarsus as "having taught righteousness to the whole world, and come to *the extreme limit of the west*." Legend and Christian tradition interpret that statement as proof that the Apostle Paul had completed a journey to Iberia, a plan he mentioned around 50 CE in his letter to the churches in Rome.[4] By the early fourth century—sometime around 313 CE—Christian churches in Iberia met as a local council, or synod, in the town of Elvira (also referred to as Illiberis and Elliberis) outside of present-day Granada. As one of the three early synods that would serve as an antecedent to the larger ecumenical or general Council of Nicaea I in 325 CE, this Synod of Elvira focused on many of the distinctions and tensions within Christianity, and between Christianity and the other religious practices and beliefs of the region, and the effects on converts from and to all of them.[5]

However later legends set the date of the arrival of Christianity much earlier, with stories of the Apostle James, or *Santiago* in Spanish, also traveling to Iberia in the early decades of the Christian movement, thus making the pilgrimage route across Europe and northern Iberia to his supposed tomb in Compostela, Galicia, one of the major events of the medieval era. However, James's travels in Iberia do not appear in writing until the 600s CE, and popular devotions did not become prominent until the 1000s CE, when he became the patron saint known as Santiago Matamoros (or Saint James the Moor-slayer) to northern Catholics battling the Muslim caliphates in al-Andalus.[6]

Early Christians in Iberia would have interacted with the other religions of the Roman Empire: local and rural religions or pagans (in the literal and technical sense of the term), Judaism, and older Israelite religions. While some midrashic readings of the Book of Jonah understand the place of Tarshish as the ancient western Mediterranean seaport of Tartessus on the Iberian Peninsula, Iberian Jews self-identified as part of the exiled community from Jerusalem to a land the Book of Obadiah called Sepharad.[7] Despite modern scholarly debates on the demographics in ancient Roman Hispania and the formation of the community of el-Sepharad during the first century BCE or after the destruction of the Second Temple in Jerusalem around 70 CE, a highly significant and influential Jewish population flourished in southern Iberia until the sixteenth century.[8] This interreligious confluence would come to bear in a particular way on Dominican thought in general but especially in northern Iberia by the 1530s. For example, the works of Moses ben-Maimon—also known as Maimonides, a rabbi, physician, and Aristotelian philosopher—as well as by Muslim Aristotelian scholar Abu al-Walid Muhammad bin Ahmad bin Rushd, or Averroes, both from thirteenth-century Córdoba, would later become essential sources for Thomas Aquinas's theological scholasticism.

However, even within the formation of Iberian Christianity, or Christianities, there was always a notable diversity. For Iberia, the most influential early Christianities arrived via the migration of Visigoth (western Gothic), Suevi, Vandal, and Alan Arian Christians from central Europe between 409 and 416 CE. Theological tensions grew between the Trinitarian grammars of Arian Christianity (which held that the second *persona* or "person" of the Trinity—the Son—was subordinate to the Father) and Nicaean Christianity (which held that all three *personae* of the Triune God were coequal, coeternal, and consubstantial). By around 589 CE, however, discord eased when King Reccared, Visigothic magistrates, and Arian Christian bishops adopted the previously unpopular Roman Catholic Nicaean position. As a result of this agreement in the early seventh century, prominent Christian theologians like Isidore of Seville and Ildephose of Toledo began to lead liturgical reforms to unify the various Christian religious practices, if not also their significance, of late ancient Hispania.[9] At the same time, a series of reforms by a line of Iberian Visigothic kings reconciled ancient Roman and Gothic customs and legal systems in unified codes like the *lex romana visigothorum*. By the time of the northern migration of Muslim Berbers led by Tariq ibn Ziyad from across the Straits of Gibraltar in 711 CE, these contemporaneous reform efforts established a basis for a policy of religious coexistence, or *convivencia*, and a distinct Christian worshiping community under Muslim rule in southern Iberia—the Mozarabs.[10]

Within a matter of decades, rival north African Berber and Arabic forces (though later consolidated under exiled Syrian caliphs—the Ummayads under 'Abd al-Rahman I, displaced from Damascus) held part of southern Gaul and most of Iberia except for the northern mountainous territories of Asturias and Cantabria. While the fluctuating border between a Catholic-governed north and a Muslim-governed south gradually moved southward until 1492, the demarcation facilitated two notable religious distinctions. First, the political and linguistic differences between the Latin north and Arabic south severed early attempts for unified Christian discourses. The Hispano-Catholicism in the northern Iberian kingdoms gravitated toward the later reforms of the Carolingians, the Bishop of Rome (also later called a Pope), the Benedictine Order, and the Cluniac reformation. The Hispano-Catholicism in the southern Muslim caliphates and emirates conserved the initial rite of Roman Visigothic Latin while engaging with both Byzantine, or Hellenistic, Christianity and the wider Islamic milieu for a distinct Arabized Christianity and Mozarabic liturgy.[11]

Second, the demarcation's slow change meant some distinctions were murky: the various polities and elites not only competed against each other, often despite religious affiliation, but also frequently switched "sides," with "Catholic" forces sometimes led by Muslims and "Muslim" forces sometimes led by Catholics. For example, even the heir-apparent to the throne of Castile-Leon, Alfonzo VI, spent nine months in self-exile in Muslim-ruled Toledo under the protection of the caliph al-Ma'mun; and the legendary "El Cid" Rodrigo Díaz of the Catholic north served for five years in the forces of Ahmad al-Muqtadir and Yusuf al-Mu'tamin, the consecutive rulers of the ta'ifa of Zaragoza.[12] In fact, until the final decree of expulsion in 1609 by King Felipe III of Spain, *mudéjares,* or Spanish Muslims, lived, worked, and contributed to the culture in the Catholic territories and spoke their own dialect of Castilian Spanish, referred to as *aljamía,* which they wrote in Arabic characters rather than a Latin-based script.[13] Some of these *mudéjar* populations consisted of skilled migrants who were hired out, thus, then considered as a kind of labor tariff, in addition to other monies, paid to Christian rulers by Muslim rulers.

In essence then, technological and intellectual skills crossed and remade the religious boundaries as often as military action did. For example, in the tenth century CE the caliph of Córdoba, 'Abd al-Rahman III, and his son and successor al-Hakam, assembled a community of scholars in their court; the group included a Greek Christian monk named Nicolas sent by Byzantine emperor Constantine Porphyrogenitus and at least one Jewish scholar, Hasdai ibn Shaprut.[14] The Archbishop Raimundo of Toledo, a strong advocate of *convivencia,* created a translation school in the early twelfth century that attracted a diversity of scholars and their works and libraries, including texts on "astrological science" and "magical art" from around Iberia.[15] Thirteenth-century King Alfonso X the Learned continued the war of the *Reconquista* ("Reconquering") to the south. But his court also sponsored an intellectual exchange that coincided with the emergence of the Kabala's *Zohar* by Rabbi Moisés de León in Catalonia and an interest in alchemy from al-Hakam II's emirate of Córdoba, along with translations of Arabic works on physics, medicine, and astronomy.[16] The Catholic and Muslim milieux also each maintained highly religiously, linguistically, and culturally diverse populations among the local peoples and elites. Castilian-speaking rulers maintained a policy of *convivencia,* and Arabic-speaking rulers recognized both *musalim,* or converts to Islam, as well as the *dhimmi,* or the non-Muslim "protected people," namely Christians and Jews. Under Muslim rule in the ninth century, for instance, there were eighteen dioceses and twenty-three bishops, and by the eleventh century, the Mozarabic population consisted of 30 percent of the general population in these areas.[17]

By the fourteenth century, however, various trends began to impinge upon these pockets of Iberian cosmopolitanism. In the Muslim-dominated south, beginning in 1040 CE, religiously conservative schools of Islam such as the Almoravids migrated north across the Straits of Gibraltar—some from as far south as present-day

Senegal—determined to redress any apparent laxism among Andalusian Muslims. In the Christian-dominated north, economic crisis, wider intolerance of religious differences within Catholicism, an increased perception of Iberian Sephardic and *mudéjar* populations as a fifth column for the Turks during the gradual defeats of the Byzantine Empire, and the Crusades in the eastern Mediterranean all culminated in the massacres of Iberian Jews in 1391, even in historically cosmopolitan cities like Toledo. Increased pressure for conversions and religious uniformity in late medieval western Christianity gave rise to new religious orders. Some, such as Francis of Assisi's Order of Friars Minor (O.F.M., or "Franciscans"), rejected monastic hermiticism in favor of a peripatetic engagement with the local public as mendicants, friars, or "begging monks." Others, such as Domingo de Guzmán y Aza's Order of Preachers (O.P., or "Dominicans"), emphasized preaching in particular. Both began in the early thirteenth century.

Gradually, an ethos of *limpieza de sangre* or "pure [Christian] blood" won out over traditions of *convivencia* in Catholic Iberia and increased attention to converts as well as to distinctions between New Christians and Old Christians. Among New Christians, terminology developed to distinguish between general converts (*converso*) and converts from Islam, called *morisco* (those from "Morocco," even though they were actually from Iberia). Pejoratively, Jewish and Muslim converts to Christianity—who were switching from religions that forbade eating pork to a religion that used one's willingness to eat it as a trial for the sincerity of the conversion—were also referred to as *marranos* or "pigs." In Iberian Hebrew, divisions could also be drawn between Sephardic Jews who willingly converted to Christianity, or *meshumadim*, and those who were forcibly converted, the *anusim*. Furthermore, the distinction between Old and New Christians depended not only on one's own subscription to Christianity but also on how far back one could trace pure Christian "blood" before locating a *converso* on the family tree. Therefore, not only were *ladinos*, *mudéjares*, *moriscos*, *meshumadim*, and *anusim* suspect, so were other Hispano-Catholics, such as Mozarabs. The Mozarabic rite in Toledo was successfully defended from complete imposition of the Roman rite in a series of struggles in the 1100s CE, but the use of the rite was restricted to six parishes. Thus, as more parts of al-Andalus fell under Christian control, subsequent Mozarabic populations in southern Iberia needed to relocate to Toledo if they did not want to convert to the Christianity endorsed by kingdoms of north Iberia.[18]

An emerging concern not only for conversion but for graduating New Christians into Old Christians across the generations did not immediately replace the religious diversity under *convivencia* with a concern with *limpieza de sangre*, but it did make the religious landscape more complex. The result was a range of terms, questions, and approaches to addressing religious, cultural, and linguistic diversities.

This pattern's roots are in the 313 CE Synod of Elvira, when Hispano-Catholicism began recognizing religious others and valuing their distinctiveness. Early on, specific attention fell on addressing, critiquing, and coexisting with a diversity of customs, laws, rites, and teachings, as well as spoken languages and scripts. Initially in Iberia and later in the Americas, late fifteenth-century Christian Iberian thinkers employed the specific resources of classical humanism and a renewed interest in scholasticism to frame the major debates on how to navigate between cultural and religious differences.

Schools of Translation: Humanism, Nominalism, and Thomism

Development of the Salamanca School

Historians of Europe debate about when the Renaissance began. Scholars of French history, for example, commonly prefer dating the "rebirth" of Western civilization to the Carolingian Kingdom. Yet, the roots of intellectual "renewal" and the "rediscovery" of ancient Greco-Roman thought runs deep in Iberia, too, especially in the kingdoms and caliphs closest to the Mediterranean Sea. It may be difficult to argue for a "rediscovery" of Aristotle in a region where Jewish and Muslim intellectuals like Maimonides and Averroes lived and taught. In the Christian regions of Aragon and wider Catalunya, mendicants inspired by the likes of Ramon Llull strove to master not only Latin to access classic Christian and non-Christian texts but also Arabic and Hebrew. The tasks of textual studies—composition, interpretation, translation, grammar, and philology—along with theology as part of a liberal arts curriculum were integral to a renewed emphasis on the craft of preaching and theories of religious conversion. The Order of Preachers, the Dominicans, in particular developed a network of language schools, or *studia*, in southern and eastern Iberia in the thirteenth century specifically dedicated to training the friars in Arabic, Hebrew, or both.[19] And while there is no direct link between these medieval Dominican language schools in Iberia and the language schools dedicated to Castilian, Greek, Latin, Nahuatl, and other indigenous Mesoamerican languages that Franciscans and Dominicans established in New Spain, they do speak to an ethos of language ideologies among Iberian mendicants that disposed them toward valuing non-Christian cultural sources and thought in general.

In the wake of the spiritual reforms of later mendicants, but specifically of the *devotio moderna* and the reforms in philological and critically historical studies of textual development related to humanism, the Renaissance in Iberia began to crystallize with Diego de Deza, O.P., when he served as *prima* chair of theology at the University of Salamanca from 1480 to 1486.[20] Deza is better known for his later tenure as head of the Spanish Inquisition and conflicts with humanists like Antonio de Nebrija, but his earlier reforms at Salamanca influenced the first Dominicans who arrived on the island of Hispaniola in 1510—namely, Pedro de Córdoba and Antonio Montesinos. They condemned the abuses against indigenous Caribbean peoples, and in 1522 persuaded then Father Bartolomé de las Casas, owner of slaves and a large estate in Cuba, to join the Dominicans. The distinctive Dominican model of evangelization was grounded in the scholastic theology already characteristic of the 1510 Dominicans' "preachers only" method of evangelization, which excluded soldiers and entrepreneurs. It set up the model later followed by Las Casas, Vico, Luis de Cáncer, and others of their cohort, foregrounding a concern with *how* to see their Christian god's presence among indigenous cultures and practices. Relatedly, Tommaso de Vio Cajetan, one of the most influential interpreters of the works of Thomas Aquinas, was master general of the Dominican Order when Dominicans first arrived to Hispaniola. He thus provided much of the initial Thomistic theological support for the Dominican model of evangelization in his commentary on the *Summa theologiae* (IIaIIea, q. 66, a. 8).

The major impact and reception of Thomistic scholasticism, especially widely influenced within the Dominican Order by Cajetan and as shaped at the University of Paris by Peter Crockaert, did not occur in Iberia until the 1520s. For example, Córdoba's catechism was posthumously translated and published in Nahuatl, becoming one of the first books published in the Americas, but there is no evidence that he or others in his early Dominican cohort wrote catechisms or sermons in Taíno, thus marking a distinction between the early waves of Dominican missionaries prior to the 1530s and those of the next decades, influenced by Friar Francisco de Vitoria, O.P. As Erasmus's popularity reached its apex at Iberian universities in Salamanca and Alcalá in the late 1520s, Vitoria returned from Paris, where he had studied the works of Aquinas in the wake of the tenure of Peter Crockaert in particular.[21] Crockaert himself, a student of John Mair, thus began as a nominalist influenced by the philosophical theology of William of Ockham. But he converted to Thomism, joined the Dominican Order, and moved to teach at the University of Paris, where his influence later initiated the second rise of Thomism in 1524. By virtue of his academic pedigree, Vitoria was named the *prima*, or principal chair, of theology at Salamanca once held by Deza and, in turn, fostered an influential blend of the previously established humanism in northern Iberia with his newly imported Thomostic scholasticism that then spread to the universities in Valladolid, Seville, Evora, Alcalá de Henares, and Coimbra.[22]

Notably, however, the dominance of Crockaert on Vitoria mitigated the rigidity of Cajetan, who not only read Aquinas's understanding of analogy as strictly analogy of proportion but also promoted it as a reigning theological method for establishing commensurability through much of European Catholic theology from

1511 into the twentieth century.[23] While Aquinas in his *summae*—*Summa contra gentiles* and *Summa theologiae*—explicitly defined analogical understanding in terms of proportional relations, he did not limit his use of analogy in his theological writings to only this kind. Aquinas's use and understanding of his logic of analogy was more nuanced, broad, and flexible than that developed by Cajetan. Whereas Cajetan focused on the relationship between names and the essence and existence of things in general, but especially as related to making claims about the names or attributes and the being of the Christian god within Aquinas's theology and theory of signification, Aquinas also focused on *actus*, the actions and works of the Christian god.[24] The students of Vitoria at the University of Salamanca—such as Vico, as evidenced in his *summa*, the *Theologia Indorum*—also did not seem to limit their understanding and use of analogical thinking strictly in terms of proportional relationships when considering the Americas as part of the divinely created world, or when comparing and contrasting Catholic and indigenous thought. Vitoria was influential for other clergy in addition to Dominicans, such as Franciscans like Bernardino de Sahagún, who also studied at the University of Salamanca during this period of humanism and scholastic reform. However, Franciscans would not have resided at the Dominican convents of San Esteban and Santo Domingo de la Cruz. More often, theological formation for Franciscans—as well as for other mendicants, like Augustinians from the monastery in Valladolid, who would missionize the Otomí in northern New Spain—occurred not at the universities but in the various conventual schools specifically for their respective novitiates. Thus, depending on the religious order, the specific region in Iberia, and the particular period during these reforms in the educational and theological curriculum, clergy leaving for the Americas were schooled in any variety of often competing theories of signification, translation, and theological method.

In addition to the development of a particular strand of Thomistic humanism, or humanist Thomism, as part of the early Salamanca school under the reforms of Vitoria, two other related contexts played into the shift from a late medieval to an early modern world for Iberian mendicants: theories of translation and theories of signs or semiotics, both of which dovetailed with theories of interpretation or hermeneutics of not only scripture but also of cultures. Regarding the former, the most influential treatise on translation published between the late medieval period and early modernity, Étienne Dolet's 1540 essay, *La manière de bien traduire d'une langue en autre*, outlined five basic principles for translation.[25] Historians of translation theory have argued that these principles were already used in Iberia by the fourteenth and fifteenth centuries, especially translations of Jewish and Muslim texts from classical languages into Castilian and Catalan.[26] Furthermore, the influence of Erasmus's humanism—which stressed rhetoric and philology, critical interpretation of texts, and studies of classical and vernacular languages—led to the production of the first systemic grammars and lexicons in Iberia on Latin, Castilian, and Arabic around the turn of the sixteenth century.[27] Attention to humanist language ideologies coincided with the political consolidation of Spain and conversion efforts toward historic Jewish and Muslim populations.[28] As these early translators attempted to apply the humanism of the *Reconquista* in Spain to the peoples of the *Conquista* in New Spain[29] and Peru, they began to develop new translation strategies for a distinct register of doctrinal and pastoral discourse as they also had done in Arabic, but now with unfamiliar non-Indo-European and non-Semitic languages, few of which had language ideologies that involved writing.[30]

Simultaneously and related to this shift in translation theories are also the significant changes in book and writing culture in Iberia during the sixteenth century. While historians often survey the inventories of the early printing presses—especially the earliest in the Americas in Mexico City, Lima, and Santiago de Guatemala—Spain by the 1550s had developed a practice of the *corre manuscrito*. Not limited to a specific genre, this kind of manuscript text allowed for privacy among its limited circle of readers, thus avoiding review by authorities like the Holy Office, but also structurally remained flexible for revisions and the incorporation of additional material.[31] Furthermore, much of university education, especially in the early universities in the Americas, such as in Mexico City, Lima, and Santiago de Guatemala, involved students who were often seminarians, copying *verbatim* and by hand the texts of their courses in order to have personal manuscript copies of their readings of Aristotle, Ovid, Cicero, Augustine, Aquinas, and the like. For early transatlantic mendicants, both of these practices within a manuscript-oriented but developing book culture built off of the prior development by Franciscans, Dominicans, and other mendicant orders and their small, highly portable *vade mecum* ("go with me") genres. All of which may help explain the curious development and limited circulation of the manuscripts of Vico's *Theologia Indorum* in the Guatemalan highlands.

Competing Semiotics: Aquinas and Bacon Come to Mesoamerica

The second, and perhaps most fraught, of the wider intellectual shifts in Iberia leading up to and during the period of first contact between mendicants and indigenous American peoples were the debates within scholasticism between Thomistic and nominalistic semiotics. In brief, the roots of the division went back to many of the classical sources that Christian scholars rediscovered in the middle medieval period and subsequently in movements like the Renaissance and humanism. Prior to Latin Christian philosophers, ancient Greek thought, namely Aristotle (384–322 BCE) and Stoicism (such as Zeno of Citium, ca. 334–ca. 262 BCE), distinguished between signs and words. By late antiquity, however, Augustine of Hippo (354–430) in his taxonomy subsumed words (*voces*) as a species or subset of signs (*signa*). Slightly later Boethius (480–524), whose Latin translations of Plato and Aristotle would be authoritative until Arabic works used by Christian thinkers corrected his limitations, conflated Aristotle's key Greek terms of *symbolon* (the symbolic relation between a word and letters) and *semeion* (the iconic relation between a concept and a thing), considering both to be *nota*.[32] The result of both on early Christian thinkers in the Latin west was to conflate distinctions between the internal (or mental) and the external (or material, natural) dimensions of the acts of referencing, signification, interpretation, and translation. However, beginning with the *Dialectica* of Peter Abelard (1079–1142), western Christian thought began to distinguish the intentional—emphasized by Augustine and his semiotics of signification—from an extensional aspect of semantics in the relation between the word and things in the world as it pertains to defining and naming.[33]

The Franciscan Roger Bacon (ca. 1214–1292), especially in his later writings on signs, would later contribute to an understood shift of the locus of a referent as being, not in the mind, but rather in the objects and structure of a divinely created reality. Bacon's classification of the different kinds of signs to systematize and reconcile these distinct historical strands marked the shift away from a philosophical interest between the internal motivations and intentionality, on one hand, and emitted vocal sounds, like words, on the other, for a more concerted focus on the relation between words and states of the world, the expression-content relationship.[34] As an extreme realist, Bacon's contribution to the shift in western Christian thought of signification from an intentionalist to an extensionalist understanding coincided also with his locating universals in the singular particulars of the world, the beginnings of a shift away from an ontological status of universals for eventually the particularist position of nominalism like that of William of Ockham, O.F.M. (ca. 1287–1347).[35]

Prior to Ockham, though, John Duns Scotus, O.F.M. (ca. 1266–1308) further built on the latent extensionalism of Abelard, breaking with the traditional Latin reading (or misreading) of Aristotle to instead shift the locus of universals from the ideational concept to the *res* ("thing"), or particular object. For Scotus and then for Ockham and later nominalists, words signified things rather than concepts or ideas. While in part it is an overgeneralization to say that Franciscans were nominalists and Dominicans were realists, nominalism developed in the thirteenth century, led largely by Franciscans in reaction to the perceived controversies of Aquinas's use of Aristotle and to the dominance of the Dominican faculty at the University of Paris.[36] So, such a distinction is at least heuristically helpful. But, case in point, Bacon was an extreme realist—in contrast to the modified realism of Aquinas—and in Iberia an anonymous contemporary of Bacon thought to have been a Castilian Dominican called simply "Peter of Spain" prepared an Iberian reception for nominalism with his theory of, not signification, but rather supposition, which focused on the arrival of names from individual things as a class of generalizations based on accidents.[37]

The 1540s arrival of Dominicans trained in the new Thomistic humanism of the University of Salamanca presented a different semiotic ideology than that held by previous Dominicans or Observant Franciscans. For one, *Salmanticenses* Dominicans did not generally share the apocalyptic millenarianism typical of most Observant Franciscans. But, in terms of their theory of signs, as Thomistic realists they also understood an ability to disassociate a *res significata* (i.e., the thing signified or referred to, such as a meaning of a word) and the *modus significandi* (the means of signifying, such as the image, gesture, or word). The increased dominance of the Dominicans' realism corresponded to wider intellectual shifts begun latently in the late writings of Peter Abelard, Roger Bacon, and Peter of Spain that gradually considered the locus of a referent as not internal to the rational human mind (and thus universally to the mind of God) but rather as external and in the fabric of the world. For Dominicans, the physical realm was linked to the metaphysical as the very existence of both came together in being predicated on the being of God, with God's existence understood by Aquinas as God's essence. In this sense God was understood as being in and of itself. For Dominicans a sign, including words, was less natural or essentially connected to what it referenced and it thus was increasingly arbitrary, established as it was by human convention or culture.[38]

By contrast, in reaction to Thomism, nominalists regarded this central focus on the issue of the being of God along with the belief in universals as a threat to the idea of the absolute sovereignty or autonomous will of God. For nominalists there were no universals but only generalizations as names from particulars. Whereas Franciscans following William of Ockham's nominalism generally held that a signifier and the signified were intrinsically linked (*universalia sunt nomina post res*), Dominicans following Aquinas's moderate realism generally held that univocal if not also analogical signifiers could replace each other to signify the same referent—that is, using other words to mean the same or at least similarly enough—since ultimately meaning was understood as associated with universals (*universalia sunt realia ante rem*).[39] For example, mendicants working to convert Muslims in southern Iberia in the early sixteenth century debated whether "Allah" could appropriately be used in place of "Deos" or "Dios" in Arabic-language Christian pastoral literature, such as catechisms. Mendicants influenced by the Thomism generally supported such strategies of doctrinal translation while mendicants more influenced by nominalism did not. Similar translation strategies, and their respective theories of signification, readily appear in the intertextual analyses of the written record by both mendicants and the native Mesoamericans.

Thus, the missionary import of the *Salmanticense* Thomistic humanism was twofold. First, it could positively affirm for its proponents, mostly Dominicans, the understood divine presence in foreign cultures. Second, it could effectively engage the unbaptized through a peaceful ethic of persuasion. With respect to the latter, learning native languages was absolutely crucial to this endeavor among Dominicans, who were retrieving classical models of rhetoric in Cicero and Aristotle during the Renaissance. Las Casas's treatise on *De unico vocationis modo* (or *The Only Way*) was exemplary in this regard, as was his *Apologética historia sumaria*, to which his Dominican recruits, like Vico among the Highland Maya, must have made ethnographic contributions, given Las Casas's brief stay in Guatemala. But Vico's *Theologia Indorum* is shown in the following chapters to be a masterful Thomistic humanist case in point. And so, with respect to the importance of positive affirmation of foreign cultures, Vico's early work as well as that by the Dominican school within southern Mesoamerica indicates a distinctively constructive theological method by which some mendicants engaged indigenous religious and cultural customs. Their efforts contrasted with a broadly Franciscan approach, which in general adhered to an Augustinian view focused exclusively on the demonic origin of idolatry.[40] The early sixteenth-century Iberian Thomistic-Aristotelian, and even Ciceronian account of natural law and natural inclinations, understood as present in all human beings, highlighted the distinct Dominican approach regarding anthropology and the human cognition in the Americas, and Mesoamerica in particular, at least prior to the arrival of the Catholic Reformation.[41]

Mendicants' Introduction of a New World, 1520s–1570s

Analogical Reasoning, Alterity, and Seeking Commensurabilities

The mendicant missionaries who arrived in the Americas with Iberian soldiers in the first half of the sixteenth century brought with them the institutional and conceptual armature of the Hispano-Catholic Church: catechism dramas for popular education and conversion; devotional practices and effigies for discipline; orders of confraternities for laity-leadership; and episcopal inquisitions for enforcement. These first missionaries to Mesoamerica had also often been renowned Latinists, theologians, and canonists in Spain, and many had contributed to the budding fields of modern natural sciences, mathematics, practical astronomy, botany, and medicine.[42] These missionaries mediated the personal and interpersonal challenges of Mesoamerica—the cultural, linguistic, and religious difficulties of relating humanity to understandings of their god, relating one discipline to another, and of understanding their own relations to Spain and to the new other—using the classical humanist and scholastic understandings of an analogical relationship between signs and referents or meanings.

While analogical thinking was initially or primarily a focus for biblical exegesis, by the beginning of the fourteenth century mendicants and their students began to see it as a broader interpretive strategy. Whereas in the thirteenth century Thomas Aquinas presented a scholastic codification of the various "literal" and "spiritual" senses of interpretation that dated back to late antiquity in Christian thought, his late contemporary, Dante Alighieri, shows in his letter to Can Grande della Scala that these conventional principles of symbolic meaning were also applied beyond scripture.[43] When confronted with radical differences in their encounters abroad, Franciscan and Dominican missionaries sought understanding through analogical thinking, seeking similarities amidst differences. For example, Friar Diego Durán, O.P., one of the first historians of the mendicants in the Americas, saw the natives of Mesoamerica as direct descendants of the "ten lost tribes of Israel," viewed the residents of the Mexica hub of Texcoco as analogous to the refined Castilians of Toledo in Spain, and viewed other rural natives as comparable to the common peasants in remote Castile.[44]

The use of analogical thinking during these early decades of encounters between Iberians and Mesoamericans was one of the most evident modes of attempts to relate and understand this land mass that stood in the way of a direct water route between Europe and Cipango (Japan), Cathay (China), and the Spice Islands. In many respects, analogy was formalized as a theological strategy for scholastic mendicant clergy to interpret the Bible and discern affirmative predicates for the divine in a doctrine of god. Analogy thus also served as a basic mode for negotiating understandings between cultures and establishing commensurate meanings across languages. Specifically, many early Hispano-Catholic theologians used analogy to identify the American cultural and religious other of the *Conquista* with the Iberian cultural and religious other (Iberian Muslim and Sephardic Jewish) of the *Reconquista*. For example, at the First Synod of Mexico in 1555, the second archbishop of Mexico, Alonso de Montúfar, O.P., declared that the Church should suppress indigenous customs in the same way that the Church had decided to suppress Iberian Muslim customs the previous year at the Synod of Guadix, Spain, which Montúfar had also attended.[45] At the congregational level, friars considered others substitutable: they put on the pedagogical festive drama "Dance of the Moors," which clergy later adapted as the "Dance of the Conquest."[46]

However, until the arrival of the implications of the Council of Trent and subsequent synods that articulated the sixteen-century Catholic or "Counter" Reformation, early contact involved a huge degree of flux and creativity in attempts to establish cross-cultural, multilingual, and theological understandings. Mendicants from southern Iberia did not conflate contemporaneous Jews with the Israelites of the Bible, as they had concrete, historical, and interpersonal, if not also intrafamiliar understandings of Jews, Muslims, and converts from both. Unlike other regions in Europe, Iberia did not tend to exoticize or demonize the otherness of Judaism or Islam. The analogous understandings, therefore, were exacting and particularized. For example, in one of the earliest critiques of Spanish maltreatment of local indigenous populations of the Caribbean, Dominican Friar Antonio de Montesinos's sermon of 1511 compared, not the natives, but rather the Spanish residents to abusive slave-owning Moors and Turks.[47] Likewise, in his 1550 debates with the humanist Juan Ginés de Sepúlveda, the scholastic bishop Bartolomé de las Casas argued that the Spaniards in the Americas were more akin to Aristotle's notion of "barbarians" than were their Native American subjects, due to the settlers' cruel and inhumane behavior.[48] The issue is not *whether* the mendicant missionaries related analogically to the indigenous peoples of the Americas, but rather *in what ways* they did so as they drew from their theological training and European cosmology.

Following centuries of *Reconquista*-thinking concerned over the process of conversion to Christianity, the debates between Iberian Dominicans and Franciscans often centered on the practical need for, and efficacy of, punishing perceived Mesoamerican heterodoxy.[49] In the Americas these debates focused on the physical manifestations of indigenous effigies and not on the beliefs or meanings associated with them.[50] Theological concerns, insights, and implications emerged, however, in the most famous series of these debates between Sepúlveda and Las Casas in the Spanish city of Valladolid. According to Las Casas, the indigenous concept of "idols" consisted of multiple facets of the Christian god, meaning effigies were intermediaries between worshipers and the divine virtues of that one true god. Thus, the Highland Maya did not "idolize" sticks and stones but rather venerated reflections of the divine in and through those objects and images.[51] Redefining these "idols" as symbols of the supernatural, over and against the questionable existence of the preternatural as the locus of witchcraft or demonology, Las Casas stressed an inherent human need to enter into relation with the divine, just as the Church had only recently recognized indigenous peoples as persons endowed with reason and souls.[52] For Las Casas's Iberian audience, demons were beside the point: Iberians were already relatively skeptical of, and focused very little on, Satan or any demonic involvement.[53] But the Maya were not considered properly religious, either; when Las Casas argued that indigenous peoples shared in a common theological anthropology—an argument that contained the first written appearance of the term "human rights," which Las Casas derived from his Thomistic cosmology—he portrayed Mesoamerican idolatry as originating out of ignorance of the true Christian god. Thus, an understanding of true divinity, according to theologians like Las Casas, remained beyond indigenous comprehension simply because they lacked exposure to Christianity.[54]

Ethnographic Attunement for Doctrines of Idolatry to Cosmogony

In Spain and the emerging colony of New Spain, Las Casas's appeals convinced mendicants to attempt to understand indigenous peoples in order to help native peoples understand Christianity. Las Casas represented the wider urge on the part of the mendicants to understand the roots of indigenous beliefs in an effort to prevent a fusion between the "ancient rites and superstition [in the Americas] with our divine law and Christian religion."[55] This attempt to better understand the indigenous worldview led these friars to condemn the earlier, overzealous missionaries who had destroyed hieroglyphic codices and temple complexes, thereby leaving later clergy ill-equipped for the task of distinguishing between forms of heresy in native quotidian practices. Furthermore, the brethren became increasingly sensitive to merely banishing local effigies. Catholic education in the emerging "Counter" Catholic Reformation heightened the role of ocular symbols in devotionalism, and taught that the sight of such symbols imprinted ritualized messages onto the human memory. While they could not abandon Hispano-Catholic symbols—such as icons, relics, and the elevated host—mendicants recognized the need to find analogous substitutes among the native cultures, religions, and languages of Mesoamerica.[56] Friar Bernardino de Sahagún, O.F.M., collaborated with the last generation of Mexica scribes at three different sites—Tepepulco in 1558–1560, Tlatelolco in 1561–1565, and Mexico City proper in 1565–1569—to produce an encyclopedic work that represents the most extant in breadth and depth of this new ethnographic approach that Sahagún created in the mission field:[57]

> hay entre ellos muy más graves y que tienen gran necessidad de remedio. Los pecados de la idolatría . . . no son aún perdidos del todo. Para predicar contra estas cosas, y aun para saver si las hay, menester es de saber cómo las usavan en tiempo de su idolatría, que por falta de no saber esto en nuestra presencia hazen muchas cosas idolátricas sin que lo entendamos.

> there are many other sins among [the natives] much more serious and greatly in need of remedy. The sins of idolatry . . . are still not entirely lost. For preaching against these things, and even to know if they exist, it is necessary to know how [the natives] were using them in the time of their idolatry, because due to not knowing this they do many idolatrous things in our presence without our understanding it.[58]

Sahagún's work, which explicitly stressed a missionary approach predicated on ethnographic and linguistic appreciation for autochthonous cultures and spiritualties, emerged from pastoral concerns:

> El medico no puede acertadamente aplicar las medicinas al enfermo sin que primero conozca de qué humor o de qué causa procede la enfermedad . . . Los predicadores y confesores, médicos son de las ánimas; para curar las enfermedades espirituales conviene tengan esperitia de las medicinas y de las enfermedades espirituales.
>
> The physician cannot successfully apply the remedies to the sick without first knowing the humor or preceding cause of the disease . . . The preachers and confessors are physicians of souls, to cure the spiritual ills it is necessary for them to have experience of the spiritual remedies and illnesses.[59]

Mendicant missionaries' attempts to diagnose a mixture of beliefs and practices proved futile without direct dialogue with native parishioners.[60] Because the local languages, ecologies, and ways of living all contained elements of indigenous religious belief, mendicants found that they would have to translate and analogize successfully if they were to carry out the work of evangelism, thus increasing the need to carry out linguistic and ethnographic studies.[61] The tasks of the first ethnographies in the Americas consisted of compiling data and then, through comparative study and interpretation, sorting out and indexing diverse cultural but not exclusively religious forms, in order to identify idolatry. After Las Casas's debate with Sepúlveda in the 1550s, Dominicans working among the Highland and Lowland Maya began to collect often contradictory information on local culture and beliefs, with the hope of preventing further blending of Hispano-Catholic and indigenous American religious expressions.[62] The effort to penetrate the perceptions and conceptions of local traditions and transform them into meaningful notions with Hispano-Catholicism helped the mendicant reader convey Catholic narratives and ideas in terms the recently "converted" could understand. For mendicants, this meant direct and extensive dialogue with Maya parishioners in order to learn how best to relate Maya spatiotemporal notions with Hispano-Catholic ones; when to accommodate or suppress such themes as death, purgatory, hell, resurrection and salvation of the soul, and paradise; and how to translate specific doctrines, such as the triune Christian god (three-in-one according to the Trinitarian grammar established in the first ecumenical councils of late antiquity), "the first cause," or "being" itself.[63] Clergy, such as Friar Domingo de Ara, O.P., often treated these themes in their sermons by resorting to aspects of local cultural life for metaphorical imagery and analogies.[64]

In general, the arriving mendicant missionaries did not encounter Mesoamericans' customs and languages empty-handed but rather imported their prior experiences of working with Ladino-, Hebrew-, and Andalusi Arabic-speaking Iberian converts, many of whom also knew classical Greek, Hebrew, and Arabic. For many mendicants from the former al-Andalus or Catholic Andalusia, and especially for those who hailed from the archdiocese of Granada, where Archbishop Hernando de Talavera encouraged clergy to learn and use Arabic, one book, Friar Pedro de Alcalá's 1501 Arabic grammar, lexicon, and catechism manual, became a model.[65] The 1560s and 1570s witnessed a prolific endeavor on the part of mendicant missionaries among the Highland Maya. Based on their education in Spain, they continued to assume that natural phenomena did not exist strictly alone but also in human perception, and thus warranted interpretation by those trained to classify perceptions within a framework. The natural world, in this sense, never existed as an object of mere passive observation but also as a mental process that converted nature into cultural structures of thought that were, in turn, embodied in local religions.[66] Dominican friars' writings were constantly concerned with transforming indigenous concepts into corresponding or conflicting Christian counterparts.[67] For example, the Maya cosmology stressed a network of unbreakable connections between the world on the surface of the earth and the other world—often symbolically represented as the celestial realm or underground—which illustrated a more fluid conception of a reality through multiple aspects in constantly redefined images.[68] Concepts of a stratified or layered cosmos are found in European literature such as Dante's *Divine Comedy* or Aquinas's *Summa theologiae*, both of which drew from early Neoplatonic Christian theology, particularly that of Pseudo-Dionysius the Areopagite. Under the influence of such conceptions brought to Mesoamerica by mendicant missionaries, the Maya cosmos grew to have between nine to thirteen layers.[69]

Erasmus to Mesoamerica: Philology, Orthography, and Translation Strategies

Unlike their predecessors and contemporaries who evangelized to win converts in Iberia and northern Africa and who had had centuries to adapt (and adapt to) the non-Christian religious systems in their area, mendicants in Mesoamerica encountered non-alphabetic writing systems, non-Indo-European languages and cultures, and religious systems entirely new to them.[70] Furthermore, the mendicants working in Mesoamerica were not unified in their attempts at theological translation. Christian thought had begun developing explicit theories and understandings of signification as well as interpretation, or semiotic ideologies and hermeneutics, since late antiquity with, for example, Origen's *De Principiis* and Augustine of Hippo's *De Doctrina Christiana*. By the late medieval period, the different schools of scholasticism presented competing semiotics or theories of signs and signification due in part to a general philosophical division between the humanism of Spanish Franciscans and Dominicans.[71] Where Scotist and voluntaristic nominalism generally favored by Franciscans argued that a word in one language could never merely substitute a word in another language since they could never really denote the same things or ideas, the Thomistic and intellectualistic scholasticism generally favored by Dominicans argued that a concept was distinct and thus separable from the word that expressed it.[72]

In general, then, Spanish Dominicans thought more optimistically that local terms and images or new phrases constructed from non-Christian understandings could be used to speak and write about Christian concepts. Spanish Franciscans, most of whom were strict Observant rather than Conventual Franciscans, disagreed, believing that local terms and images, intimately bound with their non-Christian milieux, could not readily be incorporated into Christian use without risking confusion, contradiction, and heresy. While they were exceptional linguists and authors of the first grammars and dictionaries in Mesoamerican languages, the Franciscans' and Dominicans' differing semiotic ideologies—their differing understanding of how signs related to meanings, referents, or even other signs including words, material objects, and gestures—inflected their discernment of analogical relationships between the various cultures or language groups, and their ability to perceive predicates for or construals of the divine. These different applications of humanism in turn affected the Christian educational and devotional writings in those languages.[73]

Over the course of the sixteenth and seventeenth centuries mendicants moved between three basic solutions to this problem of translation. The first proposed solution involved the simple use of Spanish or Latin words for "God," "Holy Spirit," "sacrament," "saint," "angel," and other terms fundamentally important in Catholic doctrine rather than risk accommodating indigenous terms that would inadvertently conserve local ideas and practices through multiple meanings. At times it did become necessary to use some Maya terms for translation of most of the religious instruction given; this was a second solution. Though, the use of Maya words in this sense where often restricted to the most literal, such as the first and second characters of the triune god in a "father" and "son" relationship or the Devil as the "bringer of pain." Mediating between these extremes, a third solution was to use circumlocutions and accept native terms that did not completely convey all of the meaning of the Spanish or Latin phrases. However, given the integration of Maya cosmology and daily practices such as farming, weaving, cooking, and the like, many benign Maya analogies were already loaded with religious connotations; this third solution thus could have unexpected results. As the mendicants gradually gained knowledge of indigenous languages and produced their grammars and lexicons they became more willing to use local terms rather than approximate translations.[74]

In order to convey Hispano-Catholic concepts, friars found they needed more than dictionaries: they also required an understanding of indigenous ceremonial practices and daily life, and their research generated not only the first but among the best linguistic and some ethnographic work of the era. Ethnography required developing a transliterative orthography based mostly on Latin but also some Arabic script—namely by Friar Francisco de la Parra, O.F.M., working in Guatemala—since hieroglyphics used by native Mesoamerican peoples seemed too complicated for the Spaniards and was seen as not efficient for colonial administrative recordkeeping.[75] Because this alphabetic script was not exclusive to the Catholic clergy—Maya nobility and elite commoners with mission-school educations also learned it—its propagation effectively broke any monopoly on literacy previously enjoyed by Maya scribes and priests, but also provided them with a means by which to preserve their postcontact voices.[76] With the development of a European script to phonetically capture the Mayan languages, Dominicans and Franciscans made rapid progress in this area within the first quarter-century after their arrival into the mission fields.[77] The linguistic talents of these mendicant missionaries, many of whom were educated in and even taught the humanism and Thomistic scholasticism of the University of Salamanca, caused their early chroniclers to compare them favorably with major Renaissance figures, such as Pico della Mirandola.[78] And the missionary grammars of Mayan languages relied largely on a Latin grammatical framework, and most often used Antonio de Nebrija's 1481 Latin grammar as a template.[79] Even as the influence of other humanists like Italian Augustinian Ambrogio Calepino grew to compete with that of Nebrija, especially among Franciscans among the Lowland and Highland Maya, Nebrija still continued to serve into at least the eighteenth century as a basic template for clergy who favored the Salamanca school.[80]

However, both Spanish humanism and the uniqueness of Maya phonetics prevented the mendicants from merely using Nebrija's framework as a prefabricated model for studying and elaborating guides to these non-Indo-European languages. The *artes* ("grammars") and *vocabularios* ("lexicons") by Dominicans and Franciscans working with the Highland Maya used the same rubrics as Nebrija to break a language down into functioning parts, while also noticing the degrees to which elements of these non-Indo-European languages did not entirely fit with the linguistic concepts based on Romance languages. For example, even when designing a syllabary or orthography, mendicants relied on their knowledge of Romance and Semitic languages, through Alcalá's Arabic grammar or through their own Andalusian heritage. Franciscan Friar Francisco de la Parra appears to have resorted also to using at least two Arabic characters as the basis for designing new letters to accommodate a few of the unique sounds in K'iche'an speech. Specifically, Parra borrowed the Arabic *aiyn* <ع> for the *tresillo* <ꜫ> as the K'iche'an glottalized <q>, and the Arabic *waw* <و> for the *cuartillo* <4> as the K'iche'an glottalized <k>.[81] From these two new characters Parra could then accommodate all four of the phonemes that posed a challenge to other mendicants in the region: the <q'> as <ε> (a *tresillo*), the <k'> as <4> (a *cuartillo*), the <tz'> as <4,> (a *cuartillo* with a comma), and the <ch'> as <4h> (a *cuartillo* with an <h>).[82] This is not to say that other phonemes in the Mayan languages did not also pose a challenge, but Parra managed to accommodate them with letters from Latin script, namely the glottalized <t> written as <tt> and the combined sound of <t> and <s> or <ts> written as <tz> or <tç>.[83] As late contemporaries of Parra and other clergy worked among the Highland Maya through the eighteenth century, the <4> gradually shifted to become written as a <q> or <¢> and the <ε> gradually shifted with some Maya scribes to appear as <g>. Yet, taking Parra's linguistic meticulousness and interest in general applicability as a model—after all, Parra's alphabet could be used for all of the K'iche'an if not also all of the Mayan languages—the dictionaries and grammars produced on Mesoamerican languages surpassed the quality of the language studies and aides on European vernaculars of the same time period.[84] Their previous knowledge of and value for non-Christian populations, personal histories from polyglot communities in southern Iberia, and humanist education in universities like Salamanca allowed many early mendicant missionaries to comfortably draw from other Iberian and native Mesoamerican cultures in efforts to convey their own.

This drive to learn about local languages and cultures began almost immediately on the part of the first religious or regular clergy, those who took vows to enter into a religious order and adhere to a specific rule or *regula*, such as the rules of St. Francis and of St. Dominic. While there were no clergy on Columbus's first voyage in 1492, there were a handful on his second voyage a year later: three Benedictines, one Franciscan, and Ramón Pané of the Order of Saint Jerome. The Hieronymite friar Pané stayed behind in the Caribbean for six years, attempting to learn the local languages, customs, and beliefs; his account of this time is the first European-language book written in the Americas.[85] If Pané was the first ethnologist in the Americas, Sahagún was arguably the first anthropologist: he mastered the Nahuatl language and worked with three groups of Nahua scribes and elders fluent in both Nahuatl and Castilian Spanish to collect, authenticate, translate, and illustrate a book of Nahua knowledge and beliefs.[86] Sahagún's multivolume "general history" is a nearly comprehensive—and contentious—encyclopedia of Mexica religion, "rhetoric and moral philosophy," medicine, and botany, which the Holy Office, or Spanish Inquisition, confiscated in 1577, and its whereabouts were unknown until 1779. While few models existed in Europe for sociocultural study aside from attention to the customs and laws of other peoples, Pané, Sahagún, and a few contemporaries appear to have been influenced by their training at home and by their encounters in Mesoamerica. Erasmus of Rotterdam's insistence that theological learning move away from dialectics for philology and history played out directly for mendicants as they confronted radical alterity in the Americas.[87]

Messaging Teaching Authority: Ceremonial Discourse and Pastoral Genres

Sahagún exemplifies an approach taken by others of his mendicant cohort, and raises a concern that would be echoed by the secular clergy and the Catholic Reformation in the 1570s. In brief, this approach by these early mendicant missionaries trained in both the classical humanism and the new Thomistic scholasticism of the 1530s—a distinct humanistic Thomism or Thomistic humanism of the early Salamanca school—led them to seek to become fluent in, fully engage, and thus incorporate indigenous discourses and knowledge into the production of Christian theology. More specifically, not only Dominicans but also other clergy who studied at Salamanca during this period, like the Franciscan Sahagún, focused not only on the daily lives and language of indigenous Mesoamericans but recognized and valued the high register of formal and ceremonial speech genres referred to in Nahuatl as *huehuetlatolli*.[88]

Therefore, in addition to an ethnographic understanding of Mesoamerican customs and life and a linguistic appreciation of Mesoamerican languages, the mendicant missionaries of the early sixteenth century also intentionally engaged the moral, mythic, and reflexive worldview of indigenous Mesoamericans. All three of these fields—ethnography, linguistics, and theology—served as resources from which mendicants drew as they attempted to translate and convey their Hispano-Catholicism to Mesoamericans. Because they often understood their Mesoamerican congregations as similar to their fellow brethrens' Iberian *converso* parishes, early attempts at local Christian theologies among Mesoamericans consisted of texts and genres imported from Europe, mostly results from the popular movement of modern devotionalism. Based on scholarly surveys of printing records of the first printing press in the Americas—in Mexico City—and early colonial library catalogues, the common genres included collections of sermons (*sermonarios*), lectures or lessons (*pláticas*), songbooks (*cantos*, *coplas*, and *psalmodias cristianas*), booklets of prayers (*cartillas*), confession manuals (*manuales* or *confesorios*), and catechisms (*catecismos* or *doctrinas cristianas*).[89] Many of these early texts were either bilingual, in Castilian Spanish and an indigenous Mesoamerican language, or monolingual in a widely spoken indigenous language like Nahuatl, Otomí, Yukatek, or Kaqchikel. Furthermore, like the high quality of mendicant linguistic work on indigenous American languages as earlier noted, the surviving early musical manuscripts also indicate a heavy pedagogical and liturgical reliance on song in local languages, especially by Dominicans in Guatemala—such in Chuj, Q'anojob'al, and Q'eqchi'—which drew upon the latest and best music by European clerics.[90] Where illiteracy or semiliteracy was high, or where populations had no traditional writing system—the case, for instance, of the Quechua and Aymara in the Andes, who communicated across time and distance through *khipus,* or strings of tied knots—mendicants rendered pictographic texts for their indigenous New Christians.[91] However, among Mesoamericans and their use of various writing systems prior to the development of an alphabet by mendicants, the elaboration of pictographic or hieroglyphic religious doctrinal literature, such as the catechism attributed to Friar Pieter van der Moere, O.F.M. (also known as Pedro de Gante in Spanish), may have appeared later and by indigenous elites, rather than by clergy, in an effort to establish simultaneously their Christian and prehispanic authorities.[92]

Many of these multilingual texts also took the form of dialogues, using either cues-and-responses or questions-and-answers. Sometimes these texts were simply called *diálogos* but dialogues also helped to structure liturgical plays like the Passion drama performed during Holy Week, and often appeared in or as other genres of popular theology, such as *coloquios* and *cartillas*. Both dialogic and monologic mendicant texts written for Mesoamerican audiences positioned the friars as either the authors of or the authoritative speakers in the texts, the *tlamatinime,* or "keepers of the word," and banked on the traditional "speech of the ancestors," or *huehuetlatolli.*[93] Therefore, despite the reliance on Iberian genres for written texts, these early popular theologies were produced in many of the terms (i.e., in their languages and concepts) and rules (i.e., according to their grammar, rhetoric, and speech genres) of native Mesoamericans, albeit in relatively unequal or limited ways.

Of the mendicant genres, the most common appears to have been the catechism as either *cartillas* or *doctrinas cristianas*—basic Christian doctrines or teachings.[94] Catechisms were among the most important tools of the Christian conversion and popular education, both in Spain with the local Muslim population and in New Spain with indigenous Americans since the early but especially toward the end of the sixteenth century.[95] Far from a historically set genre, the concept of the catechesis (a period of self-reflection and Christian instruction prior to the rite of baptism) dates back to late antiquity. By the early fifth century Augustine of Hippo wrote the first doctrinal texts—*De catechizandi rudius* and his *Enchiridion* (or "Handbook")—which aligned basic Christian education and the "spiritual" or theological virtues by teaching of a baptismal creed (regarding proper faith), the Pater Noster (or Lord's Prayer, regarding the virtue of hope), and the double-love commandment toward the biblical god and one's "neighbor" (regarding the virtue of charity).[96] Over the centuries, the catechisms were complemented by the Apostles'

Creed and the various virtues and vices by the ninth century and later expanded to include the Ave Maria (Hail Mary) prayer as well as explications of the Decalogue (Ten Commandments), such as in 1273 with a catechism by Thomas Aquinas. As teachings meant to be memorized, especially given the high rates of illiteracy by the general public, this popular genre often included mnemonic devices by which to learn the basic prayers and practices, such as the twelfth-century Hugh of St. Victor who structured his catechism by groups of seven—seven Beatitudes, seven deadly sins, seven gifts of the Holy Spirit, seven virtues, and so on.[97]

Centuries prior to their arrival to the Americas, the mendicant orders—namely Franciscans, Dominicans, and Augustinians—began as a reformation movement concerned with perceived heresies in southern Europe and a lack of attentiveness to the needs of popular education among local populations. This made these new religious orders particularly instrumental in the further development of vernacular theological genres like the catechism, breviary, and songs like *coplas*. Specifically, by the late medieval period, with growing concern over the influence of perceived heretical movements among the laity in Europe, like the Cathars in southern France and the Waldensians in the Alps, as well as a poorly educated clergy in general, the catechism crystallized into a distinct genre of a popular theological compendium. Written not in Latin but rather in local vernacular languages spoken in Europe, including Arabic, the catechism became one of the most widely spread forms of conveying the basic teachings of officialized Christian beliefs. Shortly prior to the sixteenth century, the vernacular catechisms served an integral role in the wider effort to codify and increase laity understanding and liturgical participation, a popular reformation referred to as the *devotio moderna,* or modern devotional movement. As a key leader of the *devotio moderna,* Jean Gerson, rector of the University of Paris, in 1395 wrote his *Opus tripertitum* or "Tripartite Catechism," which became highly influential for all catechisms especially in Spain and its expanding territories.[98] Later modern devotional leaders included Augustinian friar Martin Luther, later mendicants, and founders of the Protestant Reformation.

As one for the first missionaries on the island of Hispaniola, Friar Pedro de Córdoba, O.P., produced one of the first of catechisms before his death in Santo Domingo in 1521. In the vein of the modern devotional movement of the previous century, Córdoba appears to have adapted but closely adhered to one of the first popular catechisms, that of Gerson. Popular modern devotional texts, such as Gerson's work and Thomas à Kempis's *The Imitation of Christ*, were brought to New Spain during this period, as were popular secular literature such as Thomas More's *Utopia* and the novel *Amadis de Gaul.* However, unlike the books written in Europe, Córdoba's catechism was printed in Mexico City by 1544 not only in Castilian Spanish but also in Nahuatl. As more mendicants worked with more

Mesoamerican languages they produced more catechism manuals. However, aside from slight changes in the order of presentation, their newer works were nearly the same as Gerson's in terms of content and brevity (see table 2.1).[99]

Regardless of its authorship, a catechism served as a memory aid only: whether produced by an archbishop such as Juan de Zumárraga y Arrazola, O.F.M., in Nahuatl, a bishop such as Francisco Marroquín in Kaqchikel, or a friar in the countryside such as Juan de Guevara in Wastek, a catechism usually contained little explanation of prayers or rites, but rather listed information to be memorized and recited by New Christians. Given the consistent dearth of clergy in Mesoamerica, it is likely that authors of these catechisms intended not only mendicant readers, who would have struggled with the Mesoamerican vernaculars, but also local indigenous leaders, such as *fiscales*, in charge of church buildings, prayer services, and Christian education.[100]

Therefore, the coproduction of local theologies with and for the indigenous peoples of Mesoamerica and even the Andes remained limited in breadth and depth. More detailed catechisms, longer devotional literature, scripture, the liturgical missal, pastoral letters, papal bulls, and more expository theology such as Thomas Aquinas's *Summa theologiae* remained in Castilian Spanish or Latin. Among these first theologies in the Americas, only two works appear explicitly identified as "theology." The only one ever to be printed is an unknown work listed as *Mística theología*, purportedly written by Bonaventure.[101] Unfortunately, most of the documentation on these imported or locally produced theological works—and almost any work that was printed and published rather than handwritten—focuses on central New Spain, the *audiencia* of Mexico, and the work of Observant Franciscans. Because Franciscans were the first (and ultimately most numerous) mendicant missionaries to arrive, and because Mexico City had the only printing press in New Spain until 1659, Franciscan work is often mistakenly understood to be representative of all mendicant work in early colonial Spanish America.

However, not only did mendicants differ in their semiotic ideologies, the languages and cultures they worked with, and the degrees to which they critiqued the abuses of the Spanish soldiers and settlers, they also had theologically divergent understandings of their old world and of the emergence of a new world. Unlike other mendicants such as the Dominicans, and as a legal version of the Spiritual Franciscans, many Observant Franciscans interpreted the loss of central Europe to the rising heresies of Protestantism and the perception of a *tabula rasa* in the Americas as part of a millenarian interpretation of the Book of Revelation begun centuries prior by Joachim de Fiore.[102] For many Observant Franciscans, the "discovery" of the Americas in the early sixteenth century allowed for a turning away from what they understood as a corrupted European church. Thus Mesoamerica at the turn of the sixteenth century, according to them, was the place and time

Table 2.1. Notable catechisms of New Spain in the sixteenth century

Jean Gerson (d. 1429) French, Castilian (1526 in Spain, 1544 in New Spain)	**Pedro de Córdoba, O.P. (d. 1521)** Castilian, Nahuatl (1544 printed)	**Juan de Zumárraga, O.F.M. (1468–1548)** Castilian, Nahuatl Short Catechism (1539)	**Juan de Zumárraga, O.M.F (1468–1548)** Castilian, Nahuatl *with "Supplement" (1546)
Epistolary (Preface)	(Prologue)	Opening	Prologue
1st Part		Colophon	
Man Created by God			
Descendent from Eve and Adam		14 Articles of Faith	14 Articles of Faith
Redeemed by God		Sign of the Cross	Sign of the Cross*
		Our Father	Hearing Mass*
		Hail Mary	Devotion to Sacred Images*
	14 Articles of Faith	(short) Creed	Protestations*
10 Commandments	10 Commandments	Hail, Holy Queen	
		Symbol of Athanasius	
	7 Sacraments	7 Sacraments	7 Sacraments
		10 Commandments	10 Commandments
		4 Commandments of the Church	
Mortal Sin		7 Mortal Sins	7 Capital Sins
Remedy of Confessing			Enemies of the Soul*
Works of Mercy and Virtues			Virtues*
	7 Corporal Works of Mercy	14 Works of Mercy	14 Works of Mercy
	7 Spiritual Works of Mercy	Theological and Cardinal Virtues	
	3 Crosses: Forehead, Lips, Breast		
	Sign of the Cross		
			5 Senses, 3 Powers, and Virtues*
			7 Mortal Sins*

continued on next page

Table 2.1—*continued*

Jean Gerson (d. 1429) French, Castilian (1526 in Spain, 1544 in New Spain)	**Pedro de Córdoba, O.P. (d. 1521)** Castilian, Nahuatl (1544 printed)	**Juan de Zumárraga, O.F.M. (1468–1548)** Castilian, Nahuatl Short Catechism (1539)	**Juan de Zumárraga, O.M.F (1468–1548)** Castilian, Nahuatl *with "Supplement" (1546)
2nd Part			
Confession			4 Moral Documents*
7 Sins			Short Moral Doctrine*
Absolution			
3rd Part			
A Good Death			
4 Warnings			
6 Questions	Sermon to the Baptized		What Parents Teach Children*
Good Prayers	Short History of the World		What Children Owe Parents*
Rules for Using Manual	Blessings before and after Meals (Latin)		Blessing of the Table*
			Conclusion of the Work*
(Colophon)	(Colophon)		(Colophon)*

Alonso de Molina, O.F.M. (1513–ca. 1579) Nahuatl, Castilian (1546)	**Orden de St. Domingo** Nahuatl, Castilian (1548)	**Francisco Marroquín (1499–1563)** Kaqchikel, Castilian (1556)	Quechua pictographic, e.g., Huntington Library (various 1500s–1900s)
Prologue	Opening Prayer	Prologue	
Sign of the Cross		Sign of the Cross	
Creed			
Our Father		Our Father	Our Father (4)
Hail Mary		Hail Mary	
		Creed	Apostles' Creed (1)
Hail, Holy Queen		Hail, Holy Queen	Hail, Holy Queen (3)
14 Articles of Faith	14 Articles of Faith	14 Articles of Faith	Articles of Faith (7)

continued on next page

Table 2.1—*continued*

Alonso de Molina, O.F.M. (1513–ca. 1579) Nahuatl, Castilian (1546)	**Orden de St. Domingo** Nahuatl, Castilian (1548)	**Francisco Marroquín (1499–1563)** Kaqchikel, Castilian (1556)	Quechua pictographic, e.g., Huntington Library (various 1500s–1900s)
10 Commandments	10 Commandments of God	10 Commandments	10 Commandments (5)
5 Commandments of the Church		5 Commandments of the Church	Commandments of the Church (6)
7 Sacraments	7 Sacraments of the Church	7 Sacraments	7 Sacraments (2)
9 Venial Sins		9 Venial Sins	
		Mortal Sin, defined	
		4 Things that Pardon Mortal Sins	
7 Mortal (Capital) Sins		7 Mortal (Capital) Sins	7 Deadly Sins and Remedies (20)
Virtues opposed to Capital Sins			
3 Theological Virtues			Theological and Cardinal Virtues (19)
4 Cardinal Virtues			
		Enemies of the Soul (see Molina)	
		Works of Mercy, defined	7 Corporal Works of Mercy (8)
7 Corporal Works of Mercy	Works of Mercy	7 Corporal Works of Mercy	7 Spiritual Works of Mercy (9)
7 Spiritual Works of Mercy		7 Spiritual Works of Mercy	Catechism Questions: (10–18)
			Q: Existence and Nature of God
			Q: Nature of Trinity
7 Gifts of the Holy Spirit			Q: Nature of Christ
5 Senses			Q: Humanity and Death of Christ

continued on next page

Table 2.1—*continued*

Alonso de Molina, O.F.M. (1513–ca. 1579) Nahuatl, Castilian (1546)	**Orden de St. Domingo** Nahuatl, Castilian (1548)	**Francisco Marroquín (1499–1563)** Kaqchikel, Castilian (1556)	Quechua pictographic, e.g., Huntington Library (various 1500s–1900s)
3 Powers of the Soul			Q: Christ, and the Last Judgment
	Soul and Levels of Hell		
3 Enemies of the Soul (see Marroquín)			Q: Nature of Eucharist
8 Beatitudes			Q: Administration of Eucharist
4 Qualities of the Glorified Body			Q: Sacrament of Penance
Obligation of Godparents			Q: Salvation
Formula for General Confession		General Confession	The Confiteor (21)
	Guarding of Virginity		
	Virginity and Martyrdom		
	The Unity of the Church		
	Meaning of the Cross		
		How to Listen to Mass	
		How to Enter a Church	
		How to Take Holy Water	
		How to Kneel	
		Words before Taking the Eucharist	
		Words after the Chalice is Offered	
		Words while the Host is Raised	

continued on next page

Table 2.1—*continued*

Alonso de Molina, O.F.M. (1513–ca. 1579) Nahuatl, Castilian (1546)	**Orden de St. Domingo** Nahuatl, Castilian (1548)	**Francisco Marroquín (1499–1563)** Kaqchikel, Castilian (1556)	Quechua pictographic, e.g., Huntington Library (various 1500s–1900s)
		Words after Host Raised, the Creed	
		Words after Host Raised Second Time	
		Words while Receiving the Host	
		Words after Receiving the Host	
13 Questions before Baptism	For the Newly Baptized		
Exhortation to Newly Baptized			
	Creation of the World		
	7 Mortal Sins (see Marroquín)		
Blessings before and after Meals (Latin)		Blessing before Meals	
	Sunday Prayer	Thanks Given after Meals	
		Declaration of Faith	
		Act of Contrition	Act of Contrition (22)
	Salutation	"Alabado" Hymn	
Colophon	(Colophon)		

Note: Numbers in parentheses with Huntington pictographic catechism indicate the page in which a topic begins.

Sources: Durán (1984), Córdoba (1970), Gerson (1949), Jay and Michell (1999), Marroquín (1905). For an additional comparison between Pedro de Alcalá's catechism in Arabic and Molina's contemporaneous catechism in Nahuatl, see Zwartjes (1999, 24). For comparison with catechism material in Vico's *Theologia Indorum* (volume II, chapters 24–51, 61–93), such as listed in Sparks (2017a, 41–46), see appendix A, this volume.

* Indicates the material added later to Zumárraga's longer catechism from his "Supplement" published in 1546.

for the establishment of the purely "spiritual" or "primitive" Church, to be led by those who honored vows of strict poverty—the third and final Church before the second coming of Christ.[103] Critical scholarship on the mendicant paper trail, therefore, raises many questions regarding the theological production in the early postcontact Americas that, although left unpublished by non-Observant mendicants, had been created with the collaboration of indigenous Mesoamericans, and then was responded to by native peoples once it was read and in their hands. The other voices in these mendicants' texts sought dialogues. Amidst these questions, within this transatlantic context, and with an augmented appreciation for the Highland Maya during this period, resides the first explicit "theology" listed in the bibliographies—the *Theologia Indorum* by Friar Domingo de Vico, O.P.

EMERGENCE OF PASTORAL REGISTERS OF DISCOURSE IN THE AMERICAS

After developing an alphabetic script with native-speaking collaborators, mendicants produced translations of popular devotional literature such as catechisms, confessional aids, and sermons for educated native elites and fellow clergy. They also taught classical European languages, Greek and Latin, to indigenous elites and, with their collaboration, produced translations of non-Christian classic texts, like those by Ovid, into native Mesoamerican languages, such as Nahuatl.[104] In both central Mexico and the Andes this occurred through the establishment of schools for children of indigenous nobility beginning in the 1530s. In other places, such in the *reducciones* of the Yucatán, this occurred through the training of native consultants by clergy, who each strove for bilingual competency.[105] However, among the Highland Maya no formal system of education like that of the Mexican (Aztec) *calmecac* existed for mendicants to build upon. Nonetheless, mendicant schools were established in the Guatemalan highlands: for example, by Franciscans in Salcajá (near present-day Quetzaltenango or Xe' Lajuj No'j in K'iche') between 1535 and 1540, and by Dominicans at the Colegio Santo Tomás de Aquino in 1563, both of them in the vein of the Franciscan Colegio de la Santa Cruz established in 1533 in Tlatelolco, Mexico, for Nahuatl speakers. These schools allowed many Highland Maya elites to work closely with mendicants and their writings in K'iche'an languages, such as catechisms and sermons.[106]

These formal and even informal schools, though, only provided one venue for discursive exchange in flux; the second venue consisted of genres. As peripatetics, mendicants, or "begging clergy," traveled light and thus developed genres of texts that could travel with them—*vade mecum,* or literally "go with me" texts—of which the catechism was a favorite. Therefore, many of what are now thought of as standard, classical, or traditional pastoral genres were, in fact, relatively new and not standardized by the turn of the sixteenth century, like the genre of the catechism as just discussed. Other genres were not only especially favored by mendicant clergy but developed as hybrid genres, mash-ups of previously established kinds of texts. For example, the *sacramentum* could include elements of the liturgical calendar, including summaries of scheduled scriptural and hagiographic readings, a "cheat sheet" for the order of mass, versions of standard prayers and refrains, if not also hymns. Furthermore, as part of the wider debates regarding the nature and sources of authority during the Reformations of the late fifteenth through sixteenth centuries, the stability, content, and approval of pastoral genres were also highly in flux. For example, another highly valued genre among mendicants, and especially Dominicans, was the breviary, another kind of written guide and handbook for the liturgical seasons. In particular the breviaries of early influential Catholic reformers were widely accepted, used, and promoted by Dominicans in Spain and other Spanish European territories like the Low Countries, such as the breviary by Cardinal Francisco Quiñones of 1536 until its papal condemnation in 1568.[107] The Council of Trent marked a shift in the variety and diversity of acceptable theological production from the previous decades or even centuries, especially at regional levels or wider.

The production of standardized doctrinal and pastoral texts in indigenous languages occurred eventually when approved by the bishops' synods for use by all clergy and then enforced by the Spanish Inquisition soon after the 1570s. The result was the development of a distinct register of language that intentionally drew upon colloquial indigenous speech as well as the formal rhetoric, poetics, and idioms used by indigenous nobility in prehispanic ceremonial discourse reserved for speaking about or to gods and ancestors. Historian Alan Durston refers to this register by Dominicans and Jesuits in colonial Peru as "pastoral Quechua," and subsequent scholars of early colonial Mexico have followed Durston in referring to the development of a pastoral or doctrinal Nahuatl by Franciscans and pastoral Q'eqchi' and K'iche' by Dominicans.[108]

However, absence of phonetic writing systems continued to cause problems among the Andean population. Clergy translated catechisms into pictographic books for indigenous readers to use as mnemonic devices that transmitted the basics of Catholicism. Pictographic doctrinal materials were also produced in central Mexico, where it has conventionally been thought that early mendicants used pictographic translations of popular Catholic texts to transition Nahua readers from a prehispanic iconography to an alphabetic mode of literacy.[109] Thus, two preliminary generalizations can be made. First, that while a pastoral register of discourse was developed in collaboration with native speakers, the functional translation of Hispano-Catholicism resulted from an imposition of ecclesial editorial control backed by coercive force where possible. Second, the general indigenous unfamiliarity with alphabetic writing presented particular translation and representational challenges for clergy. In contrast, the surviving Highland Maya literature provides a slightly different context. Due to its difficult terrain and lack of valuable natural materials, the region attracted fewer clergy and resources than central Mexico or the Andes. Furthermore, the vast linguistic diversity within such a relatively small region caused Dominican and Franciscan mission territories in the Maya highlands to overlap, resulting in intense competition among the various religious orders and their different semiotic ideologies.[110] In addition to historic contact zones between distinct Mayan languages and polities prior to 1524, Christian missions added a further layer of contact zones among the Maya but between the mendicant orders who often divided them in Guatemala.

Therefore, translation efforts of Dominicans as well as Franciscans among the Highland Maya involved the elaboration of a distinct register of pastoral or doctrinal discourse in indigenous languages to convey local construals of Hispano-Catholicism. However, unlike efforts among the Nahua and Yukatek Maya by Franciscans in Mexico and among Quechua and Aymara by Jesuits and Dominicans in the Andes, the emergence of a pastoral K'iche' was more negotiated than imposed and enforced. It was as much coauthored by K'iche'an elites and their agendas as by mendicants, as evidenced in the Maya reception ethnohistory of Hispano-Catholicism that simultaneously reconfigured their prehispanic religious worldview and correspondingly "corrected" what was presented by missionaries.

The competing semiotics between the Dominicans and Franciscans represented a wider shift from an intentionalist understanding of signification, held largely among the post-1530s Salamanca Dominicans, in favor of a more extensionalist theory. Thus early modern transatlantic mendicants differed on the existence of universals, with realist Dominicans optimistic on reason's ability to establish commensurability through analogies. Their eventual dominance with a distinction between form and content played into the emergence of a modernity now viewed as overly simplistic by postmodernity's emphasis on context, which nominalists prefigured. K'iche' authors, though, did not aim for universals but employed the translation strategies of their Dominican teachers to make instead hyperlocal claims, relevant only to a limited audience. Scholars of religion, especially religions in the Americas, who are unaware of these histories of translation theories, run the risk of conflating them, missing the differences within Hispano-Catholicism as well as among the Maya in the effort of all three constituencies to translate a Christianity into an indigenous world. More readily notable within the wider corpus of religious documents written in Highland Mayan or specifically K'iche'an languages is the intertextual evidence of a seemingly mutually informative relationship between

Maya and mendicant authors. Within the religious writings of the Dominicans who worked with the Maya of Guatemala, the documents show the development of a "Dominican school" of translation distinct from the work of mendicants elsewhere in the Americas.[111] And within the religious but also civic and legal writings of the Highland Maya, early documents show that they responded to, resisted against, and drew strategically from—and thus read thoroughly if not also helped to write—not Hispano-Catholicism in general but specifically Vico's "theology for and of the Indians."

CONCLUSION: FROM THE 1570S

The turn of the sixteenth century marked significant periods of transition for the polities of the Highland Maya and the kingdoms of Iberia in their own worlds. The encounter of the two worlds created a translocal shift that moved the Maya into a late postclassic period and Europeans into the early modern period. Historical and ethnohistorical figures who were already thinking critically and analytically, with a high degree of reflexivity, about the meanings and values in religion, language, and customs or culture became instrumental in negotiating the bridge between the highly local and the translocal. For the Europeans, religious or regular clergy—such as the Franciscans, Dominicans, and Augustinians—more often filled the roles of translating figures than did secular clergy, civil administrators, or soldiers. The Highland Maya as well as most indigenous Mesoamerican local and regional elites, such as former precontact rulers and council members, served as the mendicants' counterparts. Those mendicants fluent in Mesoamerican languages and cultures were referred to as *lenguas,* or "tongues." Correspondingly, those native Mesoamerican elites who became bilingual in Castilian and could translate between their world and that of Spanish civil and religious life were referred to by Hispano-Catholic mendicants as *ladinos.*[112] Together these Iberian and Mesoamerican constituencies drew from resources of their own old worlds to cross cultural, linguistic, and religious boundaries as they strove to establish commensurate understandings and reconfigure them in an emerging new world.

However, as the brief descriptions above about their respective old worlds highlight, there was never any simple or single religious, linguistic, or cultural other. Furthermore, for at least Hispano-Catholicism, the particular attention to religious, linguistic, and cultural alterity began as early as Columbus's second voyage in 1493 with Ramón Pané. In the early decades, however, various types of clergy came in distinct waves. Initially, most clergy accompanied sailors and soldiers as *de facto* military chaplains. With the gradual establishment of permanent or semipermanent towns in the Caribbean, such as on Hispaniola, Cuba, and Puerto Rico, the clergy's role expanded to fill the pastoral and sacramental needs of Iberian residents; that role sometimes even included official governance and legal administration of the emerging colonies for the Crown. With notable exceptions, such as the concerns regarding the abuses of power in the nascent Spanish Empire raised by friars like Córdoba and Montesinos, these initial decades, dominated religiously by these two types of clergy, were marked by destruction and loss of local religions, languages, and cultures.

This destruction was not unilateral or programmatic—in fact, many fellow friars recorded and denounced such loss in the first histories of Spanish America. But this critical strand of clergy represents a third type (and second wave) of mendicants. The missionaries, who were more interested in the indigenous American world, catalogued it descriptively. Their texts ironically preserve what their earlier brethren were destroying. The 1524 arrival of the famous twelve Franciscan missionaries to Mexico and the arrival of twelve Dominican missionaries in 1526 therefore mark a shift in Spanish-Mesoamerican relations. Educated in both the blend of humanism and the competing schools of scholasticism, subsequent waves of this third type of Hispano-Catholic clergy spread out thinly across New Spain, recording as they went. At the expense of secular clergy, mendicants both in the mission field and as most of the first bishops and archbishops of New Spain, controlled the establishment of Hispano-Catholicism and the production of theology in the first half of the sixteenth century.

By the second half of this first century of contact, however, this third type of clergy, the approaches they developed, and the social space in which they worked began to close. The number of regular or religious missionaries peaked in the 1560s. More significantly, secular clergy began to see the dearth of fully converted Native Americans as a failure of the mendicant approach, a critique that the new King Felipe II took to heart after 1556. As a result, by 1574 mendicants were required to answer directly to the viceroy and bishops rather than primarily to the priors of their orders. By 1583 the tables had fully turned: King Felipe II gave secular clergy preference in administrative and episcopal offices. This shift from religious to secular clerical control—followed also by the arrival of the Jesuits—corresponded to a shift in population: a newer generation of Spanish American priests, born to wealthy settler families, resented the mendicants' local control and their history of denouncing the abuses of local Spanish elites.

In another important shift, the newest Spanish American clergy saw Native Americans less as a religious, cultural, and linguistic other than as a labor force. When the mostly mendicant bishops of New Spain met in 1555 for the First Synod of Mexico, they stressed a paternalism that recognized the basic equality and rights of indigenous peoples, claiming they needed to be protected from exploitation.

However, by the Second Synod of Mexico, in 1565, local indigenous peoples were less frequently analogized as the "ten lost tribes of Israel" in the wake of the Assyrian invasion (ca. 722 BCE), or a remnant of either the Babylonian Diaspora (ca. 597–ca. 532 BCE) or the Roman destruction of the Second Temple (70 CE), or the Ladino-speakers of the Sephardim, or the skilled and educated *conversos* or *moriscos*, or the rural Catholic serfs of Castile. Instead, they were classified as *rudas,* or rudimentary peoples, those expected to recite the minimum amount of doctrinal knowledge. The Third Synod of Mexico in 1585 officially barred indigenous Mesoamericans—regardless of status, education, or devotion to Catholicism—from being ordained as Catholic priests and missionary friars.[113]

This shift in the comparative roles and value of mendicants and indigenous peoples within the structure of the Catholic Church in the Americas reflected the wider ecclesial and intellectual changes in the Church as the sixteenth-century Reformations rippled across the waters. Prior to the 1570s local bishops and archbishops—like Zumárraga in Mexico and Diego de Landa, O.F.M., in the Yucatán—had the authority to investigate and punish cases of heresy. In 1571 the Holy Office, or Spanish Inquisition, arrived in New Spain and even later in Guatemala by 1596.[114] A year later, 1572, a new religious order—the Society of Jesus, or Jesuits—arrived in New Spain, adding a new approach toward indigenous cultures, languages, and religions and a wave of ecclesial immigrants to the mix of mostly European-born regular clergy and increasingly American-born secular clergy. The Jesuits, took over many of the mendicant mission sites, and replaced the mendicants as ethnographers and linguists. By the 1580s the Council of Trent had effectively extended to the viceroyalties of New Spain and Lima.

These larger shifts mostly affected the wider structures, authorities, and dynamics of Hispano-Catholicism; on the local level, congregations and later parishes remained highly autonomous for no other reason than lack of means for greater oversight by clergy and relevant administrative arms of the Crown, like the Spanish Inquisition. Highland Maya elite remained authorities in many areas of civic and religious life of this new world: often it was not the influx of new clergy that shifted power structures, but rather the devastating waves of smallpox, influenza, measles, mumps, pneumonic plague, typhus, diphtheria, malaria, and yellow fever that radically changed population demographics.[115] Overall, the precontact Americas had approximately fifty-seven million inhabitants; Mexico and Central America alone had almost twenty million people.[116] By 1650 the overall Native American population for the hemisphere fell to under six million people—an 89 percent reduction that hit the central Basin of Mexico especially hard, reducing the population to 180,000 by 1607.[117] At the same time, however, only 24 percent of the land of New Spain was firmly under Spanish control; at least 45 percent still within the domain of indigenous peoples.[118] Among the K'iche' in particular, such as the region of Totonicapán—which is a site of particular importance with respect to early Highland Maya literature—the estimated 1520 population of 60,000–150,000 fell to 11,500–15,000 by 1572 and then further to 7,500–8,000 by 1689, apparently largely due to disease.[119]

Friar Bartolomé de Olmedo and Hernán Cortés's Mesoamerican landing in 1519, and the 1585 Third Synod of Mexico, circumscribe a unique moment in the production of Christian theology. These two dates delimit specific concerns around the foci of language, religion, and culture. The participants in this reflection and production were not only humanistic scholastics but also the Highland Maya. While these are artificial limits, these six decades can help clarify many of the wider interests and concerns that began in 1493 and possibly stretch into the present. Paying attention to the jointly authored theological paper trail written within these decades, and specifically to the collaborative work of Domingo de Vico and the Western K'iche' council members in the 1550s, can then secure the ethnohistorical foothold for a model of the graduated steps between local and translocal religious claims.

PART 2

Recovering Vico's K'iche'an Theology

3

Nima Ajtij Father Friar Domingo de Vico, O.P.

An Ethnobiography

Vino a Guatemala, hízose maestro en la de aquella provencia, y no pisaba pueblo, aunque su lengua fuese singular y rara, que en tres o cuatro días que se detuviese en él, no la supiese tan bien como si fuera su original y maternal, y con esta perfección supo siete diferentes lenguas.

[Vico] came to Guatemala, made himself master of all that pertained to that province, and would not be in a town for more than three or four days before he knew their language so well that he could speak it as if it were his first and mother tongue, even if it was a unique or unusual language; and with this perfection he came to know seven different languages.[1]

Xkawinaq oq tikam ajaw Don Franco oq xkam chik qatata' Fray Domingo de Vico chi la' Ak'ala'. Qitzij chi nima ajtij qatata'. Xch'ay ruma amaq'.

It was forty days after the lord Sir Francisco died when our Father Friar Domingo de Vico also died over there in Acalá. Truly, he was a great teacher, our Father, since he spoke for the [Kaqchikel] nation.[2]

(RE)READING THE AMERICAS' FIRST THEOLOGY

By the turn of the sixteenth-century, Iberia was far from the uniform and militant hierarchy that later Spanish Catholic history would want to portray. On the

DOI: 10.5876/9781607329701.c003

contrary, in the midst of long traditions of cultural, linguistic, and religious diversity, including a diversity within Catholicism, western Christianity in Iberia was again undergoing a period of reformation. However, unlike previous periods—such as with the mendicant reformation at the turn of the twelfth century or the populist reformation at the turn of the fourteenth century—the humanist reformation around the turn of the sixteenth century would eventually lead to a new schism within western European Christianity, or Christianities, between various kinds of Protestants and Tridentine Catholics. Christian missionaries who crossed the waters to the Americas from the east were trying to escape from, but also brought with them, empirical and textual discoveries, intellectual experimentation, and rational optimism that had not yet been pushed to any doctrinal limits. That was still decades away.

In the midst of this early period of first contact arrived one of the most influential clerics and critics of the abuses of empire, Bartolomé de las Casas, along with his corps of Dominican missionaries, such as Domingo de Vico. Las Casas's writings have survived and, perhaps due to their polemical nature, some were widely translated and published outside of Spain and Spanish America. The impact of his construal of a hemispheric, if not also global, cultural history, and universal human rights that valued the particularities of the local, continued to influence even native elites in the Andean region, such as in the arguments for Inkan autonomy by Guaman Poma de Ayala.[3] The writings of fellow mendicants in southern Mesoamerica, many of whom shared Las Casas's wider concerns, made just as significant an impact for good or for ill but have survived less well. Their effect and legacy are possibly noticeable throughout the colonial era and even into the Christianities of the present-day Highland Maya, but the recovery of their texts is difficult at best.

The increased constriction within the Catholic Church in both western Europe and its young colonies resulted in a destruction of many of the writings, particularly local theological and pastoral writings, produced by the first translators and conveyers of Christianity to the Highland Maya. Ironically, the Highland Maya were among the first to produce their own writings in the alphabet developed and genres imported by mendicants. Aligned and read together, the contemporaneous writings of the Highland Maya and Spanish mendicant missionaries working in the Guatemalan highlands offer crucial perspectives on the period of first contact and subsequent reconfiguration of both Hispano-Catholicism and the indigenous religion of the Maya. Based on the previously established contexts in part 1, this chapter situates the near-forgotten work and theological method of Domingo de Vico. Through the use of both Spanish and Maya historical sources, this chapter also sketches a fuller account of Vico's life, work, and legacy, ultimately demonstrating the role and value of Maya texts in his theology.

FRIAR DOMINGO DE VICO, O.P.: A BRIEF LIFE AND A LONG WORK

(Mis-)Placement in History: A Brief Biographical Sketch

Friar Domingo de Vico wrote the first explicit theology in either North or South America, called the *Theologia Indorum*—the "Theology of the Indians" or "Theology for the Indians."[4] His is also the longest single written work in any indigenous American language. And though it was never printed or translated into Latin or Spanish, it was hand copied throughout the colonial period, often by Maya parish assistants, or *fiscales*. However, the attention paid to the life and work of Vico by modern theologians and historians of the Spanish Empire is surprising not in its volume but rather in its scarcity.

Arguably, the work of Dominicans in the Spanish colonial *Audiencia de los Confines*, or "court," of the Kingdom of Guatemala within the Viceroyalty of New Spain, exceeded the geographic scope of the first seminal history on conversion efforts by Spanish mendicants in the Americas, Robert Ricard's 1933 *La "conquête spirituelle" du Mexique* and the ecclesial scope of Adriaan van Oss's 1986 *Catholic Colonialism*.[5] However, the complete absence of any mention of Vico or his *Theologia Indorum* in even more recent work is notable.[6] The minor exception to this absence in more recent scholarship is the single mention of Vico in José María Iraburu's 615-page tome *Hechos de los apóstoles de América*.[7] In contrast with these late twentieth-century and early twenty-first-century works, few nineteenth-century works that focused on the role of religion in the "conquest" of Spanish America mention Vico even in passing.[8] Even in the first earliest culturally comparative and near-global histories of the Americas written by someone with extensive firsthand experience, Bartolomé de las Casas makes no mention of Vico in either his lengthy *Historia de las Indias* or his *Apologética historia sumaria,* despite the fact that he recruited Vico, traveled with him from Seville for months across the Atlantic and into the Maya highlands, and most likely used Vico's proto-ethnographic writings on the Guatemalan Maya for those chapters in his *historias*.[9] Perhaps because of the very rare mentions of Vico and his writings in colonial-period chronicles, scholarly work on the friar has only been recent and sparse.

The two main biographical accounts of Vico and his work come nearly a century after Vico from two colonial Spanish Dominican friars, Antonio de Remesal's 1619 *Historia general de las Indias occidentales* and Francisco Ximénez's 1721 *Historia de la provincia de San Vicente*.[10] While Remesal and Ximénez offer differing but not necessarily conflicting accounts of Vico, their own sources have largely been lost or remain unknown, and virtually all of the scant mentions of Vico in later works generally recite Remesal's and Ximénez's accounts. However, both chroniclers note Vico's prolific ethnographic, linguistic, and religious writing, his facility with numerous indigenous languages, and the circumstances of his death.[11] The notable exception are the mentions of Vico in a single page by German anthropologist Karl Sapper after the turn of the twentieth century. In an early turn by a scholar to the historical value of accounts written by indigenous Americans, Sapper's source on Vico was neither Remesal nor Ximénez but rather a late sixteenth-century record written in, by, and for the Poqomchi' Maya.[12]

The notable exceptions to these oversights in historical accounts, particularly beginning in the nineteenth century, pertain to Vico's contributions to early writings on, if not also in, K'iche'an languages, such as James Constantine Pilling's 1885 *Proof-sheets of a Bibliography of the Languages of the North American Indians* and Cipriano Muñoz y Manzano Viñaza's 1892 *Bibliografía española de lenguas indígenas de América por el Conde de la Viñaza*.[13] The most influential during the beginnings of the collecting and cataloging of all-things-Native-American by, initially, European Americanists was French abbot Charles Étienne Brasseur de Bourbourg and his private library of manuscripts as listed in his 1871 *Bibliothèque Mexico-Guatémalienne*.[14] In addition to his instrumental role in the reception history of most of the early manuscripts in Highland Mayan languages—including the Popol Wuj, *Xajil Chronicle*, and *Rab'inal Achi*—as discussed in detail later, his miscataloging of Vico's texts has also led to subsequent confusion regarding Vico's authorship and the languages and genres in which he wrote. Not only Brasseur de Bourbourg's manuscript collection but his bibliography, including its errors, became foundational for other nineteenth-century studies on these colonial-era texts—such as the textual survey in German by Josef Dahlman, S.J.—and later in the catalogues of the European and US libraries that acquired them.[15]

This record just summarized above is a near-exhaustive account of writings about and mentions of Vico by non-Maya authors until the critical examination of early postcontact Maya texts in the late twentieth century.

Therefore, while few, most scholarly mentions have focused on Vico's language competency and studies, and have overlooked him as an author of an original treatise on an indigenous theology and as a proto-ethnographer. In this record, Vico is said to have compiled the first important lexicons and grammars for numerous Highland Mayan languages, as well as having done ethnographic work. These served as major touchstones for later clergy in the region during the following centuries' debates regarding Mayan languages, cultures, and religions.[16] A polyglot from Andalucía at the end of the *Reconquista*, Vico came to learn at least seven Mayan languages during his mission work in Guatemala: K'iche', Kaqchikel, Tz'utujil, Q'eqchi', Poqomam, Poqomchi', and Ch'ol.[17] As Remesal described him in the first chronicle of Dominicans in lower Mesoamerica, Vico was:

> pequeño de cuerpo, aunque abultado de carnes. De un ánimo tan grande, que parecía haber nacido para emperador. Ningún trabajo ni fatiga le cansaba, y ninguno le vió jamás desmayado por dificultades que se le ofrecían en lo que proponía o trazaba, en que tenía una extrema resolución después de haberlo mirado y consultado, porque siempre fue muy amigo de saber el parecer ajeno. Con este grande ánimo que tenía, era muy aficionado a las cosas grandes, y habíalo de ser todo lo que no fuese forzoso proporcionarse con su cuerpo. No sabía escribir en papel pequeño, ni con pluma corta . . . no soltaba la pluma de la mano, y así escribió él solo en diferentes lenguas, más que todos los demás padres de su tiempo cada uno en la que mejor sabía.

> small in stature yet rotund, and with a drive so great that it would appear that he had been born to be an emperor. No task or fatigue tired him, and he was never seen to faint due to the difficulties that presented themselves to him in what he planned or sketched out, as he had a strong resolve after having seen and consulted them, as he was always very well disposed to know how things appeared to others. With this great drive that he had, he was drawn toward great things and had to be such toward everything even if disproportionately forceful for his physique. He did not know how to write on small paper nor with a short quill . . . never was a quill lax in his hand, and in this way he only wrote in all the different languages, more so than the rest of the priests of his time, knowing those languages better than any of his cohort.[18]

Born sometime between 1485 and 1519 in the province of Jaén, in or around the towns of either Úbeda or Huelma, when the area was still also an Arabic- and Ladino-(Sephardic Castilian) speaking region of southern Iberia, Domingo de Vico studied at the Dominican convent's Colegio de San Andrés in Úbeda.[19] He continued his education at the University of Salamanca and its Dominican Colegio de San Esteban during the early tenure of Francisco de Vitoria and his seminal lectures on Thomas Aquinas's *Summa theologiae*.[20] At the time of the early sixteenth century, however, the Dominicans of San Esteban were considered too strict for some. Younger Dominican students from other parts of Iberia traveling to Salamanca for their university studies were opting, instead, to rent rooms in private homes rather than live in the community. As a result, with the financial patronage of the Duke and Dutchess of Béjar, Alonso Francisco de Zúñiga y Sotomayor and Teresa de Zúñiga y Guzmán, an alternative Dominican convent was established next to San Esteban by 1533—the convent of Santo Domingo de la Cruz—to allow less-strict Dominican students to live in the community.[21] Originally planned for thirty Dominicans, the new, short-lived convent only ever had fifteen residents at its height before reducing to eight, one of whom was Domingo de Vico.[22] The economic difficulties and then death of their benefactor placed the financial burden of Santo Domingo de la Cruz

Figure 3.1. Santo Domingo de la Cruz, Salamanca, Spain. The former convent is now a municipal exhibition hall. The belltower of the convent of San Esteban de Salamanca rises in the background. (Photo by Garry Sparks.)

on the student residents, which was difficult for not only university students in general (as it is in modern times) but especially for members of a "begging" religious order. Their inability to cover the costs led to the closure of this second Domincan convent and the acquisition of its records, property, and remaining residents by San Esteban.[23] After graduation Vico seems to have returned to the Dominican convent in Úbeda, possibly to teach at the Colegio de San Andrés.[24]

But on July 9, 1544, Vico left from Seville in one of the largest and earliest groups of mendicant missionaries to the Americas, which was spearheaded by the then newly appointed bishop of Ciudad Real de Chiapa, Bartolomé de las Casas, and included forty-six additional Dominican priests, deacons, and laymen.[25] The roster reads like a map from across the early modern united kingdoms of Iberia but also signals the early influence of Thomistic scholasticism that Vitoria brought from the Sorbonne to the Dominican college in Valladolid initially, and soon after to the Dominican college of San Esteban and the University of Salamanca.[26] In addition to Las Casas and Vico, the other members of the delegation included one of Las Casas's longtime companions from his time in Santo Domingo Hispaniola—Rodrigo de Ladrada—and two other Dominicans who had previously been in the Mexico—Andrés Álvarez and Domingo de Loyola—along with Domingo de Ara, Domingo de Azcona, Diego Calderón, Pedro de Calvo, Juan Carrión, Tomás

Casillas, Pedro de la Cruz, Juan Díaz, Martín de la Fuente, Jorge de León, Vicente Núñez, Pedro Rubio, Tomás de San Juan, Domingo de San Pedro, Jerónimo de San Vicente, and Tomás de la Torre, all from Salamanca; Augustín de la Hinojosa from Salamanca and Valladolid; Dionisio Bertabillo, Alonso Portillo Noreña, Alonso de Villalba, Alonso de Villasante,[27] and Antonio de Toledo, all from Valladolid; Juan Cabrera, Miguel Duarte, and Juan Guerrero, all from Córdoba; Pedro de los Reyes and Ambrosio Villarejo, both from Galisteo; Luis de Cuenca and Jordán de Piamonte, both from Jerez; Miguel de Frías and Mateo Hernández, both from Toro; Felipe del Castillo from Ávila; Jerónimo de Ciudad Rodrigo from Peña de Francia; Alonso de la Cruz from Toledo; Vicente Ferrer from Valencia; Diego de la Magdalena from Seville; Pedro Martín from Madrid; Cristóbal Pardavé from León; Francisco de Piña from Burgos; Francisco de Quesada from Rosa; Baltasar de los Reyes from Maesa; Pedro de la Vega from La Vera de Plasencia; and a Diego Hernández whose home convent is not given.[28]

The prestige of Las Casas—a former military chaplain, previous estate and slave owner, a legally appointed "defender of the Indians," and now only the third bishop of the new diocese of Chiapa—was not a coincidence on this second and largest Dominican expedition to the American mainland in the sixteenth century.[29] Nor was it a coincidence that nearly half of the missionaries had studied at Salamanca. Vico was one of at least eight who were originally from southern Iberia and among the thirty-seven who were already ordained priests, along with an additional six deacons and five religious laymen.[30] In response to Las Casas's petition to the Crown and Juan Valcárcel, the vicar general of the Dominican Order of Spain, Vico and Friar Diego de la Magdalena were nominated from the Dominican province of Andalucía for the new delegation to Chiapas, Guatemala, Honduras, and Nicaragua. Their home province selected the friars while Magdalena at least was still at the University of Salamanca:

> porque soy informado que cada uno de ellos en su calidad es muy provechoso para aquellas partes y enviarnos heis relación de las personas que así nombráredes para que nos los mandemos proveer de lo necesario.

> because I [Friar Tomás Casillas, vicar general of the new delegation] am informed that their [Vico and Magdalena] quality is very appropriate for those parts and in sending them you have a relationship with these persons whom you have nominated so that we send them with what they need.[31]

In other words, Vico and his cohort were chosen not as a punishment or in a moment of scarcity and desperation, but rather because the Order of Preachers sought recruits from among the best and the brightest of the time.

Beginning with a core group of seventeen who left directly from Salamanca on January 12, 1544, the majority of the missionaries arrived during an extended stay in Seville before they left from the Spanish port of Sanlúcar de Barrameda in Cádiz, Spain, on July 9, 1544.[32] With a stop on La Gomera in the Canary Islands, the delegation continued to the islands of Borinquen (Puerto Rico) and then Hispaniola (present-day Dominican Republic and Haiti). From there the delegation dissolved: four friars returned to Spain; three stationed themselves in Puerto Rico; two continued on to central Mexico; and nine died in a shipwreck off the coast of Tabasco before the remainder eventually landed in Xicalango, Campeche, on February 18, 1545.[33] Upon his arrival in Ciudad Real de la Chiapa on March 12, 1545, Vico soon became head of what would eventually be the Colegio de Santo Domingo in Chiapas and began working in the Dominican Maya region.[34]

Possibly as early as May of that same year, Vico, together with Las Casas and the Dominican friar Domingo de Azcona—who would eventually succeed Vico as prior of the Dominicans in Guatemala after Vico's death—formed a delegation of forty religious and secular clergy and laity. They left Ciudad Real for Sacapulas, Guatemala, a fortified Sakapultek Maya town on the northeastern border of the prehispanic Western K'iche' confederacy of Q'umarkaj that marked the eastern frontier with the rival Achi or Eastern K'iche'.[35] Upon their arrival into Sacapulas on June 4, 1545, Vico and Azcona met up with a previously assigned Spanish Dominican missionary, Friar Juan de San Lucas, and negotiated with the regional K'iche' leadership—the local *ajpop* (or *ajpo*), known by his Spanish honorific and baptismal name Don Juan Matal B'atz', and his son and eventual successor Juan—for a sustained Dominican presence in one of the last major Maya regions left "unconquered" by Spanish forces.[36] Given the heavily armed resistance by Achi, Q'eqchi', Ch'ol, and Poqomchi' Maya, Spanish administrators such as General Captain Pedro de Alvarado referred to the area as the "Land of Eternal War"—also known by its Nahuatl name of Tecululán, or "Place of the Owls"—and left it largely alone in order to devote resources instead toward developing colonial administration elsewhere. This meeting between Dominicans and regional Maya also soon coincided on July 2, 1545, with a confrontation between Las Casas and Francisco Marroquín Hurtado, the previously established bishop of Guatemala. Marroquín was one of the first and few secular clergy to be appointed to one of the newly created sees in the Americas. He viewed the new see of Chiapas and Las Casas's activities in the region as an infringement on his authority and the greater diocese of Guatemala. By July 10, 1545, Las Casas left the area and continued on to Honduras, but Vico and four other Dominicans remained.[37]

Following the early presence of Friar Domingo Betanzos, O.P., in 1529 and again later in 1535, the Dominicans had claimed land in the shortly lived regional capital city, now Ciudad Vieja, but the first sustained Dominican missionary presence came with Las Casas in 1536 and was small. Arriving from the south, from Nicaragua and through El Salvador, Las Casas first arrived in Guatemala accompanied by two other Dominicans he had known in Hispaniola since the 1520s, Luis de Cáncer and Pedro de Ángulo, and a third, Rodrigo de Ladrada, who arrived from Peru to help establish the Dominican convent in León, Nicaragua.[38] Between July 1536 and 1540, the four of them, both together and separately in smaller groups, traveled what would become the Dominican highlands through Oaxaca, attended the Dominican provincial chapter meeting in Mexico City in August 1538, and began to establish the basis for a more sustained Dominican presence not in the capital city of Santiago but rather among the Maya in Sacapulas, Cobán, and Rabinal. In 1538 Cáncer traveled back to Spain, and in 1540 Las Casas and Ladrada briefly returned to Spain, leaving Ángulo and a couple of other Dominicans in Guatemala.[39]

However, prior to that departure in 1538, Cáncer apparently met with Don Juan B'atz', the regional K'iche' leader, in Sacapulas in May 1537. This would later provide the foundation for their negotiated return to the region within a few years. Because while also in Spain, by arguing successfully back in Valladolid against the use of coercive force on native populations, by 1540 Las Casas had already negotiated a temporary removal of all Spanish and native allied armed groups from this Maya area. With these royal decrees (*cédulas*), Cáncer in March 1541 traveled back to Guatemala to rejoin Angulo while Las Casas and Ladrada moved to Talavera, Spain, with the royal court.[40]

Therefore, by the time of their peaceful—singing, according to legend—entrance into the K'iche'an Maya region, Dominicans had already carried out considerable advance work both legally in Guatemala and Spain and on the ground with Highland Maya political leadership. Acquisition of Mayan languages was inclusive of these preparations. Vico's initial introduction to the language of K'iche' Maya took place soon upon his arrival in 1545 with Cáncer as his teacher. In a letter to Las Casas, Cáncer described Vico as a *cosa maravillosa nunca oida ni vista* ("a wonderful thing, never heard or seen"), and related that it took Vico only a fraction of the time, weeks, to master an indigenous language, when it took the other missionaries months.[41] A set of at least fifty songs (*coplas*), is product of the collaboration between Vico, during his first years in Guatemala, and Cáncer, prior to his departure in 1546 for Mexico and then Florida. The songs were originally composed in a Highland Mayan language but survive only in K'iche' and Q'eqchi' versions.[42]

By 1547, Las Casas had returned to the Highland Maya region with Vico and at least initially three other Dominicans. The Dominicans had by then negotiated a peace settlement between the major Maya polities and the Spanish administration, warranting a name change from "Land of Eternal War" to the "Land of True Peace," or Vera Paz, known now as the Guatemalan departments of Alta and Baja Verapaz, or collectively as the Verapaces.[43] In this same year Vico's name appears in a roster of clergy assigned to the Dominican convent of Guatemala, which would have included the area of the Verapaces until a distinct convent would be established in Cobán.[44]

Vico's name also appears again later in a roster of a chapter-wide meeting of the Dominican convent of Mexico in 1550, where Friar Tomás de la Torre was elected prior, or head, of the convent of Guatemala.[45] That same year the prior La Torre accompanied Vico in an expedition to the lowland area of Acatán of the Ch'ol Maya to the north of Cobán, Verapaz, and east of Sacapulas. The Ch'ol were historically antagonistic to the Western K'iche', such as the Dominican ally, Juan Matal B'atz'. However, despite the difficulties in terrain, travel, and deep local Maya political histories, Vico learned the language and preached to the Ch'ol of Acatán in an unsuccessful attempt at religious conversion and pacification.[46] While various Dominicans came and went, such as Las Casas and La Torre, Vico appears to have continued working in the region north of Lake Izabal through 1550 to establish new Maya towns like Santa Catalina Xocoló and San Andrés Polochic.[47] According to legend, Vico christened the latter in honor of his *alma mater* back in Úbeda and as a fulfillment to a promise he made in a petitionary prayer to Saint Andrew during what was possibly a hurricane—that if he survived the storm, he would name a new Maya town after him as its spiritual patron.[48]

By 1551 he was elected prior of the Dominican convent of Guatemala, a position he held for almost three years.[49] As prior he remained in the colonial regional capital city of Santiago de los Caballeros de Goathemalan.[50] There he had close contact with Franciscan friar Francisco de la Parra, who in the mid-1540s invented an alphabet based on Latin and Arabic characters to be used by all mendicants for writing Mayan languages. In Santiago de Guatemala, Vico also most likely worked with Diego Reynoso, a K'iche' nobleman from Totonicapán whom Bishop Francisco Marroquín sponsored to study in that regional capital city.[51] As *popol winaq,* or a member of the prehispanic Western K'iche' ruling council, a minor author of the eventual Popol Wuj (ca. 1554–ca. 1558), and the principal author of a number of historically important Maya notarial documents, specifically the *Title of Totonicapán* (1554), Reynoso was probably Vico's primary consultant on K'iche' Mayan language, culture, and religion. Maya signatories of later significant Maya texts—such as the *Title of Santa Clara La Laguna* (1583)—who also bear Vico's surname as their baptismal names, indicate that he had at least a few K'iche' and Kaqchikel students who became influential Maya elites.[52] While it did not become or remain a common Spanish surname among the Highland Maya, variations do appear in at least two other notarial texts from regions where Vico spent considerable time: a Pedro de Vico of Santa Cruz del Quiché is mentioned in the 1688 section of the *Título*

Chacatz-Tojin, and two persons named Juan de Vico from Sacapulas are listed in a 1572 judicial record of tributaries.[53] And one Nahuatl notarial text by Nahua from central Mexico who arrived as allies with Spaniards and eventually settled in Santiago de Guatemala indicates that Vico may have also had students of Mexican elites.[54] However, there is no mention in the Dominican chronicles, such as those by Remesal or Ximénez, that Vico ever learned Nahuatl as one of his many languages.

During this period Vico also met the royal commissioned Spanish auditor and fellow *Salmanticense* humanist, Dr. Alonso de Zorita, in one of his initial stays in Santiago de Guatemala. Because of his education at Salamanca, Zorita favored the Dominicans' approach toward the indigenous peoples.[55] In many respects, Zorita was a close late contemporary of Vico, having also been born in Andalucía, specifically Córdoba, between 1511 and 1512. He too studied law at the University of Salamanca between 1537 and 1540, arrived in Santo Domingo as an appointed judge (*oidor*) on April 28, 1548, and was a "devoted disciple of Las Casas."[56] In his *Relación de la Nueva España,* Zorita notes that:

> En el monasterio de Santo Domingo de Guatemala traté y comuniqué muy particularmente el tiempo que allí fui oidor a Fray Domingo de Bico [*sic*] muy estimado de todos por su religión y vida ejemplar aunque a la continua andaba enfermo por la gran penitencia que hacía y por lo mucho que trabajaba en predicar a los españoles y en la doctrina y conversión de los naturales de aquella tierra y en doctrinar y predicar a los negros y a los indios que están de servicio de los españoles que son muchos los domingos y fiestas cuando se hallaba en Guatimala [*sic*] y porque nunca quería estar ocioso tenía por costumbre y por ordinario de escribir tres pliegos de papel en la lengua de los indios para su doctrina y de sermones para les predicar.[57]

> In the monastery of Saint Dominic of Guatemala, while there as the auditor, I made the effort and met for a particular time with Friar Domingo de Vico, who was held in high esteem by everyone for religion and exemplary life; although he was continuously going about sickly due to the great penitential practices he did and his extensive work in preaching to the Spaniards and the doctrine and the conversion efforts of the natives of that land as well as the doctrinal teaching and preaching to the blacks and the Indians that are in the service of the Spaniards on so many Sundays and holidays when he was in [Santiago de] Guatemala; and because he never was wanting to be idle it was his regular and customary practice to write on three sheets of paper in the languages of the Indians for their doctrinal lessons and the sermons that were to be preached to them.[58]

Therefore, like Reynoso for Vico, it is highly probable that Vico was one of Zorita's primary consultants on the Maya during his audit of the treatment of indigenous peoples of Mexico and Guatemala. In his *Breve y sumaria relación de los señores de la Nueva España*, Zorita cites at least pictographic if not also logographic records used by the K'iche' of Q'umarkaj to recount their precontact history. His account remains among the most secure evidence that K'iche' Maya had a book culture if not also writing prior to the arrival of Europeans.[59]

Due to this noted high reputation, toward the end of Vico's time in the regional capital, Bishop Marroquín commissioned Vico to write a treatise on the nature of idolatry in the wake of the heated debate between Dominicans and Franciscans regarding the use of Maya religious terms in doctrinal literature. Though Marroquín most likely intended the work to serve as a moral and confessional primer or *summa consciencia* for fellow Dominicans in Maya communities, in light of debates on the diversity of religious deviance and proscribed penances, Vico instead produced a more comprehensive theological work.[60] Like many of the titles ascribed to Vico by later chroniclers, namely Remesal and Ximénez, his supposedly separate *Tratado de ídolos* has either been lost; or it was a constituent part of his larger *Theologia Indorum* that was later excised and retitled; or it was an earlier work in progress that eventually morphed into his more extensive theology as, for example, chapter 25 of the first volume, which does focus on Maya religious effigies.

In the end, drawing upon his homiletical, linguistic, and ethnographic work, Vico wrote a theology that he must have hoped would model the ways preaching might actually incorporate Maya beliefs rather than merely condemn them. The core of the first part of this theology appears to have been drawn from fairly polished material already in use by itinerant mendicants by 1552.[61] That same year, Friar Francisco de la Parra left Guatemala for the Yucatán, perhaps as a result of the tensions between Dominicans and Franciscans and their competing theories of translation that would continue until a royal decree on January 22, 1556.[62] By 1553, though, Vico appears not to have been working in the Dominican convent in Santiago de Guatemala but rather in San Martín Jilotepeque, a rural, predominantly Kaqchikel Dominican parish to the north, close to the southern linguistic border of the K'iche'.[63] There on February 11, 1553, Vico finished the first part of his *Theologia Indorum,* which was loosely modeled on Aquinas's *Summa theologiae*.[64] On November 8 that same year, Bishop Marroquín wrote to Vico regarding the establishment of the new township and convent at Santo Domingo de Sacapulas, where Vico had first passed through with Las Casas in 1545.[65]

A year later, possibly as late as November 1554, Vico completed the second volume of the *Theologia Indorum*, styled along the lines of Jean Gerson's fifteenth-century catechism, a work of vernacular theology popular among mendicants in Europe and early New Spain.[66] Based on the surviving manuscript versions, Vico most likely initially wrote the *Theologia Indorum* in K'iche' Maya and then soon produced—or others produced for or after him—versions in at least two other related K'iche'an languages, Kaqchikel and Tz'utujil. However, as indicated in the closing section of a version of the first volume, Vico states to his K'iche' readers that he has just finished his treatise *vtçibaxic chupã y4habal yx cakcheq'l vinak yx rabinaleb yx ttçutuhileb yx 4ut 4iche vinak* ("written in your languages, you all the Kaqchikel people, you all the Rab'inal people, you all the Tz'utujil people, and you all the K'iche' people").[67] In other words, given Vico's competency in multiple Highland Mayan languages and the report by Zorita that he often composed sermons and lessons simultaneously in multiple native languages, it is also possible that he produced his theology for the Highland Maya in their various languages simultaneously.

Regardless, that same year, the new and larger Dominican Province of San Vicente was established and its regional center for the Dominicans in southern Mesoamerica moved from Santiago, Guatemala, to Ciudad Real, Chiapas.[68] In the midst of these events, Vico was elected prior of the new Dominican convent in the Verapaces and relocated again from the capital city region to Cobán. From the base of this new convent, Vico apparently tried again to convert the northern Ch'ol Maya in Acalá near the present-day boarder of Guatemala and Chiapas, Mexico. As Remesal recounts it, one evening late in November 1555, Vico lay in bed deathly ill when allied Maya from Acalá came to report that anti-Catholic Ch'ol had formed an alliance with Lakantun Maya from farther north who were also antagonistic to the new Christian religion. Together with fellow Dominican friar André Mozo López and a battalion of 300 allied Maya led by Don Juan from the Dominican town of Chamelco, Vico headed for San Marcos. Insisting on entering the town unarmed, Vico and López sent away the Maya allied forces but were both eventually ambushed and shot full of arrows, and the Dominican mission house was razed. Vico supposedly died at 7 am on Friday, November 30, 1555, the feast day of Saint Andrew.[69] Many early Spanish but also earlier Maya sources mention his assassination north of Cobán by Ch'ol and Lakantun Maya in the town of San Marcos in the Acalá region at the end of November 1555.[70] As retribution for his and López's murders, the Spanish forces allied with Don Juan Matal the younger, the new leader of the Sacapulas K'iche'—the historic enemies of the Ch'ol—returned with 400 soldiers. In various reports they killed 300 Lakantun Maya, hung another eighty Maya inhabitants of San Marcos, and sold another 180 into forced labor.[71] Vico's longtime fellow Dominican and traveler from Salamanca, Friar Domingo de Azcona, succeeded him as the prior of the new convent in Cobán.

Maya Accounts of Vico: Ethnohistorical Placement

Perhaps ironically, the accounts of Vico's martyrdom are the most abundant surviving documentation on his life. Remesal, while never explicitly cited by colonial chroniclers, also most likely used the few Spanish accounts, along with other now lost sources. Placed in chronological order of authorship dates, written accounts portray an increasingly gruesome death of Vico and López, including an ambush of arrows, decapitation, and cannibalism by the Ch'ol.[72] But the earliest and most reasonable of these accounts are by Maya authors writing in indigenous languages. By contrast, Spanish colonial sources, which are second- and third-hand, are probably based on later and increasingly elaborated oral testimonies that resemble legends and do not date until the early seventeenth century. But as early as only a decade after his death, and almost a century before the Spanish written accounts, Poqomchi' Maya noted in their *Título del Barrio de Santa Ana* (also known as *Iulihii titulo quetacque natirta*) of 1565:

> hrujúm Akalá také aj-San Marcos, ix-quimik huí ca-jáhu Santo Padre Fr. Domingo de Vico, cu-hré jenaj také hru-mam hra jáhu aj-San Marcos; xi-cansanik xi-tihuik Padre Fr. Domingo de Vico aj-Acalá . . . Hruhúm na-hok, qui tzajik qui ca-tumjik hruhúm aj-tzaj Lacantum majahok in-culik i Padre Mision Fr. Melchor, Fr. Antonio, Fr. Domingo.

> because they are from Acalá, those from San Marcos, where there died our lord the holy father Friar Domingo de Vico, those who are still the grandparents and parents of those from San Marcos; they killed him, those from Acalá ate father Friar Domingo de Vico . . . only because the terrible Lakantun persecuted and attacked, when the missionary fathers Friar Melchor, Friar Antonio, and Friar Domingo [de Vico] had still arrived.[73]

The vengeance enacted in response to the Ch'ol attack on the Dominicans was carried out by a joint Spanish and Highland Maya armed force partially led by the younger Don Juan, son of Juan Matal B'atz', who had replaced his father as a regional leader. On the one hand, the collaboration of Don Juan of Sacapulas with the Spanish attests to an older rivalry between the prehispanic Western K'iche' confederacy and the eastern Maya groups—the Ch'ol and Lakantun as well as the Eastern K'iche' or Achi—who thwarted Q'umarkaj's eastern expansion in the fourteenth and fifteenth centuries. The murder of the Dominicans, who were a historically recent but undoubtedly strategic ally, known to act simultaneously with and against the Spanish military, could have offered a convenient pretext for Western K'iche' retribution for events by the Ch'ol that predated the arrival of Europeans. On the other hand, the collaborative retribution for and early mention in Maya sources of their murder also signals the deep impact Vico and the Dominicans had had on the Maya with whom they had worked, especially the Western K'iche', Q'eqchi', Sakapultek, Poqomchi', and Kaqchikel.

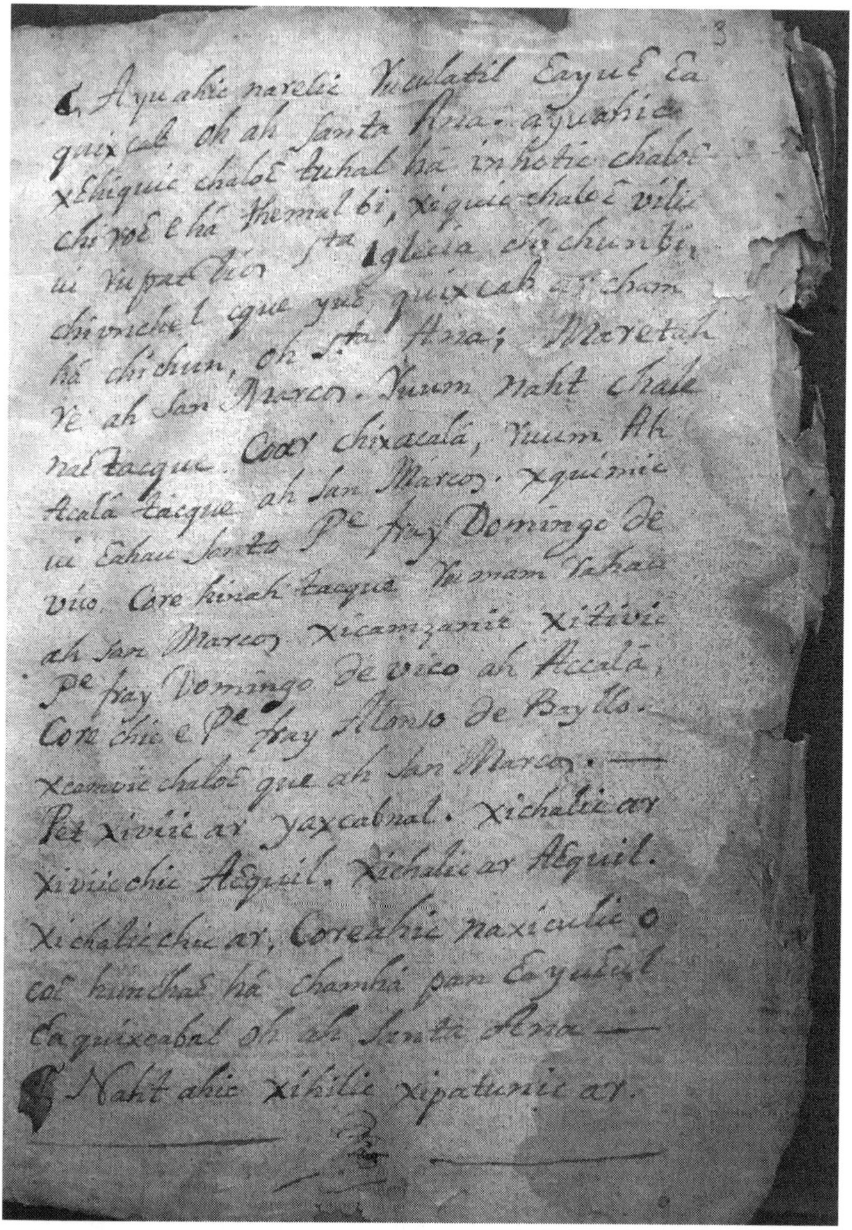

FIGURE 3.2. Garrett-Gates Mesoamerican Manuscript no. 242, fol. 3r. Note Vico's name on lines 11, 12 and 14. Princeton University Library. (Photo by Princeton University Library.)

In addition to the K'iche' Popol Wuj, *Title of Totonicapán*, and *Rab'inal Achi*, another significant Highland Maya document of this early period, the *Xajil Chronicle,* begun by Kaqchikel leadership around 1580, also speaks of Vico:

> Ja k'a ri juna' ralaxik qajawal Jesuxpto, xwuqlaj rujub'atz' ruk'in wolajuj chik chi juna' oq mixkam Don Fran. Xb'elejej oq tel wuqla'uja' roxmay. O chi B'eleje' Aj xel ruwuqla' uja' roxmay. Xkawinaq oq tikam ajaw Don Fran oq xkam chik qatata' Fray Domingo de Vico chi la' Ak'ala'. Qitzij chi nima ajtij qatata'. Xch'ay ruma amaq'. Xjuwinaq oq k'a tikam qatata' chi la' Ak'ala', toq xoqotax el P Fray Fran de la Parra kuma ajawa', obispo Ramírez.
>
> Since the year of the birth of our lord Jesus Christ, one thousand five hundred and forty and fifteen years had passed when Don Francisco [the head of the royal house of Sotz'il of the Kaqchikel Maya nation] died. It was nine days before the fifty-seven year [anniversary of the revolt by the Kaqchikel against the K'iche' Maya]. On [the day of the Maya ritual calendar] Nine Aj, forty-seven years had lapsed. It was forty days after the lord Don Francisco died, and our Father, Friar Domingo de Vico, died there at Acalá. In truth, our Father was a great teacher. He spoke for the *amaq'* [the people]. Twenty days after the death of our Father at Acalá, Father Friar Francisco de la Parra was then removed by the lords and Bishop Ramírez.[74]

Here Vico's death has parallel status with that of the former leader of one of the four prehispanic Kaqchikel noble lineages, and Vico is invoked with two other prominent clergy, the Franciscan friar La Parra and a Bishop Ramírez.[75] However, the *Xajil Chronicle* elevates Vico above the other clergy by referring to him as *nima ajtij*, a great teacher. Remesal echoes this characterization.[76]

VICO'S WRITINGS: PASTORAL, THEOLOGICAL, ETHNOGRAPHIC, AND LINGUISTIC

As noted earlier, shortly before Vico's death, Bishop Francisco Marroquín (who fostered the Dominican and Franciscan friars' work on Mayan languages and is said to have mastered a couple of the Mayan languages himself), approached Vico about writing a theological treatise, though on the nature of idolatry. Drawing upon his homiletical, linguistic, and ethnographic work, Vico wrote a theology that he must have hoped would model the ways preaching might actually incorporate local beliefs rather than merely condemn them. In addition to his earlier supposed writings on Maya grammar, vocabulary, customs, stories, and idiomatic expressions, Vico is also credited—and in some cases falsely—with having written sermons, hymns, and doctrinal material (see table 3.1). However, while much of the

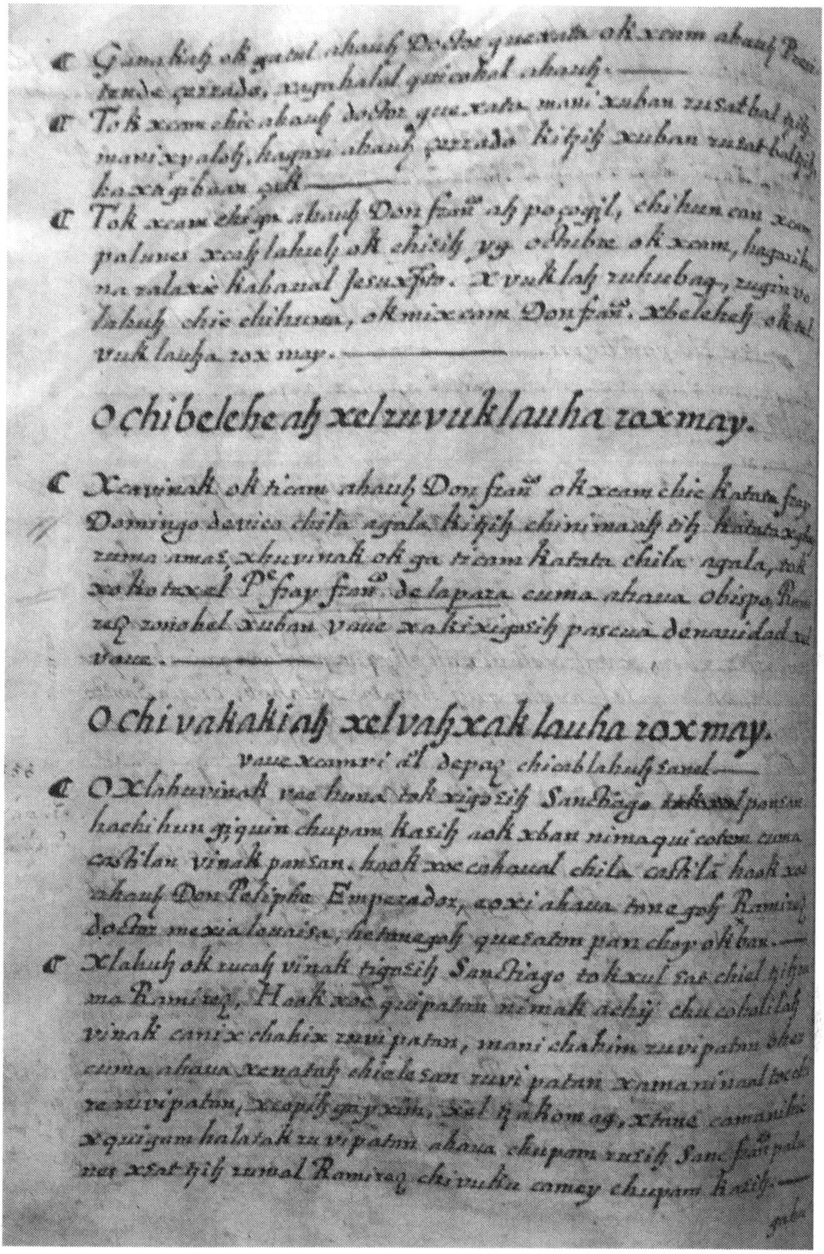

FIGURE 3.3. Berendt-Brinton Linguistic Collection, Manuscript 700, Item 221, page 66. Note Vico's name in the second line of the fourth paragraph on the page. Van Pelt Library of the University of Pennsylvania. (Photo by Garry Sparks.)

TABLE 3.1. Writings attributed to Friar Domingo de Vico, O.P.

Text	*Manuscript*	*Location*	*Language(s)*	*Date*	*Folio*	*Content*
I. PASTORAL	A. THEOLOGIES					
Theologia Indorum	GGMM no. 175	Princeton University	K'iche'	ca. 1605 [1554]	252	tome 2 (majority)
Theologia Indorum	GGMM no. 176	Princeton University	K'iche'	ca. 1600s [1554]	308	tome 2 (majority)
Theologia Indorum	GGMM no. 177	Princeton University	K'iche'	3/1/1759 [1554]	140	tome 2 (majority)
Theologia Indorum	GGMM no. 178	Princeton University	K'iche'	ca. 1500s [1553]	144	tome 1 (partial)
Theologia Indorum	GGMM no. 179	Princeton University	K'iche'	ca. 1500s [1553]	19 of 45	tome I (partial)
Theologia Indorum	GGMM no. 180	Princeton University	K'iche'	ca. 1500s [1553]	32	tome 1 (partial)
Theologia Indorum	GGMM no. 227	Princeton University	Kaqchikel	ca. 1500s [1553–54]	232	tomes 1 and 2 (partial)
Theologia Indorum	Manuscrit Américain 3	Bibliothèque nationale	Kaqchikel	ca. 1600s [1554]	275	tome 2 (complete)
Theologia Indorum	Manuscrit Américain 4	Bibliothèque nationale	Tz'utujil (or Kaqchikel)	ca. 1600s [1553]	188	tome 1 (complete)
Theologia Indorum	Manuscrit Américain 5	Bibliothèque nationale	K'iche'	9/16/1605 [1553]	185	tome 1 (complete)

continued on next page

Table 3.1—*continued*

Text	*Manuscript*	*Location*	*Language(s)*	*Date*	*Folio*	*Content*
Theologia Indorum	Manuscrit Américain 10	Bibliothèque nationale	K'iche'	ca. 1600s [1553]	105	tome 1 (complete)
Theologia Indorum	Manuscrit Américain 42	Bibliothèque nationale	Kaqchikel	ca. 1671–5 [1553]	180	tome 1 (complete)
Theologia Indorum	Manuscrit Américain 56	Bibliothèque nationale	K'iche'	ca. 1600s [1553–54]	48	tomes 1 and 2 (partial)
Theologia Indorum (as *Algunos sermones en lengua quiché de Rabinal*)	Ayer Ms 1512 Cakchiquel 33	Newberry Library	Kaqchikel	ca. 1620 [1554]	130	tome 2 (complete)
Theologia Indorum (as *Pláticas de la historia sagrada en lengua cacchi*)	Univ. of Penn. Manuscript Collection 700, Item 78	University of Pennsylvania	Q'eqchi'	ca. 1629 [1553–54]	18	tomes 1 and 2 (partial)
Theologia Indorum	Univ. of Penn. Manuscript Collection 700, Item 197	University of Pennsylvania	Tz'utujil	ca. 1700s [1554]	27 of 45	tome 2 (partial)
Theologia Indorum	Mss.497.4.Ua13 (old Indian Manuscript 178)	American Philosophical Society	K'iche'	9/16/1605 [1553]	190	tome 1 (complete)
Theologia Indorum (as "Quiché-Cakchiquel religious chants")	Tozzer Manuscript C.A.8 Q40	Harvard University	K'iche'	n.d. [1553]	54	tome 1 (partial)
	B. HOMILIES (DISPUTED)					
*Sermones en lengua achi ó tzutuhil**	Manuscrit Américain 69	Bibliothèque nationale	Tz'utujil or K'iche' (eastern Achi)	ca. 1635	173	sermons on the N.T., miracles, and prayers

continued on next page

Table 3.1—*continued*

Text	*Manuscript*	*Location*	*Language(s)*	*Date*	*Folio*	*Content*
*Sermones, oraciones y traducciones de la biblia escritos y expuestos en lengua Cakchiquel**	HSA NS3–34	Hispanic Society of America	Kaqchikel	ca. 1500s	41	sermons and lessons on the N.T.
*Coleccion de oraciones y meditaciones en lengua Quiché**	HSA NS3–37	Hispanic Society of America	K'iche'	ca. 1500s	103	lessons
	C. HYMNS (DISPUTED)					
*Varias coplas, versos é himnos en la lengua de Cobán de Verapaz**	Ayer Ms 1536, Kekchi 4	Newberry Library	Q'eqchi'	ca. 1600s [ca. 1540s]	33	songs
Las cosas de la fe católica	Kislak 1015	Library of Congress	K'iche'	1567 [1552]	42	songs
	D. OTHER (DISPUTED)					
Tratado de ídolos†	in Viana's 1577 report	[*Theologia Indorum*]	unknown			
Doctrina†	in Viana's 1577 report	[*Theologia Indorum*]	unknown			
Paraíso terrenal†	in Viana's 1577 report	[*Theologia Indorum*]	unknown			
2 *Confesionarios*†	in Viana's 1577 report	[*Theologia Indorum*]	unknown			
De los nombres grandes de los Patriarcas y Prophetas†	in Viana's 1577 report	[*Theologia Indorum*]	Rab'inal (eastern K'iche')			
Cathechismus Indorum†	in Viana's 1577 report	[*Theologia Indorum*]	Rab'inal (eastern K'iche')			

continued on next page

Table 3.1—*continued*

Text	*Manuscript*	*Location*	*Language(s)*	*Date*	*Folio*	*Content*
Euangelio de san Mateo	in Viana's 1577 report; GGMM no. 179	Princeton University	K'iche'	ca. 1500s	10 of 45	Gospel of Matthew (partial)
Los Proverbios de Salomón, la Epístolas y los Evangelios de todo el año, en lengua Mexicana†	lost; confiscated by Inquisition		Nahuatl			
II. LINGUISTIC	A. LEXICONS (DISPUTED)					
*Vocabulario en la lengua cakchiquel**	Manuscrit Américain 46	Bibliothèque nationale	Kaqchikel, K'iche', and Tz'utujil	ca. 1600s	286	lexicon
*Bocabulario en lengua Cakchi4el y 4iche otlatecas**	Codex Ind 13	John Carter Brown Library	Kaqchikel and K'iche'	ca. 1700s	353	lexicon
	B. GRAMMARS (DISPUTED)					
*Arte de Lengua 4iche ó utlatecat**	Manuscrit Américain 63	Bibliothèque nationale	K'iche'	ca. 1680s	35	grammar
	C. PHASES					
"sus frases e idiotismos"	in Remesal's 1619 *Historia*	Lost	unknown, various	n.a.	n.a.	idiomatic expressions

continued on next page

TABLE 3.1—*continued*

Text	*Manuscript*	*Location*	*Language(s)*	*Date*	*Folio*	*Content*
III. ETHNOGRAPHIC						
Todas las historias, fábulas, consejos, patrañas y errores en que vivían	in Remesal's 1619 *Historia*	Lost	unknown, most likely Spanish	n.a.	n.a.	folklore

* Disputed, especially based in large part on the dissimilarities between the pastoral discourse, terms, and phraseology of the *Theologia Indorum* and these other texts, with minor exception to parts of Kislak 1015. Furthermore, while it exceeds the scope of this book, I respectfully disagree with Ennio Bossú's conclusion that Vico wrote the *coplas*. Based on comparative analysis between the Q'eqchi' version of these *coplas* in Ayer Ms 1536 and the K'iche' version in Kislak 1015, it is possible that Vico, as a junior colleague of Cáncer briefly in the mid-1540s, did have some direct engagement with this text, but their songs' composition was most likely underway prior to the arrival of Las Casas's second group of Dominicans that included Vico; see appendix B and Sparks and Sachse (2017). However, for Bossú's position, see Bossú (1986). For comparisons between the Q'eqchi' *coplas* attributed to Cáncer with the *Theologia Indorum*, see Sparks (2011, 417–474, notes).

† Some texts attributed to Vico (e.g., by Remesal, Viana, and others) appear to have been mislabeled or misidentified sections separated from the *Theologia Indorum*: namely, a *tratado de ídolos*, a *doctrina* "grande," the *Paraíso terrenal*, a *confesionario*, another *doctrina* called *De los nombres grandes de los Patriarcas y Profetas*, and a *Cathechismus Indorum*.

‡ García Ahumada lists this work as Vico's but provides no supporting citation (García Ahumada 1994, 222). Tavárez describes a similar work—a "Proverbs of Solomon" bound with sermons in Nahuatl—held at the Hispanic Society of America, but which is Franciscan from central Mexico (possibly the same work García Ahumada attributes to Vico) and, thus, mistaken (Tavárez 2013a).

understanding of Vico's topics comes initially through Remesal's *Historia*, traces of the work may be preserved in Remesal's sources. For example, both Remesal and Ximénez undoubtedly used Las Casas's massive, nearly comprehensive description of the Americas, his *Apologética historia sumaria*, a work Las Casas began around 1552. Las Casas relied heavily, in turn, on his own experiences in the Americas but also on the experiences of other friars, such as Vico, who lived and worked extensively and intensely in specific cultural and linguistic regions. Specifically, it is most likely that Las Casas incorporated Vico's now lost ethnographic work on K'iche'an history and society into book 3 (chapters 234–241) of his *Apologética* that helped later chroniclers like Remesal.[77] Likewise, the Augustinian friar Jerónimo Román y Zamora may have also relied on Vico's ethnographic and folkloric writings for his 1575 history *Repúblicas de Indias*.[78]

While the list in table 3.1 is the most comprehensive to date, other manuscripts of the *Theologia Indorum* may still exist as either misidentified (such as the erroneous attribution of authorship to Friar Francisco Maldonado, O.F.M., to Bibliothèque nationale de France [BnF] Ms Amér 42) or bound with other contemporaneous folios (such as with sermons as in the case of University of Pennsylvania Linguistic Collection, Manuscript 700, Item 197). For example, Garrett-Gates Mesoamerican Manuscripts (GGMM, Princeton University Library) no. 227 actually consists of several different manuscripts of the *Theologia Indorum,* written by different hands and at some point all bound together. Furthermore, the William Gates photostatic copy (catalogued as Ayer Ms 1572 at the Newberry Library, Chicago) has no conclusive match with any of the known manuscripts; it remains unclear what the source manuscript was that was photocopied, perhaps one that has since been lost. Other writings attributed to other authors than Vico are included in table 3.1, such as the *Varias coplas* ascribed to Friar Luis de Cáncer, O.P., as well as those attributed to Vico but that most likely are not his, such as BnF Ms Amér 46 and 63 and Hispanc Society of America (HSA) NS3-34 and NS3-37. Also, for example, Bredt-Kriszat attributes BnF Ms Amér 56 "Algunos sermones en lengua quiche de Rabinal" to Vico; however, no systematic study has been carried out and may be as questionable of an attribution as the two lexicons and grammar.[79]

Vico's immediate impact even moved Bishop Marroquín, who in 1556 followed up on Vico's work with his own catechism, or *doctrina cristiana*, written in both Spanish and Kaqchikel Maya and published in Mexico City.[80] And while Marroquín's catechism was eventually printed, Vico's theology never was, but it also escaped suppression by the Spanish Inquisition, unlike the work of his Franciscan contemporary among the Nahua, Friar Bernardino de Sahagún.[81] On the contrary, well into the eighteenth century later clergy in the Maya highlands acknowledged, even in formal surveys submitted to the ecclesial hierarchy in Guatemala and Spain, that:

> para explicar en el Ydioma de los Naturales la Santa Doctrina, uso de los Libros que nos dejaron los Santos Padres Conquistadores, en especial de uno que se intítula Theologia Indorum, distuesto [*sic*] por el Venerable Padre Vico de me Sagrada Religión.
>
> to explain in the language of the native population the holy teachings, I use the books left to us by the holy missionary fathers, especially the one that is called the Theologia Indorum, prepared by the venerable Father Vico of my holy religion.[82]

Vico's writings were copied and passed along between later clergy long after his death and even possibly clandestinely in 1619 when Remesal wrote his history after the arrival of the institutional Catholic Reformation. Vico certainly influenced even authors who do not credit him.[83] In fact, a systematic comparison of mendicant doctrinal tracts written over the next two centuries proves how lasting an impression the *Theologia Indorum* made in the region.[84]

Regarding his linguistic work specifically, while it is possible that Vico wrote grammars and lexicons of all Mayan languages that he knew, only three have been attributed to him: a K'iche' grammar, or *arte,* and two *vocabularios* (a Kaqchikel dictionary and a combined K'iche' and Kaqchikel lexicon).[85] However, comparative analysis between the pastoral discourse in these three works on Mayan languages and that in the *Theologia Indorum* indicates that they are most likely not by Vico. Nevertheless, regardless of the veracity of these three works in particular, later seventeenth- and eighteenth-century mendicants working with Guatemalan Maya explicitly cite and quote Vico's work in their studies of Mayan languages, including Franciscan friar Thomás de Coto's Kaqchikel *Thesavrvs verborvm* (ca. 1670), Dominican friar Francisco Ximénez's *Tesoro de las tres lenguas cakchiquel, quiché y zutuhil* (ca. 1701–1704), Franciscan friar Pantaleón de Guzmán's *Diccionario cakchiquel* (1704), and the anonymous *Vocabulario en lengua castellana y guatemalteca denomido cakchikel chi.*[86] Even as late as 1813, the anonymous *Vocabulario de la lengua cakchiquel y español, con un Arte de la misma lengua* explicitly mentions Vico as an influential source.[87]

The Guatemalan mendicant texts evince a continual reception and use of Vico through most of the colonial period. But Highland Maya texts are some of the earliest postcontact indigenous literature in the Americas and illustrate various receptions of Vico among native peoples. Maya sources like the Poqomchi' *Título del barrio de Santa Ana* and the Kaqchikel *Xajil Chronicle* clarify Vico's biography and predate corroborating Spanish sources. They also help elucidate the reception of Vico's theology among the Maya. As the next sections and chapters demonstrate in greater detail, sixteenth-century Maya documents—such as the earliest text in the Kaqchikel *Xpantzay Cartulary* (erroneously dated 1524, but more likely 1552) and the Western K'iche' *Title of Totonicapán* (1554), Popol Wuj (ca. 1554–ca. 1558), *Title of the Tamub' I* or *K'iche' History of Lord Juan de Torres* (1580), *Title of the Tamub' III* or *Title of Pedro Velasco* (1592), and *Title of the Ilokab'* (ca. 1592)—echo references to Vico's theological treatise. Most of these references by Maya authors remain implicit, never mentioning Vico or his *Theologia Indorum* by name, but the 1592 Western K'iche' *Title of the Tamub' III* (or *Title of Pedro Velasco*) is quite direct:

> xpe k'ij xpe sak' wae uxenabal uticaribal kaxenabalic xojpe paraixo terrenal xa rumal uloic awas tulul rumal e wa chila paraixo terenal ta xojokotax ulok' paraixo terenal ta xepetic ri k'anabe chuch k'anabe kajaw e sanolic e puch k'atit kamam xpe k'ij xpe sak' oj umam oj ucajol atan oj umam xacab moysen abbrajan ixac xacopb xa rumal xquisach.. usuculiquil Santo wuj santo.. uloio co wi nabe wuj co wi quitsij e propeta moysen ajbrajan ixac xacapb intorum ubi nabe wuj c'o wi quica'ajolaxic k'amam k'ak'ajaw.
>
> Since the sun and since the dawn, these are the roots and the sprouting of our ancestors. We came from the Earthly Paradise because the prohibited sapote fruit was eaten by them there in the Earthly Paradise. Thus we were thrown out of the Earthly Paradise. Then came our first mother and our first father, they were naked and they were our grandmother and our grandfather since the sun and since the dawn. We are the grandsons and we are the sons of Adam; we are the grandsons of Jacob, Moses, Abraham, Isaac, and Jacob because they [the first grandparents] lost the holy rectitude of the holy book where there is the first book and where there are the words of the prophets Moses, Abraham, Isaac, and Jacob. [Theologia] Indorum was the name of the first book where there is the history of our grandfathers and fathers.[88]

The *Title of the Ilokab'* also by the Western K'iche' about 1592 is even more explicit:

> ta xetzib'an chi kut uk'ajol Moysen ta xkitzib'aj ralaxik uk'ajol Dios xa xchalax wi uk'ajol Dios xecha e propetax Moysen xcha puch propeta Balan propeta Xeremiyas xa xchalax wi q'ij xecha xa xcholax wi ch'umil xecha propetax xkitzib'aj chi uwach wuj santo Teuloxiyo Intorum k'o wi kitzij e propeta ta xa xchalax wi uk'ajol Dios xecha k'a chi ri kut xek'axtokotaj wi qamam qaqajaw chi ri Exipto.
>
> When they wrote to, then, the son of Moses, when they wrote of the birth of the son of God, "the son of God will just be born," said the prophets, Moses said thus and the prophet Balaam and the prophet Jeremiah, "the sun will just be born," they said, "the stars will just align," said the prophets when they wrote on the face of the book, the holy Theologia Indorum, there are the words of the prophets, "the son of God will just be born," they said still over there then they were cheated, our grandfathers and our fathers over there in Egypt.[89]

A century after Remesal, Friar Francisco Ximénez commented in the early eighteenth century that the majority of Vico's works could still be found among the Maya parish caretakers, or *fiscales*:

> es mucho de notar que siendo de los primeros padres que escribieron de quienes apenas se hallan ya escritos algunos, de los de el vble. padre [Vico] no se ha perdido alguno, antes de solos suyos conservan los indios teniéndolos en tanta veneración como si fuera un rico tesoro; leyéndose públicamente en la iglesia los días que comulgan, y también es cosa muy digna de reparo que siendo tan obscuros algunos escritos antiguos que hoy se hallan por haberse mudado mucho las lenguas de lo antiguo como en todas las lenguas sucede, deste ve. pe. [Vico] son tan claros para todos que parece la mesma lengua que el día de hoy se halla.

> it is important to note those first priests who wrote works here, that at least some of their writings can still be found, and that those of the venerable Father [Vico] have not all been lost but rather some of his writings are saved by the Indians who hold onto them with a veneration as if they were a rich treasure and read them publicly in church on the days that they gather; and it is a very dignified thing as I recall that there are some very obscure old writings which today seem to have been updated a great deal from the ancient languages, as in every successful language, but of those writings by this venerable Father [Vico] they are clear for everyone that they appear in the same [Mayan] language that is found here today.[90]

Clearly, in the centuries following his death, Vico's ethnographic, linguistic and theological work was a "best seller" for both Maya and mendicants.[91]

Vico's years as the Dominican prior in the capital of the *audiencia* of Guatemala placed him in a predominantly Kaqchikel-speaking area, albeit one that attracted speakers of other indigenous languages, such as K'iche' Diego Reynoso, for various commercial, legal, educational, and religious reasons. The majority of the surviving versions of the *Theologia Indorum* appear in K'iche', and the K'iche' manuscripts are the longest and most detailed, complete enough that they are the best sources to use to estimate Vico's full text. Thus, it is most likely that Vico initially began to write his theology in K'iche' and then he, or later Maya or mendicants, soon translated it into Kaqchikel, Tz'utujil, Achi, Q'eqchi', and even possibly into Sakapultek. This scholastic humanist's history—his early days in a linguistically, religiously, and culturally diverse part of the Mediterranean, his extensive fieldwork among the K'iche', his collaboration with a K'iche' *popol winaq* like Diego Reynoso, and his extended stay in the minor cosmopolitan city of colonial Santiago de Guatemala—all contributed to his vastly influential *Theologia Indorum*.

THEOLOGIA INDORUM: A THEOLOGY FROM, TO, AND FOR THE "INDIANS"

Although never published and now existing only in manuscript fragments in multiple Highland Mayan languages, all hand-copied into the late eighteenth century, a complete text of the *Theologia Indorum* can be reconstructed by comparing the eighteen surviving versions (see table 3.2).[92] A reconstructed text would consist of over 800 manuscript pages, divided between Vico's two distinct volumes of 1553 and 1554, respectively, for a total of 216 discrete units or "chapters" (including the introductions to each volume and a colophon in the first) that address a variety of religious, moral, and cultural issues. Erroneously listed in current library catalogues as a collection of sermons, a long catechism, or set of biblical translations, the *Theologia Indorum* better resembles a *summa,* or systematic theological summary or compendium, than any other genre of the early 1500s. In part, Vico used biblical narratives as a basic organizing structure. However, akin to Aquinas's *Summa theologiae*, he began the first tome by discussing the being and names of God, the creation and order of the cosmos, and then moved to stories of the Catholic Old Testament. In his second tome, structured along the books of the Christian New Testament, he incorporated but greatly expanded upon catechism material, ironically at a time when the missionaries' expectations of indigenous people were decreasing and, thus, catechisms in general were getting simpler.

Previous scholars who have worked with the *Theologia Indorum* have also mistakenly identified it as either a compilation of sermons (a *sermonario*) or the redaction of three or four separate works: "The Names of God" or "Theology of the Indians" proper (from the introduction to chapter 29 of volume one), "The Earthly Paradise" (from chapters 30–45 of volume one), "The List of Great Names of the Patriarchs and Prophets" (from chapters 46 through the remainder of volume one), and a catechism as the second volume.[93] Closer study of the second tome, however, also reveals Vico's approach of interweaving narratives from the New Testament with doctrinal material. For example, chapters 1–22 present stories of Jesus's birth, youth, and early ministry; chapters 23–32 focus on Aquinas's natural and supernatural virtues; chapters 33–41 explain the sacraments; chapters 42–60 exegete the teachings and miracles attributed to Jesus; chapters 61–93 teach specific prayers, commandments, and dogmas; chapters 94–105 shift back to present the Passion and Pentecost stories; and the final chapters, chapters 106–110, focus on the role of clergy and the final judgment.

The division of volume one of Vico's theological treatise into the three parts listed above resulted from a report to the Spanish Inquisition by Friar Francisco de Viana, O.P., a contemporary of Vico who also worked in the Verapaces region, and whose writings were also a likely source for the first historian of the Dominicans in Guatemala, Antonio de Remesal.[94] In response to the Holy Office's inquiry into the amount and types of clerical materials written in local languages,

Table 3.2. *Theologia Indorum* manuscripts: volumes, languages, conditions

Theologia Indorum, vol. I	*Theologia Indorum, vols. I & II*	*Theologia Indorum, vol. II*
APS Ms (K'iche')[A,TC]	BnF Ms Amér 56 (K'iche')[C]	GGMM no. 175 (K'iche')[B]
BnF Ms Amér 5 (K'iche')[A]		GGMM no. 176 (K'iche')[B]
BnF Ms Amér 10 (K'iche')[A,TC]		GGMM no. 177 (K'iche')[B]
GGMM no. 178 (K'iche')[B]		GGMM no. 180 (K'iche')[C]
GGMM no. 179 (K'iche')[C]		
Tozzer Ms C.A.8 Q 40 (K'iche')[C]		
BnF Ms Amér 42 (Kaqchikel)[A]		Ayer Ms 1512 (Kaqchikel)[A]
	GGMM no. 227 (Kaqchikel)[C]	BnF Ms Amér 3 (Kaqchikel)[A,TC]
BnF Ms Amér 4 (Tz'utujil [Kaqchikel])[A]		Penn Ms 700, 197 (Tz'utujil [Kaqchikel])[C]
	Penn Ms 700, 78 (Q'eqchi')[C]	

[A] Complete.
[B] Mostly complete.
[C] Fragment(s), very incomplete/damaged.
[TC] Has a table of contents (of vol. I in APS Ms; of vol. II in BnF Ms Amér 3 and 10, and Ayer Ms 1512).

on September 18, 1577, Viana sent an inventory that included a listing of writings by Vico:

> En lo que toca al negocio que v.m. me encarga y manda que aga, cierto yo quisiera scusarme, no tanto por el trabajo quanto porque lo más, o casi todo, que está scripto en estas lenguas, lo scripto yo; aunque otras scrituras ay del padre fray Domingo de Vico, pero no son tantas . . . Lo que está scripto de Sagrada Scriptura en estas lenguas es, solamente, los Euangelios de todo el año, y el Euangelio de san Mateo. No ay otra cosa scripta de Sagrada Scriptura y, ésta, ningún yndio creo yo que la tiene; pero, si alguno la tubiere, se le quitará. Los demás libros que están scriptos en estas lenguas son los siguientes:
>
> - Vna *Doctrina* algo grande por el padre fray Domingo de Vico.
> - Vn *Paraíso terrenal*, del mesmo.
> - Vn *Confesonario* para los religiosos y, otro pequeño, para los yndios.
> - Vnas *Horas* y vnos *Cantares*, y vn *Cathezismo de la fe*, brebe.
> - Ay otra *Doctrina*, que se dice *De los nonbres grandes de los Patriarcas y Prophetas*, traducida de la lengua de Rabinal, la qual scribió tanbién el padre fray Domingo de Vico en aquella lengua, y se a traducido en vna de las de acá.

- Ay otro *Cathechismus Indorum*, también traducido de la mesma lengua de Rabinal, el qual hizo el mesmo padre fray Domingo de Vico.
- El *Euangelio* de san Mateo scribió tanbién el padre fray Domingo de Vico.[95]

On the assigned task that the venerable superior charges and commands me to do, it is certain I would like to excuse myself not so much due to the amount of the work but rather because most, or almost all, that is written in these languages I wrote aside from the other writings here by Father Friar Domingo de Vico, but there is not much . . . What is written of the Holy Scriptures in these languages is only the gospels for the whole year, and the Gospel of Saint Matthew. There is nothing else written of the Holy Scriptures and of this no indigenous person, I believe, has a copy; but if someone has a copy, one will take it away. The rest of the books that are written in these languages are the following:

- a "Doctrine" somewhat large by the Father Friar Domingo de Vico,
- an "Earthly Paradise" by the same,
- a "Confessionary Manual" for the religious clergy and another small one for the indigenous laity,
- a "Book of Hours" and a "Songbook" and a brief "Catechism,"
- there is another "Doctrine" that is called "On the Great Names of the Patriarchs and Prophets" translated into the Rabinal language of which the Father Friar Domingo de Vico wrote this in that language and translated into another there,
- [and] the "Gospel of Saint Matthew" which the Father Friar Domingo de Vico also wrote.

However, a reconstructed version of the entire *Theologia Indorum* indicates Vico's theological text is highly systematic, clearly distinguished from other religious writings in both size and scope, and thus "probably the most complete theological treatise ever produced in a native American tongue."[96]

In contrast to contemporaneous mendicant texts, Vico's *Theologia Indorum* distinguished itself in four notable ways. First, Vico's theology is not a translation of a previously written European text exported to Mesoamerica, as was the case with catechisms, devotional books like Thomas à Kempis's *The Imitation of Christ*, or works on mystical theology. Instead, the *Theologia Indorum* explicitly references Maya practices and narratives, which Vico based on his direct conversation and ethnographic study among the Maya. Second, the *Theologia Indorum* was originally written in K'iche'an languages, not Latin or Castilian, and, except for 62 chapters, still remains untranslated to this day.[97] Furthermore, Vico not only wrote his treatise in K'iche' but also used a high register of moral, ritual, and ceremonial discourse attentive to traditional Maya rhetoric and poetics. Third, the *Theologia Indorum* is the first known work written in either North or South America to explicitly declare itself a theology, thus intentionally differentiating itself in terms of genre from its textual peers. Finally, and perhaps most important, while it was apparently initially commissioned as an aid for priests, the primary readers directly addressed in Vico's text are not fellow clergy but rather literate Maya, whom he refers to as *ix* ("you all") and *numi'al, nuk'ajol* ("my daughters and my sons"). This marks the *Theologia Indorum* as a direct Christian address to the Maya and a reply to their cosmogonic narratives, or "scripture," found in texts like the Popol Wuj.

Manuscripts' Overview, History, and Circulation

In general, the "disappearance" of Vico's writings and legacy from the histories of the region correspond to a general gap in the wider reception and circulation of locally produced texts, especially those by indigenous peoples in indigenous languages. Later "discoverers" of native-language manuscripts compounded this loss by misidentifying and miscataloging manuscripts, creating difficulties with which current Mayanists continue to struggle. Problems with the *Theologia Indorum*'s recirculation and reception have ultimately obscured its similarities to a *summa* and, perhaps more important, have blinded scholars to its culturally attuned theology and theological method, which in large part constitutes its uniqueness as a document.

Due to both natural decay and intentional damage to ecclesial records during the nineteenth-century Liberal periods, as well as the Guatemalan military's twentieth-century "scorched-earth" campaign, too few colonial Spanish and Maya manuscripts survive. After New Spain separated from the Spanish Empire and Guatemala declared its independence on September 15, 1821, regional political history consisted of an unstable volley between Liberal and Conservative administrations until the Liberal Revolution of 1871. As in much of former Spanish America, the positivism of French philosopher and sociologist Isidore Marie Auguste François Xavier Comte (1789–1857) provided an intellectual foundation for the political liberalism of Guatemala. Whereas the Conservative parties of the region advocated for a continuance of Roman Catholicism as the established religion of the new nation-states, liberalism carried the banner of anticlericalism.

While not as violent as the anticlericalism of the early twentieth century, such as the state policies of execution or forced marriages of Catholic clergy during the Mexican Revolution, nineteenth-century anticlerical policies by Guatemalan Liberal administrations often demanded the removal or expulsion of clergy and confiscated Catholic Church property, including parish records and archives dating back to the sixteenth century. In 1829, many of these documents were turned over to the library of the nationalized University of San Carlos, sold at auction, or given as official state gifts to foreign libraries and private collectors. In this manner, the

American Philosophical Society gained its copy of the *Theologia Indorum* along with ten other colonial texts in K'iche'an languages as a gift from the Liberal Guatemalan governor José Felipe Mariano Gálvez.[98] At one point during the late 1970s during Guatemala's genocidal armed conflict, overly zealous Maya members of Catholic Action reportedly removed *cofres* (wooden boxes) of parish records of the historic Dominican church in Sacapulas and publically burned them in the central town plaza.[99] The archive of the Dominican province of San Vicente—which would once have offered invaluable information about colonial Guatemala, Chiapas, and likely Friar Vico—has disappeared along with those of other various convents and monasteries.[100] Among those manuscripts removed from rural parishes—documents often entrusted for centuries to Catholic Maya *fiscales* or parish caretakers—and that still exist were the oldest known surviving version of the Popol Wuj and all known copies of the *Theologia Indorum.*[101]

On the one hand, the disruption of separate, isolated, and mostly forgotten repositories of colonial manuscripts in the nineteenth and twentieth centuries caused an incalculable loss of historical documents and cultural and religious patrimony, perhaps paralleled only by the destruction of prehispanic Mesoamerican texts and archives by Spanish soldiers and clergy in the sixteenth century. On the other hand, the rediscovery and dissemination of some of these manuscripts beginning in the nineteenth century coincided with and further encouraged an emerging European interest in American, especially Native American, antiquities. The birth of large private collections of colonial documents, particularly those written by Native Americans or in Native American languages, augmented the value of what had previously been considered worthless parish paperwork. The threat of intentional destruction and perceived historic neglect further propelled wealthy hobbyists initially in Europe and soon after in the United States to gather and attempt to identify and catalogue texts from the Maya highlands. Though little attempt was made to translate these texts at the time, aside from the efforts of a few notable scholars, like Brasseur de Bourbourg or Daniel Brinton, these hobbyist endeavors arguably contributed to a rediscovery of many of the most important surviving Maya texts, and those like Vico's *Theologia Indorum* that had been written in Mayan languages by colonial Spanish mendicants.

Father Charles Étienne Brasseur de Bourbourg was undoubtedly the single most significant collector of Highland Maya manuscripts during this period. Having arrived in Guatemala for the first time in 1855, during an era of a Conservative administration favorable to the return of Catholic clergy, Brasseur de Bourbourg learned Kaqchikel Maya while serving as parish priest in the highland town of San Juan Sacatepéquez. Working with Guatemalan scholars and librarians Mariano Padillo and Juan Gavarrete of the University of San Carlos's library, Brasseur de Bourbourg encountered many colonial manuscripts written by Highland Maya or in Mayan languages, including a version of the Popol Wuj redacted by Dominican friar Francisco Ximénez in the early eighteenth century. Padillo and Gavarrete purportedly gave Brasseur de Bourbourg many documents held at the library and other state-operated archives, and Brasseur de Bourbourg began to translate one of these gifts, the *Xajil Chronicle*, a sixteenth-century history by Kaqchikel Maya.[102]

On a subsequent trip to Guatemala, where he also later served as parish priest in the Eastern K'iche'-speaking town of Rabinal by invitation of Guatemalan Archbishop Francisco García Peláez, Brasseur de Bourbourg learned K'iche' and claims to have discovered many other Maya documents, including other versions of texts copied in Ximénez's hand including manuscripts of Ximénez's own study of K'iche'an languages and a copy of the only prehispanic drama in the Americas by indigenous authors—the Achi or Eastern K'iche' *Rab'inal Achi*. Brasseur de Bourbourg claims to have been given these colonial manuscripts in Mayan languages by the parish caretaker or *fiscal*, Ignacio Coloche, who was also of local noble K'iche'-Achi lineage in Rabinal.[103] A subsequent, yet more unlikely story, has a Colonel Juan Galindo—an Anglo-Irish mercenary who served during the Liberal administration of General José Francisco Morazán Quezada in the 1820s—take a copy of the Popol Wuj, most probably the one housed at the University of San Carlos, to Europe where it eventually landed in Brasseur de Bourbourg's possession.[104] Galindo's presence in this account is more important than any degree of historical validity, for it helps to illustrate the questionable circumstances under which many of Brasseur de Bourbourg's documents, and the Popol Wuj in particular, left libraries and archives in Guatemala.[105]

By the time of his death, Brasseur de Bourbourg's immense library of Mayan language documents—including the *Xajil Chronicle*, the *Rab'inal Achi*, the Popol Wuj, the *Title of Totonicapán* and other *títulos*, various *artes* and *vocabularios*, along with numerous versions of the *Theologia Indorum*—were scattered through auctions to wealthy collectors, many of whom were US industrialists.[106] Daniel G. Brinton, for example, bought the *Xajil Chronicle*, attempted the first partial English translation of that text, and included it in his groundbreaking late nineteenth-century study of comparative Native American literature. Hubert Howe Bancroft bought numerous Brasseur de Bourbourg documents, including those of Ximénez once housed at the library of the University of San Carlos and now to be found at the library of the University of California at Berkeley.[107] William Edward Gates, a self-trained Mesoamerican scholar, purchased Brasseur de Bourbourg and others' libraries and attempted to make Maya studies profitable by selling photostatic or photographic copies of many manuscripts to academic and research libraries. While never a financially lucrative investment for Gates, many libraries' special collections use his copies of the *Theologia Indorum*. However, Gates's collection of original manuscripts of the *Theologia Indorum*, the largest extant, also resides in the United States; his library moved in bulk to the Firestone Library of Princeton University through the donation of collector Robert Garrett.[108]

Despite such dispersals and massive transfers to other countries like the United States, the bulk of Brasseur de Bourbourg's Mesoamerican library remained in France, including the portion purchased by Alphonse Louise Pinart. Although Pinart eventually sold most of his collection to the Parisian Bibliothèque nationale de France (BnF), many invaluable manuscripts—such as the ca. 1701–1704 version of the Popol Wuj (the oldest known), the then-only-known copy of the *Title of Totonicapán*, and versions of Vico's works—were purchased by Count Charles-Félix-Hyacinthe G. de Charencey. However, even these documents once held by Charencey eventually arrived into the Manuscrit Américain collection of the BnF when his widow donated his collection.[109] Most of those manuscripts of Vico's work not purchased by Gates from Brasseur de Bourbourg and eventually donated or sold to libraries in the United States remain in the BnF by way of Pinart and then Charencey's donations. However, before his death, Charencey did sell several key manuscripts to other collectors, which is how Ximénez's copy of the Popol Wuj and a Kaqchikel version of the *Theologia Indorum* ended up in the possession of US railroad baron Edward Everett Ayer. Beginning in 1911, Ayer donated his entire collection of maps, Native American artifacts, and manuscripts to the Newberry Library of Chicago. The donation also included a near-complete collection of Gates's photostats of Vico's writings.[110]

While none of the surviving versions of Vico's *Theologia Indorum* appears to be written in his own hand, and thus none is first generation, the currently known, positively confirmed eighteen manuscript versions of it (tables 3.1 and 3.2) may be summed up in three ways. By their present-day locations, seven are at Princeton University, six are at the Bibliothèque nationale de France in Paris, two are at the University of Pennsylvania, one at the American Philosophical Society in Pennsylvania, one at the Newberry Library in Chicago and one at Harvard University. According to the languages in which they appear to be written, eleven are in various dialects of K'iche' Maya, four are in various dialects of Kaqchikel Maya, two are in Tz'utujil Maya, and one is in Q'eqchi' Maya; however, many of the manuscripts also show indications of more than one language and, given the history of changes within and between Mayan languages, other language variants, such as dialects of Sakapultek or Poqom, may also be in these manuscripts. Finally, based on content, eight of the manuscripts are versions (in whole or in part) of volume one, completed in 1553, which consists of 105 units in fully reconstructed form and ranges between 300 and 350 leaves; seven manuscripts (on whole or in part) are versions of the second volume, finished in 1554, which consists of 111 units in fully reconstructed form between 250 and 350 leaves; and three versions are fragments that have combined parts from both volumes one and two, often by various hands and divergent scripts.

However, given the variance in handwriting and script, the various length and number of leaves of each version make estimations of the size of the entire text difficult to assess. For example, even complete versions of the first volume in Kaqchikel and Tz'utujil are shorter in length, but not number of units, than versions in K'iche'. Future comparative analysis between versions of the same volumes, or even same chapters, may disclose not insignificant differences in terms of the content of each. Furthermore, in addition to the fact that no version appears to be a first-generation manuscript, variations between versions may also reflect attempts by local Maya scribes or even priests to accommodate the particular variant of a specific locale—such as the K'iche' of San Sebastián de Lemoa rather than of Totonicapán, or the Kaqchikel of San Martín Jilotepeque rather than of Sololá—as well as changes within and between K'iche'an languages diachronically over the course of the sixteenth, seventeenth, and eighteenth centuries. Therefore, no single manuscript contains the whole *Theologia Indorum*, which must, therefore, be reconstructed from these pieces.[111]

Preliminary Solutions to Problems in the Identification of Vico Texts

As in the late nineteenth century, current scholarly reception of Vico's work has consisted of three points of confusion: the identification of (1) Vico as the actual author of a manuscript version, (2) the original or primary languages of his theology, and (3) his writings' proper genre, and thus its role. Unfortunately, these three concerns have overshadowed more important lines of inquiry, such as, (1) the explicit and implicit claims Vico makes in his theology regarding Hispano-Catholic and Maya religion and culture, (2) how he makes his claims and thus how he relies on religious, cultural, and specifically linguistic resources, and (3) how such content impacted, or was received by, his wider contemporaneous Maya audience. Before advancing to these latter concerns regarding the substance of Vico's theological work and method, these enduring initial confusions must be addressed—always with an eye, however, to genre and language use, which do tie these questions of categorization to the more intricate concerns of Vico's contemporary implications. The wider context of mendicant work in Mesoamerica outlined in chapter 2, and the circulation history detailed in the above section, begin to correctly identify and clarify Vico's work. Therefore, before presenting a reconstruction, summary, and analysis of the content of (the claims and method in) his *Theologia Indorum*, such as in the next chapter, one should begin to address and correct some problems by previous scholarship of this text that has led to its misidentification and underappreciation.

Unlike most subsequent collectors of colonial Maya texts, but like Ximénez over a century before and René Acuña a century after him, Brasseur de Bourbourg had a working knowledge of Highland Mayan languages based on his time as parish priest in the Verapaces area, specifically among the Achi of Rabinal.[112] He appears to have done most of the initial identification and cataloging of the writings by Domingo de Vico himself. His catalogue contains many errors that (because of subsequent collectors' illiteracy with regards to Highland Mayan languages) persist all the way down to present-day library collections. Some cataloging errors pertain to the difficult task of distinguishing between the various Highland Mayan languages—languages that still change, grow apart, and swap words through continued mutual contact—as spoken in disparate communities during the colonial era, a difficulty which leads to the misidentification of the languages of the various versions of the *Theologia Indorum*. For example, colonial Kaqchikel and K'iche' among elites and especially in proximate contact zones were linguistically not as distinct as they are today by modern speakers. And the Tz'utujil identified within Vico's texts appears to modern Maya readers to have a high degree of Kaqchikel interference, as if it were from colonial variants near Kaqchikel-speaking areas around Lake Atitlán.

In some cases, this lack of familiarity with Mayan languages has also been compounded by previous cataloguers' inability to distinguish between Vico's authorship and the names of manuscript copyists as well as those of subsequent translators of the *Theologia Indorum* into other Mayan languages, thus falsely attributing Vico's work to someone else. For example, Ennio María Bossú's analysis exemplifies a case of double mistaken authorship as he attempted to attribute a sixteenth-century set of songs or *coplas* in Q'eqchi' to Vico. As he aimed to better recognize and expand Vico's written catalogue, Bossú's argued that Vico was more the likely author of the manuscript *Varias coplas, versos é himnos en la lengua de Cobán de Verapaz sobre los misterios de la religión para uso de los neofitos de la dicha provincial.* The text had initially been attributed to another Spanish Dominican and early contemporary of Vico who also worked in the Verapaces, Friar Luis de Cáncer, O.P.[113] However, according to sociolinguist Sergio Romero, the Q'eqchi' text, at least the surviving manuscript, appears to be newer than the *Theologia Indorum* by a few decades, to about the late sixteenth century.[114] Furthermore, based on close comparative analysis between the pastoral discourse and rhetoric in *coplas* in Q'eqchi' and the *Theologia Indorum* in K'iche' and Kaqchikel, three notable differences emerge that tend to serve as hallmarks of Vico's work. The first is the extensive use of Highland Maya ceremonial discourse and rhetoric of Maya poetics rather than European strophic patterns, such as the tight four-line stanzas of *coplas*. The second is Vico's use of ancient Maya phrases in parallel structure that are also found in classic-era logosyllabic texts, like *q'anal raxal* ("yellowness, greenness" to signify "splendor and abundance" or, especially for Dominicans, "glory"), but also neologisms or the incorporation of traditional K'iche'an words in new and distinctively Catholic uses.[115] The third is the appropriation of a few distinctively Highland Maya names for deities also found in K'iche' religious texts like the Popol Wuj but used in the *Theologia Indorum* for the Christian god. The pastoral discourse in these two texts is different enough to consider that the *Theologia Indorum* may have influenced the Q'eqchi' *coplas* but that Vico was not the author of them. Romero, thus, also disagrees with Bossú's claim that Vico rather than Cáncer is the real author of the *coplas* and argues instead that the *Theologia Indorum* influenced the later production of other Dominican doctrinal texts in K'iche'an languages, like the Q'eqchi' *coplas*.[116]

However, recently a K'iche' version of the *coplas* has been discovered within a small manuscript held in the Jay I. Kislak Collection of the US Library of Congress.[117] In addition to being written in K'iche' rather than Q'eqchi', the K'iche' *coplas* are more extensive and thus provide many additional chapters missing in the Q'eqchi' version. The K'iche' version also shares much more of the phrasing, terms, and ideas also found in the *Theologia Indorum*, such as identifying the fruit forbidden to Adam and Eve explicitly as sapote (*tulul*). Also, unlike the Q'eqchi' *coplas*, the K'iche' version provides a colophon with dates that seem to indicate that they were composed between 1544 and 1552, dates that encompass the end of Luis de Cáncer's time in Guatemala before leaving for Florida and the arrival of Vico from Spain.[118] The additional material found in the K'iche' *coplas* along with the Q'eqchi' *coplas* compared to both volumes one and two of the *Theologia Indorum* provides evidence of a closer degree of correspondence between these two texts (see appendix B). While it is possible that a version of these songs, possibly initially composed by Cáncer and his cohort of early Dominicans into the Maya highlands, was one of the mendicant antecedents for Vico's theology, there is no conclusive evidence as to which language was the original for the *coplas*. The later Q'eqchi' manuscript now at the Newberry Library in Chicago may, in fact, present a preserved copy of an initial version later elaborated by Vico's cohort into K'iche'. Or, Cáncer and later Vico may have originally composed or translated as a set of *coplas* into K'iche' that were subsequently refashioned into Q'eqchi'. Regardless, the *coplas* and other pastoral texts elaborated by Dominicans in K'iche'an languages—such as catechisms as analyzed by linguistic anthropologist Frauke Sachse—show the development of what sociolinguist Romero calls a "Dominican school" of translation, of which Vico was a key intellectual figure, that was distinct from the work of mendicants elsewhere in the Americas.[119]

Likewise, of the three colonial-era manuscripts in the collection at the Hispanic Society of America in New York that were written in Highland Mayan languages by mendicants, two are attributed to Vico.[120] A manuscript titled a *Colección de oraciones y meditaciones en lengua Quiché*, which is actually in Kaqchikel, is said in the catalogue to be a work that is "original and unedited without a doubt written in the hand of the author, the Friar Domingo de Vico."[121] However, the language, particularly the language used for elaborating a doctrine of the Christian god, is simply *Dios* and is not consistent with that of the *Theologia Indorum*, which is explained in detail in the next chapter. Furthermore, for a manuscript thought to have been written in the sixteenth century, the highly refinded Gothic script is completely different from that of any of the early versions of the *Theologia Indorum* or what is thought to be Vico's grammar or lexicon. Based simply on the differences in handwriting, only one of these two HSA manuscripts, the *Colección* or the *Sermones*, can possibly be written by Vico. More likely, neither one of them is, since with the possible exception of the lexicon in Kaqchikel, all eighteen versions of the *Theologia Indorum* as well as the other language studies appear to be at least-second generation copies.

The second manuscript of the three—*Sermones, oraciones y traducciones de la biblia escritos y expuestos en lengua Cakchikquel*—is also thought to be by either Vico or Franciscan friar Francisco Maldonado and is a collection of sermons. It is written in various hands, most likely from different manuscripts but eventually bound together into a single codex.[122] As is pointed out below, this is not the only time that the works of Vico and Maldonado have been confused. A thorough understanding of the *Theologia Indorum* can aid comparative textual analysis and help correct the catalogue histories of early documents in Mayan languages. Beyond that, the comparative analysis between collections of sermons (*sermonarios*), lessons (*lesiones*), talks (*pláticas*), catechisms (*doctrinas*), and other pastoral texts helps to clarify that the *Theologia Indorum* is not, in fact, a collection of homilies or any other of these common pastoral genres.

In addition to these pastoral and linguistic texts erroneously or at least suspiciously thought to have been authored by Vico, some documents identified as a *Theologia Indorum* have also suffered misattributions. For example, in the early nineteenth century, J. M. Beristain y Souza attributed a Kaqchikel version of Vico's *Theologia Indorum* of the Bibliothèque nationale de France, Ms Amér 42, to the seventeenth-century Spanish Franciscan friar, Francisco Maldonado, and Eleanor B. Adams repeated Beristain y Souza's mistake in 1952.[123] In fact, Adams attributes enormous linguistic competence and output—over thirteen manuscripts—to Maldonado instead of Vico. However, again, close comparative analysis between the purported Maldonado *Theologia Indorum* and those earlier versions known to be by Vico show that they are exactly the same text and, therefore, that Vico is also the author of that Kaqchikel version, one that Maldonado likely copied during his time at the Convento de San Francisco in Guatemala a century later. Likewise, the only manuscript of the *Theologia Indorum* in the collection of the Newberry Library of Chicago—Ayer Manuscript 1522, Cakchiquel 33—was mistakenly listed as written by Friar Francisco Gonsales rather than Vico.[124]

Finally, Enrique García Ahumada also attributes an early Nahuatl text to Vico, *Los Proverbios de Salomón, las Epístolas y los Evangelios de todo el año, en lengua mexicana* ("The Proverbs of Solomon, the Letters and Gospels of the whole year, in the Mexican tongue"), which the Holy Office prevented from publication.[125] However, this is highly unlikely for two reasons. First, the polyglot Vico learned at least seven Mayan languages, but there is no mention that he also learned a non-Mayan language such as Nahuatl. Unlike Chiapas, Guatemala did have a historic precontact Nahuatl-speaking population, referred to as the Yaki by the K'iche' Maya and later as the Pipil after the arrival of Spaniards with their Nahuatl-speaking allies from central Mexico—such as the Tlaxcaltecas, Cholultecas, Acolhuas, amd Tenochcas. However, there is no indication that Vico or other Dominicans worked in that southern coastal region near present-day El Salvador.[126]

Furthermore, Spanish Nahua allies did settle in neighborhoods around the second and third capital cities of Guatemala—present-day Ciudad Vieja and La Antigua, respectively—and Vico thus may have had some contact with Nahuatl-speakers or even students during his time at the convent in Santiago de Guatemala (present-day La Antigua). Yet he does not appear to have invested in learning Nahuatl, let alone writing in it. Las Casas was impressed by the work that the Franciscans in central Mexico did with the Nahua, such as their Colegio de Santa Cruz in Tlatelococo, and with the Nahua Christian leadership, such as the singers introduced to him by Bishop Juan Zumárraga in 1538, which possibly inspired the use of song by Dominicans among the Maya in the Verapaces.[127] Furthermore, while Vico may have also traveled at least once up to Mexico City, Nahuatl, unlike Kaqchikel (*lengua guatemalateca*) or K'iche' (*lengua utlateca*), was not the lingua franca in Guatemala as it was farther north in New Spain. Finally, the Holy Office did not arrive into New Spain until slightly more that fifteen years after Vico's death. However, in the possibility that García Ahumada is correct that the Inquisition did eventually suppress a text by Vico by the 1570s, or at least a text many of his late contemporaries thought to have been by him, this may have provided the reason for concern by Friar Francisco de Viana, O.P., and the dividing up and relabeling of the *Theologia Indorum* as the various shorter treatises and catechisms in his list to the Holy Office.

Conversely, a couple of manuscripts written by mendicants other than Vico have also been designated as a copy of, a version of, or simply another *Theologia Indorum*. Based on Andre Saint-Lu's history of the Dominicans in the Verapaces region, Israeli historian Amos Megged attributes a *Theología de los indios e industriación de ellos en la fe Católica, ceremonias sobre la vida de Cristo, evangelios y fiestas de santos, en lengua indiana* to Friar Viana, which Megged also describes as a manual of sermons composed in K'iche' and Kaqchikel with Vico.[128] However, the location of such a *Theologia Indorum* by Viana has not been verified and this is most likely another result of misinterpreting Viana's letter to the Holy Office.[129] Similarly, the Tozzer Library of Harvard University listed a *Theologia indorum en la lengua otomi*, a non-Maya indigenous language spoken in northeastern Mexico. However, again based on close comparative analysis with positively identified versions of Vico's *Theologia Indorum*, this is not an Otomí translation of Vico's theological treatise. In fact, with respect to both genre and content, it is actually a *sancturale hiemale* for the winter liturgical season that begins with the Feast of Saint Andrew on November 30 and appears, instead, to be a copy of a text written by Franciscan friar Pedro Oroz, also held at the Bibliothèque nationale de France, Ms Amér 6.[130]

One of the questions to be examined here is how far the reach of Vico's *Theologia Indorum* extended. Any translation of his work into non-K'iche'an languages would help to show the expanse or geographical limits of his work's influence. However, despite the fact that the Dominican Province of San Vincente encompassed both Guatemala and Chiapas, knowledge of, let alone use of, Vico's *Theologia Indorum* does not seem to have traveled as far north as Chiapas and Oaxaca to fellow Dominicans working among the Highland Maya and other indigenous peoples, like the Zapotecs. For example, the recently discovered elaborate and lengthy sixteenth-century *doctrina* by Dominicans in the Chocho language of northern Chiapas bears no similarity or even theological influence of Vico or the Guatemalan "Dominican school," thus perhaps helping to demonstrate a northern limit of Vico's approach.[131]

A second error has resulted in a failure to properly recognize the correct genre of Vico's text. This mistake affects content and thus value, which makes it far more egregious than its misattribution. Presently many libraries that hold at least one of the eighteen versions of the *Theologia Indorum,* as well as photostatic or microfilm copies, falsely identify Vico's work as a "collection of sermons" despite its explicit title as a "theology."[132] In fact, until recently many collections and scholarship did not recognize that the various manuscripts consisted of only one of the volumes of a two-volume text. In part, this may be because most of the versions of volume two are missing the first folio. None of the manuscripts held at Princeton and none of any of the versions of volume two in K'iche' have a complete first page; only two of the versions of volume two in Kaqchikel have a first folio and one of those was misidentified with Gonsales as author rather than Vico, thus furthering the confusion.[133] And yet, the opening lines of these two surviving versions of volume two in Kaqchikel clearly states: "This is the second tome of the grand title, the *Theologia Indorum*. Thus called the teaching of those who are Christian Indians in the language of God, the great lord" (*Wa'e rukam ruwujil nimaq b'i'j Theologia Indorum rub'ina'am tijob'al kichin Indio Cristiano pa ruch'ab'al Dios nimajaw).*[134] Because of this confusion, some catalogues, especially those that hold versions of the second volume of the *Theologia Indorum*, also classify the work as a catechism, or *doctrina cristiana* or *cartillas* in Spanish. As elaborated in the previous chapter, the vast majority of Spanish mendicant missionary writings produced during the sixteenth century in Mesoamerica did consist of catechisms and *sermonarios*. However, Vico's two-volume treatise clearly distinguishes itself in both size and scope.

Except for rare and notable exceptions—such as Franciscan Friar Bernardino de Sahagún's twelve-volume *Florentine Codex*, an encyclopedia of pre- and early postcontact Nahua knowledge and practice—few contemporaneous mendicant works approach the size of Vico's theology. Admittedly, sections of Vico's *Theologia Indorum* could possibly read like a sermon, as the explicit audience or readership is a K'iche'-fluent group; Vico's theology directly addresses *ix*, the informal plural second-person pronoun, or "y'all," in K'iche', and calls his readership *numi'al, nuk'ajol*, "my daughters, my sons" in the hierarchical if not patronizing voice of a priestly "father." However, where there do appear to be copies of sermons attributed to Vico and other mendicants in the region, such as the fragment found following the abbreviated version of the second part of his *Theologia Indorum* in Tz'utujil Maya at the University of Pennsylvania, these sermons or lessons are clearly titled as *sermones* or *pláticas* rather than as a enumerated units or chapters in a systematic theological treatise.[135] Therefore, to reduce the *Theologia Indorum* to either a catechism or a mere collection of sermons is to ignore the important claim the text makes for itself as a "theology"—the first text written in the Americas to do so—and to ignore, in turn, the degree to which the text includes and builds from previous and contemporaneous sources, exceeding any single genre. Vico's theology incorporates religious writings by fellow mendicants, such as catechisms and sermons, but also includes nonreligious sources, such as then-recent linguistic and ethnographic research (including his own work in these genres), and uses these other sources to establish analogies for theological meaning. Furthermore, Vico's theology does not limit itself to mendicant works. It may include Highland Maya sources, such as a proto-version or earlier versions of what eventually became the Popol Wuj. As Vico's theology encompasses the information and, in the case of Sahagún, a culturally attuned method of his mendicant and Maya peers, the *Theologia Indorum* approximates a kind of a theological compendium, or *summa*.[136]

In the wider sense of the term, *summae* or *summulae* (*summa* in the singular) refer to summary works that systematically collect not only theological but also philosophical, legal, ethical, and other thought into references or textbooks. Arguably, the Christian production of such compendia date back to late antiquity, such as *peri archon* (or *De Principiis* in the Latin) by Origen of Alexandria (ca. 185–ca. 254) or *De Trinitate* by Hilary of Poitiers (ca. 310–ca. 367). These works were used during the rise of the "schools" in the medieval era. By the thirteenth century the genre took a very specific scholastic form as Thomas Aquinas (1225–1274) combined the *disputatio* and *quaestio* modes of discourse in his *Summa contra gentiles* and *Summa theologiae* not only to systematically summarize Western Christian understanding but also to constructively engage and build upon the pre-Christian classical past and the intellectual advances made by other religions, especially by Jewish and Muslim intellectuals from southern Italy and Iberia. However, despite a common historical misunderstanding that Aquinas primarily wrote his *Summa contra gentiles* for use by mendicants in Iberia to convert Iberian, Italian, and north African Muslims, the intellectual reception of Aquinas's scholasticism did not arrive until Friar Francisco de Vitoria returned from his studies at the University of Paris for theology appointments at Valladolid, first, and then eventually Salamanca in the 1520s-1530s.[137] As one of the first students to learn Aquinas's *Summa* in Iberia and directly from Vitoria at Salamanca, Vico most likely had this exemplary genre in mind as a model of an inclusive, systemic, near-encyclopedic theological compendium. However, Vico was not bound by the specific structure of Aquinas's *summae*. He was dedicated instead to drawing "scientifically" upon explicit non-Christian sources (Jewish and Muslim in the case of Aquinas and Highland Maya in the case of Vico) with the assumed optimism that apparent contradictions between these sources could be resolved or reconciled, as in classic scholastic work since Peter Lombard's *Book of Sentences* (ca. 1150), which Aquinas's *Summa theologiae* evetually replaced as the curricular standard, or even the slightly earlier *Sic et Non* (ca. 1117) by Peter Abelard.

CONCLUSION: A *SUMMA THEOLOGICA AMERICANA* AND SETTLING A QUESTION OF GENRE

Unfortunately, literature about or by Vico is so scarce that the Maya and Spanish sources cited in this brief ethnobiographic sketch and the next chapter are exhaustive. As a student at the University of Salamanca while that school competed with and aimed to distinguish itself from the more humanist-oriented University of Alcalá de Henares, Vico was among the first generation of Spanish mendicants exposed to the emerging Thomistic scholasticism. Though his "Salamanca school" would later be modified by Jesuits like Francisco Suárez and Luis de Molina, the Dominican Francisco de Vitoria imported Thomas Aquinas's writings from his own schooling at the Sorbonne and made them a curricular standard. However, as explained in the previous chapter, this early phase of Spanish Thomism at Salamanca shared with humanism the drive to learn classical and vernacular languages, and an appreciation for critical textual integrity and analysis.

Furthermore, in favoring Thomism over Scotism or nominalism, Spanish scholars and students of the early Salamanca school were not removed from the debates regarding sign theories and the locus or production of meaning and "correct" referents. When, in 1519, Carlos I of the Spains was elected Carlos V of the Holy Roman Empire as well, Salamanca became one of the most politically, philosophically, and theologically influential universities in the European world.[138] One can hear Vico's reflections on Vitoria's lectures on Aquinas's *Summa theologicae* and Vico's own early grappling with Aquinas in the friar's efforts to establish theological analogies between Catholicism and Maya culture, his categorization of Maya theological relationships as proper or improper, and in his attempt to create and organize a near-comprehensive theological work that begins by reflecting on the being and names of his Christian god.

Vico's *Theologia Indorum* is not a mere collection of sermons but rather an internally coherent and cohesively structured theological work, as evidenced by his ordering of the chapters. A few of the surviving copies contain a table of contents toward the back. These tables of contents—such as of volume one, found at the end of APS (American Philosophical Society, Philadelphia, PA) Ms, and of volume two, found in the back of Ayer Ms 1512 as well as BnF Ms Amér 3 and 10—identify and list in Spanish the sections as "chapters" in order of appearance. However, such listings lose the hierarchical ordering of these sections, which distinguish their major and minor points with also subsections, sub-subsections, and, sometimes, even sub-sub-subsections. The tables of contents are written in a noticeably different hand from the main text. A later or at least different copyist most likely compiled and added such listings. However, as the numbering in the chapter headings in the main text remain remarkably consistent in the various versions regardless of copy dates (ranging from the sixteenth to the eighteenth centuries) or of language (including at least K'iche', Kaqchikel, and Tz'utujil if not also possibly Achi, Sakapultek, Q'eqchi', and Poqomchi'), it can reasonably be concluded that this internal structure is originally by Vico and not by a later compiler or redactor. In other words, Viana or other late contemporaries of Vico more likely broke up his theological treatise into shorter works rather than combined his reported disparate works to make a larger, single collection. Perhaps because the Mayan language enumerated chapter headings were not always fully written out, nineteenth-century scholars such as Brasseur de Bourbourg assumed the volumes were an edited anthology. Basing their thinking in turn on this nineteenth-century mistake, twentieth-century ethnohistorians such as Robert Carmack and James Mondloch underappreciated Vico's influence on texts written by the Maya, a point demonstrated in greater detail in the following chapters by means of comparative analysis with the *Title of Totonicapán*.

And yet the mentions or "sightings" of Vico or his theology in the contemporaneous and later writings by both Maya and mendicants are all the more notable when juxtaposed to his virtual absence not only in later histories but even in the early postcontact record. For example, the *Title of Chajoma* (also known as the *Title of San Martín Xilotepeque*), written originally in Kaqchikel in 1555 by Maya elites and eventually translated and submitted in Spanish in 1689 with regards to a land dispute, mentions the arrival of Christianity to the area but nothing specifically of Vico or his work, despite the historic heavy presence of Dominicans in San Martín Xilotepeque (now Jilotepeque) and his own stint there when he apparently finished the first volume of the *Theologia Indorum* in February 1553.[139] Likewise, in the Verapaces region, the *Title of Kaqkoj* (or *Testamento y título de los antecesores de los Señores de Cagcoh San Cristóbal Verapaz*) regarding the sixteenth century but written by Maya in Spanish in 1785, mentions Vico's successor as prior of the Dominican convent in Cobán, Friar Domingo de Azcona, but says nothing of Vico—not his writings nor even his death.[140] To this extent, in addition to mendicant writings like the lengthy Dominican catechism in Chocho from northern Chiapas, the Highland Maya ethnohistorical record helps to fill in some of the gaps regarding the impact of Vico and demarcate the geographic and temporal limits of his legacy.

Compared to other mendicant texts at the time written in the Americas, Vico's *Theologia Indorum* is unique. The subsequent chapter here gives a summary and close analysis of the structure of the *Theologia Indorum*'s units. It pays acute attention to Vico's appropriation of K'iche' terms and formal rhetoric in order to further clarify and correct the enduring concerns regarding the genre and language of Vico's theology. In turn, settling these misunderstandings provides the basis for more substantive analysis of Vico's ethnographically and linguistically grounded theological claims. Reading Vico in this way can open understanding of his work as a culturally attuned theology predicated on dialogue with the Maya.

4

Vico's Theology *for* and *of* the "Indians"

Summary of a Summa Americana

Uae nima vuh rij theologia indorum ubinaam nima etamabel utzihoxic Dios nimahau vɛalahobiçaxic v4oheic ronohel vbanoh Dios v4utuniçaxic naypuch ronohel nimabiih 40 chupam vahabal D: u4utuniçaxic naypuch chahauaxic chetamaxic rumal vtçilah vinak Chritianos v4oheic chupam 4iche 4habal tzibam ui.

This is the large book named the *Theologia Indorum*, a great wisdom and teaching about God, the great lord, and a clarification of the existence and of everything done by God, a demonstration thus of everything of the great name that there is with the language of God, the demonstration thus of what is ruled and of what is known by good Christian people of God's existence in the K'iche' language written here.[1]

THEOLOGICAL PRODUCTION AS A HISPANO-CATHOLIC RESPONSE TO THE MAYA

This chapter focuses specifically on a reconstruction, summary, and analysis of the theology of Friar Domingo de Vico. A close reading of parts of Vico's *Theologia Indorum* builds from the initial conclusions of chapter 3 to clarify further Vico's text as a unique theological work more akin to a *summa theologica americana* than any other genre used by mendicants in the Americas during the centuries that followed.

In the late nineteenth century renewed appreciation for texts in indigenous American languages, especially those by indigenous peoples, initiated a systematic attempt to understand a paper trail long ignored by historians. Late

DOI: 10.5876/9781607329701.c004

twentieth-century ethnohistory strove to complicate and nuance the agency and perspectives of indigenous peoples. In particular, the emphasis developed by such movements as New Philology on language as a venue into cultural worldviews has provided critical and analytical approaches and lines of inquiry into native language texts, written and oral. These approaches allow for revisiting and settling some of the more enduring misunderstandings concerning these texts, namely the false imposition of late medieval and early modern concepts, genres, authorial attribution, and textual production onto indigenous texts.

In the first part of this chapter, close attention to the language used by Vico from the Highland Maya in the writing of his theology, joined with a treatment and analysis of this theology as an integral whole, not only settles the question of genre that is touched on in the previous chapter but also deepens insight and appreciation for the types of theological claims by Vico. In contrast with the nominalism held by many of his non-*Salmanticenses* contemporaries, mainly Franciscans in Guatemala, Vico arguably held more closely to a form/content model of the relation of culture to religion, namely via analogical commensurability. His interdisciplinary approach that appreciated Maya culture, including language, allowed him to write a theology that did not view Christianity and Maya culture as incompatible. However, neither did he simply treat Christianity as an essence nor an emerging sixteenth-century notion of culture (Iberian or Mesoamerican) as a style or vessel. On the contrary, the second part of this chapter focuses on Vico's use of appropriated Mayan language (its terms as well as its rhetoric from ritual and moral discourse) as inseparably related to the theological claims he makes. For Vico, Maya culture, like European culture, was warped and thus needed to be reconfigured or rehabituated rather than simply replaced. This implied theology of culture interlaced Vico's soteriology and not just his processes of translation and indoctrination. However, as only one surviving voice in this dialogue, Vico's theology cannot be read without the strong evidence of Maya poetics and high registers of discourse as found in contemporaneous texts—texts that testify how Vico and the Maya drew from each other. Therefore, intertextual comparison of Vico's and Maya theological claims—such as the Maya doctrine of the divine as *Tz'aqol, B'itol, nimajaw*—highlight specifically where and to what the Maya responded, on Vico's terms and their own.

RECONSTRUCTION AND ANALYSIS OF THE STRUCTURE OF THE *THEOLOGIA INDORUM*

A reconstructed summary of both parts of the *Theologia Indorum* demonstrates Vico's systematic ordering of theological and biblical themes.[2] Direct textual evidence as found within the various surviving fragments of Vico's theology indicates a more complex and integral organizational structure of the *Theologia Indorum* than scholars have previously recognized or appreciated. As evidenced in the listing below, the numbering within Vico's theology entails multiple orders of general or major points, topics, or themes and various divisions, subdivisions, and sub-subdivisions of minor points that demonstrate Vico's familiarity with K'iche' rhetoric in particular and Maya culture in general.

Vico's dual use of the K'iche' term *b'i'j* in particular has caused the few previous scholars who have worked on the *Theologia Indorum* to mistakenly identify this text as either a mere compilation of sermons or the redaction of several separate written works.[3] As explained in chapter 3, evidence can be found for the argument that Vico's theological writings emerged from his homiletic work as a parish priest and member of the Order of Preachers among the Highland and Lowland Maya—though no sermons have conclusively been confirmed to be his—and that he may have anticipated that his theology would be a source for preaching by fellow and future mendicants. This does not mean, however, that his theology was a collection of sermons. Likewise, as is apparent in the second part of this theology, Vico draws from and elaborates on catechism material that he then incorporated into the larger work. However, his *Theologia Indorum* cannot simply be labeled as or reduced to *cartillas* or a *doctrina cristiana*. Not only his specific designation of "theology" to this particular work but also his multileveled and overlapping numbering system, illustrated below, demonstrates a systematic or scholastic ordering, and thus indicates instead a cohesive project.

A listing of contents of Vico's *Theologia Indorum* reconstructed and translated from various surviving manuscripts demonstrates how he organized and numbered his treatise not merely as chapters but also according to a hierarchy of major and minor topics as well as sub-points and side-points or excurses within many of those topics. Even a cursory glance of this table of contents highlights the order of the information along the lines beyond simply "chapter" listings, such as in the appended tables of contents at the end of three of the surviving manscripts or a redacted or amalgamated anthology of previously written items, such as hypothesized based on Viana's 1577 letter.

Vico divides each of the two volumes of the *Theologia Indorum* into a presentation of enumerated major topics or key concepts. In each of the first and second volumes he presents thirty enumerated concepts that he refers to as *nimab'i'* or *loq'olaj b'i'* (see tables 4.1 and 4.2). Vico distinguishes between the major and minor points in the *Theologia Indorum* with a set of basic K'iche' words. He refers to major topics as *b'i'j* or *b'i'* (literally "name," which in current K'iche' is *b'i'aj* in its unpossessed form), usually with some sort of modifier, such as *loq'olaj b'i'j* ("beloved name") or *nimab'i'j* ("big name"), or even occasionally a combination, *nimaloq'olaj b'i'j*. For example, as demonstrated here by the addition of uppercase numerals to index these major topics

Table 4.1. Thirty major themes or concepts in the *Theologia Indorum*, volume 1 (1553)

	"Concept" (loq'olaj b'i', nimab'i'j)	*"Chapters"*	*BnF Ms Amér 5, folio*
1.	God	1–22	fol. 2r
2.	the Trinity	23–25	fol. 30r
3	Angels	26–29	fol. 36v
4.	Earthly Paradise	30	fol. 44r
5.	Adam and Eve	31–35	fol. 45v
6.	Grace	36–40	fol. 53r
7.	Sin	41–43	fol. 58v
8.	Penance	44–46	fol. 63v
9.	Cain	47	fol. 67v
10.	Abel	47	
11.	Seth	47	
12.	Hell	48	fol. 69v
13.	Enoch	49	fol. 72r
14.	Methuselah	49	
15.	Noah	49	
16.	the Flood	50	fol. 72v
17.	Shem	51–52	fol. 75r
18.	Ham	51–52	
19.	Japheth	51–52	
20.	Abraham and Melchizedek	55–56	fol. 78v
21.	Isaac	57	fol. 82r
22.	Jacob	58–61	fol. 83v
23.	Moses	62–80	fol. 90v
24.	Joshua	81–86	fol. 125r
25.	Samuel	87–88	fol. 136r
26.	David	89	fol. 139r
27.	Solomon	90	fol. 142r
28.	the Prophets: Elias, Elisha, Daniel, Susanna, Job, Isaiah, Jews in Babylon, and the wandering of the "ten lost tribes of Israel"	91–101	fol. 144r
29.	Esther (and Haman and Holofernes)	102–103	fol. 170r
30.	Mattithiah or Mattithias	104–105	fol. 174v

Table 4.2. Thirty major themes or concepts in the *Theologia Indorum*, volume 2 (1554)

	"Concept" (loq'olaj b'i', nimab'i'j)	*"Chapters"*	*GGMM no. 175**
1.	St. Joachim and St. Anne	1	p. 9
2.	St. Mary and St. Joseph	2–7	p. 16
3	Jesus as Son of God	8–11	p. 48
4.	"Christian" defined	12	p. 78
5.	Three Kings	13–14	p. 83
6.	St. Simon, St. Anne, Child Jesus in the Temple	15	p. 95
7.	Slaughter of the Innocents, Jesus to Egypt	16	p. 100
8.	Passover, Child Jesus in the Temple	17	p. 103
9.	St. John the Baptist	18–19	p. 107
10.	Defeat of the Devil by Jesus	20	p. 115
11.	"Apostles" defined	21–22	p. 120
12.	"Gospel" and "Evangelist" defined	23	p. 130
13.	3 Theological and 4 Cardinal Virtues	24–32	p. 134
14.	7 Sacraments	33–41	p. 174
15.	8 Beatitudes	42–51	p. 208

continued on next page

or themes, such as initially with IV for *Ukaj nimab'i'j*..., "The fourth concept...," as in the case of unit or "chapter" 30 of volume one of the *Theologia Indorum*:

> IV. Vcaɧ nimabi rij vbixic Parayſo terrenal vbi ruleual ɛanal raxal chue.
> IV. The fourth concept, the telling of the Earthly Paradise, its name and arrival of "yellowness and greenness" [splendor and abundance] there.[4]

However, the enumeration of a key concept does not always appear at the beginning of a chapter title and may be included with other uses of Maya ordinal or cardinal numbers; *b'i'* or *b'i'j* may also appear, but with different meanings. For example, chapter 44 introduces the Catholic concept of penance as initially "one" more theme only later identified as specifically the "eighth" concept or major theme (designated here by lowercase numerals) but in the fourteenth part (indexed with numbers, 14) of the section on Adam and Eve, which is also the fifth major theme (designated by the numeral V):

> V.14.i–viii. Vcahlaɧupaɧ tçiɧ rij vbixic hun nimabijɧ vbi penitençia v4okobal 4ux chuchaxic xuban Adan Eva nabe kachucɧ kakahau vuaɧxak nimabijɧ vae

Table 4.2—*continued*

"Concept" (loq'olaj b'i', nimab'i'j)		*"Chapters"*	*GGMM no. 175**
16.	Miracles of Jesus†	52–60	p. 237
17.	the "Gloria"	61	p. 282
18.	Prayers, Creed, and Decalogue	62–74	p. 285
19.	"Church" defined	75	p. 344
20.	3 Offices and 5 Commandments of the Church	76–82	p. 350
21.	Excommunication	83	p. 367
22.	Sin	84–90	p. 372
23.	6 Works of Grace	91–93	p. 396
24.	Pilate, Annas, Caiaphas, and the Pharisees	94	p. 407
25.	the "Passion" explained	95–102	p. 412
26.	"Resurrection" of Jesus explained	103	p. 465
27.	"Ascension" of Jesus explained	104	p. 475
28.	Arrival of the Holy Spirit	105–106	p. 479
29.	Final Judgement	107–109	n.a.*
30.	Summary and Epilogue	110	n.a.*

* GGMM no. 175 is missing the upper third of the first folio and the final few chapters. No complete manuscript of volume two in K'iche' survives. Therefore, reconstruction of the older K'iche' version requires incorporation of these sections from the Kaqchikel manuscripts: Ayer Ms 1512 and BnF Ms Amér 3.

† Inexplicably, there is no enumerated sixteenth concept in volume two; this concept is numbered in the text as the seventeenth. This is a consistent feature in the various surviving versions of the second volume and, thus, may reflect a feature of the now-lost source text. From this point on, the enumeration in this table reflects the number of concepts or major themes of volume two rather than their assigned number within the text.

> V.14.i–viii. Its fourteenth part, the telling of a major concept whose name is Penitence and its effect on the heart as spoken of and done by Adam and Eve, our first mother and our first father, this is the eighth concept.[5]

Perhaps confusingly, while *b'i'j* as *nimab'i'j* is used to indicate "concept," *ub'i'* may also mean more literally "the name of" the topic of the chapter. So, Vico occasionally introduces a key concept, which he enumerates as a *nimab'i'j*, within a chapter already numbered as a subsection of a larger major section.[6] For example, chapter 36 introduces the concept of "grace," which is designated as the "sixth concept" but within a chapter already numbered as the sixth subsection (6) of the fifth major theme or concept (V) that is about Adam and Eve:

V.6. Vvakpaɧ tçiɧ vɛalalahobiçaxic Gracia xya chire Ada(n) Eva vuakak pu nimabi gracia.
V.6. Its sixth part, the clarification of the grace given to Adam and Eve as the sixth concept is Grace.[7]

Furthermore, in the first part of his theology the use of *b'i'j* or *b'i'* becomes increasingly confusing as the latter portion of volume one is instead structured along the lines of a list of prominent character names from the Catholic Old Testament, such as Adam and Eve, Moses, and Susanna. The two uses of "name"—the first use to mean "general point," "major theme," or "concept" and the second use to refer to proper personal names—both appear. This numbering shift occurs in chapter 47 where Vico begins to introduce and number not attributes or Thomistic names for the Christian god or key doctrinal concepts—like sin, grace, and penance—but rather a cast of biblical characters. For example, chapter 47 is designated as the beginning of a new part or section distinct from the chapters that proceeded it but continuing with a sequence of numbered names, indicated here by the use of lowercase numerals that continue from the sequence last referenced in chapter 44 with penance (viii), such as:

VI.ix–xi. hupaɧ tçiɧ vbixic oxib chi bi Cain Abel Setɧ ubeleɧ vlahuh vhulaɧ bi vae
VI.ix–xi. A part telling of three names: Cain, Abel, and Seth, the ninth, tenth, and eleventh names.[8]

In other words, while *b'i'* now more specifically and literally refers to names of biblical characters or persons rather than concepts—as it is not modified with *nim(a)*—the numbering sequence continues unbroken. Perhaps confusingly, Adam and Eve are collectively the fifth concept (*nimab'i'j*) as introduced in chapter 31 rather than the first and second biblical names, but their children are each discussed as distinctly numbered names (*b'i'*) and as the ninth, tenth, and eleventh rather than, say, the third, fourth, and fifth people of the Bible.

Furthermore, perhaps adding to the confusion, even in this latter portion of volume one, Vico treats and numbers as biblical characters nonhuman items such as the Flood and hell, which he equates with the Maya otherworld of Xib'alb'a. For example, the difference between both listings of *b'i'j* or *b'i'* is further evidenced by the two different sequences of numbers. Therefore, the listing of this second use of names may be clarified by indexing them with lowercase numerals (e.g., "xii" or "the twelfth concept" for "*Ukab'lajuj nimab'i'j*") even as they pertain to the sixth major theme or point still indicated by the uppercase numeral (e.g., VI) in the latter portion of volume one, such as with chapter 48:

VI.xii. Vcablaɦuɦ nimabi vbi Infierno xibalba vbi yvumal.
VI.xii. Twelfth concept is the name of hell, Xib'alb'a is its name by you all.[9]

Without previous attention to chapter 44 and then the shift to a different, secondary kind of count of biblical names starting with chapter 47, it would be easy to mistakenly read "chapter 48" as a "twelfth concept" rather than correctly as "the twelfth concept," which is now also "the twelfth biblical character." The false understanding of a seemingly random numbering of the chapters could then lead to the erroneous conclusion that these units compose a disparate collection of various genres rather than a well-ordered, singular work.

However, where there are inexplicable breaks in the numbering sequence of the unit listings—such as the skips in the listings between chapters 52 and 55 in volume one and the absense of an enumeration of a sixteenth concept between chapters 51 and 52 in volume two—they come in places where there is no textual evidence for there to have been two separate texts then brought together either by Vico or later redactors.[10] There is no intratextual indication that content is missing or has been intentionally omitted. And, for an inexplicable reason, the dominant or initial numbering of the chapters from 55 through 104 in volume one is not of concepts or biblical characters but rather of the chapters themselves. Whereas chapter 51 begins by introducing the "Seventeenth, eighteenth, and nineteenth [biblical] names" (*Uvuklaɦ vuaɦxaklah vbeleɦlahuɦ nimabi*), chapter 52 consists of an unenumerated excursus on the tower of Babel, but chapter 55 begins by telling the reader that it is the "Fifty-fifth chapter" rather than the enumeration of the next major concepts or biblical characters:

VI.xx.a. Rolaɦupaɦ rox4al tçih vbixic vhuvinak nimabijɦ vbi Abraham Melchiʃedech.
VI.xx.a. Fifty-fifth chapter, telling of the twentieth concept whose name is Abraham Melchizedek.[11]

Finally, within specific chapters, Vico also numbers various "signs" (*etalil*) of the Judeo-Christian god through the extraordinary or miraculous workings of nature, such as the wind and waters of Noah's flood and Moses's parting of the Red Sea, earthquakes, and solar eclipses. The final chapter, chapter 105, serves as an overall summary of the biblical stories that he presents in the latter portion of volume one but also as a narrative exegesis that recaps the signs of his god back to the names of his god elucidated in the first chapters.[12] Vico argues that his biblical and thomistically doctrinal god as the creator of the natural worlds can be known by the Maya—and in fact already is implicitly known by the Maya—through the natural world.

This second use of *b'i'j* or *b'i'* as names, though, does not continue in the second volume of the *Theologia Indorum*, which addresses catechism and New Testament themes. However, an additional but integrated numbering system, of minor points or topics, still further highlights the internally coherent structure of the *Theologia Indorum*. While the second use of *b'i'j* or *b'i'* as names does not continue into the second part of the *Theologia Indorum*, the first use as a general topic or concept does continue, along with an enumeration of minor points or topics. Minor topics, including sub-subdivisions and smaller units, have a repeating numbering order as new sets of subdivisions begin within each major topic. In addition to numbering them differently, Vico distinguishes major points from minor points by referring to the latter as *paj tzij* or simply *paj*, such as in the example of chapter 44 of volume one mentioned above. A *paj* in K'iche' is a classifier that indicates a full measure of an item in question, such as a scoopful of grain, a cupful of berries, a glassful of water, or a sackful of sugar, and more commonly today refers to liquids when measuring something tangible. However, particularly in the high register of ritual discourse of contemporary K'iche', such as in giving *pixab'* (advice, counsel, rules, or laws)—itself thought by K'iche' to be ancient—*paj* can mean the "full weight of an idea," a complete thought, or a point.[13] A Highland Maya elder or ritual or ceremonial guide (such as an *ajq'ij* or a *k'amal b'e*, respectively) often begins their speech by announcing that they only have one or two points to make, *jupaj, kapaj tzij*.[14] Throughout both volumes of his *Theologia Indorum*, Vico uses this K'iche' term to designate minor points of the subdivisions within a major point or theme.

This structure, however, seems to have caused confusion among previous non-K'iche' readers of the *Theologia Indorum*, as Vico did not distinguish between a major point (containing minor points) and that major point's first minor point; they are the same. In other words, the first explicitly enumerated minor point within a major topic with subsections is actually the second minor point, as the major point also serves as the first minor point. Therefore, the second minor point of a given major theme appears listed as the first explicit minor point of that major theme. The result is the common repetition of chapter heading "*Uka paj tzij*" ("the second point") with no immediately prior listing of "*Nab'e paj tzij*" ("the first point"), such as with chapters 23–27 of volume one:

II.1. Vcab nimabi vae vbi trinidad are vɛalaɧiçaxic rij.
II.1. Second concept, this is its name of Trinity and the clarification of it.[15]
    II.2. Ucapah tçiɧ vɛalalahobiçaxic[16] roxichal vuinakil Dios n(imahau).[17]
    II.2. Second part, clarification of the three peoples of God, the great lord.
    II.3. Rox paɧ tçih vɛilic[18] vçi4ixic abaɧ che.

II.3. Third part, the worshiping and calling upon the "wood and stone."[19]

III.1. Rox nimabi rij vbi Angeles.

III.1. The third concept, the name Angels.[20]

III.2. Vcapaɦ tçiɦ rij vpoic 4hahcar angel vhal4atihic puch rumal Luçifer.[21]

III.2. Second part, the change of the messengers or angels, the transformation thus by Lucifer.[22]

Because of Vico's unique numbering system, a reader must pay acute attention to the ordering of major points or concepts, such as *b'i'j*, as well as their subsequent minor points, such as *paj*. Otherwise a sequence like second, second, third, third, and second will seem haphazard unless noting what kind or level of chapter is being numbered. Occasionally, however, the phrase *jupaj tzij*—most likely *jun paj tzij* or "one thought" rather than "first thought"—does label a couple of seemingly random chapters, such as with chapters 47 (see above) and 52 of volume one:

VI.xix.b. Hupaɦ tçiɦ vɦal4atihic 4habal vtiqueric pucɦ vçi4ixic abaɦ che rumal vinak.[23]

VI.xix.b. A short word, the changing of language and the beginning of calling upon [effigies of] "stone and wood" by the people.[24]

Such chapters of this type of minor points, though, do not disrupt the number sequence and therefore seem to designate "side points," or excurses.

This problem in failing to recognize properly the systematic numbering of various types of chapters or points within the *Theologia Indorum* is compounded by Vico's practice of not using arabic or roman numerals (as done here to help clarify this analysis). Rather, he spells out all of the numbers in K'iche', in the units according to the vigesimal, or twenty-based, Maya number system, as in chapter 104 of volume one:

VI.xxx. Ucah pah vvak4al tçiɦ rij vhuvinak lahuh nimabi vbi Mathatias ru4 naypuch 4ij chic nimabijɦ.

VI.xxx. One hundred fourth chapter, the thirtieth concept is the name of Mattithiah with also many other major names.[25]

There is little evidence that the classic Maya number writing system with lines (for denominations of fives), dots (for denominations of ones), and a "conch shell" or "flower" symbol (for zero, null set, or space holder) as used among the Lowland Maya was also used among Highland Maya. Thus Vico does not seem to have been familiar with it. Therefore, unless a reader notes and remembers the previous number of the last listed major topic, the reoccurrence of numbered smaller units will sound merely repetitive if not chaotic. For this principal reason, previous scholars have wrongly concluded that Vico's theology was an anthology of previously written documents.[26]

The use of *paj* and the designation of minor points, however, is further complicated with two other aspects of Vico's numbering system. First of all, Vico often interchanges *paj* with other common K'iche' terms for "amounts" of words (*tzij*), such as *molaj*. The rate of occurrence without disrupting the numbering sequence would indicate that he used these terms synonymously, such as in chapters 1–10 of volume one:

I.1. Uae nabe loεolaɦ bi rij ∂(ios).
I.1. This is the first beloved concept, the God.[27]
- I.2. vcab tçiɦ rij vεalaɦobiçaxic kitçiɦ tçih ui chi 4o Dioſ nimaɦau.
- I.2. This is its second part, clarification truly, certainly that God, the great lord, exists.[28]
- I.3. Rox cɦi 4u tçiɦ rij vbixic vhal4al4at[29] v4oheic Dios chi ubanoɦ.
- I.3. Its third part, telling of the change of the existence of God that is [God's] work.[30]
- I.4. vcah tçiɦ rij vεalahobiçaxic vnimal raɦauarem D(ios) vεaεal vtepeual vpuz vnaual.
- I.4. Its fourth part, the clarification of the grandeur of the reign of God and [God's] glory, sovereignty, power, and spirit.[31]
- I.5. Vae ro molah tçiɦ rij vbixic rutçil Dios nimaɦau.
- I.5. This is its fifth part, the telling of the goodness of God, the great lord.[32]
- I.6. Vae vuak molaɦ tçiɦ rij vbixic vmaui vtaneic v4olem Dios n(imahau).
- I.6. This is its sixth part, the telling of the never-ending existence of God, the great lord.[33]
- I.7. Vvuk molaɦ tçiɦ vae v4utuniçaxic ronohel 4o ui Dios nimahau.
- I.7. Seventh part, this is the appearance of everything that is, from God, the great lord.[34]
- I.8. Vuaɦxak molaɦ tçih rij vmaui vçilobic Dios nimaɦau.
- I.8. Its eighth part, the immovability of God, the great lord.[35]
- I.9. Vbeleh molaɦ tçih vbixic Reterni∂a∂ Dios vhunelic 4oheic.
- I.9. Ninth part, telling of the eternity of God, [God's] eternal existence.[36]
- I.10. Vlahu pah tçiɦ vbixic vtuquel 4oɦeic[37] Dios nimaɦau mana caib mana oxib.
- I.10. Tenth part, telling of the singularity of the existence of God, the great lord, not two and not three.[38]

Current K'iche' speakers sense a distinction in quality or level of importance between the two terms.[39] Whereas *paj* designates a full, mutually agreed upon or conventional unit of measure—be it traditional Maya, colonial Spanish, or current metric—*molaj* implies a less specified or ordered amount. Etymologically, *molaj* is related to both "time" as the unpossessed form of ordinal time, such as a "first time" (*jumul*) or a "second time" (*ukamul*), and possibly with "pile," specifically such as the piles of dirt that a mole, or *b'a*, accumulates when it digs down into the ground and makes a hole, or *jul*.[40] While the enumeration of subdivisions as either *paj* or *molaj* indicates that they are of equal quantitative value—and thus both are minor points or subdivisions of major points rather than demarcating a distinction between subdivisions and sub-subdivisions—qualitatively a "full measure of words" is of higher importance than a "pile of words" among contemporary K'iche'. This use of *molaj*, however, is only evident in the first volume of the *Theologia Indorum* and only in K'iche' versions.

Likewise, a distinction between *paj* and *molaj* was noted by the Guatemalan Franciscan friar Bartholomé de Anleo in his seventeenth-century *Arte de lengua 4iché*. According to Anleo *hupah tzih*, *capah tzih*, *oxpah tzih*, and so on was used in K'iche' "to count words or 'reasonings'" (*para contar palabras o razonamientos*), such as points (*respondeo*) made within an argument (*disputatio)* or "to narrate something" (*para narrar alguna cosa*).[41] Whereas *molah* (in Anleo's colonial spelling) is used "to count sermons, talks, shoes, clothes, or similar things" (*para contar sermones, pláticas, zapatos, vestidos, o cosas semejantes*).[42] Unfortunately, Anleo does not clarify how K'iche' may see discourses and articles of clothing as "similar things." However, based on both the content and the length of the chapters, Vico appears to use these terms interchangeably. Furthermore, within the text's chapter headings, Vico does not use any of the other fifty-seven K'iche' terms listed by Anleo for counting, such as for counting long items like poles, beams, or fish (*yacah*), round items like hens or tamales (*4olah*), or handfuls of tobacco (*bolah*).[43]

The second complication in trying to decipher Vico's use of *paj* and *molaj* is his tendency to use them to indicate either "minor points" or literally "chapters." For example, *Ukapaj tzij* for chapter 24 in volume one clearly indexes the second minor point of the general or major point introduced in chapter 23; whereas chapter 55 explicitly begins with *Rolajuj paj roxk'al tzij*. *Paj* in these two instances does not mean the same thing, thus leaving earlier unit headings, such as chapter 22 in volume one (*Ujuwinaq kab' molaj tzij)* ambiguous as to whether it is "the twenty-second chapter" or "the twenty-second minor point." This confusion between the terms *paj* and *molaj* as well as the occasional ambiguous referent of *paj* pertains more to volume one; not only does *molaj* not appear in the second volume of the *Theologia Indorum* but *paj* more clearly refers there to "minor point." Furthermore, in his Kaqchikel translations, *pixa* or *rupixa* is used in the second volume of the *Theologia Indorum* to designate the sub-sub-points in the headings only in chapters 78–82.[44]

In conclusion, Vico's multilayered numbering system for the units within his theology, therefore, clarifies three facets of the main issues regarding the *Theologia Indorum*. These three clarifications not only serve to redress some of the more enduring misunderstandings by scholars of Vico and his work but also move beyond them and toward initial substantive insight into the content and strategic style of his theological language and method. First, by the explicit distinction between major and minor topics (if not also more and less important topics), the *Theologia Indorum* has the internally consistent, well-structured, and coherent order of a theological treatise like a *summa*, a genre of medieval theological scholastic works such as Thomas Aquinas's *Summa contra gentiles* and *Summa theologicae* or even Peter Lombard's *Sentences*. All of these would have been known to sixteenth-century clergy, especially Dominicans coming from the University of Salamanca by the 1530s. Second, the order of presentation of the material in his theology, consisting of both biblical structure and that of catechism manuals, does not fully correspond to the liturgical seasons as in a missal or of the canonical hours as in a breviary, making it less likely still to have been a *sermonario*. Third and finally, his appropriation of the use of *paj* and his spelling out of Maya ordinal numbers to designate a complete idea or thought in a traditional and complex style indicates Vico's strategic use of a formal, high register of K'iche' normally reserved for ritual speeches by K'iche' elders and religious and political leaders. This implies an argument that, for Vico, Christian clergy could position themselves as Catholic *k'amal b'e,* or spiritual guides and authorities. It thus provides further evidence of the dialogicality between Vico and Hispano-Catholicism with Highland Maya culture and religion during these initial fifty years of first contact. Furthermore, the use of a more complex ordering system in the K'iche' versions, in contrast to the Kaqchikel and Tz'utujil versions, provides further evidence that Vico most likely initially composed his theology in K'iche', which he or others later translated into other Mayan languages.[45]

VICO'S ETHNOGRAPHICALLY ATTUNED THEOLOGY AND THEOLOGICAL METHOD

Having now determined that the *Theologia Indorum* has a well-ordered format of presentation that resonates with the genre of scholastic theologies that Vico would have been taught at Salamanca, and that Vico's presentation of his theology in the K'iche' language and concepts (such as numbers and rhetorical turns of phrases) begin to blur any simple distinction between form (K'iche') and content (Catholic), analysis may now focus on Vico's theology beyond chapter headings. While the reconstructed listing of Vico's topics and themes provides a general overview of his theology, the following summary examines selected exemplary chapters in more detail. This summary demonstrates that the *Theologia Indorum* has an internal logic or rationale, focused on three key aspects: (1) Vico's construal of the divine, or doctrine of God (such as in the proemium through chapter 24 of volume one), (2) his theological approach or method with regard to Maya religion and culture (such as chapter 25 of volume one), and (3) his use of both medieval Christian cosmology, including angelology and demonology (in chapters 26–30 of volume one), and biblical narratives (through chapter 104 of volume one and the majority of volume two) not as mere translations or even summaries of Christian scripture but rather to focus on moral concerns.

This summary of Vico also demonstrates more specifically how his theology is in the vein of Aquinas and, in turn, how his incorporation of K'iche' moral and ritual discourse altered the *summa* genre and approach. With regard to a summary of his theology, however, the concern here is less on a question of genre and more on theological production and meaning. Specifically, Thomistic theological claims that influenced local theologians like Vico—namely, claims regarding predicates for his god—fall into three basic kinds: univocal or positive, cataphatic statements (such as synonymous or equating statements, like God's essence is Being), equivocal or negative, apophatic statements (such as statements addressing opposition, like God is not finite, or, thus, is infinite), and analogical statements or positive statements made in terms of similarity-in-difference (like God is Good but only understood from a limited and finite human understanding of goodness). As is argued below, for Vico and others facing the challenge of how to translate recondite understandings of Christianity across and through other languages, cultures, and religions, these three kinds of claims (especially analogy broadly understood) and the conventional modes of biblical interpretation served as immediate models for translation in general and in establishing commensurate meanings.

Combined Sources for Theological Claims and Rhetorical Resonances

As demonstrated above, the basic structure and outline of his theology highlights the variety of Catholic sources and their respective genres from which Vico pulled, and that he promoted. While the majority of the first volume and nearly half of the second volume consist of chapters or units summarizing basic biblical narratives, presented in the order of the Catholic Old and New Testaments, Vico also integrated additional material into his *Theologia Indorum*, such as doctrinal or catechism topics in the latter portion of volume two. Comparison between Vico's catechism material (as found in chapters 23–51, 61–93, and 107–110 of volume two) and those topics in *doctrinae cristianae* or *cartillas* of early and later contemporaries (as presented in table 4.2) highlights the degree to which Vico maintained that genre and order as originally popularized by French theologian Jean Gerson at the turn of the fifteenth century. However, Vico's lengthy elaboration of each topic—most notably the four cardinal and three spiritual virtues systematized by Thomas Aquinas in his *Summa theologicae*—indicates the strong influence of the early Salamanca school of humanistic scholasticism as well as an incorporation of and step beyond the simple *doctrina cristiana* or *cartilla* genres. On one hand, this step beyond by Vico entailed his incorporation of the genres and linguistic work of his mendicant peers among the Ladino and Moorish *conversos* in Iberia and indigenous peoples in Mesoamerica.

On the other hand, like the work of Aquinas with Arabic and Jewish philosophical sources in the medieval era or Paul of Tarsus and subsequent Christian intellectuals in late antiquity with Hebraic and Greco-Roman sources, this shift by Vico incorporated Maya material and concerns. Also as noted in the analysis of the reconstruction of his theology's table of contents, Vico's hierarchy of written units or topics occurs along the lines of K'iche' ritual discourse and required his intimate knowledge of it. Like the Castilian custom of indexing sections with headings or brief summaries—such as in the most popular Castilian novel read in the late fifteen century (*Amadis de Gaul*) and in historical reports (such as the first published firsthand account of the Spanish arrival, Bernal Díaz del Castillo's *Historia de la conquista de Nueva España*)—Vico employs an analogous traditional Maya literary convention at the beginning of every unit. For example, regarding the opening lines of almost every chapter, Vico uses the introductory *uae* as "this (one) here is," which goes back to the Maya classic era's (ca. 250 CE–ca. 900 CE) use of *a-lay, a-hay, a-b'ay,* and later *a-way* as found in ancient logosyllabic texts in archaeological cites.[46] Vico's incorporative efforts in the scholastic vein, and thus a demonstration of his theological method, become more evident within the particular sections and their claims.

As Aquinas hinged his theology on the "being" of the Christian god—with God as Being—Vico begins his own theology not on the rituals or prayers of the Roman Catholic Church or the first book of the Bible, Genesis, but rather on the being and names of his god. While not exactly the same as Aquinas's focus on the essence and *esse* or existence of God, where God's essence or nature was defined as "existence," the first 22 chapters of Vico's *Theologia Indorum* explain the presence and qualities of his god—such as good, enduring, merciful, sovereign, singular, authoritative, and moving but not movable—through quotidian examples, terms, and phrasing familiar to the Highland Maya. On one hand, Vico deploys his ethnographic and linguistic knowledge of the Highland Maya to establish analogical relationships to provide affirmative statements about his god, such as "wealthy" in chapter 22, as well as equivocal, negating, or apophatic statements to say what his god is not, such as "unending" in chapter 6, "immovable" in chapter 8, or "invisible" in chapter 11.[47] On the other hand, in chapters 23 and 24, Vico attempts to present Catholic doctrinal Trinitarian grammar in K'iche' in order to, in his K'iche' phrasing, "clarify" or "illuminate" (*-q'alajisaj*; *-q'alajob'isaj*) that his god who is "one" is triune. The result in K'iche' is to speak literally of the three "peoples" of this god, rather than the three "persons" (*personae*) of the Christian god, as the K'iche' term *winaq* in the sixteenth century functioned as a collective singular rather than an individual one.[48] Notably, neither Vico nor any other mendicant missionaries attempted to employ a literal translation of *persona*—originally a Latin theatrical term for "mask," akin to the Spanish term *personaje*, meaning "character" in English—by use of the K'iche' term for "mask" (*k'oj*).

With respect to his doctrine of God, throughout these opening "chapters," however, Vico constructs a Spanish-K'iche' couplet by which to refer to his god: *Dios, nimajaw* or "God, the great lord." At this level of referencing, Vico's phrase for the Christian god is not analogical or equivocal but rather univocal. Vico is linguistically challenged to differentiate a "being" of existence from a "being" of essence in K'iche', as K'iche'an languages do not have a copula "to be" construction (such as *estar* or *ser* in Spanish, by which to refer to substance or status) but only "to be" in the sense of presence or existence, *-k'olik* (such as *haber* inflected as *hay* in Spanish).[49] For another example, and with no linguistic option in K'iche' to state "the Good," in chapter 5 Vico names the analogical dimensions of his god's "being" good through examples of "good" in K'iche'an life to indicate how his god's goodness is like and unlike that good already known to the Maya. For a more particular and widespread example throughout the first part of his *Theologia Indorum* beginning in the proemium and not just in chapter 22, Vico expounds upon how his god's wealth and reign is like and unlike those riches of the K'iche' through a series of rhetorical couplets, such as cocoa and pataxte chocolate, jade and gems, gold and silver, and blue-green feathers of quetzal and cotinga birds.[50]

These forms of wealth decompose, Vico argues, but the Christian god's wealth does not. This presumption and affirmation of knowledge on the part of the Maya by Vico allows him to establish bridge terms between Maya and Catholic thought through univocal uses of an implied copula, such as his couplet for the Christian god: *Dios, nimajaw* or "God (is) the great lord." In other words, Vico translates a Christian understanding of the divine in the K'iche' language, relying on the poetic or rhetorical terms of K'iche' ritual discourse that he correspondingly aligns with biblical construals of divinity. To accomplish that, he reconfigures K'iche' religious and mundane concepts, namely *Tz'aqol* ("builder" or "framer") and *B'itol* ("shaper" or "former") from K'iche' myths and the K'iche' religious and civic title *ajaw* ("lord") with the modifier *nim(a)* ("big," "great," or "grand").[51] Vico, therefore, creates a commensurate understanding of K'iche' concepts as he recontextualizes and reentextualizes them for translating Hispano-Catholic concepts; his analogical thought in this sense is dialogical.

Furthermore, unlike his expounding upon the various "names" of his god, Vico does not provide equivocal, apophatic, or negating statements as to how his god is not like "a great lord." In this sense, his translation or construction of a K'iche' Catholic doctrine of god is not phrased like the predicates for the divine that he explores in the first chapters of volume one of his *Theologia Indorum*. He phrases those predicates in terms that both affirm and negate claims for more explicitly Thomistic analogical understanding but also by resorting to a form of K'iche' analogical expression found in the structure of a rhetorical tercet. In this first major theme consisting of the proemium through chapter 22, Vico argues for what his god "is" from what his god "does" or "has done" and the evidence of the deeds of his god, which are evident not only to Vico's contemporaneous K'iche' readership but also in the teachings of their ancestors. For example, in the opening of chapter 1, Vico explains that

> Dios cɧucɧaxic kumal oɧ padres tçakol bitol re uinak tçakol re vinak bitol re vinak banol ke vinakiriçay ke xa xoɧubano xa xoɧuuinakiriçaɧ xoɧutçakō xoɧubito oɧ utçakom oh ubitom vtçiniçanel vinakiriçanel xohutzinic rumal xoɧuinaki rumal.

"God" spoken of by us [Catholic] priests,
"Framer and Former" by the [K'iche'] people, is
    Framer of the people,
    Former of the people,
    Doer of us all, and
    Creator of us all;
        only [God] made us and
        only [God] made us people,
            sculpted us and
            carved us;
                we have been sculpted and
                we have been carved,
    by the one who perfects and
    by the one who creates
                we were perfected and
                we were created.[52]

The K'iche' root or stem *-tz'aq-* literally refers to constructing something, such as a building a foundation or a wall, often out of stone, and may connote female qualities, whereas the K'iche' root or stem *-b'it-* refers to working with clay such as pots, jars, or bowls and may connote male qualities.[53] However, as the second half of the above quote implies, *b'itol* also refers metaphorically to the raising of children,[54] such as humans, who are the "children of God." Based on his knowledge of K'iche' cosmogonic narratives, Vico selects a traditional K'iche' couplet for the divine, one that is analogous to "Creator" in Genesis, and establishes it as highly analogous if not the same as, equivalent, or univocal to the Hispano-Catholic *Dios*.

Rhetorically, Vico's univocal shift from *Dios, nimajaw* for *Tz'aqol, B'itol, nimajaw* augments his Spanish-K'iche' couplet for a tercet. Both forms, along with quatrains and longer forms of parallel or chiastic structure, are extremely common in the formal or high register of spoken and written K'iche'an languages (as is explained in greater detail in chapters 5 and 6 on the K'iche' texts). The formation of these juxtaposing parallel constructions was not only common in Maya thought and speech before the arrival of Europeans but also influenced the construction of Maya-Spanish bilingual semantic couplets with mendicant missionaries working throughout the Maya region.[55] Vico's shift from a couplet for a tercet is actually twofold as his replacement of *Tz'aqol B'itol* or "Framer and Former" for the first part of his own couplet—the "Dios" in *Dios, nimajaw*—is already in parallel form and thus a couplet. Therefore, his construction of the tercet *Tz'aqol, B'itol, nimajaw* moves both his couplet (*Dios, nimajaw*) and that of the K'iche' (*Tz'aqol B'itol*) into a tercet form. In general, a third concept or term—in this case *nimajaw*—is added within formal K'iche' rhetoric to add nuance to the first two terms neither through analogous complementarity nor necessarily equivocation but rather through subtle difference.[56] This use of a third term, or the shift of rhetorical context of *nimajaw* from the second term of his couplet to the third term of his tercet, allows Vico to establish and use analogies not only on scholastic grounds, namely as Aquinas did, but also on K'iche'an grounds and a native understanding of similarity-in-difference or analogy.

As also demonstrated in the above quote from the beginning of chapter 1, Vico's use of the high register of K'iche' language in the *Theologia Indorum* is not limited merely to couplets and tercets but rather spans the panorama of K'iche'an poetics and rhetorical structure.[57] Furthermore, in K'iche' poetics or rhetoric, a fourth term or phrase added before or after a tercet restores evenness to form either a quatrain or a pair of couplets.[58] For example, after establishing the univocal relationship between his "God" and the K'iche's' "Framer and Former," Vico moves his list of what his god does into a quatrain. He begins by not only reaffirming traditional K'iche' religious language and teaching but reiterates the *-tz'aq-* and *-b'it-* roots as the first couplet of his quatrain, followed by a second couplet of his god as one "who does" (*b'anol*) and as one "who creates" (*winaqirisanel*). By beginning his theological treatise with the construction and combination of couplets not only lexically but also according to heightened structures of K'iche' speech, Vico incorporates concepts and modes of meaning intelligible to his scholastic humanist cohort and the Maya culture of his audience.

In this regard, Vico's use of Maya culture and language as a theological resource is not merely symbolic or a negotiation of the form of his discourse. As in the construction of the second couplet to his divine quatrain, Vico strategically pulls together a quotidian word with the common stem "to do" (*-b'an-*) together with a highly technical and specialized word of "to create" (*-winaq-*) now used only by K'iche' rhetoricians.[59] The root of this verb, *-winaq-*, refers simultaneously to "people" and to "twenty," however the verb does not mean "to people or populate" or "to make into twenty." Rather, this verb means "to create for the first time," "to originate," or possibly even "to conceive" such as at the level of ideas. It is uniquely used, most commonly in colonial and current K'iche' discourse, affirmatively for an activity by a divine agent. However, when used in reference with a human agent, the connotation is not positive "to create" or "to make" but rather negative as in "to make up," "to fabricate," or "to fib." The positive human counterpart is *-k'isanik*, "to invent" or "to raise or rear a child."[60]

The result by Vico here is a classic K'iche' quatrain wherein (1) the first two terms are of a high register and complement each other like two sides of a coin: (a) "to sculpt" or "to make" (*-tz'aq-*) and (b) "to carve" or "to model" (*-b'it-*), with each implying female and male complementarity, respectively, as well as child rearing; (2) the third term (*-b'an-*) for "to make," which differentiates it as a more ordinary or low register term; and (3) the fourth term (*-winaq-*) again raises the register as a term uniquely applied to the divine in K'iche', like the first two terms, but complementing the non-specified type of "making" as a general term, like the third term. The implications of ending with this particular stem leaves an increased impact on a potential K'iche' reader as *winaq*, also meaning "twenty," denotes completion of a round within the Maya vigesimal number system. Vico's quatrain and initial presentation of an understanding of the divine as negotiated between Hispano-Catholic and K'iche' worldviews is, at least implicitly, "complete." Vico's ability to convey complex ideas of God—not by merely translating a European catechism, sermon, or *quaestio* into a Mesoamerican language but rather negotiating in, through, and with Maya concepts, style, and discursive rules—demonstrates the highly technical contextualization enterprise he engaged in as well as his need for an interdisciplinary theological method that appreciated and understood historical Maya sources and mendicant ethnographies.

Negotiating Religious Construals: Divine Agencies and Attributes

The second major theme or concept in the *Theologia Indorum* appears to formulate a large tercet with chapters 23–25. As mentioned previously, chapters 23 and 24 mark a move by Vico from using terms and images familiar to Maya, in order to elaborate on the being and names of his god, toward introducing distinctively

Christian concepts pertaining to the divine, such as Trinitarian grammar and "divinity." However, with no sixteenth-century K'iche' word for "person," Vico still employs a high degree of cultural awareness and linguistic knowledge as he presents these topics in K'iche'.[61] Building from the lines of argument and foundation laid in the previous chapters, specifically chapter 10 on the singularity of God, Vico explains the three "peoples" of his one god: *oxib' uwinaqil Dios chupam xa hun uk'oje'ik* ("three peoples of God within only one being of [God])."[62]

In chapter 24, Vico explicates each "people" of his triune god with an analogical method. Both the "fatherhood" (*qajawixel*) and "sonship" (*k'ajolaxel*) in his Trinitarian grammar can be presented and explained through Maya cultural references, understandings, and expectations of ideal familial relations. The use of these two familial terms for doctrines of, respectively, God the Father and God the Son are so literal to even be acceptable among Franciscans as evident in their sermons in and language guides on K'iche'an languages. However, with regard to the third "people" of the Christian god, Vico also uses a more culturally and religiously loaded term of *uxlab'* along with the Spanish, *Espíritu Santo*, and even occasionally Latin, *Spiritu Sancto*.[63] Arguably, to the extent that *ruxlab'* (with <r-> as the third-person singular possessive prefix before a vowel) refers to one's breath, Vico aligns a K'iche' term that most closely approximates Latin *spiritu* in (e.g., "to breathe" or related to "spirit," as in English words like "respiration" and "to inspire"), Greek *pneuma* (e.g., "breath" and later "spirit" or "soul"), and Hebrew *ruah* (e.g., the "breath," "wind," or "spirit" of God in Genesis 1:2) or *nishmat* (e.g., the "breath" or "spirit" of life from the LORD God in Genesis 2:7). In K'iche', though, the term also relates to scent or smell, which Vico later leans into in discussing the "sweet smell" of his god's good presence. Nominalist-oriented mendicants, namely Franciscans in Guatemala, condemned the use of *ruxlab' Dios nimajaw* for the third "person" of the Trinity and other such interpretive moves made by Vico. They insisted that only the Latin or Spanish could be used. Likewise, they also initially resisted the Dominican proposal of *winaqil* (even with the abstractive suffix <il>) for each of the three "peoples" or "nationhoods" of God to instead accommodate the Latin or Spanish semantically within, for example, the Kaqchikel Mayan languge (e.g., *rupersonail*, with the abstractive suffix and third-person singular possessive prefix).

This example of Dominicans' willingness to find analogous terms even for doctrinal terms, such as *uxlab'* for "spirit," even with awareness of such terms' wider connotations among the Maya, and Franciscans' suspicion of this translation strategy, marked an early salient boundary between their respective production of a pastoral register and doctrinal and linguistic materials in K'iche'an languages during the course of the colonial period. However, while *uxlab'* and other terms like *k'ab'awil* (*k'ab'awilab'* in the plural) remained contested between Dominican realists and

Franciscan nominalists, debates regarding other key terms, such as *winaq*, did eventually abate. The abatement, though, did not occur because one camp gradually conceded to the other or because authoritative meetings like the Council of Trent settled the debates between the competing semiotic ideologies for clergy at the local and hyperlocal environs. The division between these interpretive and philological schools of thought in Guatemala would only gradually move further into the background by the eighteenth century as the population of locally born, or *criollo*, and locally educated clergy filled the ranks of the Guatemalan Catholic church. For example, Franciscan friar Thomas de Coto's *Thesavrvs verborvm*, written a century after the *Theologia Indorum* but also explicitly citing Vico throughout, agrees with Vico that *winaqil* is the most appropriate K'iche'an term for the three "persons" of the doctrine of the Trinity. Though, per his reasoning, this was not because Franciscans like Coto accepted a teaching of the three "peoples" of the triune god but rather that by then the semantic domain of *winaq* had sufficiently shifted to also mean a "person."

Vico continued with this analogical approach not only in his attempts to explain to his Maya readership what his god was but also what his god was not. To the extent that chapters 23 and 24 complement each other in this shift in clarifying not only *that* his god is but also *what* his god is (triune), chapter 25 introduces what his god is *not* through a discussion of "effigies" as the K'iche' notion of *k'ab'awil*. As one of the last chapters before Vico begins to summarize and use biblical narratives as a source, organizing motif, and springboard for proper worship and behavior, chapter 25 closes the second concept or major theme and introduces the pastoral and ethical concerns that run throughout the remainder of the *Theologia Indorum*.

For an examination of mendicant theology toward the religious ideas and traditions of the Highland Maya in the sixteenth century, chapter 25 of the first volume of *Theologia Indorum* is among the most important.[64] In the opening lines, Vico begins by describing the various forms of idolatry followed by a historical argument against the antiquity of the listed divinities and ritual practices. Here Vico argues that the precontact Maya worshiped only the true god, *Tz'aqol B'itol,* or "Framer and Former." Furthermore, in his *ad hominen* argument in the next lines, Vico asserts that the current Maya are the same witnesses to and sages of this true ancient tradition. Next he urges the Maya to return to this pure form of worship. He discredits the current religious practices of the Maya in his second historical argument, which points out that the syncretic rituals are only fifty years old, since the time of first contact with Europeans. As a result of this deviation from the precontact religion, Vico proclaims, those who began the syncretizing are now in Xib'alb'a, as he equates the K'iche' otherworld with the Christian hell. In the next lines Vico repeats his plea for the current Maya to abandon any innovations and return to the religion of their ancestors with, echoing Paul's argument in Acts 17:22, "*Tz'aqol*

B'itol praised by your ancestors is the same God that we [Christians] pray to." In the remainder of chapter 25 Vico repeats his equation of *Tz'aqol B'itol* with the god of Christianity and aims to systematically discredit the "cult of the erected stone," stelae, or effigies carved of wood or stone and worshiped by his contemporary Maya.

As discussed previously in chapter 2, many mendicants, mostly Observant or Spiritual Franciscans from Spanish territories in Europe, believed that the indigenous peoples of the Americas descended from the ancient Israelites, namely the "ten lost tribes" otherwise unaccounted for after the Assyrian invasion and then diaspora during the Babylonian exile.[65] Many notables in the "pro-Indian" party, such as Dominican friar Bartolomé de las Casas, did not seem to share this position among mendicants. Furthermore, due to their affiliation with the millenarian worldview of Joachim of Fiore and Gerardo da Borgo San Donnino, Spanish Franciscans were more likely than Dominicans to hold this idea but not all mendicants necessarily linked the idea of the establishment of the apostolic primitive church in the Americas with an apocalypticism. For example, spending his life educating Nahua leadership and extensively documenting Mexica language and culture, Franciscan friar Bernardino de Sahagún was a leading spokesperson for the "pro-Indian" camp who did not share the apocalyptic worldview of many of his Franciscan cohort.[66] Finally, the widespread influence of Thomas More's *Utopia* among mendicants, and even with Jesuits working in New Spain after 1572, provided non-millenarian idealistic visions for both those who shared in the Observant Franciscans' understanding of primitivism and those who opposed it.[67]

The downside of the relation sought between ancient Israelites and indigenous peoples in the Americas was the link between their status as a biblical people and the virtue of poverty within the ideal "primitive church" of the apocalyptic or Spiritual Franciscans. This link between poverty as a virtuous or meritorious state and socioeconomic consequence of the *conquista* could be construed, or misconstrued, as ideological facet that kept Mesoamericans impoverished by some mendicant clergy to help ensure their salvation. The identification, critique, and break from this link also occurred early on by such notable mendicants as Spanish Dominican friars Antón Montesino and Pedro de Córdoba in the Americas as early as 1511, Francisco de Vitoria at the University of Salamanca and his critique of empire back in Spain, and later, the "defender of the Indians," Las Casas, in his famous debates with Juan Ginés de Sepúlveda in 1550. However, the upside of the attempt to establish an analogical, or even univocal, relationship between the ancient peoples of the Bible and the ancient peoples of the Americas was that it granted an initially high degree of credibility to local indigenous wisdom, teachings, and practices.[68] As in the case of Vico, it provided at least an implied warrant to invest in studying and building from local cultures, including native languages and their rhetoric and references.[69] There are only occasional and faint references throughout both volumes of the *Theologia Indorum*, such as to "nine or ten tribes" in chapter 25. However, close to the end of volume one, in chapter 101, Vico explicitly states to his Highland Maya audience that "you all are Israelites who came from over there, you all are the descendants of the grandsons and sons of Abraham, Isaac, and Jacob" (*ahiſrael yx petinak ui yx camic umam v4ahol Abra(ha)m yſaac Jacob*).[70]

Furthermore, Vico's education in the scholastic humanism of the early Salamanca school under Vitoria and the likes fostered a sense of skepticism shared by later Dominicans during Iberia's witch craze.[71] Just as fellow and later Dominicans in Iberia—such as inquisitor Dominican friar Alonso Salazar de Frías, who argued against the existence of witches and the notion of the preternatural that metaphysically supported such a belief—Vico appears to have resisted the notion that the Maya practiced idolatry as devotion antithetical to true worship. Rather than treat *k'ab'awilab'*, or effigies, as idolatry in the sense of demonic, in chapter 25 Vico related the *k'ab'awil* images explicitly to their observable form and material. Rather than agree with the Maya that *k'ab'awil* are protective tutelary spirits like a patron saint in Catholicism, or with many of his Franciscan peers that *k'ab'awil* are "idols," Vico clarifies that they are images of "wood and stone," as expressed in the K'iche' lexical couplet *che' ab'aj*.[72] In fact, the entry under *4abauil* (*k'ab'awil*) in the *Vocabulario en la lengua Cakchiquel y 4iche o utlatecat* attributed to Vico recognizes the Franciscan understanding of it as *idolo* [*sic*] ("an idol") but only as one definition and only listed after the more neutrally descriptive gloss of it as *estatua* ("a statue") as related to *che abah* (effigies of "wood or stone").[73] Furthermore, Vico also seems to have used the word *-k'ab'awilaj* in chapter 25 as a verb, not as "to idolize" or as "false worship" but rather more generally as "to venerate," raising the question, then, of the object of veneration: whether the divine is the referent ultimately signified, or whether the physical effigy is not only the signifier but also the signified. More directly, could the K'iche'an term *k'ab'awil* eventually come to mean "sacred," "holy," or "divine," much like the mendicant K'iche'anized neologism *diosil* (the Spanish word *Dios*, for "God," with the K'iche'an abstractive suffix <-il>)?[74] Realists like Vico seem to have officially lost the debate against the nominalists when Bishop Marroquín unilaterally silenced any further discussion on the matter and later colonial lexicons on K'iche'an languages listed *k'ab'awil* as "idol" and *-k'ab'awilaj* as "to make into an idol" or "to idolize." Unofficially, however, the disagreement seems to have continued well into at least the late seventeenth century. Most notably, for example, the entry for *cabauilah* (*-k'ab'awilaj*) in one of the most influential and significant colonial K'iche'–Spanish dictionaries—the *Vocabulario Quiché* by Dominican friar Domingo de Basseta, completed on January 29, 1698—defined the term as *idolatrar* ("to idol worship") and *ahcabauil* (*ajk'ab'awil*) as *idólatra* ("idolater").[75] However, writing in a different hand in the margin immediately to the right of the entry, a later reader of the lexicon disagreed:

> cabauil quruq rib, Dios esta en si mismo.
> ([cabauilah] significa adorar.) Cabauil se decia antig.[uamen]te
> para Dios y signi-
> fica tambien la
> est[r]ella vaga.
>
> *K'ab'awil k'u ruk' rib'* is "God being within Godself."
> *K'ab'awilaj* means "to worship."
> *K'ab'awil* was said in ancient times for "God" and also to mean "wandering star."[76]

This marginalium appears only in the BnF Ms Amér 59, the K'iche' version of Basseta's lexicon and not in any other earlier Kaqchikel versions, which he produced by relying heavily on older Franciscan Kaqchikel-Spanish dictionaries.[77] And, so, it is not part of Basseta's original listing or even a modification on his part. Specifically, BnF Ms Améri 59 notes that it was once in the possession of Sebastián Ramos, a local parish caretaker or *fiscal* who, as often was the case with *fiscales*, was most likely K'iche' Maya. While no date is given indicating when Ramos owned this manuscript copy, it does provide some evidence that Vico's reluctance to simply equate the term *k'ab'awil* with "idol" continued at least within a hyperlocal ecology of Highland Maya religious understanding and reflection.

However, according to Vico the practice of presenting offerings to the *che' ab'aj* or *k'ab'awil* was not ancient but rather a confusion between Maya and Spaniards as a consequence of the immediately preceding violent encounter and cultural destruction by earlier mendicants and soldiers. Prior to this encounter, as the descendants of the ancient Israelites, the ancestors of the Maya until the sixteenth-century correctly referred to and worshiped the true God, according to Vico. In this regard, Vico expressed his concerns less for proper forms and terms for instead proper referents and clearer understanding. *K'ab'awil* and *che' ab'aj* understood correctly as mere carved wood or stone effigies were less of a concern for Vico than their role in "proper" Catholic devotional practice and morality, and thus as signs that pointed to true divinity, which he, Las Casas, and other fellow Dominicans saw as a more authentic meaning of the Highland Maya term *k'ab'awil*.

Negotiating Ethical Discourse and Concerns
Vico's Use of Scripture

Throughout the remainder of the first volume of his *Theologia Indorum*, in chapters 26–104 (until the summary chapter 105 and colophon) and many of the nondoctrinal chapters in the second volume, Vico uses narratives to structure a historical framework for his theology but also as reference points from which to shift toward moral discourse and more normative claims regarding daily ethical behavior. Most of these narratives are biblical, beginning with the garden narratives of Genesis through chapter 30, but chapters 27–29 present extracanonical or nonbiblical material of the European popular and intellectual imagination, such as the war between Lucifer and God and the nine levels of the heavens as expressed in the *Celestial Hierarchy* by Pseudo-Dionysius the Areopagite and included more elaborately in Thomas Aquinas's *Summa theologicae*, John Milton's *Paradise Lost*, and Dante Alighieri's *Divine Comedy*. However, these later chapters do not represent Vico's attempt to translate the Bible into K'iche'an languages, which would have put him in opposition with the Church hierarchy, as the Synod of Guadix, Spain, in 1554 prohibited Bible translations into Arabic and the First Synod of Mexico in 1555 prohibited the same for native Mesoamerican languages.[78] Instead, these summaries by Vico serve to establish both a common platform between mendicants and Maya (especially as elaborated by Vico in K'iche'an languages and cultural terms) and as a jumping-off point from which to shift into more normative or ethical discourse.

Specifically regarding this shift to normative discourse, chapter 47 in particular exemplifies Vico's use of biblical stories and his moral concerns.[79] The first several lines connect the stories of Adam and Eve, told by Vico in the previous chapters, and the birth of all other human beings, namely Cain and Abel. Despite only explicitly naming Cain, Abel, and Seth as the children of Adam and Eve, Vico mentions both sons and daughters in the next lines. In the subsequent lines Vico further clarifies that humans were not made by a single woman (such as the K'iche' story of the divine grandmother Xmukane making humans out of maize dough, as told in the Popol Wuj) nor by a divine council (as also told in the Popol Wuj) but rather by a single God called *Tz'aqol B'itol* (the name of one of the principle creator deities in the Popol Wuj). Furthermore, the "Framer and Former" did so not out of maize dough, as told in the Popol Wuj, but rather mud, as told in the Judeo-Christian cosmogonic myth found in Genesis 2:7. However, Vico does state that *Dios, nimajaw* is both "our mother and our father but not two or three gods," thus referring back to previous chapters like 23 and 24. Finally, Vico ends the introductory lines that link chapter 47 with the previous ones by explicitly affirming the teachings of the Maya ancestors and exhorting his readership to know what they have said.

The next lines recount Genesis 4 and the stories of Cain, Abel, Seth, and Lamech. However, Vico does not mention the intervening generations of Enoch, Irad, Mehujael, and Methuselah, thereby implying that Lamech is a son of Cain. Furthermore, Vico makes no distinction between Cain's profession as a farmer and Abel's profession as a shepherd, nor does he attribute motivation for God's preference of Abel's offering over that of Cain. Vico merely specifies that Abel's murder resulted from Cain's envy and desire for his own "good existence." However, Vico introduces and condemns as another "sin" the polygamy of Lamech with his two wives. Toward the end of the story about Lamech, Vico has the young man who initially attacked Lamech state that he is doing so because Lamech is "evil." Before explaining his moral discourse into common K'iche' images and ideas, Vico sums up his main point as he urges his Maya readers to do like Abel and Seth rather than like Cain and Lamech, as the former are "true [to the] teaching of the existence of the ancestors."

The closing of the generational gap between Cain and Lamech and the liberties taken with the story of Lamech allow Vico to link the sin of killing with the sin of polygamy over the remaining lines, even though the theme, let alone the "sin," of polygamy is not part of the biblical account or conventional exegesis. However, the use of the summary of the biblical narrative allows Vico to address two issues regarding ritual and moral practices. First, Vico argues for an understanding of immoral practices as they are related to each other and not as isolated incidents in either the Bible or the lives of the Highland Maya. For example, Vico seems to imply that Cain's "first sin" of murder later resulted in Lamech's sin of martial "excess." Later still, Vico inverts this and argues for a relation between polygamy or adultery and the deaths of infants and young children. Second, Vico clarifies that, at least in part, the immorality is not only in the action or results of the act but is also related to the internal disposition of the actor, such as Cain's envy and desire for his own "good existence" over and against that of another, which leads him to kill his brother, and Lamech's "evilness," which leads him to have more than one wife. Vico engages in this moral discourse not merely by translating a Bible story into K'iche' and following it with exhortations, but rather through the selection of two sets of terms fundamental to K'iche' ethical and ritual discourse.

Maya Moral Discourse

Vico introduces the first set of terms, which pertain to ritual practices with the root *-mayij-*, by summarizing Cain and Abel's offerings to God in the beginning of chapter 47. The root or stem *-mayij-* implies a sacrificial offering with the passive construction *-mayixik* actually meaning "to be killed," presumably by bloodletting rather than murder, *-kamisaxik*.[80] This verb stem pertains to a larger set of K'iche' verbs that refer to ritual offerings: *-toj-* "to pay," *-sipaj* "to give as a present," *-ya'oj-* "to gift," and *-mayij-* "to sacrifice." In contrast, *-pus-*, which in ancient Maya ritual may etymologically relate "to cut," for postclassic Highland Maya seemed to pertain only to a spiritual sacrifice rather than to a material sacrifice, as the object to be "sacrificed" with *-pus-* is implied to no longer be physically present but persists only as a memory of something otherwise forgotten, rotten, or deceased or something of extraordinary power germane to ritualized activity. Vico's use of *-mayij-* in chapter 47 and elsewhere in the *Theologia Indorum* refers to objects still present or in the possession of a person. However, like the shift in understanding *-pus-* to not mean literally "cut," Vico seems to imply that the "sacrifice" of a material object to the Christian god, if done with *-mayij-*, is done spiritually or as a matter of disposition of the agent and thus is more of an "offering" in the sense of a gift than it is a "sacrifice," as of a voluntary loss and forsaking.[81] Again, by slight contrast, he employs the traditional lexical couplet *pus nawal* in volume two as the K'iche' phrase for "miracles," such as those performed by Jesus.

The second set of terms, "good" and "evil," Vico mentions when he refers to the character or dispositions of the agents in the Bible story, namely Cain and Lamech. In general, K'iche' ritual and moral discourse can involve three distinct but interrelated pairs of concepts. While "good" (*utz*) is a common term both in written texts in K'iche', such as the *Theologia Indorum* and those authored by the K'iche' Maya, and in modern spoken K'iche', "evil" (*itz*) rarely appears in Maya publications and, when discussed, is spoken of in more hushed tones or through circumlocution.[82] In this first pair or couplet, morality is usually referred to as "good" (*utz*) and "not good" (*man utz taj*, *na utz taj*, or *utz taj*). Maya may also contrast "good" with a variety of euphemisms instead of "not good," such as "dirty" (*tz'il*), thereby referring to "not good" through analogies of undesirable states or conditions. The specifics of desired or undesired conditions are referred to with another pair of terms: "hot" (*q'aq'*) and "cold" (*tew*). However, among Highland Maya an object's "hotness" or "coldness" at the level of moral discourse has little or nothing to do with temperature or spice. Colors, bodily activity, medicinal herbs, and even food are categorized as "hot," such as maize, and "cold," such as beans. In this regard, this couplet refers to an understood essential aspect of an object or activity. The aim in moral teachings and "correct" daily practices is to achieve and maintain a balance between "hot" and "cold" aspects with neither one necessarily mapping onto conceptions of "good" and "bad."[83]

Whether it occurs through compensation in other daily activities, like drinking a medicinal tea or through ritual activities like taking a sweat bath, the correction of imbalance between "hot" and "cold" involves a third pair of terms: *moxq'ab'* ("left hand") and *wikiq'ab'* ("right hand"). In particular, "hot"/"cold" and "left"/"right" relate K'iche' understandings of correctness, prosperity, and health to perceived cosmological patterns, cosmogonic narratives, social structures, and quotidian life. However, neither set maps onto Maya understanding of "good" and "not good." "Good" and "not good" reflect an undisclosed facet of a person's character that, at best, becomes manifest as a result of various conditions of imbalance. While desired "good" may be exhorted and seemingly sought through activities witnessed by a larger public, such as family and community, failures and resulting imbalance or illnesses are usually discussed through circumlocutions as they refer to other, conflicting, dangerous desires. As a result, "evil" (*itz*) is rarely explicitly referred to, even by K'iche' elites and ritual specialists. However, by declaring Lamech "evil" and identifying a flaw in Cain's desire for proper "good," Vico makes clear to his K'iche' readership that the locus of sin is subjectively internal, deep within dispositions, and a character expressed in behaviors.

Vico appears even more concerned with moral behaviors, such as polygamy and murder, than he does with ritual practices, giving the latter some benefit of the doubt, depending on the dispositions and intentions of practitioners and the understood referents of their terms and images. Vico does not merely condemn the local offerings and sacrifices of the Maya but stipulates that they need to be done like that of Abel, who was "good at heart." Vico specifically lists traditional items, such as chocolate pods, large chickens, and even children, that may be offered or dedicated—not "sacrificed" except in the spiritual sense—to the Christian god. Like his concern with effigies as the stone or wooden *k'ab'awil* in chapter 25 and the K'iche' language in general, Vico's theological method focuses on a deep appreciation of K'iche' culture through which many dimensions and meanings are affirmed. Those that were not, which Vico condemned, were replaced with Hispano-Catholic references. Both of these tasks required not necessarily a replacement of K'iche' culture but an augmentation by translating linguistically and conceptually Hispano-Catholicism into a K'iche' cultural framework. This process, in turn, allowed K'iche' culture not only to contextualize but theologically to open Hispano-Catholicism to K'iche' responses. Finally, this theological approach by Vico required an advance toward an interdisciplinary method in which he could draw from the resources of the other emerging human sciences and also make original if not also enduring contributions to them on their own grounds.

Whereas chapters 1–22 Vico's doctrine of god and more specifically his doctrine of *ajaw* drew upon quotidian and regal Highland Maya imagery and ideas, chapters 23 and 24 involved his attempt to then explain the distinctive Christian understanding of a triune god. By means of juxtaposition, chapter 25 contrasts his Christian doctrine of *ajaw* with the condemned devotionalism of *che' ab'aj* ("idols") by Highland Maya but not necessarily in conflict with his reconfigured understanding of *k'ab'awil* as interpreted as "divinity." This triadic juxtaposition conceptually forms a Maya tercet, a kind of analogical thinking but on Maya terms and rationale of similarity-in-difference, which Vico uses as a bridge to his Thomistic emphasis on analogical modes of understanding. In this sense, Vico's chapter 25 discloses the most on his theological method—how he understood Maya religious signification to align, independent of any Christian signification for the production of a systematic Christian Maya theology. Chapters 26–46 then transition into cosmogenesis and the creation and ordering of the heavens, earth, and human nature or theological anthropology, thus laying the narrative groundwork for a focus on both devotional and ethical practices beginning with chapter 47. The remaining chapters until 105 present stories from the Catholic Old Testament for both a biblical history and a renewed moral understanding for the Maya.[84] He continues this line of presentation through the second volume of his *Theologia Indorum* but with the use of stories from the New Testament and catechism through chapter 109 of volume two. As indicated in appendix A of this volume, the order of the presentation and use of the biblical material seems to correspond more to the order of hagiographic readings and themes during the late medieval liturgical year than simply the order of the respective books within the Christian Bible.

Chapter 105 of volume one, and in parallel fashion also chapter 110 of the second volume, consist of thematic summaries of each of the respective tomes. Vico assumes that his K'iche'an readers will have thoroughly read all of the preceding sections, and he repeats the history but as a set of "signs."[85] The final units, therefore, before the colophon, introduce a hermeneutic of reading "the signs of the times" of not only the biblical past but their postcontact present as well as the future until the Last Judgment. The *Theologia Indorum*, therefore, far from being a collection of sermons, is an autodidactic manual to teach its Maya readers not only a Hispano-Catholic moral and religious worldview on Maya terms but also a semiotic of how to read, akin to the Popol Wuj, as explained subsequently here in chapter 6.

CONCLUSION: A SUMMARY OF VICO'S *SUMMA*

Vico's obvious aim pertains to the conversion of the Maya to Catholicism. His strategy built off Las Casas's argument of a shared theological anthropology and the natural disposition to commune with the divine even in apparent idolatry, and thus it also affirmed dimensions of precontact Highland Maya religiosity. As Vico argued against the autonomous mixing of Maya spiritual practices with Catholic devotionalism, he did not altogether rule out a mixture of Catholic theology and indigenous culture. Rather, he provided an argument and precedent for another kind of mixture. First, he employed K'iche'an languages in which he makes his argument and assumed a literate Maya readership, in addition to fellow Catholic clergy, along with an intimate knowledge of highly formalized K'iche' vocabulary and rhetoric reserved for speaking about the sacred, *toj tzij*.[86] Second, Vico appears acutely aware of the analogical dimension within K'iche' language and thought as he selects his K'iche' terms for "God": *Tz'aqol B'itol* and even *Alom K'ajolm* (Bearer and Begetter). His K'iche' sources, such as an early version of narrative source material that went into the Popol

Wuj, use a variety of titles to refer to the cosmogonic creator(s) appearing in couplet or tercet forms, but Vico selects the titles that are most analogous to the creator god in Genesis over others, such as *Tepew Q'ukumatz* (Sovereign Plumed Serpent).

However, in addition to appropriating a classic K'iche' couplet for his god—or from the early postcontact K'iche' perspective, the creator gods—Vico yoked on his own phrase, *nimajaw* ("great lord"). If he did not coin the phrase himself, his *Theologia Indorum* is among the earliest writings in which it appears, and subsequent Catholic documents in K'iche' picked it up. To the same degree that the *shema* in the Tanakh and Christian Old Testament redacts a couplet with *'elohim* ("God") and YHWH (conventionally rendered as "Adonai" in spoken Hebrew or "LORD" in English translations), Vico forms a rhetorical K'iche' tercet by joining *nimajaw* as the third phrase of the K'iche' couplet *Tz'aqol* and *B'itol*. *Ajaw* in colonial and modern K'iche', and presumably in prehispanic K'iche', literally translates to "lord" or owner of an estate or title, like "landlord" in modern English or the title *don* or *señor* in medieval Spanish.[87] Vico merely added the augmenting modifier of *nim* or *nima*, "great," to distinguish between a quotidian owner and the Owner or LORD. Just as with other kinds of K'iche' rhetorical tercets, the third line is not synonymous with the first two words or phrases, like the first two lines or words may be synonymous with each other in a K'iche' tercet or even couplet. In this regard, just as the *shema* asserts that the LORD (YHWH) is, and is the same as, God and is thus one, Vico's tercet for the divine is not an alternative Trinitarian formulation but rather an assertion that the God who creates is also known as the God who builds and forms (be it called *Dios* or *Tz'aqol B'itol*), and thus is the same as the great lord (*nimajaw*).

Vico adopts Maya terms to convey a relationship between ideas of the divine held by Highland Maya and Iberian Christianity, but his construction and use of the phrase *Tz'aqol, B'itol, nimajaw* for "the LORD God" in K'iche'an languages also circumvents, in a Spanish Dominican fashion, one of the hotter theological debates of his day. As discussed previously in chapter 2, the difference in linguistic ideologies or semiotic theories between Spanish Franciscans and Dominicans undergirded the respectively different approaches mendicants took to convey Catholic theology to indigenous Mesoamericans. Whereas Spanish Franciscans, for the most part, held that a sign could not be divorced from its referent and thereby replaced with another sign, Spanish Dominicans, influenced more by scholastic Thomism rather than nominalism like the Franciscans, sought to establish theological analogies for Catholic concepts with Mesoamerican terms and images. As a result, Franciscans advocated for the use of Latin or Castilian (Spanish) words for distinctively religious ideas that they did not want to risk contaminating with Mesoamerican meaning. Therefore, Franciscans working among the Highland Maya—such as the

Kaqchikel, the far Western K'iche' in Quetzaltenango, and the Tz'utujil in Santiago Atitlán—promoted the use of a K'iche'anized form of "Dios," *Tyox*, for God rather than use any Maya term for the divine. Based on their differing semiotic ideologies, Franciscans translated local terms and images, like the *k'ab'awil* in K'iche' and Kaqchikel, as false divinities or "idolatries."[88]

In contrast, Dominicans working in New Spain commonly used ethnographic and linguistic research to find terms that might be appropriated. One of their initial proposals was the K'iche'an term *kab'awil* or *k'ab'awil* as "pure divinity" and the indigenous intended reference for wood or stone effigies used in Maya rituals.[89] For example, even Las Casas argued that the name "for the common and supreme god over everything" in the language of Guatemala was "Cavovil" [*k'ab'awil*] and in that of Mexico it was "Teutl" [*teotl*].[90] While generally in favor of mendicant ethnographic, linguistic, and theological work, although he himself was secular clergy and thus neither a Franciscan nor a Dominican, Bishop Marroquín nonetheless found the debates between Dominicans and Franciscans regarding the meaning of *k'ab'awil* so disruptive to civil life in Guatemala that he placed a moratorium on the issue. Marroquín sided with the Franciscan use of *Tyox* for "God" to restore harmony among the clergy in his diocese but he did not explicitly approve of the linguistic ideology or theological method of the Franciscans over and against that of the Dominicans.[91] On the one hand, Vico honors Marroquín's decision by not using *k'ab'awil* to refer to "God" but he does not concede to the Franciscans that the term should be translated as or considered to refer to only as an "idol," and thus did not concede to the perspective that the religious practices of the Maya are always idolatry. Instead, Vico employs another term altogether to refer to the stone and wood effigies: *ab'aj che'*. On the other hand, Vico does not concede the Spanish Dominican theological approach to either the bishop or his contemporaneous Franciscan opponents as he appropriates, augments, and clarifies another K'iche' term for the divine, *Tz'aqol, B'itol, nimajaw*.

However, Vico does not use *Tz'aqol B'itol* analogously to the God of the Bible but rather univocally or synonymously as he also does with the term for the Maya otherworld, Xib'alb'a, univocally as the Christian notion of "hell." As Xib'alb'a does not carry the same fearful force of permanence as "hell," Vico, ironically may have undermined the persuasiveness of the doctrinal threat of eternal punishment. However, his univocal move legitimized a common move by later mendicants who had equated the otherworld with hell, the afterlife with death and resurrection, spiritual debt with original sin, and confession with sacramental penance.[92] Even a century later, in the 1650s, Franciscans debating about the difficulties of translating the notion of *persona* in the Trinitarian grammar into Kaqchikel Maya (because *winaq* only referred to the plural "people," "nation," "humanity," or a class of "living beings") appealed to Vico's arguments for and illustration of such use.[93] This problem of interpretation and translation would also affect how the missionaries such as Vico understood, or misunderstood, Maya notions of the divine as strictly plural with little underlying metaphysical or cosmological unity.[94] On the other hand, like the humanistic skepticism shared by most Spanish mendicants toward the idea of the preternatural, Vico's long appeal within the wider linguistic and ethnographic approach to arrive analogically at a new theological lexicon and rhetoric was not uniformly agreed upon.

Along the lines of this translation but also reconfiguration strategy, Vico drew from the poetic high register of K'iche'an moral and ritual discourse as the language of his theology. The abundant splendor of heaven, the prelapsarian Eden, and future reign of his god on earth was "yellowness and greenness" (*q'anal raxal*).[95] In chapter 30 of volume one the Christian concept of a singular "soul" or *anima* is introduced in relation to the Highland Maya concept of a person's *ninuch' natub'* ("shadow and shade").[96] In contrast, Franciscans strove to replace *natub'* with the Latin term *anima*, which, like their neologism *Tyox,* is now incorporated as *anima'* in many Highland Mayan languages to mean one's "soul" or "spirit" along with the Dominican-approved *ruxlab'*.[97] In chapter 47 of volume one, but also well into the second volume, Vico uses the couplet *pus nawal* to explain and discuss the extraordinary power of properly oriented prayers and offerings, such as that "miracles" of Jesus.[98] And along the way Vico not only translates his god as "divine" (*k'ab'awil*), but never as concretized in stone or wood effigies (*ab'aj che'*), but also through the mendicant Maya couplet of *Dios nimajaw* and with the classic K'iche' couplets of *Tz'aqol B'itol* (Framer and Former), *Alom K'ajolom* (Bearer and Begetter), and *qachuch qaqajaw* ("our mother and our father"). Thus, he presents not a doctrine of God the Father but rather a divine creator both feminine and masculine, who is always balanced and whole according to Maya theogonic terms.

By 1577 a royal order, preceded by a ruling at the first Synod or Council of Mexico in 1555 and the arrival of the Inquisition to Guatemala in 1571, forbade writing about the religious customs and spiritual beliefs of the Indians in any language and, thus, prematurely terminated Friar Sahagún's work in Mexico with an official confiscation.[99] Although this order was rarely enforced, which thus allowed missionary scholars to continue to study indigenous languages and religious customs, the infamous burnings of Maya libraries in Franciscan friar Diego de Landa's *auto de fé* in Yucatán in 1562 and the trials that ensued discouraged Maya from freely discussing prehispanic rites and ceremonies.[100] Like Sahagún's confiscation, the divisions between and among Franciscans and Dominicans regarding theological work outside of Latin, Greek, or Hebrew might also have influenced Marroquín's defiance of the ban on theological work in Mayan languages and the subsequent sheltering of Vico from Sahagún's later fate.[101] Vico's approach laid a foundation not only for his immediate Maya readers but also anticipated that of the Jesuits even slightly later and elsewhere, such as Mateo Ricci in China, and for mendicants' and Jesuits' inculturation work with Highland Maya in the late twentieth century. Yet, the impact of Landa's trials and the Inquisition, as well as colonization in general, largely limited Maya religious writings until its public reemergence in the Pan-Maya or Maya Activist Movement beginning in the 1970s.

Thus, during this roughly fifty-year period (1520s–1570s) of theological creativity as well as collaboration between mendicants and Mesoamericans, Vico marshaled and developed new disciplinary skills by which to use Maya conceptual and intellectual resources for his theological approach. Chief among those resources were Maya texts, both oral and written, in various phases of reconfiguration and redaction in light of changes of the early sixteenth century, changes including a rapid 80 percent population decline due to new diseases, new colonial legal and labor structures, alternative cosmogonic narratives accompanied by ritual institutions, and a different way of writing Mayan languages. Vico's new theology and other mendicant work simultaneously drew from and influenced those Maya texts, a mutual influence examined in detail in the following chapter.

5

Use of Maya "Scripture"

Vico's Theological Method and Doctrine of Ajaw

xawi xere xa jun Dios,
nimajaw,
ri Tz'aqol,
B'itol xecha
ichuch,
iqajaw,
xawi xere b'anol
kaj
ulew,
Tz'aqol re,
B'itol re ronojel
k'o chi kaj,
k'o chi uwach ulew . . .

. . . there is only one God,
the great lord;
the Framer
and Former that
your mothers and
your fathers spoke of,
the only maker

DOI: 10.5876/9781607329701.c005

of the sky and
of the earth,
the Framer of it and
the Former of everything that
there is in the sky and
there is on the face of the earth . . .[1]

POPOL WUJ AND TALKING ABOUT TALK ABOUT "GOD"

Unlike what is often stereotypically thought of as the work of a Christian missionary among non-Christians, Vico did not use only biblical stories for the cosmogonic, theogonic, and moral construals in his theology. He also drew from the various historical, legendary, and mythological epics told by Highland Maya. Furthermore, this appeal to Maya religious narratives drew from both the content and rhetoric of K'iche'an speech to and about the divine. Within only a year or so after the completion of the first volume of the *Theologia Indorum*, perhaps in part due to the appearance of the first part of Vico's theology, K'iche' elites schooled by mendicants began to write down versions of their prehispanic worldview, such as in notarial texts like the *Title of Totonicapán*.

Fortunately, the *Title of Totonicapán* and later documents by other factions of the Kaweqib' and the Nija'ib' lineages and the Tamub' and Ilokab' branches of the Western K'iche'—discussed in the previous chapters for an ethnohistory of the K'iche' Maya and ethnobiography of Domingo de Vico—are not the only reservoir of sixteenth-century Highland Maya voices in the intertextual conversation with Vico's *Theologia Indorum*. Despite the Inquisition, intentional book burnings, the corrosive elements of time, and the still incomplete intelligibility of ancient Maya logosyllabic texts, the Popol Wuj contains the most complete account of history from cosmogony through the establishment of the Spanish Empire from any indigenous American perspective. In this regard, the Popol Wuj stands as the most important native-language text in all of the Americas due to the prehispanic character of both its style and content.[2] Furthermore, the development of the alphabetic version of the Popol Wuj makes it a response to the mendicant missionaries. The precarious manuscript history, as detailed in the previous chapters, has raised questions regarding not only the antiquity of the narratives but also the authorship of the text, especially with regard to the few but highly notable references to Christianity as corruptions to the Maya stories. While archaeological evidence proves both the indigenous authenticity and prehispanic antiquity of the narratives contained in the Popol Wuj the oldest surviving version, that copied and translated by Friar Francisco Ximénez, O.P., dates between 1701 and 1703 or 1704.[3]

Most but not all of these concerns have been resolved with recent interdisciplinary work between archaeologists, ethnohistorians, and linguistic anthropologists, but the lack of scholarly contributions from religious studies, namely the histories of Christian thought, has left the written references to Christianity relatively unexamined and assumed to represent either the K'iche' elite's reactionary resistance against or its parroting deference to Catholic clergy.

In light of the evidence examined in the previous and subsequent chapters, it is most likely that the few abstract references to "Christendom" and "utterances about God" in the Popol Wuj are not only general comments regarding the presence of Hispano-Catholicism but were made specifically regarding the *Theologia Indorum*, just as was done by other later contemporaneous K'iche'an texts. An intertextual understanding of these documents together helps solidify both one of Vico's principal sources of Maya religion and a principal source of Christianity for the authors of one of the most important indigenous American texts. Like the previous analysis given to the *Theologia Indorum*, attention to the Popol Wuj in this and the next chapter with specific attention to its rhetoric and content examines explicit key aspects of Highland Maya culture that influenced Vico, his "Indian" theology, and the opening of further Maya and Christian theological responses.

More specifically, this chapter continues to describe the contents of the *Theologia Indorum*, not topically according to modern doctrinal themes (e.g., cosmology, angelology, demonology, doctrine of god, moral anthropology, christology, etc.), but rather how Vico presented his theological work to Highland Maya through a particular order or hierarchy of ideas influenced by Thomistic scholasticism and late medieval popular devotionalism. In part, however, this does entail further examination of his construction of a doctrine of god, or more appropriately a Christian doctrine of *ajaw*, in the midst of the mendicant debates at the time and in the region regarding false gods or idolatry, namely the use of the terms *k'ab'awil* and *che' ab'aj* for effigies of wood or stone. Just as integrally related to the appropriation of Maya moral and ritual discourse, Vico's conveyance of understandings about his god moved to his understandings of the cosmic and human condition and to proper devotional and moral practices. For these latter sections of the *Theologia Indorum*, Vico moved away from scholastic sources in favor of biblical stories as well as precontact Maya source material that would soon contribute to the Popol Wuj.

MANUSCRIPT REDACTION OF THE POPOL WUJ

Ethnohistorical Context

While the Ximénez manuscript (Ayer Ms 1515) does not break up the text into distinct units, most translators and editors recognize between four to six sections or main narrative arcs redacted into a whole (see table 5.1).[4] Furthermore, the Popol Wuj provides clear evidence that its transcription into the mendicant orthography and its compilation into a single corpus was the work of a committee of Western K'iche' elite: council members or *popol winaq* of the K'iche' confederacy based around the prehispanic city of Q'umarkaj. Despite the use of first person plural narrative voice—*oj* ("we")—and the final genealogy of nobles ending with the then still-living leaders, the only name explicitly mentioned as an author-redactor of the Popol Wuj is Cristóbal Velasco, a *nim ch'okoj* or "master of ceremonies."[5]

Of the various ranks and offices of the council, the *nim ch'okoj* were ceremony officials and stewards of the dances who not only recited or enacted occasional scenes of the cosmogonic myths and legends, but also parts of K'iche' national history from the vantage of the different governing branches or lineages. As described in chapter 1, each of the four governing lineages that composed and led the confederacy had an order of *nim ch'okoj*. The only surviving example of such political dramas though is the *Lord of Rab'inal* of the Eastern K'iche', which tells of their victorious resistance to the incursions of Western K'iche' decades before the arrival of the Spaniards.[6] It was most likely the members of these specific offices from the respective lineages who were charged with compiling, transcribing (from maps or *lienzos*, calendar charts, oral and dramatic performances, and possibly glyphic texts), and redacting into a single tome stories regarding the emergence of the world and everything in it down to the K'iche' nation. This writing and editing process occurred in light of and under pressure from (1) the devastating attack on Highland Maya society by joint Spanish and Nahua forces and European diseases from the north, (2) revolt from within and attacks from outside the confederacy by groups like the Eastern K'iche', Tz'utujil, and Kaqchikel but also earlier by the Ilokab' branch, and (3) continued internal dissent throughout the confederacy in the wake of the junior Kaweqib' rebellion within the dominant royal house from the 1470s. Diego Reynoso is credited with being a member of the council and at least a minor author of the Popol Wuj, not in the text itself but rather in K'iche' oral history conveyed to Ximénez.[7]

Mendicant Contact Influence

The actual transcription and redaction of the current text from its supposed logosyllabic and oral predecessors probably occurred between 1554 and 1558, making it both a late contemporary with the *Theologia Indorum* but most likely an early one with the *Title of Totonicapán*.[8] However, the impact of the political but also religious—specifically the theogonic rather than the cosmogonic—narratives of the Popol Wuj are obvious in both the *Title of Totonicapán*, whose genealogy

TABLE 5.1. Narrative arcs in the Popol Wuj

Unit	*Contents*	*Folios*
Preamble	Introduction to the "prior word."	1 recto–1 verso
Cosmogonic creation	Measuring out of the cosmic order by divine agents; first three attempts at creating humans: animals, people of mud, and people of wood.	1 verso–5 verso
Defeat of nonhuman lords in the world by the Hero Twins	Defeat of Wuqub' Kaqix and his family by the Hero Twins: Jun Ajpu and Xb'alanke.	5 verso–12 recto
Defeat of nonhuman lords of the otherworld by the Hero Twins	Defeat of the father/uncle of the Hero Twins by the lords of the otherworld Xib'alb'a; the birth of the Hero Twins; the journey into and defeat of the Xib'alb'a lords by the Hero Twins; the reemergence of the Hero Twins and their father/uncle.	12 recto–32 verso
The first eight true human beings	Creation of people of maize, four couples; their migration from "the east" and the first (new) dawn for the fourth age of the world.	32 verso–38 recto
K'iche' nation as direct descendants	Genealogy and sociopolitical history and structure of the K'iche' nation until 1554–1558.	38 recto–56 verso

of K'iche' rulers aimed to "correct" the list in the Popol Wuj, and the *Theologia Indorum*, whose similarities of formal language and knowledge of "gods" has led some scholars erroneously to attribute authorship of the Popol Wuj to Vico or other Dominicans, such as, even later, Francisco Ximénez.[9] Instead, Vico's detailed knowledge of Maya myths should indicate that he had access to many of the same source narrative materials that the Kaweq-dominated K'iche' Maya eventually redacted into the Popol Wuj and gave to Ximénez a century and a half later. Given the fact that he was a prominent teacher (*ajtij*) of Highland Maya gentry in and around Santiago de Guatemala through 1553, at the same time and place Diego Reynoso also studied there, Vico most likely had extensive exposure to these K'iche'an oral traditions from Reynoso if not also other Highland Maya students that he may have taught.

Differences between the contents in the Popol Wuj and what Vico implicitly cites from these Maya stories indicate that he interpreted them for his own theological agenda. Furthermore, many of his sources were possibly alternative or additional versions than those compiled into the Popol Wuj eventually received by Ximénez, Brasseur de Bourbourg, and Edward Ayer. One such detailed example is Vico's listing of K'iche' characters from the cosmogonic stories in chapter 25 of volume one of the *Theologia Indorum,* in which he addresses the K'iche' about their mythic past:

1 Nim chi xib'ij iwib' rumal,
2 Nim chi uwach Xib'alb'a,
3 nim chiwach: Jun Ajpu, Xb'alankej,
4 Tasal Junrakan, Q'eteb' Pub'a'ix,
5 Jun Junajpu, Wuqub' Junajpu,
6 Jun Kame, Wuqub' Kame,
7 Kik' Re', Kik' Rixk'aq,
8 Mam Iq', Cho'a,
9 Wok, Jun Ajpu.
10 Are xixk'ab'awilaj ojer,
11 are xiwokikaj chi inimal, chi ajawarem
12 are xitz'onoj wi ronojel xraj ik'u'x . . .

1 Greatly you all were scared because
2 greatly before you all is Xib'alb'a,
3 greatly before you all is: Jun Ajpu and Xb'alankej,[10]
4 Tasul Juraqan[11] and Q'eteb' Pub'a'ix,
5 Jun Junajpu and Wuqub' Junajpu,
6 Jun Kame and Wuqub' Kame,
7 Kik' Re' and Kik' Rixk'aq,
8 Mam Iq' and Cho'a, and
9 Wok and Jun Ajpu.[12]
10 You all venerated [God] long ago,
11 you all believed in your greatness, in the reign,
12 to whom you all pleaded from all of your hearts . . .[13]

While certain names in this list—Jun Ajpu and Xb'alankej (the Hero Twins), Jun Junajpu and Wuqub' Junajpu (the father and uncle of the Hero Twins), and Jun Kame and Wuqub' Kame (the lords of the otherworld, Xib'alb'a)—are major characters in the Popol Wuj, other names, such as Kik' Re' and Kik' Rixk'aq (Bloody Teeth and Bloody Claws of Xib'alb'a) and Wok (falcon, messagner of the cosmogonic deities) are only minor characters. Some names are not only absent in the Popol Wuj but seem to have slipped away from modern K'iche' oral tradition altogether.[14] Vico appears to have had access to an earlier set of K'iche' narratives that contained details or even whole stories later dropped by the K'iche' editors of the Popol Wuj in the 1550s or possibly in later redactions until the early 1700s.

THEOLOGICAL METHOD: CONSTRUCTING A DOCTRINE OF *AJAW*

Vico's Use of Maya Poetics

As discussed previously in the introduction, theology may be simply understood as a community's critical, analytical, and evaluative reflection on their religious thought, practices, and institutions—a kind of second-order or metadiscourse to the extent that prayerfully reciting the Nicaean Creed or the Shema, chanting the Psalms or verses of the Qur'an, spinning a prayer wheel or counting through the 260 days of the Maya ceremonial calendar during a *kotz'i'j* (fire offering) ceremony would be first-order discourse. Furthermore, the extent to which the word, "theology," predates Christianity by at least a couple of centuries—and that early Christian intellectuals like Justin Martyr abhorred it, associated it with paganism, and preferred to be called instead a Christian philosopher or "lover of wisdom"—there is nothing inherently Christian or even Jewish about the word. However, within modern theology the specific attention on how theological thought is or ought to be produced is called theological method and is often considered third-order discourse (reflexive thought on second-order discourse, on theology). Such methodological concerns attend not simply to the construction of religious doctrines or ideas but to how they are constructed, how the source materials (such as the Christian Bible) engages with the thought and other resources of the wider world, including even other religions. The first 24 enumerated sections or "chapters" of the *Theologia Indorum* focus on Vico's explication of the existence and characteristics of his god. Chapter 25 more explicitly portrays how he understands a productive engagement between Hispano-Catholicism and K'iche' religiosity—ritual devotionalism, ceremonial rhetoric, and theogonic construals and stories, particularly as also written down by Highland Maya authors at the time.

The relationship between these three documents—the *Theologia Indorum*, the Popol Wuj, and the *Title of Totonicapán*—as close intertextual interlocutors is further supported by the fact that Diego Reynoso and another K'iche' scribe and *nim ch'okoj*, Cristóbal Velasco, are both associated with the authorship and redaction of the Popol Wuj and the *Title of Totonicapán* in the 1550s.[15] Furthermore, Diego Reynoso was brought to the capital of Guatemala in 1539, learned Parra's mendicant alphabet, and in the 1550s began to assist with texts in K'iche', possibly with Vico's *Theologia Indorum* being one of them. Like the *Title of Totonicapán*, the Popol Wuj's exclusive audience undoubtedly was other K'iche' Maya. Beginning in the first folio, the Popol Wuj makes explicit the analogical understanding of divinity also argued for in the *Title of Totonicapán,* as it acknowledges that it must still make clear the "root of the ancient word" (*uxe' ojer tzij*) even in the midst of the "talk of God, in Christendom thus" (*uch'ab'al Dios, pa christiano'il chik*).[16] The Popol Wuj's emphasis on and invocation of an *ojer tzij*—an "ancient word"—is implicitly juxtaposed with or differentiated from the numerous *paj tzij* or "themes" found in the *Theologia Indorum* and also cited in the first seven folios of the *Title of Totonicapán*. Furthermore, this distinction made in the Popol Wuj augments the use of *tzij* as it is further juxtaposed with or differentiates from *ch'ab'al*. As is detailed in the next chapter, while *ch'ab'al* literally refers to "language," most commonly spoken language, *uch'ab'al Dios* may imply "talk about God," such as in sermons, or it may refer specifically to Catholic doctrines, such as those found in *cartillas*, catechisms, and the second part of the *Theologia Indorum*, or it may have been an early Dominican neologism to literally convey "theology" (*theos-logia*, talking about a god). In either case, the Popol Wuj begins by establishing a contrasted relationship between the "word" by the Maya and "utterances" by mendicants like Vico.

However, this conceptual contrast pair between "word" and "utterance" should not be understood as merely an argumentative foil or reactionary conflict of Maya religion over and against Christianity in general, given the Maya propensity toward expanding complementary opposites articulated in various kinds of parallelism. In fact, later K'iche' *títulos* refer to Christianity as both *utzij Dios* ("word of God") and *uch'ab'al Dios* ("utterance of God"), apparently interchangeably and complementarily, such as in the *Title of the K'oyoy*, or exclusively as *utzij Dios*, such as in the *Title of the Ilokab'*.[17] Instead, the Popol Wuj argues for a Maya analogical understanding against the mendicant univocal or equating conceptualization on three main points, as explained in greater detail in the next chapter, chapter 6.

The first point of assertion of difference within this set of similarities-in-differences pertains to Vico's terms for the divine. Whereas Vico treats the term *k'ab'awil* explicitly as the generic K'iche' term for wood or stone images of the divine or the tutelary spirits of the ruling K'iche' lineages and implicitly as the early Dominican attempt by the likes of Las Casas to translate God with this term, the Popol Wuj explicitly refers to the divine epithet *Uk'u'x Kaj* (Heart of Sky), the Hero Twins, and the tutelary spirits of the ruling K'iche' lineages (but not the lords of Xib'alb'a) as a *k'ab'awil*.[18] More important, this insistence on the use of *k'ab'awil* to refer to divinity by the Maya authors of the Popol Wuj is over and against its predominantly Franciscan referent as "idol" as well as their corrective neologism *Tyox* (the phonetically K'iche'anized variation for "Dios").[19] Furthermore, in agreement with the *Title of Totonicapán*, the Popol Wuj pairs *Uk'u'x Kaj* with *Uk'u'x Ulew* ("Heart of Earth") to form a couplet for the divine that complements in parallel structure *Tz'aqol B'itol* or "God" as the "Framer and Former." The Popol Wuj also counters the Christian Trinitarian formula by parsing out *Uk'u'x Kaj* as a tercet: *Kakulja Juraqan* ("Lightning One-Leg"), *Chipakakulja* ("Youngest Lightning"), and *Raxakakulja* ("Green Lightning").[20] The text further clarifies how *Uk'u'x Kaj* is a *k'ab'awil* in this refusal to accommodate Christian terms, as the Popol Wuj later alludes to the three ruling lineages' tutelary spirits—*Tojil*, *Awilix*, and *Jakawitz*—in another structure parallel to the "lightning trinity."[21] Likewise, perhaps in an effort to counter mendicants' concern for idolatry or demonology within native Mesoamerican religions, the K'iche' author-redactors of the Popol Wuj also explicitly state that the lords of Xib'alb'a such as Jun Kame ("One Death") and Wuqub' Kame ("Seven Death")—are not divine (*mana k'ab'awil*).[22]

The second example of similarity-in-difference that the Popol Wuj asserts pertains not to terms for the divine but to rather how the divine creates humanity. Like the couplets formed for names of divinity, K'iche' rhetoric plays with the formation of compound words or pairs of antonymic synecdoches, such as the title *chuchqajaw* ("mother–father") in the *Title of Totonicapán*. The creation of *juyub'-taq'aj* "(mountain–plain") by the K'iche' "trinity," as another example of this type of merismus in the Popol Wuj, metaphorically refers not only to the face of the earth but also to the human body.[23] Instead of Genesis's lone Eve, the first four human women in the Popol Wuj are created after the first four men but they are not derived from the men, thus emphasizing a crucial difference with Vico's catechistic account of creation, while also underscoring the notion of gender complementarity as found in the terms for the divine, specifically *chuchqajaw* and *Tz'aqol B'itol*.[24] Furthermore, unlike Genesis's single creation event articulated in two distinctive versions (e.g., Genesis 1–2:4a and Genesis 2:4b–25), creation of true human beings according to the Popol Wuj entails four attempts, with only the second unsuccessful attempt involving people made of mud, before the first eight human beings are successfully fashioned out of maize. K'iche' traditionalists, in the twenty-first and possibly also sixteenth centuries, see religious change not as a matter of replacement or accommodation, or even fulfillment, but rather one of accumulation.[25] Just as the text of the Popol Wuj recounts the measuring of the cosmos, the text refers to itself as an *ilob'al*, or instrument for seeing, or "seer," such as the ritual crystals and mirrors used by modern day K'iche' spiritual guides, or *chuchqajawib'*.[26] Maya who possessed such codices in the sixteenth century remained able to interpret them but also went on adding new chapters because the more they added to the account of known events the more they might have not only hindsight but also foresight if not also insight.[27] For contemporary K'iche' Maya spiritual guides, especially *ajq'ijab'* or *chuchqajawib'*, ritualized recounting of the past (or postdiction) is coupled with a ritualized reflection and diagnosis of the present (syndiction) toward a possible ritualized foretelling or anticipation of the future (prediction).[28]

While an attempt to "hear" an old prose text is not the same as an attempt to break it into metrical or parallel verses, considerations of verse do matter, for oral performances or public recitations of texts with pauses and intonation show determined versification.[29] While on one level, a speaker will repeat important phrases two or three times, regardless of the formality of the speech or utterance, to give an appropriate amount of emphasis, this type of straight repetition is not the same as parallelism. Couplets, while not only synonymous, aim to show two unique perspectives on a single event or idea, such as the way "Heart of Sky, Heart of Earth" may refer to aspects of a single divinity. The relationship between the two words, phrases, or perspectives is more analogous as each term may also be used independently without referring to the larger idea. For example, "Heart of Sky" used outside of the couplet with "Heart of Earth" might also serve as shorthand for the divine or might refer explicitly to the lower three stars in the constellation of Orion: Saiph (*Kappa Orionis*), Rigel (*Beta Orionis*), and Sigma Orionis (or possibly Alnitak [or *Zeta Orionis*]).[30] When a third term is added in formal K'iche' rhetoric, it gives nuance to the first two terms to form a tercet, neither through analogous complementarity nor necessarily equivocation but rather through subtle difference. A fourth term or phrase added after a tercet restores evenness to form either a quatrain or a pair of couplets.[31] The general tendency in the realm of contemporary Maya moral and ritual discourse is to treat duality as part of the nature of the primordial world and anything that will possibly exist in the created world. However, these dualities are somehow complementary rather than strictly contrary, and they are usually contemporaneous rather than sequential.[32] In general, K'iche'an poetry or high register speech relies on the syntactic and semantic parallelism of the words and verses rather than on meter, vowel length, or number of accented syllables.[33] The second and third opening lines of the Popol Wuj presented below in stanza form illustrate a couplet and verse parallelism:

1 Are' uxe' ojer tzij
2 waral K'iche' ub'i'.
3 Waral xchiqatz'ib'ij wi,
4 xchiqatikib'a' wi ojer tzij
5 utikarib'al,
6 uxe'nab'al puch ronojel xb'an
7 pa tinamit K'iche'
8 ramaq' K'iche' winaq.[34]

This is the root of the ancient word,
here [in this place] called K'iche'.
Here we shall write it,
we shall implant the ancient word,
the sowing and also
the tapping into everything done
in the citadel of K'iche' and
the people of the K'iche' nation.[35]

Lines 3–4 form a syntactic and semantic couplet ("we shall write, we shall implant"; phonetically marked with the repetition of <xchiqa-> <-ib'-> <wi>) but also framed by repetition of the final phrase *ojer tzij* in lines 1 and 4 to form a larger quatrain. The following lines 5–6 then form a second couplet ("the sowing [of the seed], the tapping [by the root]") with lines 7–8, picking back up with the theme of place in lines 2–3 for a closing third couplet of lines 8–9 ("in the citadel of K'iche', in the people of the K'iche' nation") that further specifies the initially general "here" (*waral*). In contrast, the later lines in the cosmogonic narrative section of the Popol Wuj, which describes the initial primordial soup, illustrate a variation of the couplet form where a third line (lines 4 and 7 below) breaks with the pattern that is set and repeated in the two preceding lines (lines 2–3 and 5–6, respectively):

Are utzijoxik wa'e	This is the account, here it is,
k'a katz'ininoq,	it is still rippling,
k'a kachamamoq,	it is still murmuring,
katz'inonik,	it ripples,
k'a kasilanik,	it still sighs,
k'a kalolinik,	it still hums,
katolona puch	and it is also empty,
upa(m) kaj.[36]	the belly of the sky.[37]

In this example, lines 4 and 7 vary the pattern by not repeating the full phrasing of the previous two lines but by also not breaking the established meaning. This instead builds off a couplet form to make a tercet.[38] Therefore, the parallelism in lines 2–3 and 5–6 of this second example is not merely a couplet of two lines but rather a pair or couplet of tercets: lines 2–4, 5–7.

With four-line stanzas, the pairing of two-line couplets does occur in the Popol Wuj, in which two successive couplets appear antithetical to each other.[39] More often, however, quatrains appear, in which sound and meaning established in the first two lines are broken in the third line, as in a traditional tercet, but gets reestablished in the fourth line.[40] For example, again in the text's opening section, the Popol Wuj deploys a notable quatrain in one of the rare moments it not only refers to itself as a text ("We shall bring it out . . . a Council Book") but also further makes explicit its ritual role to the recounting of the cosmogonic narrative:

Xchiqelesaj rumal majab'i chik
ilb'al re Popo(l)[41] Wuj,
ilb'al saq petenaq ch'aqapalo,
utzijoxik qamujib'al,
ilb'al saq k'aslem; chucha'xik.[42]

We shall bring this forth because there is not anymore
a way to see it, the Council Book,
a way to see brightly that which came from the other side of the sea,
the account of our place in the shadows, and
a way to see the dawn of life, as may be is said.[43]

Lines 2–5 form a classic Maya rhetorical quatrain with lines 2–3 in particular forming the foundational couplet by juxtaposing the "see" of the "Book" (the way to "see" or what is to be read) and the "light" (the object of what is to be read about and the means by which to "see" the book). The third phrase, line 4, moves the couplet to become a tercet by not complementing or building further on "a place to see" but rather opening the topic to what may not be seen, "shadows." Line 5 restores balance initially established in the parallel of lines 2–3 by reintroducing the emphasis on "to see" but also building off line 4's topic of "shadows" by closing the theme off with that which is between "light" and "shadow"—"dawn."

The Popol Wuj's account of cosmogenesis also entails a classic Maya quatrain form:

Nim upe'oxik
utzijoxik puch,
ta chi k'is tz'uq ronojel kaj ulew:
ukaj tz'uquxik,
ukaj xukutaxik,
retaxik,
ukaj che'xik,[44]

It takes a long performance
and also account

3 to complete the lighting of the entire sky and earth:
4 the fourfold siding,
5 the fourfold cornering,
6 measuring, and
7 the fourfold staking,[45]

The section opens with a classic rhetorical couplet in lines 1–2. Line 3 follows with conceptual parallel structuring in the form of the antonymic synecdoche, *kaj-ulew* ("sky–earth") to refer not merely to both the sky and the earth but also to the cosmos as a whole. The quatrain of the emergence of the cosmos opens in lines 4–5 with a couplet of "preparation" metaphors that refer simultaneously to both Maya weaving and farming, practices respectively by women and men. The tercet phrase of the quatrain in line 6 appears with no mention of "fourfold" but rather a notion of "measuring" in general that may apply to bolts of fabric or plots of land but that also extend beyond quadrilaterals in and of the cosmos. The fourth phrase, line 7, restores rhetorical and conceptual harmony by reintroducing the refrain "fourfold" and a specialized verb akin to those used in lines 4–5 but also a verb that moves the stanza beyond mere preparation toward a more definitive act of doing or making—"staking."

Although he was not as rhetorically elaborate or extensive, Vico appears to have understood, appropriated, and employed not only K'iche'an concepts and terms but also the high register of Highland Maya moral and ritual discourse in the elaboration of his theology, as described in chapter 4 of this volume. For example, in one of the few places in the *Theologia Indorum* where the text refers to itself, these aspects of K'iche' parallelism appear:

1 Wa'e nimawuj ri *Theologia Indorum* ub'ina'am
2 nima'eta'mab'al
3 utzijoxik
4 Dios,
5 nimajaw,
6 uq'alajob'isaxik
7 uk'oje'ik
8 ronojel ub'anoj Dios
9 uk'utunisaxik naypuch
10 ronojel nimab'i'j k'o
11 chi upam uch'ab'al Dios
12 uk'utunisaxik naypuch

13 chajawaxik
14 cheta'maxik
15 rumal utzilaj taq winaq christianos uk'oje'ik
16 chi upam K'iche' ch'ab'al tzib'am wi.
17 Wa'e k'astajib'al wach,
18 k'astajib'al pa uk'u'x
19 chi rech utzilaj winaq
20 ilol wuj
21 ta'ol pu re loq'olaj b'i'j
22 k'o chi upam ri nimawuj.

1 This is the great book which is called the *Theologia Indorum*,
2 a great knowledge
3 and discourse
4 about God,
5 the great lord,
6 and a clarification
7 of the existence of and
8 all of the acts of God,
9 as well as a demonstration of
10 all of the great name that there is
11 within the language of God,
12 as well as a demonstration of
13 what shall be necessary and
14 what shall be known
15 by good Christian people who exist
16 as it is written here in the K'iche' language.
17 This is the means to revive the self and
18 the means to revive also the heart
19 of the good people,
20 those who are readers of the book
21 as well as listeners of the beloved name
22 that is in the great book.[46]

On one hand, lines 1–3 appear as a tercet between "theology," "wisdom," and "teaching." On the other hand, line 3 also parallels line 6—"teaching" and "clarification"—which in turn with the next large couplet of lines 9 and 12—"demonstration"—contributes to a larger quatrain. The intermittent lines 4–5, 7–8, 10–11, and 13–14 form distinct couplets, with the first three explicitly and the fourth implicitly speaking about God. Lines 15–16 form a transition couplet that relates the topic of God to the topic of humans—Christians and K'iche'—and the ability to talk of God. Lines 17–18 continue to explicate the topic of humanity or a theological anthropology in a couplet referring to one's "self," or literally "face," (*wach*) and heart (*k'u'x*), thus both one's more public exterior image and subjective interiority. Finally, a quatrain with lines 19–22 relates the topic of humanity back to the introductory topic of the "book" (*wuj*), with people described as "good," "readers," and "listeners" or even implicitly penitents. Poetically Vico further underlies this opening relation between the ruling idea of his book, beginning in line 1, and his anthropology or understanding of human nature, beginning in line 17 with the parallel use of "*Wa'e* . . ." ("This thing here immediately before the reader or listener is . . ."). Vico's mastery of high register K'iche' discourse runs throughout both volumes of his theological treatise.[47]

Furthermore, this K'iche' rhetorical and conceptual parallelism found in the sixteenth-century Popol Wuj and the *Theologia Indorum* is not limited to the post-encounter K'iche' Maya but is also found in both the colonial Lowland Mayan language, Yukatek, and in the surviving logosyllabic sequences.[48] However, the utility of the Popol Wuj to elucidate both Highland Maya rhetoric and poetics expands beyond simple parallelisms and couplets, tercets or triplets, and quatrains. Allen Christenson's recent research has demonstrated that over ten different types of parallelism are found in the Popol Wuj, in addition to merismus or antonymic synecdoches, which include not only couplets, triplets, and quatrains but also sextets and longer parallel series, often for larger chiastic structures.[49] This is the linguistic manner in which the Highland Maya, if not also Maya in general, ritually spoke and some continue to speak about their world, its emergence, and their role in and relation to it. The establishment of commensurate theological understandings by Vico occurred in this form of K'iche' speech.

However, in regards to thematic content, just as the creation of the "mountains and plains" (*juyub' taq'aj*) parallels and alludes to the creation of female and male humans by a holy "mother–father" (*chuchqajaw*)—a term that refers to either a god like *Tz'aqol B'itol* or a Maya spiritual guide, an *ajq'ij*—the creation account foreshadows a larger allegorical move throughout the Popol Wuj. As Dennis Tedlock argues, the central problem dealt with in the larger Maya narrative is not the need to create light but that light is hidden. The larger narrative structure moves from the hiddenness of light, to a false dawn, to the rising of the morning star, and finally to the rising of the moon and true sun.[50] This threefold cosmological narrative allegorically parallels the three previous incomplete approximations of humans and their speech as they become fully articulate religious people.

This close relationship between K'iche'an anthropology—or understandings of being human—and an understanding of language constitutes the third aspect of the Popol Wuj's response (in addition to the responses of other Highland Maya texts) to mendicant "Indian" theology. The Popol Wuj, unlike other Maya texts, highlights the close relationship between the Maya notion of reading in the sense of literacy and reading in the sense of divination (namely postdiction as an aid for syndiction or the clarification or reconfiguration of a current state of affairs but also with a concern toward possible prediction).

Just as the Popol Wuj refers to itself as an *ilob'al*, a way of seeing, to correct for the shortening of human vision in the beginning of creation—as shown above in the extensive quote—a "reader" is considered an *ilol* or "seer."[51] Such divination, a primary means by which the K'iche' interpreted and discerned how to participate in their encounter with Hispano-Catholicism, is grounded in a K'iche' conception of language or linguistic ideology. From this intertextual dialogue with mendicant missionaries a Maya notion of language, along with its implied hermeneutics and epistemology, emerges dialogically—a Highland Maya notion of "dialogue."

Vico's Use of Maya Scripture

From Highland Maya religious discourse, Vico engaged his theological training in scholastic humanism from Salamanca in an attempt to overcome the seemingly insurmountable problem of translating Catholicism into Mesoamerica. In this respect, Vico drew from K'iche'an scripture to accomplish three tasks in his *Theologia Indorum*: constructive appropriation of Maya construals of divinity, condemnation of construals he deemed incompatible, and establishment of analogies between the terms of the Highland Maya and Hispano-Catholicism. Just as Aquinas hinged his theology on the being of God—with God as the essence of existence or Being—Vico begins his own theology not with the rituals or prayers of the Roman Catholic Church or with Genesis, but rather with the being and names of God. While not exactly the same as Aquinas's focus on the essence and *esse* (existence) of God, the first twenty-two chapters of Vico's *Theologia Indorum* explain the presence and qualities of God—the first cause, good, enduring, merciful, sovereign, singular, authoritative, bountiful, and so on—using quotidian examples and rhetoric familiar to the Highland Maya.

Therefore, Vico deploys his ethnographic and linguistic knowledge of the Highland Maya to establish analogies and provide affirmative statements about the Christian god. In this effort, as discussed in the previous chapter regarding his elaboration of a doctrine of god in the near absence of a like "being" in K'iche' as in Latin, Vico seems acutely aware of not only the limitations of language but also how the particularities of Mayan languages resisted attempts to translate Catholic religious ideas, both linguistically and conceptually. In fact, early in the *Theologia Indorum* Vico explicitly stated his awareness of the insufficiency of human language, including the K'iche'an languages, to talk about God and argues that—similar to Aquinas's affirmative claims about a god predicated on Aristotelian notions of analogy—perspectives on God made from an understanding of the created world to its Creator cannot truly speak of divine essences. Furthermore, as if to stress the point that this is not due to his lack of facility with K'iche', Vico elegantly expresses this limitation in the high register of K'iche' poetic couplets, tercets, and quatrains to make his case more intelligible and persuasive to a K'iche' audience, both literate K'iche' elites—such as *fiscales*, scribes, and choir masters—and a wider illiterate population for whom such rhetoric would still signal an authoritative text. For example, by chapter 4 of the first volume of the *Theologia Indorum,* Vico says:

Chiqatzukuj wakamik juk'ulaj tzij
uk'ulel chi upam ich'ab'al,
chiq'alajin wi unimal rajawarem puch Dios nimajaw.
Qitzij nab'e chi nim uq'aq'al uja'al Dios nimajaw
xa ich'ab'al mawi janik latz',
uk'oje'ik ich'ab'al.
mana keje ajawarem waral chi uwach ulew
rajawarem Dios nimajaw.
majab'i xchap chi ajawarem
majab'i chapol re
k'o ta xworonik,
k'o ta xkaqowik,
k'o ta xitanik,
k'o ta xpwaqinik
utem,
uch'akat,
k'o ta ajchoq' chi xuq'alib'ej,
q'alib'al koj,
q'alib'al b'alam,
mujim q'uq',
mujim raxon.
K'o ta ajtatil,
k'o ta ajq'anab'aj,

24 k'o ta ajtz'ikwil koj,
25 tz'ikwil b'alam,
26 k'o ta ajchoq' q'aq'al,
27 k'o ta ajchoq' ja'al.
28 Xya ta chi re ma k'u keje ta re, xax nim . . .

1 Let us now examine a pair of words
2 that are contradictions in your language,
3 which shall clarify the greatness and also the realm of God, the great lord.
4 Truly, first is that great is the fieriness and wateriness[52] of God, the great lord.
5 It is just that your language is not that extended,
6 the existence your language.
7 An estate here on the face of the earth
8 is not like the realm of God, the great lord.
9 [God] is not one who took hold of such an estate,
10 there is not such a [divine] taker,
11 there is no [God] who pierced [Godself],
12 there is no [God] who painted [Godself],
13 there is not [God] who bejeweled
14 nor who gilded in precious metals
15 their chair or
16 their banquet,
17 there is no master who is enthroned
18 on a throne of lion pelts
19 or a throne of jaguar pelts
20 under a canopy of quetzal feathers
21 and a canopy of cotinga feathers.
22 There is no wreathmaker
23 nor is there a goldsmith,
24 there is no keeper of the lion claws
25 nor a keeper of the jaguar claws,
26 there is no owner of the fire
27 nor an owner of the waters,
28 Nothing was given like that to [God], who is alone is great . . .[53]

Vico explains in classic Maya parallelism and native symbols of powerful authority and sovereignty the limitations of human language in trying to comprehend characteristics of his god.

Yet Vico also argues that human language is only part of the conundrum, the rest being the radical unknowability of his god. To illustrate this point and to address the affirmative concepts of divine sovereignty and splendor, Vico draws from the sacred and legendary stories of the Highland Maya. In the section of the Popol Wuj that transitions from the mythico-historical chapters of the first eight human beings created out of maize dough by the divine grandmother, Xmukane, to the listing of the various genealogies of K'iche' elites from antiquity to the 1520s, the Popol Wuj tells a brief story of pilgrimage by the first rulers of the K'iche' nation. The result of their journey, possibly east from the highlands along the Motagua River down to the classic Maya city of Copán (in present-day Honduras), was that the K'iche' leaders received ancient titles and emblems of nobility and license to establish and rule over a Highland Maya nation. As articulated in the Popol Wuj:

1 Xk'is uya' uloq Nakxit[54]
2 uwachinel rajawarem.
3 Are' taq ub'i',
4 wa' mu'j, q'alib'aj;
5 su' b'aq, chamcham;
6 tatil, q'ana ab'aj;
7 tzikwil koj, tzikwil b'alam;
8 jolom, pich kej;
9 makutax, t'ot' tatam;
10 k'us b'us, kaxkon;
11 chiyom, astapulul.

1 The lord Nakxit finished by giving them [the K'iche' regents]
2 his emblems of lordship.
3 These are their names,
4 this, a canopy and a throne,
5 a bone flute and a rattle,
6 obscure and golden powder,
7 lion claws and jaguar claws,
8 a deer head and hooves,
9 bracelets and a shell rattle,

a tobacco gourd and a food bowl, and
macaw feathers and snowy egret feathers.[55]

According to Vico in chapter 4 of the first volume of his theology, God is like a regent, but not like those made regents on earth, as told in the stories of the Popol Wuj, in which the lord Nakxit approved the regents of the prehispanic K'iche' confederation. Furthermore, the Maya forms of material wealth and social signs of status listed in the Popol Wuj and *Theologia Indorum* decompose, Vico argues, whereas God's power and splendor do not. Thus, by establishing analogies Vico recognizes but also strives to circumvent linguistic and conceptual challenges of relating Maya and Catholic religious knowledge, specifically for positive construals of divinity.

Vico further mines this particular mythic history of the investiture of the first K'iche' leaders to circumvent the theological and linguistic difficulty of describing what God is by discussing instead what his god does, such as create and rule. Beginning in the proemium of volume one of his *Theologia Indorum,* Vico references these pairs of signs of power and status as he begins to claim that "God, the great lord" created all that exists, including these prestigious items, thus establishing the theological notion of *Dios* as the creator god of all that the K'iche' know and have. Vico further adds to this list additional Maya objects of wealth, such as gold and silver, quetzal and cotinga feathers, diamonds and emeralds, jade and obsidian, cacao and pataxte, and so on.

By chapter 22 of the first volume he summarizes these local objects of status and wealth with the traditional Maya concept of *q'anal raxal,* which literally means "yellowness and greenness" but alludes to the abundance and splendor of a fertile and bountiful harvest, as well as to the colors of precious metals, gems, and other rare decorative trade items like feathers.[56] Vico uses this phrase repeatedly, and seventeenth- and eighteenth-century mendicants continued to use it to express God's glory. But it also appears most notably in the Popol Wuj in a K'iche' prayer to "Heart of Earth, Heart of Sky" (a K'iche' euphemism for a creator god in Maya cosmogenesis) as well as *k'an yax* in the logosyllabic writings of the earlier classic and postclassic Maya centuries.[57] Vico borrows these basic motifs from centuries of Maya literature throughout the opening chapters of the *Theologia Indorum.*

By this approach, as discussed previously in chapter 4, Vico buttresses his construction of a Christian-K'iche'an concept of God by using various names and euphemisms for divinities found in Maya cosmogonic narratives and prayers. Affirming and drawing on local Maya knowledge and through traditional Maya ceremonial language, he establishes a hybridic bridge discourse between Maya and Catholic thought not only analogically but also univocally.

More notably, if not also more boldly, Vico does not naively allow aspects of a Highland Maya understanding of the divine to push back upon and infuse his doctrine of God. As evidenced in the Popol Wuj, K'iche' Maya used various euphemisms, almost always in couplets that also include both female and male qualities, to refer to their ideas of divine agency. Throughout the *Theologia Indorum,* Vico appropriates and repeatedly used *Tz'aqol B'itol* as distinct from other K'iche' names for divinity found in the Popol Wuj, such as *Uk'u'x Kaj, Uk'u'x Ulew* (Heart of Sky, Heart of Earth), *Tepew Q'ukumatz* (Sovereign Plumed Serpent), or *Juraqan* ("Hurricane," or literally "One Leg"), whom Vico relegates, along with the Hero Twins and other seemly incompatible characters, to Xib'alb'a. However, in so doing Vico also affirms for the K'iche' Maya that his construal of God was not strictly male—such as with the concept of God the Father—because the pair *Tz'aqol B'itol* implies both female and male connotations.[58] Vico actually emphasizes a dual-gendered understanding of God in chapter 1 of the first volume where he also referred to God as *Alom K'ajolom* (Bearer and Begetter), a couplet that also appears at the beginning of the Popol Wuj where divine names are listed.[59] Beyond a simple use of K'iche' names or titles for divinity, Vico goes further to accept the Maya emphasis on gender balance as idealized in their construal of the sacred and even explicitly proclaims throughout the *Theologia Indorum* to his K'iche' readership that God, and not just Eve and Adam, is both *qachuch qaqajaw* ("our mother and our father").

Through chapter 22 of the first volume, Vico argues on the basis of the deeds of God, which he believed were not only apparent to contemporaneous K'iche' but also evident in the teachings of their ancestors as found in their sacred stories. From this descriptive work, Vico then gradually established commensurate understandings between the Highland Maya worldview and the worldview of Hispano-Catholicism, working toward a univocal understanding of their construals of a supreme deity. This comes to an explicit head by chapter 25 of volume one, where Vico explicitly claims that:

1 Xawi xere ri xa jun Dios nimajaw,
2 ri Tz'aqol B'itol,
3 xecha ichuch iqajaw,
4 xawi xere e b'anol kaj ulew,
5 Tz'aqol re, B'itol re,
6 ronojel k'o chi kaj, k'o chi uwach ulew,
7 mixk'isqab'ij . . .

1 There is only just the one God, the great lord,
2 the Framer and Former,

3 which your mothers and your fathers spoke of,
4 the only maker of the sky and of the earth,
5 the Framer and the Former of it,
6 of all that there is in the sky and that there is
on the face of the earth,
7 as we [priests] have just finished explaining . . .[60]

In this section Vico also begins to incorporate the names of other mythical and legendary characters from the K'iche' narratives that would later appear in the Popol Wuj. Rather than appropriate them affirmatively, as he does with the terms "Framer and Former" and "Bearer and Begetter," he instead relegates them to hell.

To do this, Vico draws on the Maya stories that have many of the characters at some point in their story inhabit the Maya otherworld of Xib'alb'a while equating Xib'alb'a with the Christian notion of hell, a place of eternal but just punishment. Such as in the previously examined quote from chapter 25 of volume one, he poetically lists these damned deities as a traditional K'iche' storyteller would:

1 Nim chi xib'ij iwib' rumal,
2 Nim chi uwach Xib'alb'a,
3 nim chiwach: Jun Ajpu, Xb'alankej,
4 Tasal Junrakan, Q'eteb' Pub'a'ix,
5 Jun Junajpu, Wuqub' Junajpu,
6 Jun Kame, Wuqub' Kame,
7 Kik' Re', Kik' Rixk'aq,
8 Mam Iq', Cho'a,
9 Wok, Jun Ajpu.
10 Are xixk'ab'awilaj ojer,
11 are xiwokikaj chi inimal, chi ajawarem
12 are xitz'onoj wi ronojel xraj ik'u'x . . .

1 Greatly you all were scared because
2 greatly before you all is Xib'alb'a,
3 greatly before you all is: Jun Ajpu and Xb'alankej,
4 Tasul Juraqan and Q'eteb' Pub'a'ix,
5 Jun Junajpu and Wuqub' Junajpu,
6 Jun Kame and Wuqub' Kame,
7 Kik' Re' and Kik' Rixk'aq,

8 Mam Iq' and Cho'a, and
9 Wok and Jun Ajpu,
10 You all venerated [God] long ago,
11 you all believed in your greatness, in the reign,
12 to whom you all pleaded from all of your hearts . . .[61]

The Popol Wuj, though, clearly distinguishes between those characters deemed *k'ab'awil*—or "divine" per Las Casas and some Dominican understandings—such as the Hero Twins Jun Ajpu and Xb'alanke and those of Xib'alb'a, which the Popol Wuj explicitly states are *mana k'ab'awil*, "not 'divine.'"[62] Furthermore, while Vico reconfigures the K'iche' pantheon to place those characters in hell who could not align with the biblical god, the Popol Wuj also clearly narrates the victory over and departure from Xib'alb'a of Jun Ajpu and Xb'alanke, who then become the moon and true sun.[63]

In chapters 27 and 28 of the first volume of his *Theologia Indorum*, the last sections dealing with cosmogony before his theology shifts to focus almost exclusively on narratives from the Catholic Old Testament, Vico further clarifies for his K'iche' readers that these characters from prehispanic Maya scripture are now in Xib'alb'a, reinterpreted by him as hell. For example, he states:

1 Are ri Xib'alb'a kixcha pa ich'ab'al,
2 are usak'ulikil chi la', chi kaj xepe wi ri Xib'alb'a,
3 xtaqchi'in iwe
4 rumal xe'utaqchi'j chajkar *angeles* chi mak, chi lab'al chi la' chi kaj;
5 xixul k'ut utaqchi'j chik waral chwach ulew chi mak, chi lab'al;
6 Xib'alb'a ub'i' chupam ich'ab'al,
7 xawi xere k'ab'awil ub'i':
8 Jun Junajpu, Wuqub' Junajpu,
9 Jun Kame, Wuqub' Kame;,
10 Tasal Juraqan, Wok, Jun Ajpu,
11 Jun Ajpu, Xb'alankej,
12 Mam Iq', Cho'a,
13 kixcha chupam ich'ab'al.

1 This is the Xib'alb'a spoken of by you all in your language,
2 this is rightly to where from the sky they arrived to there, the Xib'alb'a,
3 having tempted you all
4 because of tempting by that group of angels

in sin and in war there in heaven;
5 fallen, thus, is temptation still here on the face of the earth,
in sin and in war;
6 Xib'alb'a is its name in your language,
7 just like *k'ab'awil* is the name of:
8 Jun Junajpu and Wuqub' Junajpu,
9 Jun Kame and Wuqub' Kame,
10 Tasal Junraqan, Wok, and Jun Ajpu,
11 Jun Ajpu and Xb'alankej, and
12 Mam Iq' and Cho'a,
13 called by you all in your language.[64]

Again, Vico uses many of the same legendary characters from Maya cosmogenesis who would appear later as major characters in the Popol Wuj. Later, Vico further reiterates his claim again in chapter 48 of volume one that this Maya cast of legendary characters are in hell (*infierno* rather than Xib'alb'a in one of his rare uses of Spanish in the *Theologia Indorum*), and particularly the Hero Twins—Jun Ajpu and Xb'alankej—as also again stated in chapter 51.[65] In these earlier and middle chapters of volume one Vico interweaves Christian extracanonical or legendary material with Maya stories, such as establishing an analogy between the fallen angels who sided with Lucifer and such a list of characters from the Popol Wuj. By the later chapters, though, Vico begins to weave together references from Maya scripture with the histories of the Old Testament. For example, in chapter 65 he declares one of the brothers of the Hero Twins, Jun Ajpu, and one of the names for the primary creator god, Tasal Juraqan, to be *ajmak* ("sinners") and relates them to the destructive influences of the Pharaoh in Exodus and the devil (*diablo*), as well as to the idea of constructing effigies (*k'ab'awil*).[66]

However, Vico's justification for placing them in Xib'alb'a and equating Xib'alb'a with hell is also based on Maya mythology. As stated in the Popol Wuj, Jun Kame (One Death) and Wuqub' Kame (Seven Death) ruled Xib'alb'a and killed the Hero Twins' father and uncle, and—after a series of high-stakes ball games and a challenging sequence of houses of darkness, rattles, jaguars, bats, blades, coldness, and flames—had the Hero Twins kill themselves, before the brothers' transformations into celestial objects.[67] Vico, however, states that all those in Xib'alb'a, located spatially below the earth, justly fell because of *Tz'aqol, B'itol, Dios, nimajaw* (the Framer, Former, God, the great lord), to where there are the houses of suffering and torment, disease and flames, consuming and burning, cold and heat, hunger and thirst, poverty and owners of cacao plantations, blood and malarial fever and chills, sorrow and humiliation, and darkness and night.[68] Therefore, Vico combines aspects of the Maya notion of the otherworld (a domain according to the Popol Wuj pacified by the Hero Twins in the final preparation of the earth for the first true human beings) with medieval Hispano-Catholic images of hell as well as some of the suffering felt by sixteenth-century Highland Maya especially with the arrival of Spaniards. This appropriated and reconfigured notion of Xib'alb'a, according to Vico, is not a realm domesticated by the likes of the Hero Twins but rather the place of righteous punishment for those who go against the Creator of the cosmos. After having selected which aspects of Maya scripture to use and which aspects to relegate to hell (both literally and literarily), Vico then proceeds to present the narratives of Christianity in the remainder of the first volume, followed by the prayers and practices of Catholicism in volume two.[69]

And, just as announced in the proemium and later rooted in his use of biblical history in chapters 26–104 of volume one, Vico expects that the rhetorical and informative effect of reading his *Theologia Indorum* will affect his K'iche' readers. To underscore this message, he again appears to draw from a Catholic understanding of affective theology that began in the fourth century, flourished in the medieval era (such as Aquinas's beatific vision), and persisted through the end of the sixteenth century (with the likes of Teresa of Ávila and John of the Cross), but also also drew from K'iche' Maya tradition. For example, in chapter 5 of volume one Vico places into the mouths of hypothetical skeptical Maya readers the words that are similarly said by the Popol Wuj characters Wuqub' Kaqix (Seven Macaw) and his two sons, Sipakna (Crocodile) and Kab'raqan (Earthquake) prior to their defeat by the Hero Twins. In the Popol Wuj, Wuqub' Kaqix and then his sons proclaim:

> "In nim kik'oje chik chuwi winaq tz'aq, winaq b'it. In uq'ij. In pu usaq. In nay pu rik'il. Ta chuxoq! Nim nusaqil. In b'inib'al. In pu chakab'al. In pu chakab'al rumal winaq, rumal pwaq ub'aq nuwach xa katiltotik chi yamanik, raxa k'uwal nay pu we rax kawokoj chi ab'aj keje ri uwa kaj. Are k'u ri nutza'm saq julujuj chi naj keje ri ik'. Pwaq k'ut nuq'alib'al, k'a saq pak'e uwach ulew ta kinel uloq chuwach nuq'alib'al. Keje k'u in q'ij wi, in pu ik' . . . In wa', in q'ij!" xcha' Wuqub' Kaqix. "In wa', in b'anol ulew!" xcha' ri Sipakna. "In chi k'ut chinkiyow kaj, chinwulij ronojel ulew!" xcha' ri Kab'raqan.

> "I am great and dwell high above the people who have been framed, the people who have been formed. I am their sun; I am also their light; I am also their moon. May it be so! Great is my brightness. I am the walkway and I am also pathway for the people because of my eyes of shiny metal and teeth of emeralds that just sparkle, turquoise as well as blue stones that glow like the face of the sky. And this, my beak shines bright far way like the moon. Since my throne is precious metal, when I go forth I light up the face of the earth. As thus then I am the sun and also the moon . . . Here I am, I

am the sun!" said Wuqub' Kaqix; "Here I am, I am the maker of the earth!" said Sipakna; "And thus then I bring down the sky and cause the whole earth to tumble down!" said Kab'raqan.[70]

Vico has his hypothetical unrepentant readers saying:

We k'o cha' chi we,
"nutukel utzil, nutukel cha'omal,
in utz, in cha'om,
in jeb'elik, in ajaw,
in nim, in al,
in q'aq', in ja',
in uwa'l xit, in uwa'l pwaq,
in pu uwa'l qoq'ol,[71] xtekok" . . .[72]
"Yanq'e! ajroq!
in ajmak, in itzel."

If there is anyone who says to you all,
"On my own I am goodness and preciousness,
I am been good and fine,
I am beautiful and a lord,
I am grand and weighty,
I am fire and water,
I am the juices of jade and silver,
and I am the juices gems and rubies" . . .
"Oh what shame! Woe is me!
I am a sinner and I am evil."[73]

Thus, for a K'iche' audience familiar with this ancient Maya literature, Vico has established an analogical relationship also between those who resist his god and the mythological family of Wuqub' Kaqix, who resisted *Tz'aqol B'itol* and the Hero Twins. As will be demonstrated further in chapter 7 here, Vico's Maya readers will invert this dynamic in their own theologies and collaborate in placing the words of gratitude to *Tz'aqol B'itol,* spoken by the first true human beings made of maize in the Popol Wuj, in the mouth of Adam instead.

By means of a brief contrast, Vico's use of Highland Maya cosmogonic narratives differs from his use of narratives drawn from the Catholic Bible. As noted earlier, the first volume of the *Theologia Indorum* uses mostly biblical material from the Catholic

Old Testament, especially in chapters 30–104, which cover the stories of Adam and Eve in an "Earthly paradise" (based on Genesis 2) through the dealings of the ancient Israelites with the Neo-Babylonian military leader Holofernes (from the deuterocanonical Book of Judith). Like the Maya stories, Christian scripture was a resource for Vico, an interpretive springboard rather than simple evidence. His move from scriptural presentation and exegesis into other discourses—such as the moral philosophy also found in book six of the *Florentine Codex* by his fellow mendicant friar Bernardino de Sahagún, O.F.M., among the Nahua—involved considerable redaction of Catholic scripture in addition to linguistic and conceptual translation.[74]

CONCLUSION: FROM MAYA TO MENDICANTS BACK TO MAYA

The sixteenth-century transatlantic worlds, particularly in Mesoamerica and Iberia, afford scholars of religion possibly the earliest record in the history of Christianity via missionary texts geared toward an indigenous audience along with contemporaneously written replies. Little exists, for example, to tell about the experiences of Nestorian Christians in China, Arian Christians among the Goths, or Scotti Christians among the Jutes and Saxons; similarly, contemporaneous responses by religious others are absent in the history of Christian thought until the 1550s with its arrival into New Spain. Furthermore, while many scholars, namely ethnohistorians, have attended to the presence of mendicant influences in early postcontact indigenous writings (such as the Popol Wuj), intertextual analysis of key mendicant writings and their treatment of Maya religion, like Vico's *Theologia Indorum*, reveals a more explicitly mutual influence than previously assumed.

In fact, a systematic comparison of mendicant doctrinal tracts written over the following two centuries proves how long-lasting the impression was that the *Theologia Indorum* made in the region.[75] Perhaps more ironically, because Vico's theology was never published, it escaped inspection and probable suppression by the Spanish Inquisition beginning in the 1570s, sparing the *Theologia Indorum* the fate of similar works, such as that by Friar Bernardino de Sahagún, O.F.M.[76] On the contrary, well into the eighteenth century, later clergy working in the Maya highlands continued to copy and use Vico's theological work. Even the third Archbishop of Guatemala, Pedro Cortéz y Larraz, admitted that "to explain in the language of the native population the holy teachings, I use the books left to us by the holy missionary fathers, especially the one that is called the *Theologia Indorum*, prepared by the venerable Father Vico of my holy religion."[77] Furthermore, as noted previously in chapter 3, the famed first translator of the Popol Wuj, Friar Francisco Ximénez, O.P., commented in the early eighteenth century that some of Vico's works could still be found among the Maya. Thus, combined with the inscription dates in a few of the surviving manuscripts of the *Theologia Indorum*, it is evident that Vico's writings were copied and passed down among later clergy long after his death.

Clearly, despite his disappearance from the annals of early modern Christian thought and histories of Latin American religions, including ethnohistories of religion, in the centuries following his death Vico's ethnographic, linguistic, and theological work was immensely popular among both Maya and mendicants, a legacy traceable through the Highland Maya paper trail in the next chapters of part 3.

PART 3

Tracing Vico in K'iche' Religious Texts

6

Use of the *Theologia Indorum* in the Popol Wuj

A Maya Response

Wa'e xchiqatz'ib'aj
    chi upam chik uch'ab'al Dios,
    pa christiano'il chik.[1]

Here we [the K'iche' Maya] shall write about this
    in the midst now of the language of God,
    in Christianity now.[2]

PARSING "WORD"

In arguably one of the most popular English translations of the Popol Wuj from the original sixteenth-century K'iche' Mayan language, Dennis Tedlock acutely notes the juxtaposition made by the Popol Wuj's authors between their religious narratives and those of the freshly arrived Catholic clergy.[3] In the opening lines of the Popol Wuj, the K'iche' authors announce that their text and the cosmogonic and political histories that it contains are "the root of the ancient [or prior] word" as opposed to the new "preaching of God" now in their midst in the 1550s.[4] According to Tedlock, this distinction that the Maya authors made between their "ancient word" on one hand and the "preaching" about *Dios* or God on the other hand allowed them to set up Hispano-Catholicism as a foil against which to contrast and reaffirm the previously existing Maya religion and, furthermore,

DOI: 10.5876/9781607329701.c006

the legitimacy of Maya religious narratives, practices, and authorities (such as themselves) in terms of difference, or distinctiveness, and antiquity.[5] In other words, for Tedlock as well as other late-twentieth-century scholars of indigenous Mesoamerica influenced by critical and postcolonial theories, this treatment of Maya religious narratives found in the Popol Wuj in opposition to Christianity is an act of indigenous resistance to the hegemony of Christendom or colonial Christianity and the nascent Spanish Empire during the period of first contact between Europeans and indigenous Americans.

And except for the use of the Spanish word for "God" (*Dios*) and the K'iche' Mayanized word for "Christianity" (*christianoil*) on the first page, there is no further explicit evidence of Christian influence throughout the remainder of the Popol Wuj until the end, where the K'iche' elite mention their Spanish baptismal names alongside their prehispanic K'iche' titles.[6] While a superficial comparative reading between the Popol Wuj and the Christian Bible would note some common images—such as stories of cosmic creation and order, a flood, people made out of mud, virgin births, defeat of hubris, death and the lords of the underworld, and the return of the dead—any in-depth analysis quickly reveals that such similar motifs do not mean the same in their respective texts; in fact, the Maya narratives of the Popol Wuj seem agnostic of any such possible parallels in the biblical stories.

One could even make the case that the Maya writers of the Popol Wuj, who were familiar with biblical stories by the 1550s, rather than showing how their Maya stories are the same as, equal to, or on par with Christian religious narratives, instead rank the new narratives at a lower level than the cosmic reality portrayed in the Popol Wuj. For example, the Popol Wuj's cosmogonic story tells of four attempts to create the world and true human beings: a first attempt that resulted in animals; second and third attempts that resulted in people made of earthen clay and of wood, respectively; and the final attempt that resulted in people made of maize, the Maya people.[7] By relating the destruction of the clay people and the second world by tropical rains (but not a flood, which was the end of the later wooden people), the Popol Wuj conceivably interpreted the Christian book of Genesis as having been only part of the true story of creation—not so much wrong as merely incomplete and deficient compared to the story provided more fully in the Maya narrative tradition. The crucial distinction between either of these or other possible strategies of understanding the Popol Wuj, as well as many other early postcontact indigenous Mesoamerican writings, rests on how the Popol Wuj is understood to relate to Christianity, namely the extent to which the text either articulates a continuation of a prehispanic worldview, or is an early product of an emerging colonial Christian milieu, or is some kind of direct indigenous response to, and possibly against, Christendom.

However, the placement of the Popol Wuj within such a seemingly sliding scale between the poles of Iberian Catholicism at one end and a precontact, middle postclassic period (ca. 1200–1524)[8] Highland Maya worldview at the other end depends on at least two comparative contexts: first, the authenticity of the elements of Mesoamerican antiquity in the Popol Wuj—such as narrative themes and styles—and, second, the specific facets, variations, and presentations of Hispanic Catholicism accessible to Highland Maya by the early and middle sixteenth century. While much scholarship by ethnohistorians, anthropologists, and Mayanists in general has focused on the former, the latter has remained largely neglected, with many scholars working off of precarious assumptions if not flat-out stereotypes of Christianity and the mendicant missionaries who came to the Americas.

The Popol Wuj, to this extent, serves as the exemplary indigenous Mesoamerican text. Thus, its relationship to both a prehispanic Highland Maya world (prior to 1524) and the Hispano-Catholicism translated overwhelmingly by Iberian Dominican and Franciscan friars prior to the Third Synod of Mexico (1585) provides a waypoint for placing and understanding other, later indigenous Mesoamerican documents within these comparative contexts, especially those native writings that contain either oblique or explicit religious references and perspectives. This indicates a second weakness to previous scholarship on these early indigenous writings: while ethnohistorians and social scientists have studied these texts for their political and social import, they have virtually ignored or dismissed the extent to which indigenous authors relied on or simultaneously articulated a religious understanding. With very rare exceptions, these documents are not analyzed as also local, if not hyperlocal, indigenous theologies.

The Popol Wuj is exceptional in this respect, as most of it consists of Maya religious narratives, although it also explicitly refers to the presence of a Christianity. It is not alone in representing indigenous religious discourse, especially if the contemporaneous Maya textual corpus under consideration were expanded to include seemingly nonreligious genres such as notarial documents like land deeds (*títulos*) and wills or affidavits (*testamentos*), as is examined in the next chapter. Finally, for both of these concerns—the relationship of indigenous Mesoamerican texts to Hispano-Catholicism and reading them, in part, for and as hyperlocal religious discourse—the examination of as wide of a collection as possible of specifically Highland Maya texts is instrumental, because sixteenth-century K'iche'an Maya appear very reflective on language. As detailed below, late postclassic K'iche'an Maya (1524–ca. 1650) appeared highly attuned to their traditional language ideology that included awareness of rhetorical strategies, poetic styles, the value and meaning of writing, and distinguishing between different registers of discourse.

All three of these concerns relate specifically to the significance of the two key terms that K'iche'an Maya use when speaking about language, the two terms that appear on the first page of the Popol Wuj referring explicitly to the authority of different religious narratives and claims: *tzij* ("word") and *ch'ab'al* ("speech"). Aside from the general difficulty of reading a centuries-old document and discerning how to translate words of the text that are no longer in use in a current dialect of that language, both *tzij* and *ch'ab'al* present translators with the opposite problem: each word stem has a variety of uses and meanings in the family of Highland Mayan languages widely spoken today—such as K'iche', Kaqchikel, and Tz'utujil—as well as apparently conflicting and overlapping meanings in colonial documents, such as lexicons (*vocabularios*) and grammar guides (*artes*) written by clergy. The possible meanings of this set of Maya terms for language or types of speech is compounded beginning in the sixteenth century, both in mendicant texts written in Highland Mayan languages and in texts written by literate Highland Maya elites engaging with Hispano-Catholicism. Particularly pertinent in this regard is Christianity's commitment to the "doctrine of the Word"—the confessional belief that Jesus of Nazareth is the incarnate *Logos* ("Word") of God—as stated in the opening lines of the Gospel of John of the New Testament, on one hand, and the liturgical and devotional practice of recognizing Christian canonical scripture as "the word of the Lord," on the other hand.

Furthermore, beginning in twelfth-century Europe, reformation efforts such as the mendicant movement focused a great deal of attention on revitalizing the craft of preaching, most notably among the Order of Preachers, or Dominicans, who were later the most prominent clergy in the central Maya highlands during the colonial period. As the first mendicant friars attempted to learn these non-Indo-European languages to preach, teach, and translate recondite doctrinal concepts to Highland Maya, language manuals, catechisms, and homilies in Highland Mayan languages demonstrate a lack of fixed understanding as to which word to use for "word," especially depending on the sense of "word." Conversely, a survey of how *tzij* and *ch'ab'al* variously appear in documents written by Highland Maya, especially in reference to aspects of Hispano-Catholicism, demonstrates a negotiation and apparent lack of agreement among Highland Maya on how to speak about and thus treat Christianity and its stories, practices, and representatives. Therefore, merely reading a twentieth- or twenty-first-century meaning of *tzij* or *ch'ab'al* back into a colonial Highland Maya text runs the risk of silencing the contested-ness of either of these terms and obscuring any apparent differences between them held by Highland Maya or mendicant authors, like Domingo de Vico, that were rendered in the documents during their respective times.

HIGHLAND MAYA LANGUAGE IDEOLOGY: *TZIJ* AND *CH'AB'AL*

A brief survey of how various influential translators have rendered these two terms on the first page of the Popol Wuj highlights both the ambiguity of each term and the effort to accent the distinction between them even though they both refer to language. In general, most of the translations treat the more curious and contested phrase *uch'ab'al Dios* in one of three senses (see table 6.1). Beginning with the first non-Maya reader and copyist of the Popol Wuj, Friar Francisco Ximénez, O.P., in his ca. 1701–1704 bilingual manuscript, translated *uch'ab'al Dios* as "la ley de Dios" (the law of God).[9] After the rediscovery of Ximénez's manuscript as the oldest known version of the Popol Wuj, almost simultaneously but independently in the 1850s by Carl Scherzer and Charles Étienne Brasseur de Bourbourg, who then published German and French translations, respectively, that then served as the sources for the first Spanish translations.[10] Later, subsequent editions, like Adrián Recinos's 1947 Spanish translation, Delia Goetz and Sylvanus Morley's 1950 and 1954 English translations (working from Recinos's Spanish translation), and Allen Christenson's 2003 English translation (working, like Recinos and most other scholars, from Ximénez's K'iche' manuscript), also preferred a legal sense of *uch'ab'al Dios* as "law of God."[11]

Another group of widely read translators of the Popol Wuj preferred religious rather than legal meanings of the term, and reasonably so, as *uch'ab'al* modifies *Dios* (God) and the K'iche' writers situated this *uch'ab'al Dios* in a time of Christianity or Christendom (*christiano'il*). In 1913 Noah Elieser Pohorilles translated this phrase as *der Lehre Gottes* ("the doctrine of God"), whereas Leonhard Schultze-Jena's 1944 translation as *der Veründigung Gottes* ("the proclamation or preaching about God"), Dennis Tedlock's 1984 translation and 1996 revised edition as "the preaching of God," and Luis Enrique Sam Colop's 2011 translation (only one of two translations by native-K'iche' Maya speakers) as *la prédica de dios* ("the preaching about God") all lean into the idea that the sixteenth-century K'iche' writers were referring to the specific religious speech performances by clergy, specifically the homilies by Dominicans in the region.[12] Notably, neither Schultze-Jena nor Pohorilles even imply that by *uch'ab'al Dios* the K'iche' writers might have meant a Catholic doctrine of the word as *Wort Gottes* ("Word of God"). By contrast, Georges Raynaud in his 1925 French translation that highly influenced the forebearer of Latin American literary Magical Realism—Guatemalan Nobel literature laureate Miguel Ángel Asturias—did render this phrase as *la Parole de Dieu* ("the Word of God"), and Villacorta Caldarón and Rodas Noriega likewise translated it as *la palabra de Dios* ("the word of God") but their lack of capitalizing "word" possibly distinguishes their use much like that of Edmonson.[13]

Munro Edmonson's 1971 English translation was the first attempt to translate the Popol Wuj not only with respect to how the language corresponded with colonial

Table 6.1. Translations of *tzij* and *ch'ab'al* on fol. 1r of the Popol Wuj

Translator (date)	*ojer tzij (page)*	*uch'ab'al Dios (page)*
Francisco Ximénez (ca. 1701–4) (Ayer Ms 1515)	*antiguas historias* (1 recto) (ancient stories)	*la ley de Dios* (1 recto) (the law of God)
Charles Étienne Brasseur de Bourbourg (ca. 1855) (BnF Ms Amér 57)	*antiguas historias* (2) (ancient stories)	*le* [*sic*] *ley de Dios* (2) (the law of God)
Carl Scherzer (1857)	*antiguas historias* (5) (ancient stories)	*la ley de Dios* (5) (the law of God)
Noah Eileser Pohorilles (1913)	*die alte Geschichte* (1) (the ancient history)	*der Lehre Gottes* (2) (the doctrine of God)
Georges Raynaud (1925)	*l'antiqua historie* (3) (the ancient history)	*la Parole de Dieu* (3) (the Word of God)
Miguel Ángel Asturias and José Manuel González de Mendoza (1927)	*la antigua historia* (1) (the ancient history)	*la Palabra de Dios* (165) (the Word of God)
José A. Villacorta Caldarón and Flavio Rodas Noriega (1927)	*la antiguas verdad* (163) (the ancient truth)	*la palabra de Dios* (1) (la word of God)
Leonhard Schultze-Jena (1944)	*der alten Kunde* (3) (the old account)	*der Verkündigung Gottes* (3) (the preaching of God)
Adrián Recinos (1947 [2012])	*las antiguas historias* (165) (the ancient stories)	*la ley de Dios* (167) (the law of God)
Delia Goetz and Sylvanus G. Morley (1950)	the old traditions (77)	the law of God (79)
Delia Goetz and Sylvanus G. Morley (1954)	the old stories (1)	the Law of God (2)
Dora M. de Burgess and Patricio Xec (1955)	*tradiciones antiguas* (3) (ancient traditions)	*el lenguaje ya de Dios* (3) (the language of God)
José A. Villacorta Caldarón (1962)	*la antigua Verdad* (15) (the ancient Truth)	*del habla de Dios* (16) (of the talk of God)
Munro Edmonson (1971)	the former word (3)	the word of God (6)
Dennis Tedlock (1985, 1996)	the ancient word (63)	the preaching of God (63)
Adrián Inéz Chávez (1997)	*la antigua palabra* (1) (the ancient word)	*en lengua Dios* (1) (in God talk)
Allen Christenson (2003, 2007a)	ancient traditions (I, 59)	law of God (I, 64)
Allen Christenson (2004, 2007b)	ancient word (II, 13)	his voice God (II, 14)
Luis Enrique Sam Colop (2011)	*la antigua historia* (1) (the ancient history)	*la prédica de dios* (2) (the preaching of god)

dictionaries but also entirely in Maya poetic verse, specifically parallel-structured stanzas. He translated *uch'ab'al Dios* as "the word of God" and appears to accept *ch'ab'al* as a Maya metaterm for language, a word for "word."[14] Also in this third group, Dora de Burgess and Patricio Xec in their 1955 translation with *el lenguaje ya de Dios*, Adrián Inéz Chávez (the first native K'iche'-speaker to translate from the Ximénez manuscript) with his 1997 translation as *lengua de Dios*, and Allen Christenson's 2004 literal translation as "his voice God," all imply the sense that the term *ch'ab'al* refers to speech or language in general rather than to a specific genre, like sermons or doctrine.[15]

CORRESPONDING MENDICANT TEXTUAL SOURCES IN AND ON HIGHLAND MAYAN LANGUAGES

However, none of these understandings of *ch'ab'al*, let alone *uch'ab'al Dios*, appears in the mendicant writings in or on K'iche'an languages (see table 6.2). In other words, whereas many of these translators argue—explicitly in their commentaries and notes as well as implicitly in their choice of types of words (legal, doctrinal, verbal, or otherwise) in which to translate—that the K'iche' writers of the Popol Wuj refer to a specific Christian aspect or genre of Hispano-Catholicism, they are not referred to as *ch'ab'al* in the colonial mendicant writings. For example, the K'iche' dictionary attributed to Friar Domingo de Basseta, O.P., completed in 1698 (BnF Ms Amér 59), and the catechism in K'iche' attributed to Father José Antonio Sánchez Viscaíno and dated 1790 (BnF Ms Amér 60), both translate *ley* (law) as *pixab'*, such as *upixab' Dios* for *mandmiento* or "commandment."[16] *Pixab'*, appropriately in this sense, is the K'iche'an term that generally refers to catechism and thus further distinguishes *upixab' Dios* as "commandment" from *kojb'al* as "article of faith" (*artículo de la fe*).[17] However, more significantly, the Basseta lexicon explicitly distinguishes *pixab'* as counsel or advice regarding moral or social norms such as that given by Maya elders to a young couple at a wedding or apparent in Maya aphorisms and fables. Sánchez Viscaíno distinguishes between "law" from *ch'ab'al* as "language" and, furthermore, *ch'ab'al* as "language" (*lengua*) from *tzij* as "word" (*palabra*).[18] Furthermore, in the earlier bilingual lexicon by Friar Thomás de Coto, O.F.M., of the mid-1600s—one of the most commonly consulted colonial dictionaries for current investigators of Highland Mayan language texts—also lists *tzij* as "word" (*palabra*) and *pixa'* in Kaqchikel as "law" (*ley*), "to order" (*mandar*), and "rule" (*regla*) but also lists "sermon" (*sermón*) as both *tijonik* and *tijob'al*.[19] So, neither *ch'ab'al* nor *tzij* seems to appear as "law" or even as related to preaching in colonial mendicant texts in the K'iche'an Mayan languages.

Likewise, similar discrepancies or lack of correspondence between their modern renderings from colonial Highland Maya texts and their actual treatment within

Table 6.2. Mendicant treatment of K'iche'an Mayan language for language

Document (date)	*tzij (tzih)*	*ch'ab'al (4habal, chabal)*	*other related terms*
Vocabulario by Vico BnF Ms Amér 46 (n.d., ca. 1550s)	tzij (*palabra o presepto* =[word or precept]) rutzij Dios (untranslated, supposedly "precept of God") tutzijoj kumatz (*encantar la culebra* [snake enchantment]) tzijol (*plática o memoria de tiempo* [chat or meeting minutes])	ch'ab'al (4habal) (*la habla* [speech])	
BnF Ms Amér 63 (ca. 1550s, pub. 1622)	tzijolonik (c'iholonic) (as *lesiones* [lessons])		
BnF Ms Amér 59 (n.d.)	tzij (as *palabra* [word])	chabal (as *lengua* [language, speech])	pixab' (as *ley* [law]) tijob'al, tijonik (as *doctrina* [doctrine])
Arte in K'iche' BnF Ms Amér 62 (n.d.)	qatzij Dios xari qatzij winaq uk'oje'ik (as *Jesucristo* [Jesus Christ]; literally: "truly God, truly human being" [Jesus as fully divine and fully human])		
BnF Ms Amér 60 (1790)			upixab' Dios (as *mandamiento* [commandment]) kojb'al (as *artículos de la fe* [articles of faith])

continued on next page

Table 6.2—*continued*

Document (date)	*tzij (tzih)*	*ch'ab'al (4habal, chabal)*	*other related terms*
catechism in K'iche' BnF Ms Amér 2 (1752)			tijonik (tihonic) (as *enseñazas* [teachings])
Peticion Vuq ahau Presidente BnF Ms Amér 13 (1794)	loq'olaj tzij qatzij chi nim chajawaxik (beloved word[s], truly that greatly desired) ri utzij Dios (as *doctrina* [doctrine]) utzij upixab' (as *mandamiento* [commandment])		utzij upixab' (as *mandamiento* [commandment])
Sermons in K'iche' BnF Ms Amér 11 (ca. 1796)	uloq'olaj tzij (literally: beloved word; possibly scripture) Dios utzij ri profeta kitzij (literally: God's word[s] and the prophets' words)		
Vocabulario BnF Ms Amér 64 (ca. 18th–19th cent.)		ch'ab'al (as *palabra* [word])	tzokotojib'al (as *lesión* [lesson])
Vocabulario in K'iche' and Kaqchikel BnF Ms Amér 14 (1833)	tzij (*palabra* [word]) itzel tzij (*palabras suçias* [dirty words])	ch'ab'al (*palabra* [word]) itzel ch'ab'al (*palabras suçias* [dirty words])	tijonik, tijob'al, tijtantib'al (*doctrina que se enseña* [doctrine that teaches])

continued on next page

Table 6.2—*continued*

Document (date)	*tzij (tzih)*	*ch'ab'al (4habal, chabal)*	*other related terms*
	xa'et tzij (*palabras de aca y de alla* [words of over here and there])	chi ch'ab'al (*doctrina que se enseña* [doctrine that teaches]; *doctrinar* [to indoctrinate])	tanch'ijon, tanch'awti'an (*doctrinar* [to indoctrinate])
	tzij ajtzij, titzijun kuma[tz] (*palabras de hechiceros, para enhechizar* [words of witches, to bewitch])		tijom, tijotajinaq (*doctrinado* [indoctrinated])
	qitzij (kitzih) (*lengua de propio* [language of truth])		tijom, tijonem, tijob'al (*enseñado* [instructed])
			ajtij, tijonel, tijoy richin (*enseñador* [instructor])
			tihonik, tijonem, tijob'al (*enseñança* [instruction])
			tij tijonik (*lec*[*ció*]*n del que lee* [lesson that one reads])
			tij (*sermón* [sermon])
			kitijon (quitihon) (*sermonar* [to preach])
Vocabulario Kaqchikel BnF Ms Amér 7 (1837)	qatzij (katzih) (truly, in truth)	ch'ab'al (4habal) (*habla* [talk])	pixa' (pixa) (*ley generalment*[*e*] [law in general])
	tzij (tzih) (*palabra* [word])	ch'ab'al (4habal) (*palabra* [word])	

continued on next page

Table 6.2—*continued*

Document (date)	*tzij (tzih)*	*ch'ab'al (4habal, chabal)*	*other related terms*
	kitzih quitzih (qitzij kitzij) (*lenguaje propio* [language of truth])	jumolaj chi ch'ab'al kich'aw kich'ach'ot pa castilan chi kitzijtzot pa latin chi (*hablar en otro lenguaje* [to talk in another language])	
	ajtz'ib' (ah4,ib) retal tzih tz'ib'ay tzij (4,ibay tzih) (*escrivano* [scribe])	ma kich'ab'al kitzojon (*hablar cosas sin conçierto o sin proprosito* [to talk of things without knowledge or point])	
	kich'aw, kitzijon (qui4hao, quitzihon) (*hablar* [to talk])	tinhal k'atij ruch'ab'al (*hablar en lengua estraña* [to talk in a strange language])	
	ki mayij tzijon, ki loq' tzijon (*hablar elegantemente* [to talk elegantly])		
	mayij tubij, mayij tutzijoj (*hablar de cosas altas* [to talk of high things])		
	tzij, ajtzij, titzijon kumatz (*palabras de hechizeros pa[ra] enhechizar* [witches' words to cast a spell])		

colonial mendicant texts in Highland Mayan languages appear with regards to "doctrine," "teachings," "lessons," "scripture," "preaching," "sermons," or "homilies." Mendicant texts in the early part of the colonial period, from the sixteenth and seventeenth centuries, in general tend to use Castilian Spanish headings for most of these genres, such as *pláticas* (talks), *lecciones* (lessons), and *sermones* (sermons or homilies). The K'iche' Maya word *tijonik* commonly appears in titles or headings as a Highland Maya term used by mendicant authors to refer to a lesson or doctrine. Infrequently, *ch'ab'al* appears to refer to "doctrine"; however, even within early Highland Maya literature, this use does not appear. Instead, for example, the *Xajil Chronicle* even uses the word *doctrina* in a rare use of Spanish for that text.[20] This is especially notable given that this Kaqchikel text comes from an area of Lake Atitlán largely within the Dominican, rather than Franciscan, mission territory. Furthermore, *ch'ab'al* never seems to refer to "sermon" despite the fact that in both colonial and modern use it tends to designate spoken language, or speech, in particular, or a language in general, such as *uch'ab'al K'iche'* to mean "the K'iche' language." By the later colonial mendicant documents, *ch'ab'al* appears to have settled into this general use as the word for language in K'iche'an Maya languages but not for any specific types or genres of speech.

By contrast, the K'iche' word *tzij* appears to shift over the centuries of use through the colonial mendicant texts to refer to diverse but increasingly specified types of genres. Beginning in the sixteenth and seventeenth centuries, earlier mendicant documents in or on K'iche'an Maya languages regularly use *tzij* in three basic ways: (1) literally as "word" and often possessed, such as *tzij* ("word" as found in BnF Ms Amér 59), *nutzij* ("my words"), or *kitzij profeta* ("the prophets' words"); (2) in the common idiomatic phrase for "in truth," "truly," or "really" (usually in colonial and modern K'iche'an languages as *qitzij* or *qatzij* and *qastzij*); and (3) as accompanied with an ordinal number designating a unit or "chapter" of written or spoken discourse, such as *nab'e tzij* (the "first word" or chapter) or *ukab' paj tzij* (the "second chapter"). However, gradually the word *tzij* joined with specific modifiers—possessors or predicates—designates special genres or qualitatively distinct kinds of speech, such as *utzij Dios* (God's word). However, there is little consistency among the usages in the mendicant texts from which to derive a stable, conventional meaning. In other words, unless a particular mendicant text explicitly states that *utzij Dios* means "doctrine"—such as in the 1794 *Peticion Vuq ahaw Presidente* (or roughly "How to write a legal request to the court in K'iche' Maya," BnF Ms Amér 13)—or "scripture," "commandment," and so on, the range of possibilities is too varied and wide to support intertextual comparison of the mendicant K'iche'an-based record.[21] Furthermore, in none of these later mendicant texts does *utzij Dios* appear to mean, ironically, literally "Word of God" in the sense of the doctrine of *Logos* as Jesus Christ.

Therefore, in these uses, early postcontact writings by both colonial mendicants and Highland Maya as well as in present-day K'iche'an languages, *ch'ab'al* and *tzij* can make three different kinds of distinctions: between (1) a linguistic whole (language) and a composing part (word); (2) specific people's speech (such as the K'iche' language, Kaqchikel language, or Spanish language) and specific genres or jargons (ancient narratives, legal speech, moral jeremiads, or proverbs); or (3) common, quotidian low register discourse and formal, ritual, ceremonial, moral high register discourse. Whatever *uch'ab'al Dios* or *utzij Dios* might mean within the myriad of possible references within the colonial ecclesial documents, the Catholic priests who wrote texts in K'iche'an languages during the colonial period appear to have steered away from the explicitly theological claim. Instead, *uch'ab'al Dios* or *utzij Dios* seem to designate a general distinction between types or genres of discourse and, just as important, at least two qualitatively different kinds or registers of discourse. On this particular point alone the use of *ch'ab'al* and *tzij* in the wider Highland Maya body of texts, beginning with the Popol Wuj, agree with the contemporaneous mendicant texts that *ch'ab'al* and *tzij* are two Highland Maya words that designate and differentiate kinds of discourse by K'iche' speakers and writers.[22]

Beyond this general distinction, however, if the usages of *ch'ab'al*—specifically as *uch'ab'al Dios*—or *tzij* contradict the various understandings and definitions in the mendicant documents, then either the K'iche' Maya writers of the Popol Wuj, as native-speakers, use *ch'ab'al* and *tzij* in ways that non-native speakers like the mendicants were still not able to understand until much later, if ever, or they used *uch'ab'al Dios* in a particularly mendicant way prominent by the 1550s but that eventually shifted away as mendicant texts continued to negotiate their apparent understandings and uses of *ch'ab'al* and *tzij*. With the Popol Wuj compiled and written between 1554 and 1558, only one mendicant text in the K'iche'an Maya languages appears to have existed and been widely enough circulated to be accessible to Highland Maya literate elites during this period—Vico's *Theologia Indorum*.

INTERTEXTUALITY BETWEEN THE POPOL WUJ AND THE *THEOLOGIA INDORUM*

In most occurrences the *Theologia Indorum* uses both *tzij* and *ch'ab'al* in the more conventionally established senses of the terms. For example, in both volume one of the *Theologia Indorum*, completed in February 1553, and volume two, completed over a year later in 1554, *tzij* appears most commonly as "truly" (*qitzij*) and in unit headings to announce to a reader a new chapter. For example, the second numbered section after Vico's introduction or proemium in volume one is announced as *Ukab' tzij, ri uq'alajob'isixik qastzij tzij wi chi k'o Dios, nimajaw* ("The [*Theologia Indorum*'s] second words [chapter], the clarification of the true word that there is God, the great lord").[23] Note that the first of use of *tzij* with the ordinal number "second" (*ukab'*) signals that the section is the "second chapter" of the text while the second and third uses of *tzij*—a repetition in native Maya rhetorical strategy used to add emphasis or to stress importance—expresses the speaker's validity and adamancy.

As discussed previously in chapter 4, this frequent use of *tzij* with an ordinal number is also often modified with the K'iche' Maya expression *molaj* or *paj* to designate a well-organized "amount" or "measure." In this sense it distinguishes an "alignment" or "order" from a looser aggregation. For example, the prefix *chol-* is found in the Highland Maya term of the 260-day ritual calendar, *cholq'ij* (literally, an ordered alignment of "days" or "suns"), and the neologism for a dictionary, *choltzij* (literally, an ordered alignment of words), in contrast to a general, less descriptive "pile." Yet, particularly in the high register of ritual discourse of contemporary K'iche' such as *pixab'* ("advice" or "counsel")—itself thought by K'iche' to be ancient—*paj* can mean a "full measure of an idea," a complete thought, or a point. The enumerations *tzij*, *molaj tzij*, or *paj tzij* are functionally the same in announcing to a listening audience or readership a well-ordered, formal presentation of a theme. Present-day formally trained Highland Maya rhetoricians often begin a public speech, such as at a wedding or graduation, with the phrase that she or he only wants to say "one or two words," *jun keb' tzij*, followed, ironically instead, by an extremely long and florid lecture peppered with archaic idiomatic expressions and poetic turns of phrases.

Likewise, *ch'ab'al* in the *Theologia Indorum* most often appears to refer to "language" or "speech" in general, such as *ich'ab'al* ("their languages") or *ch'ab'al K'iche'* (the K'iche' language, which Vico explicitly states in his proemium that he will use almost entirely throughout several versions of the *Theologia Indorum*).[24] Only in the second volume of his theology, which focuses on the narratives and lessons derived from the Christian New Testament, does Vico specifically refer to *uch'ab'al Jesucristo* ("the sayings of Jesus Christ")[25] but in both volumes he uses *uch'ab'al Dios* to refer to the *Theologia Indorum,* as is addressed in detail further below.

On this score Vico also uses *tzij* and *ch'ab'al* in his *Theologia Indorum* in at least three notable ways not readily apparent in the wider body of mendicant literature written in Highland Mayan languages after the 1550s. First, Vico uses *tzij* in a manner more akin to how it appears in both colonial Highland Maya documents and current Highland Maya use; *tzij* for Vico indicates special kinds of speech rather than speech or talking in general. Vico, for example—like the Popol Wuj will also state at least a year after Vico completed the first volume of his theological treatise—refers to the ancient stories and sayings of the Highland Maya as *tzij ojer*.[26] Vico also emphasizes attention on personal and social ethical concerns through *utzilaj tzij*, literally a "very good word."[27] Finally, and perhaps more confusingly, by the second volume of the *Theologia Indorum*, Vico yokes *tzij* and *ch'ab'al* together in constructions of traditional Highland Maya lexical couplets or parallel-structured phrases, the formal rhetoric also used by the K'iche' Maya writers of the Popol Wuj.

For example, in his proemium to volume two, Vico begins by making it clear that he plans to build off of the previous points he made in volume one, that the

Theologia Indorum is a sustained treatise in two parts and that he hopes that his K'iche' and Kaqchikel Maya congregations have heard or read, and will remember, "this here Godly word and also Godly message that I [Vico] shall made clear and also demonstrate to you all [Maya readers]" (*wa'e Diosil tzij Diosil ch'ab'al puch xchinq'alajisaj xchink'utunisaj puch chiwe*).[28] However, rather than conflate or confuse any distinction between these two terms—*tzij* and *ch'ab'al*—Vico's pairs them together in a Maya rhetorical couplet to present them as two different sides of the same coin, language, in order to make a larger statement about "everything" stated about the Christian god by him both in fancy, high registers of discourse according to Highland Maya rhetoric and poetics, as well as in more quotidian, low registers of discourse or K'iche'an Maya prose. His occasional use of *Diosil tzij Diosil ch'ab'al*, such as in the previous example, or *utzij uch'ab'al* or *xa ch'ab'al xa pu tzij* later in volume two of the *Theologia Indorum* expresses an idea of a larger, more comprehensive totality of how or what may be said about his god. That trope resembles how K'iche' Maya elsewhere in their own writings as well as in their speech might refer to larger wholes by their paired but distinct parts, or technically a merismus, like "parents" as literally "mothers and fathers" (*chuch qajaw*), "waters" as literally "seas and lakes" (*cho palo*), or "cosmos" as literally "sky and earth" (*kaj ulew*).[29] For example, in the second volume of the *Theologia Indorum*, Vico applies this use of a couplet to express the comprehensiveness of the New Testament Christian message, stating that "the gospel as it is called by us, the gospel thus is called the word and speech [*utzij uch'ab'al*] of our lordship Jesus Christ, the son of the God, the great lord."[30] And while this expression *utzij uch'ab'al* does specifically mean "gospel" in the *Theologia Indorum*, its use and other similar couplets demonstrates Vico's relative mastery of formal, high register K'iche'an ceremonial, ritual, and moral discourse, or *tzij*, in general.

Therefore, whatever *uch'ab'al Dios* let alone *utzij Dios* might mean for Vico, based on his introductory section from the second volume of 1554, he claims that he has already established or at least begun its understanding or meaning in the previous first volume of the *Theologia Indorum* of 1553. Thus, no ferreting out what Vico means by these two key K'iche'an metalinguistic terms is possible without careful attention to the first volume of his theological treatise, especially since in his introduction to his second volume he explicitly states that he is building off and continuing from the first volume.[31] Furthermore, both *utzij Dios* and *uch'ab'al Dios* appear—albeit separated and not as a couplet—in his introductory section of the first volume. Although the Bible was not translated into K'iche'an languages by the 1550s—and would not be fully translated until the twentieth century, first by Protestants and then by Catholics—Vico could possibly still be referring to Christian scripture with the phrase *utzij Dios*.

Given, however, the almost pedantic and long-winded written measures he takes—on Highland Maya rhetorical grounds—to ensure that his Highland Maya readership knows to what he refers, it would appear odd that Vico would point to an object, namely the Bible, to which his audience would still not yet have access. Unfortunately, other than simply talk about, or speech by, the Christian god, the phrase *utzij Dios* as rendered in Highland Maya ceremonial speech remains obscure. Likewise, Vico's use of the phrase *uch'ab'al Dios*, which appears many lines earlier in the text than *utzij Dios*, remains equally obscure except that it immediately precedes both his announcement that he will present everything that "very good Christian people" (*utzilaj taq winaq christianos*) need to know and believe, and will do so in the K'iche' language (*K'iche' ch'ab'al*).[32]

Furthermore, while Vico never defined it in either his *Theologia Indorum* or the K'iche'an grammar and lexicons attributed to him, later in the second volume of the *Theologia Indorum* he briefly elaborated on his understanding of the affective means of *uch'ab'al Dios*. In chapter 12 of the second volume of 1554 he states:

Keje ta k'u ik'u'x chi re uta'ik uk'u'xlaxik Dios,
keje ri p[a]lo k'i nimaja' chok chi upam,
mawi chisipojik,
mapu chinojik,
xawi ka'ok chupam ronojel b'enal ja',
xax uk'olib'al wi ronojel ja'.
Are ta k'u keje ik'u'x
chi re ub'ixik
uta'ik puch uch'ab'al Dios nimajaw.
Chucho'oj ta rib',
chupolonaj ta rib' uch'ab'al Dios,
chik'u'x,
mata k'u kixnojik,
mata naypu kixsipojik.
Are inojik
we chiq'ayo uta'ik,
we pu kixkos chuta'ik,
we ix saq'or,
we ix q'e'ay chi re uta'ik rutzil uch'ab'al Dios.
Are pu isipojik.
we kixnimarisan iwib',

22 we ix chik'u'x,
23 we pu nim chi iwetamb'al chik'u'x,
24 we chinimarisaj iwib' chuwi'
25 iwatz
26 ichaq'.
27 Mata k'u keje chib'ano,
28 mixnojik,
29 mixsipojik puch.
30 Uch'ab'al Dios nimajaw chuxik
31 chik'u'x,
32 keje ta kixnumik,
33 keje ta pu chichaqij ichi'
34 china'o
35 chi rech uta'ik
36 ri nimapus
37 nimanawal,
38 kicholo
39 kilem puch
40 chik'u'x,
41 chixikinala'.[33]

1 Like that then all of your hearts are toward hearing the sentiments of God,
2 like the sea and so many large waters that arrive into it
3 but do not either sink it
4 or over fill it,
5 but is just taking within it all of the arriving waters
6 as the only place for all of the waters.
7 It is thus like that, all of your hearts
8 toward being told and
9 also hearing the talk of God, the great lord.
10 May it gush and
11 may it flow up, the talk of God,
12 may you all take it to heart,
13 as you all will not then fill up
14 nor will you all swell up.

This is your being full:
if you all would only partially hearing it
and also if you all are then tired of hearing it,
or if you all are being lazy
or if you all are weak at hearing of the favorable talk of God.
This will be then your swelling up:
if you all aggrandize yourselves,
if you all take yourselves to heart
and then would enlarge your knowledge that you take to heart,
and if you would aggrandize yourselves above
your sisters and
your brothers.
But may you all then not do like that,
may you all not full up
and may you all not swell up.
The talk of God, the great lord, should be heard
and you all should take it to heart,
and likewise should you all should hunger
and you all should thirst
and you all should understand
the hearing about it
the great extraordinary force
and great extraordinary power[34]
that you all align
and also that reflect upon
taken in to all of your hearts and
taken in to all of your ears.[35]

In this brief but still insightful reflection in the middle of the section on the doctrine of the incarnation, Vico elaborated not so much what the "talk of God" is but rather what it does, as the means by which a relationship with the New Testament god is internalized, by which conversion and rehabituation of the moral character of the listener or reader occurs. In line with the wider literature favored by mendicants during the fifteenth and sixteenth centuries, this use of "talk" and a process of interiorization by means of actively listening links the intent of a desired moral aim (in the "heart"), a signified referent (in the "mind"), and corresponding moral action. Therefore, Vico's use of Christian scripture and Maya religious narratives clearly related his linguistic ideology and moral anthropology, one of the main thematic concerns that runs throughout the *Theologia Indorum*.

Therefore, based on how Vico in his text employs both *tzij* and *ch'ab'al* in reference to God not only in K'iche'an languages but also by using traditional rhetorical strategies of the K'iche' Maya, two general provisional conclusions emerge. First, Vico demonstrates an acute awareness of, and reliance on, Highland Maya language ideology, as he writes his *Theologia Indorum* originally in K'iche' but also in stanzas of couplets, tercets, quatrains, and larger chiastic patterns—as trained K'iche' rhetoricians might speak or write—while also including traditional turns of phrases possibly appropriated from Maya religious narratives. Furthermore, Vico mixes this high register of K'iche' speech with quotidian K'iche' language and images. Thus, implicitly, Vico's text uses the language of ritual discourse—such as prayer or speech used directly to his god or reported speech from his god—while simultaneously distinguishing itself, the *Theologia Indorum*, from ceremonial or ritual language, such as a prayer or sermon.

Second, by briefly noting how *ch'ab'al* and *tzij* are currently understood and used by present-day K'iche' Maya speakers, some confirmation can be established between these two terms within Highland Maya language ideology. Namely, *ch'ab'al*, as noted earlier, refers to language, speech, or talking in general, such as the Spanish or Castilian language (*kaxlan ch'ab'al*) or a Mayan language like the Kaqchikel (*Kaqchikel ch'ab'al*).[36] While *tzij* may refer literally to "words" in a language, such as Spanish words (*kaxlan tzij*), *tzij* also stands out to designate special kinds of formal speech (see table 6.3) that employ archaic expressions and styles not used in daily Maya talk in, for example, markets, gossip, or cantinas.[37]

It may be difficult to pinpoint when many of these terms with *tzij* historically appear. However, some neologisms are obviously more recent than some other terms, and many appear in the written historical (and ethnohistorical) record as well as ethnographically among present-day Highland Maya. For example, in the introductory material of a K'iche'-Kaqchikel-Tz'utujil trilingual grammar and dictionary bundled with other papers of Friar Francisco Ximénez, including his manuscript copy of the Popol Wuj, a *Catequismo de indios* presented doctrinal material labeled as *tzonobal tzih*. This K'iche' phrase, *tz'onob'al tzij*, is still used among Maya rhetoricians to refer to ceremonial language—and thus presumably also in the time between the first decades after contact and the present-day. To this extent *ch'ab'al* in general refers to first-order speech or low registers of discourse, while *tzij* refers to second-order speech or high registers of discourse, and Vico seems to have known the difference. He attempted to employ both terms in his *Theologia Indorum* as rhetorical strategies for his theological compendium or *summa*, rather than as referring

Table 6.3. Meaning of *tzij* as specified Highland Maya discourse

tzij	word, truth, language
ajtzij winaq	public announcers, town criers
ak' taq tzij	news, notices
awas tzij	prohibition
b'amb'al tzij	lie
b'anowem tzij	verb, doing word
choltzij	dictionary, lexicon, listed words, "counted" words
itzel tzij, itzijb'al	curse
k'ab'awil tzij	idolatrous speech (colonial)
k'ak' tzij	new word, neologism
k'amb'al tzij	example, parable
k'amoj tzij	second wedding ceremony
kok tzij	excuses (lit. sweet-smelling words)
maj q'atow tzij	impunity
molon tzij	joke
ojer tzij	ancient word, prior word
pach'um tzij, keman tzij, kab' tzij	poetry, poem (lit. braided/woven words, words of honey)
paj tzij, molaj tzij	chapter (lit. stack of words)
pa utzij	in one's words, one's opinion, according to
popol tzij	counsel, agreement (colonial)
qas tzij	true, truth, truly, "it is true," really
q'atb'al tzij	judicial court (vs. ch'anel = jury)
q'atol tzij, q'atal tzij (q'alel in the Popol Wuj)	a judge, a justice
q'aton tzij	to impart justice (vs. pajb'al = justice)
q'axom tzij	translation (lit. passing over of words)
retal tzij	notarial documents (colonial)
sachom tzij, tzaqom tzij, xtzaq ri tzij	lost words, archaic words
toj tzij	sacred speech, words of offering (lit. payment words)
tzijonem	discussion
tz'onob'al tzij	ceremonial speech, petitionary speech
tz'aqb'al tzij	foundational words, lies

continued on next page

Table 6.3—*continued*

utukel tzij	soliloquy
utzij Dios, uch'ab'al Dios	doctrine, preaching, scripture [ambiguous]
utzij Jesucristo	sayings of Jesus Christ (colonial)
utzalaj tzij	good words, New Testament
utzijoxik	account
-b'ano tzij	to be in agreement
-mestaj tzij	to forget, to disobey
-nimaj tzij	to obey
-tzijonik	to talk, to give a speech
-tzijoj	to tell a story, to give an account
-tzijb'ej	to be given to know
-k'otoj tzij	to ask

to any particular Hispano-Catholic genres like scripture, homily, or doctrine, as some later translators of the Popol Wuj have wanted to infer.

This is not to say, however, that Vico's Highland Maya readers were either convinced by or agreed with his use of their terms of *tzij* or *ch'ab'al.* On the contrary, to the extent that Tedlock and other interpreters of the Popol Wuj correctly note a tone and strategy of resistance to and differentiation from Christianity by the K'iche' author-redactors, these Maya elites might also have resisted and rejected Vico's understanding of their metalinguistic terminology.

To this extent a close intertextual analysis between the Popol Wuj and any and all evidence of the articulation of Catholicism in the Maya highlands by no later than 1554 is warranted. Intertextual analysis and comparison with Hispano-Catholic documents from the region both in Castilian Spanish but also especially in K'iche'an languages runs the risk of arriving at anachronistic understandings of early postcontact Highland Maya texts like the Popol Wuj. Scholars, in other words, risk muffling the voices of the K'iche' Maya author-redactors as well as failing to appreciate the full force of their respective arguments, be it simply resistance or something more complex and nuanced. Given the possibly extensive access to the *Theologia Indorum* by literate Highland Maya in the sixteenth century—if not also the collaboration with Vico by K'iche' Maya elites, such as *popol winaq* or K'iche' council member Diego Reynoso, and Vico's strategic use of prehispanic Maya religious narratives in the *Theologia Indorum*—intertextual analysis between the Popol Wuj and Vico's theology is key to understanding either text, and both.

Unlike with later mendicant documents written in or on the K'iche' language, an intertextual analysis between the first lines of the first volume of Vico's *Theologia Indorum* (1553) alongside the first lines of the Popol Wuj (ca. 1554–ca. 1558) reveals a surprisingly high degree of correspondence. For example, the original K'iche' of these two respective texts reads:

	Theologia Indorum, folio 1 recto[38]	Popol Wuj, folio 1 recto[39]
1	Wa'e nimawuj	Are' uxe' *ojer tzij*
	ri *Theologia Indorum* ub'ina'am	
2	nima'eta'mab'al	waral K'iche' ub'i'.
3	utzijoxik	Waral xchiqatz'ib'aj wi,
4	Dios,	xchiqatikib'a' wi
5	nimajaw,	*ojer tzij*,
6	uq'alajob'isaxik	utikarib'al,
7	uk'oje'ik	
8	ronojel ub'anow Dios	uxe'nab'al puch ronojel xb'an
9		pa tinamit K'iche',
10		ramaq' K'iche' winaq.
11		Are' k'ut xchiqak'am wi
12	uk'utunisaxik	uk'utunisaxik,
13	k'ut ronojel **nimab'i'j** k'o	uq'alajob'saxik,
14		utzijoxik puch
15		ewaxib'al
16		saqirib'al rumal
17		**Tz'aqol, B'itol,**
18		**Alom, K'ajolom kib'i'.**
19		**Jun Ajpu Uch', Jun Ajpu Utiw**
20		**Saqinima'aq, Sis**
21		**Tepew, Q'ukumatz,**
22		**Uk'u'x Cho, Uk'u'x Palo,**
23		**Ajraxalaq, Ajraxatzel,**
24		chuchaxik,
25		rach b'ixik,

26		rach tzijoxik
27		**ri Iyom, Mamom,**
28		**Xpiyakok, Xmukane ub'i'.**
29		**Matzanel, Chukenel,**
30		**kamul Iyom, kamul Mamom**
31		chuchaxik pa K'iche' tzij.
32		Ta xkitzijoj ronojel
33		ruk' xkib'an chik
34		chi saqil k'olem,
35		saqil tzij.
36		Wa'e xchiqatz'ib'aj
37	chi upam uch'ab'al Dios	chi upam chik uch'ab'al Dios,
38	uk'utunisaxik naypuch	
39	chajawaxik	
40	chetamaxik	
41	rumal utzilaj taq winaq christianos uk'oje'ik	pa christiano'il chik
42	chi upam K'iche' ch'ab'al tzib'am wi.	
43	Wa'e k'astajib'al wach,	xchiqelesaj rumal majab'i' chik
44	k'astajib'al pa uk'u'x	ilb'al re *Popo(l) Wuj*,
45		ilb'al saq petenaq ch'aqa palo,
46		utzijoxik qamu'jib'al
47		ilb'al saq k'aslem; chuchaxik.
49	chi rech utzilaj winaq	
50	ilol wuj	K'o nab'e uwujil
51	ta'ol pa re loq'olaj b'i'j	ojer tzib'am puch.
52	k'o chi upam ri nimawuj.	Xa ewal uwach, ilol re,
53		b'isol re.
54		Nim upeyoxik,
55		utzijoxik puch.

and translated into English as:

	Theologia Indorum, folio 1 recto[40]	Popol Wuj, folio 1 recto[41]
1	This is grand book called the *Theologia Indorum*,	This is the *root of the ancient word*
2	a great knowledge	here [in this place] called K'iche'
3	and discourse	Here we shall write it,
4	about God,	we shall implant
5	the great lord,	the *ancient word*
6	and a clarification	the sowing
7	of the existence of and	
8	all of the acts of God,	and also the tapping into everything done
9		in the citadel of K'iche' and
10		nation of the K'iche' people.
11		And here we shall take up the
12	and also a demonstration then	demonstration,
13	of everything of **the great name**	clarification,
14	that there is	and also account
15		from the place of obscurity and
16		the way of enlightenment by
17		the **Framer and Former,**
18		**named Bearer and Begetter,**
19		**Jun Ajpu Possum and Jun Ajpu Coyote,**
20		**Great White Peccary and Coati,**
21		**the Sovereign and Plumed Serpent,**
22		**Heart of the Lake and Heart of the Sea,**

23		**Plate Shaper and Bowl Shaper**
24		as they are called,
25		together named, and
26		together described as
27		**the Midwife and Negotiator,**
28		**named Xpiyakok and Xmukane,**
29		**Defender and Protector,**
30		**twice a Midwife and twice a Negotiator,**
31		as is said in the K'iche'word.
32		They accounted for everything,
33		and did it too,
34		as enlightened beings,
35		in enlightened words.
36		We shall write about this here
37	within the language of God,	in the midst now of language of God,
38	as well as a demonstration of	
39	what shall be necessary and	
40	what shall be known	
41	by good Christian people of what exits	in Christianity now.
42	as it is written in the K'iche' Maya language.	
43	This is the means to revive the self,	We shall bring it forth because there is not anymore
44	the means to revive the heart	a way to see it, the *Council Book*,
45		a way to see brightly that which came from the other side of the sea,
46		the account of our place in the shadows,
47		and a way to see the dawn of life,

48		as it may be called.
49	of the good people,	
50	those readers of the book,	There is the original book
51	and hearers of the beloved name	and also the ancient writings.
52	that is in the grand book.	But the face is hidden of the one who sees,
53		the one who laments.
54		It takes a great performance
55		and also speeches.

In the opening lines of the *Theologia Indorum*, Vico announces the title of his book and establishes the status of his text as a "grand," "great," or simply a very "large" text (line 1 in both the modern K'iche' transcription and following English translation above). In parallel form Vico further asserts that his "grand book" is also the vessel of "great knowledge" (line 2). He then proceeds to state that the main subject of his text will be about a thing called "Dios," but Vico then immediately identifies "Dios" for his K'iche' readership as not simply any lord, ruler, or owner (*ajaw* in K'iche') but rather as the "great" lord, ruler, or owner (*nimajaw*). Vico, thus, construes the Christian god to his K'iche' readership through traditional K'iche' rhetoric of a couplet form with the first phrase of the couplet being the Spanish word for "God" (*Dios*) and the second phrase the K'iche' word for "lord" but modified or specifically intensified with the predicate "great." In other words, Vico states from the outset that while he and other Iberian clergy may say "Dios" and K'iche'an Maya speakers may say "ajaw," "Dios" is the same as the "great lord" for the K'iche'. If Vico was not the first to construct this couplet, these opening lines of his *Theologia Indorum* are nonetheless among the first written evidence of this phrase that subsequent clergy and Maya authors used in the centuries that followed.[42]

In a wider couplet affiliated with his references to his god, Vico states that this access to knowledge about his god will be obtained through knowing about the "discourse" about and "clarification" of his god (lines 3–6), or more specifically the being and doings of his god—another embedded couplet—and, thus, knowledge of God is indirect and mediated through words and the result or effects of actions (lines 7–8). In traditional Highland Maya rhetorical strategy, Vico then shifts this large couplet to become a tercet by adding the clause that this will serve to demonstrate or teach to his contemporaneous Maya readership the ubiquity of this god as it extends even into the known world of the Highland Maya and through quotidian language about this god but also, as he further states, in the language of the Highland Maya. Ironically, but probably not unconsciously, Vico articulates this declaration of the availability of knowledge about his god even in local K'iche' culture, worldview, and language (*ch'ab'al*; i.e., lines 37) through a high register of formal K'iche' ceremonial discourse (*tzij*).

Vico then closes these opening lines by returning explicitly to references of the "grand book" (line 52). The readers of the book, he declares, will participate in an "revival," "renewal," or "awakening," which is qualified as "good" (lines 43–44, 49–51). While the specific book to which he refers may be obscure, let alone what he means by "good" or "heart," it is as argued above unlikely that he gestures to the Bible. From their origins, most mendicant orders from the late medieval period forward needed and used smaller editions of written and later printed works to facilitate their mobility: *vade mecum* or literally in Latin, "go with me" texts.[43] Most of these works were either practical genres for the specific tasks of preaching, teaching, and leading worship—such as confessional manuals, sacramenta, breviaries, or catechisms—or hybrid works that combined aspects of these genres, which often also included the Psalter and other frequently used sections of scripture.[44] However, given its girth, the Bible was not a book carried by individual priests or friars in the mission-field or kept in rural sites. Therefore, Vico's reference to "the grand book" or *ri nima wuj* (line 52) most likely refers back to the same use of this phrase as found in the opening line—these lines in the *Theologia Indorum* refer to the *Theologia Indorum* itself, emphasizing its importance to Maya readers.

As illustrated in the dual-column, side-by-side layout of the *Theologia Indorum* and Popol Wuj above (with the similitude of key word-stems more evident in the K'iche' versions than in the English translations but underlined in both), the Popol Wuj's opening lines follow a near-exact order of presenting information. Whereas Vico's text in 1553 began by announcing that "this is a grand book," the Popol Wuj of ca. 1554 begins by announcing that "this is the root of the ancient word" (line 1) with the K'iche' using the word *uxe'* (literally "below," or "root" when used with plants) as an agricultural metaphor characteristic of maize farmers. In contrast to Vico's "knowledge" and "discourse" about and "clarification" and "demonstration" of "everything done by God," the author-redactors of the Popol Wuj claim that through their text the "root" and its "word" (*tzij*) is not only to be "written" but also "implanted"—a furtherance of the agricultural metaphor in the form of a traditional K'iche' rhetorical couplet—as it is both "sowing" of and "tapping" into also "everything done" (lines 2–8).[45]

Vico then introduces the relationship between the work of his text ("clarification" and "demonstration"), the world ("everything") as known to him and the Maya, and his god ("the great name" of *Dios, nimajaw*, placed in bold above in lines 12–13). The author-redactors of the Popol Wuj specify in parallel stanzas that the "demonstration, clarification, and account" afforded them by the "seed" and "taproot" of their ancient stories is about the deeds of their principal divinity and auxiliaries (correspondingly also highlighted in bold above) almost all presented in female–male engendered couplets in a larger chiastic form of tercets (lines 12–30). Vico further specifies that while he will apparently address his readership in their native language and through the rhetorical and poetic strategies—*tzij*—of a K'iche' authority, such formal ceremonial discourse is only one mode by which to reflect upon, talk about, and thus aim to know his god. Instead, Vico's text will also draw upon the wider and quotidian world of language—*ch'ab'al*—to speak and write about his god, *uch'ab'al Dios*, for "good Christian people" (lines 37–41). In turn and response, the writers of the Popol Wuj recognize that their redaction and penning down of their ancient histories occurs in the face of Vico's *uch'ab'al Dios* and the arrival of Christianity (lines 36–41). Finally, both of these opening pages close with additional self-referential remarks about the status of their respective texts as written works, before preceding in greater depth to their own recitations (lines 42–55).

In other words, as illustrated in the enumerated and stanza-formatted dual-column sections above, it appears more apparent how the Popol Wuj's opening lines follow a near-exact order of presenting information through the same basic argumentative moves Vico makes in the opening lines of volume one of the *Theologia Indorum*. In line 1, where Vico declares the value of his text ("grand"), the K'iche' author-redactors counter with the value of their text ("ancient"). Whereas Vico then states the aim and scope of this subject matter ("discourse" about "everything done [by God]"), the K'iche' author-redactors counter with their aim of writing down in the missionary script of Vico their cosmogonic narratives that also account for "everything done" through lines 8. Whereas Vico then declares that the focus of his text will facilitate a "demonstration" that "everything" is an act of "God, the great lord," the K'iche' author-redactors counter that the "demonstration" and "clarification" of their text through line 30 reveals the acts of their pantheon. Whereas Vico then specifies that he will do this by talking about his God for Christians, the K'iche' author-redactors of the Popol Wuj simply acknowledge through lines 42 their new time and predicament of having to write down their texts confronted by Vico's god-talk and the presence of a Christianity. Finally, whereas Vico establishes the relationship between the value of his book and the enhanced value of its Highland Maya readers, the group of his K'iche' elite readers indirectly reply through lines 55 that they too have a book—but an "ancient" and "original" book (*wuj*)—that they will now transliterate and re-present in the sixteenth-century orthography of the mendicants in the following folios of the Popol Wuj.

THE *TITLE OF THE K'OYOY*: GEO-THEOLOGICAL LIMITS OF VICO'S INFLUENCE

In contrast to the use of the phrase *uch'ab'al Dios* in the first volume of the *Theologia Indorum* by February 1553, and then in the Popol Wuj sometime no earlier than 1554, another contemporaneous K'iche' text, the fifty-six-page *Title of the K'oyoy*, does not use this phrase in this way.[46] Like the Popol Wuj, the *Title of the K'oyoy* was written sometime in the 1550s–1560s, possibly as late as 1570, by K'iche' elites allied specifically with the Kaweq lineage and the rest of the upper-division leadership in the K'iche' capital city of Q'umarkaj. The principal author or K'iche' figurehead identified in this Maya land deed is lord (*don*) Juan de Penonias de Putanza of the K'oyoy. Like the Popol Wuj but unlike the *Title of Totonicapán*, the *Title of the K'oyoy* contains very little evidence of influence by or references to Christianity. However, like the *Title of Totonicapán*, the *Title of the K'oyoy* also follows a nearly classical pattern found in the genre of colonial indigenous *títulos*—narratives of ancient migrations by the four lineage patriarchs of the Western K'iche' (B'alam Kitze', B'alam Aq'ab', Majukutaj, and Ik'i B'alam), genealogies and descriptions of significant historical events to establish the authors' credibility, and clarification of territorial boundaries of the local polity at issue.

However, for ethnohistory, this *título* differs in notable ways from its Kaweq textual contemporaries. First, unlike either the Popol Wuj with classic Maya material or the *Title of Totonicapán* with biblical and European Catholic material, the *Title of the K'oyoy* does not contain a detailed cosmogenesis myth. Second, while the other Maya documents mention the arrival of *conquistadores* like Pedro de Alvarado and his central Mexican allies, the *Title of the K'oyoy* also recounts this but in much more extensive detail about the northern invasion and military confrontation against K'iche' forces, details substantiated in the two surviving indigenous pictographic renderings of these events: the *Lienzo de Quahquechollan* and the *Lienzo de Tlaxcala*.[47] Furthermore, the K'oyoy *título* also describes the devastating physical and conceptual changes that occurred in Highland Maya life in the immediate aftermath of Spanish military victories—changes bemoaned and denounced by these K'iche' authors. In this respect, the tone of the K'oyoy land deed places it in league with the Popol Wuj and in contrast with the *Title of Totonicapán*, but the level of postinvasion description is more akin to what is found in still greater detail in the later *Xajil Chronicle* by Kaqchikel Maya elites in Tz'oloj Ya' (present-day Sololá on Lake Atitlán).

But, perhaps more important, the Kaweq-affiliated authors of this text—specifically the K'oyoy Saq Korowach lineage of the Kejnay branch of the K'iche'—were not in the central Q'umarkaj, Ismachi', and Chi Uwi' La' (present-day Santa Cruz del Quiché and Chichicastenango) plateaus. They were instead much farther west, around Xe' Lajuj No'j (present-day Quetzaltenango), even past the western area of the authors of the *Title of Totonicapán*, the Yax clan of the K'iche' around Chi Miq'in Ja' (present-day Totonicapán). Because of this distance toward the far west, the authors of the *Title of the K'oyoy* were also farther from the heavier presence of the Dominican friars in general, the *Theologia Indorum* in particular by Vico, and its use by other mendicants and friar-friendly K'iche' like Diego Reynoso. In this respect, again like the Popol Wuj but unlike the *Title of Totonicapán*, the *Title of the K'oyoy* does not try to accommodate Christianity but only to describe and narratively account for its arrival along with that of the joint Iberian and northern indigenous military forces led by Pedro de Alvarado.[48]

The references to Christianity in the *Title of the K'oyoy* are few and occur toward the end of the manuscript. Most notably, God is referred to not primarily as *uch'ab'al Dios* but rather as *utzij Dios*. For example, in the manuscript the first mention, let alone influence, of Christianity appears not until page 35, which tells of the entrance of the Spaniards from the north into K'iche' territory:

> wa'e rulik nimajaw Adelantado Capitán Don Pedro Albarado conquistador utaqom uloq qanimajawal Dios rey Castilla ya'ol re utzij Dios pa qawi' oj K'iche' winaq[49]
>
> this here is about the arrival of the great lord, Advancement Capitan Sir Pedro de Alvarado, military commander, sent here by our great lordship God and the king of Castile, who is the one who gives the word of God over us, we the K'iche' nation[50]

And then on the immediately following page:

> Don Pedro de Albarado conquistador kape España ruk' qanaimajawal Dios rey[51]
>
> Sir Pedro de Alvarado, the military commander, arrives from Spain with our great lordship God and the king[52]

The final reference appears a few pages later, on page 40, when recounting the K'iche' military defeat near Xe' Lajuj No'j by the Spaniards and their indigenous Mexican allies:

> rumal kik'. Are ru . . . a'aj kik'el. Keje' k'u xban . . . qamam qak'ajol. Keje' pu qach'a[b'al] . . . ri'. Keje k'u . . . qokik ri' chi xptia . . . chupam uch'ab'al Dios rumal nimacapitan, Don Pedro Albarado[53]
>
> because of the blood; this is . . . the bloodiness; like this it then happened . . . our grandfathers and our sons; and like this in our language. . . ; like this then . . . we were placed among Christians . . . amidst the language of God by the great captain, Sir Pedro de Alvarado[54]

The first mention of the talking about God or Christian language is the phrase *utzij Dios*. And while the manuscript is severely damaged on page 40, the phrase *uch'ab'al Dios* does appear but not paired together in a couplet—as it is in the second volume of Vico's theology, like *utzij Dios, uch'ab'al Dios*—since these two terms are separated by a few pages here in the K'oyoy title. Furthermore, in neither context of this K'oyoy K'iche' document does either phrase appear in a rhetorical pattern corresponding to the opening lines of Vico's treatise where the *Theologia Indorum* possibly refers to itself as *uch'ab'al Dios*, which the Popol Wuj seems to echo in its opening lines. However, interestingly enough, the *Title of the K'oyoy* does appear to acknowledge that the language of the friars—although Franciscans rather than Dominicans, according to the K'oyoy—qualifies as both *ch'ab'al* and *tzij*, even if it is not clear what this particular Maya document means by these two K'iche' metalanguage terms.

Nevertheless, what is clear is that *uch'ab'al Dios* in the K'oyoy text does not refer to the *Theologia Indorum*, as it does in the Popol Wuj. Finally, this insight is further supported by the complete absence of any other key phrasing distinct to Vico, such as the phrase for his god—*Dios, nimajaw*—as either a simple couplet or joined with traditional K'iche' phrases for their god as a tercet or quatrain, such as *Tz'aqol, B'itol, nimajaw* or *Tz'aqol, B'itol, Dios, nimajaw*, respectively, as Vico also does in his writings. While the Spanish word for God, *Dios*, does appear on pages 35 and 36, it is not as *Dios, nimajaw* but rather *qanimajawal Dios* ("our great lordship [and] God"), a phrase found more often in K'iche' and Kaqchikel writings by or under the influence of Franciscans rather than Dominicans. Just as significantly, although the phrase *nimajaw* does appear on page 35 it does not refer to or modify *Dios* but rather Pedro de Alvarado. The phrase "great lord" here is not a theological claim but rather a K'iche' civic title for gentry applied with literal meaning to a recent immigrant.

In this sense, the *Title of the K'oyoy* appears to demarcate the outer western limit of the influence of the Dominicans, of Domingo de Vico's approach, and of the *Theologia Indorum*, even in Maya hands. On one hand, it indicates that while this K'oyoy title was signed by the Kaweq lords still based in Q'umarkaj (Santa Cruz del Quiché) who thereby continued to hold enough authority among Western K'iche' gentry to confirm traditional local status and estates as far west as Xe' Lajuj No'j (Quetzaltenango), it was most likely writen by K'iche' gentry in Franciscan-dominated Quetzaltenango rather Dominican-dominated Santa Cruz del Quiché.

On the other hand, however, the impact from the central K'iche' region toward the east continued. In the initial Maya area into which Vico and fellow Dominicans entered in the 1540s, evidence from even decades afterwards shows continued use of Vico's theology, even beyond Dominican work with the K'iche'. For example, in the

Ch'olti' Maya colonial grammar, catechism, and lexicon—*Arte y vocabulario de la lengua cholti*—attributed to Friar Alonso Morán, O.P., but most likely finalized by Joseph Ángel de Zenoyo between 1691 and 1692, Vico's *Dios nimajaw* appears frequently in a Ch'olti' variation as *Dios noh-noh ahaw* or *Dios nonohau*.[55] Curiously the K'iche'an word for "owner" or "lord" (*ajaw*) is used in this couplet for "God" rather than the Ch'olti' word *yam*, as defined in the lexicon section of this manuscript and, as a consequence, *Dios noh-noh yam* never appears in the text, which may indicate the continued implied privileging of the K'iche' couplet as originally written in the *Theologia Indorum*.[56] Likewise, the appearance of a variant of this couplet in Nahuatl—*Dios vei tatoyani*—also appears in a letter written to King Felipe II from a Nahua subject in the 1570s, from a Dominican mission area of Nahuas in the regional capital city of Santiago de Guatemala (present-day La Antigua).[57] This petition is accompanied by another supporting letter, also written in Nahuatl from the 1570s, stating that a "Friar Domingo [affiliated with the Dominicans of Las Casas and thus possibly Vico] first taught [us Nahuas] with the divine words of God," thus possibly marking the most southern expanse of Vico's influence beyond the K'iche'an Maya.[58]

In other words, despite the many similarities between the ethnohistorical content and the K'iche' authors—namely their close, common prehispanic alliance and shared distance toward Christianity—the *Title of the K'oyoy* helps to illustrate a possible limit to the reach of and engagement with the *Theologia Indorum* by K'iche' Maya, especially by those geographically removed from the early territory of the Dominicans. Just as important, the use of *uch'ab'al Dios* and *utzij Dios* in the *Title of the K'oyoy* helps to highlight the extent to which (1) the ambiguity of the meaning of these two terms in K'iche' writings in the mid-sixteenth century remains vague for translators, or (2) the extent to which the status of Christian teaching and moral claims were or were not on a par with that of K'iche' religious and moral discourse and thus remained a matter of debate among K'iche' Maya beginning by the 1550s.

In the centuries that followed, the debates between realism and nominalism faded into the background, especially as the preference for mendicant clergy under King Carlos I waned in favor for secular clegy and Jesuits under King Felipe II, and particularly in contact zones where historic Dominican and Franciscan territories blurred and competed, such as around Lake Atitlán or Momostenango in Guatemala. Later, Dominicans and Francisans drew upon, copied, and "corrected" each others' Mayan language materials, occasionally even citing their sources from other orders, such as the Franciscan friar Coto with Vico's works, or the Dominican friar Basseta with Franciscan lexicons.[59] In this sense, their competing pastoral registers eventually overlapped even on the same page. For example, pasted on the opening page of BnF Ms Amér 7 is a petitionary prayer to St. Francis, thus presumably marking the document as a Franciscan Kaqchikel-Spanish dictionary, but the prayer is written in K'iche' and refers to God as *Dios nima Ahauh* (rather than *nimajawal Dios*) and to the third member of the Christian Trinity combined as *Dios uxlabixel Espiritu Santo* (rather than simply the latter).[60] Later Highland Maya notarial documents also often used Catholic phrases from both Franciscans and Dominicans, such as the set of affidavits from Momostenango in K'iche' related to a property case dated 1696 that use *qanimajawal* to refer to both God and the king of Spain but also uses *Dios nimajaw*.[61] Furthermore, one of the litigants, Maria Sanchez, compares her legal opponents to both Judas Iscariot and the devil, and accuses them of devotion to a stone "idol" (*kik'ab'awil*), related to a malevolent spirit that took the form of an owl.[62] The presentation of some European popular Catholic associations of Judas with owls appears presented and translated to K'iche' at least as early Vico's second volume of the *Theologia Indorum* (1554).[63] For Highland Maya, and even for mendicants striving to establish analogies, such associations were ripe with precontact layers of meaning as, like in the Popol Wuj, owls were the messengers of the lords of Xib'alb'a, and the legendary K'iche' old country of Teculutlán or "Place of the Owls" (now Alta Verapaz) was thought to also have a portal down into Xib'alb'a. At least at their various hyperlocal religious ecologies, the initial debates between mendicants and Highland Maya elites did not abate but continued to shift.

CONCLUSION: RESISTING BABEL

As highlighted here and in the previous chapters, Vico employed common, everyday K'iche' language and images, in addition to K'iche' religious discourse, narratives and symbols, to convey his Catholic theology to his Highland Maya audience. Vico drew from all aspects of K'iche'an culture, including religion and language ideology, to establish analogies between Hispano-Catholicism and the Maya worldview. However, regardless of what Vico might have meant by *uch'ab'al Dios*—speech or language of God in his *Theologia Indorum*—the K'iche' editors and writers of the Popol Wuj seem to have employed this phrase not to mean either talk in general about the Iberians' *Dios* or any particular genre or speech acts by them, such as sermons or catechism lessons. Instead, in contrast to how translators of the Popol Wuj have treated this phrase, in the opening lines of the Popol Wuj—as it follows a near move-by-move reply if not rebuttal to Vico's opening lines—*uch'ab'al Dios* refers specifically to the *Theologia Indorum*.

Furthermore, intertextual analysis between the opening lines of the Popol Wuj and the first volume of the *Theologia Indorum* demonstrates that the K'iche' writers of the Popol Wuj had read and were responding specifically to the *Theologia Indorum*, at least volume one, just as Vico drew from some of the same Mesoamerican source materials for his theological writings as the writers of the Popol Wuj did. However, unlike the middle sections of the *Theologia Indorum*, in which Vico reconfigures and re-presents K'iche'an cosmogonic and theogonic elements, the middle sections of the Popol Wuj show no explicit influence of Vico's theology. In other words, what has been argued here is not that those stories found in the Popol Wuj that bear resemblance to those in the Christian Bible, especially as presented in the *Theologia Indorum*, are Mayanized versions of Christian myths. Nor is it claimed that Dominicans like Vico wrote, supervised the editing of, or were even an intended audience for the Popol Wuj.[64] The Popol Wuj is not a product of Christianity in this sense. However, this is not to say that many of the dominant themes of the *Theologia Indorum* did not provide an implied set of rubrics that may have influenced the K'iche' writers of the Popol Wuj. In being presented with a book, the *Theologia Indorum*, by the Dominicans, K'iche' authors explicitly state that they, too, have a book (*wuj*). Their selection of ancient stories—of cosmogony, a threefold creator deity, people made of mud, destruction by a flood, arrogant creatures who think themselves gods, eating of forbidden fruit, a virgin birth, defeat of lords of death by the return of self-sacrificing sons of gods, linguistic divisions among peoples, and seminomadic migrations of a people who form a confederated union of tribes—may very well have also been part of their response to Vico's theology. Just as Dominicans employed analogical reasoning to navigate translation between their Catholic world and that of the Highland Maya, some K'iche' elites may have also noticed their own analogical understanding between biblical stories and those of their ancestors—stories that were in some superficial respects similar and yet still significantly different and thus were worth preserving, while other stories that maybe did not align as much with those told by the missionaries, were perhaps less worthy and thus not included in the Popol Wuj.

While other contemporaneous K'iche' texts, such as the *Title of Totonicapán*, and later sixteenth-century Highland Maya texts (discussed in detail in the next chapter) explicitly reference, cite, and even mention the *Theologia Indorum* or Vico by name, the Popol Wuj only confronts him and his text implicitly—acknowledging enough of his work's presence and impact to warrant an indirect response but not seen as significant enough to mention by name, address explicitly, or consider on a par with the Highland Maya textual, ceremonial, ritual, and discursive traditions. To the extent that the Popol Wuj may be articulating Highland Maya resistance, it is not resisting Hispano-Catholicism in general nor a specific discourse genre like preaching or doctrinal catechesis, and neither is it merely rejecting or resisting. Instead, the phrase *uch'ab'al Dios* in the proemium of the Popol Wuj refers specifically to the *Theologia Indorum*, in part because that is how Vico also refers to his text in his proemium. The phrase confirms that—from the perspective of

K'iche' elites, namely of the Kaweq lineage based in the area of the former K'iche' capital city Q'umarkaj (near present-day Santa Cruz del Quiché) of the 1550s—the *Theologia Indorum* is only *ch'ab'al*, or babble, about that *Dios*. Despite Vico's efforts to write the *Theologia Indorum* in *tzij*-style, his volumes were not *tzij*—prestigious, authoritative, revered talk—to be truly heeded according to the Popol Wuj.

Therefore, no elaboration of the historical context in which some Kaweqib' and other K'iche' elites by 1554 decided to compile their prehispanic narratives into the Popol Wuj can be complete without fuller appreciation of the influence of Vico's *Theologia Indorum*. The Popol Wuj, furthermore, as one of the earliest autonomously written postcontact Mesoamerican texts represents only the first response among a series by Highland Maya to the arrival and transmission of a Christianity in general but also to the *Theologia Indorum* specifically. Placed within a wider ethnohistorical context with other K'iche'an documents of the sixteenth and early seventeenth centuries, the Popol Wuj and this wider Highland Maya textual corpus that engaged with Vico's theology can help provide an indigenous reception history, or perhaps more appropriately a reception ethnohistory, in the next chapter—the first of its kind not only in the Americas but also within the histories of Christian thought in general—to balance out the transmission history written by mendicant missionaries and their later ecclesial successors.

7

Maya Notarial Genres as Hyperlocal Theology

The Title of Totonicapán

Keje' k'ut kipetik
  wa'e ch'aqa cho, ch'aqa palow
          Pa Tulan, Pa Sewan.
  Wa'e k'ute kib'i' nab'e winaq,
  wa'e nab'e K'iche'
    e kajib' chi winaq:
      are nab'e ajaw B'alam Kitze'
        ri qamam qaqajaw oj Kaweqib';
      are k'ut ukab' ajaw ri B'alam Aq'ab'
        umam uqajaw ajaw Nija'ib';
      rox k'ut ajaw ri Majukutaj
        ri kimam kiqajaw e Ajaw K'iche';
      ukaj k'ut ajaw ri Ik'i B'alam . . .
  Xa uq'anawinaq rib' chupam wa'e wuj.

Xa e junelik uloq
      ch'aqa cho, ch'aqa palow,
      releb'al q'ij
      Pa Tulan, Pa Sewan . . .
Xa jun kitzij,
xa pu jun kiwach

DOI: 10.5876/9781607329701.c007

chi oxib' amaq' chi K'iche',
e ral uk'ajol Israel,
oj K'iche' winaq,
ta xujpe Babiloniya
releb'al q'ij.

Like that then they arrived
here from across the lake, across the sea
from Pa Tulan, Pa Sewan.
Here are then the names of the first people,
here are the first K'iche' . . .
and they were four in the nation:
the first lord was B'alam Kitze',
our grandfather and our father, of us Kaweqib';
then the second lord was B'alam Aq'ab',
grandfather and father of the Nija'ib' lords;
the third lord then was Majukutaj,
their grandfather and their father of the Ajaw K'iche';
the fourth lord then was Ik'i B'alam [who had no heirs] . . .
Just the golden people themselves in this here book.

Only they arrived once and for all from
across the lake, across the sea,
in the east,
Pa Tulan, Pa Sewan . . .
Only one was their word,
and also only one was their front,
the three lineage tribes of the K'iche',
they were the children, the sons of Israel,
and we were the K'iche' nation,
when we came from Babylon
in the east.[1]

THE INTERTEXTUALITY OF MAYA REPONSES TO HISPANO-CATHOLICISM

Thus far Highland Maya documents written between the mid-sixteenth and early seventeenth centuries have been used to help elaborate an ethnohistorical context of the region prior to the arrival of Europeans, an epoch argued here in chapter 1 as the middle postclassic period (ca. 1200–1524). Furthermore, aside from one Dominican report back to Spain shortly after Vico's murder, this same corpus of early postcontact Maya literature also contains the earliest surviving references to Domingo de Vico until the seventeenth century, when Friar Antonio de Remesal, O.P., wrote his multivolume history of the Dominican order in Guatemala and Chiapas, Mexico. To this extent, any thorough biography of Domingo de Vico and his theological work can and must also be an "ethnobiography"—an account from local, indigenous perspectives. Therefore, a closer examination is now required of these late postclassic (1524–ca. 1650) Maya texts—material written by Highland Maya elites, in the mendicant orthography for K'iche'an languages, and primarily for a contemporaneous Maya audience and their posterity. Reflecting on and strategically redacting their past to adapt and make sense of their tragically new present, which included not only Hispano-Catholicism in general but also the work of mendicant missionaries like Domingo de Vico in particular, Highland Maya elites composed some of the earliest known and most significant postcontact autochthonous texts in the Americas, like the Popol Wuj, or "Council Book," as discussed in detail in the previous chapter.

Similar to the ability of some of these key texts to provide Highland Maya perspectives on Vico's arrival and work, many of these documents help compose a reception history of the impact of Vico's *Theologia Indorum* among K'iche'an Maya of the central highlands of Guatemala. A handful of them contain not only implicit but also explicit references to the unique turns of phrases and concepts in the *Theologia Indorum*, and a couple of texts even cite the *Theologia Indorum* as a principal source. Arranged chronologically, these Highland Maya texts sketch a shift in the status of Hispano-Catholicism among some literate indigenous elites according to the evaluative criteria of their Maya language ideology—*tzij* and *ch'ab'al*—detailed in the previous chapter. In turn, outlining the mutual engagement and influences between Maya and mendicant texts in Mayan languages better appreciates the various ways and degrees that each authoring constituency drew from both sets of sources to translate, accommodate, differentiate, and reconfigure their otherwise rapidly shifting worldviews.

However, the textual sources consulted require widening the scope of documents typically read for insight into a religious worldview. Until the twentieth century—unless collaborating with clergy in the translation or even the writing of a sermon, catechism, or possibly even the *Theologia Indorum*—Highland Maya did not write exclusively religious texts, with the first two-thirds of the Popol Wuj a notable exception. The bulk of late postclassic Highland Maya writings—with the exceptions of the Popol Wuj, *Xajil Chronicle*, and *Lord of Rab'inal*—appear as indigenous adaptations of Iberian notarial genres such as the land deed (*título*) and will or affidavit (*testamentos*).[2] What they do all share, though, is a common stock language, like K'iche' or Kaqchikel, written in variations of the colonial Parra orthography and a highly local perspective from roughly the same geographic contact zone and historical period. Furthermore, while accommodating a new sociopolitical environment, set of genres, and writing system, many of these early postcontact texts also draw from precontact indigenous genres such as pictographic or cartographic histories (akin to postcontact *lienzos*, or large and highly descriptive maps painted on animal hide); *res gestae* or "accounts of deeds"; and continuous year-count annals, along with the formal rhetoric and poetics of high registers of ceremonial discourse (*tzij*).[3] In many cases, they share the same relatively small, often competing but also overlapping circles of Highland Maya scribal or authorial families—many of whom learned Castilian Spanish, the Parra alphabet for their Mayan languages, and Catholic stories and concepts together in early Franciscan and Dominican schools, as evidenced in the reoccurrence of names on the signatory pages of these legal and extralegal texts.

Furthermore, as discussed previously toward the end of chapter 1 and in chapter 2, early mendicant missionaries were instrumental in importing Iberian legal genres that also had direct or overlapping relevance with the religious world. For example, the will or last testament, while a legal assessment and redistribution of material wealth, did not merely allocate property to posterity but also to the local church or monastery, such as in alms and donations for a funeral mass. Not surprisingly, even indigenous peoples' wills were peppered with Catholic religious phrases of beseeching, blessing, and proclamation of a Christian faith. In fact, for example, Franciscan friar Alonso de Molina's 1569 *confesionario* for Mexica included a section in Nahuatl on how to write a will.[4] Among the mendicants and indigenous Americans in the sixteenth century, the teaching of doctrinal and notarial genres was not so separate. For Dominicans in particular—such as Cajetan and Vitoria in Europe and Las Casas in Mesoamerica—theology and governance overlapped, such as Vitoria's arguing for a higher "law of nations" between and above that of individual monarchs, or the first formulation of an idea of universal human rights by the "defender of the Indians," Las Casas. During the early period of contact, Dominicans in particular stood out as advocates for defending the rights, including property rights, of indigenous American peoples—the apologetics they engaged in was based on their understanding of natural law as fundamentally rational and the natural inclination in all humans. Their defense of indigenous property rights occurred both back in Spain before the royal court and in theological debates—such as the famous 1550 debate in Valladolid between Las Casas and Juan Ginés de Sepúlveda—but also in New Spain, implicitly if not also directly, as articulated in *títulos* by native elites.[5] With Franciscans like Molina and Dominicans like Las Casas incorporating new theories of natural law and teaching legal genres to native elites, it should be little surprise that the earliest postcontact literature by indigenous Americans explicitly assumed a legal form rather than, for example, confessional or homiletic genres.

Ethnohistorians have recently mined these documents for their sociopolitical content to foster the elaboration of the first century of contact with Europeans from indigenous perspectives as well as early indigenous reflections of a prehispanic era. Yet, these documents still remain largely overlooked and underappreciated, especially with regards to their explicit and implicit articulations of native theological understandings.[6] Religious—both Catholic and Maya—terms and significance pepper the texts but also frame and ground their legal arguments regarding their ownership of lands and sociopolitical authority. The recent scholarship on later Lowland Maya texts in Yukatek has begun a correction to also read indigenous texts, ostensibly legal, for their explicit and implicit religious material; this chapter extends that approach to the earlier Highland Maya notarial literature.[7] The distinction here is that many of these early Maya texts can and should be read as theologies, and as highly local—hyperlocal—theologies at that. They should also be regarded as Maya theological responses, not only to Hispano-Catholicism in general, but to, against, and with Vico's *Theologia Indorum* in particular.

In other words, mendicant theological texts in indigenous languages—be they in Nahuatl, Otomí, or Mayan languages, and be they catechisms, sermons, devotional lessons, hagiographic stories, hymns, or other popular genres of Catholic religious and moral reflection—aimed to make universal statements about their one, true god. The mendicants understood such statements ultimately to transcend the particularities and differences noted in their linguistic and ethnographic studies of indigenous peoples. The Highland Maya texts, by contrast, did not strive to make universizable or possibly even translocal theological claims for a religious understanding accessible beyond a highly local communicative ecology of K'iche'an elite families.[8] In contrast to the efforts by mendicants to explain the catholicity of their theologies, Highland Maya produced hyperlocal theologies and their notarial texts, in part, should be read as such. Their hyperlocal religious perspectives gradually shifted over the course of the sixteenth and early seventeenth centuries, as indicated, for example, in a shift in their understanding of Catholicism from *uch'ab'al Dios* to *utzij Dios*. Those perspectives increasingly drew from Hispano-Catholic material, such that a Maya reception history, or more accurately a reception ethnohistory, emerges to counterbalance the dominant transmission histories of Christianity in the Americas written by later chroniclers and historians.

In this sense, this chapter provides a comparative analysis of Vico's work with respect to two of the most important pieces of early Native American writing: the *Title of Totonicapán* and the Popol Wuj, both by the K'iche' Maya of the Guatemalan highlands. As discussed in previous chapters, ethnohistorians and linguistic anthropologists—such as Burkhart among the Nahua; Tedlock, Sam Colop, Carmack and Mondloch, and Christenson among the K'iche'; and Hanks among the Yukatek—paid attention to the rhetoric, poetics, genres, and claims by comparing contemporaneous indigenous and nonindigenous (e.g., Spanish) texts and often through collaboration with present-day indigenous religious leaders and elders. The analyses of the life and work of Vico in chapter 3 and his *Theologia Indorum*, or "'Indian' Theology," in chapters 4 and 5 of this volume in particular, have employed a similar approach to the study of a Spanish priest and his theological text. Despite popular images of Hispano-Catholic imperial imposition and drive for religious homogeneity, almost all early evidence regarding Vico's life and work appears not in Spanish documents but rather those written by Highland Maya.

As the previous chapters demonstrated, rather than presenting mere doctrinal or ritual formulas of Hispano-Catholicism for Highland Maya to memorize, Vico's theology appears remarkably original in both content and method in light of Mayan languages, culture, and religion. During Vico's time the new field of linguistic analysis, namely as philology, for Iberian clergy in the Americas served as an early template for mendicant studies of Mesoamerican languages.[9] For example, even the later, eighteenth-century dictionary on Wastek—the Mayan language spoken historically around the area of Veracruz, Mexico, also referred to as Tenek—still followed the basic structure and rubrics of Nebrija's late fifteenth-century *Introductiones Grammaticae*.[10] And while their models grew to include other influential lexicographers, like the Augustinian Ambrogio Calepino, Iberian missionaries had few similar types of templates for their studies of Mesoamerican cultures and religions. Except for travelers' journals, the previous work done on the laws, customs, or practices of other civilizations in Renaissance period "ethnographies" had not yet assumed a specific genre, nor had taxonomy-like language studies by humanists yet appeared.[11] The work of mendicant ethnographers, like Franciscan friar Bernardino de Sahagún's twelve-volume *Florentine Codex* about the Nahua, is a unique work that seemingly invents ethnography in the field. These first missionary-theologians appear to have had the popular theology of Jean Gerson and other works from the populist *devotio moderna* movement in mind if not also on hand, many of which were translated into Nahuatl at the Franciscan Colegio de Santa Cruz in central Mexico.[12] Yet the arrival of the second wave of mendicants schooled in the new humanism and Thomistic scholasticism of the University of Salamanca held Aquinas's analogical method and the compendium genre or *summa* approach more in the fore. However, neither theology nor ethnography had the templates like those of linguistics or law for these early mendicant missionaries in Mesoamerica. While study of local and indigenous languages was more established and acceptable, study and production of ethnographies in general and theologies in the Americas was less developed, more in flux, and consequently increasingly suspect by the 1570s with the arrival of the Catholic, or "Counter," Reformation.

The analysis of intertextual connection between two of the most important K'iche' texts and the *Theologia Indorum* will resolve some of the enduring questions regarding these Highland Maya documents. While the linguistic anthropologist William Hanks has begun similar analysis of intertextual relations between mendicant texts, namely Franciscan, and those of the Yukatek Maya from the sixteenth and seventeenth centuries, treatment of Highland Maya texts with contemporaneous mendicant texts has remained severely neglected.[13] Furthermore, Hanks's impressive work has not attended to the different schools of thought and debates among the mendicants nor the rapid changes within Europe and abroad occurring in Catholic thought and theology during the mid-sixteenth century.[14] While these early missionaries to Mesoamerica were becoming increasingly ethnographically attuned, treatment of their work by most historians and social scientists has remained theologically ignorant in terms of the period's shifts in pastoral genres, rhetorical strategies, scientific ideologies, ecclesial authorities and structures, interdisciplinary methods with and within Christian theology, and understandings for what qualifies as "orthodox" thought at the time.

Suffice it to say that little in the sixteenth century was definitively orthodox, since that was precisely the core question at issue initially within the Catholic Church and then between it as well as among the increasingly separate schools of that Reformations period. Reading anachronistically the canons of the Council of Trent (1545–1563) back into theological experiments of the earlier decades does not resolve any questions of the "orthodoxy" or "heterodoxy" of the positions articulated, but rather erases the complexity and variances of the respective arguments that were held near and dear. Rather than focus on diversity of popular Christianity within Europe during this period, this chapter will home in on the emergence of a popular Catholicism, or Catholicisms, within the indigenous Americas.

This chapter begins with a brief description of the Spanish colonial legal genre of *título* ("title" or "deed") and its appropriation by indigenous Mesoamerican elites, particularly the Highland Maya, in the beginning in the early sixteenth century. It demonstrates that through playing with and mixing colonial Spanish genres, Maya made distinct legal, historical, and theological claims that differed from but did not necessarily contradict those also made by Hispanic authorities. *Títulos* were a means of reasserting their own authority while reconfiguring their own Maya identities and worldview. The *Title of Totonicapán* (ca. 1554), the "mother title" for many K'iche' intellectuals today, exemplifies the appropriated use of this genre by late postclassic Highland Maya. By way of comparison, this chapter argues that the

Popol Wuj (ca. 1554–ca. 1558) does not attempt to emulate this genre but rather consists of a unique Highland Maya response to Vico. Analysis of intertextual relations between the *Theologia Indorum* (1553, 1554) and the *Title of Totonicapán* (ca. 1554), as well as between the latter and other late postclassic Highland Maya notarial documents, provides wider background for the dialogicality between the Popol Wuj and the *Theologia Indorum* as well as the reception of Hispano-Catholicism by Highland Maya. This analysis, in turn, illustrates the pervasiveness of Vico's theology with the Highland Maya who read it closely, as well as the indirect Maya theological replies to Vico and, thus, to Hispano-Catholicism in general—an impact that persists unknowingly among present-day readers of the Popol Wuj, both Maya and non-Maya.

In sum, this chapter demonstrates that a complete reading of any one of Vico's *Theologia Indorum*, or the *Title of Totonicapán*, or the Popol Wuj is impossible without also reading the other two: their intertextuality is distinctively and tightly triadic. In this regard, ethnohistorians and linguistic anthropologists must read the K'iche' texts in light of Vico, and scholars on religion can only read Vico in light of these late postclassic (early postcontact) Highland Maya writings. Furthermore, because Mayanists need these insights, too, in addition to parsing out important points of contact between Vico and the K'iche' political and religious leadership, comparative and intertextual analysis demonstrates that Maya did not simply acquiesce or reject Catholicism but rather offered a constructive correction to mendicant claims and Vico's theological method.

HIGHLAND MAYA *TÍTULOS* IN INTERTEXTUAL DIALOGUE

A result of the alphabet developed by mendicants in the Americas was that literate Maya quickly generated a body of indigenous literature. And while literature in Nahuatl written by Franciscan missionaries farther north in Mexico does predate the earliest alphabetic texts in Highland Mayan languages from the 1540s, texts written by K'iche'an authors consist of some of the earliest postcontact indigenous American literature. Elsewhere, indigenous literature in, by, and for Zapotec, Mixtec, Nahua, and Yukatek Maya, for example, does not seem to date prior to the mid-to-late 1550s and is still fewer in number compared to that of the Highland Maya.[15] One notable exception is the *Historia Tolteca Chichimeca*, whose composition in Nahuatl by and for Nahua elites possibly began as early as the late 1540s.[16]

Farther north in Anglophone America it would be over another century before native peoples—such as Cockenoe-de-Long Island, Job Nesuton, and James Printer—learned an alphabet and wrote in English and indigenous languages at the behest of Christian missionaries but also for legal defense of native peoples.[17]

Arguably, New England would not see native literature like that of New Spain until 1790 with Samson Occom's written presentation of pre-Christian indigenous civization and defense of native autonomy.[18]

In contrast, the surviving colonial documents authored by Highland Maya in the missionary script represent their voices in their encounters with Hispano-Catholicism. Along with the mendicant missionaries, indigenous Mesoamericans were not passive recipients of conversion efforts but active participants and initiators of religious changes that, in turn, transformed their culture. As their voices "fixed" from oral narratives or transcribed from pictographic or even logosyllabic texts and oral speeches into the colonial script and in interaction with missionary materials (such as catechism manuals, scripture, sermons, and passion plays), these documents illustrate a larger, longer conversation that evinces active Maya involvement in the reshaping and maintaining of their cosmology and corresponding religiosity.[19]

Most of the postcontact native documents from the highlands may have eventually served legal and political purposes and functioned as land titles before the Spanish Crown or local courts.[20] Among the K'iche' Maya, the largest of the highland sociopolitical and linguistic groups, the prehispanic social order, noble genealogies, calendrics, history, and creation of the cosmos are detailed in approximately forty notarial documents that still exist as annals, testaments, appendices, and fragments, in addition to the Popol Wuj and a play, the *Lord of Rab'inal*.[21] This does not include other indigenous documents in Nahuatl or descendants of indigenous allies of the Spaniards from central Mexico who settled in Guatemala.[22] These early postcontact K'iche'an writings contain many clues of the sixteenth-century Highland Maya point of view.[23] Read intertextually, these documents—with the Popol Wuj, the *Xajil Chronicle*, the *Title of Totonicapán*, the *Xpantzay Cartulary*, the *Title of the Yax*, and the *Lord of Rab'inal* among the most important—help reconstruct much of Highland Maya society, history, and religion prior to contact with Europeans and Christianity. More important, for an ethnohistorical understanding of the production and transmission of religious construals, many of these written texts contain references to Christianity, with the *Title of Totonicapán*, the *Title of the Tamub' III*, and the *Title of the Ilokab'* as the most notable.

Although they were recognized as unique documents rather than mere land deeds in indigenous Mesoamerican languages, the *Title of Totonicapán* and other texts like it did not receive careful scholarly attention until the 1970s and 1980s. Despite the fact that the *Title of Totonicapán* was among the first of these indigenous texts to be rediscovered in 1860, most studies have focused primarily on the *títulos* from central Mexico, leaving the *títulos* from the Maya highlands largely overlooked except by a handful of scholars.[24] *Títulos* written in Nahuatl—one of the most widely spoken administrative and trade languages in Mesoamerica until the establishment of Castilian—overall comprise the largest amount of *títulos* written in the Americas, beginning within the first decades of the arrival of Europeans.[25] Despite the appearance of the word *título* in the opening lines of many of these indigenous postcontact manuscripts, earlier historians initially dismissed and questioned their authenticity because many of their signed dates have been proven inaccurate or even deliberatively faked because the apparent authors wrote earlier dates to make their land claims seem older and therefore more valid. However, recent ethnohistorians have used a comparative intertextual approach to look past such dates to corroborate the unique content of the texts. They accordingly can appreciate the emergence of a borrowed, hybrid, and then distinct genre of indigenous writing, often referred to as *títulos primordiales*—that is, as "indigenous deeds" or "quasi-notarial" genres—to distinguish them from their Iberian counterparts.[26]

In general, Mesoamericans such as the Mexica (aka Aztec), other Nahuatl speakers, Mixtec, Zapotec, and other language groups in New Spain adapted the Spanish colonial legal genre of a "land deed" or "title" to record older narratives in the alphabetic script invented by mendicant missionaries, particularly for their own native purposes. While many of these older narratives might have existed previously and been conveyed in oral genres, many of them were also represented visually.[27] Early and contemporaneous "pictographic texts," or *lienzos*, painted on large rectangular hides, as well as archaeological images from the classic Maya and Teotihuacan eras (ca. 200 CE–ca. 900 CE), help corroborate the precontact themes and styles in many *títulos*.[28] These documents had been used to serve prehispanic concerns of the official collective memory of a particular native polity, lineage, or nation.[29] *Títulos*, therefore, were more than merely a population's attempt to argue for land rights and legal privileges (or *fueros* as they were historically called back in Spain) in a genre imposed upon them by colonial authorities, because they argued from the basis of their ancient traditions and sources.[30] In other words, the boundaries negotiated in these *títulos* were not only legal and geographic but also conceptual, cultural, and religious.[31]

On one hand, the adoption of a legal Iberian genre led to some common features, namely that they portray an ethnic and religious identity through the description and geographic inventory of a specific locale—such as a hamlet, village, or community—incorporating concepts of the lineages of the residential elites through time.[32] The perspective of local elites encompassed not only their native understandings of space, time, customs, and social structures but also formal rhetoric and high register speech.[33] These poetic textual features are evidence that most of the *títulos* were written or commissioned by lineage heads, elders, and the last generation of independent indigenous leaders or their direct descendants.[34] Based on surviving signatory pages or other references to specific authors of some of these texts, these *títulos* were written as committee documents by groups of indigenous Mesoamericans and share a general formal structure of (1) mentioning a time of founding, (2) tracing the origin and succession line of rulers, and (3) describing the features of the territory.[35] The Highland Maya texts such as the *Title of Totonicapán*, the *Title of the Yax*, and the Popol Wuj (though not a *título*) distinguish themselves by including mentions of cosmogonic narratives and ancestral stories that are absent in the other Mesoamerican *títulos*. Furthermore, in addition to being written in indigenous languages, these texts spoke directly to a Highland Maya readership and audience, as they did not directly address themselves to Spanish colonial authorities, nor were they always presented to Spanish officials. In this sense they are not mere variations on a legal deed but rather rearticulations of Maya history, including their cosmogonic histories.[36] The degree to which these documents were (and still are) revered, guarded in a town's *caja real*—the "royal chest"—or *cofre* often kept in the local church building, and annually paraded by Maya community leaders, even well into the twenty-first century, testifies to how many Highland Maya understood these texts as authoritative if not also as something "sacred" and thus approximating the status of religious "scripture."[37]

On the other hand, the use of this appropriated colonial genre changed both across the region (given the territorial and social differences between communities) and over time. By the mid-seventeenth century, the Spanish Crown affirmed that native peoples could submit pictographic maps and narratives or *lienzos* as legal affidavits or evidence, and increased pressure to transliterate them into written forms in Spanish or an approved "official" native language. This later finalization of indigenous texts by native scribes and their adoption of other genres—such as annals, wills, and testimonies—provide some of the last evidence of Highland Maya written contributions until the twentieth century.[38] Despite this gap, however, these Mesoamerican texts in general and Maya texts in particular demonstrate some patterns of speech, thinking, and beliefs whose continuation is carried out by current Highland Maya ritual and rhetorical specialists: *chuchqajawib'* and *k'amal b'e*.

LATE POSTCLASSIC MAYA THEOLOGICAL RESPONSES

Context of the *Title of Totonicapán*

No other Maya document contains as much traditional information and as many references to Christianity as the *Title of Totonicapán*, which ranks as the third-most important Highland Maya text, according to ethnohistorian Robert Carmack.[39] As briefly described previously, until the late twentieth century the only known copy of this text was the eighteen-page version made by Abbot Charles Étienne Brasseur de Bourbourg on his second visit to Guatemala in 1860.[40] Through the hands of Alphonse Pinart and later Count Hyacinthe de Charencey, who was the first to produce and publish a non-Spanish-language translation—French—in 1885, Brasseur de Bourbourg's copy eventually landed in the Bibliothèque nationale de France as Manuscrit Américain 77.[41] His copy, however, was already at least third generation, since he used as his master version an earlier copy, a translation from K'iche' into Spanish by a parish priest of Sacapulas, Father Dionisio José Chonay. Chonay was approached only decades earlier in 1834 by members of the Yax family to translate their colonial *título* so that they could submit it to the local Guatemalan civil court as evidence of their ownership of land in an ongoing property dispute.[42] Chonay finished and submitted his translation on September 14 that same year but intentionally omitted the first seven folios (or fourteen pages) because, as he stated in his appended translator's note to the court,

> they are on the creation of the world, of Adam, the Earthly Paradise in which Eve was deceived not by a serpent but by Lucifer himself, as an Angel of Light. It deals with the posterity of Adam, following in every respect the same order as in Genesis and the sacred books as far as the captivity of Babylonia. The manuscript assumes that the three great Quiché nations with which it particularly deals are descendants of the Ten Tribes of the Kingdom of Israel, whom Shalmaneser reduced to perpetual captivity and who, finding themselves on the border of Assyria, resolved to emigrate.[43]

Until the late twentieth century, with the apparent loss of Chonay's translation and copy of the K'iche' original, Brasseur de Bourbourg's version was the only copy in known existence. Ethnohistorians, like US anthropologist Robert Carmack, suspected that the Yax clan of Totonicapán had an additional copy if not the original of what the Yax referred to as the "mother *título* of the town."[44] Fortunately, in 1973 the Yax family presented Carmack with a document that proved, based on close comparison with Brasseur de Bourbourg's version housed in the BnF, to most likely have been the original used by Chonay but that still contained the previously untranslated initial seven folios, which makes up 20 percent of the document.[45]

The appropriation of the legal genre of *título*, land title or deed, as well as of legal wills or affidavits (*testamentos*) by Highland Maya like the K'iche' was not an uncommon event amidst the ongoing legal disputes over land between Spaniards and Maya nobility as well as among the various rivalries of Maya elites.[46] The *Title of Totonicapán*, to this extent, is no exception.[47] As the document is written in K'iche', it is most likely to have had a primarily exclusive readership among the K'iche' but while addressing an indigenous audience in the form of the Spanish colonial administration by Highland Maya elites, which the Spanish Crown recognized as local gentry, absolved from paying tribute, and allowed to hold estates of indigenous labor forces. However, unlike their Spanish and Nahua counterparts, the Maya deeds could not base their arguments on conscripted service and armed victory in the name of the Catholic Monarchs, like the Holy Roman Emperor Carlos V or Felipe II, since the Maya were the militarily subjugated population.[48] Instead most of these Highland Maya notarial texts make their legal claims of rightful ownership and privileges from an argument of divinely sanctioned prior possession that drew upon prehispanic accounts of cosmogony—or creation of the cosmos—and migration of the Highland Maya into the region centuries prior to the Iberians. In this way, like the Popol Wuj, the *Title of Totonicapán* grounds the legitimacy of its claims within an argument from antiquity; however, unlike the Popol Wuj, the *Title of Totonicapán* demonstrates references not only to traditional Maya religious narratives but also explicit incorporation of, if not also "corrections" to, the version of Genesis offered in Vico's *Theologia Indorum*, specifically volume one, which Vico completed in February 1553.[49]

Not surprisingly, the high regard for Vico's work by mendicant missionaries led to a fairly rapid dissemination of his theological work in the Maya highlands not only among priests but also among Highland Maya authorities and scribes.[50] Evidence for this dissemination appears in later mendicants' references to Vico's theology and the number of existing copies over the centuries as well as, more notably, the *Theologia Indorum*'s correspondence to Maya texts like the Popol Wuj. Though there is no evidence that the Highland Maya had a formal system of education like the Mexican (Aztec) *calmemac*, which mendicants could simply replace or build upon. But regardless, the establishment of mendicant schools in the Guatemalan highlands[51] allowed many Highland Maya elites to work closely with early mendicants like Vico and their writings in K'iche'an languages such as catechisms and sermons.[52] Many of these K'iche' and Kaqchikel student collaborators from these schools, while most likely anonymous ghost writers or coauthors of mendicant pastoral texts in Highland Mayan languages, appear as signatory authors or later copyists of some of the most important early Maya documents in the colonial alphabet.[53]

The adoption of the Spanish surname "de Vico" by the later two K'iche' authors most likely further indicates the extent of the tight collaboration between, admiration for, if not also patronage of Domingo de Vico with his K'iche' students in Santiago de Guatemala. According to historian Owen Jones, the Maya surname "Tavico" in Rabinal may also evince patronage with a scribal family in that part of the Verapaces.[54] The K'iche' lord Juan Matal B'atz' of Sacapulas collaborated with Las Casas and other Dominicans in their entrance into the Eastern K'iche' (or Achi) region of the Verapaces, and his son and heir, also Juan de Sacapulas, later persecuted the Ch'ol Maya for their assassination of Vico. Dutch ethnohistorian Ruud van Akkeren argues that the elder Juan de Sacapulas may also have been the father of Ajpop K'amja (or "vice regent") Juan Cortés, a coauthor of the Popol Wuj, and thus have been sympathetic to Reynoso's pro-Dominican leanings, and also a contributor to the *Title of Totonicapán*.[55] To this extent, it should come as little surprise that Vico's two students who were also writers of the *Title of Totonicapán*—namely Popol Winaq Diego Reynoso but also a Sir (or *don* in Spanish) Cristóbal—were immediately familiar with at least the first volume of the *Theologia Indorum*, or that the *Title of Totonicapán* is also so familiar with much of the prehispanic content that was also compiled into the Popol Wuj. In fact, Reynoso in particular but possibly other Highland Maya students as well may have been more coauthors with Friar Vico of this theology than explicit textual evidence would support. Regardless, in the case with some parts of the *Title of Totonicapán*, the K'iche' Maya authors, like Diego Reynoso, clearly cited and adapted Vico's theological treatise.[56]

And according to US anthropologist Allen Christenson, the orthography—including even irregular spellings of basic words—remain shared between the *Title of Totonicapán* and some early versions of the first volume of the *Theologia Indorum*, specifically BnF Ms Amér 5 and APS Ms, thus providing some additional evidence of a tight relationship between some of the coauthors or at least scribes of these texts.[57] Among the eighteen versions of the *Theologia Indorum*, BnF Ms Amér 5 and APS Ms are the only two produced by the same Maya scribe—a Don Juan Gómez, *fiscal*—with both copies dated 1605.[58] He might be the same K'iche' writer whose name appears in other early K'iche' documents—the Nija'ib' *títulos*—from Momostenango within the Totonicapán region. If so, he would be of the Roqche' lineage of the Ilokab' branch of the K'iche', and thus a relation of Diego Reynoso, and also possibly related to a family of established K'iche' scribes that included a Pedro Gómez, Alonso Gómez Us, Domingo Gómez Us, and a Don Francisco Gómez.[59] These names also appear as signatures in the Nija'ib' texts and Don Francisco Gómez is specifically identified as the *primer ahzip quiché*, the first or highest ranked K'iche' *ajtz'ib'* (scribe) and namesake to a now lost *Título Gómez Ajtz'ib'*.[60] A later possible descendant, Juan Matías Gómez, is a signer of the 1640 copy of the *Title of Santa Clara La Laguna* along with a Cristóbal Reynoso, Gregorio de Vigo, and Gabriel de Vico.[61] Therefore, if correct, the scribe of at least two copies of volume one of the *Theologia Indorum* was a descendant of a prominent family of K'iche' scribes who were also distantly related to one of Vico's main K'iche' collaborators, all of whom were from the Totonicapán region.

In general, the *Title of Totonicapán* consists of three sections: (1) an account of biblical creation followed by the biblical genealogies and migration stories; (2) a genealogy of K'iche' rulers since their mythical migration from "across the waters" in the east and into the Guatemalan highlands; and (3) the verbal mapping out of the territory specifically attributed to the Yax clan, due in part to their alliance and participation with Ajpop (or regent) K'iq'ab' and his expansion of the Western K'iche' confederacy based in Q'umarkaj. The signature page towards the end of the document contains the names of the then still living K'iche' nobility residing both in Totonicapán and the area of Q'umarkaj, the middle postclassic-period K'iche' capital near present-day Santa Cruz del Quiché and Chichicastenango (or Chi Uwi' La', in the K'iche' Maya language).

For the most part, the scholarly value of the document is its correspondence to genealogies in other *títulos* and the final sections of the Popol Wuj whereby a prehispanic K'iche' national history can be reconstructed from the perspective of the K'iche' Maya from the thirteenth century through the 1550s.[62] However, in addition to this correspondence, the few but marked differences between the genealogies found in the Popol Wuj and those in the *Title of Totonicapán* also provide valuable historical insight on intra-K'iche' tensions. Most notably, the account of the pilgrimage back to the east by two ruling brothers in the Popol Wuj does not recount the failure of the second brother to reach his destination and attain symbols that would later legitimate his reign among the Western K'iche'. The *Title of Totonicapán* not only tells of his failure but also of the adulterous affair that occurred between this failed brother and his sister-in-law, the wife of the brother who did complete his pilgrimage and return with official titles and emblems of lordship bestowed on him by the well-established ruler Nakxit (a variation of Quetzalcoatl or Plumed Serpent) by which to authentically rule the nascent K'iche' polity.[63] Unlike the Popol Wuj, the *Title of Totonicapán* describes this stain within the ancient noble lineage history of the rulers of the K'iche' confederacy at Q'umarkaj, thus indicating—at the very least regardless of its factual veracity—a breach between the leadership of Q'umarkaj and Totonicapán at the time these two manuscripts were written in the 1550s, the Popol Wuj by the former and *Title of Totonicapán* by the latter.

Despite the names on the signature page, the only name to appear within the body of the document and that discloses information about one of its authors is that of Diego Reynoso, a K'iche' nobleman, or *popol winaq*. His father, Lajuj No'j, most likely achieved elevated status not only through his purported noble lineage from his maternal side—of the Roqche' clan of the Ilokab' branch and a royal house of the K'iche' ruling polity—but also in collaboration with the expansion of the K'iche' confederacy into Totonicapán under the reign of Ajpop K'iq'ab' in the mid-fifteenth century. Ajpop K'iq'ab' is noted in the Popol Wuj and the *Xajil Chronicle* for having had a particularly long reign but also for an expansion program that brought the K'iche' confederacy to its apex, extending it even into present-day southern Mexico.[64] The rapid growth, including increased wealth in Q'umarkaj, came at a high price. A revolt around 1470 by lower nobility, possibly even from within his own household such as his sons, forced K'iq'ab' out of power and resulted in an abuse of power by the new rulers. The abuse of power provoked a permanent waning of Western K'iche' regional influence as the Kaqchikel, at the behest of the dethroned K'iq'ab', abandoned their center near Q'umarkaj, Chiawar (near present-day Chichicastenango), and moved south to establish their own independent nation with a new capital city of Iximche' (present-day Tecpán).[65] The emerging Kaqchikel nation, within the next fifty years as it expanded, would not only rival Q'umarkaj but form an alliance by 1524 with the joint Spanish–Nahua force arriving from the north for a definitive military defeat, followed by pillage and scorching of Q'umarkaj, the capital city of the Western K'iche'.

The post-1470 leadership in Q'umarkaj continued until the arrival of the Spaniards and Nahuas from the north in early 1524 but faced internal opposition from remnants of the previous local leaders favorable to K'iq'ab', like Lajuj No'j and his son Diego Reynoso in Totonicapán. Reynoso's *título*, with its occasional deviations from the official narrative of Q'umarkaj leadership found in the Popol Wuj, casts doubts on the legitimacy of those post-1470 rulers by relating them, not to the descendants of the older brother who ages ago proved himself physically and spiritually worthy of his title and office, but rather to the offspring of the adulterous affair of a loser whose lineage took power by betrayal. While it confirms or augments much of the last portion of the Popol Wuj as well as other *títulos* that mention aspects of prehispanic (specifically middle postclassic-period) K'iche' Maya history and political society, the *Title of Totonicapán* also consists of a minority report that is subversive of the Popol Wuj, the official narrative written by Q'umarkaj leadership, and it specifically offers an unflattering perspective on the royal house of the Kaweqib'.

In addition to this particular political tension just before the arrival of the Franciscan missionaries who accompanied the Spanish–Nahua forces from central Mexico, two additional and older tensions may have contributed to the differences between these two important Western K'iche' texts. First, as discussed earlier in chapter 1, shortly after founding the first Western K'iche' capital city of Pa Ismachi' (near present-day Estancia) in the mid-1300s, the Ilokab' branch of the Western K'iche' confederation rebelled against the Nima K'iche' branch, whose Kaweq lineage dominated the top two positions of the confederacy by holding both the offices of *ajpop* and *ajpop k'amja* (or regent and vice-regent). The rebellion by leadership of the Ilokab' branch was initiated in particular by its Roqche' clan, that of Reynoso's father's maternal lineage. While the Ilokab' remained one of the three principal branches of the Western K'iche' confederacy (along with the Tamub' and Nima K'iche'), they were expelled from Pa Ismachi' and then prevented from settling in the new capital city of Q'umarkaj just across the ravine to the north. Instead, the Ilokab' formed a separate city much farther to the north of Q'umarkaj, called Pa Ilokab' (near present-day San Antonio Ilotenango in the Department of El Quiché).[66]

This political battle took place a century prior to the 1470 overthrow of Ajpop K'iq'ab'. A second old tension, though, was also manifest in the structure of the confederacy, which allowed the Nima K'iche' to hold the top two positions of *ajpop* and *ajpop k'amja* over the Ilokab' and Tamub'. Furthermore, these offices were more specifically held by the major lineage Kaweqib' within the Nima K'iche' branch. The Popol Wuj, while a committee document composed by ruling members of the various lineages and branches, as a text redacted in Q'umarkaj it reflects the perspective of the Kaweqib', specifically a new guard who overthrew Ajpop K'iq'ab' and the Kaweq old guard, more so than any of the other contributors. By contrast, *títulos* from the regions like Totonicapán, including the *Title of Totonicapán*, and even farther west reflect the perspectives of at least one of the other major lineages within the Nima K'iche' branch, that of the Nija'ib', Reynoso's paternal lineage.[67] Thus, although he was a member of the Nima K'iche' elite, Diego Reynoso was a member of the competing Nija'ib' house in the Nima K'iche' and was also related to the older rebellious Roqche' house of the Ilokab'. He therefore had numerous historical bases of suspicion against the new Kaweqib' leaders in Q'umarkaj and their account of national history in the Popol Wuj, including its place within Maya cosmogony.

Unlike the Popol Wuj and more like the majority of other Highland Maya documents written in the sixteenth century, the genre of the *Title of Totonicapán* assumed a colonial Spanish legal form. Whether Diego Reynoso intended for it to be originally submitted to colonial Spanish authorities as legal registration of geographic dominion is unknown, as no record exists of any such submission until that of Chonay's translation in 1834. Rather, given that it was originally written in K'iche', it is more likely to have had a primary if not exclusive readership or audience among the Highland Maya (as with also the Popol Wuj, *Lord of Rab'inal*, and *Xajil Chronicle*). It addressed them by authors who were historic Maya landed gentry but in a genre of the new, larger polity of the Spanish Empire. Like the Popol Wuj, however, the *Title of Totonicapán* stands out because it makes theological interpretations as it fuses mythical and historical narratives to ground its claims of rightful land ownership and identity. Furthermore, unlike the Popol Wuj or almost any other Maya notarial document, the *Title of Totonicapán* uses narratives indigenous to the Maya—specifically those of cosmogenesis, genealogy, and migration—as well as the Bible and popular western European Catholic thought. In this respect, use and redaction of Catholic devotional material in this text consist of one-fifth of the whole document, and thus is no minor source.

Folios 1–7: The First Maya Christian Account

Written in 1554—the same year that Vico completed the second part of his *Theologia Indorum*—the first seven folios of the *Title of Totonicapán* consist of a summary of Vico's treatment of the Catholic Old Testament and consistently reiterates the K'iche' phrases Vico used for "God"—namely *Dios, nimajaw* ("God, the great lord") and *Tz'aqol B'itol* ("Framer and Former"). By the eighth folio, however, the *Title of Totonicapán* signifies a shift and incorporates elements from traditional, prehispanic Maya narratives, such as the cosmogonic histories also found in the Popol Wuj. In some parts of the *Title of Totonicapán* the authors literally recite from the first part of the *Theologia Indorum*, which Vico had completed a year earlier in 1553, while in other places they either changed his pastoral K'iche' or substantially adapted his message to fit better into their traditional Maya understanding. In this sense, while the *Title of Totonicapán* does not negate or resist Vico's appropriated K'iche' names for God or his theology in general, it does use many other divine names, as if to correct Vico's univocal use and equation of K'iche'an and Catholic concepts for the divine and an analogical use in reconciling these understandings of a "creator" divinity. On one hand, this Maya text recognizes and validates Vico's accommodation to Maya culture and religiosity. On the other hand, the Maya authors, such as Diego Reynoso, in turn accommodated Vico but in a way that did not allow his theology to overwrite theirs, thereby crafting an indirect Maya response or correction to the *Theologia Indorum*.

Intertextual analysis of the first seven folios in light of the internal structure of the *Theologia Indorum* clarifies how the K'iche' authors of the *Title of Totonicapán* redacted and incorporated Vico's work into their own context.[68] For example, the opening line of the *Title of Totonicapán* begins with what has previously been translated as "This is the second chapter" (*Uae vcab tçih* or *Wa'e ukab' tzij*), leading some interpreters to speculate that either a first chapter from an earlier version is missing or that its K'iche' authors misquoted or miscopied directly from the first part of Vico's *Theologia Indorum*. The latter is more likely, since the word-final <h> or <ɧ> and <b> in the colonial mendicant script appear similar, and this opening line of the *Title of Totonicapán* begins by describing the "Earthly Paradise," the topic of chapter 30 in the first volume of *Theologia Indorum*. Vico did not divide and number the units within the *Theologia Indorum* into conventional chapters but rather, like Aquinas's *Summa theologiae*, into major and minor themes, with the thirtieth unit in volume one enumerated as the fourth major theme or concept (*Vcah nimabi* or *Ukaj nimab'i'*), where the "Earthly Paradise" is first introduced by Vico. In other words, where Vico numbered his thirtieth unit in K'iche' as *vcah* (*ukaj*, "fourth"), the authors or scribes of the *Title of Totonicapán* instead possibly wrote *vcab* (*ukab'*, "second"). Therefore, based on such comparative analysis between an alignment of the listing of sections, subsections, and sub-subsections as "chapter" units in the *Theologia Indorum* and those "chapters" (*paj tzij*) explicitly mentioned in the first seven folios of the *Title of Totonicapán*, it becomes increasingly obvious that the K'iche' authors did not merely copy but read and further redacted chapters 26–101 of the first volume of the *Theologia Indorum* into their own text as a critical appropriation of and correction to Vico's theological narratives.

An example of this pointed revision occurs when the *Title of Totonicapán* discusses the "nine groups and levels of angels" from chapter 29, or the "fourth subsection of the third major theme" in the *Theologia Indorum*. In this section from volume one of the *Theologia Indorum*, Vico introduces the Christian "celestial hierarchy" developed by Dionysius the Areopagite (called Pseudo-Dionysius after the sixteenth century), which was incorporated into Aquinas's *Summa theologiae* (Ia, q. 108), most likely Vico's principal source for his cosmogony.[69] For Vico and the medieval European Catholic cosmos, in the uppermost realm beyond the ninth level of heaven lay the unrevealed side of God, to be encountered only via a mystical union (*unio mystica*) and as an ultimate mystery. According to the spirituality of medieval Christian mysticism, such as that begun by Pseudo-Dionysius and other neo-Platonic Christians, God could be spoken of only in paradoxical terms like "brilliant darkness" or Aristotle's "unmoved mover."[70] According to Vico's cosmogony in chapter 30, "there, within thus the tenth level up above, nothing may move; there is only the eternal throne, house, and citadel of God, the great lord" (*ulajuj tas chi k'ut k'o aq'anoq puwi' majab'i chisilob'ik xa junelik kub'ulik rochoch utinamit Dios nimajaw*).[71] The *Title of Totonicapán* reproduces these lines almost verbatim with two subtle but highly significant exceptions, that the tenth level is not motionless but dynamic and does not point to God but rather to the sun: "the tenth level thus shall move, the eternal throne, house, and citadel all day" (*ulajuj tas k'ut chisilob'ik junelik kub'ul rochoch utinamit chi ronojel q'ij*).[72] According to the Popol Wuj, Jun Ajpu was transformed after defeating the lords of the otherworld Xib'alb'a and ascended as the new dawn for the ancient Maya people. The identification of the new sun with Jun Ajpu and the moon with the other Hero Twin, Xb'alankej, within Highland Maya cosmogony is made explicit on folio 7 verso of the *Title of Totonicapán*.

So, while modern ethnography on Maya religion describes various Maya understandings of multilayered upper and lower worlds—respectively above and below this world—it is highly likely that this notion was not indigenous to the Maya prior to contact with Hispano-Catholicism, given the dearth of such cosmologies in the archaeological record.[73] For example, even the early postcontact Popol Wuj does not describe either the sky (*kaj*) or underworld (Xib'alb'a) as containing various layers; Xibalba, instead, holds various houses (*ja*) of trials implying a vertical rather than horizontal structure. Furthermore, the mendicant material that was presented to Mesoamerican converts, which also incorporated popular understandings from Catholic Europe, was not consistent. For example, Franciscan literature in Yukatek Maya described an eleven-layered heaven.[74] The *Title of Totonicapán*'s clear referencing of the *Theologia Indorum* helps to clarify some of the specific sources developed by clergy by which to convey the Catholic worldview and religious doctrines to local populations, and indicates how and when in the relatively early historical periods and conditions the Maya began to appropriate some of these concepts. As this concept of angels in a heavenly hierarchy is introduced as another "*[u]kaj paj tzij*," interpreters of this early K'iche' document often misunderstand this as another listing of a "fourth chapter" of the *Title of Totonicapán*, instead of recognizing that the authors of the *Title of Totonicapán* are explicitly citing one of their principal sources, the *Theologia Indorum*.

Not all of Vico's sections are explicitly referenced through the first 65 lines of the *Title of Totonicapán*, for the K'iche' authors combined and redacted chapters 26 and 29 of the *Theologia Indorum* before then moving to chapter 31, which is enumerated as the "fifth chapter [major theme]" (*ro' paj tzij*) and addresses Adam and Eve as the first human beings. Chapters 27 and 28 of the *Theologia Indorum*, which tell the story of the fall of Lucifer, are not mentioned until line 70 of the *Title of Totonicapán,* where they are then condensed with chapter 38. Therefore, this apparent move from a "fourth chapter" (*ukaj paj tzij*) to a "fifth chapter" (*ro' paj tzij*) has mistakenly led interpreters to read these section headings as "chapters" proper to the *Title of Totonicapán*, rather than as K'iche' Maya author-redactors' explicit citations of the *Theologia Indorum*. In discussing the relationship between Lucifer, Adam, and Eve, by line 103 the *Title of Totonicapán* again cites an "*[u]kaj paj tzij*" but it does so as the fourth subsection of the fifth major theme, or "chapter" 43 of the *Theologia Indorum*, giving the false impression that the K'iche' authors have lost count of their own "chapters" as they move from a "fourth" unit to a "fifth" unit and then to a "fourth" unit again.[75]

As illustrated in table 7.1, in the *Title of Totonicapán* the K'iche' authors strategically selected sections about creation and migration, such as the flood, the tower of Babel, Exodus, and exile stories from the Catholic Old Testament, to construct a Catholic summary to integrate with their own cosmogonic and migration narratives. Their choices were not unlike Vico's own use of Highland Maya cosmogonic narratives—such as his use of paired names from the creator pantheon like *Tz'aqol B'itol* and *Alom K'ajolom* and his inclusion of the Hero Twins Jun Ajpu and Xb'alankej and the lords of otherworld Xib'alb'a in his theological summary or *summa*.[76]

As written during the initial years of mutual encounter from the 1520s and the 1570s, the texts illustrate the space for this dialogue opened up by Vico and

Table 7.1. "Chapters" from Vico's *Theologia Indorum* in the *Title of Totonicapán*

Contents	*Folio of TT*	*Line in TT*	*"Chapters" of Vico's TI*	*Unit Number in Vico's TI**
Seven days of creation and the Earthly Paradise	1 recto	1	30	Fourth major theme
Nine levels of angels and their names	1 verso	36	29 (and 26)	Fourth part of the third major theme
Adam, Eve, Lucifer, the two trees of Paradise	2 recto	66	31 (27, 28, 30, 35)	Fifth major theme
Adam names animals, creation of Eve from Adam's rib, Devil has Eve eat the forbidden fruit	3 recto	103	34 (35–44, 46)	Fourth part of the fifth major theme
Cain, Abel, and Seth and their descendants	4 recto	164	47	Ninth, tenth, eleventh names of the sixth major theme
Methuselah and Noah and Noah's sons: Shem, Ham, and Japheth	4 verso	185	49, 51	Fourteenth and fifteenth; seventeenth, eighteenth, and nineteenth names of the sixth major theme
Building a tower, scattering of languages, and the flood	4 verso	186	52, 50	Sixteenth name and a word of the sixth major theme
Shem, Ham, Japheth's sons: Abraham, Isaac, Esau, Jacob	4 verso	197	55, 57	Twentieth and twenty-first names of the sixth major theme
Jacob and his sons and the journey to Egypt	4 verso	198	58 (59–61)	Twenty-second name of the sixth major theme
Moses in Egypt	5 recto	206	62 (60, 63)	Twenty-third name of the sixth major theme
Moses and Aaron confront the pharaoh	5 recto	223	(64, 65)	
Arrival at and crossing the sea	5 verso	250	(66, 76)	
Journey in the wilderness	5 verso	259	(67, 68)	
Defeat of Amalech	6 recto	264	(69)	
Arrival of children of Jacob; Death of Myriam	6 recto	265	(72)	

continued on next page

TABLE 7.1—*continued*

Contents	*Folio of TT*	*Line in TT*	*"Chapters" of Vico's TI*	*Unit Number in Vico's TI**
Death of Moses in Moab	6 recto	267	(77, 80)	
Jericho defeated and Joshua as ruler	6 recto	269	81 (82–84)	Twenty-fourth name of the sixth major theme
Death of Joshua	6 recto	270	(86)	
Samuel	6 recto	272	87	Twenty-fifth name of the sixth major theme
Saul	6 recto	274	88	Second part of the twenty-fifth name of the sixth major theme
David	6 recto	273	89	Twenty-sixth name of the sixth major theme
Solomon	6 recto	275	90	Twenty-seventh name of the sixth major theme
Listing of prophets and patriarchs: Elias, Elisha, Daniel, Isaiah, and Jonah	6 recto	273	91 (92–95, 99)	Twenty-eighth "name" of the sixth major theme
Diaspora of Jerusalem by Babylon and Assyria	6 verso	280	100	Tenth subsection of the Twenty-eighth "name" of the sixth major theme
Diaspora of the ten tribes of Israel by Assyria	6 verso	283	101	Eleventh subsection of the twenty-eighth "name" of the sixth major theme
Journey through the Sinai, summary of the Hebrews	7 recto	299	(67, 70, 105)	

* Underlined words for numbers in the last column are those that explicitly appear in the *Title of Totonicapán* with exception to the first "fourth" (*ucah* or *ukaj*), regarding creation, since it appears in the text as "second" (*ucab* or *ukab*') due to a scribal error.

Highland Maya elites. While the citation of the numbered headings of sections or "chapters" from the *Theologia Indorum* indicates that the K'iche' authors had closely read Vico's text, the K'iche' authors' autochthonous revisions of biblical accounts demonstrates that they not only understood them thematically but also as evidence of the persuasive force such stories bore for Spanish ecclesial and colonial authorities. Furthermore, while there is no textual evidence that the Pauline epistles from the New Testament were a strong focus in early sermons and doctrinal lessons, the K'iche' authors of the *Title of Totonicapán* could be said to have inverted Paul of Tarsus's approach to appropriating other religions: Whereas in his letter to the Christian community in Rome Paul argued that non-Jews could be "grafted onto" (e.g., Romans 11:17–24) and thus included into the messianic movement of Jesus of Nazareth,[77] the K'iche' author-redactors, possibly influenced by Vico's method of reinterpreting prehispanic K'iche' rituals in chapter 25 of the *Theologia Indorum*, integrated medieval cosmogony and Christian biblical history into their worldview.

To do this the *Title of Totonicapán* does not merely summarize the first volume of the *Theologia Indorum*, it also uses two additional, possibly corrective strategies beyond Vico's theology. The first corrective strategy consisted of altering Vico's translated biblical stories to be understood by a wider K'iche' audience.[78] For example, in his rendition of the story of the garden of Eden, Vico specifies that the two trees placed in the "Earthly Paradise" by God—the tree of eternal life and the tree of knowledge of good (*utz*) and "not good" (*mawi utz* but not necessarily "evil" [*itzel*])—were *tulul* or sapote trees (*Pouteria sapota* or *Manilkara sapota*).[79] The *Title of Totonicapán* in a near-verbatim quote states:

> K'ate k'ut ub'anik ka'ib' chi nimaq tulul xub'an Dios nimajaw chi unik'ajal Parayso Terenal, jun tulul k'aslemal tulul. "Achinaq chilo'on uwach jun elik chik'ase'ik rumal," xcha' Dios nimajaw. Jun chi tulul etamab'al tulul ub'i'. Are ub'ina'am wi etamab'al tulul achinaq chilowik, chiretaj utz chiretamaj utz, chiretamaj mawi utz. Keje k'ut uk'oje'ik ka'ib' tulul ri' . . . ta xulkik'axtok'okoj ri Eva chulo'ik awas tulul.
>
> Suddenly then two large sapote trees were made, made by God, the great lord, in the middle of the Earthly Paradise, one sapote was a sapote tree of life. "Whoever would take from the fruit should live because of it," said God, the great lord. Another sapote tree was the sapote of knowledge, that was its name. It was called the sapote tree of knowledge since whoever would eat it would signal good, would know good, and would know not-good. Just like that the two sapote trees came to be . . . and when he [the Devil] came to bear pain upon Eve she partook of the prohibited sapote.[80]

Because apples were a European crop imported later, Highland Maya would have had little to no cultural understanding of the popular, non-biblical Western European notion of these two trees mentioned in Genesis as apple trees (*Malus domestica*) let alone a philological basis in K'iche' to comprehend the pun between "evil" (*mălum*) and "apple" (*mālum*) made from the hermit monk Jerome's Latin translation of Genesis for the Vulgate in the fourth century. The sapote, on the other hand, in the story of the creation of humans found in the Popol Wuj, accompanies maize, the sacred plant from which the first humans were made.[81]

Likewise, Vico took liberty to designate the burning bush that confronted Moses as a *tukan* in K'iche'—a *mora*, bush in Spanish, which includes raspberry, boysenberry, blackberry, and other types of thorned berry-bearing shrubs.[82] And again, as with Vico's use of the sapote, the ninth page the *Title of Totonicapán* also states that

> Katajin k'ut Moyses yuq'ul chij, ta xsik'ix rumal Dios nimajaw k'o pa tukan. Mawi kak'ataj, kaporotaj taj puch uxaq tukan k'o wi Dios nimajaw.

> Moses was pasturing sheep when he was called by God, the great lord, there in a thorned berry bush. Not even did it burn nor scorch, thus, the leaves of the thorned berry bush as God, the great lord, was there.[83]

In addition to their use as common food sources, *tukan* bushes are still commonly used by K'iche' as property border markers against human or animal intruders. Such an example might highlight not only the border of a particular parcel of land but also a conceptual boundary between the domesticated and the divine, a border groped for by mendicant missionaries but better explained and translated by K'iche' scribes to a Highland Maya audience. The initiative by Vico to specify the two sapote trees as well-known, prized fruit native to the highlands and associated with Maya indigenous cosmogony, and the burning shrub as a commonly used sign of different domains, reduced the unfamiliarity of the biblical narratives for a wider Highland Maya audience—a creative license that Maya authors adopted in their own writings.

K'iche' elite authors furthered the practice of altering biblical narratives for their newly Catholic commoners in four other notable examples. As mentioned above, the first folio of the *Title of Totonicapán* in the K'iche' summary of the nine-layered celestial realm changed the static tenth level for a dynamic one and replaces the Catholic *Dios* with the sun, possibly a reference to Jun Ajpu from Maya native cosmogony. Additionally, line 178 of the *Title of Totonicapán* states that Cain after killing Abel was later eventually slain in his *ab'ix*, a typical farming plot of traditional foodstuffs such as maize, beans, and squash of many Mesoamerican and North American indigenous peoples, also known as *milpa* in Spanish.[84] Lines 176–178 of the *Title of Totonicapán* state:

> Keje k'ut uya'ik uk'axel umak Cain. Xa wi ma utzilaj kamik xok chi rech, xa xk'aq rumal jun casador k'o pa rab'ix.

> Just like that then the pain and the sin of Cain was given. Only there was not a very good death that came to him, just hunted down by a hunter there in his *milpa*.[85]

However, chapter 47 of the *Theologia Indorum,* in which Vico recounts the story of Cain and Abel, does not specify in what kind of field Cain's death took place and, thus, does not use the term *ab'ix*. For these early K'iche' exegetes, therefore, Cain was not simply killed in a generic field but rather on his own land, presumably connoted as a safe place by average Mesoamerican agriculturalists. For a Highland Maya audience, this additional contextualization makes Cain's death at the hand of Lamech, as Vico in chapter 47 conveyed this non-biblical but yet medieval interpretation of the story, more poignantly because Cain was killed working in his own field and doing work that all "good" men do.

A third instance of their contextualization of Vico's biblical history involves the story of the tower of Babel and the changing and scattering of different languages. Whereas Vico in the *Theologia Indorum* did not state which or how many languages came about, the authors of the *Title of Totonicapán* specify that thirteen groups of mutually unintelligible languages resulted from the judgment of "God, the great lord":

> Ta xeq'il rumal Dios nimajaw, ta xuq'at tzij Dios pa kiwi', ta xuljalk'atij Dios nimajaw kich'ab'al. Oxlajuj ch'ob' chi ch'ab'al kich'ab'al, xuxik. Ma chichi xkita' kich'ab'al chi kib'al kib'.

> Then they were chastised by God, the great lord; then God judged them; then God, the great lord, changed forever their language, thirteen groups of languages is what their language became. Afterwards they did not hear the languages of each other.[86]

Rather than from any other Judeo-Christian biblical or Catholic doctrinal source—which more likely would have either carried over the idea that there were 70–73 languages distinguished in Genesis 11 or stressed the symbolism of the number twelve, such as references to the twelve ancient tribes of Israel or the twelve disciples and later apostles of Jesus—the K'iche' authors drew from their prehispanic history of the nascent K'iche' confederation once united with the thirteen other distinct polities (*amaq'*) within the Maya highlands. As written in the Popol Wuj around the same time as the composition of the *Title of Totonicapán*:

1 Ox ch'ob' chinamit
2 chi uk'oje'ik,
3 mawi sachel ub'i' umam,
4 uqajaw.
5 Are poq'ol,
6 k'irol chi la'
7 releb'al q'ij,
8 xawi xere xpe wi Tamub',
9 Ilokab'

ruk' oxlajuj uq'a amaq',
oxlajuj tekpan[87]

There were three groups of [K'iche'] lineages
that existed
and the names of their grandfathers
and their fathers are not forgotten.
They multiplied and
increased over there
in the east.
But there also arrived the Tamub'
and the Ilokab' [incorporated into the K'iche' nation]
along with the thirteen allied nations,
thirteen royal households[88]

But after their arrival to the primal city of Tulan they linguistically developed:

Ta xok chi k'ut ronojel amaq' . . .
Chi ri' k'ut xjalq'atij uch'ab'al ri amaq';
jalajoj kich'ab'al xuxik.
Mawi q'alaj chik xkita'o chi kib'il kib'
ta xepetik chi Tulan,
chi ri' k'ut xkipaxij wi kib'.[89]

When all the nations then entered [Tulan] . . .
Over there the language of the nations changed;
their languages shifted to be different.
Never again would they hear each other clearly
when they came from Tulan,
over there then they split apart among themselves.[90]

The prehispanic K'iche' tradition as recorded in the Popol Wuj later tells of separation along linguistic lines as a result of tensions regarding local religious differences and access to power and resources, symbolized as the acquisition of fire, but does not explicitly link these divisions by the lines of the "thirteen" *amaq'*. Furthermore, given the thirteen cofficients that align with the twenty days to compose the Mesoamerican 260-day ceremonial calendar, the use of thirteen here in the Popol Wuj may be more symbolic than historic. On the other hand, the *Title of Totonicapán* explicitly relates the development of language differences among the Highland Maya between the so-called thirteen highland polities once unified in an idyllic past. Unlike the Popol Wuj, the *Title of Totonicapán* attributes the divisions to divine justice rather than political disloyalty. Furthermore, the Popol Wuj portrays the K'iche' confederacy as having symbolically recovered from this loss by later prospering under the reign of thirteen generations of K'iche' rulers (*ajpop*), whereas the *Title of Totonicapán* instead emphasizes a correspondence between the thirteen ancient peoples of K'iche'an history and the "thirteen" ancient peoples they read into Vico's biblical history. In all three of these examples, the K'iche' author-redactors of Vico's theology further contextualized the biblical narratives in their own terms to make them more familiar and culturally accessible for a wider K'iche'an audience, a criterion that would not be apparent in a mere resistant document or a text exclusively dedicated to property rights.

But, a second kind of contextualizing strategy unique to the *Title of Totonicapán* correlates prehispanic indigenous narratives to the biblical accounts from Vico, including his construals of the divine in K'iche' Maya. For example, in the first seven folios, which contain a redaction of Genesis, this occurs most notably in their treatment of the creation of the first human being made of clay. The Maya cosmogonic literature articulated in the Popol Wuj tells of not one but rather four attempts by divine creators like *Alom K'ajolom* (Bearer and Begetter) to fashion the first generation of true humans, with clay used in a second attempt, following the creation of animals and before people of wood and then true people finally, successfully created from maize. Rather than explicitly address the discrepancy between a narrative of true humans being made from mud in only one initial attempt, as in Genesis 2:7, or of mud people existing only as a second mistaken effort, as in the Popol Wuj, the *Title of Totonicapán* reconciled this tension, in part, by stating, like Vico, that their Adam was not made merely from earth but also with the other three basic elements—fire, water, and air. Drawing on Vico's use of Aquinas's *Summa theologiae*, the K'iche' authors of the *Title of Totonicapán* stated that, during the creation of the first human person,

> Kajib' chuyujik xok uti'ojil: ulew, q'aq', ja', kaq'iq'. Ulew xok wi unimati'ojil, ja' k'ut uq'anal, ukik'wl puch, q'aq' k'ut xel puch umiq'inal, uk'atinal. Kaq'iq' k'ut xokesax ruxlab'. Keje k'ut chi kaj molaj wi xokesax winaqil ti'ojil.

> Four elements came about, mixed then in the flesh: earth, fire, water, and air. Earth came in the compiling of humanity, water then in the maturity, in the blood then, and fire then taken thus for its heat and its brightness. Air then became the breath. Just like that then in four groups of elements were made into human flesh.[91]

While Adam here is not from a previous Maya epoch of animal creatures or wooden people, or an eventual moment of maize people, he is also not only of clay but of an additional three elements that qualifies him as complete and thus still fully human, as truly *winaq*.

Furthermore, in the *Title of Totonicapán*, Adam fulfills the sole divine command issued in the Popol Wuj. After the first attempt to create people, which resulted in the animals, the Maya creator deities ask their creation to fulfill only one request:

> Ta xe'uchax chi k'ut ri kej tz'ikin rumal Tz'aqol, B'itol, Alom, K'ajolom "Kisch'awoq kixsik'inoq! Mixyonolikinik mixsik'inik! Kixch'awajetaj chi jujunal, chu jutaq ch'ob'il, chi jutaq molajil," xe'ucha'xik ri kej, tz'ikin, koj, b'alam, kumatz. "Chib'ij na k'ut ri qab'i', kojiqajarisaj oj ichuch, oj iqajaw . . . Juraqan, Ch'ipikaqulja, Raxakaqulja, Uk'u'x Kaj, Uk'u'x Ulew, Tz'aqol, B'itol, Alom, K'ajolom. Kixch'awoq kojisik'ij kojiq'ijila'!" xe'ucha'xik.[92]

> Then the deer and birds were told by the Framer, Former and the Bearer, Begetter, "Speak and proclaim! Don't moan or cry out! May you all talk, each one to each other, within each kind, within each group," they were told—the deer, birds, lions, jaguars, and serpents. "You all, name then our names and praise us. We are your mother, we are your father . . . Hurricane, Youngest Thunderbolt, and Green-Blue Thunderbolt, Heart of Sky and Heart of Earth, the Framer and Former, and the Bearer and Begetter. Speak! Call upon us! And keep our days!" they were told.[93]

However, the efforts to create people who could comply with this command were suspended after the third attempt due to the need to finish preparing the surface world (*uwach ulew*), including rebalancing it within a new cosmic order with the forces of the otherworld, Xib'alb'a. When the theme of human creation is resumed by the Maya pantheon and the first people of maize eventually come about, the Popol Wuj states:

> Wa'e kib'i' nab'e winaq xetz'aqik xeb'itik [B'alam Kitze', B'alam Aq'ab', Majukutaj, and Ik'i B'alam] . . . Xech'awik xetzijon puch, xemukunik xeta'on puch, xeb'inik xechapanik. E utzilaj winaq . . . K'ate puch xk'iskil ronojel uxe' kaj. K'ate k'ut kik'amowanik ri chi re Tz'aqol, B'itol.[94]

> These are the names of the first people who were fashioned and who were formed [B'alam Kitze', B'alam Aq'ab', Majukutaj, and Ik'i B'alam and their respective wives] . . . They spoke and they also had words. They looked and they also listened. They walked and they worked. They were good people . . . And suddenly then they also saw everything under the sky. And suddenly then they thanked the Framer and Former.[95]

However, in the *Title of Totonicapán*, Adam is the first creature to successfully fulfill the first divine command—not that of the Christian Bible to procreate as stated in Genesis 1:28, but to praise. After summarizing from the *Theologia Indorum* the creation of Adam, the *Title of Totonicapán* elaborates:

> Jeb'elik xuxik rumal Dios. K'ate k'ut ta xk'amowan chi rech Tz'aqol B'itol: "K'amo chech lalaj nuchuch, lalaj nuqajaw, mixitz'aq laj, mixib'it laj," xcha' chi rech Dios.
>
> [The first human] was beautiful because it was by God. Suddenly then thanks were given to the Framer and Former: "Thanks to you all my great mother and my great father, who just fashioned me and just formed me," [Adam] said to God.[96]

After the creation of Eve, the *Title of Totonicapán* states that while Adam was told by an angel to wake up and speak to his new companion he instead speaks directly to God on Eve's behalf, thus again fulfilling the divine command of the Popol Wuj to give praise and state the name of the creator god as *Tz'aqol B'itol*:

> Ta xuk'amowaj chi rech Dios: "K'amow chi rech la lal Tz'aqol B'itol wech. Mixya' laj wachb'al," xcha'chi rech Dios nimajaw.
>
> Then [Adam] gave thanks to God: "Thanks be to you, you the Framer and Former of me. You have just given me my partner," he said to God, the great lord.[97]

As the *Title of Totonicapán* never clarifies that this command to thank the divine creator came not from the Christian Bible à la the *Theologia Indorum*, a K'iche' audience to a public reading would already most likely have been familiar with its understood divine origin and significance from ancient Maya cosmogonic stories that also eventually composed the Popol Wuj.

As highlighted above, the authors of the *Title of Totonicapán* retained the names of K'iche' divine creators appropriated by Vico in the *Theologia Indorum* to elaborate a doctrine of the Christian god in the K'iche' language—that is, *Tz'aqol B'itol* (Framer and Former)—while also omitting the other names for Maya gods, such as *Uk'u'x Kaj, Uk'u'x Ulew* (Heart of Sky and Heart of Earth), found in the Popol Wuj. Like the *Theologia Indorum*, the *Title of Totonicapán* alternates between the K'iche' phrases and the Spanish *Dios*, including at times Vico's couplet *Dios, nimajaw*, which places the biblical *Dios* and Maya "Framer and Former" in not merely an analogical but a synonymous relationship. However, notably, the K'iche' authors of this *título* never replace *Dios* with *Tz'aqol B'itol* (as in Vico's tercet *Tz'aqol, B'itol, nimajaw*) or pair them together (as in Vico's quatrain *Tz'aqol, B'itol, Dios, nimajaw*), both of which appear in the first volume of the *Theologia Indorum*. Nor do the K'iche' authors use the other main traditional couplet *Alom K'ajolom* (Bearer and Begetter) also found in the Popol Wuj and appropriated by Vico to also refer to biblical creator deity. Despite this narrower use, the authors of the *Title of Totonicapán* reaffirm the Maya view of the creator god serving as both a divine mother and divine father, also articulated by Vico and in the Popol Wuj.

Toward the end of the first seven folios the K'iche' authors make a second major constructive move that not only further contextualized Vico's theological worldview but also correlated his late medieval cosmology and biblical history with stories in the Popol Wuj about ancient Maya migration into the highland region. While the first seven folios consist of an edited version of Vico's theology, folio eight of the *Title of Totonicapán* identifies the migration of the four principal founders of the K'iche' nation—B'alam Kitze', B'alam Aq'ab', Majukutaj, and Ik'i B'alam, fashioned from maize by the divine grandmother Xmukane in the Popol Wuj—with the proverbial "ten lost tribes" of ancient Israel, a result of the invasion of ancient Assyrian Empire into the northern kingdom of Israel (ca. 722 BCE) but also popularly conflated with the diaspora due to the invasion by Babylonia in the southern kingdom of Judah (ca. 597–ca. 532 BCE). Even if further contextualization of these biblical narratives existed prior to the *Title of Totonicapán*, such as in sermons by other mendicants in their attempts to translate this material for a K'iche'an congregation, the K'iche' elite would still have drawn from a variety of written and oral sources, K'iche' and mendicant, to write their *título*.

This second constructive move enabled the authors of the *Title of Totonicapán* to make three original interpretive claims that entailed mapping Tulan, the Mesoamerican mythical place of origin, onto the biblical Babylon. Such a relocation placed the legendary ruler Nakxit (a Maya variation of Plumed or Feathered Serpent, or Quetzalcoatl, as called in Nahuatl) in the biblical Babylon and identified this Babylon as the place where the K'iche' learned about devotional practices to effigies, *ab'aj che'* (literally a "stone tree"), that Vico condemned in chapter 25 of his *Theologia Indorum*. The K'iche' elite authors of the *Title of Totonicapán* accomplished this through their strategy of grafting the Maya religious narratives and devotional tradition onto the late medieval Christian biblical history in the *Theologia Indorum*—again inverting the Pauline motif to instead graft the K'iche' Maya tradition onto that of ancient Israel.

By chapter 101 (or more appropriately, according Vico's hierarchical numbering of units within his theology, the "eleventh subsection of the twenty-eighth 'name' of the sixth major theme" of the first volume) of the *Theologia Indorum*, Vico picks up this topic again as he attempts to relate the K'iche' Maya more directly to the ancient biblical Israelites.[98] While some clergy and explorers proposed that the indigenous peoples of the Americas were not only descendants of Adam and Eve, and thus part of the human family, the notion that they were more specifically from the diaspora in the wake of the Assyrian or later Babylonian invasions of the kingdoms of Israel and

Judah was strongly contested, especially among clergy. These early debates regarding the origins and identities of native peoples of the Americas, as explained in chapter 2 of this volume, is further complicated by clergy, who often made comparisons and analogies between "Indians" and Muslims, peasant Christians, and Jews, either ancient and biblical or contemporaneous and Iberian. Later scholars run the risk of reading an early mendicant missionary's text literally where he is, instead, establishing an analogical relationship between Jews and native peoples rather than a univocal relationship. Furthermore, any mendicant as intimately familiar with Maya—or even Nahua or wider indigenous Mesoamerican—narratives, such as Vico, would have needed to reconcile the tension between the supposed journey of ancient Jews through Babylonia and across the rest of Asia to the "Indies"—in other words from the west—and the explicit native Mesoamerican idea that the mythical place of origin and return is in and from the east. Vico did not resolve the apparent contradiction, and neither did the K'iche' authors of the *Title of Totonicapán* or other early Highland Maya texts that presented further versions of this idea. But the *Title of Totonicapán* did explicitly cite Vico's "eleventh" subsection (*ujulajuj paj tzij*) and, also like Vico in chapter 101, explicitly related biblical Babylon with the ancient mythical places for native Mesoamerican peoples, like Tulan.

German linguistic anthropologist Frauke Sachse has noted that the trope of "from the east," "from across the waters," the "city among the reeds" (i.e., Tula, Tulan, Tollan, and so on in Nahuatl), and the place of "seven caves" or "seven canyons" is pervasive throughout not only Maya but wider ancient Mesoamerica. Narratives of origins and migration, including those of the Mexica, shaped not only their theological anthropologies and cosmogonies but also grounded their respective centralized political authorities, public rituals, and civic infrastructures.[99] Sachse argues that this common trope is less a factual datum of ancient Mesoamerican history than a mythical literary motif that oriented both cosmogonic narratives and religious ceremonial practices toward where the sun always enters the world. While the archaeological sites of some Tulans, such as the ancient cities of the so-called Olmec, are on the eastern Mexican coast, others are farther north and central-inland; and sixteenth-century Highland Maya texts, like the *Xajil Chronicle*, even note that there were multiple Tulans, including the place of origin.[100] Other late contemporaneous K'iche' *títulos* also specified the area of the sapotes as on the western Pacific coast, such as the prehispanic cities called Chi Tulul ("Place of the Sapotes," or Zapotitlán in Nahuatl) perhaps further reinforcing the idea that Maya understood multiple places of origins, especially those associated with the four cardinal points.[101] In many of these stories, these places represented the various and often distinct origins of the cosmos, maize and basic foodstuffs, true human beings, divinely sanctioned political leadership, and national or ethnic histories often conflated with the east but also symbolically located along the other three cardinal points: south, west, and north. Depending on a story's context, these various points of "origin"—of mythical migration from, or of legendary pilgrimage toward—may be conflated or notably distinguished by the indigenous authors.

For example, the Popol Wuj says that the creation of the first true human beings occurred where maize was created, a place called *Pan Paxil, Pan K'ayala'*.[102] From there the first eight human couples procreated, diversified into different lineages and polities, and then collectively migrated west "from the east" or "from where the sun arrives" (*releb'al q'ij* in K'iche') across grasslands (*pa k'i* in K'iche') to arrive at a mountainous area called *Tulan Suywa, Wuqub' Pek, Wuqub' Siwan*.[103] There the Popol Wuj claims that the K'iche'an Maya emigrants acquired lineage patron deities (*k'ab'awil*) and effigies (*ab'aj che'*) related to them. From there they traveled farther west and crossed over the waters (*uloq pa palo* in K'iche') to begin a settlement pattern farther into the central Guatemalan highlands. After a period of political consolidation, establishment, and institutionalization, the Popol Wuj tells of the pilgrimage by heads of the three leading lineages—the Kaweqib', Nija'ib', and Ajaw K'iche'—who traveled back east "across the waters" to have their leadership offices sanctioned by a better-established ruler, Nakxit, before returning to the Western K'iche' plateau with new official titles and signs of office.[104] In other words, for the K'iche' authors of the Popol Wuj, *Paxil, K'ayala', Tulan Suywa*, and quite possibly the city or "Tulan" of the lord Nakxit were distinct places, with "the waters" simply marking the far eastern border of the K'iche' geopolitical territory.

The contemporaneous K'iche' authors of the *Title of Totonicapán*, however, realign *Paxil K'ayala'* and *Tulan Suywa, Wuqub' Pek, Wuqub' Siwan* from the Maya material as well as with Genesis's earthly paradise, Exodus's Mount Sinai, and the biblical milieux of the ancient Assyrian and Babylonian empires. Specifically, while distinguishing between the Earthly Paradise (as the place of origins) and *Paxil K'ayala'* (the place of human creation in the Popol Wuj) the *Title of Totonicapán* conflates *Paxil K'ayala'* with *Tulan Suywa, Wuqub' Pek, Wuqub' Siwan* and then equates both with Mount Sinai. For example, in folio seven it tells of

> xa xkipo', xa xkijalk'atij kitzij <u>Wuqub' Pek, Wuqub' Siwan, Siwan Tulan</u>, xecha' chi rech. <u>Pan Parar, Pan Paxil, Pan K'ayala'</u>, xecha'. Are' k'ut ri Pan Paxil, Pan K'ayala' xekib'ij are' ri chi upam <u>Parayso Terenal</u> xojtz'aq wi, xojb'it wi rumal Dios nimajaw . . . Are' k'u ri <u>Siwan Tulan</u> xkib'ij cha k'ut usik'ilikil <u>Sineyeton</u>. Are' k'u ri Wuqub' Pek, Wuqub' Siwan ri tzij wi re' ri pa pek, pa siwan xewar wi chi la' chi <u>releb'al q'ij</u>.

> how they broke and changed their words of <u>Seven Caves, Seven Ravines, and Siwan Tulan</u> as they said it there, <u>"Parar" Place, Split Place, and Bitter Water Place</u>, as they

> said. It was then in Split Place and Bitter Water Place that they were told about the center of the Earthly Paradise, their being formed there, their being shaped there by God, the great lord . . . It was then at Siwan Tulan they said, it is told, the story of Mount Sinai. This was thus the Seven Caves and Seven Ravines, truly it was in caves and canyons where they slept over there in the east.[105]

In the *Title of Totonicapán*, *Paxil K'ayala'* is not the same as the Earthly Paradise but rather where their ancestors first learned about their creation by God, the great lord (*Dios, nimajaw*)—who is also the Framer and Former (*Tz'aqol B'itol*)—and received their true "word" or laws from which they later deviated. Their "Sinai," however, is not a mountain as it is in the Book of Exodus but rather a set of "seven caves" reminiscent of the legendary cities of origins of the ancestors of the Mexica, Yukatek Maya, and K'iche' Maya of Q'umarkaj. Their Tulan though, like the mountains the K'iche' say they encountered on the western journey in the Popol Wuj, also consists of signs of wealth, rendered as a memory of what was lost or left behind because of the Assyrian Emperor Shalmaneser V.

They then state a couple of lines later in the *Title of Totonicapán*:

> Xa kejunelik uloq, xa pu e jusa chik, ta xesach chi la' Asiriya rumal Salmanazar . . . wa'e uk'oje'ik ajawarem, uxe' puch tzij ri ub'ixik ri q'analaj juyub', raxalaj juyub' ri Pa Siwan, Pa Tulan xkib'ij utzib'al pek, utzib'al siwan Tulan, xecha'. Ta xenimataj chupam ri tz'aqb'al tzij, ta xecha' chi rech ri q'ij, ik' jun q'apoj, jun k'ajol xecha'. Jun Ajpu xecha' chi rech ri q'ij, Xb'alankej chuchax ri ik' kumal.

> Only they left there and then before they would arrive many got lost there in Assyria due to Shalmaneser [V] . . . this is the existence of the dominion, the root of the word told of the mountain of "yellowness" and the mountain of "greenness" in Pa Siwan and Pa Tulan, they said as written in the caves and written in the canyons of Tulan, as they have said. Then they aggrandized in the lies. Then they spoke about the sun and moon as a young woman and a young man. They spoke of Jun Ajpu as the sun, Xb'alankej was spoken of as the moon by them.[106]

What they claim to acquire, though, during this previous ancient period of residing in caves was a set of written knowledge, the ceremonial or true "word" (*tzij*) that echoes the "root of the ancient word" (*uxe' ojer tzij*) proclaimed also in the opening lines of the Popol Wuj, including also the stories of the Hero Twins (Jun Ajpu and Xb'alankej) and their transformation into the new dawn: the sun and his sibling, the moon. In other words, the authors of the *Title of Totonicapán* place the cosmogonic Hero Twins' ascension from death in the otherworld of Xib'alb'a into the sky, as told more fully in the Popol Wuj, within their own Sinai moment, while also claiming that cosmogonic association with the legendary Hero Twins is false, as Vico had done in the *Theologia Indorum*. Like Vico's attempt to incorporate aspects of Highland Maya cosmology, theogony, and ceremonial discourse into his Catholic theology for the Maya, the similar attempt by the K'iche' authors' of the *Title of Totonicapán* to produce a Mayanized Christianity indicates the extent to which such efforts were works of thought in process, not yet resolving conceptual tensions between these two worlds by the 1550s.

Before transitioning from the redaction of biblical narratives culled from Vico's *Theologia Indorum* and moving into the political history and noble genealogies of the K'iche' nation, the *Title of Totonicapán* weaves together two last elements of the two traditions. Distinguishing historically and geographically between Assyria and Babylonia, its K'iche' authors, while seemingly condemning Shalmaneser V of Assyria, locate Babylon as the residence of the Maya lord Nakxit. The same gesture also allows the K'iche' authors to assert that they are not only descendants of this noble Maya lineage but also of "Saint Moses" and the Israelites. The end of the seventh folio states:

> Oj umam oj uk'ajol ajIsrael, Santo Moysen. Chupam kichinamital ajIsrael xel wi' e qamam, e qaqajaw, ta xepe chi releb'al q'ij. Chi la' pa Babelonia kowisanoq ajaw Nakxit ri uxe' qamamaxik, qak'ajolaxik.
>
> We are the grandchildren and sons of Israelites and holy Moses. From the center of the tribes of the Israelites left our grandfathers and our fathers, when they came from the east, from over there in Babylonia had been covenanted the lord Nakxit, the root of our grandsons' and our sons' lineage.[107]

The area for these locales is in the east and across the waters. As the *Title of Totonicapán*'s authors say of their now quasi-biblical Maya ancestry on the next folio:

> Keje k'ut kipetik wa'e ch'aqa cho, ch'aqa palow Pa Tulan, Pa Siwan. Wa'e k'ute kib'i nab'e winaq, wa'e nab'e k'iche' . . . Xa uq'ana winaq rib' chupam wa'e wuj. Xa e junelik uloq ch'aqa cho, ch'aqa palow, releb'al q'ij Pa Tulan, Pa Siwan . . . e ral uk'a Israel oj K'iche' winaq ta xujpe Babelonia releb'al q'ij.
>
> Like that then they arrived here from across the lake, across the sea from Pa Tulan, Pa Siwan. This is then the names of the first people, these are the first K'iche' . . . Only these are the golden people themselves within this here book. Only they arrived once and for all from across the lake, across the sea, from the east, from Pa Tulan, Pa Siwan in the east . . . they were children of Israel and we are the K'iche' nation, then we came from Babylon in the east.[108]

In almost the same breath, the *Title of Totonicapán* argues that the Highland Maya, and especially the Kaweq lineage of the K'iche' Maya, descend from the first four maize people, whose sons journeyed back "to the east" to have their authority legitimized by older Lowland Maya nobility and

> chi konojel aj Israel, aj Kanan, aj Eb're'os, ke'uchaxik, e qamam . . . qelik puch uloq releb'al q'ij . . . oj umam uk'ajol Adan, Eva, Enok, Ab'rajam, Isa'ak, Jakob'.
>
> of them all: Israelites, Canaanites, and Hebrews, as they are spoken of, our grandfathers . . . our departure then from the east . . . us the grandsons and sons of Adam, Eve, Enoch, Abraham, Isaac, and Jacob.[109]

On one hand, by exploiting the popular misunderstanding by many of the Spanish missionaries that the indigenous peoples of the Americas were descendants of the "ten lost tribes," these K'iche' elite grounded the legitimacy of their cultural and religious worldview on popular mendicant terms. On the other hand, based on the commonly accepted authority of this misunderstanding, the K'iche' thus proceeded not only to unfold their national history after the "migration from the east"—with the Maya mythic place of origin of Tulan and biblical Babylon now one and the same—but also to reassert the validity of their own prehispanic cosmogonic narratives, such as of the Hero Twins' cosmic ball game with the lords of the otherworld of Xib'alb'a. While the K'iche' author-redactors of the *Title of the Totonicapán* further contextualized Vico's biblical stories, they simultaneously reconfigured their own religious stories. Throughout the course of this dual process, they referred repeatedly to God, affirming the common use of Vico's K'iche' term for the triune but dual-gendered God and adding to it in defense of their other terms regarding precontact understandings of divine agency and K'iche'an relations with it.

CONCLUSION: FROM A MESOAMERICAN DOMINICAN SCHOOL TO A "TOTONICAPÁN" SCHOOL

As discussed in this chapter and summarized in table 7.2 below, both the contextual and constructive moves made by the likes of Diego Reynoso and other Maya coauthors in the *Title of Totonicapán* articulates only the first—though most lengthy and elaborate—evidence of the reception of a Christianity, via a particular theological text, from an indigenous people's perspective. This Maya reception of a notion of biblical antiquity strategically albeit implicitly raised the validity, authenticity, authority, and general value of prehispanic Maya beliefs and practices, an act of translation that allowed for acceptance of Vico's theology and the beginnings of a conversion to a Catholicism without an overwriting of their own worldview. The influence of these moves made in the *Title of Totonicapán*, based on the reception of Vico's theology, did not stop there, though, for they are further apparent in later

Maya notarial texts in the decades if not also centuries that followed, as is discussed in greater detail in the next chapter.

Within their efforts to translate and transmit Catholicism to Mesoamerica—unlike Latin, Greek, Arabic, and Hebrew—the American languages that mendicants used did not have phonetic writing systems, with the exception of the Lowland Maya.[110] Instead, indigenous civilizations such as the Mexica and Mixtec recorded their histories in pictographic books or elaborate cartographies, while the Inka kept records via *khipus* (multicolored strands of tied knots), which can only be considered "writing" with, as Elizabeth Hill Boone has argued, an expansion of the conventional definition.[111] The language ideologies in Mesoamerica and the Andes thus posed unique puzzles for early mendicant translators. After developing a mostly Latin-based script with native-speaking collaborators, mendicants produced translations of popular devotional literature such as catechisms, confessional aids, and sermons for educated native elites and fellow clergy. In central Mexico and the Andes this occurred through two main regulatory mechanisms: the establishment of schools for indigenous nobility and the production of standardized doctrinal and pastoral texts in indigenous languages approved for use by all clergy in these regions through consensus by bishops or synods and enforced by the Spanish Inquisition. The result was the development of a distinct register of language that intentionally drew upon colloquial indigenous speech as well as the formal rhetoric, poetics, and idioms used by sixteenth-century indigenous nobility in prehispanic ceremonial discourse reserved for speaking about or to gods and ancestors. Historian Alan Durston refers to such speech by Dominicans and Jesuits in colonial Peru as "pastoral Quechua," and subsequent ethnohistorians and sociolinguists of early colonial Mexico have followed Durston in referring to the pastoral or doctrinal Nahuatl developed by Franciscans and the pastoral Q'eqchi' and K'iche' by Dominicans.[112]

However, the absence of prior cultural understanding of phonetic writing systems continued to cause problems among the Andean population. Clergy resorted to translating catechisms into pictographic books for indigenous readers to use as mnemonic devices that transmitted the basics of Catholicism. In the Andean region these doctrinal texts were produced throughout and after the colonial period.[113] Pictographic doctrinal materials were also produced in central Mexico, where it has been conventionally thought that early mendicants used pictographic translations of popular Catholic texts to transition Nahua readers from a prehispanic iconography to an alphabetic mode of literacy.[114] However, recent work by Louis Burkhart has discovered that the doctrinal content of these pictographic catechisms could not have dated prior to the 1650s and were likely written not by clergy but by seventeenth-century Nahua elites.[115]

Nevertheless, two preliminary generalizations can be made. First, that while a pastoral register of discourse was developed in collaboration with native speakers,

Table 7.2. Comparative places of Highland Maya origins, migrations, and authority

Text (Date)	*Place of Origin and Authority of the K'iche' Maya*
Coplas in K'iche' (1544–1552)	HUMAN ORIGINS IN: "Earthly Paradise" [Eden] DESCENDANTS OF: Adam and Eve
Xpantzay I (1552?)	DIRECT DESCENDANTS OF: Adam, Abraham, Isaac, Jacob MIGRATION FROM: Canaan, then Babylon where languages divided MIGRATION TO: Tulan, Wuqu' Pek, Wuqu' Siwan CONTINUED MIGRATION: "across the waters"
Theologia Indorum (1553, 1554)	HUMAN ORIGINS: "Earthly Paradise" [Eden] DESCENDANTS OF: Adam and Eve
Popol Wuj (ca. 1554–ca. 1558)	HUMAN ORIGINS IN: Pan Paxil, Pan K'ayala' BEGINNING OF RELIGION IN: Tulan Suywa, Wuqub' Pek, Wuqub' Siwan WESTERN MIGRATION: "other side of the waters" in the east GRANT OF POLITICAL AUTHORITY BY: lord Nakxit back in the east of the tribes of the: Kaweqib', Nija'ib', and Ajaw K'iche' DIRECT DESCENDANTS OF: B'alam K'itze, B'alam Aq'ab', Majukutaj
Title of Totonicapán (1554)	HUMAN ORIGINS IN: "Earthly Paradise" [Eden] BEGINNING OF HISTORY IN: Tulan Siwan and, Wuqub' Pek, Wuqub' Siwan = Pan Parar, Pan Paxil, Pan K'ayala' = Mount Sinai "in the east" MIGRATION AWAY: lost into Assyria due to Shalmaneser V WESTERN MIGRATION: from "other side of the waters" in the east = Pa Tulan, Pa Siwan = Babylon, the land of lord Nakxit OF THE TRIBES OF THE: Israelites, Canaanites, Hebrews; and Kaweqib', Nija'ib', Ajaw K'iche' DIRECT DESCENDANTS OF: Adam, Eve, Enoch, Abraham, Isaac, Jacob; and B'alam Kitze', B'alam Aq'ab', Majukutaj
Title of the Tamub' I (1580)	MIGRATION FROM: "across the waters" MIGRATION TO: Babylon where divided into 18 languages
Title of Santa Clara La Laguna (1583)	MIGRATION FROM: "across the waters" OF THE TRIBES OF THE: Kaweqib', Nija'ib', Ajaw K'iche', Saqik'

continued on next page

Table 7.2—*continued*

Text (Date)	*Place of Origin and Authority of the K'iche' Maya*
Title of the Tamub' III (1592)	HUMAN ORIGINS IN: "Earthly Paradise" [Eden]
	MIGRATION TO: Babylon where lost moral ways
	DIRECT DESCENDANTS OF: Adam, Abraham, Isaac, Jacob, Moses; and B'alam Kitze', B'alam Aq'ab', Majukutaj, Ik'i B'alam
	OF THE TRIBES OF THE: Egyptians, Israelites
	BEGINNING OF RELIGION (BLOODLETTING): in the east with Yaki (the Nahua)
	WESTERN MIGRATION: "other side of the waters" in the east
Title of the Ilokab' (1592)	HUMAN ORIGINS IN: "Earthly Paradise" [Eden]
	MIGRATION FROM: Egypt, Babylon where divided into 13 languages, Tulan
	BEGINNING OF RELIGION IN: Egypt
	WESTERN MIGRATION: from Egypt, "other side of the waters" in east
	DIRECT DESCENDANTS OF: Adam, Jacob, Moses; and B'alam Kitze', B'alam Aq'ab', Majukutaj, Ik'i B'alam

the functional translation of Hispano-Catholicism resulted from an imposition of ecclesial editorial control backed by coercive force where possible. Second, the indigenous unfamiliarity with alphabetic writing presented translation and representational challenges for clergy. In contrast, the surviving Maya literature provides a slightly different context for several reasons. First, the Lowland Maya were the only indigenous people with a complex logosyllabic writing system prior to contact with Europeans.[116] Furthermore, due to its difficult terrain and lack of valuable natural materials like gold, the region attracted fewer clergy and resources than central Mexico or the Andes. Finally, the vast linguistic diversity within an area smaller than the rest of New Spain caused Dominican and Franciscan mission territories in the Maya highlands to overlap, resulting in intense competition and discord among the various mendicant orders and their competing semiotic ideologies.

So, the translation efforts of Dominicans as well as Franciscans among the Highland Maya also apparently involved the elaboration of a distinct register of pastoral or doctrinal discourse in indigenous languages to convey local construals of Hispano-Catholicism, as is evident among the Nahua by Franciscans and Augustinians in Mexico and among Quechua and Aymara by Jesuits and Dominicans in the Andes. However, unlike those two regions, the emergence of a Maya pastoral register of speech was more organic and negotiated than imposed and enforced, just as much coauthored by K'iche'an elites and their agendas as by the mendicants—as evidenced in the Maya reception ethnohistory of Hispano-Catholicism that simultaneously reconfigured their prehispanic religious world-view and, correspondingly, from their perspective, correctively rewrote what was presented by mendicant missionaries.

8

A Reception Ethnohistory of a Christianity

Other Early Maya Hyperlocal Theologies

oj umam
oj ucajol atan
oj umam xacab
moysen
abbrajan
ixac
xacop
xa rumal xquisach..
usuculiquil Santo
wuj santo..
uloio co wi nabe wuj
co wi quitsij e propeta
moysen
ajbrajan
ixac
xacapb
intorum ubi nabe wuj
co wi quica'ajolaxic k'amam k'ak'ajaw.

We are the grandsons and
we are the sons of Adam, and

DOI: 10.5876/9781607329701.c008

we are the grandsons of Jacob,
        Moses,
        Abraham,
        Isaac, and
        Jacob
because they [the first grandparents] lost
    the holy rectitude and
            the holy book;
    where there is the first book,
            where there are the words of the prophets:
            Moses,
            Abraham,
            Isaac, and
            Jacob.
    [Theologia] Indorum, the name of the first book
        where there is history of our grandfathers and fathers.[1]

VICO AND REYNOSO'S LEGACY

The transmission of ideas is only part of any intellectual history, with the other part being the reception of those ideas. Survival of any evidence of such transmissions—whether written, drawn, dramatic, sculpted, and so on—depends on who is doing the receiving, and especially on the extent to which the receiving hosts have a language ideology that prioritizes writing. As many scholars of texts written by indigenous American authors have pointed out, these postcontact native documents, even when written in indigenous languages, were often composed and revised under the gaze of friars. As often indicated by the direct address of "you all" or "my sons" by the Maya authors, the primary readership or audience of many of the early Highland Maya texts was other Highland Maya and only secondarily or later, if ever, for a nonindigenous audience, be it ecclesial or civil. In this sense, the concerns, claims, and even relative accessibility of the texts' intelligibility did not extend beyond a rather narrow constituency—a hyperlocal communicative ecology. However, as these early documents often attest, the Highland Maya elites were by no means homogenous. In the decades prior to the arrival of Europeans, the Western K'iche' confronted both external and internal tensions as their dominance in the region waned.

Externally, the precontact Western K'iche' elite confronted continued and growing resistance by either those who did not join their expanding confederacy (such as with the Eastern K'iche', as evidenced in the *Rab'inal Achi*) or those former member groups within the K'iche' confederacy who broke away to establish their own polities (such as the Kaqchikel, as evidenced in the *Xajil Chronicle*). Internally, the Western K'iche' governing leadership harbored tensions between competing governing linages (such as illustrated in the failed takeover by the Ilokab' against the dominant Kaweqib' of the Nima K'iche') and between older and younger generations within that ruling Kaweq lineage (such as between allies of the prerevolt "old guard" of the regent Ajpop K'iq'ab' and the victorious "new guard" rulers of K'iq'ab's descendants who had ousted him). Both the old guard and the ruling new guard confronted the joint Iberian and Mexican forces in 1524, but the precontact tensions between them played into the different approaches these K'iche'an elites took toward mendicant missionaries (as evidenced in the differences between the Popol Wuj and the *Title of Totonicapán*). Whereas the Popol Wuj, as discussed in chapter 6 of this volume, articulates a kind of resistance to Hispano-Catholicism that did not simply ignore or reject it but rather accommodated it as inferior and incomplete to that of ancient Maya truth, the *Title of Totonicapán* took a much more conciliatory approach, as discussed in chapter 7.[2]

However, as also discussed in the previous chapters, mendicants drew from the knowledge of their indigenous students and language coaches, but their indigenous aides may actually have had more of an editorial if not also authorial hand and voice in pastoral writings than the mendicants themselves and later scholars have fully understood. To this extent, a collaborator like Diego Reynoso, working closely with Domingo de Vico prior to 1554, would not only have been extremely familiar with at least the first volume of the *Theologia Indorum* but may have also had a considerable say in its composition.

The use or threat of coercive force by non-Maya in the region, in conjunction with the increased death toll among Highland Maya due to new communicable diseases, and any strategic political and socioeconomic benefits deriving from cooperation with the friars and their new religion, should not be dismissed. However, comparative and intertextual analysis of the early Highland Maya documents composed during the sixteenth century provides a traceable shift in at least one strand or approach the K'iche' Maya took toward Christianity, namely the approach strongly instigated and promoted by Diego Reynoso. The reception of a version of the Popol Wuj via Friar Francisco Ximénez, O.P., at the turn of the eighteenth century while working as the parish priest in Chi Uwi' La' (or Chichicastenango), and the later ethnographic evidence of modern Maya cultural activists, provide evidence that the approach taken by the dominant author-redactors of the Popol Wuj critical of Christianity continued well past the 1550s. Though, a number of the other early Highland Maya texts written in the immediately subsequent decades into the seventeenth century illustrate a furtherance of the reception of a Christianity along the lines of a Maya "Totonicapán school."

By widening the pool of analysis of early Highland Maya documents, including those in ostensibly notarial genres but especially those that use religious discourse or tropes, a more nuanced reception history by Maya emerges in documents written initially and mostly for Maya. The legacy of Vico's *Theologia Indorum* continues not only in the later documents by fellow clergy, as noted in writings of Friars Viana, Remesal, Coto, Delgado, Ximénez, and others, but also in documents by Highland Maya influenced by the approach taken by Reynoso, the *Title of Totonicapán*, and other Maya legal documents to which he directly contributed. Furthermore, to the extent that they critically reflected upon and constructively engaged Christian construals, albeit in notarial genres, many of these early indigenous American texts can nonetheless be read as a kind of theology—a Maya theology, a possibly developing Catholic theology, but a theology whose claims were nevertheless limited in scope, impact, and import to the hyperlocal rather than translocal or universal realms.

OTHER CORROBORATING *TÍTULOS*: HYPERLOCAL MAYA CHRISTIAN THEOLOGIES

The *Title of Totonicapán* stands out for the degree to which it draws from—in quoting, citing, paraphrasing, augmenting, summarizing, "correcting," and so on—the first part of Vico's *Theologia Indorum*. It is a unique Highland Maya text in degree, but not necessarily in kind, as other late postclassic-period Maya texts also straddle and emerge from the seismic faultline of the sixteenth century. However, despite the intertextual relations with Vico's *Theologia Indorum*, the *Title of Totonicapán* neither mentions him nor his writings explicitly. This close relationship and influence of Vico's theology on Highland Maya texts is only apparent through an intertextual reading between the *Title of Totonicapán* and the *Theologia Indorum* in light of its use of the *Theologia Indorum*'s numbering system for "chapters," as explicated earlier.

Many of the other Highland Maya texts were authored by Maya elites like Diego Reynoso, and another couple of texts appear to have been signed by him in particular, such as the 1583 *Title of Santa Clara La Laguna*. Using the *Title of Totonicapán* as the "mother title," or standard for the K'iche' Maya, one can clarify that the *Theologia Indorum* was a specific source that other highland texts used for their references to Christianity, and one can appreciate as well the extent to which the approach taken in the *Title of Totonicapán* toward Vico's theology extended beyond Reynoso, the Yax clan, and the area of Totonicapán (or Chi Uwi' Miq'in Ja' in K'iche'). Furthermore, this intertextual reading and insights into dialogue are only available through analysis of key parts of Vico's theological opus. For example, the grafting of the K'iche' noble genealogical history onto an understanding of Tulan as Babylon appears in the 1579 K'iche' *Title of the Tamub' I*:

E puch b'elej chi nim ja.
Wa k'ute kib'i' xujpoqowik xujkirow puch
Kopichoch ub'i'
Jun Kur ub'i' rixoqil,
Kochojlan ub'i' jun chik
Xb'it Ku ub'i' rixoqil.
Chi la' k'ut xepe wi
chi releb'al q'ij,
ch'aqa cho,
ch'aqa palo,
ta xelik
chi la' naypuch Babilonia ub'i'.

There were nine noble lineages.[3]
Here thus are their names:
Kopichoch one was called
and his wife Jun Kur,
Kochijlan the other was called
and Xb'it Ku was his wife's name.
From over there they came
from the east,
the other side of the lake,
the other side of the sea,
when they left from
over there as well, Babylon is its name.[4]

However, as discussed in chapter 3, the *Theologia Indorum*'s translation into other Highland Mayan languages like Kaqchikel and Tz'utujil and its spread into the hands of many Maya political and religious leaders also makes the approach taken to it in the K'iche' *títulos* possible beyond the K'iche' area. With Reynoso's time and study in the colonial capital of Guatemala, where he most likely met and worked with Prior Domingo de Vico, his Highland Maya approach to reading the *Theologia Indorum* may have been closely (if not also personally) attached to the writing and spreading of the text beyond the K'iche' territory. The Kaqchikel Maya mention

Vico by name as a "great teacher," or *nima ajtij*, in the *Xajil Chronicle*. And in the "Origins and Lands of the Xpantzay," the first document of the *Xpantzay Cartulary*, possibly dating as early as 1552 (the same year Vico may have helped to complete the songs recently found in Kislak 1015 that are possibly an antecedent to the first volume of the *Theologia Indorum*), this *Xpantzay* document states:

> Oj ajawa' wa'e' qatitulo ri kipetik qati't qamama' ri toq xepe chi q'equm, chi aq'a'. Oj ri', oj riy, oj rumam Abraham, Isaac, Jacob ke'uchex; oj na wi pe ajIsrael; oj ri xk'oje' qati't qamama' chi ri' Canaan chupam ri jo'om ulew chi re Abraham rumal Dios, nimajaw. Xawi k'a oj ri xojk'oje' chi ri' Babilonia, ri xb'an wi nimajay, nimatz'aq ruma ronojel winaq. Xnik'ajar aq'anej kaj rutza'm ri tz'aq kuma ronojel winaq. Xa k'ak'a' jun oq kich'ab'al chi nima konojel. Ri toq xepaxin ki', ri q'eqal xeb'e je chi kochoch xewar. Xcha k'a Dios, nimajaw, "Xax kiwach wi', xax kik'ojlem wi ri [kal]k'wal ri Atan. Xax je wi ajmak. Utz xa t'injalk'atij kich'ab'al, k'iya molaj kich'ab'äl tux xcha k'a Dios, nimajaw, chi ke. Ri toq xujalk'atij kich'ab'al. Qitzij k'iya molaj kich'ab'al xux ja ok xek'ulu ki k'o chi kaq'ayan. Mani chi k'a tikak'axaj kich'ab'al chi kib'il ki'; ri toq xkiq'ijala' ki'. Xa keb'ereloj chik chi kib'il ki'. Ke re' k'a toq xepaxin ki', xeb'e konojel xekaj. Xb'e kina'oj je chik kijuyub'al kitaq'ajal, toq kipetik k'a qati't qamama', toq k'ulik k'a nik'aj palow. Xe nimajayin k'a chi ri', je k'a molan, k'oj kitrompeta, k'oj kicheremiyas, k'oj kiplaute, kixul, kib'ix, je molan xenimajayin chi ri'. Ja k'a toq xeyakataj pe, ke re' k'a rub'inatisaxik kan kumal ri nik'aj palow Wuqu' Pek, Wuqu' Siwan, rikim Tulan, rajsik Tulan," xecha chi re.
>
> We are the lords and this is our land deed of the arrival of our grandmothers and our grandfathers when they came from blackness and from night. We are the ones, we are the grandchildren of the women and the men of Abraham, Isaac, and Jacob as they are called. We are the ones from the Israelites. We are the ones who had our grandmothers and our grandfathers over there in Canaan, within the promised land to Abraham by God, the great lord. Only then we who existed over there in Babylonia, where was made the large house, the large building by all the people. It ascended up among the sky, the tip of the building, by all the people. Only was there scarcely then one language among the great lot of them all. Then they spread out into darkness, they went then to their homes, and they slept. Then spoke God, the great lord, "Only this is their image, only this is their essence, the children of Adam. They are only sinners. It is good that only I divide up their language, that their language becomes many groups," thus said God, the great lord, to them. Then [God] divided up their languages. Truly, their language became many groups when they suffered and there was their spoilage. Never again then are their languages understood as they speak to each other, as when they communicated with each other. In speaking to each other now they only go sounding frayed. Like that then they divided up among themselves, they went, everyone under the sky, they went so they would know again their mountains and their plains, when

> comes then our grandmothers and our grandfathers, when arriving then from across the sea. They were a great household then over there, thus then together there were their trumpets, their chirimiyas,[5] their flutes, their recorders,[6] and their songs thus together as a great household over there. But then they rose up to come like that then to what was named by them as: the side of the sea, the Seven Caves and the Seven Ravines, under[7] Tulan and above Tulan, as they spoke of it.[8]

While this famous Kaqchikel text does not use Vico's K'iche' phrase for God—*Tz'aqol, B'itol, nimajaw*—it does use his alternative phrase, which appears in the Kaqchikel version of the *Theologia Indorum*—*Dios, nimajaw* rather than the Francinscan *nimajawal Dios*, which tends to be more common in writings in Kaqchikel. As also seen in the *Title of Totonicapán* but evident in the *Theologia Indorum*, this use of Vico's Maya term for the divine occurs in this passage along with the grafting of Kaqchikel noble genealogy onto the "major names" and events of ancient Israel, which the authors most likely also acquired via the *Theologia Indorum*.

One could argue that, despite the close similarities, these references to and uses of Hispano-Catholic material in late contemporaneous Highland Maya religious writing does not necessarily mean a direct relation with or response to the *Theologia Indoru*, or even indirectly via the *Title of Totonicapán*, as none of them mentions Vico's theology. Thus, one other piece of evidence is necessary to conclude that the Highland Maya were not only responding to Hispano-Catholicism in general but specifically with and to the *Theologia Indorum*. The 1592 Western K'iche' *Title of the Tamub' III* (also known as the *Title of Pedro Velasco*) presents similar information as the other Maya texts but explicitly mentions its source as Vico, filling in a citation left blank:

1 wae uxenabal
2   uticaribal kaxenabalic
3 xojpe
4   paraixo terrenal
5   xa rumal uloic awas tulul rumal e wa
6 chila paraixo terenal
7   ta xojokotax ulok'
8   paraixo terenal
9 ta xepetic ri
10   k'anabe chuch
11   k'anabe kajaw
12 e sanolic

13 e puch
14 k'atit
15 kamam
16 xpe k'ij
17 xpe sak'
18 oj umam
19 oj ucajol atan
20 oj umam
21 xacab
22 moysen
23 abbrajan
24 ixac
25 xacopb
26 xa rumal xquisach..
27 usuculiquil Santo
28 wuj santo..
29 uloio co wi nabe wuj
30 co wi quitsij e propeta
31 moysen
32 ajbrajan
33 ixac
34 xacapb
35 intorum ubi nabe wuj
36 c'o wi quica'ajolaxic
37 k'amam
38 k'ak'ajaw ta xeopon babilonio
39 ri k'anabe chuch
40 k'ak'ajaw xeopon babilonio ubi tinamit

1 This is the tapping and
2 the sprouting of our ancestors.
3 We came
4 from the Earthly Paradise
5 because the prohibited sapote fruit was eaten by them,
6 over there in the Earthly Paradise.
7 Then we were thrown out

of the Earthly Paradise.
Then came from there
our first mother and
our first father,
they were naked and
they were
our grandmother and
our grandfather
since the sun and
since the dawn.
We are the grandsons and
we are the sons of Adam;
we are the grandsons
of Jacob,
Moses,
Abraham,
Isaac, and
Jacob
because they [the first grandparents] lost
the holy rectitude of
the holy book,
where there is the first book, and
where there are the words of the prophets
Moses,
Abraham,
Isaac, and
Jacob.
[The *Theologia*] *Indorum* was the name of the first book
where there is the history
of our grandfathers and
fathers who then arrived at Babylon.
Our first mothers and
fathers arrived at Babylon, the city's name.[9]

Therefore, other Highland Maya texts from the mid- to late-sixteenth century written after the *Title of Totonicapán* also appear to take the same approach to Vico's theology as Reynoso, especially if they are *títulos* on which Reynoso may have had some direct influence.

As *títulos*, these texts seem to emerge as community documents, written if not also signed by local or regional K'iche' elites. For ethnohistorians, these perspectives from local historical vantages on roughly contemporaneous events and K'iche' sociopolitical history and myth are of particular value because they emerge from both groups favorable to the former Kaweqib' rulers of Q'umarkaj as well as also from Tamub', Ilokab', and allies of dissenting Kaweqib' elites within the former K'iche' confederacy. Unfortunately, very little additional information exists regarding the specifics of these authors and their motives. Read as local theologies, however, these various *títulos* illustrate how K'iche' elites—like Reynoso as argued in the previous chapter—neither simply resisted Vico's theology nor merely surrendered to Hispano-Catholicism in general. Furthermore, these Highland Maya texts help illustrate the enduring influence of both Vico's theology and the initial approach to it by elites like Reynoso. To the extent that this intertextuality is an instantiation of dialogicality in the surviving paper trail—and dialogically entextualizes theology as metadiscourse or second-order reflection on the religious life—the intertextuality between these specific documents' claims on a people's construal of a divine agency, place in the cosmos, and responsiveness to others is theological. This is of particular significance for the intertextual and comparative analysis between the *Theologia Indorum* and the *Title of Totonicapán* in chapter 7 and in this chapter, as well as with the Popol Wuj, discussed in chapters 5 and 6. Whereas neither the *Title of Totonicapán* nor the Popol Wuj explicitly cites Vico or his theology by name, enough of these small and later K'iche'an texts do provide evidence of Vico's voice within these texts as highland local theologies.

This is not to say, however, that Highland Maya elite were either beholden to Diego Reynoso personally or wed to the *Title of Totonicapán* for the continued use of this Iberian genre in their furthered attempts to reconcile a traditional Maya worldview with a history from Hispano-Catholicism. For example, the 1592 *Title of the Ilokab'* echoes many of the biblical genealogies from the *Theologia Indorum* that are also later redacted in the *Title of Totonicapán* as the Ilokab' title's author, Juan Álvarez, claims that he is

retal ztayul
ecum
tepepul
ilocab
k'ucumaz
xepe tulan

7 chila chak'a cho
8 chak'a palo
9 oj ralcwal xacob
10 moysen
11 ta xojpe pablionio
12 ixraeletos oj
13 cut ucajol xacob

1 the sign of Iztayul,
2 Tekum,
3 Tepepul,
4 the Ilokab', and
5 the Plumed Serpent
6 who came from Tulan,
7 from over there on the other side of the lake,
8 the other side of the sea.
9 We were the children of Jacob and
10 Moses
11 when we came from Babylon.[10]
12 We were Israelites and
13 thus sons of Jacob.[11]

After this grafting of the noble K'iche' lineage onto that of the patriarchs of the Catholic Old Testament and conflating Tulan and Babylon, Álvarez, like Reynoso before him, proceeded with his own redaction of biblical narratives about Abraham, the flood, Sodom and Gomorrah, Lot, Jacob, Moses, Joshua, and the Egyptians.[12]

This late *título* illustrates the enduring influence of Vico's work and the approach by Reynoso toward the *Theologia Indorum* in his *Title of Totonicapán* understood as a theological text. Later K'iche' author-redactors continued not only to write in a colonial Spanish genre but also independently used Catholic source materials on their own terms, as Reynoso had, but not necessarily in the same way. For example, the redaction or editing of the biblical narratives in the *Title of the Ilokab'* is not as extensive as that of the *Title of Totonicapán* but it is more extensive than most of the other *títulos*. However, this particular summation of biblical names and stories in the *Title of the Ilokab'* is obviously not a mere copy from the *Title of Totonicapán* but rather another unique editing by K'iche' elites. Specifically, whereas the *Title of Totonicapán*'s biblical summary corresponds to the chronological order found in both the Catholic Old Testament and Vico's *Theologia Indorum*, the summary in the *Title of the Ilokab'* is alinear and thus shares a narrative characteristic more akin to the layered or looping chronological order of events in the Popol Wuj or the final summary chapter of the first volume of the *Theologia Indorum*. Furthermore, by page 6 of the *Title of the Ilokab'*, Álvarez mentions additional themes like *santismisa trinitat* ("Holy Trinity") from other chapters from the first volume of the *Theologia Indorum* absent in the *Title of Totonicapán*—namely chapter 24—or possibly even from the doctrinal material from the second part of the *Theologia Indorum*, which Reynoso may not have had access to when he wrote the *Title of Totonicapán*.[13]

Finally, like its close 1592 contemporary—the *Title of the Tamub' III*—as mentioned earlier in chapter 3 of this volume, the *Title of the Ilokab'* is the only other Maya text that explicitly cites the *Theologia Indorum* as one of its principal mendicant sources. Curiously, though, it does not mention Domingo de Vico by name but rather lists the secular bishop of Guatemala, Marroquín, and the Franciscan missionaries who arrived a few years after the Spanish *conquistadores* in early 1524. Among these later Franciscans to arrive was Friar Pedro de Betanzos, O.F.M., who wrote a K'iche' grammar, lexicon, and catechism and was opposed to the K'iche' term *k'ab'awil* for "God" that was proposed by Dominicans.[14] As discussed, Vico's use of *k'ab'awil* in volume one of his *Theologia Indorum* distinguished him from Marroquín, Franciscans, and some of his fellow Dominicans in the polemical use of that term. Mendicants engaged in heated debates regarding their different approaches and understandings of language, culture, and theology, such as the appropriateness of the term *k'ab'awil* for "divinity," "idol," or simply "effigy." A later *título* like the *Title of the Ilokab'* appears to continue to engage in an increasing variety of Highland Maya materials (e.g., previous *títulos* like the *Title of Totonicapán* and the Popol Wuj narratives and style) as well as later Dominican (e.g., the second volume of Vico's *Theologia Indorum*) and Franciscan materials. In these respects, later *títulos* like the *Title of the Ilokab'* illustrate the fact that, as the engagement between Hispano-Catholicism and the K'iche' continued past the generation of Vico and Reynoso, their mutual responses, respective sources, and increased diversity of positions further developed dialogically and intertextually.

On this issue in particular, Álvarez's *título* differs the greatest from Reynoso's, as the *Title of the Ilokab'* asserts that the Maya use of effigies, or *k'ab'awil*, in rituals did not originate in Babylon as "Tulan," the place of "true religion" according to the *Title of Totonicapán*, but rather in Egypt.[15] It thus appears to echo the increasingly dominant Franciscan understanding of *k'ab'awil* as an "idol" rather than (1) a mere "effigy," as treated by Vico, (2) an aspect of "true religion," as treated in the *Title of Totonicapán*, or (3) as defined yet differently in the Popol Wuj, as discussed below. But, Álvarez still maintains and builds off the approach used earlier by Reynoso—a classic Maya method of accumulation or augmentation rather than negation or replacement—by having the *título* genre incorporate both parts of the *Theologia Indorum* as well as other Hispanic source materials, such as later, Franciscan-influenced work.

On the other hand, implied references to or tracings of Vico's *Theologia Indorum* in the *Title of the Ilokab'* are also evident. Most notably, on page 4 of the manuscript, the *Title of the Ilokab'* uses not only the joint Spanish and K'iche' term for "God" in couplet form—*Dios, nimajaw*—but also follows up by clarifying that this God is also the "Framer and Former"—*Dios ajtz'aq, ajb'i[t]*.[16] Furthermore, like the *Title of Totonicapán*, the *Title of the Ilokab'* references many of the same units or "chapters" in the first volume of the *Theologia Indorum*, such as chapter 30, regarding the Earthly Paradise; chapter 56, pertaining to Joshua; chapter 74, on the journey from "across the sea"; and chapter 101's relationship between the Maya and the ancient Israelites.[17] However, reference to chapter 55, which tells of the destruction of Sodom and Gomorrah, does not appear in Reynoso's *título* but it does in the *Title of the Ilokab'*. Furthermore, the reference to the "Holy Trinity," and thus possibly to the more doctrinal or New Testament–oriented language of the second volume of the *Theologia Indorum*, indicates that Álvarez and later K'iche'an author-redactors still read and drew directly from mendicant theological work, yet not at the expense of the moves made by Reynoso and others beyond Vico's theology. For example, the *Title of the Ilokab'* also claims that the "holy" tree in the Earthly Paradise was the sapote tree—the same extracontextual move made initially in the *Theologia Indorum* and further in the *Title of Totonicapán*.[18]

Scholars such as René Acuña and Adrián Recinos did not have access to the first seven folios of the *Title of Totonicapán*, as Father Dionisio José Chonay considered them to consist of only a brief summary of the Old Testament from the seven days of creation through the Babylonian exile. Even later ethnohistorians, like Robert Carmack and James Mondloch, have characterized these folios as a biblical summary that appears copied or paraphrased from Vico's catechism with erroneous understandings on the part of the K'iche' author-redactors as to what Vico's theology means.[19] However, as demonstrated previously, rather than verbatim patches from Vico's theology, the authors of the *Title of Totonicapán* wrote their own redaction of biblical history, using Vico's *Theologia Indorum* as a primary source, just as he used their cosmogonic narratives for one of his sources. In this respect, having to read as well as understand enough of the *Theologia Indorum* to select what they considered to be of importance, the K'iche' writers of the *Title of Totonicapán* can be seen as authoring their own edited version of Vico's theology.

Furthermore, the seventh folio of the *Title of Totonicapán* provides a transition wherein the K'iche' authors rearticulate Vico's later Pauline argument (chapter 25 of the first volume of the *Theologia Indorum*) while simultaneously resisting it and adding nuance.[20] Affirming that they are human beings originally created by

God, the Framer and Former (*Tz'aqol B'itol*) in the "Earthly Paradise" and thus are descendants of "Saint Moses" as Israelites, they assert that the Maya belief of the Hero Twins, Jun Ajpu and Xb'alankej as the Sun and the Moon, respectively, is an untruth.[21] In this regard, Reynoso and other Western K'iche' elite agree with Vico's appropriated use of a K'iche' couplet for "God" as well as a literal understanding of traditional Maya texts, namely cosmogonic narratives. However, while these Maya authors do predominately use Vico's name for God, *Tz'aqol B'itol*, the authors of the *Title of Totonicapán* not only use other names but also employ the dual-gendered title *chuchqajaw* ("mother–father") over and against the Christian "Father."[22] While Vico does explicitly maintain the Maya notion of gender complementarity implicit in the couplet *Tz'aqol B'itol* by declaring God another Maya couplet—"our mother and our father" (*qachuch, qaqajaw*)—Vico does not use the compound word *chuchqajaw*, which now also refers to K'iche' spiritual guides and Maya ritual specialists. Finally, folio 7 ends with the authors of the *Title of Totonicapán* locating the lord Nakxit, who bestows royal titles on the first line of K'iche' rulers, not in the eastern Honduras city of Copán, as a "Tulan" (as implied in the Popol Wuj), but rather in Babylon, where they claim that their noble lineage began with "true religion."

The eighth folio of the *Title of Totonicapán* drops all biblical references and direct influence of the *Theologia Indorum* in order instead to rearticulate parts of the creation story and history of K'iche' nobility that are found in the Popol Wuj. While the use of *Tz'aqol B'itol* is not dropped, by folio 18 other names for God, if not other gods, such as *Tojil* and *Uk'u'x Kaj, Uk'u'x Ulew* (Heart of Sky, Heart of Earth), are put forward specifically in reference to Nakxit's prayer.[23] In this respect, K'iche' sociopolitical and religious leaders, through their appropriation of a genre originally designed as a legal appeal to the Spanish Crown regarding land ownership, refute Vico's equation of the Christian god of the Bible with the Maya understanding of divinity. On one hand, they agree with Vico that God is like *Tz'aqol B'itol* but, on the other hand, God is not limited to *Tz'aqol B'itol*. Vico uses his ethnographic and linguistic research to construct analogical or commensurate meanings between Hispano-Catholic and K'iche'an cultural concepts and images, but also univocal or synonymous understandings of *Tz'aqol B'itol* as the same as the God of the Bible. K'iche' Maya intellectuals argue back for an analogical or commensurate construal of God from the basis of a more univocal or equating understanding between Maya and biblical migration narratives. Whereas Vico argues for an equivalent or univocal understanding of *Tz'aqol B'itol* as God, K'iche' Maya intellectuals argue back for an analogical understanding. The result is a documented exchange between at least two linguistically, culturally, and religiously distinct groups drawing from each other's source materials to reflect upon, translate, and negotiate ideas about the divine and how to speak of it—theology (*theos-logia*).

A RECEPTION ETHNOHISTORY OF A CHRISTIANITY

Placed chronologically in order to compose a larger, jointly authored intertextual corpus written in K'iche'an languages, the early mendicant and Highland Maya literature provides a reception history of a Christianity, namely Hispano-Catholicism, from a highly local indigenous perspective that nuances if not counterbalances the dominant transmission histories derived exclusively from Eurocentric sources. As charted in figure 8.1, the *Theologia Indorum* specifically played a highly influential role in the reception of Hispano-Catholicism among Highland Maya elites, especially as they assumed autonomous interpretive license with Vico's text. While other mendicant materials also undoubtedly contributed to the configuration of Christianity for, among, and by the Maya, the *Theologia Indorum* leaves the most noticeable footprint in the highlands. However, as evidenced in the explicit and implicit theological statements that Highland Maya elites wrote among themselves, Vico's work, including his cross-cultural theological method, helped to foster the production of the first indigenous Christianities in the Americas.

Therefore, by taking into account all of earliest documents written in Highland Mayan languages by both K'iche'an elites and mendicant missionaries, there can begin to be constructed a flow of events to more clearly determine who pulled from and responded to whom. Based on archaeological evidence as well as the ethnohistorical sources, there was a common, related, but highly varied pool of religious narratives shared within the Maya region from at least the preclassic era in the third century BCE. The arrival of Franciscans and Dominicans and their new training in humanism and scholasticism introduced ecclesial genres from Europe as well as the production of texts in indigenous languages in an alphabet by the 1540s. This encounter with Iberians also introduced distinct legal genres by not only religious but also political and social elites. Vico's *Theologia Indorum* as a *summa* or theological compendium introduced a new genre that allowed Vico to draw together his and other mendicants' previous linguistic, ethnographic, and doctrinal works (as shown by the thin solid arrow pointing from "mendicant texts" to "*Theologia Indorum*, I" in figure 8.1) as well as, particularly in the first volume, the prehispanic religious material specifically from the Maya highlands (as shown by the thin dash-dot-dash arrow extending from "precontact Maya source material" to "*Theologia Indorum*, I" in figure 8.1) to present a Catholic Maya theology on Maya terms.

One year after the completion of the first volume of the *Theologia Indorum*, K'iche' Maya elites of the prehispanic ruling class began to compile and write down in the missionary script their version of the prehispanic religious, social, and political worldview (as shown by the thick solid arrow extending from "precontact Maya source material" to "Popol Wuj" in figure 8.1) to become the Popol Wuj as, in part, an indirect response to Vico's text (as shown by the small-dotted arrow extending from "*Theologia Indorum*, I" to "Popol Wuj" in figure 8.1), with only the final portion, if any, of the Popol Wuj borrowing only slightly from the Mayanized land-deed genre (as shown by the small-dotted arrow extending from "Iberian notarial texts" to "Popol Wuj" in figure 8.1). That same year (1554), K'iche' who worked with Vico wrote the *Title of Totonicapán* as their own account of prehispanic myths and political history in which they drew from both the first volume of the *Theologia Indorum* and the Maya material also found in the Popol Wuj that they agreed with (as shown respectively by the thick dot-dot-dash arrow extending from "*Theologia Indorum*, I" to "*Title of Totonicapán*," and the short, dashed arrow extending to the same box from "Iberian notarial texts" in figure 8.1). Their text, however, explicitly took the form of a legal land claim and title (as represented by the very short arrow from "*Title of Totonicapán*" to "30+ K'iche'an notarial texts" in figure 8.1).

Over the course of the next few decades other Highland Maya documents were produced, all taking the form of colonial legal genres but being intended primarily for local Maya use. A few drew upon the strategy of the *Title of Totonicapán* directly, if not also from the Popol Wuj and the *Theologia Indorum*. By the final epidemics through the Maya highlands by the turn of the seventeenth century, this indigenous paper trail decreased but did not completely end. Instead, the Highland Maya documents written primarily for a Maya audience generally shifted in terms of their use as notarial genres. As ethnohistorian Owen Jones has argued, there was a shift away from *títulos* and toward an increase of wills by the late seventeenth and eighteenth centuries, and a change in the hyperlocal issues addressed also occurred.[24] While still in many respects community documents, as a genre, wills focused more on individual holdings, the dispersal of those items after one's death, and securing prayers and a mass for one's soul, in contrast to the narrative history and description of a community's land in a *título*.[25] However, few major translocal texts were written by the Highland Maya again until the 1970s. And, Dominican and Franciscan literature in Highland Mayan languages of Guatemala further developed the ecclesial genres while also continuing to use the *Theologia Indorum*.

For example, while most likely not begun by Vico, the *Coplas*, or hymns, in Q'eqchi' Maya attributed to his early Dominican contemporary Luis de Cáncer show either a shared theological hermeneutic with Vico—an early *Salmanticense*-influenced but notably Mesoamerican Dominican school—or it bears the strong influence of his *Theologia Indorum*. This is further confirmed in the recently discovered K'iche' version of the *Coplas* found embedded within Kislak 1015 that, unlike the Q'eqchi' version of the *Coplas*, shares more discursive features with the *Theologia Indorum*, namely use of Maya poetics and theogonic names.[26] At the least, some of the rhetorical and conceptual commonalities between Vico's theology with the *Coplas*, and also with later texts like sermons in the eastern and southern highlands

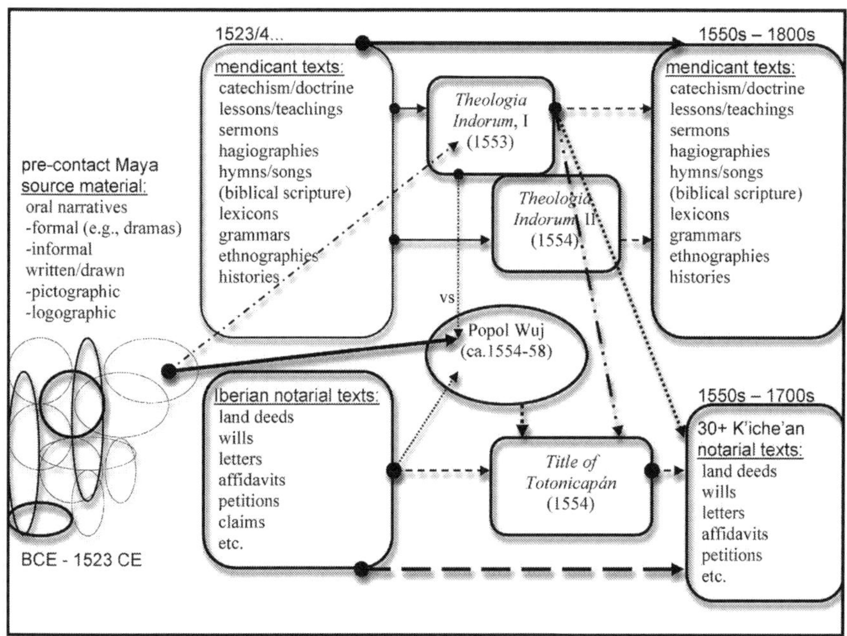

FIGURE 8.1. A Maya and mendicant intertextual reception history.

among the Q'eqchi' and Kaqchikel, mark spheres of influence in contrast to that of the *Title of the K'oyoy* in the far western highlands, as discussed in the prior chapter. Furthermore, handwritten copies of the *Theologia Indorum* continued to be made, most likely by Maya parish caretakers or *fiscales*. Finally, according to some colonial mendicant sources, the *Theologia Indorum* was used not only by local priests but also independently by local Maya into the 1700s.

THE MORLEY MANUSCRIPT: CONTRAST WITH FRANCISCAN YUKATEK NOMINALISM

As a brief contrast to the adaptation by Diego Reynoso and other Highland Maya elites of Vico's Dominican theology in the *Title of Totonicapán*, the Morley manuscript provides an insight into the translation, contextualization, and adaptation of Observant Franciscan theology by literate Lowland Maya. Named after the famous twentieth-century Mayanist Sylvanus Morley who bequeathed it to the Museum of New Mexico, the surviving manuscript copy dates to the latter half of the eighteenth century, 1760–1780, but the content and composition of much of the text appear to correspond to around the only date appearing within the document, 1576.[27] Similar to the *Title of Totonicapán*, which combined redactions of the first volume of the *Theologia Indorum* with the genealogical section of the Popol Wuj and is thus understood as a midpoint between translated Catholic doctrinal or devotional texts imported from Europe and the later autochthonous seventeenth- and eighteenth-century Maya *Books of Chilam Balam*,[28] the Morley document, written in a single hand, consists of three sections in Yukatek Maya, two of which drew upon notable Spanish sources from the sixteenth and seventeenth centuries. More specifically, pages 22–70 of the first section of the manuscript is a Yukatek translation of *Las preguntas que el emperador Adriano hizo al infante Epitus*, a book of popular Catholic doctrine as riddles that was published in Burgos, Spain, in 1540 but was eventually condemned by the Spanish Inquisition in 1559.[29] Most likely, the initial text of the Morley manuscript was longer, since the first twenty-one pages of the manuscript are missing and page 22 begins in midsentence.[30] Broken into two parts, the second and final part of the manuscript, consisting of pages 234–346, contains an incomplete copy of a catechism and hagiographic material written in Yukatek in 1620 by Franciscan friar Juan Coronel—the *Discursos Predicables*—which drew upon Gregory the Great's *Dialogues*, Jacobus de Voragine's *The Golden Legend* (particularly its Spanish translation *Flos sanctorum*), and Clemente Sánchez de Vercial's *The Book of Tales by A.B.C.*[31] The heavy reliance on these identifiable European sources helps to confirm the extent to which the manuscript's content is an early postcontact Lowland Maya text and a late but still comparable contemporary with the Highland Maya corpus, such as the *Title of Totonicapán*.

However, manuscript pages 70–213 in the first part consists of material not readily identifiable in previous Spanish-authored sources and includes use of indigenous Mesoamerican religious references more akin to what is found in the *Theologia Indorum* and *Title of Totonicapán*. And while the Morley manuscript does not in general share the same Maya poetic style with *Title of Totonicapán* or *Theologia Indorum*, like the beginning of the *Theologia Indorum* it does directly address its Maya readers by strategically using a Mayan language as the primary means to translate Catholic thought. Specifically, on manuscript page 149, the section identified as "On Holy Scripture," the author of the Morley manuscript states that

> these things only are recorded here, so you mourn for the true, only son of God the ruler, that is Christ, that you may earn eternal life in His blessed name, by taking that to hear. This Christian wisdom that we will give and we will translate into your Mayan language, you who are Maya [people] here, is in order that you come to know the one-ness of God, that you worship, you serve, and you love Him most above everything.[32]

Likewise, as previously examined, decades earlier Vico wrote in the first page of his *Theologia Indorum*:

1 Wa'e nimawuj ri *Theologia Indorum* ub'ina'am
2 nima'eta'mab'al
3 utzijoxik
4 Dios,
5 nimajaw,
6 uq'alajob'isaxik
7 uk'oje'ik
8 ronojel ub'anoj Dios
9 uk'utunisaxik naypuch
10 ronojel nimab'i'j k'o
11 chi upam uch'ab'al Dios
12 uk'utunisaxik naypuch
13 chajawaxik
14 cheta'maxik
15 rumal utzilaj taq winaq christianos uk'oje'ik
16 chi upam K'iche' ch'ab'al tzib'am wi.
17 Wa'e k'astajib'al wach,
18 k'astajib'al pa uk'u'x
19 chi rech utzilaj winaq

1 This is the great book which is called the *Theologia Indorum*,
2 a great knowledge
3 and discourse
4 about God,
5 the great lord,
6 and a clarification
7 of the existence of and
8 all of the acts of God,
9 as well as a demonstration of
10 all of the great name that there is
11 within the language of God,
12 as well as a demonstration of
13 what shall be necessary and

what shall be known
by good Christian people who exist
as it is written here in the K'iche' language.
This is the means to revive the self and
the means to revive also the heart
of the good people[33]

While not directly influenced by Vico's theological tome, the voice of the Morley manuscript, at least in this section, by referring to the Yukatek language in the second-person—"your Mayan language"—grounds its source in Spanish clergy speaking to Maya parishioners.

At the same time, the language throughout the whole Yukatek manuscript consistently expresses more of a Franciscan nominalist translation strategy than a Dominican realist approach. For example, and most notably, the Yukatek Maya author-translator consistently uses the Spanish term *Dios* to refer to the god of Catholicism and only modifies the term when explaining the Trinity or the role of cosmic creator or ruler along literal rather than analogical lines, such as *Dios yumbil = Dios mehenbil. Dios espiritu Santo* ("God the Father, God the Son, God the Holy Spirit"), *Dios ah chaabtah = ah sihsah = ti caanob* ("God the creator, the birth giver, for the heavens"), and *ah tepal. U sihsah babalil. tulacal* ("the ruler, the creator of all things").[34] Unlike in the *Theologia Indorum* or *Title of Totonicapán*, *Dios* is not joined with an analogous Maya term and constructed into a couplet such as *Dios, nimajaw* let alone loan indigenous terms like *Tz'aqol B'itol* (Framer and Former) or *Alom K'ajalom* (Bearer and Begetter). Furthermore, like Franciscans in Guatemala, loaded terms related to the Trinitarian grammar such as "Holy Spirit" and "person" that would be problematic to translate literally are retained in Spanish rather than using the local Lowland Maya term for "person," *uinic*, as Vico did with the K'iche'an term *winaq*. Finally, unlike Franciscans in Guatemala who eventually Mayanized *Dios* into *Tyox*, even the orthography is strictly maintained throughout even this later copy of the Morley manuscript.

However, variation, especially as adaption and accommodation, though, does occur within the text and particularly in the bulk of the first part, pages 70–213, which do not appear as mere translation of a previously written Spanish or Latin text. For example, the Spanish and Latin word *persona* appears in the translated section of *Las preguntas*—such as *oxtul persona = huntuli* ("three persons in one")—but, similar to what Franciscans do with the term in Kaqchikel (*rupersonail*), it is subtly inflected as if it were a Yukatek word, such as *personasile*, *personayl*, and *personaob* (for "persons" rather than *personas* or *personae*).[35] And it is in these sections of the Morley manuscript where significant variation and modification of Hispano-Catholic material appears, which indicates more than a mere copyist at work, but rather display further contextualization by a Maya authorial hand, for other Maya.

In contrast to that in the first section of the first part, in manuscript pages 22–70, based on *Las preguntas* and the second part based on *Discursos*, in manuscript pages 234–346, the voice in these later sections of the first part also uses direct address to its readership similar to the style of the *Theologia Indorum*, sixteenth-century Highland Maya texts like the *Xajil Chronicle*, and later Lowland Maya texts like some of the *Books of Chilam Balam*. For this reason, it is thought that this section might consist of sermons translated and adapted or even written by a Yukatek pastoral assistant.[36] However, just as the various parts of the *Theologia Indorum* have been mistakenly catalogued as a collection of sermons or *sermonario*, it is also possible that the Yukatek author simply employed a classic Maya voice used in traditional ceremonial and moral discourse, just like Vico also aimed to employ in his *Theologia Indorum* a Maya authorial voice traditional to a precolumbian indigenous noble class and as also found in later Yukatek works like the *Book of Chilam Balam of Chumayel*.[37] Furthermore, in this regard, the correspondences between these later sections of the first part of the Morley manuscript and the first half of the first volume of the *Theologia Indorum* are striking (see table 8.1). Much of this material rearticulates portions of the cosmogonic narratives of the Judeo-Christian Book of Genesis, but additional, nonbiblical, later European Catholic material also appears—for example, the four basic elements of creation: air, fire, earth, and water appropriated from classic Hellenistic thought.[38]

However, upon closer intertextual comparison, further differences in the content in these sections and the *Theologia Indorum* stand out. For example, the Morley manuscript and correspondingly the Yukatek *Book of Chilam Balam of Ixil* describe the created order of the cosmos in eleven layers, whereas the *Theologia Indorum* and correspondingly the *Title of Totonicapán* present a nine-layered order of the heavens.[39] In contrast, as a rearticulation of the prehispanic Maya worldview, the Popol Wuj does not describe a stratified cosmic hierarchy beyond the world of the "surface of the earth," or *uwach ulew*, and the otherworld of Xib'alb'a, which can relate to both the celestial sky at night and an underworld during the day. Again, this difference between these trajectories of translating and adapting Hispano-Catholicism stem from and highlight the distinction between Franciscan and Dominican sources, in addition to their respective translation theories. The Morley manuscript most likely was influenced by Voragine's *The Golden Legend* and Gonzalo de Berceo's Spanish rhymed version in general and specifically Pedro de Medina's 1561 *Suma de cosmographía de Sevilla*, regarding the eleven layers of the cosmos, whereas the *Title of Totonicapán* was more influenced by the nine orders of heaven and angels as found in the *Summa theologiae*'s use of Pseudo-Dionysius the Areopagite but by means of Vico's *Theologia Indorum*.[40] Finally, the frequent name-dropping of major Christian writers such as Augustine of Hippo and John of Damascus and proof-texting references to New Testament verses without exposition in the Morley manuscript also indicate reliance on mendicant liturgical texts such as a breviary or missal, both of which were hybridic *vade mecum*, or portable "go with me" genres, highly popular among peripatetic clergy, given their small size but also the focus of debates and subject to much revision during the sixteenth century Reformations. The Morley manuscript refers explicitly to the *kulem Dzib* ("Holy Scripture") to ground its authority, whereas the *Theologia Indorum* makes no explicit references to the Bible but only to what the Catholic god has said and done as taught by the clergy and summarized in the *Theologia Indorum*. Later K'iche'an texts, like the *Title of Totonicapán*, rooted their authority in the *Theologia Indorum* as *utzij Dios* ("truth about God" or "words about God") as well as the *ojer tzij* ("ancient truth" or "ancient word") of their Maya ancestors.

The modifications, therefore, in the Morley manuscript of Catholic interpretations of biblical stories are not the same as those found in the *Title of Totonicapán* but are no less significant. For example, the Morley manuscript does not Mayanize the two forbidden trees in *Parayso Terenal* ("Earthly Paradise"), as the *Theologia Indorum*, the *Title of Totonicapán*, and other later Highland Maya texts do, when declaring them sapote trees. But the Morley manuscript does change them to be only one tree, rather than two, and declares them to be "[God's] tree of grace, life, and peace of mind" (*U cheel gracia = cuxtal = yt. toh olal =*).[41] However, the Morley manuscript further elaborates that the result of eating its fruit brought "great wisdom . . . vision will reach everywhere . . . [Eve and Adam] will become like God."[42] This version of creation of the first true human beings echoes less of Genesis and more of the ancient Maya cosmogonic story as written beginning in 1554 in the Popol Wuj, where the creator gods worry about their creatures-of-corn's ability of sight and proclaim:

1 Xa ta naqaj chopon wi kimuqub'al.
2 Xa ta sqaqi'n uwach, uwach ulew chikilo.
3 Mawi utz ri kakib'ij.
4 Mawi pa xa tz'aq, xa b'it, kib'i'?
5 . . . Xa qayojo chi sqaqi'n chik,
6 k'o chi karaj.
7 Mawi utz kaqana'o.
8 Xa pa xchijunamataj kib'anoj quk',

TABLE 8.1. Comparison between the *Theologia Indorum* and the Morley manuscript

Morley Manuscript (ca. 1576)	*Theologia Indorum, Volume I (1553)*
On Confession (pp. 70–100)	in the fourth major theme: chapter 45
15 Signs before Final Judgment (pp. 101–106)	[not in *Theologia Indorum*, vol. I]
True and False Wisdom (pp. 106–125)	proemium
Hun Ahau as Lucifer (pp. 125–129)	[not in *Theologia Indorum* (chapters 27–28)]*
On Holy Scripture (pp. 129–150)	[not in *Theologia Indorum* (chapter 20)]†
God as One and Three (pp. 151–164)	in the second major theme: chapter 24 (and 23)
God as Creator (pp. 164–169)	in the first major theme: chapters 1–3
The Descendants of Adam (pp. 169–174)	in the sixth major theme: chapter 47 (49–105)
About the Creation of Eve (pp. 174–175)	in the fifth major theme: chapters 31, 34 (32–33)
About the Heavens (pp. 178–189)	in the third major theme: chapter 29 (and 26–28)
About the Earthly Paradise (pp. 194–195)	in the fourth major theme: chapter 30
About the Creation of Adam (pp. 195–198)	in the fifth major theme: chapters 31 (32–33)
About Eve's Fall (pp. 199–213)	in the fifth major theme: chapters 38, 39 (35–37, 40)

Sources: Whalen (2003, 42–170); BnF Ms Amér 5; APS Ms; and BnF Ms Amér 10.

* There are no distinct chapters exclusively dedicated to Lucifer but rather chapters that recite Christian folklore, such as these, about the celestial heirarchy and war in heaven, as well as later chapters that conflat him with the serpent in the garden with Eve and Adam.

† While not about the Bible, chapter 20 of volume one is about God's "Book of Life" as a version of Aquinas's *Summa theologiae* (Ia, q. 24).

9 ri najt kopon wi keta'mab'al,
10 kilon ronojel.

1 [What humans see] should only be what comes about closely, and
2 they should only see superficially on the face of the earth.
3 Since it is not good what they say [about having near-infinite sight];
4 Since are they not just "framed" and "formed," as they are called?
5 . . . We should then just decompose them a bit,
6 that is what is desired.
7 Since it is not good what we discovered,
8 since their deeds could become equal with ours,
9 and their knowledge arriving too far,
10 and they would see everything.[43]

The concern, therefore, in the Morley manuscript, like that in the Popol Wuj—but unlike that in Genesis, the *Theologia Indorum*, or the *Title of Totonicapán*—was not human disobedience to the creator god but rather godlike insight and foresight among humans.

In one other notable variation in the telling of the creation of the first human beings, the Morley manuscript earlier describes in detail how "our lord God" (*Ca yumil ti dios*)

> spat in the palm of His hand, and saliva was placed on his [Adam's] mouth, and his mouth became open; and then the saliva was placed and was anointed upon his ears, both of them, and then his ears became open and his mouth became open; then he began to speak, while he gives thanks to God his creator[44]

Aside from the sharp difference between *Dios*'s use of saliva in the Morley manuscript and "the LORD God's" (YHWH 'elohim) use of breath in Genesis 2:7, the Morley manuscript here again echoes the Maya tradition also found in other autochthonous Maya texts like the Popol Wuj on two main points. First is the story of the conception of the Hero Twins—Jun Ajpu and Xb'alanke—who eventually finish setting the world and cosmic order in place for final preparation for the creation of humanity. Their fathers—Jun Junajpu and Wuqub' Junajpu—were killed by the lords of the otherworld, Xib'alb'a, who hung the severed head of Jun Junajpu in a tree, where it took the form of a large gourd. Through the saliva from Jun Junajpu's former head the brothers essentially together impregnated Xkik', a daughter of one of the lords of Xib'alb'a, by spitting into her hand, telling her that "It is just a sign I have given you, my saliva, my spittle. This is my head, [it] has nothing on it . . . After that, his son is like his saliva, his spittle, in his being, whether it be the son of a lord . . . Rather, he will leave his daughters and sons . . . Keep the word."[45] This comes around nearly full circle again at the end of the Xib'alb'a story with the Hero Twins resuscitating their fathers but now through reconstructing Wuqub' Junajpu's head. To finish the process Wuqub' Junajpu must speak all of the names of his head, such as his mouth, nose, and eyes.[46]

A second echo of Maya tradition concerns the cosmogonic stories of the Popol Wuj. The command to "keep the word," as stated by the head of Jun Junajpu, or to "give thanks to God," as stated in the Morley manuscript, appears also earlier in the Popol Wuj as arguably the only divine commandment given in the whole text. According to the Popol Wuj, the fashioning of true human beings out of maize by Xmukane was only the fourth and final attempt to create people.[47] Previously, after the first attempt, which produced birds and animals, the Maya creator gods declared that the new creatures should "Name now our names, praise us. We are your mother, we are your father. Speak now . . . speak, pray to us, keep our days." However, the creatures "just squawked, they just chattered, they just howled. It wasn't apparent what language they spoke."[48] Like the *Theologia Indorum* and *Title of Totonicapán*, The Morley manuscript clarifies from the outset that the creation of the first person by the Christian god implicitly fulfills this Maya divine command to speak, praise, and give thanks to the cosmic creator(s).[49]

This is not to say that the middle section of the Morley manuscript tries to thoroughly accommodate Hispano-Catholicism to the prehispanic Lowland Maya worldview. Like the *Title of Totonicapán* but in a distinctive way, the Morley manuscript explicitly and literally demonized the main characters of traditional Maya mythology, as the clergy did in their own writings and discourses. However, again, the distinctive influence of Franciscan and Dominican translations and adaptations of the Maya worldview emerge respectively in Lowland and Highland Maya Catholic texts. Specifically, the Morley manuscript equates the Maya legendary character Hun Ahau with Lucifer as the sign of the planet Venus.[50] The *Title of Totonicapán*, however, merely states that ancient Maya erroneously believed that the Hero Twins were the sun and the moon, a belief also affirmed as correct in the Popol Wuj.[51]

The *Title of Totonicapán* appears either to echo the *Theologia Indorum* or, possibly, to find an ambiguous compromise between Vico's treatment of the Hero Twins and the treatment later found in the Popol Wuj. Because, as Vico states in chapters 25, 27–28, 48, and 51 of the first volume of the *Theologia Indorum*, from his Catholic perspective the Hero Twins as well as other key legendary Maya figures are in hell (*infierno*), which he equates with the Maya notion of Xib'alb'a—stating, "Greatly you all were scared because, greatly before you all was this Xib'alb'a, greatly before you all was Jun Ajpu and Xb'alankej"—an understanding of Xib'alb'a not necessarily shared by the K'iche' authors of the Popol Wuj.[52] Although Jun Ajpu is in hell, according to the *Theologia Indorum*, he was thought of as the true sun of the present age by ancient Maya, according to a belief condemned in the *Title of Totonicapán* but affirmed in the Popol Wuj. Likewise, his brother Xb'alanke is the moon ("evening sun") or Venus (evening and morning star). The Morley manuscript exclusively relates Hun Ahau as the Maya version of the ancient but nonbiblical story of Lucifer as the fallen angel of light found in popular medieval European lore, like Dante's *Inferno*.[53] To this extent the Morley manuscript shared in a wider Franciscan understanding and strategy of establishing univocal relationships between indigenous Mesoamerican cosmology and Hispano-Catholic demonology, much as the Franciscan Bernardino de Sahagún who equated Lucifer with the Nahua god Tezcatlipoca. But Franciscans in Mesoamerica were in general opposed to such a univocal or analogical approach toward possible native terms for Christian theology unless justifiably limited to literal domains of signification, for example, God as the "father" or the "son" and Jesus as the "savior." In contrast, Highland Maya texts influenced by the Dominican *Theologia Indorum* more abundantly established analogical if not also univocal understandings for commensurability between Christian and non-Christian worldviews.[54]

This is not to say, however, that Franciscans did not borrow from local indigenous cultures to translate Catholicism in Europe, the Americas, and Asia. However, particularly for those Franciscans still harboring the suspicion of Thomas Aquinas's semiotic moderate realism and analogical method for developing theology, especially as further and more strictly construed by later highly influential Thomists like Thomas Cajetan's *De Nominum Analogia* (1498), the use of establishing analogical relationships between Catholic and non-Catholic religious terms, such as names for their god, was generally rejected. As ethnohistorian Mark Christensen has pointed out, the second part of the Morley manuscript, based on Coronel's *Discursos*, also contains notable uses of Maya culture, such as conveying time in the *katun*s, or the 20-year count.[55] But these are cultural and not religious concepts translated presumably by Coronel, perhaps with a Yukatek pastoral assistant.

Gretchen Whalen, modern transcriber and translator of the Morley manuscript into English, strongly speculates that the translator-redactor of the first section was Gaspar Antonio Chi Xiu, a Yukatek *maestro*—schoolmaster and pastoral assistant—to friar and later bishop of the Yucatán, Diego de Landa, O.F.M., whose fear of unorthodox Catholic teachings instigated his *auto de fé* and the burning of at least twenty-seven precolumbian Maya codices.[56] Given its early date, its use of eventually condemned Catholic material from Spain, and its unique modifications in eloquent Yukatek, the first part of the Morley manuscript was possibly one of Chi Xiu's own writings. Since neither the *Title of Totonicapán* nor the Popol Wuj came into non-Maya hands for centuries after their composition—1834 and 1973 for the former and ca. 1701 and 1851 for the latter—and since the *Theologia Indorum* was never officially condemned (either because it was never published and thus never subjected to scrutiny by the Inquisition, or never read outside of the small circle of Highland Maya and mendicants who were literate in K'iche'an languages), Reynoso and other Highland Maya authors, such as those of a native *Salmanticense* "Totonicapán school," never suffered the same end as Gaspar Antonio Chi Xiu and Lowland Maya authors.

This is not to say, however, that these respective autochthonous Maya translations of Hispano-Catholicism had limited impact. The apocalyptic millenarianism of the Observant Franciscans in the Yucatán continued to be reconfigured and contextualized in later nonecclesial Yukatek works by Yukatek scribes exclusively for Yukatek readers, such as the *Book of Chilam Balam* of Tusik, Kaua, Chan Kan, and Ixil, and the "Teabo Manuscript."[57] This was a worldview not shared generally by Dominicans or even by a majority of Franciscans in Europe, but particularly not if they had studied at the University of Salamanca, as Domingo de Vico and Bernardino de Sahagún had. Therefore, this was not a feature appropriated in either the Highland Maya texts or some of the important early Nahua texts.

CONCLUSION: GETTING OVER TRANSMISSION HISTORIES

Like the Popol Wuj, this other set of K'iche' texts more in the "Totonicapán" strand of Reynoso also seems agonistic as to whether clergy or the courts would consider their worldview "true." But unlike the Popol Wuj school of thought among Kaweq elites based in Q'umarkaj, analysis of the wider corpus of K'iche'an texts illustrates a shift away from an understanding on the part of Maya of Catholicism as merely *uch'ab'al Dios* (babel of God) toward, instead, Catholicism increasingly spoken of as *utzij Dios* (truth of God). Likewise, in concert with this shift in terminology, these same K'iche' elites, in their religious histories, also moved back the point of origin of their devotional or ritual practices with *k'ab'awil* (effigies), as dating back to a Tulan as Babylon, but then to an even more ancient time of a biblical Egypt. On one hand, whereas Vico in chapter 25 of the first volume of the *Theologia Indorum* blamed the first postcontact in the 1490s with indigenous peoples for devotion toward wood and stone effigies, these Maya authors cast their responsible ancestors far back into ancient biblical times. And, on the other hand, like the import of antiquity for their stories of the founders of the four principal lineages of the Highland Maya, making the devotional practices more ancient implicitly also makes them more authentic and more valid. They are then not construed as recent innovations, as Vico claimed, but rather part of an ancient (*ojer*) Maya tradition, which Vico also wanted to argue as once being true.

Within the history of Christianity there is no paper trail jointly authored by Christian missionaries and contemporaneous responses by local Asian Minor, Asian, African, or European population prior to the sixteenth century. This wider group of texts by Spanish mendicants together with the Highland Maya is arguably the first. What has briefly been argued for is an understanding and treatment of these writings via a dialogical appreciation. What gradually emerges is a more complex portrait of mendicants prior to the arrival of the Inquisition and the Catholic Reformation, who did not simply condemn indigenous religiosity but also tried to strategically accommodate aspects of it, and indigenous elites, who did not simply resist Iberian Catholicism but also employed the new genres and orthographies for the reconfiguration of their indigenous worldviews. However, for any of this to occur, scholars of religion need to move beyond the dyadic model of either passive acquiescence or reactionary resistance by indigenous peoples during colonialism. Only then can there begin to develop a clearer transmission history of religious ideas. A clarity enhanced by a reception ethnohistory, in turn, further augments the role and value of indigenous intellect and agency, specifically the Highland Maya but also indigenous American peoples in general.

9

Intertextuality, Hyperlocalism, and the Continued Dialogic Emergence of Theologies

China'o ta puch ik'u'x chirij ri loq'olaj wuj.
  Mixutzinik
  utz'ib'axik chupam ich'ab'al
    ix Kaqchikel winaq
    ix Rab'inaleb'
    ix Tz'utujileb'
    ix k'ut K'iche' winaq
  xax skaqin ujalq'at ich'ab'al,
  xa jun uti'ojil ich'ab'al
  xa xoloxoxinaq iwumal.

May you all think when, thus, your heart is behind the beloved book.
  It has just been quieted,
  written in your language,
    you all the Kaqchikel people,
    you all the Rab'inal,
    you all the Tz'utujil,
    you all, thus, the K'iche' people,
  only a few changes of your language,
  only one corpus of your language,
  only intertwined by you all.[1]

—From the final chapter of the *Theologia Indorum*, vol. I (February 11, 1553).

DOI: 10.5876/9781607329701.c009

> Xere k'ut uk'oje'ik K'iche' ri'
> rumal majab'i chi ilob'al re.
> K'o nab'e,
> ojer
> kumal ajawib' sachinaq chik.
>
> This was it then about the existence of the K'iche'
> because there is no longer a way to see it.
> There is the original [book],
> the ancient [book]
> by them, lords, which is now lost.[2]
>
> —CLOSING LINES OF THE POPOL WUJ (CA. 1554–CA. 1558).

> "Kiwil na ri man qilom taj,
> Kita na ri man qatom taj."
>
> "You all shall see what we have not seen,
> you all shall hear what we have not heard."
>
> —A PRESENT-DAY K'ICHE' PROVERB THAT GRANDPARENTS SAY TO THEIR GRANDCHILDREN.

The intertextual analysis between the earliest set of contemporaneous missionary and indigenous writings allows for the construction of a thicker historical context, including an ethnohistorical context. It also allows for wider studies of colonial and modern Mesoamerica, Maya, and religious movements in general in the Americas as well as histories of Christian thought, especially during the advent of early modernity. Texts by *Salmanticenses* Dominicans in Mesoamerica may be placed in a dialogical relationship with the wider diverse corpus of late medieval and early modern Christian debates, and also with the first autonomous postcontact Native American writings. This thus allows for an alignment of the dominant transmission histories side by side with reception microhistories of a Christianity. Many of these early postcontact Highland Maya texts critically and creatively reflected upon and engaged construals of religious history, cosmogony and geography, theogony, and moral or legal anthropology—from both Christian and Maya perspectives—in their various efforts to reconfigure their traditional religious world and respond to that presented by mendicants. Those texts should therefore be read as containing their hyperlocalized theologies. Neither the mendicant documents nor the early K'iche'an writings can be understood fully on their own but rather must be read intertextually. Finally, the ethnohistorical lenses by which to read the literature of this period of first contact also provides an ethnohistorical basis for understanding later and present-day Christianities in the Americas. The legacy of Vico's theology is not limited to only the late postclassic period of the Highland Maya. The reconstruction and understanding of Vico's *Theologia Indorum* may very well bear on how Highland Maya continued to think about and are still reflecting on and worshiping within their Christianity.

Like the adage regarding history, theology is also written by the victors. To this extent, the retrieval of the *Theologia Indorum* ought to have focused just as much on figures like Diego Reynoso as it did on Domingo de Vico in order to consider the transatlantic and Highland Maya milieux of its production, the strands of late medieval Hispano-Catholic humanism and scholasticism, the contemporaneous reception of the theologies, and the reconfigurations of the Maya worldview in their late postclassic period (1524–ca. 1650). Reynoso's biography, including ethnobiography, is even more difficult to cull out of the sparsely written record than that of Vico, but he seems to have been a minor author of the Popol Wuj, a major author of the *Title of Totonicapán*, a coauthor on other later Highland Maya notarial texts, a student of and influential consultant on K'iche' language, religion, and culture for Vico, and quite possibly an amanuesis on at least the first volume of the *Theologia Indorum*. While years in the making prior to their completion dates of 1553 and 1554, changes in how some key concepts are used by the second volume compared to the first volume indicate that Vico's understanding may have changed as his locale shifted between the central highlands for the western slopes of the Verapaces, across various Highland Mayan languages and communities in which he worked (many of whom harbored long antipathies between each other), and as his associations with his Maya collaborators correspondingly changed, especially after 1553.

One of the other shifts then seems to have been the departure of Reynoso from Santiago de Guatemala back to Totonicapán by 1554. As studies on later pastoral and doctrinal writing in Yukatek have noted, Franciscan clergy relied on local collaborators as language coaches and translators but also as ghost coauthors, if not full authors, of pastoral texts. The working arrangements between clergy among the Highland Maya even as early as the initial decades of first contact would most likely not have been much different. Therefore, the absence of Vico and his writings from modern histories of Latin America, Catholicism, and religion in general is matched by the rare preservation of someone like Reynoso and his writings within even the hyperlocal record given the period in the Americas in which these records were written. Militating against the survival of the records were the perennial and increasing bias against indigenous peoples from the sixteenth century through the present day, the lack of investment in archival preservation in Central America, the intentional destruction of local records, especially parochial records as a result of anticlericalism beginning in the early nineteenth century, and the genocide against the Maya during the thirty-six-year war in the late twentieth century.

And yet, it would be disingenuous to conflate Vico's voice, agenda, worldview, and translation of his Hispano-Catholicism with that of Reynoso's, let alone have them serve as mere tokens of their respective mendicant or Highland Maya cohorts. While there is sufficient evidence to suggest that they were not unique or that their work was *sui generis*, there is also not enough evidence to support the idea that either of them represents a hidden, previously unknown majority at the time. Their respective schools of writings stand out because they were distinct and influential but not necessarily unique, and thus their significance is not related to any dominance nor necessarily to any pat resistance. Instead, their writings stand out with respect to their strategies of drawing from both Maya and Hispano-Catholic materials, employing similar resources presented in the same K'iche'an language and high register of ceremonial discourse for similar Maya audiences but via different approaches, genres, local contexts, additional specific constituencies, and overall aims. Vico and other mendicants through their pastoral genres strived for construals and messages that they thought to be not only translocal but definitively universal in import, while Highland Maya elites like Reynoso conveyed messages as indirect and implied responses to the mendicants but that were not designed to have any significance beyond a hyperlocal domain of intelligibility. Even though so much of their new worlds overlapped, their respective texts emerged from and spoke to different communicative ecologies. The mutual influences are of import not simply from the fact *that* their new worlds engaged each other, but rather in *how* they did, thus making the respective written positions highly dialogical.

These varying positions, though often bothersome to many modern scholars, are as theological as they are ethnographic, linguistic or philological, historiographic (including epic, legendary, and mythic), or sociopolitical. "Theology" is meant here not in the more narrowly understood confessional, doctrinal, dogmatic, or apologetic sense of the term but rather as a people's second-order or metadiscourse on their religious contruals, be they explicitly or even implicitly religious. And with "the religious" understood here as a people's articulation through discourse (high and low registers), practices (ritualistic, ethical, and quotidian), and symbols that convey their understandings of proper or normative orders of values, their selection and ordering of those values (over all other possible values and structural dynamics of ordering), and even their discernment of the criteria for that selection and of their understanding of what is to be understood as "proper." In this sense, the scholarly errand of culling out a people's theology—be it explicitly or implicitly religious, in whole or in part—is also a kind of theology, albeit a descriptive theology, descriptive of "their" theological and religious worldviews regardless of the extent to which a scholar subscribes to, likes or dislikes, or agrees or disagrees with it. The scholarly mission is thus concerned with the intersection between axiology (claims of value), epistemology (claims of truth), and hermeneutics (methods and modes of interpretation and claims of meaning or signification).

Among the mendicant-authored lexicons (*vocabularios*) and grammars (*artes*) written on Highland Mayan languages during the colonial period, several stand out as not only the more substantial in terms of entries and information covered—and thus the most insightful for present-day scholars of Highland Mayan languages and culture—but also among the more influential among later mendicant authors working among and with Highland Maya. Along with the philological or linguistic works by Thomás de Coto, O.F.M., Francisco Ximénez, O.P., Bartholomé de Anleo, O.P., and even possibly Domingo de Vico, O.P. (one of the most copied and deferred to, and thus arguably more often read and used by Catholic clergy in Guatemala, even if the linguistic works attributed to him are erroneous) is the 1698 *Vocabulario* by Friar Domingo de Basseta, O.P. In Basseta's K'iche'–Castilian Spanish lexicon the entry for *k'ab'awil* is translated as "idol," and in a separate, later, handwritten comment to the side of this entry is the contestation that this entry is wrong and instead "this means 'to worship'" (*significa adorar*) and that "*k'ab'awil* was anciently said for God and also means the wandering star" (*cabauil, se decia antig. te para Dios y significa tambian la Estrella vaga*).[3] Apparently the debate that began in the early-to-mid sixteenth century between Dominicans and Franciscans—or more precisely between those who subscribed to a more realist or Thomist semiotic ideology and those who subscribed to a more nominalist or Scotist semiotic ideology—regarding the understanding of *k'ab'awil* as "idol" or "true divinity," or as "idolatry" or simply "worship," continued long after Bishop Marroquín's decree banning the arguments over the term—centuries longer than previously suspected.

Most likely the translation, negotiation of meaning, reconfiguration, efforts for commensurability, and, as written evidence illustrates, intertextuality of various other basic religious concepts of Hispano-Catholicism or of the Highland Maya worldview were in similar degrees of recontextualization. Given the changing understandings of the world—literally—but also of understanding the world of human understanding (such as the crisis and preoccupation with the regrounding of epistemological certainty)[4] by peoples on both sides of the Atlantic in the sixteenth century, such seismic shifts in religious construals, let alone in understanding how a religion may be construed, is part of a broader transatlantic context. However, the effect did not consist of a unilateral European transition from its late medieval worldview into its early modernity through a period of Reformations that then gradually came to bear in pockets of the Americas, such as upon the Highland

Maya. Rather, the change was multidirectional. Mendicant work among indigenous peoples of the Americas in general but also among the Highland Maya in particular traveled back to Spain through writings, such as those by Bartolomé de las Casas, who seems to have included the works of fellow Dominicans like Vico into his own, as well as through peoples, such as K'iche' Ajpop Juan Cortés's travel from Guatemala to Spain in 1557 with his written *títulos* and the hope of making his case for recognition of his indigenous sovereignty before King Felipe II.[5] The K'iche' regent's affidavits and land deeds were, unfortunately, lost when the Spanish ship he was on was attacked by a French ship, most likely seeking Spanish gold. What kinds of K'iche'an writings Don Juan Cortés brought with him to present directly to the Crown will probably never be known, and even less is known about his time in Spain before returning to Guatemala, since he was never granted an audience with Felipe II. But, his time most likely was spent in Valladolid, Spain, with Las Casas and other Dominicans familiar with the Highland Maya and the plight of indigenous Americans.

Though faint, the traces of their impacts "across the sea" and "to the east" in Europe can still be seen today well beyond Europe or Mesoamerica. For example, there are at least three K'iche' loan words trafficked most probably through the Lowland Maya and Caribbean peoples to European sailors, settlers, and traders: *sik'* (meaning "tobacco," and related to the words "cigar" and "cigarette"), *juraqan* (meaning "hurricane" but literally "one leg" in K'iche', as distinct from the K'iche' phrase "two legs," or *kab'raqan*, to mean "earthquake"), and *kakow* (meaning "cacao" or, to use the Nahuatl loan word, *chocolatl*—also known globally as "chocolate"). Items, ideas, and terms from Europe were appropriated, such as *wakax* for "cows" (or *vacas* in Spanish), *alemonax* and *alanxax* for "lemons" and "oranges" (or *limones* and *naranjas* in Spanish, but prefixed with the Arabic definite article *al*, as was common in sixteenth-century southern Iberia).[6] However the impact of the encounter with Highland Maya went more than one way and was profound beyond lexical borrowings. Las Casas's writings attest to the first use of the phrase "human rights," which he applied to Europeans and especially indigenous Americans—and later in his life to Africans. It was based largely on his personal experiences in the Caribbean and Mesoamerica but also the written firsthand experiences of others throughout the Americas. Likewise, Francisco de Vitoria, O.P., chair of theology at the University of Salamanca and influential teacher to many Dominicans in New Spain, like Domingo de Vico, developed his legal theory of a "law of nations"—arguably the first doctrine of modern international law—highly influenced by the reports of Las Casas and other clergy who worked in the Americas.

And yet, from the vantage point of current postmodernity and more complex theories of signification and translation, the dyadic understanding between signs and referents along a simple binary distinction between form and content similar to that held by Vico and others of the early Salamanca school in Mesoamerica seems overly simplistic if not also naive. And the nominalism (minus the millenarian apocalypticism) of their Observant Franciscan competitors now seems semiotically more sophisticated though politically more antagonistic toward indigenous worldviews at the time. Such anachronistic evaluation of their semiotic and language ideologies risks missing the point of the direct and even explicit legacy of Vico's *Theologia Indorum* on the hyperlocal formulation of Christian thought among the Highland Maya of Guatemala, as well as Maya reconfiguration of indigenous religious thought—and the extent to which some of them, like Reynoso, may not have seen these two legacies as mutually exclusive.

These twinned legacies are identifiable in the earliest writings in K'iche'an Mayan languages, by K'iche'an Maya authors, exclusively for their Maya readers. It is also apparent in contemporaneous mendicant writings in and on K'iche'an Mayan languages, thus allowing for the elaboration of an ethnohistorical context, albeit relatively limited in temporal and geographic scope. The Highland Maya paper trail shifts around 1650—for example from preference by Maya authors for *títulos* toward *testamentos* and ledger accounts of local confraternities—and also decreases in sheer volume. On the other hand, mendicant writings—both pastoral, such as sermons and catechisms, and language studies, like lexicons and grammars of Mayan languages—provide evidence of the continued influence of Vico's work among both mendicants and Maya during the subsequent centuries. However, by the nineteenth century—while, ironically, his works were being collected and catalogued, if not also misidentified, by the likes of Brasseur de Bourbourg—and through the early-to-mid-twentieth century, Vico seemed lost to history.

By the 1960s, in large part due to the impact of the increased influence of Protestantism within the region, three notably distinct strands of Catholic thought that intentionally and constructively aimed to engage local culture emerged simultaneously in Latin America: liberation theology, charismatic Catholicism or Catholic Renewal, and inculturation or "Indian" theology. Until recently, scholars of religious movements in Latin America generally viewed liberation theology as the outgrowth of Catholic ecumenical engagement with liberal Protestantism (specifically the Social Gospel movement), a critically constructive rapprochement with Marxism housed within Neo-Scholasticism along with emphasis on Catholic social teachings leading up to and in the wake of the Second Vatican Council (1962–1965). Likewise, many students and scholars of late modern Latin America—including religious, indigenous, and revolutionary social movements—view charismatic Catholicism as a reaction against liberation theology but also as a critically constructive engagement with evangelical Pentecostalism. Inculturation theology is seen as a spinoff or subset of liberation theology that privileges analysis of racism and colonialism over Marxist class analysis and, thus, is a constructive engagement with indigenous "spirituality." And while the first two understandings have been a large and growing subject of scholarly investigations—recently leading to a more historical understanding of liberation theology and charismatic Catholicism as beginning simultaneously rather than consecutively in the 1960s in Latin America—inculturation theology or *teología India* (including *teología Mayense* among the Maya of Mexico and Guatemala) still remains highly understudied.[7]

Furthermore, with particular respect to the religious worlds of indigenous peoples, one of the perennial concerns within liberationist thought, both political (as evinced, for example, by Che Guevara in his Bolivian diary) and religious, beginning in the late 1960s and into the mid-1980s, was the virtual dearth of interest, sympathy, or participation by indigenous activists and intellectuals, especially in areas like Guatemala and Bolivia, where native peoples are an ethnic majority as well as historically, if perhaps nominally, Christian.[8] For many indigenous Americans, such as the Highland Maya of Guatemala, the primacy of class analysis over race analysis in liberation theology seemed inherently racist, if not also a furtherance of a program of ethnocide, in that "liberation" ultimately required assimilation by indigenous peoples into the dominant *ladino*, mestizo, or Anglo culture of the Americas.[9] In contrast, another perennial question among historians and social scientists of religion in Latin America is why so much of the recent growth and active participation and even leadership within charismatic strands of Christianity, including not only Pentecostalism but also Catholic Renewal, has included indigenous peoples, especially indigenous women. Little scholarly analysis on these contemporary religious movements—and the extent to which they have and have not attracted indigenous American peoples—has placed them within a thick historical context that includes the decades of first contact, and none within an ethnohistorical context.[10]

Despite the misperception that inculturation theology in Latin America began as an offshoot of the second phase of liberation theology of the mid- to late 1980s, Dominicans and Jesuits among the Highland Maya in the Catholic diocese of San Cristóbal de las Casas in Chiapas, Mexico, initiated attempts to Mayanize Catholicism even prior to Vatican II. This pastoral and theological work, which sought to constructively engage both local Maya culture and leadership as well as the social sciences, namely ethnography and sociolinguistics, began prior to the arrival of Bishop Samuel Ruiz García, but his tenure provided support for the emergence of what is now called "Indian theology" hemispherically and "Maya theology" regionally.[11] Furthermore, not only in the Highland Maya region but also throughout Latin America, the Popol Wuj has become one of the key indigenous textual sources that Catholic inculturation theology engages in an effort to identify analogical points of contact between Christian theology and Native American "spiritualties."[12] Ironically, little of this new "Indian" theology in Latin America, with the large participation of indigenous peoples, makes any explicit use of Vico's theology of and for the "Indians" of the sixteenth century. In this sense, curiously, current inculturation or "Indian" theology does not build off of Vico's ethnographically and linguistically attuned interdisciplinary theological method or his efforts at establishing a commensurable, mutually informative rapprochement between Christian and Maya religious worldviews, nor construe his work as a kind of historical antecedent to theirs today, nor understand their current theological work as even within an implied tradition of the production of Latin American Christian indigenous thought since the 1550s.[13] Though the present-day inculturation project by Dominicans in the Verapaces—the Ak' Kutan Center outside of Cobán, Guatemala—recognizes the theological work of Domingo de Vico, they only do so mainly due to his history as a Dominican in that historically Dominican mission but not directly due to his *Theologia Indorum*.[14] Vico and his theological treatise have all but disappeared except in name even among those who would arguably benefit the most from understanding his legacy, for good and for ill.

And yet, with respect to present-day Highland Maya and even more specifically among those K'iche'an Maya who participate in the Maya Movement or Maya Renaissance, scholars of religion should critically reassess the possible extent to which even an implied legacy of Vico, his Mayanized theology, and the creative work of Maya elites who engaged it, like Reynoso, persist. The present recovery of the writings of Vico and an intertextual analysis of his *Theologia Indorum* with contemporaneous Maya literature now allows for a thicker ethnohistorical context by which to study current sociopolitical and religious movements among indigenous peoples in the Highland Maya region and perhaps beyond—and to better appreciate the extent to which such movements may not be as new as scholars or even the indigenous participants themselves currently realize and write about.

Appendix A

Comparison of the Structures between Aquinas's Summa theologiae, *Late Medieval Liturgical Year Readings, and Vico's* Theologia Indorum

Summa theologiae by Thomas Aquinas (1225–1274)	*liturgical-year structure* of hagiographic readings of the *Legenda sanctorum* (ca. 1260) aligned with annual readings of biblical scripture; **additional material used by Vico in bold.**	*Theologia Indorum* by Domingo de Vico (d. 1555)
Prima Pars, Ia (written between 1266–1268)		Volume I (February 11, 1553)
1. Introduction: *sacra doctrina* (q. 1)		1. Proemium for Volume I
2. Proving God's existence (q. 2)		2. Names (attributes) of God (chapters 1–22)
3. How God exists (qq. 3–13)		
a. Essential attributes (qq. 3–11)		
b. How God is known (qq. 12)		
c. How God is named (qq. 13)		

DOI: 10.5876/9781607329701.c010

4. Divine operations (qq. 14–26)		
a. God's knowledge (qq. 14–18)		
b. God's will (qq. 19–24)		
c. God's beatitude (q. 26)		
5. The Trinity (qq. 27–43)		
a. The procession of the divine persons (q. 27)	**use of Maya material:** *k'ab'awil*	3. The divinity of God (chapters 23–25)
b. The divine relations (q. 28)		a. Clarifying God as three "peoples" (chapter 24)
c. The three persons (qq. 29–43)		
6. Production of creatures from God (qq. 44–119)		b. Contrast of devotion to effigies (chapter 25)
Various kinds of creatures including angels (qq. 47–102)	**use of Maya material:** *Xib'alb'a and the hero twins*	4. Creation of angels (chapters 26–29)
		a. Change of Lucifer from an angel (chapter 27)
		b. Place of Lucifer in Xib'alb'a (chapter 28)
		c. Nine levels of heaven and angels (chapter 29)
	Winter: Septuagesima-Easter	5. Creation of Earthly Paradise (chapter 30)
	A time of deviation, turning away from the right way	
	From Adam to Moses	
	Readings: Genesis	
Secunda Pars, IaIIae		6. About Adam and Eve (chapters 31–46)
(written between 1268–1272)		
1. Introduction: Beatitude as goal of humanity (qq. 1–5)		
2. Human acts in themselves (qq. 6–48)	*Spring: Advent-Nativity*	7. On the Patriarchs and Prophets (chapters 47–104)
3. The principle of acts (qq. 49–114)	A time of renewal, of being called back to God	
a. Intrinsic principles: powers and habits	From Moses to the birth of Christ	
b. Extrinsic principles: God's law and grace	Readings: Isaiah and faith of the prophets	
Secunda Secundae, IIaIIae		8. Summary of Volume I on the existence of God (with Book of Judith and Holofernes; Books of Maccabees) (chapter 105)
1. Acts pertaining to all conditions of humanity (qq.1–170)		

9. Colophon

Winter: Christmas-octave of Epiphany

Volume II

(finished in late 1554)

A time of reconciliation

1. Proemium for Volume II

use of New Testament

2. Life of Saints Joachim and Anne (chapter 1)
3. Life of Saints Joseph and Mary (chapters 2–7)
4. Birth and infancy of Christ (chapters 8–17)
5. Life of John the Baptist and baptism of Christ (chapters 18–19)
6. Fasting of Christ during Passover, anticipating the Eucharist (chapter 20)
7. About Apostles and evangelists (chapters 21–22)
8. About the law and commandments (chapter 23)
9. About the 3 theological, 4 cardinal virtues, and humility (chapters 24–32)

   a. Theological virtues: faith, hope, charity
   b. Cardinal virtues: prudence, justice, fortitude, temperance

2. Acts pertaining to a special manner (qq. 171–189)
   a. Graces freely given, spiritual charisms
   b. Active and contemplative lives
   c. Ecclesiastical offices

Tertia Pars, IIIa

(written between 1271–1273)

1. Christ in himself (qq. 1–59)
   a. The appropriateness of the Incarnation
   b. The mode of the union
   c. Consequences of the union
   d. The mysteries of Christ's life and death

	Summer: Easter-Pentecost	
	a time reconciled by Christ	
	readings: Book of Revelation and mystery of reconciliation fully read	
2. Christ active in the sacraments (qq. 60–90)		10. About the 7 sacraments (chapters 33–41)
a. Sacraments in general	**use of catechism material**	11. About the Beatitudes (chapters 42–51)
b. Sacraments in particular		
–Baptism		12. About the miracles of Jesus (chapters 52–61)
–Confirmation		
–Eucharist		13. About the meaning of the "gloria" (chapter 62)
–Penance		
Supplementum		14. About prayers, creeds, and biblical commandments (chapters 62–74)
(compiled posthumously)		
1. Sacraments in particular, continued (qq. 1–68)		
a. Penance		
b. Extreme unction		
c. Holy orders		15. On the church, ecclesiastical offices, commandments of the church (chapters 75–82)
d. Matrimony		
		16. About sin, 7 vices, 7 virtues, and grace (chapters 83–93)
	Autumn: octave of Pentecost	17. About the "passion" of Christ and the Pentecost (chapters 94–106)
	-Advent	
2. Last things and eternal life (qq. 69–99)	a time of pilgrimage	18. About the Final Judgment and last things (chapters 107–108)
	the present life	
a. Resurrection of the body and last judgment	readings: Books of Kings and of Maccabees at the end of *TI* Vol. I, not Vol. II	19. Final exhortation by a priest to faithful Christians (chapter 109)
b. Heaven		20. Summary of works of Christ and of Volume II (chapter 110)
c. Hell		

Sources: Van Akkeren (2011, 88); Aquinas, *Summa theologiae*; McGinn (2004, 74–79); Ryan (1993, 3–4); APS Ms; BnF Ms Amér 5; BnF Ms Amér 3.

Appendix B

Comparison between the Content and Themes found in the Coplas *in Q'eqchi' (Ayer Ms 1536) and in K'iche' (Kislak Ms 1015) and the* Theologia Indorum

34 chapters and 5 hymns in the Q'eqchi' Coplas (n.d.)	*Kislak 1015, folios 17r–68v (1544–1552 [1567])*	Theologia Indorum *(vol. I 1553, vol. II 1554)*
[Proemium, first hymn, and opening lines of Chapter I missing.]	¶Here begins the succession of the things of the Catholic faith from the beginning until the end by means of hymns, psalms, or plain songs so that the Indians may sing them at their festivals.	(Proemium)*
	¶The first chapter on the excellences that we owe our lord for the many aspects that pertain to that in creation.	(Part I, Chapters 1–22)*
Chapter II: On the creation of all the things in the order of the days.	¶The second chapter on the creation of the creatures in the order of the days.	Part I, Chapter 30
Chapter III: On the sin and fall of the angels.	¶The third chapter on the sin and fall of the angels.	Part I, Chapters 27, 28
Chapter IV: On the creation of Adam and Eve.	¶The fourth chapter on the creation of Adam and Eve.	Part I, Chapter 31

DOI: 10.5876/9781607329701.c011

34 chapters and 5 hymns in the Q'eqchi' Coplas (n.d.)	*Kislak 1015, folios 17r–68v (1544–1552 [1567])*	Theologia Indorum *(vol. I 1553, vol. II 1554)*
Chapter V: On the natural light that God put in the mind of man and custody of the angels.	¶The fifth chapter on the natural light that God put in the mind of man.	Part I, Chapter 35
Chapter VI: On the sin of Adam and Eve and the expulsion from the Earthly Paradise.	¶The sixth chapter on the sin and fall of Adam and Eve and the expulsion from Earthly Paradise.	Part I, Chapter 39
Chapter VII: On the miseries that man incurred and the approval that there is one God.	¶The seventh chapter on the miseries that man incurred and the approval that there is only one God.	Part I, Chapter 42
Chapter VIII: On the [illegible] of Adam and the promise of Christ.	¶The eighth chapter on the penance of Adam and promise of Jesus Christ.	Part I, Chapters 46, 47 (Part II, Chapter 8)*
Chapter IX: On the death of Adam and the places for the souls.	¶The ninth chapter of the four places of the souls.	Part I, Chapter 48
Second hymn on the Flood.	¶The second hymn on the Flood until the incarnation of Jesus [with chapter 10].	Part I, Chapter 50 (Part II, Chapter 8)*
Chapter X: On the increase of the peoples and the Flood.		
Chapter XI: On the division of the languages.	¶The eleventh chapter on division of the languages.	Part I, Chapter 52
Chapter XII: On the beginning of idolatry.	¶The twelfth chapter on the beginning of idolatry.	Part I, Chapter 52
Chapter XIII: On the election of Sodom and Gomorrah.	¶The thirteenth chapter on the election of Abraham and the destruction of Sodom and Gomorrah.	Part I, Chapter 56
Chapter XIV: On the prophets and [illegible]	¶The fourteenth chapter on the prophets and petition of Moses for a messiah and the prophecies of him.	Part I, Chapters 58, 62, 89, 92, 99
Chapter XV: On the grace of God that came to redeem the world.	¶The fifteenth chapter on the mercy of God that came to redeem the world.	Part II, Proemium
Chapter XVI: On Saint Joachim and Saint Anne and the birth of the holy Mary.	¶The sixteenth chapter on Saint Joachim and Saint Anne and the birth of Holy Mary.	Part II, Chapter 1

34 chapters and 5 hymns in the Q'eqchi' Coplas (n.d.)	*Kislak 1015, folios 17r–68v (1544–1552 [1567])*	Theologia Indorum *(vol. I 1553, vol. II 1554)*
Third hymn on the Saint John the Baptist with.	[no third hymn or equivalent with chapter xvii]	Part II, Chapters 4, 6, 7
Chapter XVII: On Saint John the Baptist and his birth and the incarnation of Christ.	¶The seventeenth chapter on Saint John the Baptist and on the incarnation of the son of God and on the visitation of Saint Elizabeth.	
[fourth hymn missing; presumably on the nativity of Jesus]	¶Singing the nativity, a continuation of the procession.	
Chapter XVIII: On the birth of Christ.	¶The eighteenth chapter on the birth of Jesus Christ, our lord.	Part II, Chapters 8, 9
Chapter XIX: On the circumcision and naming of Jesus Christ and why people call themselves Christians.	¶The nineteenth chapter on the circumcision and naming of Jesus Christ and why men call themselves "Christians."	Part II, Chapters 11, 12
Chapter XX: On the arrival of the three kings, magi, to adore Christ.	¶The twentieth chapter on the arrival of the three kings, magi.	Part II, Chapters 13, 14
Chapter XXI: On the purification of Saint Mary.	¶The twenty-first chapter on the purification of Holy Mary.	n.a.
Chapter XXII: On the journey to Egypt.	¶The twenty-second chapter on the departure of Jesus Christ our lord to Egypt.	Part II, Chapter 16
Chapter XXIII: On the investment of the temple.	¶The twenty-third chapter on the investiture of Jesus in the temple.	Part II, Chapters 15, 17
Fifth hymn on the greatness of Jesus Christ.	¶Fifth hymn on the grandeur of Jesus Christ.	
Chapter XXIV: On the baptism of Saint John and the baptizing of Christ.	¶The twenty-fourth chapter on the baptism of Saint John and how Christ was baptized.	Part II, Chapter 18, 19
Chapter XXV: On the fasting of Christ that were temptations and the return of Christ to where Saint John was.	¶The twenty-fifth chapter on the fast of Christ and the temptations and Christ's return to where Saint John was.	Part II, Chapter 20
Chapter XXVI: On the election of the apostles.	¶The twenty-sixth chapter on the election of the apostles.	Part II, Chapter 21

34 chapters and 5 hymns in the Q'eqchi' Coplas (n.d.)	*Kislak 1015, folios 17r–68v (1544–1552 [1567])*	Theologia Indorum *(vol. I 1553, vol. II 1554)*
Chapter XXIX: The law of Christ announced by others previously.†	¶The twenty-seventh chapter on the announcing that there would be a Christ.	Part II, Chapter 22
Chapter XXVIII: On the teaching of Christ [in the Trinity].	¶The twenty-eighth chapter on [Trinitarian] delegates with Christ.	n.a.
Chapter XXVII: The teachings of Christ.†	¶The twenty-ninth chapter on the elaboration of Christ's teachings.	Part II, Chapters 42–51
[sixth hymn missing; presumably on the miracles of Jesus].	¶Sixth hymn on the miracles of Jesus Christ.	
[Chapters XXX–XXXIII missing]	¶Chapter thirty on the miracles of Jesus Christ, firstly, that which is called a "miracle."	Part II, Chapter 52
	¶Chapter thirty-one on the miracles in particular.	Part II, Chapters 53–57
	¶Chapter thirty-two, a continuation on the miracles.	Part II, Chapters 53–57
	¶Chapter thirty-three on the Canaanite woman, the miracle of the breads.	Part II, Chapter 58
Seventh hymn on the transfiguration of Christ and on other miracles.	¶Seventh hymn on the transfiguration of Jesus Christ and other miracles.	
Chapter XXXIV: On the transfiguration.	¶Chapter thirty-four [on the transfiguration].	Part II, Chapter 59
Chapter XXXV: [On healing the blind man].	¶Chapter thirty-five on the man born blind.	Part II, Chapter 60
Chapter XXXVI: On the woman who [Jesus] healed and on the ten lepers.	¶Chapter thirty-six on the woman that Jesus healed and the ten lepers.	Part II, Chapter 60
Eighth hymn on the resurrection of Saint Lazarus and on the death of Christ, our lord.	¶Eighth hymn on the resurrection of Saint Lazarus and of Jesus Christ.	
Chapter XXXVII: [On the death and resurrection of Lazarus and of Jesus].	¶Chapter thirty-seven on the resurrection of Saint Lazarus.	Part II, Chapters 95, 100

34 chapters and 5 hymns in the Q'eqchi' Coplas (n.d.)	*Kislak 1015, folios 17r–68v (1544–1552 [1567])*	Theologia Indorum *(vol. I 1553, vol. II 1554)*
Chapter XXXVIII: On the destruction of Jerusalem by the death of Jesus Christ.	¶Chapter thirty-eight the song of the "enlivenment," the Easter of the Resurrection.	Part II, Chapters 101, 102
	[chapter 39 initial part missing as folio xxxii is missing, presumably it is on the resurrection or Jesus' time in hell]	[Part II, Chapters 102–103]
	¶Chapter forty on the Ascension.	Part II, Chapter 104
	[chapter 41 (xli) omitted; with possibly a ninth hymn]	
	¶Chapter forty-two on the arrival of the Holy Spirit and Pentecost.	Part II, "Chapter" 105
	¶Chapter forty-three on prophecies on the occasion on the arrival of the Holy Spirit.	Part II, "Chapters" 105
	¶Tenth song on the gifts of the apostles.	
	¶Eleventh hymn on the apostles and on the preaching to the world.	
	¶Chapter 44 on Saint Peter and Saint Andrew and Saint James and Saint John and Saint Philip and Saint Bartholomew.	Part II, "Chapter" 106
	¶Chapter forty-five on the faith of the apostles.	Part II, "Chapter" 106
	¶Chapter forty-six on Saint Paul and Saint Barnabas and Saint Luke and Saint Mark.	Part II, "Chapter" 106
	¶Chapter forty-seven on exhortation for the Indians.	Part II, "Chapter" 109
	¶Chapter forty-eight on how fire will consume everything and how the dead will resurrect.	Part II, "Chapter" 107
	¶Twelfth hymn on the faithfulness of the world.	

34 chapters and 5 hymns in the Q'eqchi' Coplas (n.d.)	*Kislak 1015, folios 17r–68v (1544–1552 [1567])*	Theologia Indorum *(vol. I 1553, vol. II 1554)*
	¶Chapter 49 on how He will descend [again], Jesus Christ.	Part II, "Chapter" 107
	¶Chapter fifty on the penalties of the damned and on the glory of the good ones [text date 1552, copydate 1567].	Part II, "Chapter" 108
	¶This here is a song on Saint Michael and Saints Gabriel and Raphael thus with all the angels.	
	¶This here is an excursus about Lucifer.	
	¶A song of Goliath with David.	
	¶A song of the Holy Mary, our mother.	
	¶This is the beloved clarification, a song for the Holy Cross.	
	[text ends here but *Tabla* on folio 89v lists eight additional chapters on songs, thus at least 11 folios missing on:]	
	¶Body of Christ.	
	¶Saint Francis.	
	¶Saints Simeon and [illegible].	
	¶Saint Augustine, Saint Jerome.	
	¶Saint Ambrose, Saint Gregory.	
	¶Saint Louis, Saint Anthony.	
	¶On [illegible].	
	¶Saint Andrew.	

Sources: Bossú Z. (1986); Kislak 1015; BnF Ms Amér 3; BnF Ms Amér 5; and GGMM no. 175.

* Indicates that while there appears to be topical or thematic similarities with these chapters, with respect to the content its treatment, or location within the structural order of the work these units are notably distinct.

† In Ayer Ms 1536, Chapters 27–29 appear in their enumerated order, but Chapters 27 and 29 have been inverted here to illustrate how the contents of these texts correspond.

Notes

INTRODUCTION: (RE)READING A FIRST COAUTHORED PAPER TRAIL

1. The title of the Popol Wuj appears in italics in many publications, but it does not do so here. As sacred Maya literature or scripture, it remains capitalized but not italicized, as is the convention with the titles of other religious texts such as the Bible, Qur'an, I Ching, and Upanishads (see Tedlock 2010, 300). Because the other texts in this book have not attained the status of scripture or other "canonized" works, their titles are in italics.

2. In general, the writing of postcontact Highland Maya autochthonous literature predates that by other indigenous groups, such as the texts by Zapotec, Yukatek, or Nahua authors; however, the dating of many of the early writings in central New Spain is difficult to affix with certainty. For example, the composition of the *Historia Tolteca Chichimeca,* written in Nahuatl by Mexica elders for Mexica readers, may have begun as early as the late 1540s but not have been completed for another decade (Townsend 2017, 31, 265n62). In contrast, a number of key K'iche' texts are clearly finished by the early-to-mid 1550s, making them at least contemporaneous if not slightly earlier.

3. As historian Heiko Oberman has argued, despite their polemically anti-tradition rhetoric, those Christian thinkers eventually identified by the sixteenth century as Protestants during the Reformations period also engaged tradition but more as informative than as strictly authoritative (for example, Oberman 1992, 280–296).

4. For a concise history of the various scriptural canons and gradual process of canonization in early Christianity see Ehrman (2003, 330–342).

5. For examples of such kinds of assessment of early colonial indigenous Mesoamerican religious texts, see Hanks (2010) and Christensen (2013, 2014). However, arguably one of the earliest scholarly studies to explicitly put forward the idea of a plurality of "Christianities" was Smith (1990), in the field of history of religions.

6. This is arguably true for not only Christianity throughout its intellectual history since late antiquity but also other dominant religions in the world; see Henderson (1998).

7. See, for example, Hoffmann (1987).

8. See, for example, Bettenson and Maunder (2011, 1–5) for English translations of Tacitus's *Annales*, xv.44.2–5 (1), Suetonius's *Vita Claudii*, xxv.4 and *Vita Neronis*, xvi (2), Pliny the Younger's letter to Emperor Trajan (3–4), and Trajan's response to Pliny the Younger (5); as well as Whiston (1974, 11, 20, and 140) for an English translation of Flavius Josephus's *Antiquities of the Jews* XVIII, iii:3, v.2, and ix.1.

9. See, for example, Murphy (1992) and Talbot (1954).

10. See, for example, Ehrman (2003). It should be pointed out that while much of the early ecumenical councils' work tried to negotiate generally inclusive positions on the diverse Trinitarian grammars (like the councils of Nicaea I [325 CE] and Constantinople I [381 CE]) and Christologies (like the councils of Ephesus [431 CE] and Chalcedon [451 CE] but also Constantinople II [553 CE] and III [680–681 CE] and Nicaea II [787 CE]), the wider variety of non-Nicene-Chalcedonian Christians never considered themselves less Christian, let alone heterodox, and continued even well after being condemned by the imperially sponsored councils.

11. For examples of the former, see England et al. (2002, 3–27, 79–80). For the latter, see Dawson (1955).

12. Hanks (2010, 17–19).

13. Hanks (2000, 2010).

14. Sparks (2017a).

15. In addition to the formative scholarship in the historical study on this period of the Reformations by Oberman (1981, 1992), see Eire (2016, especially 3–129).

16. Despite Pope Gregory XIII's bull *Inter gravissimas* (Februrary 24, 1582), which specified the adoption of the reformed, modern calendar to take place on October 1582, and King Felipe II's decree of agreement (September 29, 1582) for all the territories of his realm, the change did not officially take place in New Spain until nearly two years later. No scholarly investigations have examined the effects of this change with respect to local liturgical devotions, the dating of early postcontact indigenous literature, or temporal worldviews. There is considerable debate among scholars about the size of the human population in the Americas prior to 1492; for an example of one of the more conventionally mentioned numbers, see Butzer (1992, 345–368).

17. In this respect, linguistic ideology is treated here as a subset or type of semiotic ideology. See Keane (2007, 5, 13–21, 42, 59–60). For a more detailed treatment of the seismic

shifts in semiotic ideologies in Europe during the sixteenth century and its encounter with South Asia, see Yelle (2013).

18. García-Ruiz (1992, 89–92).

19. While the *Salmanticense* theological school of thought did not technically begin until the publication of *Complutenses* at the Universidad de Alcalá in 1570, I use the phrase "Salamanca school" here to distinguish the Thomistic thought by Salamanca Dominicans in relationship with Spanish humanism from the Thomism or humanism in other parts of Europe. For a more detailed account of the *Salmanticenses*, see the entry under "Salamanque (théologiens de)" in Amann et al. (1939, 1017–1031) as well as the *New Catholic Encyclopedia* (1967, 126–135). For recent scholarship on Francisco de Vitoria and the curricular changes he made at the University of Salamanca based on Aquinas's *Summae* in the 1530s, see Piñón (2016) and Valenzuela-Vermehren (2013).

20. Hernández de León-Portilla (2009, 57–58).

21. García-Ruiz (1992, 91–94), Brinton (1881, 630). As is explained in greater detail in the next chapter, throughout this book "K'iche'" refers specifically to the various dialects of the K'iche' Maya language found in the central and western Guatemalan highlands, the post-classic civilization of the Western K'iche' based in this locale, and their literature. "K'iche'an" refers to the linguistic macrofamily of the Western K'iche' and related language groups in the wider region, such as Kaqchikel, Tz'utujil, Achi (or Eastern K'iche'), Sakapultek. Also, notably, the term *k'ab'awil* has various spellings (e.g., *k'ab'awil, kab'awil, k'ab'owil,* and *kab'owil*) and proposed etymologies in both colonial and modern K'iche'an languages but has been rendered consistently throughout this book to avoid confusion for the reader despite any possible disconnection from the primary sources.

22. Sáenz de Santa María (1974, 369), Carmack and Mondloch (1985, 242).

23. While outside the scope of this study, the fourth classic medieval mode of Christian biblical exegesis—anagogical—was on the wane due in part to the transition away from the historical dominance of Neoplatonism that resulted from the gradual, critical influence of Aristotelianism. As a result, the sixteenth century consisted of the final articulation of classic western Christian mysticism such as through exemplary representatives like Nicholas of Cusa, Theresa of Ávila, and John of the Cross. Though, compared to the affective theology of the *devotio moderna* and pietism, the Franciscan *iluminismo* of the likes of Francisco de Osuna, or the development of Ignatius of Loyola's critically introspective kind of spirituality, the mysticism of biblical anagogy had run its course and was, at best, reconfigured in light of sixteenth-century humanism and the Reformations. By and large Iberian Dominicans and those who came and worked in Mesoamerica, such as Vico, exhibit little to no influence or interest in mysticism or "spirituality" as historically understood in this sense.

24. Restall (1997, 246–254), Megged (1995, 62).

25. Carmack (1973, 18; 2012).

26. Tedlock (1996, front cover).

27. Farhi (1991).

28. Garfield and Giordano (2010).

29. Koenig (2012a, 2012b); *This American Life* (2012); Greenslade (2012).

30. Khondker (2004, 12–20). For an example of use of "glocalization" in religious studies, particularly regarding Hispanic religious expression, see Vásquez and Friedmann Marquardt (2003, 56–58, 208–215).

31. Hartley (2010), Garfield and Jarvis (2009), Garfield and Marymont (2007).

32. See, for example, Durston (2014, 162–163) regarding such dimensions in the *Huarochirí Manuscript*, and Shoaps (2009), specifically for her coining the term and explicating the concept of a "communicative ecology."

33. Shoaps (2009).

34. Ibid.

35. The present volume can only touch lightly upon this topic in the limited region of Mesoamerica (which requires its own extensive attention in subsequent research); however, for the Andean region, Rolena Adorno examines in greater detail and analysis the impact of Salamancan legal humanism by native elites (Adorno 2007).

36. For example, in her 2009 TED Talk, "The Danger of the Single Story," Nigerian author Chimamanda Ngozi Adichie quotes Palestinian poet Mourid Barghouti: "if you want to dispossess a people, the simplest way to do it is to tell their story and start with 'secondly'"; see http://www.ted.com/talks/chimamanda_adichie_the_danger_of_a_single_story#t-612173, minute 10:19 (accessed July 2019).

37. See, for example, Hill (1992).

38. Dary (1997, 229–236). This, of course, excludes the more recent "revitalization" efforts and rhetoric of the Maya Activist Movement in Guatemala since the 1970s; the uprising in Chiapas, Mexico, by the Zapatista Army of National Liberation (Ejército Zapatista de Liberación Nacional, or EZLN) since 1994; or the much earlier Caste Wars by Yukatek Maya in the nineteenth century.

39. It escapes the scope of this book, but the still highly understudied flow of influences, beginning in the sixteenth century, among Asia, the Pacific Islands, the Spanish Americas (including what eventually became the southern United States), and Spain should not go completely unmentioned.

40. In general, exemplary scholarly studies on the arrival of Catholicism to Mesoamerica—such as those by Ricard (1966), Phelan (1970), Hanks (2010), Lopes Don (2010), and Christensen (2013)—have focused overwhelmingly on the Franciscans as too generally representative of the transmission and translation efforts of all of colonial Christianity. Studies on the work of Dominicans, such as that of Megged (1996), focuses after the Third Synod of Mexico (1585) in Chiapas, which has little to no Maya literary history, and does not distinguish that venue from various other scholastic, mendicant, and diocesan approaches.

A notable attempt to diversify perspectives on Catholicism in the Americas is the history of secular clergy in early colonial Mexico by Schwaller (1987).

41. Studies on early Dominicans in the Americas have tended to focus on the specific person of Bartolomé de las Casas—for example, Hanke (1974) and Gutiérrez (1993)—or concentrate on the Dominican arrival and work in the Andean region, such as the exemplary scholarship by MacCormack (1993) and Durston (2007). That latter approach helps to contrast the work of Dominicans in Guatemala and illustrate that even this order was not a monolithic whole. Tavárez (2011) devotes attention to Dominicans in central New Spain among the Nahua, Zapotec, and Mixtec, though mostly after the arrival of the Spanish Inquisition as does the recent books by Farriss (2014, 2018) on Dominicans among Zapotec; for some perspective on Dominicans north of the Highland Maya prior to 1571, see Tavárez (2011, 26–61).

CHAPTER 1: MESOAMERICANS SHAPE A NEW WORLD

1. Popol Wuj: Ayer Ms 1515, fol. 23v. English translation based on Tedlock (1996, 116); Christenson (2003, 160; 2004, 116–117, 286); Sam Colop (1999, 92; 2011, 81) but with slight modifications in the English translation, K'iche' orthography, and stanza formation, but based on Sam Colop (1994, 2012) and Christenson (2003, 26–42).

2. While the name of the first brother of the Hero Twins is most clearly a date on the 260-day ritual calendar and more likely translates to One Blowgunner, the etymology and thus subsequent questionable translations of the second brother is more precarious. With the initial /x-/ usually understood to mean a diminutive marker ("little") rather than the other option of indicating feminine ("she"), *balan* in the colonial script is often read as *b'alam* ("jaguar"), and the final letters as either "sun" (if it is from Lowland Maya derivation, such as *k'in*) or "deer" (if it is from Highland Maya derivation, namely *kej*). In the Popol Wuj the name appears as Xb'alanke (Xbalanque; without a final <h>), and for scholars of the Popol Wuj it is more often understood to mean "little jaguar (or dark) sun" (i.e., Venus or the moon) rather than "little jaguar deer"; see Tedlock (1996, 361), Janssens and Van Akkeren (2003, 34), and Van Akkeren (2012, 126–130). Furthermore, in mendicant texts like those by Vico this name usually appears with a final <h> (Xbalanqueh; or Xb'alankej in the modern orthography); for this reason the spelling varies throughout this book depending on what texts are quoted or discussed. In Maya cosmology Jun Ajpu is associated with the sun (specifically the sun of the fourth age, of people made from maize) or Venus (namely as the Morning Star) and Xb'alanke is associated with Venus as well as the moon (or specifically the full moon); see, for example, Milbrath (1999, 96–100, 130–135).

3. Sam Colop (2011, 221n149).

4. Literally, the root for this term, *koj*, can mean "to wear" or "to put on" and might be better translated here as "belief," especially given the historic affective theological

understanding of "spirituality" in Christian thought until the early modern period or the more therapeutic understanding currently imputed to the term with the development of the New Age movement. However, Maya religious leaders and cultural activists translate *kojb'al* as *espiritualidad Maya* and, thus, as other studies have done, it has been rendered here in English as they use it in Spanish; for example, see Molesky-Poz (2006) and Hart (2008).

5. The estimated 90 percent population decline suffered by indigenous Americans, due largely to warfare, labor exploitation, and, most significantly, communicable diseases, is discussed in greater detail in the conclusion of chapter 2. Historians of Native America (such as David E. Stannard) and Native American intellectuals including theologians (such as Vine Deloria Jr. and George E. Tinker) have used the term "genocide" in regards to the massive population loss during the decades of initial contact between the indigenous peoples of the Americas and Europeans; for example, see Stannard (1992) and Tinker (1993). While not denying that some policies were intended to reduce if not eliminate Native American populations, on my read most of the programs—such as Christian denominationally operated boarding schools in the United States for Native American children—aimed to eliminate not Native Americans as individual persons but rather Native American cultures. Therefore, I apply the term "ethnocide" rather than "genocide" or even "cultural genocide" to this phenomenon. Regarding the systemic human rights violations against the Highland Maya during Guatemala's thirty-six-year internal war (1960–1996) and the efforts to document and charge genocide as well as other war crimes against former members of the Guatemalan armed forces, see Oficina de Derechos Humanos del Arzobispado de Guatemala (ODHA) (1998), especially Volumen II: *Los mecanismos del horror*; Comisión para el Esclarecimiento Histórico (CEH) (n.d.); United Nations Verification Mission in Guatemala (MINUGUA) (2002, especially page 2, paragraph 6); and Garrard-Burnett (2010), which was written prior to General Ríos Montt's trial and conviction of genocide and other crimes against humanity by a Guatemalan court in May 2013.

6. This chapter is designed to provide a general overview for non-Mayanists that based on both primary sources (written by Highland Maya since the 1500s) and influential secondary scholarship that will serve as a foundation for more detailed analysis of many of these same sources in the subsequent chapters. However, even among scholars of Mesoamerica, or even of, the Lowland Maya, sufficient specific understanding of the distinctiveness of the Highland Maya is too often thin as a result of overgeneralizing and importing understandings from the milieux of the Nahua or Yukatek (predominantly Franciscan mission territories), for example, onto the Maya highlands and the approaches taken there by some schools of Dominicans.

7. For analysis of this kind of engagement in a comparative but very different cultural and historical setting, namely between Lakota and French Jesuits, and with respect to these same three rubrics, see White (1991). However, beyond the classic if not stereotypical story of Hernán Cortés and Malinalli Tenepatl in Mexico—or even Pedro de Alvarado and

Tecuelhuetzin "María Luisa" Xicoténcatl in Mexico and later Guatemala—also see Herrera (2007, 127–144).

8. Jones (1998). For the most part, except where noted, names for Maya peoples (such as the Itza' Maya) are spelled according to the modern orthography of the Mayan Language Academy of Guatemala (Academia de Lenguas Mayas de Guatemala, ALMG) whereas toponyms of the region, even those derived from Nahuatl if not also in Spanish, are rendered as they appear on local maps (such as Petén Itzá). Accent marks in Nahuatl-derived toponyms (such as Totonicapán, Sololá, Atitlán, etc.) appear as they are currently spelled on Guatemalan maps and literature and are not indicative of how they were once pronounced in Nahuatl.

9. Dary F. (1997, 229–236); also see Smith (1990).

10. Díaz del Castillo (1956, 9, 40).

11. Schele and Freidel (1990, 26).

12. Regarding the former, other variations on this name include "Gonzalo de Aroca" or "Gonzalo de Aroza"; regarding the latter, which also appears as "Jerónimo de Aguilar," some histories claim that Aguilar was a friar or deacon.

13. Díaz del Castillo (1956, 45–52).

14. Ibid. (66–68). Other sources refer to her as "Doña Marina" and "La Malinche." For a recent historical reevaluation of Malinalli Tenepatl and her invaluable role in negotiations between Cortés and Motecuhzoma Xocoyotzin in 1520, see Restall (2003, 77–99) and especially Townsend (2006).

15. For a recent scholarly analysis of these Yukatek texts and their relationship with Spanish Franciscan writings in the area, see Hanks (2010, 283–364). While outside the scope of this book, four of the nine *Books of Chilam Balam* have been translated into English—Edmonson (1982), Edmonson (1986), Gubler and Bolles (2000), and Bricker and Miram (2002)—as have two sets of other significant late postclassic period Yukatek texts: Roys (1939, 1965). Though the legal or notarial genres used by Mesoamericans and Highland Maya in particular are discussed in greater detail in later chapters, regarding these kinds of texts among Lowland Maya, see Restall (1995), Christensen and Truitt (2016), and Christensen and Restall (2019).

16. Wastek, Tenek, or the historic "Greater Wastekan" branch north of Veracruz, Mexico is both geographically and historically distant and is thus outside of these five branches.

17. See, for example, Asselbergs (2004) but also Universidad Francisco Marroquín (2007), Van Akkeren (2007), Oudijk and Restall (2007, 28–64), Matthew (2007, 102–126; 2012, especially 1–131).

18. Schele and Freidel (1990, 56).

19. Ibid. (57), but also see Wolf (1959, 21–151) and Coe (1992, 54–60). By comparison, the size and density of these Maya city-states far surpassed European contemporaries such as London (25,000–50,000) and Paris (40,000–80,000).

20. Schele and Freidel (1990, 51–55); Coe and Van Stone (2001, 14–15).

21. Schele and Freidel (1990, 58).

22. For correlative development in the Guatemalan highlands, see Sanders and Murdy (1982, 23–47).

23. Tedlock (1996, 149–160), Carmack and Mondloch (2007, 64–67), and Maxwell and Hill (2006, 2–7). "Popol Wuj" is a modernized title of a K'iche' manuscript, and is translated by modern scholars as the "Council Book" or "Book of the Council." The titles for other important Highland Maya texts do not appear within their manuscripts, and modern scholars have given various titles to them. Recently Maya activists and Mayanists, such as Carmack and Maxwell, have helped advocate for titles in the languages of current Highland Maya speakers or the original languages of their texts: for example, *Uwujil Kulewal aj Chwi Miq'ina'* (*Title of Totonicapán*) and *Kiwujil Xajila'* (*Xajil Chronicle* or *Annals of the Kaqchikel*). For the latter, see Maxwell (2010, 216) and most recently Matsumoto's (2017) proposed renaming of Princeton University Library's Nija'ib' documents. While I agree with the politics of these new titles and hope that the new names eventually become conventional, I have retained the most familiar titles of these texts here.

24. Carmack (1981b, 54–55), Brown (1982, 35–47). For particular focus on archaeological evidence, see Popenoe de Hatch (1998, 93–115).

25. Carmack (1981b, 52).

26. Tedlock (1996, 45).

27. Van Akkeren (2012).

28. Fox (1977, 82–83).

29. Frauke Sachse has argued the theme of "across the waters from the east" is a common feature in many ancient Mesoamerican myths and thus may be much more a symbolic motif in native religious literature than a historical reference; see Sachse (2008).

30. Fox (1978, 16). For a general but detailed overview of the archaeological record of the prehispanic K'iche' urban area of Q'umarkaj, see Babcock (2012).

31. Carmack (1981b, 130–134), Fox (1978, 16–68), Tedlock (1996, 183–184). For the character of Quetzalcoatl in myth and his possible historical antecedents, see Carrasco (2000). It is said that directly below Q'umarkaj are three separate caves with their entrances from the northern ravine of the city. The first and most easily accessible is an active ceremonial site that consists of a labyrinthine set of tunnels, including a deep pit, each leading to an offering site or altar. The second cave is farther down the ravine and consists of a single long, narrow tunnel. Both of these show signs of being human-made rather than natural formations. Despite various attempts since 1998, I have never been able to locate the third supposed cave and, despite the hearsay of its existence, have never met an *ajq'ij* (ritual calendar priest) who has actually visited it either, which is not to say that it does not or has not existed.

32. For an ethnohistorical examination of this same period focused on the Tz'utujil, see Orellana (1984). However, Van Akkeren (2000) also presents a different understanding of

the western migration of the main lineages of the rulers (*chinamit*) over the K'iche' from the lowlands and Verapaces region and their merger with populations that migrated from the southern Pacific coast.

33. There is considerable debate among Highland Mayanists regarding the best translation of K'iche'an social terms like *amaq'*, *winaq*, and *chimamit*, and the extent to which they designate lineages or class- or caste-based units; see, for example, Carmack (1981b, 148–180; 2001a, 73–104; 2001b, 110–250) in contrast to Braswell (2001, 2003a, 2003b). Translations here should be considered loose and for heuristic purposes only.

34. Fox (1977, 85), Tedlock (1996, 149–150, 172–173), Carmack and Mondloch (2007, 108–109).

35. Carmack and Mondloch (2007, 100–103), Tedlock (1996, 193–198).

36. Van Akkeren (2003, 252–253).

37. For similar analysis of a major Tamub' citadel, see Van Akkeren, (n.d., 223–234).

38. Carmack (1981b, 164–179, 181–211), Wallace (1977, 23–54).

39. For an assement of the various waves of settlement of Nahuatl-speakers prior to the sixteenth-century and their engagement with Highland Maya, see Bove et al. (2012).

40. Fox (1977, 85; 1978, 69–175).

41. Smith (2005, 404).

42. Tedlock (1996, 185–191; 2003), Fox (1977, 84; 1978, 230–269), Carmack (1981b, 134–141), Carmack and Mondloch (2007, 130–145), Maxwell and Hill (2006, 179–215), Recinos (1987, 132–149). For more detailed description on the archaeological record drawn from the establishment and development of the independent prehispanic Kaqchikel Maya and their capital city, see Guillemín (1965) and Nance et al. (2003).

43. Fox (1977, 94–95; 1978, 176–229), Maxwell and Hill (2006, 215–255).

44. For one of the notable exceptions of Kaminal Juyu', see Alvarado Galindo (2012).

45. For a more elaborate explanation of these indigenous Mesoamerican genres, see Boone (2000).

46. Such as, for example, the denunciations of Diego Columbus's administration of Hispaniola by Friars Pedro de Córdoba and Antonio Montesinos, Friar Francisco de Vitoria's development of a "law of nations" or early international law, and Friar Bartolomé de las Casas's doctrine of "human rights."

47. Carmack (2012, 356).

CHAPTER 2: MENDICANTS SHAPE A NEW WORLD

1. Governor of Cuba Diego de Velázquez's orders to Hernán Cortés before the latter's departing for *la tierra firma* in 1519, as quoted from Cuevas (1928, 107); my translation into English, emphasis added.

2. See, for example, Christensen (2013).

3. See Irenaeus of Lyon's "Against Heresies" in Roberts and Donaldson (1996, 331). The full quotation is: "For the Churches which have been planted in Germany do not believe or hand down anything different, nor do those in Spain, nor those in Gaul, nor those in the East, nor those in Egypt, nor those in Libya, nor those which have been established in the central regions [e.g., Palestine] of the world."

4. See Clement's "The First Epistle of Clement" in Roberts and Donaldson (1996, 6, emphasis added) and Romans 15:22–24: "But now, with no further place for me in these regions, I desire, as I have for many years, to come to you when I go to Spain."

5. The other two early synods, or local church councils, are the Synod of Arles ca. 313 and the Synod of Ancyra ca. 314. For more early sources regarding Christianity in Spain see Mullen (2004, 248–259).

6. Gómez-Ruiz (2007, 14).

7. Jonah 1:3 and Obadiah 20, respectively.

8. Gómez-Ruiz (2007, 14).

9. Ibid. (19).

10. Ibid. (18). The term is derived from *mozárbes*, the Hispanicized version of the Arabic word for "Arabized": *musta'rib* or "Arabized" Christians (Payne 1984, 11).

11. Ibid. (20).

12. Fletcher (1990, 125–126).

13. Likewise, the Sephardic Jewish population in Catholic territories spoke their own Castilian dialect eventually called *ladino*. To this day *ladino* remains both a ceremonial and quotidian vernacular language among pockets of Sephardic Jews in places like Bosnia-Herzegovina and Turkey.

14. Fletcher (1990, 52).

15. Martínez-Pereda Rodríguez (1991, 96).

16. Ibid. (98–99).

17. Gómez-Ruiz (2007, 24). For an overview of religious identities in medieval Iberia, see Payne (1984, 3–24).

18. Gómez-Ruiz (2007, 28–31). Today, in addition to the noon mass in the cathedral of Toledo, only two parishes continue with the Mozarabic rite: Santa Eulalia y San Marcos and Santas Justa y Rufina; Ibid. (3).

19. Bollweg (1995), Vose (2009, especially 94–130), but also Szpiech (2013).

20. For example, regarding the early impact of the theological legacy of scholastic humanism at Salamanca, see Belda Plans (2009).

21. Regarding Vitoria's instrumental role in the introduction of the second school of Thomism into Iberia, initially Valladolid and then Salamanca, see McGinn (2014). Regarding his influence on the Salamanca school, impact in New Spain, and the influence of Dominican missionary reports on him, see Pagden (1982, especially pages 57–108).

22. *New Catholic Encyclopedia* (1967, 133).

23. Vio Cajetan (2000). Regarding the reexamination of Aquinas's understanding of analogical reasoning and the shift away from the influence of Cajetan, see, for example, McInerny (1961) and Burrell (1979) in addition to McGinn (2014). I am especially grateful to Thomas Maloney for his pointing out this shift in interpreting Aquinas and providing me with the work of Burrell and McInerny.

24. Burrell (1979, especially 55–67).

25. Dolet argued for five fundamental principles of translation. First, a translator needs to perfectly understand both the content of the text and the intention of the text's author. Second, a translator needs to have a thorough knowledge of both the language from which, and the language into which, a text is to be translated. Third, a translator should avoid the tendency to translate word for word, as this would strip original text of meaning and rhetorical beauty. Fourth, a translator should use speech contemporary to the readers of the translated text. Fifth, a translator must produce and maintain an appropriate tone achieved by strategic diction and syntax in the translation. See Dolet (n.d., 5–7) and Bibliothèque nationale de France, département Littérature et art (8-Z-16203-(1–3), 13–19).

26. Cartagena (2009, xi–xlii). Also see López Carrillo et al. (1995, 123–130) and Pons Rodríguez (2006, 9–17).

27. See Antonio de Nebrija's *Introducciones latinas contrapuesto el romance al latín* of 1488, *Grammatica de la castellana* of 1492, *El ortografia castellano* of 1517, and Pedro de Alcalá's *Arte para ligeramente faber la legua arauiga* of 1504. Although Andrew Laird (2018) confirms the influence of Nebrija's *Introducciones Latinas,* he questions that of his *Gramática castellana*.

28. Meyerson (1995).

29. For example, even the eighteenth-century dictionary on Wastek—the Mayan language spoken historically around the area of Veracruz, Mexico, also referred to as Tenek—still followed the basic structure and rubrics of Nebrija's *Introductiones Grammaticae*. See Quirós (2013, 19–22, 55, 75).

30. Strictly speaking, only the Lowland Maya had developed a logographic syllabary or logosyllabic writing system based on phonemes prior to the arrival of Europeans (Coe and Van Stone [2001, 18–25]; Coe [1992, 289]); however, if the understanding of writing were to be expanded, the *khipu* of the Inka and other systems such as that of the Mexica could also be considered; see Boone (1994).

31. Bouza (2004, especially 51–53).

32. Eco et al. (1989, 4–10).

33. Eco (1989, 51–53).

34. Eco et al. (1989, 4–10, 22).

35. See, for example, Roger Bacon's *On Signs* (2013); on his universals, see Maloney (1989); and on his semiotics, see Maloney (1983, 120–154). I am especially grateful to Thomas Maloney for his assistance through personal conversations in helping clarify for me these shifts in medieval theories of signs and semiotics.

36. Courtenay (1974) and Oberman (1960, 47–76).

37. Eco (1989, 57–58).

38. For a more detailed account of the shift in European semiosis during the sixteenth century, especially with regards to the Protestant Reformation, colonialization, and later structuralism, see Yelle (2013).

39. Regarding this difference of sign theories among mendicants in New Spain, see García-Ruiz (1992, 89–9)2. Regarding this difference in medieval and early modern signification between realists and nominalists, such as between Dominicans and Franciscans, see Kelly (1979), Eco (1989), Eco et al. (1989), and Carré (1946).

40. For the contrasting Observant Franciscan approach, see, for example, Cervantes (1997) and Lopes Don (2010), as well as Rubiés (2006) regarding the intellectual shifts, chiefly as a result of Thomism, undergirding understandings of "idolatry" in wider Europe, Iberia, and the Americas.

41. There appear to be important differences between those Dominican missionaries who were recruited by Las Casas for southern Mesoamerica and those who went to the Andean region; for the latter in particular, see MacCormack (1991).

42. Scholes (1952, 392).

43. For Thomas Aquinas, see his *Summa theologicae* Ia, q. 1.9–10, such as in Pegis (1948, 15–19). And for Dante Alighieri's "Letter to Can Grande della Scala," especially paragraph seven, see Richter (2007, 122). For more on the use of figurative, symbolic, metaphorical, or analogical thinking beyond scriptural hermeneutics, see Carruthers (1998, 117–129) and Minnis and Scott (1988, 373–394, 439–458).

44. Durán (1967, I, 3; 1994, 14).

45. Garrido Aranda (1980, 94–104).

46. While the term "Moors" is commonly used in English-language scholarship regarding the historic Muslim populations of Iberia, it is an English translation from the Spanish term *moro* or *morisco* that is understood to mean "someone from Morocco." In this sense, it implies that the religious other, mainly Muslims but also Jews, did not belong to Iberia but rather were considered alien to Europe by Christians (even though Muslim migration to Iberia predated by centuries that of Christian groups, such as the House of Habsburg). Furthermore, in many places today, such as Germany, the term is used as a racial epithet, such as against Europeans of African ancestry. For this reason, the term has been used sparingly here in favor of more accurately descriptive phrases like "Iberian Muslims."

47. Bartolomé de las Casas, *Historia*, Book II, Chapter IV, cited in Jay (2002, 18–19).

48. Las Casas (1974, 37–49). While often understood that, historically, Las Casas won this debate with Sepúlveda, officially there was no conclusion to the junta by the jury of scholars.

49. Garrido Aranda (1980, 67).

50. Ibid. (65).

51. Las Casas (1973, 204–205, fol. 86v–87v, and 293–294, fols. 167v–168r).

52. Pope Paul III's papal bull *Sublimis Dei* (May 29, 1537a), unequivocally declared the indigenous peoples of the Americas to be rational beings with souls and, thus, entitled to rights of liberty and property (as well as evangelization); Paul III reaffirmed this message only a couple days later in his papal encyclical to Cardinal Juan de Tavera, Archbishop of Toledo, *Veritas ipsa* (June 2, 1537b).

53. Christian (1981, 195–196).

54. Martínez Portorreal, "Bartolomé de las Casas inventó término 'Derechos Humanos,'" Con la pluma como espada (blog), July 16, 2007, http://www.conlaplumacomoespada.com/2007/07/16/bartolome-de-las-casas-invento-termino-derechos-humanos/; also see Gutiérrez (1993, 44, 386, 594n53).

55. Durán (1967), "Libro," 1, 5; my translation.

56. Megged (1995, 69–70).

57. Temprano (1990, xii–xviii).

58. Bernardino de Sahagún, *Historia general de las cosas de Nueva España*, Juan Carlos Temprano, ed. (Spain: HISAPAT, S. A., 1990 [ca. 1569]), 1; my translation.

59. Ibid.; my translation.

60. Megged (1995, 69).

61. Scholes (1952, 398).

62. Megged (1995, 68).

63. Ibid. (71, 82).

64. Ibid. (75, 80).

65. Zwarijes (1999, 17–18, 35–36). Also see, for example, Alcalá (1928).

66. Megged (1995, 70).

67. Ibid. (77).

68. While based on ethnographic study of contemporary K'iche' Maya, C. James MacKenzie's application of Eduadro Viveiros de Castro's concept of native "multinatural perspectivism" within the Highland Maya religious worldview may be also particularly insightful, at least heuristically, with respect to native Maya religion during the period immediately prior to and during first contact (2016, 64–112). Likewise, comparatively with respect to the native relgious worldview of other early colonial Mesoamericans, namely Zapotecs, also see Tavárez (2011, 9–13).

69. See, for example, Nielsen and Sellner Reuert (2009, 399–413; 2015, 25–54). While their articles focus specifically between the transmission of this cosmology by Franciscans to the Mexica, later chapters here argue for the slightly different multilayered cosmology conveyed by Dominicans to the Maya.

70. Zwartijes (1999, 21–22).

71. For Origen's *On First Principles*, see Butterworth (1973, especially Book IV, 256–288), and for Augustine's *Teaching Christianity: De Doctrina Christiana* regarding references on things (*res*) and signs (*signa*), respectively, see Hill (1996, 106–107, 129–162).

72. García-Ruiz (1992, 89–92).

73. León-Portilla (2009, 57–58). In this respect, linguistic or language ideology is treated here as a subset or type of semiotic ideology, a concept that I draw from Keane (2007, 5, 13–21, 42, 59–60).

74. Scholes (1952, 402). For a detailed analysis of the development and use of the linguist work by Spanish Franciscans among the Yukatek Maya in the late sixteenth and seventeenth centuries, see Hanks (2010, 118–156).

75. Scholes (1952, 399–400), Vázquez (1937, 125–126).

76. On the development of prehispanic Maya literacy, but mainly among the ancient Lowland Maya, see Houston (1994).

77. Scholes (400).

78. Vázquez (1937, 125).

79. See, for example, Hamann (2015, 60) regarding the work by mendicants with Highland Mayan languages like Kaqchikel. Nebrija, a Spanish humanist, also published the first Castilian grammar in 1492 (Scholes 1952, 403); he is also called "Antonio de Lebrixa" in Zwartijes (1999, 20). For examples of Nebrija's works, see Nebrija (1926, 1996). This simultaneous critical attention to the classical languages—Latin, Greek, Hebrew, and Arabic—of ancient texts and local vernaculars not only placed Nebrija among the top representatives of Iberian humanism but also established him as among the first modern linguists. Followers like Alcalá in Andalusia and Friar Alonso de Molina, O.F.M., among the Nahua saw his work as paradigmatic; see Lope Blanch (1997, 39–45) and Alvar (1992, 313–339).

80. Chuchiak (2017); Sachse (2018). Also see Hamann (2015, 42) regarding Nebrija and Calepino.

81. Ximénez (1993, xii); Chinchilla argues that these two Arabic letters are the *ayin* for the tresillo and the *waw* for the cuatrillo; however, orthographically, this is maybe a *waw* <و>, but phonetically based on a Kufic *qaf* <ق>. I am endebted to Perry Wong's close comparison between the Arabic script of *aljamía* or Spanish *aljamiado*, Iberian Andalusi, and Kufic of North Africa; Wong also suggests that these early mendicants used the Andalusian *fa'* <ڢ>, which traditionally wrote the dot below the character for the Parra letter <4,> (*cuartillo* with a comma for <tz'>). Perry Wong, "Parra and the Orthography of al-Andalus in Guatemala," (unpublished paper, 2009). Brinton's earlier work recognizes that these two characters by Parra were likely based on Arabic script, however Brinton erroneously thought that Parra drew upon Arabic numbers; Brinton (1884, 358–360). If this were the case, they would most likely have been the Arabic number nine <٩> for the *cuartillo* <4> and number four <٤> for the *trecillo* <ɛ>, which would probably have confused those mendicants already familiar with Arabic. These two letters are now written as <q'> and <k'>, respectively.

82. These latter two characters are now written as <tz'> and <ch'>, respectively, in the current Maya orthography.

83. These two characters are now written as <t'> and <tz> in Guatemala or also <ts> in Mexico for the latter, respectively, in the current Maya orthographies.

84. Scholes (1952, 411).

85. See, for example, Pané (1999).

86. For the former, see Constantino Bayle as cited in Pané (1999, xviin1), and for the latter, see León-Portilla (2002) and Baird (1993, 14–18). However, Victoria Ríos Castaño (2014) has critiqued this attribution to Sahagún and has argued the extent to which Sahagún's ethnographic approach drew from investigative methods used by prosecutors in the Spanish Inquistition back in Salamanca.

87. Baird (1993, 7).

88. Ebacher (1991, 136, 158, 162n18).

89. Among the bibliographies and catalogue listings surveyed here are Chinchilla M. (1993, xxvii–xxix), García Icazbalceta (1954), Solano Pérez-Lila (1963, 319–3490), and Streit (1924, 284–330). For early notable use of music in Guatemala, particularly by Dominicans, see Bossú Z. (1986) and Romero (2017).

90. Stevenson (1964, 341–352), Stevenson (1966, 91–94).

91. See, for example, Jay and Michell (1999). Pictures also often accompanied written text; in general, however, mendicant missionaries preferred written texts over picto-ideographic writings; Ebacher (1991, 148).

92. Burkhart (2014, 167–206).

93. Ebacher (1991, 156–157); for specific scholarly attention to the development and use of catechisms in Yukatek by Franciscan missionaries in the late sixteenth and seventeenth centuries, see Hanks (2010, 242–276).

94. The correct plural is *doctrinae christianae*, but the more Hispanicized version is more common in bibliographies and secondary literature in both Spanish and English.

95. Rodríquez (1998).

96. Marthaler (1995, 10). However, as mentioned earlier, Augustine's *De doctrina christiana* ("On Teaching Christianity"), despite the title, should not be confused with a catechism; it is, instead, a treatise on semiotics (theory of signs) and hermeneutics (theory of interpretation), especially with regards to how a Christian should read scripture.

97. Ibid. (11).

98. See, for example, McGuire (1998, 1–58).

99. Also see, for example, Smith Stark (2010).

100. There is little scholarly attention to the office of *fiscal* as developed and used by Dominican missionaries among the Highland Maya. For detailed analysis of Franciscan missionaries among the Yukatek or Lowland Maya, however, see Hanks (2010, 59–84). For detailed analysis of mendicant catechisms written in and for, if not also with, Highland Maya such as the K'iche' and Kaqchikel, see Sachse (2016, 2017d).

101. García Icazbalceta (1954, 86), Rodríguez Demorizi (1945, xx). Despite this interpretation of García Icazbalceta's bibliography by Rodríguez Demorizi, given the popularity of Gerson's works in the previous century and the lack of greater specificity as to which text in particular by Bonaventure that this could be, I suspect that this text is not by Bonaventure but is Gerson's *On Mystical Theology*. For examples of these texts by Gerson, see McGuire (1998, 262–364).

102. Phelan (1970, 44–58).

103. McGinn (1979, 97–112).

104. Tavárez (2013, 203–235).

105. Hanks (2010, 15–21).

106. On these early schools in Guatemala, see Van Akkeren (2010, 33; 2011, 102), Remesal (1988, II, 337–338). For their counterparts by the Franciscans with the Yukatek, see Hanks (2010), or by the Dominicans and later the Jesuits among the Quechua in the Andes, see Durston (2007).

107. Legg (1908), Bonniwell (1945).

108. Durston (2007), Romero (2012a, 2012b).

109. See, for example, Resines (2007) as well as Resines (2002). However, recent work by Louis Burkhart has discovered that the doctrinal content of these pictographic catechisms could not have dated prior to the 1650s and were likely written, not by clergy, but by seventeenth-century Nahua elites (Burkhart 2014).

110. Again, I am treating language ideology or linguistic ideology (a constituency's local understanding of language) as a subset or type of semiotic ideology (a constituency's understanding of signification), a concept developed by and borrowed from anthropologist Keane (2007, 5, 13–21, 42, 59–60).

111. Romero (2015a).

112. Hanks (2010, 19–20).

113. Poole (1989, 13).

114. Regarding the Holy Office's arrival to Guatemala, see Chuchiak (2012, 24).

115. Butzer (1992, 351).

116. Denevan (1992, 370; 1996, 392), Butzer (1992, 347).

117. Denevan (1992, 371).

118. Butzer (1992, 354).

119. Veblen (1977, 494–498).

CHAPTER 3: *NIMA AJTIJ* FATHER FRIAR DOMINGO DE VICO, O.P.

Sections in this chapter regarding Vico's biography and description of his *Theologia Indorum* have previously appeared as more truncated versions in English in Sparks (2017a, 25–33) and in Spanish in Sparks (2014a, 93–108; 2017b). Based on subsequent research and findings, this more expanded chapter corrects parts of those prior summaries regarding Vico's life and work.

1. Remesal (1966b, IV, 1497); English translation mine.

2. Maxwell and Hill (2006, 301). Orthography has been modified to accord with the ALMG; English translation mine.

3. See, for example, Adorno (2007, 21–98).

4. There are, of course, two other possible translations of this title from the Latin: "Theology of the Indies" or "Theology for the Indies" (in other words a *Teología de las indias* rather than *Teología de los indios*). However, as argued in this chapter, Vico seemed primarily concerned with the religious, linguistic, and cultural phenomena of the Highland Maya rather than also the diversity and history of flora and fauna of the Americas, as Indorum is used by other writers.

5. Ricard (1966), Van Oss (1986). The colonial Kingdom of Guatemala stretched from present-day Chiapas, Mexico, down through Costa Rica. Guatemala was considered a subdivision within the Viceroyalty of New Spain (Spanish North America) but had its own *audiencia* (Spanish juridical court or council).

6. Including such work as that of anthropologist and former Catholic priest to Guatemala, John D. Early (2006) *The Maya and Catholicism: An Encounter of Worldviews*; historian James Muldoon, ed. (2004), *The Spiritual Conversion of the Americas*; Ricardo Bendaña Perdomo (1996) *La iglesia en Guatemala: Síntesis histórica del catolicismo*; historian John Frederick Schwaller's (2011) more hemispheric *The History of the Catholic Church in Latin America: From Conquest to Revolution and Beyond*; Josep Ignasi Saranyana's (1999) four-volume edited history of theology in Latin America from 1493 to 2001, *Teología en América Latina*; or the very focused and detailed study of Dominican missionaries in the sixteenth-century Americas, *Los predicadores novohispanos del siglo XVI* by María Teresa Pita Moreda (1992).

7. Iraburu (2003, 118).

8. Such as, for example, St. John Fancourt (1854, 182–183), Helps (1857, 337) quoting from Villagutierre Soto-Mayor (libro I, capitulo 10). Even André Saint-Lu's (1968) highly focused tome on Dominicans in the region of the Verapaces, where Vico carried out the bulk of his missionary work, has very few mentions of Vico's life, work, or writings.

9. This absence is even more curious given Remesal's close affinity with Las Casas a century later; see, for example, MacLeod (1970).

10. Especially chapters 6 through 10 of book X of Remesal (1966a, I, 420; II, 297), Ximénez (1977, especially II, 523–525).

11. Remesal and Ximénez's possible sources include Bartolomé de las Casas's, *Apologética historia sumeria*, a text to which Vico most likely contributed. Ximénez may also have consulted the slightly earlier contemporaneous work by Juan de Villagutierre Sotomayor, *Historia de la conquista de la provincia de el Itza*.

12. Sapper (1907, II, 427).

13. Pilling (1885, 786–787), Muñoz y Manzano Viñaza (1892, especially 258–259).

14. Brasseur de Bourbourg (1871); for specific entries regarding Vico, see pages 136, 152–154, 164, 166, and 180; for the false attribution of a *Theologia Indorum* to Franciscan friar Francisco Maldonado, O.F.M., see page 94.

15. See Rojas (1893, 179–180) regarding the erroneous attribution of the *Theologia Indorum* to copyist Friar Francisco Maldonado.

16. For example, the following Maya grammar and lexicons are questionably attributed to Vico: BnF Ms Amér 46 (Kaqchikel), BnF Ms Amér 63 (K'iche'), and Codex Ind. 13 (Kaqchikel and K'iche') at the John Carter Brown Library, Brown University.

17. These languages were K'iche', Kaqchikel, Tz'utujil, Q'eqchi', Poqomam, and Ch'ol (Lakantun or Lacandon), according to Ximénez and Poqomchi', according to Biermann (Ximénez 1929, I 58; Biermann 1964, I, 128). Also see the letter to the Audiencia de los Confines from Dominicans of May 14, 1556, Archivo General de Indias (Seville, Spain), expediente Guatemala, Legajo 168 (i.e., the records on Guatemala, file 168), as cited in Bredt-Kriszat and Holl (1997, 176).

18. Remesal (1966a, II, 296–297); English translation mine.

19. According to Ruud Van Akkeren, the earlier date is more widely mentioned but not formally documented in popular literature (Van Akkeren 2009, 4; 2011, 84). However René Acuña arrives at the later date in order to place Vico in school at a more plausible age by before 1544 (Acuña 1985, 281). For examples of some of the more recent and often cited popular references to Vico (which often use the earlier date of his birth), see the *Gran Enciclopedia de Andalucía* (1979, 32, 59), Jarra Torres Navarrete (2002, II, 659), Mesansa (n.d.). See also the only book in the Archivo General de Centro América in Guatemala City that mentions Vico, which claims that Vico was not martyred but rather elected bishop of Verapaz between 1560 and 1566 and died a septuagenarian. On the web, see the Guatemalan Catholic Archdiocese of Los Altos's website http://arquidiocesisdelosaltos.org/content/view/15/34/ (accessed June 2009; no longer active); the Spanish and French language website dedicated to the biographies of mendicants who worked among the Maya, http://moines.mayas.free.fr (accessed July 2019); and the more recent Swiss-Guatemalan development project among Q'eqchi' Maya in Cahabón, Alta Verapaz, the Instituto Agroecológico de Educación Bilingüe "Fray Domingo de Vico," http://www.guatesol.ch/lwschule_es.html (accessed July 2019). I agree with Van Akkeren and Acuña that the later year, 1519, is more likely. Furthermore, his birth place as Úbeda is most likely attributed to Remesal's mention of his being a "son of Saint Andrew's convent of the city of Úbeda in Andalucía" (*hijo del convento de San Andrés de la ciudad de Úbeda, en Andalucía*; Remesal 1966b, 1481). However this citation specifically refers to Vico's education rather than birth. In the decades leading up to the fifteenth century the Vico surname was more prevalent in Huelma, only around twenty-five miles south of Úbeda; see, for example, Sáez Gámez (1979, 107–108). Friar Tomás de la Torre

lists Vico as from Úbeda; however the designation of towns for the other members of this mission are not places for birth but rather of their convents prior to joining this delegation in either Salamanca or Seville (Torre 1985, 59–60).

20. Unfortunately, due to the passage of time and the destruction of ecclesial property due to the anticlericalism during the Napoleonic Wars and then Spanish Civil War, the records of the University of Salamanca prior to the seventeenth century are sparse. As a result there appears to be no record of Vico in the Archivo Histórico de la Universdad de Salamanca (person communication, July 2018, with Victoria Barcina Cuevas, Jefa de sección del Archivo Histórico). However, while the handwriting is difficult to read, there may remain some mention of him in some of the early sixteenth-century documents (http://ausa.usal.es/ausa_pruebastestificales.php; accessed July 2018).

21. Cuervo Angulo (1914, II, 579). Cuervo Angulo's history of the Dominicans who went to Guatemala with Las Casas in 1544 appears to be largely based on the chronicle by Remesal. However, Remesal makes no mention of the Convent of Santo Domingo de la Cruz in general let alone Vico's residence there instead of at the Convent of San Esteban. In this respect, Cuervo Angulo possibly supplemented Remesal's history with now-lost records once in the archives at Salamanca. According to Father Lazáro Sastre, O.P., the loss of clerical archives and property—such as the tomb of Las Casas at Nuestra Señor de Atocha in Madrid—throughout Spain during the Peninsular War (1807–1814) and later its Civil War (1936–1939) was extensive (personal communication, July 2018), similar to the loss of colonial Highland Maya records once kept in local churches that were damaged during Guatemala's internal armed conflict and genocide (1960–1996).

22. Ibid. (254, 580, 600). The surviving archives of Santo Domingo de la Cruz are sparse and are now held at San Esteban but contain no mentions of Vico. Likewise, the archives of San Esteban has a six-volume work of roughly 1,300 pages each that lists chronologically the names of Dominicans who studied at the University of Salamanca. Unfortunately, volume three, which covers 1537–1564, has been lost and Vico's name does not appear in volume two. At the very least this indictes that Vico arrived to study at Salamanca and reside at the Convento de Santo Domingo de la Cruz by no earlier than 1537, further supporting Acuña's later birthdate for Vico. I am endebted to the assistance of Father Lazáro Sastre, O.P., head archivist at the Convento de San Esteban, for his assistance in examining the records for Vico's name and showing me the archives in July 2018.

23. In subsequent centuries the former Convento de Santo Domingo de la Cruz was used as a warehouse and stable, and fell into general disrepair. It is now municipal property, restored by the local government of Salamanca, and since 2002 has been used as the Sala de Exposiciones Santo Domingo de la Cruz for concerts and gallery shows.

24. Unfortunately, there are apparently no available documents at the Dominican convent in Úbeda prior to the early eighteenth century (Huerga 1992, 289–291).

25. Not to be confused with the understanding of Christian laity as persons who are neither ordained clergy nor take religious vows of a particular order, mendicant laity (*legos*) consist of non-clergy men and woman (i.e., not priests or friars [the "first order"] nor nuns [the "second order"]) as the "third order" of people who commit to live according to the rules and ideals of a particular religious order (e.g., the rules of Saint Dominic de Guzmán or of Saint Francis of Assisi).

26. Even nearly 150 years later Ximénez noted the influence of Vitoria on these early cohorts of Dominican missionaries to Guatemala (Ximénez 1977, 374).

27. Alonso de Villafante also appears in Torres's account, but this appears to be an orthographic error and, thus, the same person as Alonso de Villasante (Torre 1985, 50).

28. Torre (1985, 22, 59–60).

29. Ciudad Suárez (1996, 29–31n66). More details and dates regarding this specific delegation of Dominicans are found in the account by one of its own members, Dominican friar Tomás de la Torre; see Blom and Torre (1973, 429–526). This account, however, ends with the delegation's arrival into Chiapas, Mexico, and does not provide details of Vico's life in Guatemala. While often mistakenly identified as the first bishop of Chiapas, Las Casas actually succeeded Juan de Arteaga y Avendaño, who was appointed the second bishop of Ciudad Real de Chiapas on February 15, 1541, but died shortly afterwards on September 8, 1541. Similarly, Arteaga y Avendaño had followed the first bishop of Chiapas, Juan de Urteaga, O.S.H., who died in 1540, less than a year after being appointed in March 1539. Las Casas was appointed bishop on December 19, 1543, consecrated as bishop on March 30, 1544, and served until his resignation on September 11, 1550 when back in Spain.

30. Ciudad Suárez (1996, 30, 54, 125). However, the delegation's designated chronicler, Torre, does not list Vico as one of the friars who leaves directly from the Dominican house in Salamanca on January 12, 1544. Vico first appears in a longer listing of the delegation in Andalucía, and Torre only notes that the friar is from Úbeda (Blom and Torre 1973, 433–434, 466–467).

31. Archivo General de Indias (Seville, Spain), Guatemala 402, book T.2, folios 105v–106v, as cited in Ciudad Suárez (1996, 24); for bracketed information see page 160n43; translation mine.

32. Cuidad Suáez (1996, 31).

33. Ibid. (31–32n67, citing Torre 1985, 87–89), Van Akkeren (2009, 4; 2011, 84), Torre (1985, 137).

34. Remesal (1966a, II, 289–292).

35. Fabié (1879, 185–186).

36. Pérez Fernández (1981, 672–673), Van Akkeren (2010, 4–5; 2011, 84–85). The Lowland Izta' Maya in Tayasal, or present-day Flores, on Lake Petén Itzá in the El Petén rainforest, were the last major Maya group to be militarily defeated by the Spanish, on March 13, 1697 (Jones 1998).

37. Saint-Lu (1968, 177, 566).

38. According to Giménez Fernández, who relies largely on Remesal, Cáncer was part of this early cohort (Giménez Fernández 1971, 89–92). However, according to Biermann, who draws on Bataillon's scholarship and critique of Remesal's account, Cáncer did not enter the region until 1542 (Biermann 1971, 450, 453). Therefore, for this period, also see Bataillon (1951).

39. Biermann (1971, 455–456), Giménez Fernández (1971, 89–91). Again, Bataillon and therefore Biermann deny this early presence of Cáncer in Guatemala, as is accepted by other scholars of Las Casas.

40. Giménez Fernández (1971, 92–93).

41. As quoted from Biermann (1971, 465) from a source that he cites as *Colección de documentos inéditos relativos al descubrimiento, conquista y colonización de las posesiones españoles en América* (or CDIAm), ser. VII, (1864–1884), 151–154 (Biermann 1971, 482n780).

42. Respectively, Kislak 1015, fols. 17r–59r, 89 in K'iche' and Ayer Ms 1536 in Q'eqchi'. See Sparks and Sachse (2017).

43. Saint-Lu (1968, 378). Romero disputes this common understanding and argues that Spaniards misunderstood the name in Nahuatl for the region, which was instead called the "Place of Owls," Tecolotlán or Teculutlán (Romero 2017, 170).

44. Remesal (1988, II, 161).

45. Ibid. (271).

46. Ibid. (169).

47. Saint-Lu (1968, 314–315, note 163), Van Akkeren (2009, 4–5). These new towns were known administratively to Dominicans as "congregations" (*congregaciones*) or "doctrines" (*doctrinas*) and to the Spanish colonial *audiencia* as "reductions" (*reducciones*). For comparative understanding in the Spanish Americas, see Lovell (1990, 289–290, note 3), and specifically on the Franciscans in the Yucatán, see Hanks (2010).

48. Remesal (1988, II, 361).

49. Akkeren (2009, 7; 2011, 87). Perhaps in an ironic twist of history, the colonial Dominican convent where Vico was the prior and based in present-day La Antigua, Guatemala, is now a five-star luxury hotel: Hotel Casa Santo Domingo, at the eastern end of the colonial city (3a Calle Oriente, no. 28A). The archaeological ruins of the colonial Dominican monastery may be visited as part of the private museum of the hotel and are presented in a related children's book, *Let's See Santo Domingo in Antigua Guatemala / Conozcamos Santo Domingo en La Antigua Guatemala* by Elizabeth Bell (2010).

50. Santiago (or Saint James) built in the Panchoy Valley was the third of four attempts to establish a regional capital for Guatemala after Iximche' (Tecpán), then Ciudad Vieja (San Miguel Escobar), and then the most enduring capital city of Guatemala to date, currently La Antigua. The fourth and current capital—La Nueva Guatemala de la Asunción, or Ciudad de Guatemala (Guatemala City)—was established in the 1770s near the prehispanic city of Kaminal Juyu' (ca. 1500 BCE–ca. 1200 CE) in the Valley of La Ermita.

51. In this sense, as is discussed in Chapter 8, Diego Reynoso for Dominicans in Guatemala is comparable to Gaspar Antonio Chi for Franciscans later in the Yucatán.

52. Namely the Kaqchikel baptismal names of *popol winaq* Gregorio de Vigo and Gabriel de Vico; Recinos (2001, 180–181), Van Akkeren (2009, 84).

53. Carmack (1973, 367, 393).

54. See Lutz and Dakin (1996, 12–13, 94n8) identifying "Memoria 3" as referring to Dominicans, though it does not specify who is the mentioned "Fray Domingo." These Mexican Nahuatl speakers are distinct from the historic Guatemalan population of Nahuatl speakers referred to as "Yaki" in the K'iche'an literature and "Pipil" in the colonial Spanish documents. For discussion of postcontact Nahua history in early Guatemala see Matthews (2012).

55. Lovell (1990, 286).

56. Vigil (1976, 502, 503, 505–506).

57. While the Spanish is fairly straightforward here, the different spelling of Vico's name is noteworthy, "Bico," and the other various ways that it appears, like "Vigo," in both Spanish and Maya documents, may also account for how he has disappeared from modern historical accounts.

58. Zorita (1999, 708). I am indebted to Ruud van Akkeren for directing me to this source. However, there is a historical puzzle in that some claim that Zorita (also as Zurita) did not arrive to Guatemala until March 1555, only a few months before Vico's death, although this may indicate that Vico was still in Santiago rather than relocated to Cobán in early 1555 or there are discrepancies by Zorita in his dates; see, for example, Keen (1994, 35). Ralph Vigil, however, claims that Zorita arrived in Guatemala on September 20, 1553, and left in April 1556 to be in Mexico City by July 9 that same year (Vigil 1976, 508).

59. Keen (1994, 217–223).

60. Scholes (1952, 400). Also see Megged (1995, 68n21).

61. Based on comparative textual analysis conducted in March 2015 of Kislak 1015 (pages 29–80).

62. Vázquez (1937, I, 128), Lovell (1990, 285).

63. Also spelled "Xiltoteqeque"; however, not to be confused with the predominantly Poqomchi' town of San Luis Jilotepeque farther east in the region of Jalapa.

64. As the date indicated, for example, in APS MS, fol. 185r; BnF Ms Amér 5, fol. 185r; and BnF Ms Amér 10, fol. 101r. Remesal also notes the similarities in the approach taken by Aquinas and that later of Vico in Guatemala among the Maya (Remesal 1966a, II, 298).

65. Remesal (1988, II, 353), Lovell (1990, 285).

66. Acuña (1983, XXIX); while Van Akkeren also agrees with Acuña's analysis and hypothesis for this date (2010, 10; 2011, 88), there is no clear composition date apparent in any of the known surviving versions of volume two of the *Theologia Indorum* as there is with volume one.

67. APS Ms, fol. 185r; colonial orthography maintained but English translation mine. Also see Sparks (2017a, 166).

68. Van Akkeren (2011, 87).

69. Remesal (1966a, II, 294–295).

70. Confusingly, his death has also been claimed to have occurred on November 22 and November 28, 1555. Given the lack of primary sources from the 1550s, it is also possible that Remesal took poetic license in having Vico martyred on the feast day of the saint whom he so closely identified with as his patron and protector.

71. Remesal (1966a, II, 196–198, 292–298, 312), Saint-Lu (1968, 424, 426–427n227), Recinos (1953, 140n281), Thompson (1966, 29), and Biermann (1971, 478). According to Biermann, the Dominicans sent an account dated May 14, 1556, that reported the details of Vico's and López's deaths, which may have been one of Remesal's sources but that has not been located.

72. Among these sparse yet still extant early Spanish sources are León Pinelo (1986), Morán (2000), Salazar (2000), and Tovilla (2000).

73. Sapper (1906, 373–381), Stoll (1906, 375, 377); due to the date of transcription and paleography of this document, the orthography has been left as it was published by Sapper and Stoll; the translation from Sapper and Stoll's Spanish translation of the Poqomchi' is mine. The catalogue of Princeton University Library lists this *título* as written in Q'eqchi' and Spanish. While it does contain various loanwords and personal names in Castilian, presumably based on the typed notes by William Gates included with the *título*, both Stoll and Sapper identity the document as Poqomchi'.

74. Maxwell and Hill (2006, 300–302); orthography in the Kaqchikel has been changed to accord with the Academia de Lenguas Mayas de Guatemala (ALMG), namely the ALMG's 2008 decision to use only five unmarked vowels.

75. Franicisco Marroquín was still bishop of Guatemala at the time of Vico's death and La Parra's transfer to the Yucatán. This mention most likely refers instead to Juan Ramírez de Arellano, O.P., the fourth bishop of Guatemala from 1600 to 1609, and is a historical conflation by the Kaqchikel authors that, thus, evinces the composition period of this Maya text.

76. Ibid. (301).

77. Las Casas (1967, 499–528), Bredt-Kriszat (1999, 193), and Biermann (1964, 130).

78. Christenson (2016, 85–86).

79. See Bredt-Kriszat (1999, 185n9).

80. Scholes (1952). Marroquín's catechism is often misidentified as written in K'iche' (Utlateco)—for example in Dahlmann (1893, 149), Muñoz y Manzano Viñaza (1892, 11), and University Library, University of North Carolina at Chapel Hill https://archive.org/details/doctrinacristianoomarr (accessed May 2018)—but it is actually in Kaqchikel (Guatemalteco); see Marroquín (1905).

81. Marshall Peterson erroneously claims that not only was Vico's *Theologia Indorum* published but that it was printed in 1544, ten years before Vico even completed the first volume or had even arrived to the Americas; see Peterson (1999, 31n5).

82. Cortéz y Larraz, "Respuesta del Padre Cura de Xocopilas," 1771, Archivo General de Indias, cuaderno 2, fols. 35v–43r, Seville, Spain, found at http://afehc-historia-centro americana.org /index.php/_fichiers/index.php?action=fi_aff&id=1739 (accessed on June 2009, no longer active) and https://www.afehc-historia-centroamericana.org/index_action _fi_aff_id_1739.html (not active) orthography left uncorrected, English translation mine; also see Solano Pérez-Lila (1963, 330).

83. Remesal (1966a, II, 298); Sáenz de Santa María (1974, 369).

84. For comparison of these sources see Sachse (2007, 2; accessed June 2009).

85. BnF Ms Amér 46 (Kaqchikel), BnF Ms Amér 63 (K'iche'), and Codex Ind. 13 (Kaqchikel and K'iche') at the John Carter Brown Library, Brown University; however, based on language use within the *Theologia Indorum* and these philological works, Vico's attributed authorship to the latter two needs further critical, comparative examination for confirmed verification similar to that carried out on BnF Ms Amér 46 by Bredt-Kriszat and Ursula Holl (1988) and Hernández (2008). Until then Vico's authorship of BnF Ms Amér 63 and Codex Ind. 13 is questionable.

86. See, for example, Chinchilla M. (1993), Guzmán (1984), and Pläschke (1995, VIIn23), as cited in Bredt-Kriszat and Holl (1997, 188n16).

87. BnF Ms Amér 47, fol. 88r.

88. Carmack and Mondloch (1989, 140–141, 173). Due to the poor resolution of the photocopy version of this folio, Carmack and Mondloch's paleographic analysis and older orthography have been maintained; however, the English translation is mine from their K'iche' and Spanish versions.

89. Carmack and Mondloch (1985, 236); my English translation and punctuation from Carmack and Mondloch's transcribed K'iche' and Spanish translation. I have retranscribed the K'iche' version to agree with the ALMG orthography.

90. Bredt-Kriszat (1999, 184), Ximénez (1985, 43); my English translation from Ximénez's Spanish.

91. Bredt-Kriszat (1999, 185).

92. Based on my survey of the various collections, seventeen partial manuscripts of the *Theologia Indorum* in the respective languages in which they are written are, of volume I: APS Mss.497.4.Ua13, previously Indian Manuscript 178 (hereafter APS Ms; in K'iche' Maya); BnF Ms Amér 4 (in Tz'utujil Maya); BnF Ms Amér 5 (in K'iche' Maya); BnF Ms Amér 10 (in K'iche' Maya); BnF Ms Amér 42 (in Kaqchikel Maya); Garrett-Gates Mesoamerican Manuscript (hereafter GGMM) nos. 178 (in K'iche' Maya) and 179 (in K'iche' Maya); of volume II: GGMM nos. 175–180 (in K'iche' Maya); Butler Ayer Manuscript 1512 Cakchiquel 33 (hereafter Ayer Ms 1512; in Kaqchikel Maya); BnF Ms Amér 3 (in Kaqchikel Maya);

Berendt-Brinton Linguistic Collection, Manuscript 700, Item 197 (in Tz'utujil Maya); and of portions of both volumes I and II together: BnF Ms Amér 56 (in K'iche' Maya), GGMM no. 227 (in Kaqchikel Maya), and Manuscript 700, Item 78 (in Q'eqchi' Maya). John Weeks lists another two manuscripts attributed to the Princeton University Library and an additional four photostatic copies whose whereabouts presently remain unknown or are lost; see Weeks (1990, 197–199) and Bredt-Kriszat (1995, 218). In bibliographies and catalogue listings of the nineteenth and twentieth centuries, BnF Ms Amér 42 is erroneously attributed not to Domingo de Vico but rather to the manuscript's copyist, Friar Francisco Maldonado, O.F.M.; see, for example, (Adams 1952, 47), who cites Beristain y Souza (1947) and Dahlmann (1893, 179–180), who cites Pilling (1885) and Leclerc (1867). BnF Ms Amér 59, which is a manuscript copy of Dominican friar Domingo de Basseta's 1698 bilingual K'iche'-Castilian dictionary, contains a brief mention from chapter 25 of Vico's *Theologia Indorum*; however, this fragment appears too insignificant to include in the above list; see BnF Ms Amér 59, fols. 246r–247v. In November 2019 Frauke Sachse and I discovered an eighteenth manuscript at the Tozzer Library of Harvard University (Tozzer Ms C.A. 8 Q 40); however, due to production time for this book I have listed it here but we have not yet closely studied it.

93. See Acuña (1985, 19; 1989; 1992, 137); and Remesal (1966a, II, 297). Remesal most likely used Viana as his source, hence the similarity. Rather than reconstructing the text based on the various surviving manuscripts, Acuña relies on Remesal but also Ximénez. See Acuña (1985, 283) regarding the overall structure and contents of Vico's theology.

94. Cited as Archivo General de la Nación, Inquisición, vol. 83, exp. 24, fols. 305–306 (as cited and quoted in Acuña 2004, 23); also see Acuña (1992, 137). Also consulted was Acuña's original typed manuscript in La Antigua, Guatemala: Centro de Investigaciones Regionales de Mesoamerica (CIRMA, 1989, 3); and Acuña (2004, 19). As I highlight later, the designation of the units or sections in the *Theologia Indorum* as "chapters" is precarious, hence my use of scare quotes.

95. Cited as AGNM, Inquisición, Vol. 83, exp. 24, fols. 305–306; however, neither a copy of the original nor a fuller citation was available but is as cited and quoted in Acuña (2004, 23); my English translation.

96. Brinton (2011, 19).

97. For these recent translations of selected chapters, see Acuña (1983, 1–16; 1985, 281–307; 1989; 1992, 136–148; 2004, 17–45); López Ixcoy (2010, 2011, 2013, 2017); Sachse (2017a); Sparks (2011, 417–621; 2017a, 47–120, 126–167); and Zimmermann and Riese (1980, 612–617). A critical transcription and translation of both volumes—the entire *Theologia Indorum*—is currently underway by Sparks, Sachse, López Ixcoy, and Romero.

98. Ten of these eleven K'iche'an language manuscripts remain in the collection of the American Philosophical Society, including not only a version of the first volume of the *Theologia Indorum*, a collection of sermons, and various grammars and dictionaries but also of

Coto's *Thesavrvs verborvm*. As part of the recognition (and Maya critique) of the 500th anniversary of Columbus's first landing in the Americas, in 1990 the APS repatriated the *Calepino en lengua cakchikel*, attributed to Friar Francisco de Varea, to Mariano Gálvez University at the request of the university's rector, Álvaro Rolando Torres Moss, and David F. Oltrogge, then director of the university's new School of Linguistics. While until 2018 the exact whereabouts of this *Calepino en lengua cakchikel* manuscript remained unknown, it was confirmed by Torres Moss to still be held uncatalogued at Mariano Gálvez University (personal communication, June 2018). A transcription edited by Judy Garland de Butler was published by the university in 1997. Similarly, six colonial mendicant texts specifically in K'iche', some of which may relate to Vico's work, once held at the Pius XII Memorial Library of St. Louis University have also been lost (personal communication with Gregory Pass in March 2018; see, Landar 1967, 77–78). If ever found, any one of these now missing six mendicant texts in K'iche', supposedly written in the 1550s, could provide additional insight on Vico's work or his wider philological context.

99. Personal communication by Robin Shoaps, July 2008.

100. Ciudad Suárez (1996, 2).

101. During my field and archival research in Guatemala in the summer of 2008, I searched the following institutions for any possible remaining fragment of work by or about Domingo de Vico: the Archivo General de Centroamérica, the Biblioteca Nacional (including its rare books catalogue, the Fondos de Libros Antiguos), and the Archivo Eclesiástica del Arzobispado Metropolitano de Guatemala (all in Guatemala City), and the library and archives of the Centro de Investigaciones Regionales de Mesoamérica (CIRMA) in La Antigua, Guatemala. These searches were fruitless.

102. Recinos (1950, 41).

103. Ibid. (55, 43n68). His name also appears as "Coloché" in some Spanish-language sources.

104. Tedlock (1996, 27), Coe (1992, 75–76).

105. Recinos (1950, 43–44). For a more thorough account of Brasseur de Bourbourg, see Sainson (2017).

106. Recinos (1950, 45).

107. Ibid., may be found as: Francisco Ximénez, "Manuscrito antiguo Kiche encontrado a principios del siglo XVIII entre los indios del Pueblo de Chichicastenango" (Guatemala, ca. 1721), University of California, Berkeley, Hubert Howe Bancroft Collection, BANC MSS M-M 439.

108. For a more detailed account of this transfer from Gates to Princeton University via Garrett, see Basler and Wright (2008, 29–55). For a detailed cataloguing of Gates' collection in and beyond the library holdings of Princeton University, especially of versions of Vico's *Theologia Indorum*, see also Weeks (1985, 1990).

109. Recinos (1950, 45). For a precise listing of the works of Vico and others included in this transfer, see Omont (1925, 91–93, 99–100, 104–107). While an earlier, complete version of the *Title of Totonicapán* surfaced in the late twentieth century, still in possession by the Yax family, the copy obtained by Brassuer de Bourbourg now resides in the BnF as Ms Amér 77.

110. This version of the Popol Wuj in Ximénez's hand is generally agreed by scholars to be the oldest surviving copy and appears to be Ximénez's working copy and translation that he made directly from the purported K'iche' manuscript that has since been lost or is still guarded by K'iche' Maya religious leadership. It is currently catalogued as: "Empiezan las historias del origen de los indios de esta provincia de Guatemala," Francisco Ximénez, trans., ed., Newberry Library, Chicago, Illinois, Butler Ayer Manuscript 1515. As early as at least Daniel G. Brinton, scholars have read Ximénez as claiming that there were multiple written versions of the Popol Wuj read by colonial K'iche' elites (Brinton 2011, 21). I am indebted to John Aubrey and Analu López—respectively the former and current librarians for the Edward Ayer Manuscript Collection at the Newberry Library—for their notes and assistance in clarifying some of the reception history of the Popol Wuj and Vico documents.

111. For analysis of four of the manuscripts of the *Theologia Indorum* held at the BnF, also see Lladó (1990); however, not only does Lladó miss the other two manuscripts in her survey, it is also unclear whether she is examining different versions of two distinct volumes of the same work.

112. His own book on the K'iche' language testifies to Brasseur de Bourbourg's competency; see, Brasseur de Bourbourg (1961).

113. For Bossú's analysis, see Bossú Z. (1986). The original manuscript is Butler Ayer Manuscript 1536 (hereafter Ayer Ms 1536), Newberry Library, Chicago, Illinois. However, comparison of the rhetoric between these two texts by Vico and Cáncer raise doubts of Vico's authorship. See, for example, Sparks (2011, "Appendix One," notes).

114. Romero (2015a).

115. Sachse (2016).

116. Romero (2015b, 91–96).

117. Sparks and Sachse (2017).

118. Kislak 1015, fols. 17r–59r.

119. Sachse (2016); Romero (2015a).

120. These three manuscripts are: HSA (Hispanic Society of America) Ms NS3/11 (*Sermones varios predicados en lengua quiché, y trasladados para el uso de los padres de la orden de S.Domingo en Rabinal*), HSA Ms N53/34 (*Sermones, oraciones y traducciones de la biblia escritos y expuestos en lengua Cakchikel*), and HSA Ms NS3/37 (*Colección de oraciones y meditaciones en lengua Quiché*). My deep gratitude to Dr. John O'Neill of the HSA for identification and access of these manuscripts as well as explanation of the catalogue history within the HSA.

121. "Obra original é inédita sin duda escrita de la mano del autor el Fray Domingo de Vico": catalogue entry on front inset of HSA Ms NS3/37. More specifically this work appears to be a collection of Lenten lessons and reflections, though not sermons, on the sacraments.

122. HSA Ms N53/34. The third manuscript mentioned here, HSA Ms NS3/11, is also a set of later sermons written in K'iche' from the seventeenth and eighteenth centuries and mostly attributed to Friar Damián Delgado, O.P., but at least two are thought to be of Friar Domingo de Basseta, O.P.

123. Beristain y Souza (1947, originally published Mexico, 1816–1821; 2nd ed., Amecameca, 1883) as cited in and used by Adams (1952, 47). While the current website of the Guatemalan Catholic Archdiocese de Los Altos does not clearly cite sources in its mission history of the region, it is most likely referring to Beristain's work as well when it claims that Franciscans wrote their own *Theologia Indorum*, which clergy used in addition to that of Vico: http://arquidiocesisdelosaltos.org/content/view/15/34/.

124. For my evidence and comparative analysis of Vico's *Theologia Indorum* as found in BnF Ms Amér 5 and 10 and the purportedly Maldonado *Theologia Indorum* as Ayer Ms 1502, see Sparks (2011, 418n55). I am grateful to the Newberry Library for allowing me to verify my analysis and in correcting its catalog listing of Ayer Manuscript 1522, Cakchiquel 33.

125. García Ahumada (1994, 222). Unfortunately, García Ahumada does not provide any citation or documentation to support his assertion regarding this text or its attribution to Vico. Despite this lack, it is one of the more widely circulated factoids regarding Vico currently on the Internet (e.g., https://en.wikipedia.org/wiki/Domingo_de_Vico as of March 2018). Based on Távarez's research, this Nahuatl text mentioned by García Ahumada was most likely written not by Vico but rather by Franciscan friar Luis Rodríguez, as mentioned in Gerónimo de Mendieta's *Historia eclesiástica Indiana*, and is currently held at the Hispanic Society of America in New York (Tavárez 2013a).

126. According to Sergio Romero, the historic, precontact Nahuatl-speaking population of Central America consisted of speakers of at least two distinct dialects, which are distantly related to two distinct regional variants farther north in Mexico. The older of the two, eventually labeled as "Pipil," was spoken largely in El Salvador and southwestern coastal Guatemala and shared features with other eastern or "peripheral" variants, such as those spoken in Veracruz, Mexico. The later, second dialect, now called "Central American Nahuatl," was related more closely to, but was still notably distinct from, variants from central Mexico, such as the speakers of Central Mexican Nahuatl, who arrived after 1521 as Nahuatl-speaking allies ("mexicanos") of the Spaniards. K'iche'an documents that reflect on their precontact histories refer to both Pipil and Central American Nahuatl speakers as "Yaki" (personal communication with Romero on March 2018; also see Matthew 2012, 77–92; Braswell 2003b, 297).

127. Biermann (1971, 458).

128. Megged (1996, 107–106n13, 167).

129. I am grateful in personal communications with both Amos Megged as well as Louise Burkhart in their efforts to try and clarify the bibliographic entry on Megged (1996, 167).

130. This may also correspond with Oroz's *Lectionarium* in Otomí located in the US Library of Congress, Container 57. I am deeply grateful to Frauke Sachse of the University of Bonn and Janet Steins of Harvard University's Tozzer Library for their collaboration in analyzing this document and its entry. I am especially grateful to Pam Beattie of the University of Louisville and her expertise on medieval Iberian Franciscan literature in helping to read the Latin and positively identify the genre and content of the text.

131. See for example Van Doesburg and Swanton (2008). I am grateful to Sebastián van Doesburg for his preliminary comparative analysis between this early colonial Dominican *doctrina* in Chocho and my translations of Vico's *Theologia Indorum*; personal communication in 2012.

132. Based on my library and archival searches, these libraries are the Bibliothèque nationale de France, the Firestone Library of Princeton University, the American Philosophical Society in Philadelphia, the University of Pennsylvania Library, and the Newberry Library in Chicago, Illinois.

133. GGMM no. 175 is the only one that has even a surviving fragment of folio one in K'iche' but the upper third is missing.

134. Based on comparative analysis of the surviving fragment of GGMM no. 175, fol. 1; BnF Ms Amér 3, fol. 1r; and Ayer Ms 1512, fol. 1r.

135. For example, see University of Pennsylvania Manuscript Collection 700, Item 197, fols. 29v, 188r, and 199r; also see "Appendix One" of Sparks (2011) for how this Tz'utijil version corresponds to the fuller table of contents of the second part of the *Theologia Indorum*, and University of Pennsylvania Manuscript Collection 700, Item 78.

136. Recinos (1950, 31).

137. Vose (2009, 52–54).

138. Until the coronation of Carlos I/V's son, Felipe II, "Spain" consisted of four Iberian kingdoms—Castilla y León, Navarre (which included the Basque country and language of Euskara), Aragon (which included Catalunya and the language of Catalá), and Portugal (which briefly became part of the Spanish Empire)—with relatively powerful courts whose ancient rights and privileges, or *fueros,* monarchs swore to honor upon their coronation. Extended territories—such as the Low Countries, Naples, Sicily, Sardinia, the Canary Islands, Andalucía, and the Americas—came under the ownership of these Iberian kingdoms; the Americas (except Brazil) were part of the Castile kingdom.

139. See, for example, Cabezas Carcache (2008, 155–163).

140. See, for example, Bossú (2008, 93–105).

CHAPTER 4: VICO'S THEOLOGY *FOR* AND *OF* THE "INDIANS"

1. BnF Ms Amér 5, fol. 1r; transcription of the colonial orthography and English translation mine.

2. The reconstructed complete table of contents of both volumes one and two of the *Theologia Indorum* is based on comparative study of various partial versions in K'iche' and Kaqchikel; see Sparks (2017a, 33–46).

3. The term may be simply *b'i'* with a predicate like *nim(a)* ("big" or "grand") or *loq'olaj* ("beloved"), or a truncation of the term as unpossessed *b'i'aj* (versus term of possession, such as *ub'i'* [her or his name]) in the modern orthography. In the manuscripts it appears as *biih, bijh,* and even *biitz* in the colonial scripts. For its possible, though unlikely, treatment as *biitz,* see López Ixcoy (2017, 21n1).

4. APS Ms, fol. 44r; paleography of the colonial orthography and translation mine.

5. APS Ms, fol. 63v; paleography of the colonial orthography and translation mine.

6. In such cases, these concepts are not designated with capital numerals, for the specific chapter has already been designated with a different hierarchical value as a subsection.

7. APS Ms, fol. 53r; paleography of the colonial orthography and translation mine.

8. APS Ms, fol. 67v; paleography of the colonial orthography and translation mine.

9. APS Ms, fol. 69v; paleography of the colonial orthography and translation mine.

10. These two skips in the numbering sequence within these two particular sections remain inexplicable, leaving for the moment only two plausible yet unsatisfactory explanations, based on evidence in the scant secondary literature and in the text of the *Theologia Indorum* itself: (1) there were other chapters initially written by Vico and almost immediately removed early on by him or one of the earliest copyists (again, there is no sustainable evidence that any of the surviving manuscripts are in Vico's own hand), or (2) the skip in count is an early scribal or copyist error repeated by later copyists.

11. APS Ms, fol. 80r; paleography of the colonial orthography and translation mine.

12. See, for example, Sparks (2017a, 132–166).

13. Notably, mendicant colonial catechisms use the term *pixab'* to mean "commandments," as in reference to the Decalogue and the commandments of the Catholic Church.

14. Linguistically, this feature is merely a numerical classifier common in Mayan languages. Based on my work with the K'iche' Maya beginning in 1998, this opening of formal speech by elders or a *k'amal b'e* remains true today.

15. APS MS, fol. 30v; paleography and translation mine.

16. The repetition of <*la*> here is most likely a scribal error since it is already in the previous line to form the word with *vɛalahobiçaxic* and it appears as well in BnF Ms Amér 5, fol. 30v; BnF Ms Amér 10, fol. 18v; and GGMM no. 178, 57.

17. Vico may be using the *uq'alajob'isaxik* to mean something more like "revelation"; however, the root is "clear" or "clarity" and, as is discussed in detail in chapter 6, his use seems to correspond to its use by K'iche' writers in the opening lines of the Popol Wuj.

18. The term <vɛilic> appears twice here in APS MS but is most likely a scribal error since it already appears at the end of the previous line and does not appear twice in other versions. Therefore, it has been omitted here.

19. APS Ms, fol. 33r; paleography and translation mine.

20. APS Ms, fol. 36v; paleography and translation mine.

21. The use of *4hahcar* here is obscure but most likely relates to *ch'ab'* (*4hab*) "one (who is) sent" or "messenger," such as *enviado de Dios* (Dürr and Sachse 2017, 208).

22. APS Ms, fol. 76v; paleography and translation mine.

23. While *usik'ixik* has been translated here more literally, Vico more likely aims for it to mean "pray to" and, thus, is only further evidence of the extent to which he and others in his Dominican school of translation are comfortable using such Maya terms if not synonymously then at least analogously for Catholic ideas.

24. APS Ms, fol. 33r; paleography and translation mine.

25. APS Ms, fol. 174v; paleography and translation mine.

26. Later notarial documents written by K'iche' scribes use similar numbers, especially in bills of sale for lands and houses (Owen Jones, personal communication, May 2017).

27. APS Ms, fol. 2r; paleography and translation mine.

28. APS Ms, fol. 3r; paleography and translation mine.

29. In this section head, BnF Ms. Amér. 5 has written *vhal4at,* indicating that the <4al-> is a scribal error, especially since the apparent <l> is crossed out here (fol. 5r).

30. APS Ms, fols. 4v–5r; paleography and translation mine.

31. APS Ms, fol. 6r; paleography and translation mine.

32. APS Ms, fol. 7r; paleography and translation mine.

33. APS Ms, fol. 9v; paleography and translation mine.

34. APS Ms, fol. 10v; paleography and translation mine.

35. APS Ms, fol. 11v; paleography and translation mine.

36. APS Ms, fol. 12r; paleography and translation mine.

37. The ink on this line is very faint and was thus reconstructed by comparison with BnF Ms. Amér. 5; however, this section heading in BnF Ms. Amér. 5 does not contain *4oɦeic* (fol. 14r).

38. APS Ms, fol. 13v; paleography and translation mine.

39. Personal conversation with tat Manuel Tahay in Nawalja' (Nahualá), Guatemala, June 2008.

40. I am indebted to tat Santos Par for this explanation and local etymologies; personal conversation, Chicago, Illinois, July 2009.

41. See Acuña (2002, 127, 129) or BnF Ms Amér 9, fols. 58r, 60r.

42. See Acuña (2002, 128) or BnF Ms Amér 9, 58r.

43. See (Acuña 2002, 127–132) or BnF Ms Amér 9, fols. 58r–62v.

44. This word, *pixa*, does not appear in either colonial or modern K'iche' dictionaries and does not appear to be related to *pix*, "tomato" or "flash" (*centella* in Spanish; Ximénez 1993, 130). It is possible that it is shorthand for *paj tzij* or, more likely, another K'iche' or Kaqchikel term of measurement since lost. However, it is more likely a shortened version of *pixab'* or "advise" as one case of *rupixab'* does appear in BnF Ms Amér 42. While *paj* and *molaj* are recognizable in modern K'iche' speech and writings, the contemporary convention for "chapter" is *tanaj*, a "well-ordered stack," as opposed to a disordered "pile," which does not appear in Anleo (1744).

45. While unaware of this particular evidence, van Akkeren shares the conclusion that Vico originally wrote the *Theologia Indorum* in K'iche' (personal correspondence via email on September 17, 2008). René Acuña, however, has argued that Vico originally wrote the *Theologia Indorum* in Kaqchikel and translated it later; Acuña (1985, 284). However, as addressed in the previous chapter, there also appears to be some evidence in some versions of the colophon of volume one that Vico wrote his theology simultaneously in multiple Mayan languages.

46. Van Akkeren (2003, 238).

47. For an English translation of the proemium as well as chapters 1–6 and 22 of the first volume, see Sparks (2017a, 47–103).

48. See, for example, Coto's entry on *persona*, where he summarizes the debate regarding the use of *winaq* but also concedes with Vico for the use of this term in the Trinitarian grammar in K'iche'an languages (Coto 1983, 413–414).

49. Acuña (2002, 47n26). The K'iche' word *kohlem* (or *k'ojlem* in the Unified Alphabet of ALMG) appears to mean "essence"; see Brinton (1884, 373). *K'ojlem* does not appear in contemporary K'iche'.

50. Cocoa (*Theobroma cacao*) and pataxte (*Theobroma bicolor*) were two distinct species of chocolate cultivated by Mesoamerican peoples and used, among other things, as currency. Until the late twentieth century *rax* in K'iche'an languages referred to color (or colored items like gems and feathers) in the green-to-blue range. Present-day K'iche' and Kaqchikel language promoters have since proposed using *rax* for only "green" and its inverse, *xar*, for "blue"; however, this is a later convention not attested to in the colonial literature.

51. As evident in Ximénez's copy of the Popol Wuj, the complex relationship between a notion of a single creator deity with many names or facets and multiple creator deities remains unclear, as both singular and plural personal pronouns are used with *Tz'aqol B'itol* in the divine names lists, e.g., Popol Wuj, fol. 34r; see Christenson (2003, 160, 297).

52. BnF Ms Amér 5, fol. 2r. For point of contrast for culling out the use of Maya parallelism within the *Theologia Indorum,* I have merely transcribed these lines in K'iche' exactly as they appear in the manuscript. Subsequent quotes will be transcribed into the modern orthography of the ALMG, attentive to modern punctuation and strophes according to the ethnopoetics of the text.

53. Carmack and Mondloch (1983, 206n12).

54. Tedlock (1983, 267). The *-ol* suffix designates an adjectival or abstractive form.

55. See Knowlton (2009, 90–112) for evidence of this in the *Books of Chilam Balam* and the work constructed by colonial Yukatek Maya with Franciscan missionaries in particular, and Restall (1997, 239–276) in the region in general. Knowlton identifies this type of bilingual parallelism with Bakhtin's notion of "syncrisis."

56. Restall (1997, 267). Also see England (1994, 105–108) regarding parallelism in Maya poetics in general; for a case example in non-K'iche'an speech, see Brody (1988, 55–62). This textual structure not only appears in formal Highland Maya speech but also with weaving patterns, or *etz'ab'alil*. In addition to merismus, or antonymic synecdoches, ten different types of parallelism have been identified within formal K'iche' rhetoric, which contribute not only to couplets, tercets, and quatrains but also to sextets and longer parallel series often used for larger chiastic structures (Christenson 2003, 44–51). Some early mendicants to the Americas, like Vico, harbored the idea that the indigenous peoples were descendants of the ancient Israelites. Despite the modern rejection of that idea, the Maya use of parallelism described here can readily be contrasted with modern scholarly analysis of parallelism in ancient Jewish scripture, such as Kugel (1981, 1–95).

57. For a more detailed analysis of Vico's use of Highland Maya high register discourse with specific respect to the various different kinds of rhetorical parallelisms, see Sparks (2017a, 9–21).

58. Tedlock (1983, 267).

59. The unique use of the verb *-winaq-* ("to create") in Maya texts is abundantly apparent, such as in lines 9, 15, 21–23, 25–26 of the *Title of Totonicapán*'s account of the seven days of creation (Carmack and Mondloch 1983, 42–45).

60. Personal conversation with tat Santos Par, Chicago, Illinois, July 2009.

61. For this specific translation problem between *winaq* and *persona* as well as how a century later Franciscan friar Thomás de Coto defers to Vico's analysis and use of *winaq*, see Coto (1983, 414–415) and Scholes (1952, 407–410). This is also an apparent translation issue with the Lowland Maya such as the Yukatek (Knowlton 2009, 106).

62. APS Ms, fol. 30r.

63. Sachse (2017b).

64. Acuña (1983, 6). For an English translation of chapter 25 of volume one, see Sparks (2017a, 103–120).

65. Phelan (1970, 59–68, 75).

66. Ibid. (74).

67. Ibid. (70–71, 76), Ricard (1966, 299), Surtz (1964, vii).

68. See, for example, Pagden (1982, especially 59–145).

69. By the nineteenth century, initial modern scholars of the Maya past made analogies not between the Maya and Israelites but rather the Maya and ancient Greeks. Brasseur

de Bourbourg even believed that the Maya were direct descendants from the lost continent of Atlantis. However, based on her English translations of Brasseur de Bourbourg's French travel writings, Katia Sainson argues that this impression of him has been historically overstated if not misconstrued (personal communication with Sainson, 2015). While a rare idea for today, some religious organizations still seek to confirm a link between Native Americans (such as the Highland Maya) and ancient peoples of the eastern Mediterranean.

70. APS Ms, fols. 35r and 168r, respectively.

71. I am indebted to Santiago Piñón's recent work on Francisco de Vitoria, O.P., for this possible connection between Vico and the introduction of Aquinas's theology to the University of Salamanca. Fray Francisco Ximénez, O.P., indicates that Vico, his cohort, and many of his later contemporaries studied under Vitoria at Salamanca; Ximénez (1977, 374).

72. Maxwell and Hill (2006, 257). In modern K'iche' *k'ab'awil* can refer to the twenty "guiding" stones in a divining bundle and are not large stelae but rather small pieces of jade or quartz, only a few centimeters long.

73. Ayer Ms 1582, 478.

74. For example, see Vico's use of *xixk'ab'awilaj* to mean something close to "you all venerated" in BnF Ms Amér, fol. 53r.

75. BnF Ms Amér 59, fol. 168r.

76. Ibid. The transcription, which is close to how it actually appears in the manuscript, and the English translation are mine. Also see Basseta (2005, 352). *Estrella vaga*, or literally "vague star," may also be translated as "wandering star" and may refer to planets as in the ancient Greco-Roman cosmology such as Mars or Venus as morning or evening stars but also to "shooting stars." The specific connection between such "stars" and divinity within colonial Maya cosmogony may pertain to the Hero Twins in stories like the Popol Wuj (Milbrath 1999, 159–160, but also see 218–248).

77. Such as in the dictionary formerly catalogued as the Gustafson manuscript, "Vocabulary of the 17th Century" (Washington, DC: Library of Congress; photocopy from November 13, 1950, 365), which is now Biblioteca Nacional de España (BNE) MSS/23234; I am grateful to John Hessler for clarifying the transfer of this copy of Basseta's dictionary from the Library of Congress to the BNE. For detailed analysis on the genealogies of colonial mendicant dictionaries on Highland Mayan languages, see Sachse (2009, 2018) and Dürr and Sachse (2017, 9–70).

78. Garrido Aranda (1980, 94–104).

79. For an English translation of chapter 47 of volume one, see Sparks (2017a, 126–132).

80. The following distinctions were made by tat Te'k (Diego Adrián Guarchaj Ajtzalam) over the course of reading chapter 47 along with the first seven sections of the *Theologia Indorum* in August 2008. See also, for example, the title of chapter 73 of volume one of the *Theologia Indorum* translated in the table of contents in Sparks (2017a).

81. Based on personal conversations with tat Te'k, June–August 2008.

82. It should be noted, however, that even among the K'iche' Maya there is a wide amount of variation between geographical locales and between those *chuchqajawib'* who are engaged in the growing number of national associations of Maya spiritual guides and those who are not. Among *chuchqajawib'* there is a subspecialty of practitioners called *ajitzab'* (*ajitz* in the singular) or *itzel winaq*. However, these titles are usually attributed to *chuchqajawib'* in an accusatory or pejorative sense rather than claimed by an *ajq'ij*; or, if self-attributed, is discussed not in public and accompanies a number of caveats clarifying how the term *ajitz* is used. Most of the fieldwork that I conducted was with K'iche' *chuchqajawib'* in the areas of Santa Cruz del Quiché, Chichicastenango, Nahualá, and Quetzaltenango, with some comparative work with Kaqchikel spiritual guides beginning in 1995.

83. The distinctions between these three sets of terms—"good"/"not good," "hot"/"cold," and "left"/"right" and how they conceptually interrelate—are based on my work since 1996 with Highland Maya spiritual guides, *chuchqajawib'* or *ajq'ijab',* who prefer to remain anonymous, but the work was also corroborated in personal conversations with José Serech Sen in August 2003 and tat Wel (Manuel Tahay) in July 2008. For more extensive analysis of these three pairs in K'iche' moral discourse, see Sparks (2018, 107–111).

84. Also see Bredt-Kristzat (1995, 219–222), especially regarding Vico's treatment of the biblical Book of Ruth and his comparative use of the biblical character Balaam and the K'iche' word *b'alam* (jaguar), which is also found in the names of three of the four characters in the Popol Wuj who were created out of maize. Vico's use Maya mythology is examined in greater detail in the next chapter.

85. For a full English translation of chapter 105, see Sparks (2017a, 132–165).

86. Acuña (1983, 7), Mondloch (1983, 99), and personal conversation with tat Wel Tahay, May 2006.

87. The "shema" as found in Deuteronomy 6:4 is: "Hear [*shema*], O Israel, the Lord [*adonai*] is our God [*'elohim*], the Lord [*adonai*] is one."

88. García-Ruiz (1992, 91–94), Brinton (1881, 630).

89. Remesal (1966b, IV, 1454–1456), Vázquez (1937, 127–128). The Franciscan chronicler Vázquez, writing decades later, still accused Vico of being one of the leading Dominicans who advocated for the affirmative appropriation of the term *cabovil* (*k'ab'awil*). The variance between *k'ab'awil* and *kab'awil* in K'iche' (*k'ab'owil* or *kab'owil* in Kaqchikel) is due in part to inconsistent spellings in the colonial literature between *cabauil*, *cabahuil*, *cabouil*, *4abauil*, etc., with the colonial <4> or modern <k'> being a glottalized <k>. Also see Sáenz de Santa María (1974, 369)

90. "*por el dios común y superior de todos,* [n11, *que llamaban*] *que ellos decían, cuyo nombre en la lengua de Guatimala* [sic] *nombraban Cavovil, y en la de México, Teutl*" (Las Casas 1967, II, 506).

91. Sáenz de Santa María (1974).

92. Megged (1995, 78).

93. Scholes (1952, 407–408).

94. Again, as evident in Ximénez's copy of the Popol Wuj, the complex relationship between a notion of a single creator deity with many names or facets and multiple creator deities remains unclear, as both singular and plural personal pronouns are used with *Tz'aqol B'itol* in the divine names lists: for example, lines 5100–5116 of the Popol Wuj of Ayer Ms 1515, Ximénez (n.d. [ca. 1701–ca. 1704], fol.34r); see, for example, Christenson (2004, 160, 297).

95. This couplet also appears revered throughout the *Theologia Indorum* (i.e., *raxal q'anal*, "greenness and yellowness") with no apparent change in meaning.

96. In colonial K'iche'an lexicons, both of these terms are defined as *sombra*. It is unclear whether the lack of distinction between these two terms—*ninuch'* and *natub'*—is inherent to K'iche' (i.e., that for a native K'iche' speaker they would have been synonymous and only used in a poetic parallelism for rhetorical reasons) or because *sombra* in Spanish can mean either shadow or shade; see Sachse (2017c). Because they are rendered as two at least phonetically distinct words in K'iche', I have rendered them in English as two different words. Regardless, similar terms of "shadow" to mean something akin to one's "soul" are found in other non-K'iche'an Highland Mayan languages, such a *naab'l* in Mam and *ch'ulel* in Tzeltal (Watanabe 1992, 254; Pitarch 2010, 24–39; Pitarch 2012, 105).

97. Fischer and Hendrickson (2003, 81).

98. Though, unlike *pus* (*puz* in the colonial orthography), *nawal* is etymologically not a Maya word but rather derives from the Nahua term *nahualli* resultant from Nahua influence either from the Yaki (Pipil) Nahuatl-speaking population in Guatemala and El Salvador or the later "Toltec" influence on the Maya by the twelfth-century. However, rather than replace the Maya term *pus*, the Nahua term *nawal* was adjoined to it to form a lexical couplet. However, the concept of one's having a soul related to an animal spirit companion is common throughout even non-K'iche'an Highland Maya peoples, such as *lab'* among Tzeltal Maya (Pitarch 2012, 40–59). In general studies of the religions of indigenous peoples of the Americas, this is akin to the concept of *totem* (e.g., totemism) as derived originally from the Ojibwe.

99. García-Ruiz (1992, 85).

100. Scholes (1952, 413–414), Bandelier (1932, 10–12). Regarding the term *auto de fé* (also *auto-da-fé*, *auto da fe*, or "act of faith"), see Chuchiak (2012, 344).

101. García-Ruiz (1992, 87).

CHAPTER 5: USE OF MAYA "SCRIPTURE"

1. BnF Ms Amér 5, fol. 34v. Transcription from the Parra orthography into the modern Maya orthography, English translation from the K'iche', and stanza format are mine.

2. Tedlock (1983, 261).

3. Tedlock (1996, 27). Arguably, the oldest archaeological evidence of some of the mythic content written in the Popol Wuj can be found in murals of San Bartolo, which date to at least the third century BCE; regarding the archaeological record of the classic era (200 CE–900 CE) and the Popol Wuj, see, for example, Coe (1992, 220–222, 226), Freidel et al. (1993, 59–113), and especially Chinchilla Mazariegos (2011, 2017).

4. However, the Ximénez manuscript (Ayer Ms 1515) has marginalia in Ximénez's hand that may indicate that he recognized and was planning to divide his draft into chapters. I am grateful to John Aubrey, former librarian of the Edward Ayer Collection of the Newberry Library, for pointing this out.

5. Recently, however, Carmack and Mondloch have questioned the validity of Cristóbal Velasco's name on fol. 31v of the *Title of Totonicapán* and therefore his role as a contributing author (Carmack and Mondloch 2007, 9). Note that between the dialectical variations within K'iche' this title may also be *nimach'okoj,* such as the central dialect around Nawalja' (Nahualá), but has been left within the eastern dialect of the greater Q'umarkaj-Utatlán-Santa Cruz del Quiché area.

6. Tedlock (2003, 157–185); also see Van Akkeren (2000).

7. Tedlock (1996, 196, 340), Van Akkeren (2003, 237–256). Van Akkeren presents overwhelming evidence that Diego Reynoso was not the principal author of the Popol Wuj and that Q'umarkaj leadership, such as Juan de Rojas and Juan Cortés, most likely had strong influence on the *Title of Totonicapán*. In this regard he nuances and builds upon Tedlock's theory of Popol Wuj authorship. However, Van Akkeren's argument does not convincingly eliminate the theory that Reynoso was the major author of the *Title of Totonicapán* and a minor contributor to the Popol Wuj, because he does not fully dismiss the dangling account for the oral tradition regarding Reynoso as an author of the Popol Wuj; also see Benítez Porta (1999). For Reynoso as a minor author rather than coauthor of the Popol Wuj, see also Dürr (1994, 10).

8. Tedlock (1996, 56–57), Florescano (2002a, 213).

9. René Acuña is one of the more notable scholars who entertains the role of Vico as having a helping hand in the composition of the Popol Wuj; see, for example Acuña (1998, especially 44, 54, 89–94). Van Akkeren has argued the strongest and most detailed rebuttal to this hypothesis; see Van Akkeren (2003, 237–239).

10. Again, while the name of the first brother of the Hero Twins is most clearly a date on the 260-day ritual calendar and more likely translates to One Blowgunner, the etymology and thus subsequent questionable translations of the second brother are more precarious. With the initial <x-> usually understood to mean a diminutive marker ("little") rather than other option of indicating feminine ("she"), *balan* in the colonial script is often read as *b'alam* ("jaguar"), and the final letters as either "sun" or "deer." In the Popol Wuj the name appears as Xb'alanke (Xbalanque), and for scholars of the Popol Wuj it is more understood to mean "little (jaguar/dark) sun" (i.e., Venus or the moon) rather than "deer";

see Tedlock (1996, 361), Janssens and Van Akkeren (2003, 34), and Van Akkeren (2012, 126–130). However, notably in the *Theologia Indorum* as well as in the *Title of Totonicapán*, the name appears as Xb'alankej (Xbalanqueh), "little jaguar deer." In Maya cosmology, Jun Ajpu is associated with the sun (specifically the sun of the fourth age of people made from maize) or Venus (namely as the Morning Star) and Xb'alanke is associated with Venus as well as the moon (or specifically the full moon); see, for example, Milbrath (1999, 96–100, 130–135).

11. This name could be a variant of Kaqulja Juraqan (Lightning Hurricane), the first of the three lightning personalities of the god Uk'u'x Kaj (Heart of Sky) in the Popol Wuj (Ayer Ms 1515, fol. 2r) or the names of two separate characters—Tasul and Juraqan—with only the latter mentioned in the Popol Wuj and the former unknown.

12. Certain names in this list—specifically Jun Ajpu and Xb'alankej (the Hero Twins), One One-Blowgunner and Seven One-Blowgunner (the father and uncle of the Hero Twins), and One Death and Seven Death (Jun Kame and Wuqub' Kame as the lords of the otherworld, Xib'alb'a)—are major characters in the Popol Wuj. However, other names listed here by Vico, such as Bloody Tooth and Bloody Claw (Kik' Re' and Kik' Rixk'aq), are only minor characters in the Popol Wuj. More notably, the remaining names (Mam, Iq', Cho'a, and possibly Tasul) are not only absent in the Popol Wuj altogether but also seem to have slipped away from modern K'iche' oral tradition. Based on these kinds of discrepancies, such as the different treatments of the character Falcon (or Wok) here in the *Theologia Indorum* in contrast to within the Popol Wuj, Vico appears to have had access to an earlier version of the Popol Wuj or simply the same set of K'iche' narratives that contained details or even whole stories later dropped by the K'iche' editors of the Popol Wuj in the 1550s. Finally, while the Popol Wuj clearly distinguishes between these characters—namely the Hero Twins and their father and uncle on one hand versus the lords of Xib'alb'a on the other hand—Vico not only lists them all together but later, in chapters 28, 40, and 51 of the first volume of the *Theologia Indorum,* states that they are all in hell, including the Hero Twins (BnF Ms Amér 5, fols. 41r, 70r, and 76r).

13. BnF Ms Amér 5, fol. 33r; translation, paleography, punctuation, and stanza structure are mine.

14. Tasul Juraqan may be an alternative name for the storm deity mentioned in the Popol Wuj, Juraqan. According to Frauke Sachse, Mam Iq' Cho'a may be a Highland Maya variant of Mam Ek' Chuah as the classic Maya God L (personal communication, July 2018). Both tat Wel and tat Te'k had difficulty in translating Q'eteb' and Pub'a'ix, though they may relate to features of the Hero Twins such as their blowguns with the verbs *-q'etej* (to roll or squeeze) and *-pub'aj* (to shoot a blowgun); though Coto glosses a version of both together as "aziago día"; Acuña (1983, CLXXXVII, CCXXX). Furthermore, the transcription and meaning of the name of the second Hero Twin, Xb'alankej, is highly disputed and debated among K'iche' elders; both of the dominant spellings and one of the many translations is presented

here but with reservations. Vico presents lists of Maya deities and legendary characters in a few places in the *Theologia Indorum*, and, while similar, they are not identical. Acuña notes other names of Maya deities listed in the *Theologia Indorum* and absent in the Popol Wuj (Acuña 1983, 5–6). Current research by Alonso Zamora Corona strives to find remaining evidence of these other Maya religious characters in the oral traditions and prayers of present-day Highland Maya (personal communication March 2018).

15. Carmack (1973, 14).

16. Tedlock (1996, 63, 218n63), Sam Colop (1999, 21, 22).

17. Carmack and Tzaquitzal Zapeta (1993, 24, 28), Carmack and Mondloch (1985, 229).

18. Tedlock (1983, 264).

19. Sáenz de Santa María (1974, 369), García-Ruiz (1992, 107n22).

20. Tedlock (1983, 265).

21. Ibid. (264). While Tedlock provides an insightful read of implied K'iche' theology within the Popol Wuj, he overstates his argument of contrast over and against Christian doctrines of Creation with narrow readings of Genesis, probably due to a heavy reliance on Fox (1972, 9–159).

22. Popol Wuj, fol. 31v.

23. Tedlock (1983, 266).

24. Ibid. (268).

25. Ibid. (273–274). This Maya position serves as a response not only to sixteenth-century theological positions interested in other religions and cultures, like Vico's own, but also to twentieth century positions like those of Karl Barth, Karl Rahner, and David Tracy, for example; see Knitter (2002) and Bevans (1992).

26. Tedlock (1983, 279). Or even analogous to John Calvin's metaphor for scripture, as Calvin first used "spectacles" as a metaphor to refer to the role of scripture to correct the blindness of postlapsarian human reason in I.4.xiv in his *Institutes of the Christian Religion* (1559); in contrast, Friar Francisco de Osuna, O.F.M., contemporaneously elaborated an apophatic dimension of contemplative "recollection" or *recogimiento* with the metaphor of "blindness" in his letter "C" (*ciego*) of his *Third Spiritual Alphabet* (1527).

27. Tedlock (1983, 280–281).

28. I am indebted to Professor Raymond Fogelson for this threefold distinction.

29. The most extensive example of this style of versification of a text was Martin Buber and Franz Rosenzwig's German translation of the Tanakh; Tedlock (1983, 129). However, efforts by non-Maya to replicate Maya texts into couplets, such as that by Munro Edmonson, who originally saw parallelism in Maya texts, have tended to overstate the structure as too rigid or rule bound, thus losing the performative and dialogical quality of the text. Tedlock does not tend to commit this error; however, efforts by K'iche' writers, such as Luis Enrique Sam Colop and Juan Rodrigo Guarchaj, do provide more nuanced demonstrations of poeticism in the Popol Wuj and other Maya texts.

30. The particulars of this example are based on work with *ajq'ijab'* in and around Santa Cruz del Quiché between 1998 and 2001. However, it also illustrates the long tradition of cosmological and astronomical imagination within Maya thought, as noted by many other scholars on the Maya, such as Broda et al. (1991), Aveni (1992), Freidel et al. (1993), Malmström (1997), and Milbrath (1999).

31. Tedlock (1983, 267). This textual structure appears in formal Highland Maya speech but may also be seen as similar to Maya weaving patterns, or *etz'ab'alil*. In addition to merismus, or antonymic synecdoches, ten different types of parallelism have been identified within the rhetoric of the Popol Wuj, which contribute not only to couplets, triplets, and quatrains but also to sextets and longer parallel series, often for larger chiastic structures; see, for example, Christenson (2003, 44–51).

32. Tedlock (1996, 270–271).

33. Edmonson's English-K'iche' bilingual translation and transcription of the Popol Wuj was the first to attempt to render the whole text in couplet or strophic format. However, limited to only the couplet form, he attempted to impose only that stanza style of parallelism throughout the whole text; see Edmonson (1971).

34. Ayer Ms 1515, fol. 1r; Sam Colop (1999, 21), Christenson (2004, 13) consulted for moden orthography, paleography, and stanza lines, though modified.

35. Tedlock (1996, 63), Christenson (2004, 13) consulted for English translation, though modified.

36. Ayer Ms 1515, fol. 1r; Sam Colop (1999, 23), Christenson (2004, 16) consulted for moden orthography, paleography, and stanza lines, though modified.

37. Tedlock (1996, 64), Christenson (2004, 16) consulted for English translation, though modified.

38. Tedlock (1983, 222).

39. Ibid. (219).

40. Ibid. (224).

41. Sam Colop (1999, 22n1); Christenson (2004, 14n9).

42. Ayer Ms 1515, fol. 1r; Sam Colop (1999, 22), Christenson (2004, 14) consulted for moden orthography, paleography, and stanza lines, though modified.

43. Tedlock (1996, 63), Christenson (2004, 13) consulted for English translation, though modified.

44. Ayer Ms 1515, fol. 1r; Sam Colop (1999, 22), Christenson (2004, 14) consulted for moden orthography, paleography, and stanza lines, though modified.

45. Tedlock (1996, 63), Christenson (2004, 13) consulted for English translation, though modified.

46. BnF Ms Amér, fol. 1r; modern orthography, paleography, and English translation mine.

47. Both of my native K'iche'-speaking consultants—tat Wel and tat Te'k—independently and repeatedly commented on their amazement of Vico's mastery of K'iche' moral and ritual discourse even as they each strongly disagreed with what Vico said.

48. Tedlock (1983, 228–229).

49. Christenson (2003, 44–51).

50. Tedlock (1983, 268).

51. Ibid. (133).

52. This particular lexical couplet is unattested in mendicant colonial sources; however, *q'aq'al tepewal* does appear—e.g., <ɛaɛal tepeual> as *esfuerzo de Dios* "God's might" (Sachse and Dürr 2017, 273) or *magestad* "[God's] majesty" (Acuña 1983, CCXXIX)—as well as in early K'iche' literature such as the Popol Wuj (Ximénez n.d. [ca. 1701–ca. 1704]; Ayer Ms 1515, fols. 37v, 51v, and 55r). Nor is it common in current ceremonial discourse of *chuchqajawib'* (e.g., *ajq'ijab'* or daykeepers). Thus, Vico does not seem to be using here a preexistent traditional K'iche' phrase and, if an early mendicant neologism, this couplet does not seem to have been used by other later missionaries or Maya.

53. BnF Ms Amér 5, fols. 5v–6r. English translation from the K'iche' mine; stanza format also mine but in accord with the principles of Maya poetics as identified by Luis Enrique Sam Colop; see Sam Colop (1994; 1999, 15–19).

54. As with the transcription of K'iche' in general throughout this book, I have transliterated even most of the colonial K'iche' texts, including proper nouns and names, to conform to modern orthography as developed by native Maya speakers. In Ximénez's manuscript of the Popol Wuj, this name appears as "Nacxit" but it has been rendered here as "Nakxit," as it also appears in Sam Colop's (1999, 2011) and Carmack and Mondloch (2018) editions of the Popol Wuj. For a summary on the scholarly understanding of this name, see Christenson (2003, 257n688).

55. Ayer Ms 1515, fol. 48v; Sam Colop (1999, 174), Tedlock (1996, 179–180), and Christenson (2003, 225, 311) consulted for modern orthography, modified. I have translated *tatil* as "obscure" because Christenson translates it as "black" but etymologically it does not appear related to *q'eq'*, so the word is also literally obscure.

56. BnF Ms Amér 5, fols. 27v–29v.

57. Ayer Ms 1515, fol. 54r. For the historical and comparative depth of this analysis, see Sachse (2016).

58. For example, see BnF Ms Amér 5, fols. 7v, 9v, 29v, and 68r. Either of these two terms in this couplet can be translated as "Creator"; however, *Tz'aqol,* referring to stonework, possibly implies the female realm and *B'itol,* referring to work with clay or adobe, possibly implies the male realm; see Carmack and Mondloch (2007, 165n2). This couplet for the divine appears throughout both the *Title of Totonicapán* and the Popol Wuj along with other couplet and tercet references to divine agency. Vico appropriates this couplet in particular as the K'iche' phrase synonymous with the creator god of the book of Genesis.

59. BnF Ms Amér 5, fol. 3r; Ayer Ms 1515, fol. 1r.

60. BnF Ms Amé 5, fol. 34v; modern orthography, paleography, and English translation mine.

61. BnF Ms Amér 5, fol. 33r; modern orthography, paleography, and English translation are mine.

62. BnF Ms Amér 5, fol. 33r; modern orthography, paleography, and English translation are mine.

63. BnF Ms Amér 5, fol. 33r; modern orthography, paleography, and English translation are mine.

64. BnF Ms Amér 5, fol. 41r; modern orthography, paleography, and English translation mine. Coto translates *voc* as *junco* ("rush" or "reed"); see Coto (1983, CCXV). Christenson translates *Wok* as "falcon" in Christenson (2003, 65). *Wok* appears in two different contexts in Vico's *Theologia Indorum* and the Popol Wuj, thus providing evidence against Acuña's argument that Vico is the final redactor, if not major author, of the Popol Wuj. Furthermore, the unclear use of *Wok* by Vico here possibly shows that he had access to a version of the Popol Wuj, oral or written, by the K'iche' contributors to the Popol Wuj, Diego Reynoso or Cristóbal Velazquez, thus putting the Popol Wuj copied by Ximénez in closer dialogue with Vico.

65. BnF Ms Amér 5, fol. 70r; BnF Ms Amér 5, fol. 76r.

66. BnF Ms Amér 5, fols. 96v–97r.

67. Ayer Ms 1515, fols. 15r, 25r–27r. Note that, as rendered in the Popol Wuj, neither Xib'alb'a or any celestial realm is multilayered or tiered. As pointed out by Chinchilla Mazariegos, narratives of cosmogenesis and cosmogony are, in fact, rare in precontact Maya texts and art (Chinchilla Mazariegos 2017, 5).

68. BnF Ms Amér 5, fol. 41r–41v.

69. Allen Christenson has recently argued that these stories about Xib'alb'a refer not only to a single narrative event within Highland Maya cosmogony but also to the mythical establishment of the repeating cycles of life and death of both humans and agriculture (Christenson 2016). However, with the redaction of the Xib'alb'a stories into the Popol Wuj in the wake of the influence of Christian cosmogonic stories such as told in the *Theologia Indorum*, K'iche' Maya reorganize them into a linear rather than cyclical account. Frauke Sachse also argues that Xib'alb'a or "place of fear," even in the Popol Wuj, may have been a neologism crafted by Dominican missionaries in the early 1500s. It was possibly coined to convey a Christian notion of hell to K'iche' Maya, since "Xib'alb'a" is not attested to in earlier Maya sources, thus further evincing the impact of the *Theologia Indorum* in the Popol Wuj (personal communication March 2017).

70. Ayer Ms 1515, fols. 5v and 6v; Tedlock (1996, 73–74, 77–78), Christenson (2003, 92–93, 96; 2004, 38, 41, 268, 269), Sam Colop (1999, 39, 41) consulted for moden orthography, paleography, and English translation, though modified.

71. No satisfactory interpretation of "jade juice" has been found, and its pairing in couplet form with "juice of *q'oq'ol*" is also vexing and only adds to the confusion. Furthermore, no satisfactory interpretation of *q'oq'ol* could be found. While typically *q'oq'* (usually pronounced with a long <oo> in Modern K'iche') refers to *chilacayotes* in Spanish or Malabar squash (*Cucurbita ficifolia*), tat Te'k reads this as a nominalized form of *-q'oq'aj* or "to place under" or "to cover up." However with the apparent repetition of this couplet below in line 35 but instead with *qoqol*, a possible scribal error may have occurred twice in an attempt to write *qoq'ol* or "gem"; Edmonson (1965, 108).

72. According to Edmonson, *tekuh* means "spilt"; Edmonson (1965, 120). However, Guzmán lists *xtecoc* as "rubí" (ruby), *4ual* as "diamante" (diamond), *xit* as "turquesa" (turquoise), *lemo* as "cristal" (crystal), and *wo* as "vidrio" or "obsidiana" (obsidian or volcanic glass); Guzmán (1984, 21–22). Given the context of these couplets by Vico, I have gone with Guzmán.

73. BnF Ms Amér 5, fol. 8r; modern orthography, paleography, and English translation mine.

74. The following analysis is based on BnF Ms Amér 5, fols. 68r–69v.

75. For comparison of these sources, see Sachse (2007, 21).

76. Again, Marshall Peterson erroneously claims that not only was Vico's *Theologia Indorum* published but that it was printed in 1544, ten years before Vico even completed the first volume; see Peterson (1999, 31n5).

77. Cortéz y Larraz (1771), Solano Pérez-Lila (1963, 330).

CHAPTER 6: USE OF THE *THEOLOGIA INDORUM* IN THE POPOL WUJ

Sections in this chapter regarding the close intertextual relationship between the open lines of the *Theologia Indorum* and the Popol Wuj were initially presented at the Primer Seminario sobre el Popol Wuj at the Universidad Rafael Landívar in June 2014 and published in a briefer version in Spanish in Sparks (2014a, 2018).

1. Ayer Ms 1515, fol. 1r., Tedlock (1996, 63), Christenson (2004, 13) consulted for English translation, though modified. Modern orthography and stanza formation modified based on studies of Maya poetics by Sam Colop (1994; 1999, 15–19; 2012, 283–309). Most scholars of the Popol Wuj place its compilation, transcription, and redaction by K'iche' elites from older Maya source material between 1554 and 1558, though Ruud Van Akkeren, partially agreeing on this point by René Acuña, pushes this period to as late as 1563 (Van Akkeren 2003, 254–255). However, the earliest possible compilation date for the text found in Ayer Ms 1515 (i.e., 1554) is generally agreed upon by scholars.

2. Tedlock (1996, 63), Christenson (2003, 64; 2004, 14, 264); modified per Sam Colop (1999).

3. Tedlock (2010, 299).

4. Ayer Ms 1515, fol. 1r.

5. Tedlock (2010, 299).

6. See, for example, Ayer Ms 1515, fol. 55v–56r; Tedlock (1996, 95–96).

7. Ayer Ms 1515, fol. 2r–6r, 32r–33v; Tedlock (1996, 66–73, 145–146).

8. As noted in chapter 1, the postclassic era of the Maya should not be assumed to have ended simply with the arrival of Europeans. Instead, as indicated in their surviving postcontact writings, like the Popol Wuj, traditional Maya social structures, worldview, reasoning, and discourse continued well into the seventeenth century. Therefore, the postclassic era of the Maya should be understood as consisting of not merely two periods—early (ca. 900–ca. 1200) and late (ca. 1200–1524)—but rather three periods: early postclassic (ca. 900–ca. 1200), middle postclassic (ca. 1200–1524), and late postclassic (1524–ca. 1650).

9. Ayer Ms 1515, fol. 1r.

10. Ximénez (1857, 5), Brasseur de Bourbourg (n.d., 2). This is not to suggest, however, that Scherzer and Brasseur de Bourbourg based their respective translations on the same manuscript by Ximénez.

11. Christenson (2003, 64), Goetz and Morley (1950, 79; 1954, 2), Recinos (2012, 167).

12. Pohorilles (1913, 2), Sam Colop (2011, 2), Schultze-Jena (1944, 3), Tedlock (1996, 63).

13. Raynaud (1925, 3), Ángel Asturias and González de Mendoza (1998, 1), Villacorta C. and Rodas N. (1927, 164–165).

14. Edmonson (1971, 6). However, Miguel León-Portilla (1969) was the first scholar to arrange sample sections of Highland and Lowland Maya texts according to indigenous parallelism and poetic verse (Christenson 2012, 314).

15. Burgess and Xec (1955, 3), Chávez (1997, 1), Christenson (2004, 14).

16. See listings "Pixab, mandameinto. Vpixab Dios," "Ley pixab upixab Dios," and "Mandar, chinpixabah" in BnF Manuscrit Américain 59, fols. 211v, 92v, 98r, respectively; see the section heading "Vpixab Dios" for "Los Mandam.s de Dios" and "Vpixab Kachuch Sa. Yglesia" for "Los mandam.s de N.Me. Sa. Yglesia" in BnF Ms Amér 60, fol. 2r.

17. See headings "Yuikab cohbal re Dios" for "Los articulos de la fee de Dios" but also "Cohbal re Dios" for "el Credo" in BnF Ms Amér 60, fol. 1v and 3r, respectively.

18. See listings "Lengua diferente yaqui chi [Yaki chi' (i.e., Pipil or Nahuatl)] quiche chi [K'iche' chi'] cachiquel chi [Kaqchikel chi'] pokom chi [Poqom chi'] ixil chi [Ixil chi']" and "Lenguaje mío nuchabal," "Palabra tzih," and "tzih palabra, nutzih mi palabra mi dicho" in BnF Ms Amér 59, fols. 92r, 114r, and 226r, respectively.

19. Coto (1983, 398, CCLXIV–CCLXV, CLXXXIII, and 529, respectively). Interestingly, *ch'ab'al* is not listed.

20. Hill and Maxwell (2006, 291).

21. BnF Ms Amér 13, fol. 5r.

22. This distinction is similar to what Sergio Romero has noted with native K'iche' speakers in places like Santa María Chiquimula between *puro K'iche'* and *K'iche' mezclado* (Romero 2015, 59–89).

23. BnF Ms Amér 5, fol. 3r but also corresponds to BnF Ms Amér 10, fol. 2v; and APS Ms, fol. 4v.

24. BnF Ms Amér 5, fol. 1r.

25. GGMM no. 175, fol. 46r.

26. BnF Ms Amér 5, fols. 34r and 34v; in the second of these uses, the text reads "as names of their lordships of the Sotz'il and Tuquche' [leading clans of the Kaqchikel nation] they have no ancient word, nothing, not a word about the beginning nor respecting a stele effigy" (*quibi e rahaual Çotzil tukuche maha kitzih oher. mahamay maha tçih vtiqueric vnimaxic abah che*; or in the current orthography, *kib'i' e rajawal Sotz'il Tuquche' maja kitzij ojer, maja juyal, maja tzij utikirik unimaxik ab'aj che'*). Here, Vico tells his K'iche' readership that the Kaqchikel do not have the ancient myths and legends and ritual practices like he has found among the K'iche'; a couple of years later, K'iche' elites collect and write down some of those narratives to compose the Popol Wuj.

27. BnF Ms Amér 5, fol. 68r.

28. GGMM no. 175, 3r.

29. GGMM no. 175, fols. 46r and 63r for the former and 58v for the latter (Christenson 2003, 48).

30. GGMM no. 175, fol. 63r, which reads in the orthography of the ALMG *Evangelio chuchaxik qumal, evangelio puch ub'i' utzij uch'ab'al puch qajawal Jesucristo, uk'ajol Dios nimajaw* (or, as it appears in the colonial Parra orthography, *evangelio chuchaxic cumal evangelio puch vbi vtçih vchabal puch cahaual Jhuxo vcahol Dios nimahau*). Note that "gospel" is derived from "good spell" or "glad tidings" and is an older English translation of *euaggelion* (Greek, literally "good message" or "good news"), which is often presented into Spanish as not only a loanword from the Greek (*evangelio*) but translated as either "buenas noticas" or just as correctly "buenas nuevas"; it is curious that Vico's K'iche' phrase for "gospel" does not include the modifier "good" (*utzil*), so this could be a scribal error of *utzij*.

31. BnF Ms Amér 3, fols. 1r–3v.

32. BnF Ms Amér 5, fol. 1r. Notably, while the abstractive suffix <-il> is often applied to the older Spanish word *christiano* to mean "Christianity" or "Christendom," such as in the Popol Wuj (Ayer Ms 1515, fol. 1r), Vico does not seem to use the plural suffix <ib'> (e.g., *christianoib*) to Mayanize "Christians."

33. GGMM no. 175, fols. 27v–28r; the transcription from the Parra orthography to the modern Unified Alphabet of the ALMG and the arrangement in stanza formation are mine, intended to illustrate the poetics according to Maya principles as described by Sam Colop (1994, 1999, 2012), Tedlock (1983, 1995, 1996, 2010), and Christenson (2003, 2004, 2012); crossed-out lines indicate parts of the text that appear to be scribal errors.

34. While Vico in volume two of his *Theologia Indorum* as well as other mendicnats in various colonial dictionaries use the lexical couplet *pus nawal* to mean "miracles," that does not appear to be the reference here. In general, these terms in Highland Maya contexts tend to refer to extraordinary or "magical" events or relations (such as sheet, ball, or other rare forms of lightening, or between a person and their spiritual animal companion per their day according to the 260-day ceremonial calendar) and, thus, Dominicans like Vico seem to reconfigure these two terms to refer to distinctively God's power or Christian "magic."

35. English translation from Vico's colonial K'iche' mine.

36. However, this is in the K'iche'; in the Kaqchikel versions of the *Theologia Indorum* the Kaqchikel language is referred to as *Kaqchikel chi'* (*cakchiquel chi*, Kaqchikel "tongue").

37. Table 6.3 presents a general listing of types of formal discourse in K'iche' as found in either colonial or contemporaneous documents, or both, about, and by the Highland Maya. For a comparable list of kinds of speech in Tzotzil Maya and *k'op*, ("word" in Tzotzil and thus analogous to *tzij* in K'iche'), see Laughlin (2012, 471–475). The analogous understanding of the high register of discourse and rhetoric in Nahuatl (the language of the Nahua including the Mexica or Aztecs) is *huehuetlatolli*, "language of the ancestors"; see, for example, Bernardino de Sahagún, *Florentine Codex*, Book 6: *Rhetoric and Moral Philosophy* (Dibble and Anderson 1969).

38. The transcription from colonial Parra orthography into that of the ALMG, the formation into stanzas based on studies of traditional Maya poetics and rhetoric (Sam Colop 1994, 1999, 2012; Christenson 2003, 2004, 2012), and the English translation are all mine, based on comparative analysis of folio 1 of APS Ms, BnF Ms Amér 4, 5, 10, and 42. The proemium is missing in GGMM nos. 178, 179, and 227. While GGMM no. 176 is described in the Princeton University Library catalogue as being a version of volume one it is, instead, a partial version of volume two.

39. Ayer Ms 1515, fol. 1r, though this English translation is a composite and, further, a slightly modified version of that found in Tedlock (1996, 63) and Christenson (2003, 59–64; 2004, 13–14, 264) but also in consultation with Sam Colop (1999, 21–22) and Craveri (2013, 3–6). The stanza formation is mine but in accordance with the insights into traditional Maya poetics in the Popol Wuj in particular but also in Highland Maya ceremonial rhetoric or high register discourse in general; see Christenson (2003, 42–52; 2012, 311–336), Edmonson (1971, xi–xiii, 3–7), Hull (2012, 73–122), Sam Colop (1994; 1999, 15–19; 2012, 283–309), and Tedlock (1983, 123–132, 216–231; 2010, 305–306, 354, 403).

40. My English translation from the colonial K'iche'.

41. Tedlock (1996, 63–64), Christenson (2004, 13–14) consulted for English translation, though modified.

42. The other two possibly earlier attestations of this phrase are in *Xpantzay I* and Kislak 1015, each claiming much earier dating but most likely at least prior to 1552.

43. D'Avray (1980, 60–64).

44. Ibid.

45. For more on how the different language ideologies held by European missionaries to the Americas and, in contrast, by indigenous Mesoamericans, see Mignolo (1994, 293–313), and as well for Guatemala later in the seventeenth and eighteenth centuries, see Jones (2016a).

46. Carmack, who first translated this Highland Maya land deed from K'iche' into both English and Spanish versions, renders the K'iche' branch as "C'oyoi." However, according to the ALMG this final <i> must either be a <y> in the official orthography or the two contiguous vowels must be separated with a glottal stop, such as <o'i> rather than <oi> and, thus, I have gone for K'oyoy rather than K'oyoi, K'oyo'i, or the older C'oyoi. While debatable, without evidence that the second <o> is glottalized to be <o'> I have rendered the final <i> as a <y>. For Carmack's commentary see Carmack (1973, 39–41) and Carmack and Mondloch (2009, 15–17).

47. See, for example, Van Akkeren (2004).

48. Carmack and Mondloch argue that the authors of the *Title of the K'oyoy* were from the western region of Xe' Lajuj No'j (Quetzaltenango) but wrote the text in the central region with the assistance of Q'umarkaj leadership; Carmack (1973, 267) and Carmack and Mondloch (2009, 16). However, given the notable differences in the use of key phrases (e.g., *Dios, nimajaw*) that evince more Franciscan (western Guatemala) rather than Dominican (central and eastern Guatemalan highlands) pastoral registers, I think that it is more likely that the document was composed by K'oyoy (in Quetzaltenango) leadership but for authentication purposes had Kaweq leadership (in Santa Cruz del Quiché) sign off on it, possibly much like the first rulers of the K'iche' confederacy sought authenticity from and deferred to older, previously established leaders like Nakxit further in the proverbial east.

49. Carmack and Mondloch (2009, 51) and Carmack (1973, 282), modified.

50. English translation mine but also see Carmack (1973, 301).

51. Carmack and Mondloch (2009, 52) and Carmack (1973, 282), modified.

52. English translation mine but also see Carmack (1973, 301).

53. Carmack and Mondloch (2009, 56–57) and Carmack (1973, 284); modified; ellipses (. . .) here indicate corruption or illegibility of the original manuscript.

54. English translation mine but also see Carmack (1973, 303).

55. Robertson et al. (2010, 13–33) regarding the text's redaction history and authorship, and (2010, 38–39, 278, 292) for examples of "God, the great lord." In contrast, the rough contemporary lexicon and grammar on Wastek Maya (also known as Tenek) farther north around Veracruz, Mexico, by the secular priest Seberino Bernardo de Quirós appears to be suspicious of employing Aquinas's distinction between the *res signata* and *res significandi* and instead adheres almost exactly to the fifteenth-century rubrics of humanist Antonio de Nebrija. As a result, he only lists *Dios* rather than establishing analogical relations with Wastek loan-words or constructing a neologism like "God, the great lord" along Wastek rhetorical strategies; see Seberino Bernardo de Quirós, *Arte y vocabulario del idioma Huasteco* (Hurch 2013).

56. Ibid. (313 for "God" as *Dios*, 314 for "owner" as *yum*, and 322 for *nono* as "big").

57. See "Memoria 11" (Lutz and Dakin 1996, 46–47, 94n8).

58. See "Memoria 3" (Lutz and Dakin 1996, 12–13); English translation from the Spanish mine.

59. For the most detailed and authoritative analysis of the interrelated pedigrees of Highland Maya, languages, materials by mendicants, see Sachse (2009, 2009, 2018).

60. BnF Ms Amér 7, back inside of the cover; original colonial orthography maintained. While Smailus notes that Carmack dates this dictionary to the mid-sixteenth century, the opening petitionary prayer is clearly not only in another Mayan language but in another, later hand, based on the script (Smailus 1989, 11).

61. Jones (2016a, 363, 367); orthography modernized.

62. Ibid. (365); orthography modernized.

63. GGMM no. 175, 443; also see Sachse (2016, 101).

64. To this extent, not only do I disagree with Acuña's thesis that Vico (or any other comtemporanseous or later Dominican, like Ximénez) wrote the Popol Wuj—a position sufficiently countered by Van Akkeren (2003) and even Himelblau (1989)—but neither am I convinced by Chinchilla Mazariego's suggestion that Dominicans solicited the Popol Wuj, namely what has survived in the Ximénez manuscript, from their K'iche' students (Acuña 1998; Van Akkeren 2003; Chinchilla Mazariegos 2017, 43).

CHAPTER 7: MAYA NOTARIAL GENRES AS HYPERLOCAL THEOLOGY

Portions of this chapter previously appeared in Sparks (2016) and have since been expanded and revised based on subsequent research.

1. *Title of Totonicapán*, fol. 8r–8v; see Carmack and Mondloch (1983, 70–71) and Carmack and Mondloch (2007, 66–67); transcription from the colonial orthography into modern Unified Alphabet of the Academia de Lenguas Mayas de Guatemala (ALMG) and English translation (including emphasis) from the K'iche' are mine.

2. Despite the notable differences in notarial documents written by indigenous Americans beginning in the sixteenth century but also throughout the colonial period, such as incorporation of native genre elements, compared with notarial literature written in late medieval and early modern Iberia by both Christians and even Jews, the basic general or framing legal genres used by native elites have their origins in western Europe and were imported and taught to indigenous peoples. Regarding notarial writing in Iberia see Eire (1995), Peñefiel Ramón (1996), and Burns (1996).

3. Regarding the use of prehispanic genres in early Kaqchikel literature, see Hill (2012); for K'iche' literature, see Tedlock (1996, 2010); and for use of Highland Maya poetics in K'iche' early notarial texts, see Christenson (2012).

4. Cline (1998). There is, however, no such example among the mendicant writings in Highland Mayan languages, with the possible exception of the much later (e.g., 1798) set of sample of petition letters in K'iche' to ecclesial and civil authorities, the *Peticion Vuq ahau Presidente* (BnF Ms Amér 13, fols. 1–14).

5. Adorno (2007, 21–60). For example, as Rolena Adorno has argued, by the early seventeenth century Quechua nobleman Felipe Guaman Poma de Ayala employed the writings of Las Casas, especially his questioning of the Crown's correct use of Augustine's doctrine of just war, and Inkan lore to pen his "chronicles" and plead his case for his property, title, and Andean right for regional autonomy.

6. Examples of such notable scholarly treatment of these kinds of early postcontact indigenous writings are in recent edited books by Kellogg and Restall (1998), Megged and Wood (2012), Christensen and Truitt (2016), and Christensen and Restall (2019). For the most recent summary of the scholarly literature and interpretive approaches to this literature, see Matsumoto (2016, 469–472). However, except for Terraciano (1998) and Hosselkus (2016), studies of native notarial documents do not attend to the religious or theological discourse and concepts but rather instead concentrate on other topics such as autochthonous construals of memory, property, gender, and kinship. Surprisingly, also, most studies on indigenous notarial writing focus overwhelmingly on central and southern Mexico, overlooking such writing in K'iche'an languages of Guatemala, which are among the earliest and predate the arrival of the Catholic Reformation to the region. Notable exceptions to such exclusions are Hill (1998) and Maxwell (2012), as well as Jones (2016a, 2016b) on later colonial K'iche' texts.

7. See Christensen (2013, 2014).

8. For more on this concept of "communicative ecology," see Shoaps (2009). Durston notes similar features of "highly localized character of information" and the use by early seventeenth-century Quechua authors of their myths as a foundation from which to ground and present legal concerns, notably Cristóbal Choquecasa with the *Huarochirí Manuscript* but also including others, such as Felipe Guaman Poma de Ayala (Durston 2014, 162, 163).

9. Nebrija (1969, 1996), Alcalá (1928).

10. Quirós (2013, 19–22, 55, 75).

11. See, for example, Rubiés (2000).

12. See, for example, Tavárez (2013).

13. See, for example, Hanks (2010). However, studies such as Hanks, where there were only Franciscans in the Yucatán, and of Farriss (2014), where there were only Dominicans in Oaxaca, make comparison somewhat disengenuous. Regretably, Farriss's (2018) expanded study on Dominicans in Oaxaca was published too recently for attention in this book but is one of the first and few in English to focus primarily on early colonial Dominicans, rather than Franciscans, in Mesoamerica. A more apt comparison would be between contemporaneous mendicant orders' lexicographical and pastoral writings in the same indigenous

language from the same region, such as central Mexico, that is attentive to their various competing semiotic ideologies and theological preoccupations (e.g., the question of the being of God for Dominicans versus that of the will of God for Franciscans).

14. In contrast, for such a study of the work by and global influence of Jesuits in the Americas, specifically in the Southern Cone, see Prieto (2011).

15. Personal conversations with John F. Chuchiak IV, David Tavárez, and Owen H. Jones in December 2017.

16. See Townsend (2017, 31).

17. Teuton (2018, 35).

18. Ibid. (37).

19. Megged (1995, 62).

20. Carmack (1973, 19).

21. Other scholars have also provided differing counts, such as Matthew Restall's (1997, 263) and Robert Carmack's (2012, 356) reporting of up to fifty *títulos* in K'iche' alone. Although there is no comprehensive list, the various studies that have looked as this early corpus of postcontact indigenous American literature include Alvarez Arévalo (1987), Cabezas Carcache, ed. (2008, 2009), Carmack (1973, 57–80, 265–399; 1981a, 83–103), Carmack and Mondloch (1985, 213–256; 1989; 2007), Carmack and Tzaquitzal Zapeta (1993), Chinchilla Mazariegos (1999, 77–84), Crespo Morales (1956, 13–15; 1968), Hill (1989), Maxwell and Hill (2006), Matsumoto (2016), Orellana (1984, 111–136), Polo Sifontes (1979), Recinos (1984, 2001), Sapper (1906, 373–381), Tedlock (2003, 187–201), and Yamase (2002, 23–58).

22. For example, the *Probanzas de los hijos del cacique Francisco Calel vecinos de las mesas de Petapa, descendientes de yndio-conquistador de Cholula* (ca. 1582–ca. 1670), as discussed in Matthew (2012, 171–172), or the documents presented in Lutz and Dakin (1996).

23. Carmack (1973, 18).

24. Florescano (2002a, 212; 2002b, 200).

25. Florescano (2002b, 165).

26. Ibid. (180–181); also Restall (1997, 265–267). Since only *títulos* written by Native American authors are discussed in this chapter, and since part of the label pertains to historians' treatment of these documents in general as forgeries—a concern that has never been raised in regards to the *títulos* of the Highland Maya—only the term "título" appears throughout.

27. Florescano (2002a, 212; 2002b, 198–199), Restall (1997, 252).

28. Florescano (2002b, 202), Restall (1997, 247).

29. Florescano (2002b, 208). As stipulated in chapter 3, "nation" does not refer to the modern understanding of nation-state but rather more generally to a single polity or governed realm administered across a geographical region whose salient borders were mutually agreed upon by those "within" and "outside" of such a domain of identity. While a "nation" in this limited sense may map onto a single language group (either language or dialect) or

cultural identity, Maya "nations" as either classic-era city-states or postclassic polities (such as the Western K'iche' confederacy based out of the area of Q'umarkaj) were often multilingual and multiethnic (including both Highland Maya and Nahuatl-speaking Pipil, or Yaki). Therefore, "nation" here loosely adheres to the K'iche'an notion of *winaq* (as a distinct "people") and premodern European notions of *ethne* in Greco-Roman thought.

30. Florescano (2002b, 216).

31. Restall (1997, 246–247).

32. Florescano (2002b, 169, 173, 207).

33. Christenson (2012).

34. Florescano (2002, 174, 208).

35. Ibid. (184).

36. Florescano (2002a, 217). For the inclusion of sixteenth-century Highland Maya texts with this understanding of *títulos*, also see Florescano (2001, 34–38).

37. For example, among the Mam Maya of Todos Santos, see Oakes (1951, 66–68).

38. Florescano (2002a, 195–197), Carmack and Mondloch (1989, 129).

39. Carmack and Mondloch (1979, 86). While Carmack does not specify what he considers to be the two more important Highland Maya texts, most ethnohistorians of the Highland Maya would rank the Popol Wuj as the first and either the *Xajil Chronicle* or possibly the *Rab'inal Achi* as second if not also a competing third, possibly even placing the *Title of Totonicapán* as the fourth most important.

40. For Brasseur de Bourbourg's copy of Chonay's translation, see BnF Ms Amér 77; and for Charencey's bilingual Spanish and French translation based on Brasseur de Bourbourg's copy of Chonay's version, see Charencey (1885).

41. Goetz (1953, 163–164).

42. Ibid. (163).

43. Goetz (1953, 166).

44. Carmack (1973, 29).

45. Carmack and Mondloch (2007, 7).

46. Carmack and Mondloch (1983, 15).

47. For example, regarding the ethnohistorical importance of the *Title of Totonicapán*, also see Morselli Barbieri (2004) and Carmack (1966).

48. Although, according to Van Akkeren's (2007) analysis of the *Lienzo de Quauhquechollan*, Spaniards did conscript K'iche' "*conquistadores*."

49. BnF Ms Amér 5, fol. 185r; APS Ms, fol. 185r.

50. Sáenz de Santa María (1974, 368–369).

51. Schools were established by, for example, Franciscans in Salcajá (near present-day Quetzaltenango or Xe' Lajuj No'j in K'iche') between 1535 and 1540, and also by Dominicans at the Colegio Santo Tomás de Aquino in 1563 in the vein of the Franciscan Colegio de la Santa Cruz, established in 1533 in Tlatelolco, Mexico, for Nahuatl-speakers.

52. On these early schools in Guatemala see Van Akkeren (2010, 33; 2011, 1020) and Remesal (1988, II, 337–338). For their counterparts by the Franciscans with the Yukatek, see Hanks (2010), or by the Dominicans and later Jesuits among Quechua in the Andes, see Durston (2007).

53. Indigenous collaborators or authors include: the authors of the Popol Wuj Ajpop Juan de Rojas, Ajpop K'amja Juan Cortés, and Nim Ch'okoj (or ceremonial drama master) Diego de Velasco; one of the authors of the *Xajil Chronicle* Ajtz'ib' (or "scribe") Juan Pérez; one of the contributors of the *Xpantzay Cartulary* Alonso Pérez; and 1640 copyists of the 1583 *Title of Santa Clara La Laguna* Popol Winaq (or "council member") Gregorio de Vico and Gabriel de Vigo, the latter of whom also appears as a contributor to or copyist of the *Title of the Chiefs* and *Title of the Ajpop Huitzitzil Tz'unum* of 1567. Regarding the signatures of Gregorio de Vigo and Gabriel de Vico, see Van Akkeren (2010, 39–40, especially note 38); the manuscripts of *Title of the Chiefs* and *Title of the Ajpop Huitzitzil Tz'unum* could not be located for examination. It remains unclear the extent to which "Vigo" is a scribal error for "Vico." For an English translation of the *Title of Santa Clara La Laguna*, see Sparks (2017a, 251–259).

54. Personal communication with Jones, October 2017.

55. Van Akkeren (2010, 36–37; 2011, 104–106).

56. Carmack and Mondloch (1983, 13).

57. Christenson (2014).

58. APS Ms, fol. 185v.

59. Regarding the relation of Juan Gómez, see Carmack (1967, 7–1)3; regarding their names in the Nija'ib' corpus, see Matsumoto (2017, 175–176, 260–261, 266, 269, 277, 280). Matsumoto is correct in conservatively noting that there is no explicit familial link in these texts between these names (Matsumoto 2017, 261n11).

60. Carmack (1973, 76), Fuentes y Guzmán (2013, 580).

61. See, for example, Sparks (2017a, 258–259).

62. See, for example, the respective genealogies in Tedlock (1996, 179–198) and Carmack and Mondloch (2007, 94–103, 138–141, 183n159–161, 186n177, 202n292).

63. While there is not direct textual evidence, it is possible that Vico knew of this disparaging story about the two brothers and early founders of the Western K'iche' confederacy, possibly from the likes of Reynoso, and thus turned the moral lesson in his exegesis of Cain and Abel in chapter 47 of his *Theologia Indorum* on the issue of polygamy (see chapter 4, this volume). For K'iche' readers, this account of these two brothers and early coregents of the middle postclassic K'iche' stands in contrast with the moral rectitude of the mythic Hero Twins as told in the Popol Wuj. This account of adultery, and thus questionable legitimacy, within the K'iche' royal genealogy is also found later in the *anejo* (annex or appendix) of the *Relación geográfica de Zapotitlán* (1579); Acuña (1982, 59–61).

64. See, for example, Maxwell and Hill (2006, 167–174) and Tedlock (1996, 187–195).

65. Regarding Chiawar, see Fox (1978, 190–191). This might help explain why, dispite being separated by the large geography of K'iche' speakers, Sakapultek to the north of the K'iche' and Kaqchikel to the south of the K'iche' are linguistically closer to each other than they are to K'iche' (Robin Shoaps, personal communication in June 2009).

66. Carmack (1981b, 128–131).

67. Carmack and Mondloch (2007, 11).

68. For a full English translation of the first seven folios of the *Title of Totonicapán* translated from K'iche', see Sparks (2017a, 219–236).

69. For example, also see Blackfriars (1964, 182–187).

70. See, for example, Pseudo-Dionysius's "The Divine Names," "The Mystical Theology," and "The Celestial Hierarchy" in Rorem (1988, 47–191).

71. BnF Ms Amér 5, fol. 44v. For a complete translation of chapter 30 of volume one of the *Theologia Indorum*, see Sachse (2017a).

72. Carmack and Mondloch (2007, 40); my translation. See also Sachse (2014).

73. For scholars' analysis of multilayered heavens and underworlds of postcontact Highland and Lowland Maya and understandings that these comprise a precontact indigenous worldview, see La Garza C. (2012, 53–81), Sotelo Santos (2012, 83–114), León-Portilla (1988,135–142), and McGee (1990, 60–70).

74. Whalen (2003, 178–189). For a broader analysis of the possible Euro-Christian origins of an understanding of an indigenous Mesoamerican cosmology, see Nielsen and Sellner Reunert (2009, 399–413; 2015, 25–54).

75. For example, see Carmack and Mondloch (2007, 166n25, 167n33).

76. For this analysis see Sparks (2014b).

77. See, for example, Romans 11:11–24 for Paul's use of the grafting metaphor and Acts 17:16–34 as an illustration of how he might have applied it in practice.

78. I borrow the concept of K'iche'ization (or "Quicheization") from the literary and ethnohistorical analysis of the *Title of Totonicapán* and *Title of the K'oyoy* by Néstor Quiroa (2011, 316), although I disagree that this necessarily marks Maya resistance within the texts.

79. BnF Ms Amér 5, fol. 45r.

80. Carmack and Mondloch (1983, 48–49, 50–51, 52–53; 2007, 44–45, 46–47, 48–49); transcription from the Parra orthography into that of the ALMG and English translation from the K'iche' mine.

81. The Popol Wuj has two significant mentions of sapotes (or zapotes) with which to compare the use within the *Title of Totonicapán*: with other tropical fruit at the place of the origin of maize (Ayer Ms 1515, fol. 33r) and as the few foods eaten during ritual fasts by the ruling ancestors of the K'iche' Maya (Ayer Ms 1515, fol. 54r). In modern Lowland Maya poetry, it implies an erotic connotation with the sapote or custard-apple specifically related to the fertility of a young woman; see, for example, McGee (1990, 81). However, based on ethnography among K'iche' and Kaqchikel Maya, the sapote is not among the many current

euphemisms regarding female sexuality, so any wider cultural connotation of the explicit use of sapote within this Highland Maya text seems now lost.

82. BnF Ms Amér 5, fol. 91v.

83. Carmack and Mondloch (1983, 58–59; 2007, 54–55); transcription from the Parra orthography into that of the ALMG and English translation from the K'iche' mine.

84. It should also be noted that the Spanish term is not from Iberia but rather is a loanword from Nahuatl: *mil(li) pa* as "toward the field."

85. Carmack and Mondloch (1983, 56–57; 2007, 52–53); transcription from the Parra orthography into that of the ALMG and English translation from the K'iche' mine. The initial <r> on *rab'ix* in these lines of the *Title of Totonicapán* indicates third-person possessive such as "his" or "hers"; Carmack and Mondloch render it as *rabis*, in accord with the colonial Maya orthographic variation of writing <x> with only one stroke to appear as an <s>, a nonstandardized but common occurrence in some early modern Highland Maya language documents. Also notable is the use of the Spanish term for "hunter," *cazador* (rendered as *casador* but still with a <d>, which is a foreign phoneme in K'iche').

86. Carmack and Mondloch (1983, 48–49; 2007, 52–53); transcription from the Parra orthography into that of the ALMG and English translation from the K'iche' mine.

87. Popol Wuj, Ayer Ms 1515, fol. 34v. See, for example, Sam Colop (1999, 126–127) and Christenson (2004, 163, 297); modifications in the K'iche' transcription mine.

88. Also see Christenson (2003, 204) and Tedlock (1996, 149); modifications in the English translation mine.

89. Ayer Ms 1515, fol. 35v–36r. See, for example, Sam Colop (1999, 132) and Christenson (2004, 169–170, 298–299); modifications in the K'iche' transcription mine.

90. Also see Christenson (2003, 213) and Tedlock (1996, 152); modifications in the English translation mine.

91. Carmack and Mondloch (1983, 48–49; 2007, 44–45); transcription from the Parra orthography into that of the ALMG and English translation from the K'iche' mine. For use of the four basic elements from classical Greco-Roman thought in Thomas Aquinas's theology, see *Summa theologiae* Ia., q. 90, a. 1.

92. Ayer Ms 1515, fols. 2v–3r. See, for example, Sam Colop (1999, 28) and Christenson (2004, 23–24, 265–266); modifications in the K'iche' transcription mine.

93. Also see Christenson (2003, 76–77) and Tedlock (1996, 67); modifications in the English translation mine.

94. Ayer Ms 1515, fols. 33r–33v. See, for example, Sam Colop (1999, 121–123) and Christenson (2004, 156–158, 296); modifications in the K'iche' transcription mine.

95. Also see Christenson (2003, 196–199) and Tedlock (1996, 146–147); modifications in the English translation mine. Translation of the names of the first four humans is debatable—especially *Kitze'*, see Christenson (2003, 196n477)—and should normally be left in K'iche' as proper names.

96. Carmack and Mondloch (1983, 48–49; 2007, 44–45); transcription from the Parra orthography into that of the ALMG and English translation from the K'iche' mine.

97. Carmack and Mondloch (1983, 52–53; 2007, 48–49); transcription from the Parra orthography into that of the ALMG and English translation from the K'iche' mine.

98. Toward the later portion of the first part of the *Theologia Indorum*, the various manuscripts have some variance in how the chapters are numbered in K'iche' and Kaqchikel. Carmack and Mondloch note that this part of folio 6v of the *Title of Totonicapán* corresponds to chapter 99 in BnF Ms Amér 10 (Carmack and Mondloch 2007, 170n57), which is numbered as chapter 101 in BnF Ms Amér 5 and APS Ms. Though the contents are the same in all three of these manuscripts, none of them enumerates in this section as the "eleventh." However, BnF Ms Amér 4 and 42 do (e.g., *Rulaju' paj tzij*), but these latter two manuscripts are versions written in Kaqchikel rather than K'iche' thus leaving unclear, or even lost, what copy or version the authors of the *Title of Totonicapán* actually used.

99. Sachse (2008).

100. Maxwell and Hill (2006, 1–10).

101. See, for example, the *Title of the K'oyoy* (Carmack and Mondloch 2009, 15–67) or the *Survey of Zapotitlán* (Estrada and Niebla 1982, 15–61).

102. This is roughly translated as "Split Place, Place of Bitter Water"; for explanations, see Tedlock (1996, 145) and Christenson (2003, 193).

103. This is roughly translated as "Place among the rushes, seven caves and seven canyons"; for explanations, see Tedlock (996, 151) and Christenson (2003, 209–210). The phrase *ab'aj che'* in K'iche' and Kaqchikel is ambiguous and may either refer to the material from which the devotional effigies were made—stone (*ab'aj*) or wood (*che'*)—or may refer to the appearance of the effigies as vertical carved stelae, or "stone trees" or "erected stones." Either way, the phrase functions as rhetorical parallelism.

104. See Sam Colop (1999, 173–175), Tedlock (1996, 179–180), Christenson (2003, 256–259).

105. See Carmack and Mondloch (1983, 66–67, 68–69; 2007, 62–62, 64–65); transcription from the Parra orthography into that of the ALMG and English translation from the K'iche' mine.

106. See Carmack and Mondloch (1983, 68–69; 2007, 64–65); transcription from the Parra orthography into that of the ALMG and English translation from the K'iche' mine.

107. See Carmack and Mondloch (1983, 68–69, 70–71; 2007, 64–65, 66–67); transcription from the colonial Parra orthography into that of the ALMG and English translation from the K'iche' both mine.

108. See Carmack and Mondloch (1983, 70–71, 72–73; 2007, 66–67, 68–69); transcription from the Parra orthography into that of the ALMG and English translation from the K'iche' mine.

109. See Carmack and Mondloch (1983, 66–67; 2007, 62–63); transcription from the Parra orthography into that of the ALMG and English translation from the K'iche' mine.

110. Similar to many other writing systems, like ancient Egyptian and modern Japanese, the ancient Maya script is technically logographic or logosyllabic: consisting of both phonetic symbols representing simple consonant-vowel morphemes and logograms of words (but not ideas, as they may be homonyms). See Coe (1992, 233–234, 289), Coe and Van Stone (2001, 18).

111. Boone (1994, 13–22).

112. Durston (2007), Romero (2012a, 2012b).

113. See, for example, Jay and Mitchell (1999).

114. See, for example, Resines (2007) as well as Resines (2002).

115. Burkhart (2014).

116. Not counting the glyphs found at Kaminal Juyu', which predate the postclassic era, given this site's uncertain relationship with Highland Maya.

CHAPTER 8: A RECEPTION ETHNOHISTORY OF A CHRISTIANITY

1. Carmack and Mondloch (1989, 140–141, 173); paleographic analysis and orthography of this edition has been maintained, English translation and emphasis is mine; also see Carmack and Mondloch (1979, 100).

2. The presentation of written biblical stories and similar tropes may have had some determining influence not only on *what* stories the K'iche' authors collected and wrote down to become the Popol Wuj but *that* they felt compelled to write them in the mendicants' script in the first place.

3. In K'iche' this phrase for lineages is literally "big houses" and, thus should not be confused with the Nimajayib' or Nija'ib' (literally "Big Houses") lineage that also composed the Western K'iche' confederacy, along with the Tamub', based in Q'umarkaj. Here, "big houses" refers to the major familiar or clan groups that compose a specific larger geopolitical unit, such as a *chinamit*, and physically had large houses or meeting halls built around the central plaza of a prehispanic city. For the specific relationship between archaeology of postclassic Highland Maya towns and the *Title of the Tamub' I*, see Van Akkeren (2006, 223–234).

4. GGMM no. 102, 1. Also known as the *Title of the Tamub I*; my transcription, strophic formation, English translation, and emphasis. Also see Recinos (1984, 23–24), Carmack (1981a, 99), and Contreras (2008, 107–127).

5. Like an oboe but with a trumpet-like mouthpiece instead of a reed.

6. Both *plaude* (a Mayanization from the Spanish *flauta*) and *xul* here may be translated as "flute" according to Coto (for example, see Coto 1983, CCXXIV), however Maxwell and Hill (2006, 595) make the nice distinction between "flute" and "recorder" here.

7. As also noted in Maxwell and Hill (2006, 596), Coto (1983, 3) claims that *iquim* (*-ikim*) means "abajo" ("under" or "below").

8. "Trasunto de los títulos de las tierras de Tecpán Guatemala." 1658–1663 [1662]. Archivo General de Centro América (formerly Archivo General del Gobierno de Guatemala), Sig. A1, número expediente 53,957, Legajo 6062, fol. 30r; transcription and English translation mine. Also see Maxwell and Hill (2006, 592–596), Recinos (1984, 120–123), and Ivic de Monterroso (2009, 87–95).

9. Carmack and Mondloch (1989, 140–141, 173); due to the poor resolution of the photocopy version of this folio, Carmack and Mondloch's paleographic analysis and older orthography have been maintained; however, the English translation, emphasis, and stanza formation in accord with Maya poetics is mine from Carmack and Mondloch's (1979, 100) K'iche' and Spanish versions.

10. Like the integrationist approach of the *Title of Totonicapán*, the *Title of the Ilokab'* here equates Tulan with Babylon and conflates the diaspora narrative arcs of the Bible with the Mesoamerican motif of migration from where the sun rises. Although neither these texts nor any sixteenth-century advocates of the idea that indigenous Americans were the direct descendants of the Israelite or later Judean dispersal attempt to rectify the fact that the Judean exile was a demographic shift eastward, farther into Asia Minor, and the Mesoamerican migration stories tell of a westward demographic movement.

11. Carmack and Mondloch (1985, 230–231); I have retained Carmack and Mondloch's K'iche' orthography and paleography; however, the English translation, punctuation, and strophes are mine; also see Carmack (1981a, 100–101). Note that this is not the same text that Carmack and Mondloch also identified as a title of the Ilokab' in 1966, which they have since reclassified as the *Title of the Nija'ib' III*.

12. Carmack and Mondloch (1985, 231–233).

13. Ibid. (234); for the full transcription of the *Title of the Ilokab'*, see Sparks (2017a, 268–281).

14. See Vázquez (1937, 120, 127, 129) for Betanzos's treatment of *k'ab'awil* (*cabovil*). Unfortunately, Betanzos's *arte* and catechism, which Vázquez used as his sources, have not survived, and it is thus not possible to verify what Betanzos said exactly about *k'ab'awil* in his writings.

15. Carmack and Mondloch (1985, 234, 252n47).

16. Ibid. (232).

17. Ibid. (243n9, 245n19, 246n25, 247n29).

18. Ibid. (234).

19. Ibid. (214).

20. For folio 7 recto of *Title of Totonicapán* in English, see Sparks (2017a, 235–236); for Vico's chapter 25 in English, see Sparks (2017a, 103–120).

21. Carmack and Mondloch (2007, 64–65).

22. Carmack and Mondloch (1985, 207n22).

23. Carmack and Mondloch (1983, 107, 185).

24. Specifically, Owen Jones has identified and analyzed a few caches of short but ethnohistorically insightful K'iche'an wills written in the seventeenth and eighteenth centuries: fifty-two from Rab'inal, seven from San Miguel Totonicapán, five from Quetzaltenango, and one from San Cristóbal Totonicapán. However, in many respects described here and in Jones's research, these later K'iche'an Maya documents seem to illustrate further a shift from what I have called a late postclassic period to an early colonial period by around the 1650s. See Jones (2009; 2016b, 138–151).

25. Ruiz (1998, 63–90). For comparative examples of indigenous wills, see Kellogg and Restall (1998), Christensen and Truitt (2016); for the Lowland Maya in particular, see Restall (1995), Christensen and Restall (2019).

26. Sparks and Sachse (2017).

27. This date is found on manuscript page 216, below the heading; Whalen (2003, 2).

28. Knowlton (2010, 48).

29. Whalen (2003, 2).

30. The Morley manuscript begins: "*ti huntul ah miatz = Uchebal. U cambesabal = ti xoc huun = yt. ti Dzib*" ("to a wise man, in order that he be taught to read books and to write"); Whalen (2003, 11).

31. Christensen (2014, 27–30).

32. Whalen (2003, 108).

33. BnF Ms Amér 5, fol. 1r; my transcription, English translation from the K'iche', and stanza formation.

34. Whalen (2003, 152, 111, and 128, respectively).

35. Whalen (2003, 13, 109, 116, and 117, respectively). On manuscript page 158, *personasob* also appears, making the word *persona* doubly marked in the plural: <-s> for the Castilian Spanish and <-ob> for the Yukatek Maya.

36. Whalen (2003 5, 7–8, and 42, especially note 65).

37. Knowlton (2010, 43).

38. Whalen (2003, 123); *Title of Totonicapán*, fol. 2v, line 16 (Carmack and Mondloch 1983, 48–49; 2007, 44–45).

39. Whalen (2003, 111, 133–143); Carmack and Mondloch (1983, 44–45).

40. Whalen (2003, 62, 135).

41. Ibid. (166).

42. Ibid. (167).

43. Ayer Ms 1515, fol. 34r; modern orthography, English translation, and strophic form mine but in consultation with Tedlock (1996, 148), Christenson (2003, 200; 2004, 159–600), Sam Colop (1999, 124–125), and Whalen (2003, 167n259).

44. Whalen (2003, 154).

45. Tedlock (1996, 99).

46. Ayer Ms 1515, fol. 32r.

47. Ibid. (145–146).

48. Ibid. (67).

49. There is also a strikingly similar use of the image the owl in both the Morley manuscript (Whalen 2003, 78) and the Popol Wuj (Tedlock 1996, 93–94, 100–102) as a messenger from a world beyond those presently living on the face of the earth. However, without further investigation, this could be as much an influence of medieval European popular belief in the Morley manuscript as traditional Maya worldview.

50. Whalen (2003, 125–129). "Hun Ahau" is the Lowland Maya variation of "Jun Ajpu," with *hun* and *jun* both meaning "one," and *ahau* (or *ajaw* in K'iche'an Mayan languages) in the Yukatek Maya ritual calendar (the *tzolkin*) being the same day name as *ajpu* in the K'iche'an Maya ritual calendar (the *cholq'ij*).

51. Carmack and Mondloch (2007, 65).

52. BnF Ms Amér 5, fol. 34v; translation from the original K'iche' is mine. Also see fols. 41r, 70r, 76r, and 96v–97r.

53. For this understanding of Xb'alanke, see Tedlock (1996, 361) and Van Akkeren (2013, 126–130). Though Jun Ajpu is not explicitly linked with Venus in the Popol Wuj, for interpretations of his association with the morning star in the K'iche' Maya Popol Wuj and Yukatek Maya Dresden Codex, see Tedlock (1996, 24–25, 309, 344, 351).

54. Whalen (2003, 83–84, especially note 130).

55. Christensen (2014, 31–42) indicates numerous places and ways that the Catholic legendary material in the third, final section of the Morley manuscript becomes contextualized for a Yukatek readership. For this reason, also, I have focused in particular on the middle, second section.

56. Whalen (2003, 8).

57. Christensen (2014, 30).

CHAPTER 9: INTERTEXTUALITY, HYPERLOCALISM, AND THE CONTINUED DIALOGIC EMERGENCE OF THEOLOGIES

1 APS Ms, fol. 185r. Transcription from the Parra orthography into the modern Maya orthography, English translation, and stanza format mine.

2. Final lines of the Popol Wuj, Ayer Ms 1515, fol. 56v. For alternative English translations, see Tedlock (1996, 198) and Christenson (2003, 305), and for alternative stanza formation, see Sam Colop (1999, 201). Note: While Christenson is correct in that these lines do not explicitly mention a book (*wuj*), I agree with both Tedlock and Sam Colop that this is the implied referent, with the object oblique here but explicitly mentioned elsewhere on folio 1r: *rumal maja b'i chik ilb'al re Popo[l] Wuj*; see Sam Colop (2011, 199–200).

3. BnF Ms Amér 59, fol. 168r, my English translation, but the emphasis and orthography is as found in the original. The reference to the *Estrella vaga* here is not clear, though if referring to Venus, it could also mean the Evening Star or it could also be a scribal error and mean to say "estrella Vega," which is Alpha Lyrae, the Harp Star, and is often considered one of the northern polar stars.

4. See Schreiner (2003, 345–380).

5. Tedlock (1996, 56), Christenson (2016, 84–85), Carrasco (1967, 254).

6. Many thanks to Sergio Romero for these examples and the etymological analysis; personal communication in Nawalja' (Nahualá), Guatemala in 2006.

7. Regarding Latin American liberation theology, one of the most thorough accounts of its history and analysis as a social movement remains Smith (1991). Regarding the scholarly history and analysis of charismatic Catholicism in Latin America and the extent to which it did not begin in reaction to liberation theology, see Cleary (2011), but also with respect to charismatic Catholicism specifically in Guatemala, see (Thorsen 2015). Regarding Catholic inculturation theology in Latin America, most of the documentation remains in local publications almost entirely in Spanish and Portuguese, and it is rarely systematized into larger studies, such as that by Espeja (1993) and Suess et al. (1998), with extremely few translated into English, like Irarrázaval (2000).

8. Guevara (2006).

9. Leonardo and Clodovis Boff (2007, 28–29) argue that racism was only a "superstructure," subset, or even a result of the "infrastructure" of socioeconomic oppression. Their model is emblematic of much of the first phase (ca. 1968–ca. 1987) of Latin American liberation theology. Later work, such as that of Gutiérrez (2003), represents a turn toward culture or "spirituality" in a second phase of liberation theology in Latin America.

10. While an ethnography, one recent notable exception that moves in this direction is MacKenzie (2016).

11. See, for example, Sparks (2013) regarding this movement in Chiapas, Mexico. Regarding "Indian" theology in general, including its use of the pejorative term *indio*, see, for example, López Hernández (2000).

12. For example, Guatemalan Jesuit and cultural anthropologist Ricardo Falla (2013) has recently published an analysis and commentary of the Popol Wuj as the basis for a liberationist moral philosophy.

13. With the exception of García Ahumada (1994, 223) and López Hernádez (2004, 274–275).

14. See, for example, Rojas (2006), Rodríguez Cabal (1997, 31–33), and Terga (1982).

References

EDITIONS OF VICO'S WORKS CONSULTED

Vico, Domingo de. n.d. [ca. 1500s]. *Coleccion de oraciones y meditacions en lengua Quiché.* HSA NS3–37. New York: Hispanic Society of America.

Vico, Domingo de. n.d. [ca. 1500s]. *Sermones, oraciones y traducciones de la biblia escritos y expuestos en lengua Cakchiquel.* HSA NS3–34. New York: Hispanic Society of America.

Vico, Domingo de. n.d. [1553]. *[Theologia Indorum].* Garrett-Gates Mesoamerican Manuscript no. 178. Princeton, NJ: Firestone Library, Princeton University.

Vico, Domingo de. n.d. [1553]. *[Theologia Indorum].* Garrett-Gates Mesoamerican Manuscript no. 179. Princeton, NJ: Firestone Library, Princeton University.

Vico, Domingo de. n.d. [1553]. *[Theologia Indorum]* "Quiché-Cakchiquel religious chants." Tozzer Manuscript C.A.8 Q 40. Cambridge, MA: Tozzer Library, Harvard University.

Vico, Domingo de. n.d. [1553–1554]. *[Theologia Indorum] Algunos sermones en lengua quiché de Rabinal.* Manuscrit Américain 56. Paris: Bibliothèque nationale de France.

Vico, Domingo de. n.d. [1554]. *[Theologia Indorum].* Garrett-Gates Mesoamerican Manuscript no. 175. Princeton, NJ: Firestone Library, Princeton University.

Vico, Domingo de. n.d. [1554]. *[Theologia Indorum].* Garrett-Gates Mesoamerican Manuscript no. 177. Princeton, NJ: Firestone Library, Princeton University.

Vico, Domingo de. n.d. [1554]. *[Theologia Indorum].* Garrett-Gates Mesoamerican Manuscript no. 180. Princeton, NJ: Firestone Library, Princeton University.

Vico, Domingo de. n.d. [1554]. *[Theologia Indorum].* Garrett-Gates Mesoamerican Manuscript no. 227. Princeton, NJ: Firestone Library, Princeton University.

DOI: 10.5876/9781607329701.c012

Vico, Domingo de. n.d. [1554]. *Vocabulario en la lengua Cakchiquel y 4iche o utlatecat.* Edward E. Ayer Manuscript 1582. Chicago, IL: Newberry Library.

Vico, Domingo de. n.d. [ca. 1635]. *Sermones en lengua achi ó tzutuhil.* Manuscrit Américain 69. Paris: Bibliothèque nationale de France.

Vico, Domingo de. n.d. [ca. 1700s]. *Arte de lengua 4iche ó utlatecat.* Manuscrit Américain 46. Paris: Bibliothèque nationale de France.

Vico, Domingo de. n.d. [ca. 1700s]. *Bocabulario en lengua cakchiqel y 4iche o utlatecat.* Codex Ind. 13. Providence, RI: Brown University, John Carter Brown Library.

Vico, Domingo de. 1600s [1553]. *Theologia Indorum.* Garrett-Gates Mesoamerican Manuscript no. 176. Princeton, NJ: Firestone Library, Princeton University.

Vico, Domingo de. 1605 [1553]. *[Theologia Indorum] Vae nima vuh rii theologia indorum ubinaam.* American Philosophical Society Mss.497.4.Ua13 (formerly American Indian Manuscript 178). Philadelphia, PA: American Philosophical Society.

Vico, Domingo de. 1605 [1553]. *[Theologia Indorum] Vae nima vuh rii theologia indorum ubinaam.* Manuscrit Américain 5. Paris: Bibliothèque nationale de France.

Vico, Domingo de. 1600s [1553]. *[Theologia Indorum] Vae nima vuh rii theologia indorum ubinaam.* Manuscrit Américain 10. Paris: Bibliothèque nationale de France.

Vico, Domingo de. 1600s [1553]. *[Theologia Indorum] Vae nima vuh theologia indorum rubinaam.* Manuscrit Américain 4. Paris: Bibliothèque nationale de France.

Vico, Domingo de. 1600s [1554]. *[Theologia Indorum] Vae rucam ruvuhil nimak biih theologia indorum rubinaam.* Manuscrit Américain 3. Paris: Bibliothèque nationale de France.

Vico, Domingo de. 1671 [1553]. *[Theologia Indorum] Ha nima vuh vae theologia yndorum rubinaam.* Manuscrit Américain 42. Paris: Bibliothèque nationale de France.

Vico, Domingo de. ca. 1700 [1554]. *Pláticas de la historia sagrada en lengua cacchí (con un fragmento de un tratado por Fr. Domingo de Vico) [Theologia Indorum].* University of Pennsylvania Manuscript Collection 700, Item 78. Philadelphia: University of Pennsylvania Library.

Vico, Domingo de. 1700s [1554]. *[Theologia Indorum].* University of Pennsylvania Manuscript Collection 700, Item 197. Philadelphia: University of Pennsylvania Library.

Vico, Domingo de. 1700s [1554]. *[Theologia Indorum] Vae rucam ruvuhil nimac biih theologia indorum rubinaam.* Edward E. Ayer Manuscript 1512, Cakchiquel 33. Chicago, IL: Newberry Library.

OTHER SOURCES CONSULTED

Academia de Lenguas Mayas de Guatemala. "Cobertura de Comunidades Lingüísticas." http://www.almg.org.gt/index.php?option=com_content&view=article&id=12&Itemid=7. (accessed on December 11, 2010).

Acuña, René. 1982. *Relaciones geográfica del siglo XVI: Guatemala*. Mexico City, Mexico: Universidad Nacional Autónoma de México.

Acuña, René. 1983. "El *Popol Vuh*, Vico y la *Teologia Indorum*" In *Nuevas Perspectivas sobre el Popol Vuh*, 1–16. Edited by Robert M. Carmack and Francisco Morales Santos. Guatemala City, Guatemala: Editorial Piedra Santa.

Acuña, René. 1983. "Introducción." In *[Thesavrvs Verborv]: Vocabulario de la lengua cakchiq v[el] guatemalteca, nueuamente hecho y recopilado con summoestudio, trauajo y erudición*, XIII–LXI. Edited by René Acuña. Mexico City, Mexico: Universidad Nacional Autónoma de México.

Acuña, René. 1985. "La *Theologia Indorum* de fray Domingo de Vico." *Tlalocan: Revista de Fuentes para el conocimiento de las culturas indígenas de México*. X: 281–307.

Acuña, René. 1989. "Cápitulo primero, en lengua quiché, de la *Theologia Indorum* de Vico." Author's original typed manuscript. La Antigua, Guatemala: Centro de Investigaciones Regionales de Mesoamerica (CIRMA).

Acuña, René. 1992. "Cápitulo primero, en lengua quiché de la *Theologia Indorum* de Vico." In *Memorias del Primer Congreso Internacional de Mayistas: Inauguración, homenajes, lingüística; Lingüística y texos indígenas, antropología social y etnología*, 136–148. Mexico City, Mexico: Instituto de Investigaciones Filológicas, Centro de Estudios Mayas, Universidad Nacional Autónoma de México.

Acuña, René. 1998. *Temas del Popol Vuh*. Mexico City, Mexico: Universidad Nacional Autónoma de México.

Acuña, René, ed. 2002 [ca. 1670s]. *Bartolomé de Anleo, Arte de lengua 4iché: Edición paleográfica, anotada y crítica*. Mexico City, Mexico: Universidad Nacional Autónoma de México.

Acuña, René. 2004. "La *Theologia Indorum* de Vico en lengua quiché." *Estudios de Cultura Maya: Publicación Periódica del Centro de Estudios Mayas*. XXIV: 17–45.

Adams, Eleanor B. 1952. "A Bio-Bibliography of Franciscan Authors in Colonial Central America: L–Z." *The Americas* 9 (1, July): 37–86.

Adichie, Chimamanda Ngozi. "The Danger of the Single Story." http://www.ted.com/talks/chimamanda_adichie_the_danger_of_a_single_story#t-612173, minute 10:19 (accessed July 2019).

Ajpacajá Túm, Florentino Pedro. 2001. *Tz'onob'al tziij: Discurso ceremonial K'ichee'*. Guatemala City, Guatemala: Cholsamaj.

Alcalá, Pedro de. 1928 [ca. 1504]. *Arte para ligeramete saber la lengua arauiga*. New York: Hispanic Society of America.

Alvar, Manuel. 1992. "Nebrija y tres gramáticas de lenguas americanas (náhuatl, quechua y chibcha)." In *Estudio nebrisenses*, 313–339. Edited by Manuel Alvar. Madrid, Spain: Ediciones de Cultura Hispánica.

Alvarado Galindo, Carlos. 2012. "Desarrollo urbano de Kaminaljuyú." In *Ciudades Mesoamericanas*, 87–111. Guatemala City, Guatemala: Publicaciones Mesoamericanas.

Álvarez Arévalo, Miguel. 1987. *Manuscritos de Covalchaj*. Guatemala City, Guatemala: Serviprensa Centroamericana.

Amann, A., E. Mangenot, and A. Vacant, eds. 1939. "Salamanque (théologiens de)." In *Dictionnaire de théologie catholique contenant l'exposé des doctrines de la théologie catholique*, XIV: 1017–1031. Paris: Librairie Letouzey et Ané.

Ángel Asturias, Miguel, and José María González de Mendoza. 1998 [1927]. *Popol-vuh o libro del consejo de los indios Quichés*. Buenos Aires, Argentina: Losada, S.A.

Anleo, Bartholomé de. 1744 [ca. 1670s]. *Arte de Lengua 4iché*. Copied by Antonio Ramírez de Utrilla. Manuscrit Américain 9. Paris: Bibliothèque nationale de France.

Anonymous. n.d. [1567]. Kislak Manuscript 1015. Washington, DC: Jay I. Kislak Collection, US Library of Congress.

Anonymous. 1565. "Iulihii titulo quetacque natirta." Garrett-Gates Mesoameican Manuscript no. 242. Princeton, NJ: Princeton University Library.

Anonymous. 1752. *Catecismo de la doctrina Christiana en idioma kiché y castellano*. Manuscrit Américain 2. Paris: Bibliothèque nationale de France.

Anonymous. ca. 1794. *Petición Vuq ahàu Presidente*. Manuscrit Américain 13. Paris: Bibliothèque nationale de France.

Anonymous. ca. 1700s–1800s. *Vocabulario de la lengua castellana y quiche*. Manuscrit Américain 64. Paris: Bibliothèque nationale de France.

Anonymous. 1813. *Vocabulario de la lengua cakchiquel y español, con un Arte de la misma lengua*. Manuscrit Américain 47. Paris: Bibliothèque nationale de France.

Anonymous. 1833. *Vocabulario kiché, kakchiquel*. Manuscrit Américain 14. Paris: Bibliothèque nationale de France.

Anonymous. 1837. *Vocabulario de la lengua castellana y guatemalteca que se llama Cakchiquel chi*. Manuscrit Américain 7. Paris: Bibliothèque nationale de France.

Aquinas, Thomas. 1266–1273. *Summa theologiae*. http://biblioteca.campusdominicano.org/suma.htm.

Arquidiodesis de Los Altos. http://arquidiocesisdelosaltos.org/content/view/15/34/ (accessed June 2009).

Asselbergs, Florine. 2004. *Conquered Conquistadors, The Lienzo de Quauhquechollan: A Nahua Vision of the Conquest of Guatemala*. Boulder: University Press of Colorado.

Aveni, Anthony F., ed. 1992. *The Sky in Mayan Literature*. New York: Oxford University Press.

Ayer Ms 1515. Ximénez, Francisco. n.d. [ca. 1701–ca. 1704] *[Popol Vuh] Empiezan las historias del origen de los indios de esta provincia de Guatemala*. Edward E. Ayer Manuscript 1515. Chicago, IL: Newberry Library.

Ayer Ms 1536. Cáncer, Luis de. n.d. [1540s–1590s]. *Varias coplas, versos é himnos en la lengua de Cobán de Verapaz.* Edward E. Ayer Manuscript 1536, Kekchi 4. Chicago, IL: Newberry Library.

Ayer Ms 1582. Vico, Domingo de. n.d. [1554]. *Vocabulario en la lengua Cakchiquel y 4iche o utlatecat.* Edward E. Ayer Manuscript 1582. Chicago, IL: Newberry Library.

Babcock, Thomas F. 2012. *Utatlán: The Constituted Community of the K'iche' Maya of Q'umarkaj.* Boulder: University Press of Colorado.

Bacon, Roger. 2013. *On Signs.* Translated by Thomas S. Maloney. Ontario, Canada: Pontifical Institute of Mediaeval Studies, University of Toronto.

Baird, Ellen T. 1993. *The Drawings of Sahagún's Primeros Memoriales: Structure and Style.* Norman: University of Oklahoma Press.

Bandelier, Fanny R. 1932. "Biography of Fray Bernardino de Sahagun." In *A History of Ancient Mexico*, 3–17. Translated by Carlos Maria de Bustamante. Nashville, TN: Fisk University Press.

Basler, Teresa T., and David C. Wright. 2008. "The Making of a Collection: Mesoamerican Manuscripts at Princeton University." *Libraries and the Cultural Record* 43 (1): 29–55.

Basseta, Domingo de. 1695. *Vocabulario en lengua castellana cachiquel chi y quiche chi.* BNE MSS/23234. Madrid, Spain: Biblioteca Nacional de España.

Basseta, Domingo de. 1698. *Vocabulario quiche.* Manuscrit Américain 59. Paris: Bibliothèque nationale de France.

Basseta, Domingo de. 2005 [1698]. *Vocabulario de lengua quiché.* Edited by René Acuña. Mexico City, Mexico: Universidad Nacional Autónoma de México.

Bataillon, Marcel. 1951. "La Vera Paz. Roman et histoire." *Bulletin Hispanique* 53 (3): 235–300.

Belda Plans, Juan. 2009. *La Escuela de Salamanca: La renovación de la teología en el siglo XV.* Madrid, Spain: Biblioteca de Autores Cristianos.

Bell, Elizabeth. 2010. *Let's See Santo Domingo in Antigua Guatemala / Conozcamos Santo Domingo en La Antigua Guatemala.* Mixco, Guatemala: Textos y Formas Impresas.

Bendaña Perdomo, Ricardo. 1996. *La iglesia en Guatemala: Síntesis histórica del catolicismo.* Guatemala City, Guatemala: Librerías Artemis-Edinter.

Benítez Porta, Oscar. 1999. *Diego Reynoso: Popol Vinak.* Guatemala City, Guatemala: Impresos Marylena.

Beristain y Souza, J. M. 1947 [1816–1821]. *Biblioteca Hispano Americana Septentrional*, vol. II, 3rd ed. Mexico City, Mexico: Editorial Fuente Cultural.

Berlin, Heinrich. 1950. "La historia de los Xpantzay." *Antropología e historia de Guatemala* 2 (2): 40–63.

Bettenson, Henry and Chris Maunder, eds. 2011. *Documents of the Christian Church*, 4th ed. New York: Oxford University Press.

Bevans, Stephen B. 1992. *Models of Contextual Theology*. Maryknoll, NY: Orbis Books.

Biermann, Benno. 1964. "Missionsgeschichte der Verapaz in Guatemala." In *Jahrbuch für Geschichte Staat, Wirtschaft und Gesellschaft Lateinamerikas*, I: 117–156. Cologne, Germany: Böhlau Verlag Köln Graz.

Biermann, Benno M. 1971. "Bartolomé de Las Casas and Verapaz." In *Bartolomé de Las Casas in History: Toward an Understanding of the Man and His Work*, 443–484. Edited by Juan Friede and Benjamin Keen. DeKalb: Northern Illinois University Press.

Blackfriars. 1964. "Appendix 3: Ancient and Medieval Astronomy." In *Summa theologiae*, Volume 10: *Cosmogony*, 182–187. New York: McGraw-Hill Book Company, and London: Eyre and Spottiswoode.

Boff, Leonardo and Clodovis Boff. 2007. *Introducing Liberation Theology*. Translated by Paul Burns. Maryknoll, NY: Orbis Books.

Bollweg, John August. 1995. "Sense of a Mission: Arnau de Vilanova onf the Conversion of Muslims and Jews." In *Iberia and the Mediterranean World of the Middle Ages: Studies in Honor of Robert I. Burns*, 50–71. Edited by Larry J. Simon. Leiden, Netherlands: E. J. Brill.

Bonniwell, William R. 1945. *A History of the Dominican Liturgy 1215–1945*, 2nd ed. New York: J. F. Wagner.

Boone, Elizabeth Hill. 1994. "Introduction: Writing and Recording Knowledge." In *Writing Without Words: Alternative Literacies in Mesoamerica and the Andes*, 13–22. Edited by Elizabeth Hill Boone and Walter D. Mignolo. Durham, NC: Duke University Press.

Boone, Elizabeth Hill. 2000. *Stories in Red and Black*. Austin: University of Texas Press.

Blom, Frans, trans., and Tomás de la Torre. 1973. "Travelling in 1544: From Salamanca, Spain to Ciudad Real Chiapas, Mexico." *The Sewanee Review* 81 (3, Summer): 429–526.

Bossú [Zappa], Ennio [María]. 2008. "Título Cagcoh [Kaqkoj]." In *Crónicas mesoamericanas,* I: 93–105. Guatemala City, Guatemala: Publicaciones Mesoamericana.

Bossú Z[appa], Ennio María. 1986. "Un manuscrito k'eckchi' del siglo xvi: Transcripción paleográfica, traducción y estudio de las coplas atribuidas a Fray Luis Cáncer." Licenciature thesis, Universidad Francisco Marroquín. Guatemala City, Guatemala.

Bouza, Fernando. 2004. *Communication, Knowledge, and Memory in Early Modern Spain*. Translated by Sonia López and Michael Agnew. Philadelphia: University of Pennsylvania Press.

Bove, Fredrick J., José Vicente Genovez, and Carlos A. Batres. 2012. "Pipil Archeology of Pacific Guatemala." In *Fanning the Sacred Flame: Mesoamerican Studies in Honor of H. B. Nicholson*, 231–268. Edited by Matthew A. Boxt and Brian D. Dillon. Boulder: University Press of Colorado.

Brasseur de Bourbourg, M. [Charles Étienne]. 1871. *Bibliothèque Mexique-Guatémalienne précédée d'un coup d'œil sur les études américaines*. Paris: Maisonneuve & C. Libraire Éditeur.

Brasseur de Bourbourg, Charles Étienne. 1961 [1862]. *Gramática de la lengua quiché según manuscritos de los mejores autores guatemaltecos; acompañada de anotaciones filológicas y un vocabulario*. Guatemala City, Guatemala: Editorial del Ministerio de Educación Publica "José de Pineda Ibarra."

Brasseur de Bourbourg, [Charles Étienne]. n.d. [ca. 1855]. [Popol Vuh] Manuscrit Américain 57. Paris: Bibliothèque nationale de France.

Brasseur de Bourbourg, Charles Étienne. n.d. [ca. 1850]. [*Title of Totonicapán*]. Manuscrit Américain 77. Paris: Bibliothèque nationale de France.

Braswell, Geoffrey E. 2001. "Ethnogenesis, Social Structure, and Survival: The Nahuaization of K'iche'an Culture, 1450–1550." In *Maya Survivalism*, 51–58. Edited by Ueli Hostettler and Matthew Restall. Acta Mesoamericana, vol. 12. Markt Schwaben, Germany: Verlag Anton Saurwein.

Braswell, Geoffrey E. 2003a. "Highland Maya Polities." In *The Postclassic Mesoamerican World*, 45–49. Edited by Michael S. Smith and Frances F. Berdan. Salt Lake City: University of Utah Press.

Braswell, Geoffrey E. 2003b. "K'iche'an Origins, Symbolic Emulation, and Ethnogenesis in the Maya Highlands, A.D. 1450–1524." In *The Postclassic Mesoamerican World*, 297–303. Edited by Michael S. Smith and Frances F. Berdan. Salt Lake City: University of Utah Press.

Bredt-Kriszat, Cristina. n.d. [1995]. "Un texto religioso de mediados del siglo XVI en Guatemala: La '*Theologia Indorum*' de fray Domingo de Vico." In *Actas del I Congreso Internacional de Hispanistas, Del 26 al 30 de Junio de 1995, Universidad Nacional de Educación a Distancia, Centro Asociado de Melilla*, 215–233. Malaga, Spain: Corcelles-La Española.

Bredt-Kriszat, Cristina. n.d. [1996]. "Fray Domingo de Vico: Un ubetense en Guatemala." In *Actas del II Congreso Internacional de Hispanistas, Del 31 de Octubre al 4 de Noviembre de 1996 celebrado en la Universidad Internacional de Andalucía, Sede "Antonio Machado." Baeza (Jaén)*, 237–247. Malaga, Spain: Editorial Algazara.

Bredt-Kriszat, Cristina. 1999. "La *Theologia Indorum* y la respuesta indígena en las crónicas de Guatemala." In *La lengua de la cristianización en Latinoamérica: Catequización e instrucción en lenguas amerindias [The language of christianisation in Latin America: Catechisation and instruction in Amerindian languages]. Bonner Amerikanistishe Studien, Volume 32: Centre for Indigenous American Studies and Exchange*, Occasional Papers 29: 183–203. Edited by Lindsey Crickmay and Sabine Dedenbach-Salazar Sáenz. Marka Schwaben, Germany: Verlag Antón Saurwein.

Bredt-Kriszat, Cristina, and Ursula Holl. 1997. "Descripción del Vocabulario de la lenga cakchiquel de fray Domingo de Vico." In *La descipción de las lenguas amerindias en la época colonial*. Biblioteca Ibero-Americana 63: 175–192. Edited by Klaus Zimmermann. Madrid, Spain: Iberoamericana, and Frankfurt, Germany: Vervuet.

Bricker, Victoria R., and Helga-Maria Miram, trans. 2002. *An Encounter of Two Worlds: The Book of Chilam Balam of Kaua*. New Orleans, LA: Middle American Research Institute, Tulane University.

Brinton, Daniel G. 1881. "The Names of the Gods in the Kiche Myths, Central America." *Proceedings of the American Philosophical Society* 19 (109, June–December): 613–647.

Brinton, Daniel G. 1884. "A Grammar of the Cakchiquel Language of Guatemala." *Proceedings of the American Philosophical Society* 21 (115, April): 345–412.

Brinton, Daniel G. 2011 [1883]. *Aboriginal American Authors and Their Productions; Especially Those in the Native Languages: A Chapter in the History of Literature*. Lexington, KY: ZuuBooks Publications.

Broda, Johanna, Stanislaw Iwaniszewski, and Lucrecia Maupomé, eds. 1991. *Arqueo-astronomía y etnoastronomía en Mesoamerica*. Mexico City, Mexico: Universidad Nacional Autónoma de México.

Brody, M. Jill. 1988. "Discourse Genres in Tojolabal." In *The Tojolabal Maya Ethnographic and Linguistic Approaches*. Edited by M. Jill Brody and John S. Thomas. *Geoscience and Man*, 26 (July): 55–62. Baton Rouge: Geosciences Publications, Louisiana State University.

Brown, Kenneth L. 1982. "Prehispanic Demography within the Central Quiche Area, Guatemala." In *The Historical Demography of Highland Guatemala*, Publication No. 6, 35–47. Albany: Institute for Mesoamerican Studies, State University of New York at Albany.

Burgess, Dora M. de, and Patricio Xec. 1955. *El Popol Wuj: Texto del Padre Ximénez*. Quetzaltenango, Guatemala: Talleres Tipográficos "El Noticiero Evangélico."

Burkhart, Louis M. 2014. "The 'Little Doctrine' and Indigenous Catechesis in New Spain." *Hispanic American Historical Review* 94 (2): 167–206.

Burns, Robert I. 1996. *Jews in the Notarial Culture: Latinate Wills in Mediterranean Spain, 1250–1350*. Berkeley and Los Angeles: University of California Press.

Burrell, David B. 1979. *Aquinas: God and Action*. Eugene, OR: Wipf and Stock.

Butzer, Karl W. 1992. "The Americas before and after 1492: An Introduction to Current Geographical Research." *Annals of the Association of American Geographers* 82 (3, September): 345–368.

Cabezas Carcache, Horacio. 2008. "Título de Xilotepeque." In *Crónicas mesoamericanas*, Tomo I, 155–163. Guatemala City, Guatemala: Publicaciones Mesoamericanas.

Calvin, John. 1960. *Institutes of the Christian Religion*. Edited by John T. McNeill. Louisville, KY: Westminster John Knox Press.

Cáncer, Luis de. n.d. [1540s–1590s]. *Varias coplas, versos é himnos en la lengua de Cobán de Verapaz*. Edward E. Ayer Manuscript 1536, Kekchi 4. Chicago, IL: Newberry Library.

Carmack, Robert M. 1966. "La perpetuación del clan patrilineal en Totonicapán." *Antropología e historia de Guatemala* 18 (1): 3–13.

Carmack, Robert M. 1967. "Analisis histórico-sociológico de un antiguo título quiche." *Antropología e Historia de Guatemala* 18 (2): 3–13.

Carmack, Robert M. 1973. *Quichean Civilization: The Ethnohistoric, Ethnographic, and Archaeological Sources*. Berkley and Los Angeles: University of California Press.

Carmack, Robert M. 1981a. "New Quichean Chronicles from Highland Guatemala." *Estudios de Cultura Maya* XIII: 83–103.

Carmack, Robert M. 1981b. *The Quiché Maya of Utatlán: The Evolution of a Highland Guatemala Kingdom*. Norman: University of Oklahoma Press.

Carmack, Robert M. 2001a. *Kik'aslemaal le K'iche'aab': Historia social de los K'iche's*. Guatemala City, Guatemala: Cholsamaj.

Carmack, Robert M. 2001b. *Kik'ulmatajem le K'iche'aab': Evolución del reino K'iche'*. Guatemala City, Guatemala: Cholsamaj.

Carmack, Robert M. 2012. "Prehispanic K'iche-Maya Historiography." In *Fanning the Sacred Flame: Mesoamerican Studies in Honor of H. B. Nicholson*, 355–388. Edited by Matthew A. Bot and Brian Dervin Dillon. Boulder: University Press of Colorado.

Carmack, Robert M., and James L. Mondloch. 1983. *El título de Totonicapán: Texto, traducción y comentario*. Mexico City, Mexico: Universidad Nacional Autónoma de México.

Carmack, Robert and James L. Mondloch. 1985. "El título de Ilocab': Texto, traducción y análisis." *Tlalocan: Revista de fuentes para el conocimiento de las culturas indígenas de México* 10: 213–256.

Carmack, Robert M., and James L. Mondloch. 1989. *El Título de Yax y otros documentos quiches de Totonicapán, Guatemala: Edición facsimiar, transcripción, traducción y notas*. Mexico City, Mexico: Universidad Nacional Autónoma de México.

Carmack, Robert M., and James L. Mondloch. 2007. *Uwujil Kulewal aj Chwi Miq'ina' / El Título de Totonicapán*. Guatemala City, Guatemala: Cholsamaj.

Carmack, Robert M., and James L. Mondloch. 2009. "Título K'oyoi." In *Crónicas Mesoamericanas*, Tomo II: 15–67. Guatemala City, Guatemala: Publicaciones Mesoamericanas.

Carmack, Robert M., and Alfonso Efraín Tzaquitzal Zapeta. 1993. *Título de los señores Coyoy*. Guatemala City, Guatemala: Serviprensa Centroamericana.

Carmack, Robert M., and Dwight T. Wallace, eds. 1977. *Archaeology and Ethnohistory of the Central Quiche*, Publication No. 1. Albany: Institute for Mesoamerican Studies, State University of New York at Albany.

Carmack, Robert M., and John M. Weeks. 1981. "The Archaeology and Ethnohistory of Utatlan: A Conjunctive Approach." *American Antiquity* 46 (2, April): 323–341.

Carrasco, Davíd. 2000. *Quetzalcoatl and the Irony of Empire: Myths and Prophecies in the Aztec Tradition*, Revised Edition. Boulder: University Press of Colorado.

Carrasco, Pedro. 1967. "Don Juan Cortés, Cacique de Santa Cruz Quiché." *Estudios de Cultura Maya* 6: 251–266.

Carré, Meyrick H. 1946. *Realists and Nominalists*. Oxford, UK: Oxford UniversityPress.

Carruthers, Mary. 1998. *The Craft of Thought: Meditation, Rhetoric, and the Making of Images, 400–1200*. New York: Cambridge University Press.

Cartagena, Nelson. 2009. "Introducción: Las reflexiones sobre la traducción en España durante la Edad Media." In *La contribución de España a la teoría de la traducción: Introducción al estudio y antología de los siglos XIV y XV*, xi–xlii. Madrid, Spain: Iberoamericana, and Frankfurt, Germany: Vervuet.

Cervantes, Fernando. 1997. *The Devil in the New World: The Impact of Diabolism in New Spain*. New Haven, CT: Yale University Press.

Charencey, M. [Charles-F.lix-Hyacinthe G.] de. 1885. *Título de los señores de Totonicapán, Titre genealogique des seigneurs de Totonicapán.* Paris: E. Renaut-De Broise, Imprimeur.

Chávez, Adrián I. 1997. *Pop-Wuj: Poema Mito-histórico Kí-chè*. Quetzaltenango, Guatemala: Timach.

Chinchilla M., Rosa Helena. 1993. "Introducción." In *Arte de las tres lenguas kaqchikel, k'iche' y tz'utujil, por Fr. Francisco Ximénez, O.P.*, Biblioteca "Goathemala" Volumen XXXI, ix–xxxii. Edited by Rosa Helena Chinchilla M. Guatemala City, Guatemala: Academia de Geografía e Historia de Guatemala.

Chinchilla Mazariegos, Oswaldo. 1999. "Título de los Nimak Achi de Totonicapán (1545)." *Mesoamérica* 38 (December): 77–84.

Chinchilla Mazariegos, Oswaldo. 2011. *Imagenes de la Mitología Maya*. Guatemala City, Guatemala: Museo Popol Vuh, Universidad Francisco Marroquín.

Chinchilla Mazariegos, Oswaldo. 2017. *Art and Myth of the Ancient Maya*. New Haven, CT: Yale University Press.

Christenson, Allen J. 2003. *Popol Vuh: The Sacred Book of the Maya*. New York: O Books.

Christenson, Allen J. 2004. *Popol Vuh*, Volume II: *Literal Poetic Version, Translation and Transcription*. New York: O Books.

Christenson, Allen J. 2007a. *Popol Vuh: The Sacred Book of the Maya*. Norman: University of Oklahoma Press.

Christenson, Allen J. 2007b. *Popol Vuh*, Volume II: *Literal Poetic Version, Translation and Transcription. Norman*: University of Oklahoma Press.

Christenson, Allen J. 2012. "The Use of Chiasmus by the Ancient K'iche' Maya." In *Parallel Worlds: Genre, Discourse, and Poetics in Contemporary, Colonial, and Classic*

Maya Literature, 311–336. Edited by Kerry M. Hull and Michael D. Carrasco. Boulder: University Press of Colorado.

Christenson, Allen J. 2014. "'These You Deified Anciently': An Authentic K'iche' Theological Text within Fr. Domingo de Vico's Theologia Indorum." Annual Meeting of the American Ethnohistory Society, Indianapolis, IN, October 8–12.

Christenson, Allen J. 2016. *The Burden of the Ancients: Maya Ceremonies of World Renewal from the Pre-Columbian Period to the Present*. Austin: University of Texas Press.

Christensen, Mark Z. 2013. *Nahua and Maya Catholicisms: Texts and Religion in Colonial Central Mexico and Yucatan*. Stanford, CA: Stanford University Press.

Christensen, Mark Z. 2014. *Translated Christianities: Nahuatl and Maya Religious Texts*. University Park, PA: Penn State University Press.

Christensen, Mark Z., and Jonathan Truitt. 2016. *Native Wills from the Colonial Americas: Dead Giveaways in the New World*. Salt Lake City: University of Utah Press.

Christensen, Mark Z., and Matthew Restall. 2019. *Return to Ixil: Maya Society in an Eighteenth-Century Yucatec Town*. Louisville: Univeristy Press of Colorado.

Christian, William A., Jr. 1981. *Apparitions in Late Medieval and Renaissance Spain*. Princeton, NJ: Princeton University Press.

Chuchiak, John F., IV 2012. *The Inquisition in New Spain, 1536–1820: A Documentary History*. Baltimore: The Johns Hopkins University Press.

Chuchiak, John F., VI. 2017. "Sin, Shame, and Sexuality: Franciscan Obsession and Maya Humor in the Calepino de Motul Dictionary, 1573–1615." In *Words and Worlds Turned Around: Indigenous Christianities in Colonial Latin America*, 195–219. Boulder: University Press of Colorado.

Ciudad Suárez, María Milagros. 1996. *Los dominicos, un grupo de poder en Chiapas y Guatemala: Siglos XVI y XVII*. Seville, Spain: Escuela de Estudios Hispano-Americanos.

Cleary, Edward L. 2011. *The Rise of Charismatic Catholicism in Latin America*. Gainesville: University of Florida Press.

Clement I. 1996. "The First Epistle of Clement." In *The Ante-Nicene Fathers: Translations of the Writings of the Fathers down to A.D. 325*, 1–21. Edited by Alexander Roberts and James Donaldson. Grand Rapids, MI: Wm. B. Eerdmans Publishing Company.

Coe, Michael D. 1992. *Breaking the Maya Code*. New York: Thames and Hudson, Inc.

Coe, Michael D., and Mark van Stone. 2001. *Reading the Maya Glyphs*. London: Thames and Hudson, Ltd.

Comisión para el Esclarecimiento Histórico (CEH). n.d. [1999]. *Guatemala, memoria del silencio / tz'inil na'tab'al: Conclusiones y recomendaciones del Informe de la Comisión para el Esclarecimiento Histórico*. Guatemala City, Guatemala: Servigráficos, S.A.

Contreras, J. Daniel. 2008. "Historia quiché de don Juan de Torres." In *Crónicas Mesoamericanas*, Tomo I: 107–127. Edited by Horacio Cabezas Carcache. Guatemala City, Guatemala: Publicaciones Mesoamericanas.

Córdoba, Pedro de. 1970 [1544]. *Christian Doctrine.* Translated by Sterling A. Stoudemire. Coral Gables, FL: University of Miami Press.

Cortéz y Larraz, Pedro. 1771. "Respuesta del Padre Cura de Xocopilas." Seville, Spain: Archivo General de Indias, 1771, cuaderno 2. http://afehc-historia-centroamericana.org/index.php/_fichiers/index.php?action=fi_aff&id=1739 (accessed on June 2009).

Coto, Thomás de. 1983 [ca. 1670]. *[Thesavrvs Verborv]: Vocabulario de la lengua cakchiq v[el] guatemalteca, nueuamente hecho y recopilado con summo estudio, trauajo y erudición.* Edited by René Acuña. Mexico City, Mexico: Universidad Nacional Autónoma de México.

Courtenay, William J. 1974. "Nominalism and Late Medieval Religion." In *Studies in Medieval and Reformation Thought,* 26–59. Edited by Charles Trinkaus and Heiko A. Oberman. Leiden, Netherlands: E. J. Brill.

Crespo Morales, Mario. 1956. "Título indígenas de tierras: Trasunto de un título de los del pueblo San Martín Xilotepeque." *Antropología e historia de Guatemala* 8 (2): 10–15.

Crespo Morales, Mario. 1968. "Algunos títulos indígenas del Archivo General del Gobierno de Guatemala." Licenciature thesis, Universidad de San Carlos. Guatemala City, Guatemala.

Cuervo Arango, Justo. 1914–15. *Historiadores del Convento de San Esteban,* Tomos I–III. Salamanca, Spain: Imprinta Católica Salmanticense.

Cuevas, Mariano, S.J. 1928. *Historia de la iglesia en México*, Tomo I. El Paso, TX: Editorial "Revista Católica."

Dahlmann, Joseph. 1893. *El estudio de la lenguas y las misiones por José Dahlmann, S.J.* Translated by Jerónimo Rojas. Madrid, Spain: Librería Católica de Gregorio del Amo.

Dary F., Claudia. 1997. *El derecho international humanitario y el orden jurídico maya: Una perspectiva histórico cultural.* Guatemala City, Guatemala: FLACSO.

D'Avray, David L. 1980. "Portable Vademecum Books Containing Franciscan and Dominican Texts." In *Manuscripts at Oxford: An Exhibition in Memory of Richard William Hunt (1908–1979), Keeper of Western Manuscripts at the Bodleian Library, Oxford, 1945–1975, on Themes Selected and Described by Some of His Friends*, 60–64. Edited by Albinia C. de la Mare and B. C. Barker-Benfield. Oxford, UK: England Bodleian Library.

Dawson, Christopher, ed. 1955. *The Mongol Mission: Narratives and Letters of the Franciscan Missionaries in Mongolia and China in the Thirteenth and Fourteenth Centuries.* New York: Sheed and Ward.

Delgado, Damián. n.d. [ca. 1600s-1700s]. *Sermones varios predicados en lengua Quiche y trasladados para el use el los padres de la Santa Orden de N.P.S. Domingo en Rabinal.* HSA NS3–11. New York: Hispanic Society of America.

Denevan, William M. 1992. "The Pristine Myth: The Landscape of the Americas in 1492." *Annals of the Association of American Geographers* 82 (3, September): 369–385.

Denevan, William M. 1996. "Carl Sauer and Native American Population Size." *Geographical Review* 86 (3, July): 385–397.

Des moines chez les Mayas. http://moines.mayas.free.fr (accessed June 2009).

Díaz del Castillo, Bernal. 1956 [1576]. *The Discovery and Conquest of Mexico, 1517–1521.* Translated by Irving A. Leonard. New York: Farrar, Straus and Cudahy.

Dolet, Étienne. 1540. *La manière de bien traduire d'une langue en autre, d'advantage de la punctuation de la langue françoise, plus des accents d'ycelle.* Paris: Imprimerie de I. Tastu. https://gallica.bnf.fr/ark:/12148/bpt6k505680/ (accessed on July 2019).

Durán, Diego. 1967 [ca. 1580]. "Libro de los ritos y ceremonias en las fiestas de los dioses y celebración de ellas." In *Historia e las Indias de Nueva España e islas de la tierra firme,* tomo I, 3–210. Edited by Ángel Maria Garibay K. Mexico City, Mexico: Editorial Porrua, S.A.

Durán, Diego. 1994 [ca. 1580]. *The History of the Indies of New Spain.* Translated by Doris Heyden. Norman: University of Oklahoma Press.

Durán, Juan Guillermo, ed. 1984. *Monumenta catechetica hispanoamericano.* Volumen 1: *Siglo XVI.* Buenos Aires: Facultad de la Pontifica Universidad Católica Argentina.

Dürr, Michael. 1994. "El Popol Vuh, la obra de Francisco Ximénez y el Título de Totonicapán: aspectos comparativos de grafías y gramática." In *De orbis Hispani linguis litteris historia moribus: Festshrift für Dietrich Briesemeister zum 60. Geburtstag,* volume 2, 1153–1165. Edited by Axel Schönberger and Klaus Zimmermann. Frankfurt, Germany: Domus Editoria Europaea.

Dürr, Michael, and Frauke Sachse, eds. 2017. *Diccionario k'iche' de Berlín: El Vocabulario en lengua 4iche otlatecas: edición crítica.* Estudios Indiana 10. Berlin, Germany: Ibero-Amerikanisches Institut Preußischer Kulturbesitz and Gerb. Mann Verlag.

Durston, Alan. 2007. *Pastoral Quechua: The History of Christian Translation in Colonial Peru, 1550–1650.* Notre Dame, IN: University of Notre Dame Press.

Durston, Alan. 2014. "The Making of the *Huarochirí Manuscript.*" In *Indigenous Intellectuals: Knowledge, Power, and Colonial Culture in Mexico and the Andes,* 151–169. Edited by Gabriela Ramos and Yanna Yannakakis. Durham, NC: Duke University Press.

Early, John D. 2006. *The Maya and Catholicism: An Encounter of Worldviews.* Gainesville: University Press of Florida.

Ebacher, Colleen. 1991. "The Old and New Worlds: Incorporating American Indian Forms of Discourse and Modes of Communication into Colonial Missionary Texts." *Anthropological Linguistics* 33 (2, Summer): 135–165.

Eco, Umberto. 1989. "Denotation." In *On the Medieval Theory of Signs,* 43–77. Edited by Umberto Eco and Costantino Marmo. Amsterdam, Netherlands, and Philadelphia: John Benjamins Publishing Company.

Eco, Umberto, Roberto Lambertini, Costantino Marmo, and Andrea Tabarroni. 1989. "On Animal Language in the Medieval Classification of Signs." In *On the Medieval Theory of Signs*, 3–41. Edited by Umberto Eco and Costantino Marmo. Amsterdam, Netherlands, and Philadelphia: John Benjamins Publishing Company.

Edmonson, Munro S. 1965. *Quiche-English Dictionary*, Publication 30. New Orleans, LA: Tulane University Press, Middle American Research Institute.

Edmonson, Munro S. 1971. *The Book of Counsel: The Popol Vuh of the Quiche Maya of Guatemala*, Publication 35. New Orleans, LA: Tulane University, Middle American Research Institute.

Edmonson, Munro S. 1982. *The Ancient Future of the Itza: The Book of Chilam Balam of Tizimin*. Austin: University of Texas Press.

Edmonson, Munro S. 1986. *Heaven Born Merida and Its Destiny: The Book of Chilam Balam of Chumayel*. Austin: University of Texas Press.

Ehrman, Bart D. 2003. *Lost Scriptures: Books that Did Not Make It into the New Testament*. New York: Oxford University Press.

Eire, Carlos M. N. 1995. *From Madrid to Purgatory: The Art and Craft of Dying in Sixteenth-Century Spain*. New York: Cambridge University Press.

Eire, Carlos M. N. 2016. *Reformations: The Early Modern World, 1450–1650*. New Haven, CT: Yale University Press.

Elliott, J. H. 2009. *Spain, Europe, and the Wider World, 1500–1800*. New Haven, CT: Yale University Press.

England, John C., Jose Kuttianimattathil, John M. Prior, Lily A. Quintos, David Suh Kwang-sun, and Janice Wickeri, eds. 2002. *Asian Christian Theologies: A Research Guide to Authors, Movements, Sources*, Volume 1. Maryknoll, NY: Orbis Books and ISPCK/Claretian Publishers.

England, Nora C. 1994. *Autonomía de los idiomas mayas: Historia e identidad / Ukuta'miil, ramaq'iil, utzijob'aal: Ri Maya' amaaq'*. Guatemala City, Guatemala: Editorial Cholsamaj.

England, Nora C. 1999. *Introducción a la lingüística: Idiomas mayas*. Antigua and Guatemala City, Guatemala: Proyecto Lingüístico Francisco Marroquín and Editorial Cholsamaj.

Estrada, Juan de, and Fernando de Niebla. 1579. *Relación geográfica de Zapotitlán*. Benson Latin American Collection, XX-9. Austin: University of Texas.

Fabié, Antonio María. 1879. *Vida y escritos de fray Bartolomé de las Casas, obispo de Chiapa*, tomo I. Madrid, Spain: Imprenta de Miguel Ginesta.

Falla, Ricardo. 2013. *El Popol Wuj: Una interpretación para el día de hoy*. Guatemala City, Guatemala: Asociación para el Avance de las Ciencias Sociales de Guatemala.

Farhi, Paul. 1991. "Taking Local Coverage to the Limit: 24-Hour Cable News," *The Washington Post*, March 11.

Farriss, Nancy. 2014. Libana: *El discurso ceremonial mesoamericano y el sermon cristiano*. Mexico City, Mexico: Universidad Nacional Autónoma de México.

Farriss, Nancy. 2018. *Tongues of Fire: Language and Evangelization in Colonial Mexico*. New York: Oxford University Press.

Fischer, Edward F., and Carol Hendrickson. 2003. *Tecpán Guatemala: A Modern Maya Town in Global and Local Context*. Cambridge, MA: Westview Press.

Fletcher, Richard. 1990. *The Quest for El Cid*. New York: Alfred A. Knopf.

Florescano, Enrique. 2001. "Titres primordiaux et mémoire canonique en Méso-amérique." Translated by Carmen Bernand. *Études rurales* 157/158 (January–June): 15–43.

Florescano, Enrique. 2002a. "El canon memorioso forjado por los *Títulos primordiales*." *Colonial Latin American Review* 11 (2): 183–230.

Florescano, Enrique. 2002b. *National Narratives in Mexico: A History*. Translated by Nancy Hancock. Norman: University of Oklahoma Press.

Fox, Everett. 1972. "In the Beginning." *Response* 14: 9–159.

Fox, John W. 1977. "Quiche Expansion Processes: Differential Ecological Growth Bases within an Archaic State." In *Archaeology and Ethnohistory of the Central Quiche*, Publication No. 1: 82–97. Edited by Dwight T. Wallace and Robert M. Carmack. Albany: Institute for Mesoamerican Studies, State University of New York at Albany.

Fox, John W. 1978. *Quiche Conquest: Centralism and Regionalism in Highland Guatemalan State Development*. Albuquerque: University of New Mexico Press.

Freidel, David, Linda Schele, and Joy Parker. 1993. *Maya Cosmos: Three Thousand Years on the Shaman's Path*. New York: William Morrow and Company, Inc.

Friedrich, Paul. 2006. "Maximizing Ethnopoetics: Fine-Tuning Anthropological Experience," 207–228. In *Language, Culture, and Society: Key Topics in Linguistic Anthropology*. Edited by Christine Jourdan and Kevin Tuite. New York: Cambridge University Press.

Fuentes y Guzmán, Francisco Antonio. 2013 [ca. 1690]. *Recordación Florida: Discurso historial y demonstración natural, material, militar y política del Reyno de Guatemala*, Tomo II. Guatemala City, Guatemala: Universidad de San Carlos de Guatemala, Editorial Universitaria.

García Ahumada, Enrique. 1994. "La inculturación en la catequesis inicial de América." *Anuario de historia de la iglesia* 3: 215–232.

García Icazbalceta, Joaquín. 1954. *Bibliografía mexicana del siglo XVI: Catálogo razonado de libros impresos en México de 1539 a 1600*. New edition by Agustín Millares Carlo. Mexico City, Mexico: Fondo de Cultura Económica.

García-Ruiz, Jesús. 1992. "El misionero, las lenguas mayas y la traducción: Nominalismo, tomismo y etnolingüística en Guatemala." *Archives de Sciences sociales des Religions* 77 (January–March): 83–110.

Garfield, Bob, and Mary Ann Giordano. 2010. "Is Hyperlocal the Future of News? Transcript," On the Media, Friday, July 16, http://www.onthemedia.org/2010/jul/16/is-hyperlocal-the-future-of-news/transcript/.

Garfield, Bob, and Jeff Jarvis. 2009. "Post-Newspaper Journalism? Transcript," On the Media, Friday, August 21, http://www.onthemedia.org/2009/aug/21/post-newspaper-journalism/transcript/.

Garfield, Bob and Kate Marymont. 2007. "Citizenship Papers: Transcript," *On the Media*, Friday, October 12, http://www.onthemedia.org/2007/oct/12/citizenship-papers/transcript/.

Garrard-Burnett, Virginia. 2010. *Terror in the Land of the Holy Spirit: Guatemala under General Efraín Ríos Montt 1982–1983*. New York: Oxford University Press.

Garrido Aranda, Antonio. 1980. *Moriscos y indios: Precedentes hispánicos de la evangelización en México*. Mexico City, Mexico: Universidad Nacional Autónoma de México, 1980.

Garza C., Mercedes de la. 2012. "Origen, estructura y temporalidad del cosmos." In *Religión maya*, 53–81. Edited by Mercedes de la Garza Camino and Martha Ilia Nájera Coronado. Madrid, Spain: Editorial Trotta.

Gerson, Jean. 1949 [1544]. *Tripartito del cristianissimo y consolatorio, Doctor Juan Gerson de doctrina cristiana a cualquiera muy provecha*. Mexico City, Mexico: Ediciones "Libros de México."

Gerson, Jean. 1998. *Jean Gerson, Early Works*. Translated by Brian Patrick McGuire. Mahwah, NJ: Paulist Press.

Giménez Fernández, Manuel. 1971. "Fray Bartolomé de Las Casas: A Biographical Sketch." In *Bartolomé de Las Casas in History: Toward an Understanding of the Man and His Work*, 67–125. Edited by Juan Friede and Benjamin Keen. DeKalb: Northern Illinois University Press.

Goetz, Delia, trans. 1953. *The Annals of the Cakchiquels, Title of the Lords of Totonicapán*. Translated into Spanish by Adrian Recinos and Dionisio Chonay. Norman: University of Oklahoma Press.

Goetz, Delia, and Sylvanus G. Morley, trans. 1950. *Popol Vuh: The Sacred Book of the Ancient Quiché Maya*. Translated into Spanish by Adrian Recinos. Norman: University of Oklahoma Press.

Gómez-Ruiz, Raúl. 2007. *Mozarabs, Hispanics, and the Cross*. Maryknoll, NY: Orbis Books.

Gran Enciclopedia de Andalucía. 1979. Seville, Spain: Ediciones Anel, S.A.

Greenslade, Roy. 2012. "Lessons to learn from the Journatic fakery scandal," Greenslade Blog, July 17, *The Guardian*, http://www.guardian.co.uk/media/greenslade/2012/jul/17/ newspapers-digital-media.

Gubler, Ruth, and David Bolles, eds. 2000. *The Book of Chilam Balam of Na: Facsimile, Translation, and Text*. Lancaster, CA: Labyrinthos.

Guillemín, Jorge F. 1965. *Iximché: Capital de antiguo reino cakchiquel*. Guatemala City, Guatemala: Instituto de Antropología e Historia de Guatemala.

Gutiérrez, Gustavo. 1993. *Las Casas: In Search of the Poor of Jesus Christ*. Translated by Robert R. Barr. Maryknoll, NY: Orbis Books.

Gutiérrez, Gustavo. 2003. *We Drink from Our Own Wells: The Spiritual Journey of a People*. 20th Anniversary Edition. Translated by Matthew J. O'Connell. Maryknoll, NY: Orbis Books.

Guzmán, Pantaleón de. 1984 [1704]. *Compendio de nombres en lengva cakchiqvel*. Edited by René Acuña. Mexico City, Mexico: Universidad Nacional Autónoma de México.

Hamann, Byron Ellsworth. 2015. *The Translations of Nebrija: Language, Culture, and Circulation in the Early Modern World*. Amherst: University of Massachusetts Press.

Hanke, Lewis. 1974. *All Mankind Is One: A Study of the Disputation Between Bartolomé de Las Casas and Juan Ginés de Sepúlveda on the Religious and Intellectual Capacity of the American Indians*. DeKalb: Northern Illinois University Press.

Hanks, William F. 1986. "Authenticity and Ambivalence in the Text: A Colonial Maya Case." *American Ethnologist* 13 (14): 721–744.

Hanks, William F. 1987. "Discourse Genres in a Theory of Practice." *American Ethnologist* 14 (4, Novemeber): 668–692.

Hanks, William F. 1999. *Intertexts: Writings on Language, Utterance, and Context*. Lanham, MD: Rowman and Littlefield.

Hanks, William F. 2010. *Converting Words: Maya in the Age of the Cross*. Berkeley and Los Angeles: University of California Press.

Hart, Thomas. 2008. *The Ancient Spirituality of the Modern Maya*. Albuquerque: University of New Mexico Press.

Hartley, Sarah. 2010. "10 Characteristics of hyperlocal," http://sarahhartley.wordpress.com/2010/08/25/10-characteristics-of-hyperlocal/.

Hellman, Wayne J. A. 1989. "The Spirituality of the Franciscans." In *Christian Spirituality*, Vol. 2, *High Middle Ages and Reformation*, 31–49. World Spirituality: An Encyclopedic History of the Religious Quest, Vol. 17. Edited by Jill Raitt. New York: Crossroad Publishing Company.

Helps, Arthur. 1857. *The Spanish Conquest in America and Its Relation to the History of Slavery and to the Government of Colonies*. New York: Harper and Brothers.

Henderson, John B. 1998. *The Construction of Orthodoxy and Heresy: Neo-Confucian, Islamic, Jewish, and Christian Patterns*. Albany: State University of New York Press.

Hernández, Esther. 2008. "Indigenismos en el *Vocabulario de la lengua cakchiquel* atribuido a fray Domingo de Vico, MS. BnF R. 7507." *Revista de Filología Española*, 88 (1): 67–88.

Hernández de León-Portilla, Ascensión. 2009. *Las primeras gramáticas del nuevo mundo*. Mexico City, Mexico: Fondo de Cultura Económica.

Herrera, Robinson A. 2007. "Concubines and Wives: Reinterpreting Native-Spanish Intimate Unions in Sixteenth-Century Guatemala." In *Indian Conquistadors: Indigenous Allies in the Conquest of Mesoameirca*, 127–144. Edited by Laura E. Matthew and Michel R. Oudijk. Norman: University of Oklahoma Press.

Hill, Edmund. 1996. *Teaching Christianity: Translation of St. Augustine's De Doctrina Christiana, The Works of St. Augustine (A Translation for the 21st Century)*. Hyde Park, NY: New City Press.

Hill, Robert M., II. 1989. *The Pirir Papers and Other Colonial Period Cakchiquel-Maya Testamentos*. Nashville, TN: Vanderbilt University.

Hill, Robert M., II. 1992. *Colonial Cakchiquels: Highland Maya Adaptation to Spanish Rule 1600–1700*. New York: Harcourt Brace Jovanovich.

Hill, Robert M., II. 1998. "Land, Family, and Community in Highland Guatemala: Seventeenth-Century Cakchikel Maya Testaments." In *Dead Giveaways: Indigenous Testaments of Colonial Mesoamerica and the Andes*, 163–179. Edited by Susan Kellogg and Matthew Restall. Salt Lake City: University of Utah Press.

Hill, Robert M., II. 2012. *Pictographic to Alphabet and Back: Reconstructing the Pictograph Origins of the Xajil Chronicle*. Philadelphia, PA: American Philosophical Society.

Himelblau, Jack J. 1989. *Quiché Worlds in Creation: The Popol Vuh as a Narrative Work of Art*. Lancaster, CA: Labyrinthos.

Hoffmann, R. Joseph. 1987. *Celsus on True Doctrine: A Discourse against the Christians*. New York: Oxford University Press.

Hosselkus, Erika R. 2016. "Disposing of the Body and Aiding the Soul: Death, Dying, and Testaments in Colonial Huexotzinco." In *Native Wills from the Colonial Americas: Dead Giveaways in a New World*, 195–214. Edited Mark Christensen and Jonathan Truitt. Salt Lake City: The University of Utah Press.

Houston, Stephen. 1994. "Literacy among the Pre-Columbian Maya: A Comparative Perspective." In *Writing without Words: Alternative Literacies in Mesoamerica and the Andes*. Edited by Elizabeth Hill Boone and Walter D. Mignolo. Durham, NC: Duke University Press, 27–49.

Huerga, Álvaro. 1992. *Los dominicos de Andalucia*. Seville, Spain: s.n. (Madrid: Imprinta Taravilla).

Hull, Kerry. 2012. "Poetic Tenacity: A Diachronic Study of Kennings in Mayan Languages." In *Parallel Worlds: Genre, Discourse, and Poetics in Contemporary, Colonial, and Classic Maya Literature*, 73–122. Edited by Kerry M. Hull and Michael D. Carrasco. Boulder: University Press of Colorado.

Instituto Agroecológico de Educación Bilingüe "Fray Domingo de Vico." http://www.guatesol.ch/lwschule_es.html (accessed June 2009).

Iraburu, José María. 2003. *Hechos de los apóstoles de América*, 3rd ed. Pamplona, Spain: Fundación Gratis Date.

Irarrázaval, Diego. 2000. *Inculturation: New Dawn of the Church in Latin America*. Maryknoll, NY: Orbis Books.

Irenaeus [of Lyon]. 1996. "Against Heresies." In *The Ante-Nicene Fathers: Translations of the Writings of the Fathers Down to A.D. 325*, 309–567. Edited by Alexander Roberts and James Donaldson. Grand Rapids, MI: Wm. B. Eerdmans Publishing Company.

Janssens, Bert, and Ruud van Akkeren. 2003. *Xajooj Keej: El baile del venado de Rabinal*. Guatemala City, Guatemala: Cholsamaj.

Jarra Torres Navarrete, Ginés de la. 2002. *Historia de Úbeda en sus documentos*, volume II. Úbeda, Spain: Úbeda Asociación Cultural Ubetense Alfredo Cazabán Laguna.

Jay, Barbara H., and William P. Michell, eds. 1999. *Picturing Faith: A Facsimile Edition of the Pictographic Quechua Catechism in the Huntington Free Library*. New York: Huntington Free Library.

Jones, Grant D. 1998. *The Conquest of the Last Maya Kingdom*. Stanford, CA: Stanford University Press.

Jones, Owen H. 2009. "Colonial K'iche' in Comparison with Yucatec Maya: Language, Adaptation, and Intercultural Contact." PhD diss. University of California, Riverside.

Jones, Owen H. 2016a. "Language, Politics, and Indigenous Language Documents: Evidence in Colonial K'ichee' Litigation in Seventeenth-Century Highland Guatemala." *The Americas* 73 (3, July): 349–370.

Jones, Owen H. 2016b. "'One or Two of My Living Words': Seventeenth- and Eighteenth-Century K'iche' Testaments from Guatemala." In *Native Wills from the Colonial Americas: Dead Giveaways in a New World*, 138–151. Edited by Mark Christensen and Jonathan Truitt. Salt Lake City: The University of Utah Press.

Kaufman, Terrence. 1974. *Idiomas de mesoamérica*. Guatemala City, Guatemala: Ministerio de Educación, Editorial José de Pineda Ibarra.

Keane, Webb. 2007. *Christian Moderns: Freedom and Fetish in the Mission Encounter*. Berkeley and Los Angeles: University of California Press.

Keen, Benjamin. 1994. "Editor's Introduction." In *Life and Labor in Ancient Mexico: The Brief and Summary Relation of the Lords of New Spain*, 3–77. Norman: University of Oklahoma Press.

Kellogg, Susan, and Matthew Restall, eds. 1998. *Dead Giveaways: Indigenous Testaments of Colonial Mesoamerica and the Andes*. Salt Lake City: University of Utah Press.

Kelly, Louis G. 1979. "*Modus Significandi*: An Interdisciplinary Concept." *Historiographia Linguistica* 6 (2): 159–80.

Khondker, Habibul Haque. 2004. "Glocalization and Globalization: Evolution of a Sociological Concept." *Bangladesh e-Journal of Sociology*, 1 (2):12–20; http://www.bangladeshsociology.org/BEJS%201.2%20Issue%20Habibul%20Haque%20khondker.pdf.

Kislak 1015. Anonymous. n.d. [1567]. Kislak item 1015. Washington, DC: Jay I. Kislak Collection, US Library of Congress.

Knitter, Paul F. 2002. *Theologies of Religions*. Maryknoll, NY: Orbis Books.

Knowlton, Timothy. 2009. "Dynamics of Indigenous Language Ideologies in the Colonial Redaction of a Yucatec Maya Cosmological Text." *Anthropological Linguistics* 50 (1): 90–112.

Knowlton, Timothy W. 2010. *Maya Creation Myths: Words and Worlds of the Chilam Balam*. Boulder: University Press of Colorado

Koenig, Sarah. 2012a. "Swicheroo," Episode 468, June 29, *This American Life*. http://www.thisamericanlife.org/radio-archives/episode/468/switcheroo?act=2.

Koenig, Sarah. 2012b. "Updates about Journatic," July 17, *This American Life* (blog). http://www.thisamericanlife.org/blog/2012/07/updates-about-journatic.

Kugel, James L. 1981. *The Idea of Biblical Poetry: Parallelism and Its History*. New Haven, CT: Yale University Press.

Laird, Andrew. 2018. "Colonial Grammatology: The Versatility and Transformation of European Letters in Sixteenth-century Spanish America." *Language and History* DOI: 10.1080/17597536.2018.1441952 (accessed April 2018).

La Torre, Tomás de. 1985 [1545]. *Diario de viaje de Salamanca a Chiapa*. Burgos, Spain: Editorial OPE.

Landar, Herbert. 1967. "Bibliographic Note: Quiché." *International Journal of American Linguistics* 33 (1, January): 76–78.

Las Casas, Bartolomé de. 1967 [1560s]. *Apologética historia sumeria*. "Historiadores y Cronistas de Indias" Series. Volumes I and II. Edited by Edmundo O'Gorman. Mexico City, Mexico: Universidad Nacional Autónoma de México, Instituto de Investigaciones Históricas.

Las Casas, Bartolomé de. 1973 [1551]. *Apología de Juan Ginés de Sepúlveda contra Fray Bartolomé de las Casas y de Fray Bartolomé de las Casas contra Juan Ginés de Sepúlveda*. Translated by Ángel Losada. Madrid, Spain: Editorial Nacional.

Las Casas, Bartolomé de. 1974 [ca. 1552–1553]. *In Defense of the Indians: The Defense of the Most Reverend Lord, Don Fray Bartolomé de Las Casas, of the Order of Preachers, Last*

Bishop of Chiapa, against the Persecutors and Slanderers of the People of the New World Discovered across the Seas. Translated by Stafford Poole. DeKalb: Northern Illinois University Press.

Las Casas, Bartolomé de. 2002 [1561]. *Historia*, Book II, Chapter IV. In *Three Dominican Pioneers in the New World: Antonio de Montesinos, Domingo de Betanzos, Gonzalo Lucero*, Spanish Studies Volume 16: 18–22. Translated by Felix Jay. Lewiston, NY: Edwin Mellen Press.

Laughlin, Robert M. 2012. "To Speak the Words of Colonial Tzotzil." In *Parallel Worlds: Genre, Discourse, and Poetics in Contemporary, Colonial, and Classic Maya Literature*, 471–475. Edited by Kerry M. Hull and Michael D. Carrasco. Boulder: University Press of Colorado.

Leclerc, Charles. 1867. *Bibliotheca americana: Catalogue raisonné d'une très précieuse collection de livres anciens et modernes sur l'Amérique et les Philippines, classés par ordre alphabétique de noms d'auteurs*. Paris: Maisonneuve.

Legg, J. Wickham, ed. 1908. *The Second Recension of the Quignon Breviary*. London: Henry Bradshaw Society.

León Pinelo, Antonio de. 1986. *Report Made in the Royal Council of the Indies*. Translated by Doris Zemurray Stone. Edited by Frank E. Comparato. Culver City, CA: Labyrinthos Press.

León-Portilla, Miguel. 1969. *Pre-Columbian Literatures of Mexico*. Norman: University of Oklahoma Press.

León-Portilla, Miguel. 1988. *Time and Reality in the Thought of the Maya*. Norman: University of Oklahoma Press.

León-Portilla, Miguel. 2002. *Bernardino de Sahagún: First Anthropologist*. Translated by Mauricio J. Mixco. Norman: University of Oklahoma Press.

Lladó, Marie. 1990. "Theologia Indorum (1553, Cuatro Tomos) de la Biblioteca Nacional de Paris." In *Evangelización y teología en América (siglo xvi): X simposio internacional de teología de la Universidad de Navarra*, volumen segundo, 947–954. Edited by Josep-Ignasi Saranyana, Primitivo Tineo, Antón M. Pazos, Miguel Lluch-Biaxaulli, and María Pilar Ferrer. Pamplona, Spain: Servicios de Publicaciones de la Universidad de Navarra.

Lope Blanch, Juan M. 1997. "Nebrija, primer lingüista moderno." In *Memoria del coloquio La obra de Antonio de Nebrija y su recepción en la Nueva España. Quince estudios nebrisenses (1492–1992)*, 39–45. Edited by Ignacio Guzmán Betancourt and Eréndira Nansen Díaz. Mexico City, Mexico: Instituto Nacional de Antropología e Historia.

Lopes Don, Particia. 2010. *Bonfires of Culture: Franciscans, Indigenous Leaders, and the Inquisition in Early Mexico, 1524–1540*. Norman: University of Oklahoma Press.

López Carrillo, Rodrigo, Esperanza Martínez Dengra, and Pedro San Ginés Aguilar. 1995. "Étienne Dolet o los cinco principios de la traducción." In *La traducción: Metodología, historia, literatura, ámbito hipanofrancés*, 123–130. Edited by Francisco Lafarga, Albert Ribas Pujol, and Mercedes Tricás. Barcelona, Spain: Promociones Publicaciones Universitarias.

López Hernández, Eleazar. 2000. *Teología india: Antología*. Cochabamba, Bolivia: Editorial Verbo Divino.

López Hernández, Eleazar. 2004. "Teologías indias en la iglesia: Métodos y propuestas." In *En busca de la tierra sin mal: Mitos de origen y sueños de futuro de los pueblos indios. Memoria del IV Encuentro-Taller Ecuménico Latinoamericano de Teología India, Ikua Sati, Asunción, Paraguay, 6 al 10 de mayo de 2002*, 267–289. Quito, Ecuador: Ediciones Abya Yala.

López Ixcoy, Saqijix Candelaria, trans. 2010. *Theologia Indorum, Fray Domingo de Vico: Reproducción facsimilar, Transcripción paleográfica al K'iche' actual, Traducción al español*, vol. 1. Guatemala City, Guatemala: Instituto de Lingüística e Interculturalidad, Universidad Rafael Landívar.

López Ixcoy, Saqijix Candelaria, trans. 2011. *Theologia Indorum, Fray Domingo de Vico: Reproducción facsimilar, Transcripción paleográfica al K'iche' actual, Traducción al español*, vol. 2. Guatemala City, Guatemala: Instituto de Lingüística e Interculturalidad, Universidad Rafael Landívar.

López Ixcoy, Saqijix Candelaria, trans. 2013a. *Theologia Indorum, Fray Domingo de Vico: Reproducción facsimilar, Transcripción paleográfica al K'iche' actual, Traducción al español*, vol. 3. Guatemala City, Guatemala: Instituto de Lingüística e Interculturalidad, Universidad Rafael Landívar.

Lopez Ixcoy, Saqijix Candelaria. 2013b. "Una evidencia de la Resistencia lingüística a lo largo de los siglos. Saqill b'ee, Saqill k'aslemaal. . . ." *Voces: Revista semestral del Instituto de Lingüística e Interculturalidad* 8 (1, January–June): 5–32.

Lovell, W. George. 1990. "Mayans, Missionaries, Evidence and Truth: The Polemics of Native Resettlement in Sixteenth-Century Guatemala." *Journal of Historical Geography* 16 (3): 277–294.

Lutz, Christopher H., and Karen Dakin. 1996. *Nuestro pesar, nuestra aflicción, tunetulini-liz, tucucuca: Memorias en lengua náhuatl enviadas a Felipe II por indígenas del Valle de Guatemala hacia 1572*. Mexico City, Mexico: Universidad Nacional Autónoma de México.

MacCormack, Sabine. 1991. *Religion in the Andes: Vision and Imagination in Early Colonial Peru*. Princeton, NJ: Princeton University Press.

MacKenzie, C. James. 2016. *Indigenous Bodies, Maya Minds: Religion and Modernity in a Transnational K'iche' Community*. Boulder: University Press of Colorado.

MacLeod, Murdo J. 1970. "Las Casas, Guatemala, and the Sad but Inevitable Case of Antonio de Remesal." *Topic: A Journal of the Liberal Arts*, 20 (Fall): 53–64.

Maldonado, Francisco. n.d. [1553]. *[Theologia Indorum] Ha nima vuh vae theologia yndorum rubinaam.* Manuscrit Américain 42. Paris: Bibliothèque nationale de France.

Maloney, Thomas S. 1983. "The Semiotics of Roger Bacon." *Mediaeval Studies* 45: 120–154.

Maloney, Thomas S. 1989. *Three Treatments of Universals by Roger Bacon.* Binghamton, NY: Medieval and Renaissance Texts and Studies.

Malmström, Vicent H. 1997. *Cycles of the Sun, Mysteries of the Moon: The Calendar in Mesoamerican Civilization.* Austin: University of Texas Press.

Marroquín, Francisco. 1905 [1556]. *Doctrina cristiana en lengua guatemalteca.* Santiago, Chile: Imprenta Elzeviriana.

Marthaler, Berard L. 1995. *The Catechism Yesterday and Today: The Evolution of a Genre.* Collegeville, MN: Liturgical Press.

Martínez, Marcos. ca. 1565–1584. *Arte de la lengua utlateca ó kiché, vulgarmente llamado el Arte de Totonicapán.* Manuscrit Américain 62. Paris: Bibliothèque nationale de France.

Martínez-Pereda Rodríguez, José Manuel. 1991. *Magia y delito en España.* Bilbão, Spain: Laida, Editorial e Imagen.

Martínez Portorreal, Ramón B. 2007. "Bartolomé de las Casas inventó término 'Derechos Humanos'." *Con la pluma como espada* (blog), July 16. http://www.conlaplumacomoespada.com/2007/07/16/bartolome-de-las-casas-invento-termino-derechos-humanos/.

Matsumoto, Mallory E. 2016. "Recording Territory, Recording History: Negotiating the Sociopolitical Landscape in Colonial Highland Maya *Títulos*." *Ethnohistory* 63 (3, July): 469–495.

Matthew, Laura E. 2007. "Whose Conquest? Nahua, Zapoteca, and Mixteca Allies in the Conquest of Central America." In *Indian Conquistadors: Indigenous Allies in the Conquest of Mesoamerica*, 102–126. Edited by Laura E. Matthew and Michel R. Oudijk, eds. Norman: University of Oklahoma Press.

Matthew, Laura E. 2012. *Memories of Conquest: Becoming Mexicano in Colonial Guatemala.* Chapel Hill: The University of North Carolina Press.

Maxwell, Judith M. 2010. "Maya Daykeepers and the Politics of Sacred Space." In *Rethinking Intellectuals in Latin America*, 213–225. Edited by Mabel Moraña and Bret Gustafson. Norwalk, CT: Iberoamericana Vervuert Publishing.

Maxwell, Judith M. 2012. "Memory, Remembering, and the Construction of Truth among Maya Groups in Highland Guatemala." In *Mesoamerican Memory: Enduring Systems of Remembrance*, 233–248. Edited by Amos Megged and Stephanie Wood. Norman: University of Oklahoma Press.

Maxwell, Judith M., and Robert M. Hill II, trans. 2006. *Kaqchikel Chronicles: The Definitive Edition.* Austin: University of Texas Press.

McGee, R. Jon. 1990. *Life, Ritual, and Religion among the Lacandon Maya*. Belmont, CA: Wadsworth Publishing Company.

McGinn, Bernard. 1979. *Apocalyptic Spirituality: Treatise and Letters of Lactantius, Adso of Montier-en-der, Joachim of Fiore, The Franciscan Spirituals, Savonarola*. Mahwah, NJ: Paulist Press.

McGinn, Bernard. 2004. *Thomas Aquinas's* Summa theologiae*: A Biography*. Princeton, NJ: Princeton University Press.

McGuire, Brian Patrick. 1998. "Introduction." In *Jean Gerson: Early Works*, 1–58. Mahwah, NJ: Paulist Press.

McInerny, Ralph M. 1961. *The Logic of Analogy: An Interpretation of St. Thomas*. The Hague, Netherlands: Martinus Nijhoff.

Megged, Amos. 1995. "'Right from the Heart': Indians' Idolatry in Mendicant Preachings in Sixteenth-Century Mesoamerica." *History of Religions* 35 (1, August 5–12): 61–82.

Megged, Amos. 1996. *Exporting the Catholic Reformation: Local Religion in Early-Colonial Mexico*. Leiden, Netherlands: E. J. Brill.

Megged, Amos, and Stephanie Wood, eds. 2012. *Mesoamerican Memory: Enduring Systems of Remembrance*. Norman: University of Oklahoma Press.

Mesanza, Andrés. 1939. *Los obispos de la orden Dominicana en América*. Einsiedeln, Switzerland: Benziger & C., S.A.

Meyerson, Mark D. 1995. "Religious Change, Regionalism, and Royal Power in the Spain of Fernando and Isabel." In *Iberia and the Mediterranean World of the Middle Ages: Studies in Honor of Robert I. Burns*, 96–112. Edited by Larry J. Simon. Leiden, Netherlands: E. J. Brill.

Mignolo, Walter D. 1994. "Afterward: Writing and Recorded Knowledge in Colonial and Postcolonial Situations." In *Writing without Words: Alternative Literacies in Mesoamerica and the Andes*, 293–313. Edited by Elizabeth Hill Boone and Walter D. Mignolo. Durham, NC: Duke University Press.

Milbrath, Susan. 1999. *Star Gods of the Maya: Astronomy in Art, Folklore, and Calendars*. Austin: University of Texas Press.

Minnis, A. J., and A. B. Scott, eds. 1988. *Medieval Literary Theory and Criticism c.1100–c.1375: The Commentary Tradition*. New York: Oxford University Press.

Molesky-Poz, Jean. 2006. *Contemporary Maya Spirituality: The Ancient Ways Are Not Lost*. Austin: University of Texas Press.

Mondloch, James. 1983. "Una comparación entre los estilos de habla del Quiché moderno y los encontados en el Popol Vuh." In *Nuevas Perspectivas sobre el Popol Vuh*, 87–108. Edited by Robert M. Carmack and Francisco Morales Santos. Guatemala City, Guatemala: Editorial Piedra Santa.

Mondloch, James, and Robert Carmack. 2018. *Popol Wuj: Nueva traducción y comentarios*. Guatemala City, Guatemala: Publicaciones Mesoamericanas.

Monterroso, Matilde Ivic de. 2009. "Historia de los Xpanzay de Tecpán Guatemala." In *Crónicas mesoamericanas* II: 87–95. Guatemala City, Guatemala: Publicaciones Mesoamericanas.

Morán, Francisco. 2000. "Report that Friar Francisco Morán, Friar of the Order of Preachers, Made to the Very Reverend Father Master of the Holy Place Friar Nicholas Ricardi on the Conversation of the Province of the Manché and the Pagans of the Ahitzas in the West Indies." In *Lost Shores, Forgotten Peoples: Spanish Explorations of the South East Maya Lowlands*, 151–157. Edited and translated by Lawrence H. Feldman. Durham, NC: Duke University Press.

Morselli Barbieri, Simonetta. 2004. "El Título de Totonicapán: Consideraciones y comenatrios." *Estudios Mesoamericanos* 6: 70–85.

Muldoon, James, ed. 2004. *The Spiritual Conversion of the Americas*. Gainesville: University Press of Florida.

Mullen, Roderic L. 2004. *The Expansion of Christianity: A Gazetteer of Its First Three Centuries*. Boston, MA, and Leiden, Netherlands: Koninklijke Brill NV.

Muñoz y Manzano Viñaza, Cipriano. 1892. *Bibliographia española de lenguas indígenas de América por el Conde de la Viñaza*. Madrid, Spain: Tipográfico "Sucesores de Rivadeneyra."

Murphy, G. Ronald. 1992. *The Heliand: The Saxon Gospel, a Translation and Commentary*. New York: Oxford University Press.

Nance, C. Roger, Stephen L. Whittington, and Barbara E. Borg. 2003. *Archaeology and Ethnohistory of Iximché*. Gainesville: University Press of Florida.

Nebrija, Antonio de. 1926 [1492]. *Gramática de la lengua castellana: Muestra de la historia de las antigüedades de España, reglas de orthographi en la lengua castellana*. Edited by Ignacio González-Llubera. New York: Oxford University Press.

Nebrija, Antonio de. 1969 [1492 and 1517]. *Grammatica castellana, 1492; El ortografia castellano, 1517, Antonio de Lebrija*, European linguistics, 1480–1700 no. 11. Madrid, Spain: Menston, Scolar P.

Nebrija, Antonio de. 1996 [ca. 1488]. *Introducciones latinas contrapuesto el romance al latín*. Edited by Miguel Ángel Esparza and Vicente Calvo. Munster, Germany: Nodus Publikationen.

New Catholic Encyclopedia. 1967. Washington, DC: Catholic University of America.

Nielsen, Jesper, and Toke Sellner Reuert. 2009. "Dante's Heritage: Questioning the Multi-Layered Model of the Mesoamerican Universe." *Antiquity* 83: 399–413.

Nielsen, Jesper, and Toke Sellner Reuert. 2015. "Estatos, regiones e híbridos: Una reconsideración de la cosmología mesoamericana." In *Cielos e inframundos: Una revisión de las cosmologías mesoamericanas*, 25–64. Edited by Ana Díaz. Mexico City, Mexico: Universidad Nacional Autónoma de México, Instituto de Investigaciones Históricas.

Norman, William M. 1983. "Paralelismo gramatical en el lenguaje ritual Quiché." In *Nuevas Perspectivas sobre el Popol Vuh*, 109–121. Edited by Robert M. Carmack and Francisco Morales Santos. Guatemala City, Guatemala: Editorial Piedra Santa.

Oakes, Maud. 1951. *The Two Crosses of Todos Santos: Survivals of Mayan Religious Ritual.* New York: Pantheon Books.

Oberman, Heiko A. 1960. "Some Notes on the Theology of Nominalism with Attention to its Relation to the Renaissance." *Harvard Theological Review* 53 (1): 47–76.

Oberman, Heiko A. 1981. *Forerunners of the Reformation: The Shape of Late Medieval Thought*. Philadelphia, PA: Fortress Press.

Oberman, Heiko A. 1992. *The Dawn of the Reformation*. Grand Rapids, MI: William B. Eerdmans.

Oficina de Derechos Humanos del Arzobispado de Guatemala (ODHA). 1998. *Guatemala, nunca más: Informe proyecto interdiocesano de recuperación de la memoria histórica.* Guatemala City, Guatemala: Arzobispado de Guatemala.

Omont, Henri Auguste. 1925. "Catalogue des manuscrits américains de la Bibliothèque Nationale." *Revue des bibliothèques* 35: 90–110.

Orellana, Sandra. 1984. *The Tzutujil Mayas: Continuity and Change, 1250–1630*. Norman: University of Oklahoma Press.

Origen. 1973 [ca. 220-230]. *On First Principles*. Translated by G. W. Butterworth. Gloucester, MA: Peter Smith.

Oroz, Pedro. n.d. *Lectionarium*. Washington, DC: US Library of Congress.

Osuna, Francisco de. 1981 [1527]. *The Third Spiritual Alphabet*. Translated by Mary E. Giles. New York: Paulist Press.

Oudijk, Michel R., and Matthew Restall. 2007. "Mesoamerican Conquistadors in the Sixteenth Century." In *Indian Conquistadors: Indigenous Allies in the Conquest of Mesoamerica*, 28–64. Edited by Laura E. Matthew and Michel R. Oudijk. Norman: University of Oklahoma Press.

Oxlajuj Keej Maya' Ajtz'iib'. 1997. *Maya' chii': Los idiomas mayas de Guatemala*. Guatemala City, Guatemala: Editorial Cholsamaj.

Pagden, Anthony. 1982. *The Fall of Natural Man: The American Indian and the Origins of Comparative Ethnology*. New York: Cambridge University Press.

Pané, Ramón. 1999 [ca. 1498]. *An Account of the Antiquities of the Indians.* Edited by José Juan Arrom. Translated by Susan C. Griswold. Durham, NC: Duke University Press.

Paul III. 1537a. *Sublimis Dei*, May 29. http://papalencyclicals.net/Paul03/p3subli.htm.

Paul III. 1537b. *Veritas ipsa*, June 2.

Payne, Stanley G. 1984. *Spanish Catholicism: An Historical Overview*. Madison: The University of Wisconsin Press.

Pegis, Anton C., ed. 1948. *Introduction to St. Thomas Aquinas: The Summa Theologica, The Summa Contra Gentiles*. New York: Modern Library, Random House, Inc.

Peñafiel Ramón, Antonio. 1987. *Testamento y buen muerte: Un estudio de mentalidades en la Murcia del siglo XVIII*. Murcia, Spain: Academía Alfonso X El Sabio.

Pérez Fernández, Isacio. 1981. *Inventario documentado de los escritos de Fray Bartolomé de las Casas*. Edited by Helen Rand Parish. Bayamón, Puerto Rico: Centro de Estudios de los Dominicos de Caribe.

Peterson, Marshall N. 1999. "Commentary on the History of the Origin of the Indians, Fray Francisco Ximénez." In *The Highland Maya in Fact and Legend: Francisco Ximénez, Fernando Alva de Ixtlilxóchitl, and Other Commentators on Indian Origins and Deeds: From Escolias a las Historias del Origen de los Indios and De los Reyes Toltecas y su Destrucción*, 29–39. Culver City, CA: Labyrinthos Press.

Phelan, John Leddy. 1970. *The Millennial Kingdom of the Franciscans in the New World*, 2nd ed., revised. Berkeley and Los Angeles: University of California Press.

Pilling, James Constatine. 1885. *Proof-sheets of a Bibliography of the Languages of the North American Indians*. Washington, DC: Smithsonian Institution, Bureau of Ethnology.

Piñón, Santiago, Jr. 2016. *The Ivory Tower and the Sword: Francisco Vitoria Confronts the Emperor*. Eugene, OR: Pickwick Publications.

Pita Moreda, María Teresa. 1992. *Los predicadores novohispanos del siglo XVI*. Salamanca, Spain: Editorial San Esteban.

Pitarch Pedro. 2010. *The Jaguar and the Priest: An Ethnography of Tzeltal Souls*. Austin: University of Texas Press.

Pitarch, Pedro. 2012. "The Two Maya Bodies: An Elementary Model of Tzeltal Personhood." *Ethnos* 77 (1, March): 93–114.

Pohorilles, Noah Eileser. 1913. *Das Popol wuḥ, die mythische geschichte des kiče-volkes von Guatemala, nach dem original-texte übersetzt und bearbeitet von Noah Elieser Pohorilles*. Leipzig, Germany: J. C. Hinrichs.

Pons Rodríguez, Lola. 2006. "Introducción: La historia de la lengua y la historia de las transmisiones textuales." In *Historia de la Lengua y Crítica Textual*, 9–17. Madrid, Spain: Iberoamericana, and Frankfurt, Germany: Vervuet.

Poole, Stafford. 1989. "The Declining Image of the Indian among Churchmen in Sixteenth-Century New Spain." In *Indian-Religious Relations in Colonial Spanish America*, 11–53. Edited by Susan E. Ramírez. Syracuse, NY: Maxwell School of Citizenship and Public Affairs, Syracuse University.

Popenoe de Hatch, Marion. 1998. "Los k'iche's-kaqchikeles en el altiplano central de Guatemala: Evidencia arqueológica del período clásico." *Mesoamérica* 35 (June): 93–115.

Popol Wuj (*Popol Vuh*). ca. 1701–1704 [ca. 1554–1558]. By Francisco Ximénez. Newberry Library, Edward E. Ayer Manuscript 1515. Chicago, Illinois.

Prieto, Andres I. 2011. *Missionary Scientists: Jesuit Science in the Spanish South America, 1570–1810*. Nashville, TN: Vanderbilt University Press.

Quiroa, Néstor I. 2011. "Revisiting the Highland Guatemala Títulos: How the Maya-K'iche' Lived and Outlived the Colonial Experience." *Ethnohistory* 58 (2): 293–321.

Quirós, Seberino Bernardo de. 2013. *Arte y vocabulario del idioma Huasteco (1711)*, Lingüística Misionera, Vol. 3. Edited by Bernhard Hurch. Madrid, Spain: Iberoamericana, and Frankfurt, Germany: Vervuert.

Raynaud, George. 1925. *Les dieux, les héros et les hommes de l'ancien Guatémala d'après le Livre du conseil*. Paris: E. Leroux.

Recinos, Adrián. 1950. "Introduction." In *Popol Vuh: The Sacred Book of the Ancient Quiché Maya*. Translated by Delia Goetz and Sylvanus G. Morley. Norman: University of Oklahoma Press.

Recinos, Adrián. 1953. *The Annals of the Cakchiqueles, Title of the Lords of Totonicapán*. Translated by Delia Goetz. Norman: University of Oklahoma Press.

Recinos, Adrián. 1984 and 2001. *Crónicas indigénas de Guatemala*, 2nd ed. Academia de Geografía e Historia de Guatemala, Publicación Especial No. 29. Guatemala City, Guatemala: Serviprensa Centroamericana.

Recinos, Adrián. 2012. *Popol Vuh: Las antiguas historias del Quiché*. México: Fondo de Cultura Económica.

Remesal, Antonio de. 1964 [1619]. *Historia general de las Indias occidentales y particular de la gobernación de Chiapa y Guatemala*, Vol. I. Edited by Carmelo Sáenz de Santa María. Madrid, Spain: Ediciones Atlas, Biblioteca de Autores Españoles.

Remesal, Antonio de. 1966a [1619]. *Historia general de las Indias occidentales y particular de la gobernación de Chiapa y Guatemala*, Vol. II. Edited by Carmelo Sáenz de Santa María. Madrid, Spain: Ediciones Atlas, Biblioteca de Autores Españoles,

Remesal, Antonio de. 1966b [1619]. *Historia geneal de las Indias occidentales y particular de la gobernación de Chiapa y Guatemala*, Tomos I–IV. Guatemala City, Guatemala: Departamento Editorial y de Producción de Material Didáctico "José de Pindea Ibarra" Ministerio de Educación.

Remesal, Antonio de. 1988 [1619]. *Historia general de las Indias occidentales y particular de la gobernación de Chiapa y Guatemala*, Volume II. Biblioteca Porrúa. Mexico City, Mexico: Editorial Porrúa.

Resines, Luis. 2002. *Catecismo del Sacromonte y Doctrina Cristiana de Fr. Pedro de Feria: Conversión y evangelización de moriscos e indios*. Madrid, Spain: Consejo Superior de Investigaciones Científicos.

Resines, Luis. 2007. *Catecismos pictográficos de Pedro de Gante, incompleto y Mucagua.* Madrid, Spain: Fundación Universitaria Española.

Restall, Matthew. 1995. *Life and Death in a Maya Community: The Ixil Testaments of the 1760s.* Lancaster, CA: Labyrinthos.

Restall, Matthew. 1997. "Heirs to the Hieroglyphs: Indigenous Writing in Colonial Mesoamerica." *The Americas* 54: 239–276.

Restall, Matthew. 2003. *Seven Myths of the Spanish Conquest.* New York: Oxford University Press.

Ricard, Robert. 1966. *The Spiritual Conquest of Mexico: An Essay on the Apostolate and the Evangelizing Methods of the Mendicant Orders in New Spain: 1523–1572.* Translated by Lesley Byrd Simpson. Berkeley and Los Angeles: University of California Press.

Richter, David H., ed. 2007. *The Critical Tradition: Classic Texts and Contemporary Trends,* 3rd ed. New York: Bedford/St. Martin's.

Ríos Castaño, Victoria. 2014. *Translation as Conquest: Sahagún and Universal History of the Things of New Spain.* Madrid, Spain: Iberamericana, and Frankfurt, Germany: Vervuert.

Robertson, John S., Danny Law, and Robbie A. Haertel. 2010. *Colonial Ch'orti': The Seventeenth-Century Morán Manuscript.* Norman: University of Oklahoma Press.

Rodríguez Demorizi, Emilio. 1945. "Prefacio." In *Doctrina cristiana para instrucción y información de los indios, por manera de historia, Pedro de Córdoba,* x–xxi. Ciudad Trujillo, Dominican Republic: Universidad de Santo Domingo.

Rodríquez, Pedro. 1998. *El catecismo romano ante Felipe II y la Inquisición española: Los problemas de la introducción en España del Catecismo del Concilio de Trento.* Madrid, Spain: Ediciones RIALP, S.A.

Rojas, Jerónimo, S.J. 1893. *El estudio de las lenguas y las misiones por José Dahlmann, S.J.* Madrid, Spain: Librería Católica de Gregorio del Amo.

Rojas, Vernor Manuel. 2006. *Fray Domingo de Vico: Apóstol y mártir de Verapaz (s. XVI).* Cobán, Guatemala: Ak' Kutan, Centro Bartolomé de las Casas.

Romero, Sergio. 2011. "Language, Catechisms and Mesoamerican Lords in Highland Guatemala: Addressing 'God' after the Spanish conquest." *XIII European Maya Conference.* Copenhagen, Denmark.

Romero, Sergio. 2012a. "Nahuatl and Pipil in Colonial Guatemala: A Central American Counterpoint." *Ethnohistory* 59 (4): 765–783.

Romero, Sergio. 2012b. "'They Don't Get Speak Our Language Right': Language Standardization, Power And Migration among the Q'eqchi' Maya." *Journal of Linguistic Anthropology* 22 (2): 21–41.

Romero, Sergio. 2015a. "Language, Catechisms and Mesoamerican Lords in Highland Guatemala: Addressing 'God' after the Spanish Conquest." *Ethnohistory* 62 (3): 623–649.

Romero, Sergio. 2015b. *Language and Ethnicity among the K'ichee' Maya*. Provo: University of Utah Press.

Romero, Sergio. 2017. "Other Dominican Lessons in Highland Mayan Languages—Spoken and Sung: *Coplas* of Friar Luis de Cáncer, O.P." In *The Americas' First Theologies: Early Sources of Post-Contact Indigenous Religion*, 168–181. Edited by Garry Sparks. New York: Oxford University Press.

Rorem, Paul, t988. *Pseudo-Dionysius: The Complete Works*. Mahwah, NJ: Paulist Press.

Roys, Ralph L. 1939. *The Titles of the Ebtun*. New York: AMS Press.

Roys, Ralph L. 1965. *Ritual of the Bacabs*. Norman University of Oklahoma Press.

Rubiés, Joan-Pau. 2000. *Travel and Ethnology in the Renaissance: South India through European Eyes, 1250–1625*. New York: Cambridge University Press.

Rubiés, Joan-Pau. 2006. "Theology, Ethnography, and the Historicization of Idolatry." *Journal of the History of Ideas* 67 (4, October): 571–596.

Ruiz, Teofilo F. 1998. "The Businss of Salvation: Castilian Wills in the Late Middle Ages, 1200–1400." In *On the Social Origins of Medieval Institutions: Essays in Honor of Joseph F. O'Callaghan*, 63–90. Edited by Donald J. Kagay and Theresa M. Vann. Leiden, Netherlands: E. J. Brill.

Sachse, Frauke. 2007. "Documentation of Colonial K'ichee' Dictionaries and Grammars." Foundation for the Advancement of Mesoamerican Studies, Inc. (FAMSI). http://www.famsi.org/reports/06009/index.html (accessed July 2019).

Sachse, Frauke. 2008. "Over Distant Waters: Places of Origin and Creation in Colonia K'iche'an Sources." In *Pre-Columbian Landscapes of Creation and Origin*, 123–155. Edited by John Edward Staller. New York: Springer Science+Business Media, LLC.

Sachse, Frauke. 2009. "Reconstructing the Anonymous Franciscan K'ichee' Dictionary." *Mexicon* 31 (1, February): 10–18.

Sachse, Frauke. 2014. "Worldviews in Dialogue: Precolumbian Cosmologies in the Context of Early Colonial Christianisation in Highland Guatemala." 19th European Maya Conference, Bratislava, Slovakia (November 22).

Sachse, Frauke. 2016. "The Expression of Christian Concepts in Colonial K'iche' Missionary Texts." In *La transmisión de conceptos cristianos a las lenguas amerindias*, Collectanea Instituti Anthropos 48: 93–116. Edited by Sabine Dedenbach-Salazar Sáenz. Sankt Augustin, Germany: Academia Verlag.

Sachse, Frauke. 2017a. "Chapter 30." In *The Americas' First Theologies: Early Sources of Post- Contact Indigenous Religion*, 120–125. Edited by Garry Sparks. New York: Oxford University Press.

Sachse, Frauke. 2017b. "Mendicant Perspectives on Translating Christian Conceptualisations of Divinity into Sixteenth-Century K'iche'." Presentation, Colloquium "Translating God," University of Stirling, Scotland (May 4).

Sachse, Frauke. 2017c. "Of Gods and Souls: Ontological Categories in the Missionary Sources from Highland Guatemala." Presentation, 22nd European Maya Conference, Malmö, Sweden (December 15).

Sachse, Frauke. 2017d. "Other Dominican Lessons in Highland Mayan Languages—Spoken and Sung: *Doctrina cristiana* by Friar Damián Delgado, O.P." In *The Americas' First Theologies: Early Sources of Post- Contact Indigenous Religion*, 181–203. Edited by Garry Sparks. New York: Oxford University Press.

Sachse, Frauke. 2018. "Renaming Vico's Dictionary: Reconstructing the Textual Genealogy of the *Vocabulario copioso de las lenguas cakchikel y 4iche.*" *INDIANA (Journal of the Ibero-Amerikanisches Institut, Preußischer Kulturbesitz)* 35 (1): 67–95.

Sáenz de Santa María, Carmelo. 1974. "Lo Cristiano en los libros indígenas del Altiplano Guatemalteco" In *Atti del XL Congresso Internazionale degli Americanisti, Roma, 3–10 Settembre 1972*, Volume II, 365–370. Genova, Italy: Casa Editrice Tilgher.

Sáez Gámez, Mariano. 1979. *Hidalguías de Jaén*. Madrid, Spain: Instituto Salazar y Castro.

Sahagún, Bernardino de. 1969 [ca. 1575–ca. 1577]. *Florentine Codex: General History of the Things of New Spain*, Book 6, *Rhetoric and Moral Philosophy*. Translated by Charles E. Dibble and Arthur J. O. Anderson. Santa Fe, NM: The School of American Research, and Salt Lake City: The University of Utah.

Sahagún, Bernardino de. 1990 [ca. 1569]. *Historia general de las cosas de Nueva España.* Edited by Juan Carlos Temprano. Madrid, Spain: HISAPAT, S. A.

Sainson, Katia. 2017. *The Manuscript Hunter: Brasseur de Bourbourg's Travels through Central America and Mexico, 1854–1859*. Norman: University of Oklahoma Press.

Saint-Lu, André. 1968. *La Vera Paz: Esprit évangélique et colonisation, thèse, mémorial et travaux*. Paris: Université de Sorbon.

St. John Fancourt, Charles. 1854. *The History of Yucatan from Its Discovery to the Close of the Seventeenth Century*. London: John Murray, Albermarle Street.

Salazar, Gabriel. 2000. "Geography of the Lowlands: Gabriel Salazar, 1620." In *Lost Shores, Forgotten Peoples: Spanish Explorations of the South East Maya Lowlands*, 22–54. Edited and translated by Lawrence H. Feldman. Durham, NC: Duke University Press.

Sam Colop, Luis E. 1994. "Maya Poetics." PhD diss., State University of New York at Buffalo.

Sam Colop, [Luis Enrique]. 1999. *Popol Wuj: Versión poética K'iche'.* Quetzaltenango and Guatemala City, Guatemala: Proyecto de Educación Maya Bilingüe Intercultural PEMBI, GTZ and Cholsamaj.

Sam Colop, Luis [Enrique]. 2011. *Popol Wuj (traducción al Español y notas)*. Guatemala City, Guatemala: F&G Editores.

Sam Colop, Luis Enrique. 2012. "Poetics in the *Popol Wuj.*" In *Parallel Worlds: Genre, Discourse, and Poetics in Contemporary, Colonial, and Classic Maya Literature*, 283–309.

Edited by Kerry M. Hull and Michael D. Carrasco. Boulder: University Press of Colorado.

Sánchez Viscaíno, José Antonio. 1790. *Doctrina cristiana en la lengua utlateca alias 4iche.* Manuscrit Américain 60. Paris: Bibliothèque nationale de France.

Sanders, William T., and Carson Murdy. 1982. "Population and Agricultural Adaption in the Humid Highlands of Guatemala." In *The Historical Demography of Highland Guatemala*, Publication No. 6, 23–34. Edited by Robert M. Carmack, John Early, and Christopher Lutz. Albany: Institute for Mesoamerican Studies, State University of New York at Albany.

Sapper, Karl. 1906. "Título del barrio de Santa Ana, agosto 14 de 1565" In *[14th] Internationaler amerikanistenkongress, 1904*, 373–381. Stuttgart, Germany: W. Kohlhammer.

Sapper, Karl. 1907. "Choles und Chorties." In *Congrès International des Américanistes, XVe session tenue à Québec en 1906,* Tome II, 423–438. Quebec City, Canada: Dussault & Proulx, I Imprimeurs.

Saranyana, Josep Ignasi, et al. 1999. *Teología en América Latina: Desde los orígenes a la Guerra de Sucesión (1493–1715)*, Vol. 1. Madrid, Spain: Iberoamericana, and Frankfurt, Germany: Vervuert.

Saz, Antonio del. ca. 1662. *Sermones y marial en la lengua quiché.* Photostatic copy, Edward E. Ayer Manuscript 1571. Chicago, IL: Newberry Library.

Saz, Antonio del. ca. 1796. *Marial sacro y santoral: Sermones en la Lengua 4ijche escritos por varios Autores, principalm[en]te por un Indio.* Manuscrit Américain 11. Paris: Bibliothèque nationale de France.

Schele, Linda, and David Freidel. 1990. *A Forest of Kings: The Untold Story of the Ancient Maya.* New York: William Morrow and Company, Inc.

Scholes, France V. 1952. "Franciscan Scholars in Colonial Central America." *The Americas* 8 (4, April): 391–416.

Schreiner, Susan E. 2003. "Appearances and Reality in Luther, Montaigne, and Shakespeare." *The Journal of Religion* 83 (3, July): 345–380.

Schultze-Jena, Leonhard. 1944. *Popol Vuh: das heilige Buch der Quiché-Indianer von Guatemala, nach einer wiedergefundenen alten Handschrift neu übers. und erlautert von Leonhard Schultze.* Stuttgart, Germany: Kohlhammer.

Schwaller, John Frederick. 1987. *The Church and Clergy in Sixteenth-Century Mexico.* Albuquerque: University of New Mexico Press.

Schwaller, John Frederick. 2011. *The History of the Catholic Church in Latin America: From Conquest to Revolution and Beyond.* New York: New York University Press.

Shoaps, Robin Ann. 2004. "Morality in Grammar and Discourse: Stance-taking and the Negotiation of Moral Personhood in Sakapultek (Mayan) Wedding Counsels." PhD diss., University of California, Santa Barbara.

Shoaps, Robin Ann. 2009. "Ritual and (Im)moral Voices: Locating the Testament of Judas in Sakapultek Communicative Ecology." *American Ethnologist* 36 (3, August): 459–477.

Smailus, Ortwin. 1989. *Vocabulario en lengua castellana y guatemalteca que se llama cakchiquel chi: Análisis Gramatical y Lexicográfico del Cakchiquel Colonial según un antiguo Diccionario Anónimo*, Bibliothèque Nationale de Paris—Fond Américaine No. 7. Tomo I. Hamburg, Germany: WAYASBAH-Verlag Dr. Heinz Jürgen Probst.

Smith, Carol A., ed. 1990. *Guatemalan Indians and the State: 1540–1988*. Austin: University of Texas Press.

Smith, Christian Stephen. 1991. *The Emergence of Liberation Theology: Radical Religion and Social Movement Theory*. Chicago, IL: University of Chicago Press.

Smith, Jonathan Z. 1990. *Drudgery Divine: On the Comparison of Early Christianities and the Religions of Late Antiquity*. Chicago, IL: University of Chicago Press.

Smith, Michael E. 2005. "City Size in Late Postclassic Mesoamerica." *Journal of Urban History* 31 (4, May): 403–434.

Smith Stark, Thomas C. 2010. "La trilogía catequística: Artes, vocabularios y doctrinas en la nueva España como instrumento de una política lingüística de normalización." *Historia sociolingüística de México*, Volumen 1, 451–482. Edited by Rebeca Barriga Villanueva and Pedro Martín Butragueño. Mexico City, Mexico: El Colegio de México.

Solano Pérez-Lila, Francisco de. 1963. "Los libros del misionero en Guatemala (siglo XVIII)." *Missionalia Hispanica* 20: 319–349.

Sotelo Santos, Laura Elena. 2012. "Los dioses: Energía en el espacio y en el tiempo." In *Religión maya*, 83–114. Edited by Mercedes de la Garza Camino and Martha Ilia Nájera Coronado. Madrid, Spain: Editorial Trotta.

Sparks, Garry. 2011. "*Xalqat B'e* and the *Theologia Indorum*: Crossroads between Maya Spirituality and the Americas' First Theology." PhD diss., University of Chicago.

Sparks, Garry. 2014a. "Primeros folios, folios primeros: Una breve aclaración acerca de la *Theologia Indorum* y su relación intertextual con el Popol Wuj." *Revista semestral del Instituto de Lingüística e Interculturalidad* 9 (2): 91–142.

Sparks, Garry. 2014b. "Use of Mayan Scripture in the Americas' First Theology." *Numen (International Review for the History of Religions)* 61 (4): 396–429.

Sparks, Garry. 2016. "How 'Bout Them Sapotes: Mendicant Translations and Maya Corrections in Early Indigenous Theologies." *CR: The New Centennial Review* 16 (1, Spring): 213–243.

Sparks, Garry. 2017a. *The Americas' First Theologies: Early Sources of Post-Contact Indigenous Religion*. With Frauke Sachse and Sergio Romero. New York: Oxford University Press.

Sparks, Garry. 2017b. "Proemium." In *Theologia Indorum: BnF Manuscrit Américan 10 / Fray Domingo de Vico; Paleografía y traducción: K'iche'-español*, ix–xxxi. Edited by

Saqijix Candelaria López Ixcoy. Guatemala City, Guatemala: Editorial Cara Parens de la Universidad Rafael Landívar.

Sparks, Garry. 2018. "Maya Moral and Ritual Discourse: Dialogical Groundings for Consuetudinary Law." *Journal of Religious Ethics* 46 (1, March): 88–123.

Sparks, Garry, and Frauke Sachse. 2017. "A Sixteenth-Century Priest's Fieldnotes among Highland Maya: Proto-*Theologia* as *Vade mecum*." In *Words and Worlds Turned Around: Indigenous Christianities in Latin America*. Edited by David Tavárez. Boulder: University Press of Colorado.

Stannard, David E. 1992. *American Holocaust: The Conquest of the New World*. New York: Oxford University Press.

Stevenson, Robert. 1964. "European Music in 16th-Century Guatemala." *The Muscia Quarterly* 50 (3, July): 341–352.

Stevenson, Robert. 1966. "A Newly Discovered Mexican Sixteenth-Century Musical Imprint." *Anuario* 2: 91–94.

Stoll, Otto. 1906. "Titulo del Barrio de Santa Ana. Agosto 14 de 1565." In *14th International Congress of Americanists*, 383–397. Stuttgart, Germany: W. Kohlhammer.

Streit, Rob. 1924. "Appendix. 1. Dokumente ohne bestimmte Jahreszahl." In *Bibliotheca Missionum, Amerikanische Missionsliteratur 1493–1699*, 284–330. Cologne, Germany: Franziskus-Xaverius-Missionsverein.

Suess, Pablo, Juan F. Gorski, Beat Dietchy, Fernando Mires, and José Luis Gómez-Martínez. 1998. *Desarrollo histórico d la teología india,* Iglesia, Pueblos y Cultura no. 48–49. Quito, Ecuador: Ediciones Abya-Yala.

Surtz, Edward. 1964. "Introduction." In *Utopia*, vii–xxx. By Thomas More. Edited by Edward Surtz. New Haven, CT: Yale University Press.

Szpiech, Ryan. 2013. *Conversion and Narrative: Reading and Religious Authority in Medieval Polemic*. Philadelphia: University of Pennsylvania Press.

Talbot, C. H. 1954. *The Anglo-Saxon Missionaries in Germany: The Lives of S.S. Willibrord, Boniface, Sturm, Leoba and Lebuin, Together with the Hodoeporicon of St. Willibald and a Section from the Correspondence of St. Boniface*. New York: Sheed and Ward.

Tavárez, David. 2000. "Invisible Wars: Idolatry Extirpation Projects and Native Responses in Nahua and Zapotec Communities, 1536–1728." PhD diss., University of Chicago, IL.

Tavárez, David. 2011. *The Invisible War: Indigenous Devotions, Discipline, and Dissent in Colonial Mexico*. Stanford, CA: Stanford University Press.

Tavárez, David. 2013a. "A Banned Sixteenth-Century Biblical Text in Nahuatl: The Proverbs of Solomon." *Ethnohistory* 60 (4, Fall): 759–762.

Tavárez, David. 2013b. "Nahua Intellectuals, Franciscan Scholars, and the *devotio moderna* in Colonial Mexico." *The Americas* 70 (2): 203–235.

Tedlock, Barbara. 1982. *Time and the Highland Maya*. Albuquerque: University of New Mexico Press.

Tedlock, Dennis. 1983. *The Spoken Word and the Work of Interpretation*. Philadelphia: University of Pennsylvania Press.

Tedlock, Dennis. 1985. *Popol Vuh: The Definitive Edition of the Mayan Book of the Dawn of Life and the Glories of Gods and Kings*. New York: Simon and Schuster.

Tedlock, Dennis. 1996. *Popol Vuh: The Definitive Edition of the Mayan Book of the Dawn of Life and the Glories of Gods and Kings*, Revised and expanded. New York: Touchstone, Simon and Schuster.

Tedlock, Dennis. 2003. *Rabinal Achi: A Mayan Drama of War and Sacrifice*. New York: Oxford University Press.

Tedlock, Dennis. 2010. *2000 Years of Mayan Literature*. Berkeley and Los Angeles: University of California Press.

Tedlock, Dennis, and Bruce Mannheim, eds. 1995. *The Dialogic Emergence of Culture*. Urbana and Chicago: University of Illinois Press.

Temprano, Juan Carlos. 1990. "Introducción." In *Historia general de las cosas de Nueva España*, v–xlii. Edited by Juan Carlos Temprano. Madrid, Spain: HISAPAT.

Terga, Ricardo. 1982. *La Verapaz: Colonización y evangelización*. Cobán, Guatemala: n.p. [Centro Ak' Kutan].

Terraciano, Kevin. 1998. "Native Expressions of Piety in Mixtec Testaments." In *Dead Giveaways: Indigenous Testaments of Colonial Mesoamerica and the Andes*, 115–140. Edited by Susan Kellogg and Matthew Restall. Salt Lake City: University of Utah Press.

Teuton, Sean. 2018. *Native American Literature: A Very Short Introduction*. New York: Oxford University Press.

"Thomism." 1967. *New Catholic Encyclopedia*, 126–138. Washington, DC: Catholic University of America.

Thompson, J. Eric S. 1966. "The Maya Central Area at the Spanish Conquest and Later: A Problem in Demography." In *Proceedings of the Royal Anthropological Institute of Great Britain and Ireland for 1966*, 23–37. London: Royal Anthropological Institute of Great Britain and Ireland.

Thorsen, Jakob Egeris. 2015. *Charismatic Practice and Catholic Parish Life: The Incipient Pentecostalization of the Church in Guatemala and Latin America*. Leiden, Netherlands: E. J. Brill.

Tinker, George E. 1993. *Missionary Conquest: The Gospel and Native American Cultural Genocide*. Minneapolis, MN: Fortress Press.

Torre, Tomás de la. 1985. *Diario de viaje. De Salamanca a Chiapa. 1544–1545*. Burgos, Spain: Editorial OPE Caleruega.

Tovilla, Capitán don Martín Alfonso. 2000 [1630–1635]. "Relación Histórica Descriptiva de las Provincias de la Verapaz y de la del Manché." In *Lost Shores, Forgotten Peoples: Spanish Explorations of the South East Maya Lowlands*, 55–150. Edited and translated by Lawrence H. Feldman. Durham, NC: Duke University Press.

Townsend, Camilla. 2006. *Malintzin's Choices: An Indian Woman in the Conquest of Mexico*. Albuquerque: University of New Mexico Press.

Townsend, Camilla. 2017. *Annals of Native America: How the Nahuas of Colonial Mexico Kept Their History Alive*. New York: Oxford University Press.

Tugwell, Simon. 1989. "The Spirituality of the Dominicans." In *Christian Spirituality*, Vol. 2, *High Middle Ages and Reformation*, 15–30. World Spirituality: An Encyclopedic History of the Religious Quest, Vol. 17. Edited by Jill Raitt. New York: Crossroad Publishing Company.

United Nations Verification Mission in Guatemala (MINUGUA). 2002. "Report of the United Nations Verification Mission in Guatemala (MINUGUA) for the Consultative Group Meeting for Guatemala." Guatemala: n.p. 18 January.

Universidad Francisco Marroquín. 2007. *El lienzo de la conquista, Quauhquechollan: A chronicle of conquest*. Guatemala City, Guatemala: Universidad Francisco Marroquín.

Valenzuela-Vermehren, Luis. 2013. "Vitoria, Humanism, and the School of Salamanca in Early Sixteenth-Century Spain." *Logos* 16 (2): 99–125.

Van Akkeren, Ruud. 2000. *Place of the Lord's Daughter: Rab'inal, Its History, Its Dance-Drama*, Center for Non-Western Studies Publications, Vol. 91. Leiden, Netherlands: University of Leiden.

Van Akkeren, Ruud W. 2003. "Authors of the Popol Wuj." *Ancient Mesoamerica* 14: 237–256.

Van Akkeren, Ruud. n.d. [2005]. "El chinamit y la plaza del postclásico: La arqueología y la etnohistoria en busca del papel de la casa de consejo." In *XIX Simposio de Investigaciones Argueológicas en Guatemala, 2005*, 223–234. Guatemala City, Guatemala: Museo Nacional de Arqueología y Etnología.

Van Akkeren, Ruud. 2007. *La vision indígena de la conquista*. Guatemala City, Guatemala: Serviprena.

Van Akkeren, Ruud. 2009. "Título de los Indios de Santa Clara La Laguna." In *Crónicas Mesoamericanas*, Tomo II: 69–84. Edited by Horacio Cabezas Carcache. Guatemala City: Publicaciones Mesoamericana.

Van Akkeren, Ruud. 2010. "Fray Domingo de Vico: Maestro de autores indígenas." *The Mayan Studies Journal / Revista de estudios mayas* 2 (7): 2–61.

Van Akkeren, Ruud. 2011. "Fray Domingo de Vico maestro de autores indígenas." In *Cosmovisión Mesoamericana*, 83–117. Edited by Horacio Cabezas Carcache. Guatemala City, Guatemala: Publicaciones Mesoamericanas.

Van Akkeren, Ruud. 2012. *Xib'alb'a y el nacimiento del nuevo sol: Una version posclásica del colapso maya*. Guatemala City, Guatemala: Editorial Piedra Santa.

Van Doesburg, Sebastián, and Michael Swanton. 2008. "La traducción de la Doctrina Cristiana en lengua mixteca de fray Benito Hernández al chocholetco (ngiwa)." In *Memorias del Coloquio Francisco Belmar: Conferencias sobre lenguas otomangues y oaxaqueñas*, Vol. II, 81–117. Edited by Ausencia López Cruz and Michael Swanton. Oaxaca, Mexico: Biblioteca Francisco de Burgoa, AUBJO; Colegio Superior para la Educación Integral Intercultural de Oaxaca; Fundación Alfredo Harp Helú Oaxaca; and the Instituto Nacional de Lenguas Indígenas.

Van Oss, Adriaan C. 1986. *Catholic Colonialism: A Parish History of Guatemala, 1524–1821*. New York: Cambridge University Press.

Vásquez, Manuel A., and Marie Friedmann Marquardt. 2003. *Globalizing the Sacred: Religion across the Americas*. New Brunswick, NJ: Rutgers University Press.

Vázquez, Francisco. 1937 [1714]. *Crónica de la Provincia del Sántisimo Nombre de Jesús de Guatemala,* Segunda Edición, Biblioteca "Goathemala" Volumen XIV. Edited by J. Antonio Villacorta C. Guatemala City, Guatemala: Sociedad de Geografía e Historia.

Veblen, Thomas T. 1977. "Native Population Decline in Totonicapán, Guatemala." *Annals of the Association of American Geographers* 67 (4, December): 484–499.

Varea, Francisco de. 1997 [ca. 1603]. *Calepino en lengua cakchikquel.* Edited by Judy Garland de Butler. Bogota, Colombia: Panamericana Formas e Impresos, S.A.

Vico, Domingo de. *See* the list of Vico's works consulted at the beginning of the references.

Vigil, Ralph H. 1976. "Alonso de Zorita: Early and Last Years." *The Americas* 32 (4, April): 501–513.

Villacorta C., Antonio J., and Flavio Rodas N. 1927. *Manuscrito de Chichicastenango, Popol Buj: Estudios sobre las antiguas tradiciones del pueblo quiché; Texto indígena fonetizado y traducido al castellano*. Guatemala City, Guatemala: Sociedad de Geografía e Historia de Guatemala.

Villagutierre Soto Mayor, Juan de. 1983. *History of the Conquest of the Province of the Itza.* Culver City, CA: Labyrinthos Press.

Villalón, María Eugenia. 1999. "De/Recentring the Native Text: Contemporary Discourse Strategies in Christianising Latin America." In *The Language of Christianisation in Latin America: Catechisation and Instruction in Amerindian Languages*, 313–328. Edited by Sabine Dedenbach-Salazar Sáenz and Lindsey Crickmay. Bonn, Germany: Verlag Antón Saurwein.

Vio Cajetan, Tommaso de. 2000. *The Analogy of Names, and The Concept of Being.* Translated by Edward A. Bushinski with Henry J. Koren. Eugene, OR: Wipf and Stock Publishers.

Voragine, Jacobus de. 1993. *The Golden Legend: Readings on the Saints*, Volume I. Translated by William Granger Ryan. Princeton, NJ: Princeton University Press.

Vose, Robin. 2009. *Dominicans, Muslims and Jews in the Medieval Crown of Aragon*. New York: Cambridge University Press.

Wallace, Dwight T. 1977. "In Intra-site Locational Analysis of Utatlan: The Structure of an Urban Site." In *Archaeology and Ethnohistory of the Central Quiche*, Publication No. 1, 20–54. Edited by Dwight T. Wallace and Robert M. Carmack. Albany Institute for Mesoamerican Studies, State University of New York at Albany.

Watanabe, John M. 1992. *Maya Saints and Souls in a Changing World*. Austin: University of Texas Press.

Weeks, John M. 1985. *Middle American Indians: A Guide to the Manuscript Collection at Tozzer Library, Harvard University*. New York: Garland.

Weeks, John M. 1990. *Mesoamerican Ethnohistory in United States Libraries: Reconstruction of the William E. Gates Collection of Historical and Linguistic Manuscripts*. Culver City, CA: Labyrinthos Press.

Wehr, Hans. 1994. *A Dictionary of Modern Written Arabic*, 4th ed. Edited by J. Milton Cowan. Ithaca, NY: Spoken Language Services, Inc.

Whalen, Gretchen. 2003. "An Annotated Translation of a Colonial Yukatek Manuscript: On Religious and Cosmological Topics by a Native Author." FAMSI: http://www.famsi.org/reports/01017/01017Whalen01.pdf (accessed July 2019).

Whiston, William. 1988. *The Works of Flavius Josephus*, Volume IV: *Antiquities of the Jews Books XVIII–XX, Flavius Josephus against Apion, Concerning Hades*. Grand Rapids: Baker Book House.

White, Richard. 1991. *The Middle Ground: Indians, Empires, and Republics in the Great Lakes Region, 1650–1815*. New York: Cambridge University Press.

Wolf, Eric. 1959. *Sons of the Shaking Earth: The People of Mexico and Guatemala—Their Land, History, and Culture*. Chicago, IL: The University of Chicago Press.

Wong, Perry. 2009. "Parra and the Orthography of al-Andalus in Guatemala." Unpublished paper.

Ximénez, Francisco. n.d. [ca. 1701–ca. 1704] *[Popol Vuh] Empiezan las historias del origen de los indios de esta provincia de Guatemala*. Edward E. Ayer Manuscript 1515. Chicago, IL: Newberry Library.

Ximénez, Francisco. n.d. [ca. 1721]. "Manuscrito antiguo Kiche encontrado a principios del siglo XVIII entre los indios del Pueblo de Chichicastenango." Berkeley: University of California, Hubert Howe Bancroft Collection.

Ximénez, Francisco. 1857 [ca. 1721]. *Las historias del origen del los indios de esta provincia de Guatemala traducidas de la lengua quiché al castellano para mas comodidad de los ministros del s. evangelio*. Edited by Carl Scherzer. Vienna, Austria: Libreros de la Academia Imperial de las Ciencias.

Ximénez, Francisco. 1977 [ca. 1721]. *Historia de la Provincia de San Vicente de Chiapa y Guatemala de la Orden de Predicadores,* Biblioteca "Goathemala" Volumen XXVIII. Edited by Carmelo Sáenz de Santa María. Guatemala City, Guatemala: Sociedad de Geografía e Historia de Guatemala.

Ximénez, Francisco. 1985 [ca. 1701]. *Primera parte del tesoro de las lenguas cakchikel, quiché y zutuhil, en que las dichas lenguas se traducen a la nuestra, española*. Edited by Carmelo Sáenz de Santa María. Guatemala City, Guatemala: Academia de Geografia e Historia de Guatemala.

Ximénez, Francisco. 1993 [ca. 1701]. *Arte de las tres lenguas kaqchikel, k'iche' y tz'utujil,* Biblioteca "Goathemala" Volumen XXXI. Edited by Rosa Helena Chinchilla M. Guatemala City, Guatemala: Academia de Geografía e Historia de Guatemala.

Yamase, Shinji. 2002. *History and Legend of the Colonial Maya of Guatemala*. Lewiston, NY: Edwin Mellon Press.

Yelle, Robert A. 2013. *Semiotics of Religion: Signs of the Sacred in History*. New York: Bloomsbury.

Zimmermann, Günther, and Berthold Riese. 1980. "Capitel 1 aus Domingo de Vicos 'Theologia Indorum' in der Sprache de Quiché-Indianer von Guatemala." *Anthropos* 75 (3–4): 612–617.

Zorita, Alono de. 1994. *Life and Labor in Ancient Mexico: The Brief and Summary Relation of the Lords of New Spain*. Translated by Benjamin Keen. Norman: University of Oklahoma Press.

Zorita, Alonso de. 1999. *Relación de la Nueva España II: Relación de algunas de las muchas cosas notables que hay en la Nueva España y de su conquista y pacificación y de la conversión de los naturales de ella*. Edited by Ethelia Ruiz Medrano and José Mariano Leyva. Mexico City, Mexico: Conaculta, Cien de México.

Zwartjes, Otto. 1999. "El lenguaje en la catequización de los moriscos de Granda y los indígenas de Latinoamérica: Las obras de los gramáticos como vehículo entre instrucción religiosa y pensamiento lingüístico." In *The Language of Christianisation in Latin America: Catechisation and Instruction in Amerindian Languages*, 17–40. Edited by Sabine Dedenbach-Salazar Sáenz and Lindsey Crickmay. Bonn, Germany: Verlag Antón Saurwein.

Index